T0293304

CISSP Cert Guide, Fifth Edition

Companion Website and Pearson Test Prep Access Code

Access interactive study tools on this book's companion website, including practice test software, review exercises, Key Term flash card application, a study planner, and more!

To access the companion website, simply follow these steps:

1. Go to **www.pearsonitcertification.com/register**.
2. Enter the **print book ISBN**: 9780135343999.
3. Answer the security question to validate your purchase.
4. Go to your account page.
5. Click on the **Registered Products** tab.
6. Under the book listing, click on the **Access Bonus Content** link.

When you register your book, your Pearson Test Prep practice test access code will automatically be populated with the book listing under the Registered Products tab. You will need this code to access the practice test that comes with this book. You can redeem the code at **PearsonTestPrep.com**. Simply choose Pearson IT Certification as your product group and log into the site with the same credentials you used to register your book. Click the **Activate New Product** button and enter the access code. More detailed instructions on how to redeem your access code for both the online and desktop versions can be found on the companion website.

If you have any issues accessing the companion website or obtaining your Pearson Test Prep practice test access code, you can contact our support team by going to **pearsonitp.echelp.org**.

CISSP Cert Guide

Fifth Edition

Robin M. Abernathy
Dr. Darren R. Hayes

Pearson

Hoboken, New Jersey

CISSP Cert Guide, Fifth Edition

ISBN-13: 978-0-13-534399-9

ISBN-10: 0-13-534399-2

Library of Congress Control Number: 2024911820

2 2024

Trademarks

Warning and Disclaimer

Special Sales

For information about buying this title in bulk quantities, or for special sales opportunities (which may include electronic versions; custom cover designs; and content particular to your business, training goals, marketing focus, or branding interests), please contact our corporate sales department at corpsales@pearsoned.com or (800) 382-3419.

For government sales inquiries, please contact governmentsales@pearsoned.com.

GM K12, Early Career and Professional Learning
Soo Kang

Product Line Manager
Brett Bartow

Executive Editor
James Manly

Development Editor
Ellie C. Bru

Managing Editor
Sandra Schroeder

Senior Project Editor
Mandie Frank

Copy Editor
Bill McManus

Indexer
Timothy Wright

Proofreader
Donna E. Mulder

Technical Editors
R. Sarma Danturthi
Ben Mayo

Publishing Coordinator
Cindy Teeters

Designer
Chuti Prasertsith

Compositor
codeMantra

KD 10.26.2024 0420

Contents at a Glance

Online Elements

Table of Contents

Online Elements

About the Authors

Robin M. Abernathy has been working in the IT certification preparation industry for more than 20 years. She has written and edited certification preparation materials for many (ISC)², Microsoft, CompTIA, PMI, ITIL, ISACA, and GIAC certifications and holds multiple IT certifications from these vendors.

Robin provides training on computer hardware and software, networking, security, and project management. Over the past decade, she has ventured into the traditional publishing industry by technically editing several publications and co-authoring Pearson's *CISSP Cert Guide* and *CASP+ Cert Guide* and authoring Pearson's *Project+ Cert Guide.* She presents at technical conferences and hosts webinars on IT certification topics.

Dr. Darren R. Hayes has close to 20 years of academic and professional experience in computer security and digital forensics. He has authored numerous publications in these fields, including *A Practical Guide to Digital Forensics Investigations*, which is published by Pearson. He is Associate Professor at Pace University, where he is the founder and director of the Seidenberg Digital Forensics Research Lab. He holds numerous IT certifications in security and digital forensics and holds a PhD from Sapienza University in Italy and a doctorate from Pace University.

Darren is also a professional digital forensics examiner and has supported both criminal and civil investigations over the past decade and a half. He has also been declared an expert witness in federal court.

Dedications

To all those out there on a certification journey!

—Robin

To all our cyber warriors who protect our businesses and our national security. Your careers are so demanding and your ambition to gain certifications is to be commended.

—Darren

Acknowledgments

My first thanks goes to God for blessing me with the ability to learn and grow in any field I choose. With Him, all things are possible!

For me, it is hard to believe that I am on the fifth edition of this book. I appreciate my family and my friends, who have supported me in my publishing journey through three titles and multiple editions.

It is my hope that you, the reader, succeed in your IT certification goals!

—Robin

To my beautiful wife, Nalini, and my children, Aine, Fiona, Nicolai, and Shay, I cannot thank you enough for your support and love over the years. Also, to my parents, Ted and Annette, who inspired me to be an eternal learner and try to help others to gain knowledge. I would like to acknowledge my fellow teachers who make immeasurable sacrifices to see their students succeed. My sincere thanks to all of the tremendous reviewers, editors, and other staff at Pearson whom I have had the honor of working with for many years.

—Darren

About the Technical Reviewers

R. Sarma Danturthi, PhD, PMP, CISSP, has a doctoral degree in engineering from the University of Memphis, Memphis, Tennessee, and has taught graduate-level courses in engineering, microprocessors, and computer science. He has been in the IT field for more than 20 years. His earlier experience included designing processor-level boards with interfaces and programming with several languages such as C and C++ on various platforms such as Windows, Linux, UNIX, and VAX/VMS. He has been a funding proposal reviewer, scientific paper peer reviewer for universities in the USA and Taiwan, book reviewer and exam preparation subject matter expert for Pearson, (ISC)^2, and CompTIA.

His current experience includes information and cybersecurity, database security, software and application security, project team lead, and project management. He has published several papers in peer-reviewed journals and has written book chapters on software interfaces, modeling, IT security, and simulation. His interests include evolving cybersecurity, cloud computing, intelligent interfaces, and mobile application development. Besides being proficient in various programming languages, databases, information, and cybersecurity, he has certifications in Java, Project Management Institute's PMP, CompTIA Sec+, and (ISC)^2's CISSP.

Dr. Danturthi published *70 Tips and Tricks for Mastering the CISSP Exam* (Apress) in 2020. He can be contacted at danturthi@gmail. com.

Ben Mayo, CCIE No. 24861, CISSP, is the head of security and lead engineer for Montana's largest independent network and data center provider. He has more than 19 years of experience in the network and security fields. Ben's experience spans multiple industries, including electrical power generation, education, and telecommunications. Ben takes a "purple team" approach to security, applying both offensive and defensive security practices to enhance his organization's security posture. Though security is his passion, he most enjoys spending time with his three awesome kids and his amazing wife. You can follow Ben on Twitter at @ping_18024.

We Want to Hear from You!

As the reader of this book, *you* are our most important critic and commentator. We value your opinion and want to know what we're doing right, what we could do better, what areas you'd like to see us publish in, and any other words of wisdom you're willing to pass our way.

We welcome your comments. You can email or write to let us know what you did or didn't like about this book—as well as what we can do to make our books better.

Please note that we cannot help you with technical problems related to the topic of this book.

When you write, please be sure to include this book's title and author as well as your name and email address. We will carefully review your comments and share them with the author and editors who worked on the book.

Email: community@informit.com

Reader Services

Register your copy of *CISSP Cert Guide* at www.pearsonitcertification.com for convenient access to downloads, updates, and corrections as they become available. To start the registration process, go to www.pearsonitcertification.com/register and log in or create an account.* Enter the product ISBN 9780135343999 and click Submit. When the process is complete, you will find any available bonus content under Registered Products.

*Be sure to check the box that you would like to hear from us to receive exclusive discounts on future editions of this product.

Introduction

Certified Information Systems Security Professional (CISSP) is one of the most respected and sought-after security certifications available today. It is a globally recognized credential, which demonstrates that the holder has knowledge and skills across a broad range of security topics.

As the number of security threats to organizations grows and the nature of these threats broadens, companies large and small have realized that security can no longer be an afterthought. It must be built into the DNA of the enterprise to be successful. Consequently, trained professionals must be versed not only in technology security but all aspects of security. It also requires a holistic approach to protecting the enterprise.

Security today is no longer a one-size-fits-all proposition. The CISSP credential is a way security professionals can demonstrate the ability to design, implement, and maintain the correct security posture for an organization, based on the complex environments in which today's organizations exist.

The Goals of the CISSP Certification

The CISSP certification is created and managed by one of the most prestigious security organizations in the world and has a number of stated goals. Although not critical for passing the exam, having knowledge of the organization and of these goals is helpful in understanding the motivation behind the creation of the exam.

Sponsoring Bodies

The CISSP is created and maintained by the International Information System Security Certification Consortium $(ISC)^2$. The $(ISC)^2$ is a global not-for-profit organization that provides both a vendor-neutral certification process and supporting educational materials.

The CISSP is one of a number of security-related certifications offered by $(ISC)^2$. Other certifications offered by this organization include the following:

- Systems Security Certified Practitioner (SSCP)
- Certified Cloud Security Professional (CCSP)
- Certified Authorization Professional (CAP)
- Certified Secure Software Life Cycle Professional (CSSLP)
- HealthCare Information Security and Privacy Practitioner (HCISPP)

Several additional versions of the CISSP are offered that focus in particular areas:

- CISSP-Information Systems Security Architecture Professional (CISSP-ISSAP)
- CISSP-Information Systems Security Engineering Professional (CISSP-ISSEP)
- CISSP-Information Systems Security Management Professional (CISSP-ISSMP)

$(ISC)^2$ derives some of its prestige from the fact that it was the first security certification body to meet the requirements set forth by ANSI/ISO/IEC Standard 17024, a global benchmark for personnel certification. This ensures that certifications offered by this organization are both highly respected and sought after.

Stated Goals

The goal of $(ISC)^2$, operating through its administration of the CISSP and other certifications, is to provide a reliable instrument to measure an individual's knowledge of security. This knowledge is not limited to technology issues alone but extends to all aspects of security that face an organization.

In that regard, the topics are technically more shallow than those tested by some other security certifications, while also covering a much wider range of issues than those other certifications. Later, we cover the topics that comprise the eight domains of knowledge in detail, but it is a wide range of topics. This vast breadth of knowledge and the experience needed to pass the exam are what set the CISSP certification apart.

The Value of the CISSP Certification

The CISSP certification holds value for both the exam candidate and the enterprise. This certification is routinely in the top 10 of yearly lists that rank the relative demand for various IT certifications.

To the Security Professional

A security professional would spend the time and effort required to achieve this credential for numerous reasons:

- To meet growing demand for security professionals
- To become more marketable in an increasingly competitive job market
- To enhance skills in a current job

- To qualify or compete more successfully for a promotion
- To increase salary

In short, this certification demonstrates that the holder not only has the knowledge and skills tested in the exam but also has the wherewithal to plan and implement a study plan that addresses an unusually broad range of security topics.

To the Enterprise

For an organization, the CISSP certification offers a reliable benchmark to which job candidates can be measured by validating knowledge and experience. Candidates who successfully pass the rigorous exam are required to submit documentation verifying experience in the security field. Individuals holding this certification will stand out from the rest, not only making the hiring process easier but also adding a level of confidence in the final hire.

The Common Body of Knowledge

The material contained in the CISSP exam is divided into eight domains, which comprise what is known as the Common Body of Knowledge. This book devotes a chapter to each of these domains. Inevitable overlap occurs between the domains, leading to some overlap between topics covered in the chapters; the topics covered in each chapter are described next.

Security and Risk Management

The Security and Risk Management domain, covered in Chapter 1, encompasses a broad spectrum of general information security and risks management topics and is 15 percent of the exam. Topics include

- Professional ethics
- Concepts of confidentiality, integrity, availability, authenticity, and nonrepudiation
- Security governance principles
- Compliance requirements
- Legal and regulatory issues
- Investigation types
- Security policy, standards, procedures, and guidelines
- Business continuity (BC) requirements

- Personnel security policies and procedures
- Risk management concepts
- Threat modeling concepts and methodologies
- Supply chain risk management (SCRM) concepts
- Security awareness, education, and training program

Asset Security

The Asset Security domain, covered in Chapter 2, focuses on the collection, handling, and protection of information throughout its life cycle and is 10 percent of the exam. Topics include

- Information and asset identification and classification
- Information and asset handling requirements
- Resource provisioning
- Data life cycle
- Asset retention
- Data security controls and compliance requirements

Security Architecture and Engineering

The Security Architecture and Engineering domain, covered in Chapter 3, addresses the practice of building information systems and related architecture that deliver the required functionality when threats occur and is 13 percent of the exam. Topics include

- Engineering processes using secure design principles
- Fundamental concepts of security models
- Control selection based on systems security requirements
- Security capabilities of information systems
- Vulnerabilities of security architectures, designs, and solution elements
- Cryptography
- Cryptanalytic attacks
- Security principles of site and facility design
- Site and facility security controls

Communication and Network Security

The Communication and Network Security domain, covered in Chapter 4, focuses on protecting data in transit and securing the underlying networks over which the data travels and is 13 percent of the exam. Topics include

- Secure design principles in network architectures
- Network components security
- Secure communication channels

Identity and Access Management (IAM)

The Identity and Access Management domain, covered in Chapter 5 and comprising 13 percent of the exam, discusses provisioning and managing the identities and access used in the interaction of humans and information systems, of disparate information systems, and even between individual components of information systems. Topics include

- Physical and logical access to assets
- Identification and authentication of people, devices, and services
- Federated identity as a third-party service
- Authorization mechanisms
- Identity and access provisioning life cycle
- Authentication systems

Security Assessment and Testing

The Security Assessment and Testing domain, covered in Chapter 6 and comprising 12 percent of the exam, encompasses the evaluation of information assets and associated infrastructure using tools and techniques for the purpose of identifying and mitigating risk due to architectural issues, design flaws, configuration errors, hardware and software vulnerabilities, coding errors, and any other weaknesses that may affect an information system's ability to deliver its intended functionality in a secure manner. The topics include

- Assessment, test, and audit strategies design and validation
- Security control testing
- Security process data collection
- Test output analysis and reporting
- Security audits

Security Operations

The Security Operations domain, covered in Chapter 7, surveys the execution of security measures and maintenance of proper security posture and is 13 percent of the exam. Topics include

- Investigations compliance
- Logging and monitoring activities
- Configuration management
- Security operations concepts
- Resource protection
- Incident management
- Detective and preventive measures
- Patch and vulnerability management
- Change management processes
- Recovery strategies
- Disaster recovery (DR) processes
- Disaster recovery plan (DRP) testing
- Business continuity (BC) planning and exercises
- Physical security implementation and management
- Personnel safety and security concerns

Software Development Security

The Software Development Security domain, covered in Chapter 8, explores the software development life cycle and development best practices and is 11 percent of the exam. Topics include

- Software development life cycle (SDLC) security
- Security controls in development environments
- Software security effectiveness
- Security impact of acquired software
- Secure coding guidelines and standards

Steps to Becoming a CISSP

To become a CISSP, a test candidate must meet certain prerequisites and follow specific procedures. Test candidates must qualify for the exam and sign up for the exam.

Qualifying for the Exam

Candidates must have a minimum of five years of paid full-time professional security work experience in two or more of the eight domains in the Common Body of Knowledge. You may receive a one-year experience waiver with a four-year college degree or additional credential from the approved list, available at the $(ISC)^2$ website, thus requiring four years of direct full-time professional security work experience in two or more of the eight domains of the CISSP.

If you lack this experience, you can become an Associate of $(ISC)^2$ by successfully passing the CISSP exam. You'll then have six years to earn your experience to become a CISSP.

Signing Up for the Exam

The steps required to sign up for the CISSP are as follows:

1. Create a Pearson Vue account and schedule your exam.
2. Complete the Examination Agreement, attesting to the truth of your assertions regarding professional experience and legally committing to the adherence of the $(ISC)^2$ Code of Ethics.
3. Review the Candidate Background Questions.
4. Submit the examination fee.

When you are notified that you have successfully passed the examination, you will be required to subscribe to the $(ISC)^2$ Code of Ethics and have your application endorsed before the credential can be awarded. An endorsement form for this purpose must be completed and signed by an $(ISC)^2$ certified professional who is an active member and who is able to attest to your professional experience.

Facts About the CISSP Exam

The CISSP exam is a computer-based test that the candidate can spend up to three to six hours completing (depending on whether you take the CAT version that is available in English only or the linear format that is available in all other languages). There are no formal breaks, but you are allowed to bring a snack and eat it at the back of the test room, but any time used for that break counts toward the three to six hours. You must bring a government-issued identification card. No other forms of ID will be accepted. You may be required to submit to a palm vein scan.

The CAT test consists of a maximum 175 questions, while the linear format consists of 250 questions. As of May 2022, the CISSP exam will be in a computerized adaptive testing (CAT) format for those who take the English-language version, whereas all other languages have only the linear format. With the CAT format, the computer evaluates the certification candidate's ability to get the next question right based on the candidate's previous answers and the difficulty of those questions. The questions get harder as the certification candidate answers questions correctly, and the questions get easier as the certification candidate answers questions incorrectly. Each answer affects the questions that follow. Therefore, unlike the linear test format where the certification candidate can go back and forth in the question pool and change answers, a CAT format exam does *not* allow the certification candidate to change the answer or even view a previously answered question. The certification candidate may receive a pass or fail score without seeing 175 questions. To find out more about the CAT format, please go to www.isc2.org/Certifications/CISSP/CISSP-CAT#.

Although the majority of the questions will be multiple-choice questions with four options, test candidates may also encounter drag-and-drop and hotspot questions. The passing grade is 700 out of a possible 1,000 points. Candidates will receive the unofficial results at the test center from the test administrator. (ISC)^2 will then follow up with an official result via email.

About the *CISSP Cert Guide*, Fifth Edition

This book maps to the topic areas of the (ISC)^2 Certified Information Systems Security Professional (CISSP) exam and uses a number of features to help you understand the topics and prepare for the exam.

Objectives and Methods

This book uses several key methodologies to help you discover the exam topics on which you need more review, to help you fully understand and remember those details, and to help you prove to yourself that you have retained your knowledge of those topics. This book does not try to help you pass the exam only by memorization; it seeks to help you to truly learn and understand the topics. This book is designed to help you pass the CISSP exam by using the following methods:

- Helping you discover which exam topics you have not mastered
- Providing explanations and information to fill in your knowledge gaps
- Supplying exercises that enhance your ability to recall and deduce the answers to test questions
- Providing practice exercises on the topics and the testing process via test questions on the companion website

Book Features

To help you customize your study time using this book, the core chapters have several features that help you make the best use of your time:

- **Foundation Topics:** These are the core sections of each chapter. They explain the concepts for the topics in that chapter.
- **Exam Preparation Tasks:** After the "Foundation Topics" section of each chapter, the "Exam Preparation Tasks" section lists a series of study activities that you should do at the end of the chapter:
  - **Review All Key Topics:** The Key Topic icon appears next to the most important items in the "Foundation Topics" section of the chapter. The Review All Key Topics activity lists the key topics from the chapter, along with their page numbers. Although the contents of the entire chapter could be on the exam, you should definitely know the information listed in each key topic, so you should review these.
  - **Define Key Terms:** Although the CISSP exam may be unlikely to ask a question such as "Define this term," the exam does require that you learn and know a lot of information systems security terminology. This section lists the most important terms from the chapter, asking you to write a short definition and compare your answer to the glossary at the end of the book.
  - **Review Questions:** Confirm that you understand the content that you just covered by answering these questions and reading the answer explanations.
- **Web-based practice exam:** The companion website includes the Pearson Cert Practice Test engine that allows you to take practice exam questions. Use it to prepare with a sample exam and to pinpoint topics where you need more study.

How This Book Is Organized

This book contains eight core chapters—Chapters 1 through 8. Chapter 9 includes some preparation tips and suggestions for how to approach the exam. Each core chapter covers a subset of the topics on the CISSP exam. The core chapters map directly to the CISSP exam topic areas and cover the concepts and technologies that you will encounter on the exam.

How to Access the Companion Website

Register this book to get access to the Pearson IT Certification test engine and other study materials, as well as additional bonus content. Check this site regularly for new and updated postings written by the author that provide further insight into the more troublesome topics on the exam. Be sure to check the box indicating that you would like to hear from us to receive updates and exclusive discounts on future editions of this product or related products.

To access this companion website, follow these steps:

Step 1. Go to **www.pearsonitcertification.com/register** and log in or create a new account.

Step 2. Enter the ISBN: **9780135343999**.

Step 3. Answer the challenge question as proof of purchase.

Step 4. Click the **Access Bonus Content** link in the Registered Products section of your account page to be taken to the page where your downloadable content is available.

Please note that many of our companion content files can be very large, especially image and video files.

If you are unable to locate the files for this title by following the steps above, please visit www.pearsonITcertification.com/contact and select the Site Problems/Comments option. Our customer service representatives will assist you.

Pearson Test Prep Practice Test Software

As noted previously, this book comes complete with the Pearson Test Prep practice test software, containing two full exams. These practice tests are available to you either online or as an offline Windows application. To access the practice exams that were developed with this book, please see the instructions below.

How to Access the Pearson Test Prep (PTP) App

You have two options for installing and using the Pearson Test Prep application: a web app and a desktop app. To use the Pearson Test Prep application, start by finding the registration code that comes with the book. You can find the code in these ways:

- You can get your access code by registering the print ISBN (9780135343999) on pearsonitcertification.com/register. Make sure to use the print book ISBN regardless of whether you purchased an eBook or the print book. After you register the book, your access code will be populated on your account page under the Registered Products tab. Instructions for how to redeem the code are available on the book's companion website by clicking the Access Bonus Content link.

- If you purchase the Premium Edition eBook and Practice Test directly from the Pearson IT Certification website, the code will be populated on your account page after purchase. Just log in at pearsonitcertification.com, click Account to see details of your account, and click the Digital Purchases tab.

NOTE After you register your book, your code can always be found in your account on the Registered Products tab.

Once you have the access code, to find instructions about both the Pearson Test Prep web app and the desktop app, follow these steps:

Step 1. Open this book's companion website, as shown earlier in this Introduction, under the heading, "How to Access the Companion Website."

Step 2. Click the **Practice Test Software** button.

Step 3. Follow the instructions listed there for both installing the desktop app and using the web app.

Note that if you want to use the web app only at this point, just navigate to pearsontestprep.com, log in using the same credentials used to register your book or purchase the Premium Edition, and register this book's practice tests using the registration code you just found. The process should take only a couple of minutes.

Customizing Your Exams

When you are in the exam settings screen, you can choose to take exams in one of three modes:

- **Study mode:** Allows you to fully customize your exams and review answers as you are taking the exam. This is typically the mode you would use first to assess your knowledge and identify information gaps.
- **Practice Exam mode:** Locks certain customization options, as it is presenting a realistic exam experience. Use this mode when you are preparing to test your exam readiness.
- **Flash Card mode:** Strips out the answers and presents you with only the question stem. This mode is great for late-stage preparation when you really want to challenge yourself to provide answers without the benefit of seeing multiple-choice options. This mode does not provide the detailed score reports that the other two modes do, so you should not use it if you are trying to identify knowledge gaps.

In addition to these three modes, you will be able to select the source of your questions. You can choose to take exams that cover all of the chapters, or you can narrow your selection to just a single chapter or the chapters that make up specific parts in the book. All chapters are selected by default. If you want to narrow your focus to individual chapters, simply deselect all the chapters; then select only those on which you wish to focus in the Objectives area.

You can also select the exam banks on which to focus. Each exam bank comes complete with a full exam of questions that cover topics in every chapter. You can have the test engine serve up exams from all banks or just from one individual bank by selecting the desired banks in the exam bank area.

There are several other customizations you can make to your exam from the exam settings screen, such as the time of the exam, the number of questions served up, whether to randomize questions and answers, whether to show the number of correct answers for multiple-answer questions, and whether to serve up only specific types of questions. You can also create custom test banks by selecting only questions that you have marked or questions on which you have added notes.

Updating Your Exams

If you are using the online version of the Pearson Test Prep software, you should always have access to the latest version of the software as well as the exam data. If you are using the Windows desktop version, every time you launch the software while connected to the Internet, it checks if there are any updates to your exam data and automatically downloads any changes that were made since the last time you used the software.

Sometimes, due to many factors, the exam data may not fully download when you activate your exam. If you find that figures or exhibits are missing, you may need to manually update your exams. To update a particular exam you have already activated and downloaded, simply click the **Tools** tab and click the **Update Products** button. Again, this is only an issue with the desktop Windows application.

If you wish to check for updates to the Pearson Test Prep exam engine software, Windows desktop version, simply click the **Tools** tab and click the **Update Application** button. This ensures that you are running the latest version of the software engine.

Figure Credits

Figures 4.47 and 4.49: Microsoft

Figure 7.13: Ratchat/Shutterstock

This chapter covers the following topics:

- **Security Terms:** Concepts discussed include five pillars of information security (confidentiality, integrity, availability, authenticity, and non-repudiation); auditing and accounting; default security posture; defense in depth; abstraction; data hiding; and encryption.
- **Security Governance Principles:** Concepts discussed include security function alignment, organizational processes, organizational roles and responsibilities, security control frameworks, and due care and due diligence.
- **Compliance:** Concepts discussed include contractual, legal, industry standards, and regulatory compliance and privacy requirements compliance.
- **Legal and Regulatory Issues:** Concepts discussed include computer crime concepts, major legal systems, licensing and intellectual property, cyber crimes and data breaches, import/export controls, trans-border data flow, and privacy.
- **Investigation Types:** Concepts discussed include operations/administrative, criminal, civil, regulatory, industry standards, and eDiscovery investigations.
- **Professional Ethics:** Concepts discussed include (ISC)2 Code of Ethics, Computer Ethics Institute, Internet Architecture Board, and organizational code of ethics.
- **Security Documentation:** Documentation types include policies, processes, procedures, standards, guidelines, and baselines.
- **Business Continuity:** Concepts discussed include business continuity and disaster recovery concepts, scope and plan, and BIA development.
- **Personnel Security Policies and Procedures:** Policies and procedures discussed include candidate screening and hiring; employment agreements and policies; onboarding and offboarding processes; vendor, consultant, and contractor agreements and controls; compliance policy requirements; privacy policy requirements, job rotation, and separation of duties.

- **Risk Management Concepts:** Concepts discussed include asset; asset valuation; vulnerability; threat; threat agent; exploit; risk; exposure; countermeasure; risk appetite; attack; breach; risk management policy; risk management team; risk analysis team; risk assessment; implementation; control categories; control types; control assessment, monitoring, and measurement; reporting and continuous improvement; and risk frameworks.
- **Geographical Threats:** Concepts discussed include internal versus external threats, natural threats, system threats, human threats, and politically motivated threats.
- **Threat Modeling:** Concepts discussed include threat modeling concepts, threat modeling methodologies, identifying threats, potential attacks, and remediation technologies and processes.
- **Security Risks in the Supply Chain:** Concepts discussed include risks associated with hardware, software, and services; third-party assessment and monitoring; minimum security requirements; and service-level requirements.
- **Security Education, Training, and Awareness:** Concepts discussed include levels required, methods and techniques, and periodic content reviews.

The Security and Risk Management domain addresses a broad array of topics, including the fundamental information security principles of confidentiality, integrity, and availability; governance; legal systems; privacy; the regulatory environment; personnel security; risk management; threat modeling; business continuity; supply chain risk; and professional ethics. This domain carries an average weight of 16 percent, which is the highest weight of all the eight domains. So, pay close attention to the many details in this chapter!

CHAPTER 1

Security and Risk Management

Information security governance involves the principles, frameworks, and methods that establish criteria for protecting information assets, including security awareness. Risk management allows organizations to identify, measure, and control organizational risks. Threat modeling allows organizations to identify threats and potential attacks and implement appropriate mitigations. These facets ensure that security controls that are implemented are in balance with the operations of the organization. Each organization must develop a well-rounded, customized security program that addresses the needs of the organization while ensuring that the organization exercises due care and due diligence in its security plan. Acquisitions present special risks that management must understand prior to initiating purchases.

Security professionals must take a lead role in their organization's security program and act as risk advisors to management. In addition, security professionals must ensure that they understand current security issues and risks, governmental and industry regulations, and security controls that can be implemented. They also must understand professional ethics for security personnel. Security is an ever-evolving, continuous process, and security professionals must be watchful.

Business continuity and disaster recovery ensure that the organization can recover from any attack or disaster that affects operations. Using the results from the risk assessment, security professionals should ensure that the appropriate business continuity and disaster recovery plans are created, tested, and revised at appropriate intervals.

In this chapter, you learn how to use the information security governance and risk management components to assess risks, implement controls for identified risks, monitor control effectiveness, and perform future risk assessments.

Foundation Topics

Security Terms

When implementing security and managing risk, you must keep in mind several important security principles and terms, including the 5 pillars of information security; auditing and accounting; default security posture; defense in depth; abstraction; data hiding; and encryption.

Five Pillars of Information Security

The five pillars of information security are confidentiality, integrity, availability, authenticity, and non-repudiation. The first three of those pillars are known as the CIA triad. But all five terms are closely related in how they help an organization provide security for their assets.

CIA Triad

The first three fundamentals of security are confidentiality, integrity, and availability (CIA), often referred to as the ***CIA triad***. Although the CIA triad is being introduced here, each principle of the triad should be considered in every aspect of security design. The principles are equally associated and applied to every domain of the CISSP exam.

Most security issues result in a violation of at least one facet of the CIA triad. Understanding these three security principles will help security professionals ensure that the security controls and mechanisms implemented protect at least one of these principles.

Every security control that an organization puts into place fulfills at least one of the security principles of the CIA triad. Understanding how to circumvent these security principles is just as important as understanding how to provide them.

A balanced security approach should be implemented to ensure that all three facets are considered when security controls are implemented. When implementing any control, you should identify the facet that the control addresses. For example, Redundant Array of Inexpensive Disks (RAID) addresses data availability, file hashes address data integrity, and encryption addresses data confidentiality. A balanced approach ensures that no facet of the CIA triad is ignored.

Confidentiality

To ensure ***confidentiality***, you must prevent the disclosure of data or information to unauthorized entities. As part of confidentiality, the sensitivity level of data must be determined before putting any access controls in place. Data with a higher sensitivity level will have more access controls in place than data at a lower sensitivity level. Identification, authentication, and authorization can be used to maintain data confidentiality.

The opposite of confidentiality is disclosure. Encryption is probably the most popular example of a control that provides confidentiality.

Integrity

Integrity, the second part of the CIA triad, ensures that data and systems are protected from unauthorized modification or data corruption. The goal of integrity is to preserve consistency, specifically:

- **Data integrity:** Implies that the data can be trusted, is complete, consistent, and accurate.
- **System integrity:** Implies that a system will work as intended—that is, store, process, and display data correctly.

The opposite of integrity is alteration or corruption. Hashing can be used to prove (or disprove) data integrity.

Availability

Availability means ensuring that information, systems, and supporting infrastructure are operating and accessible when needed. The two main instances in which availability is affected are (1) when attacks are carried out that disable or cripple a system and (2) when service loss occurs during and after disasters. Each system should be assessed in terms of its criticality to organizational operations. Controls should be implemented based on each system's criticality level.

Availability is the opposite of destruction or denial of service. Fault-tolerant technologies, such as RAID or alternate sites, are examples of controls that help improve availability.

Authenticity

Authenticity in security refers to the assurance that data, transactions, communications, and documents are genuine and can be verified as genuine. Authenticity involves ensuring that users or entities are who they claim to be. This is often done through authentication mechanisms like passwords, biometric scans, or digital certificates.

However, authenticity is not just about verifying user identities but also about ensuring that the data has not been tampered with. Digital signatures, for example, are used to verify that a message or document is authentic and that it comes from a verified source. Authenticity is closely tied to non-repudiation, which ensures that once a transaction or communication has taken place, the parties involved cannot deny their involvement.

The concept of authenticity extends to various topics such as web security, where certificates ensure the authenticity of websites; in email security, where mechanisms help verify the authenticity of email senders; and in network security, where authentication protocols and VPNs ensure the authenticity of users and devices connecting to a network.

Non-Repudiation

Non-repudiation is the assurance that a sender cannot deny an action they have performed earlier, and can also involve the sender being sent proof of delivery, while the receiver is provided with proof of the sender's identity. This behavior is usually seen in electronic communications where one party denies sending a contract, document, or email. Non-repudiation means putting measures in place that will prevent the sender from denying that it sent a message.

A valid digital signature gives a recipient reason to believe that the message was created by a known sender (authentication), that the sender cannot deny having sent the message (non-repudiation), and when encrypted with a signature, that the message was not altered in transit (integrity).

Auditing and Accounting

Auditing and *accounting* are two related terms in organizational security. ***Auditing*** is an internal or external process of providing a manual or systematic measurable technical assessment of a system or application, whereas ***accounting*** is the logging of access and use of information resources. Auditing requires an analysis, which may be used to form an opinion. Accountability is the process of tracing actions to the source. Security professionals can perform audits of user or service accounts, account usage, application usage, device usage, and even permission usage. An audit is often used to identify corporate assets, detect risks to those assets, and improve security protocols. Regular audits should be carried out to ensure that the security policies in place are enforced and are being followed. Accounting is used to determine what changes need to be made.

Organizations should have a designated party who is responsible for ensuring that auditing and accounting of enterprise security are being completed regularly. Although computer security audits can be performed by internal personnel, such as corporate internal auditors, the audits may also need to be completed by federal or state regulators, external auditors, or consultants.

Keep in mind that in many contexts auditing can also be a third-party activity whereby an organization gains independent assurance based on evidence. With this type of auditing, the third party is usually assessing an organization's compliance with standards or other organizational guidelines or providing the organization with a non-biased assessment.

Default Security Posture

An organization's approach to information security directly affects its access control strategy. For a ***default security posture***, organizations must choose between the allow-by-default or deny-by-default options. As implied by its name, an allow- by-default posture permits access to any data unless a need exists to restrict access. The deny-by-default posture is much stricter because it denies any access that is not explicitly permitted. Military institutions and many commercial organizations use a deny-by-default posture.

Today, few organizations implement either of these postures to its fullest. Most organizations use some mixture of the two. Access control protocols enable an organization to balance both protocols. Although the core posture should guide the organization, organizations often find that this mixture is necessary to ensure that data is still protected while providing access to a variety of users. For example, a public website might grant all HTTP and HTTPS content but deny all other content.

Defense in Depth

A ***defense-in-depth*** strategy refers to the practice of using multiple layers of security between data and the resources on which it resides and securing that data from possible attackers (see Figure 1-1). It is derived from a military strategy, whereby multiple layers of defense are used rather than one line of defense, thereby slowing down the advancement of an attacker.

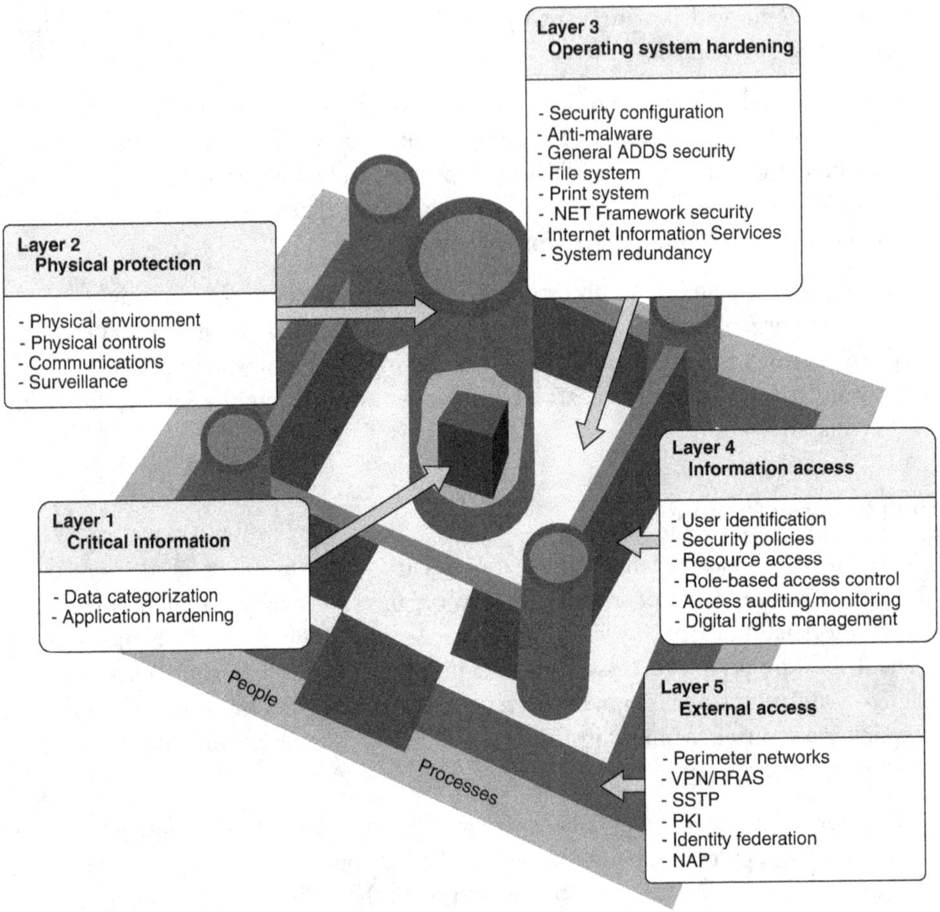

Figure 1-1 Defense-in-Depth Example

The first layer of a good defense-in-depth strategy is appropriate access control strategies. Access controls exist in all areas of an information systems (IS) infrastructure (more commonly referred to as an IT infrastructure), but a defense-in-depth strategy goes beyond access control. It also considers software development security, asset security, and all other domains of the CISSP realm.

Figure 1-2 shows layered defense-in-depth considerations.

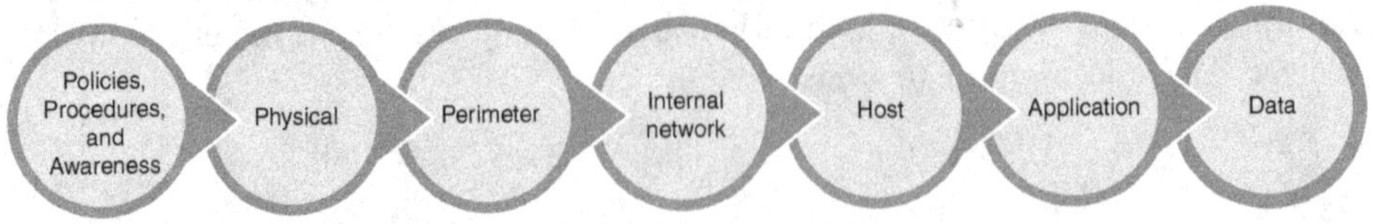

Figure 1-2 Defense-in-Depth Considerations

Abstraction

Abstraction is the process of taking away or removing characteristics from something to reduce it to a set of essential characteristics. Abstraction usually results in named entities with a set of characteristics that helps in their identification. However, unnecessary characteristics are hidden. Abstraction is related to both encapsulation and data hiding.

Data Hiding

Data hiding is the principle whereby information about a known entity is not accessible to certain processes or users. For example, a database may collect information about its users, including their name, job title, email address, and phone number, that an organization wants all users to be able to access. However, it might not want the public, or certain internal employees, to be able to access their Social Security numbers, birthdate, or other protected personally identifiable information (PII). Encapsulation is similar to data hiding; data hiding is related to data security, whereas encapsulation is focused on hiding the complexity of a system or its data.

Encryption

Encryption is the process of converting information or data into a scrambled text or an unreadable format to prevent unauthorized access. Data can be encrypted while at rest, in transit, and in use. Encryption is covered in more detail in Chapter 3, "Security Architecture and Engineering."

Security Governance Principles

Corporate governance is the system by which organizations are directed and controlled. Governance structures and principles identify the distribution of rights and responsibilities. As applied to information cybersecurity, governance is the responsibility of leadership to

- Determine and articulate the organization's desired state of security.
- Provide the strategic direction, resources, funding, and support to ensure that the desired state of security can be achieved and sustained.
- Maintain responsibility and accountability through oversight.

Organizations should use security governance principles to ensure that all organizational assets are protected. Organizations often use best practices that are established by organizations, such as the National Institute of Standards and Technology (NIST), Information Technology Infrastructure Library (ITIL), or the

ISO/IEC 27000 family of standards. Because information technology is an operational necessity, management must take an active role in any security governance initiative. In fact, more and more privacy regulations provide guidance on the responsibilities of management in information security.

Security governance assigns rights and uses an accountability framework to ensure appropriate decision-making. It must ensure that the framework used is aligned with the business strategy. Security governance gives directions, establishes standards and principles, and prioritizes investments. It is the responsibility of the organization's board of directors and executive management.

The IT Governance Institute (ITGI) issued the *Board Briefing on IT Governance*, 2nd Edition, which is available from the Information Systems Audit and Control Association's (ISACA's) website. It provides the following definition for IT governance:

> *IT governance is the responsibility of the board of directors and executive management. It is an integral part of enterprise governance and consists of the leadership and organizational structures and processes that ensure that the organization's IT sustains and extends the organization's strategies and objectives.*

According to this publication, IT governance covers strategic alignment, value delivery, risk management, resource management, and performance measurement. It includes checklists and tools to help an organization's board of directors and executive management ensure IT governance.

Security governance principles include security function alignment, organizational processes, organizational roles and responsibilities, security control frameworks, and due care and due diligence.

Security Function Alignment

The security function must align with the business strategy, goals, mission, and objectives of the organization. Every information security decision must be informed by organizational goals and be in alignment with strategic objectives. When strategically aligned, security functions as a business enabler that adds value.

It is critical that organizations implement a threat modeling program (which we discuss later in this chapter), continually reassess the threat environment, including new adversaries, and proactively adapt their information security program.

Organizational Strategies and Goals

The organizational security strategy and goals must be documented. Security management protects organizational assets using physical, administrative, and logical controls. Although management is responsible for the development of the organization's security strategy, security professionals within the organization are responsible for carrying it out. Therefore, security professionals should be involved in the development of the organizational security strategy and goals.

A strategy is a plan of action or a policy designed to achieve a major or overall aim. Goals are the desired results from the security plan. A security management team must address all areas of security, including protecting personnel, physical assets, and data, when designing the organization's security strategy and goals. The strategy and goals should change over time as the organization grows and changes and the world changes too. Years ago, organizations did not need to worry about their data being stolen over the Internet. But today, the Internet is one of the most popular mediums used to illegally obtain confidential organizational data.

Organizational Mission and Objectives

The organization's mission and objectives should already be adopted and established by organizational management and the board of directors. However, they can also be revised based on decisions made by the board of directors or management. An organization's security management team must ensure that any security strategy and goals fit with the mission and objectives of the organization. Information and the assets that support the organization's mission must be protected as part of the security strategy and goals. Senior management must ultimately determine whether the organization's security strategy aligns and compliments its business goals, while providing the necessary resources for its security strategy. The board of directors provides oversight for the organization's security and business strategy. For some companies in certain industries, the board of directors is required to review an organization's cybersecurity policy, such as New York State Department of Financial Services, 23 NYCRR 500.

The appropriate policies, procedures, standards, and guidelines must be implemented to ensure that organizational risk is kept within acceptable levels. Security professionals will advise management on organizational risks. Organizational risk is also affected by government and industrial regulations, which may force an organization to implement certain measures that they had not planned. Weighing the risks to the organization and choosing whether to implement security controls are ultimately the job of senior management.

Security management ensures that risks are identified and adequate controls are implemented to mitigate the risks, all within the context of supporting the organizational mission and objectives.

Business Case

A ***business case*** is a formal document that gives the reasons behind an organizational project or initiative and usually includes financial justification for a project or an initiative. The security management team should develop a formal business case for the overall security assessment of an organization. After the organization's security assessment is complete and its business case has been created, management will decide how to proceed.

At that point, other business cases for individual security projects will need to be developed. For example, if management wants the security management team to ensure that the organization's internal network is protected from attacks, the security management team may draft a business case that explains the devices that need to be implemented to meet this goal. This business case may include firewalls, intrusion detection systems (IDSs), endpoint detection and response (EDR), access control lists (ACLs), and other devices, and it should detail how these systems will provide protection.

Security Budget, Metrics, and Efficacy

The chief security officer (CSO), chief information security officer (CISO), or other designated high-level manager prepares the organization's security budget, determines the security metrics, and reports on the efficacy of the security program. This officer must work with other subject matter experts (SMEs) to ensure that all security costs are accounted for, including development, testing, implementation, maintenance, personnel, and equipment. The budgeting process requires an examination of all risks and ensures that security projects with this best cost/benefit ratio are implemented. Projects that take longer than 12–18 months are long term and strategic and require more resources and funding to complete.

Security metrics provide information on both short- and long-term trends. By collecting these metrics and comparing them on a daily basis, security professionals can determine the daily workload. When the metrics are compared over a longer period of time, the trends that occur can help to shape future security projects and budgets. Procedures should state who will collect the metrics, which metrics will be collected, when the metrics will be collected, and what the thresholds are that will trigger corrective actions. Security professionals should consult with the information security governance frameworks listed later in this chapter, particularly ISO/IEC 27004:2016 and NIST 800-55 Rev. 2, for help in establishing metrics guidelines and procedures.

Although the security team should analyze metrics on a daily basis, periodic analysis of the metrics by a third party can ensure the integrity and efficacy of the security metrics by verifying the results of the internal team. Data from the third party should be used to improve the security program and security metrics process.

Resources

If the appropriate resources are not allocated to an organization's security function, even the best-laid security plans tend to fail. These resources include, but are not limited to, security personnel, devices, and controls. As discussed in the "Security Budget, Metrics, and Efficacy" section, resource allocation is limited based on the security budget. Risk analysis helps an organization determine which security resources are most important and which are not necessary. But keep in mind that as the security function of the organization is constantly changing, so should the resource allocation to the security function change as needed. What may have been cost-prohibitive last year may become a necessity this year, and what may have been a necessity a few years ago may now be considered outdated and may not provide the level of protection needed. For this reason, security professionals should continuously revisit the risk analysis process to determine what improvements can be made in the security function of an organization.

Security professionals should also understand what personnel resources are needed to support any security function. Resources may include, but are not limited to, data owners, system administrators, network administrators, IT technicians, software developers, law enforcement, and accounting officers. The size of the organization will often influence the availability of resources to any organizational security function. Security professionals should work to build relationships with all personnel resources to ensure a successful security program.

Organizational Processes

To understand organizational processes, organizations must determine the work needed to accomplish a goal, assign those tasks to individuals, and arrange those individuals into a decision-making organizational structure. The end result of documenting the processes is an organization that consists of unified parts acting in harmony to execute tasks to achieve goals. But all organizations go through periods of growth and decline. Often during these periods, organizations will go through acquisitions, mergers, and divestitures. In addition, governance committees will be formed to help improve the organization and its processes.

Acquisitions and Divestitures

An acquisition occurs when one organization takes over another organization. This situation may be friendly or hostile. A merger occurs when two organizations come together to form one entity.

Security professionals should bring several considerations to the attention of management to ensure that organizational security does not suffer as a result of an acquisition or a merger. The other organization may have new data and technology types that may need more protection than is currently provided. For example, the acquired organization may allow personnel to bring their own devices and use them on the network. Although a common reaction may be to just implement the same policy as in the current organization, security professionals should assess why the personal devices are allowed and how ingrained this capability is in the organization's culture.

Another acquisition or merger consideration for security professionals is that the staff at the other organization may not have the appropriate security awareness training. If training has not been given, it may be imperative that security awareness training be deployed as soon as possible to the staff of the acquired company.

When acquisitions or mergers occur, usually a percentage of personnel are not retained. Security professionals should understand any threats from former personnel and any new threats that may arise due to the acquisition or merger. Security professionals must understand these threats so they can develop plans to mitigate the threats. Access control therefore becomes a key consideration. Employee terminations, or layoffs, should include a plan for terminating access to computer systems and physical facilities.

As part of a merger or acquisition, technology is usually integrated. This integration can present vulnerabilities that the organization would not have otherwise faced. For example, if an acquired company maintains a legacy system because personnel need it, the acquiring organization may need to take measures to protect the legacy system or to deploy a new system that will replace it.

Finally, with an acquisition or a merger, new laws, regulations, and standards may need to be implemented across the entire new entity. Relationships with business partners, vendors, and other entities also need to be reviewed. Security professionals must ensure that they properly advise management about any security issues that may arise.

A divestiture, which is the opposite of an acquisition, occurs when part of an organization is sold off or separated from the original organization. A divestiture impacts personnel because usually a portion of the personnel goes with the divestiture.

As with acquisitions, with divestitures, security professionals should bring certain considerations to the attention of management to ensure that organizational security does not suffer. Data leakage may occur as a result of exiting personnel. Personnel who have been laid off as a result of the divestiture are of particular concern. Tied to this is the fact that the exiting personnel have access rights to organizational assets.

These access rights must be removed at the appropriate time, while protocols and ports that are no longer needed should be removed or closed.

Security professionals should also consider where the different security resources and controls will end up. If security assets are part of the divestiture, steps should be taken to ensure that replacements are implemented prior to the divestiture, if needed. In addition, policies and procedures should be reviewed to ensure that they reflect the new organization's needs.

Whether an organization is going through an acquisition, a merger, or a divestiture, it is vital that security professionals be proactive to protect all organizations involved.

Governance Committees

A governance committee recruits and recommends members of an organization's governing board (e.g., board of directors or trustees). The governance committee should be encouraged to include select board members or individuals who understand information security and risks among the board members.

A board committee (generally the audit or enterprise risk management committee) is generally tasked with the oversight of information security. Management-level security professionals should make themselves available for briefings and establish a direct line of communication with the designated committee.

Organizational Roles and Responsibilities

Although all organizations have layers of responsibility within the organization, information security is generally considered the responsibility of everyone in the organization. The following sections cover the responsibilities of the different roles within an organization.

Board of Directors

An organization's board of directors includes individuals who are nominated by a governance committee and elected by shareholders to ensure that the organization is run properly. The loyalty of the board of directors should be to the shareholders, not high-level management. Members of the board of directors should maintain their independence from all organizational personnel, especially if the Sarbanes-Oxley (SOX) Act or Gramm-Leach-Bliley Act (GLBA) applies to the organization.

NOTE Regulations that are pertinent to the CISSP exam are discussed later in this chapter. Keep in mind that for testing purposes, security professionals need to understand only the types of organizations and data that these laws affect.

Senior officials, including the board of directors and senior management, must perform their duties with the care that ordinary, prudent people would exercise in similar circumstances. This is known as the prudent-man rule. Due care and due diligence, discussed later in this chapter, also affect members of the board of directors and high-level management.

Management

High-level management has the ultimate responsibility for preserving and protecting organizational data. High-level management includes the CEO, CFO, CIO, CPO, and CSO. Other management levels, including business unit managers and business operations managers, also have security responsibilities.

The chief executive officer (CEO) is the highest managing officer in any organization and reports directly to the shareholders. The CEO must ensure that an organization grows and prospers.

The chief financial officer (CFO) is the officer responsible for all financial aspects of an organization. Although structurally the CFO might report directly to the CEO, the CFO must also provide financial data for the shareholders and government entities. Financial data must conform to the CIA triad.

The chief information officer (CIO) is the officer responsible for all information systems and technology used in the organization and reports directly to the CEO or CFO. The CIO usually drives the effort to protect company assets, including any organizational security program.

The chief privacy officer (CPO) is the officer responsible for private information and usually reports directly to the CIO. As a newer position, this role is still considered optional but is becoming increasingly important, especially in organizations that handle lots of private information, including healthcare companies, insurance companies, and financial institutions. The title and position of data protection officer (DPO), which is equivalent to CPO, has become more important, especially with the introduction of privacy legislation, such as the General Data Protection Regulation (GDPR).

The chief security officer (CSO) is the officer who leads any security effort and reports directly to the CEO. Although this role is considered optional, this role must solely be focused on security matters. Its independence from all other roles must be maintained to ensure that the organization's security is always the focus of the CSO. This role designs and manages all aspects of security, including risk analysis, security policies and procedures, incident handling, security awareness training, and emerging technologies. While CSOs do not carry out the implementation, they are held responsible for such implementation.

Security professionals should ensure that all risks are communicated to executive management and the board of directors, if necessary. Executive management should maintain a balance between acceptable risk and business operations. Although executive management is not concerned with the details of any security implementations, the costs or benefits of any security implementation and any residual risk after such implementation will be vital in ensuring their buy-in to the implementation.

Business unit managers provide departmental information to ensure that appropriate controls are in place for departmental data. Often business unit managers are classified as the data owner for their business units. Some business unit managers have security duties. For example, the human resources department manager would be best suited to oversee all human resources policies and all devices that store human resources data.

Audit Committee

An audit committee evaluates an organization's financial reporting mechanism to ensure that financial data is accurate. It may also be tasked with cybersecurity risk. This committee performs an internal audit and engages independent auditors as needed. Members of this committee must participate in continuing education on a regular basis to ensure that they can oversee financial reporting and enforce accountability in the financial processes.

Data Owner

The main responsibility of the data or information owners is to determine the classification level of the information they own and to protect the data for which they are responsible. This role approves or denies access rights to the data. However, data owners usually do not handle the implementation of the data access controls. Ultimately, the CEO of an organization is the data owner for the organization.

The data owner role is usually filled by an individual who understands the data best through membership in a particular business unit. Each business unit should have a data owner. For example, a human resources department employee better understands human resources data than an accounting department employee.

Data Custodian

The data custodian implements the information classification and controls after they are determined by the data owner. Although the data owner is usually an individual who understands the data, the data custodian does not need any knowledge of the data beyond its classification levels. Although a human resources manager should be the data owner for the human resources data, an IT department member could act as the data custodian for the data.

System Owner

A system owner owns one or more systems and must ensure that the appropriate controls are in place on those systems. Although a system has a single system owner, multiple data owners can be responsible for the information on the system. Therefore, system owners must be able to manage the needs of multiple data owners and implement the appropriate procedures to ensure that the data is secured.

System Administrator

A system administrator performs the day-to-day administration of one or more systems. These day-to-day duties include adding and removing system users and installing system software and creating baselines.

Security Administrator

A security administrator maintains security devices and software, including firewalls, antivirus software, and so on. The main focus of the security administrator is security, whereas the main focus of a system administrator is the system availability and the main focus of the network administrator is network availability. The security administrator reviews all security audit data and implements appropriate and recommended countermeasures if any.

Security Analyst

A security analyst analyzes the security needs of the organization and develops the internal information security governance documents, including policies, standards, and guidelines. The role focuses on the design of security, not its implementation.

Application Owner

An application owner determines the personnel who can access an application. Because most applications are owned by a single department, business department managers usually fill this role. However, the application owner does not necessarily perform the day-to-day administration of the application. This responsibility can be delegated to a member of the IT staff, depending on the technical skills needed.

Supervisor

A supervisor manages a group of users and any assets owned by this group. Supervisors must immediately communicate any personnel role changes that affect security to the security administrator.

User

A user is any person who accesses data to perform their job duties. Users should understand any security procedures and policies for the data to which they have access. Supervisors are responsible for ensuring that users have the appropriate access rights.

Auditor

An auditor monitors user activities to ensure that the appropriate controls are in place. Auditors also make sure that the controls that are in place are functioning as intended. Auditors need access to all audit and event logs to verify compliance with security policies. Both internal and external auditors can be used.

Key Topic

Security Control Frameworks

Many organizations have developed security management frameworks and methodologies to help guide security professionals. These frameworks and methodologies include security program development standards, enterprise and security architect development frameworks, security control development methods, corporate governance methods, and process management methods. Frameworks, standards, and methodologies are often discussed together because they are related. ***Standards*** are accepted as best practices, whereas *frameworks* are practices that are generally employed. Standards are specific, while frameworks are general. Methodologies are a system of practices, techniques, procedures, and rules used by those who work in a discipline. Here, we cover all three as they relate to security controls.

The following sections discuss these frameworks and methodologies and explain where they are used:

- ISO/IEC 27000 Series
- Zachman Framework

- TOGAF
- DoDAF
- MODAF
- SABSA
- COBIT
- NIST 800 Series
- HITRUST CSF
- CIS Critical Security Controls
- COSO
- OCTAVE
- ITIL
- Six Sigma
- CMMI
- CRAMM
- FedRAMP
- PCI DSS
- Top-down versus bottom-up approach
- Security program life cycle

NOTE Organizations should select the framework, standard, and/or methodology that represents the organization in the most useful manner, based on the needs of the stakeholders.

ISO/IEC 27000 Series

The International Organization for Standardization (ISO), often incorrectly referred to as the International Standards Organization, joined with the International Electrotechnical Commission (IEC) to standardize the British Standard 7799 (BS7799) to a new global standard that is now referred to as the ISO/IEC 27000 Series. Although technically not a framework, ISO 27000 is a security program development standard on how to develop and maintain an information security management system (ISMS).

The 27000 Series includes a list of standards, each of which addresses a particular aspect of ISMSs. These standards are either published or are in development. The following standards are included as part of the ISO/IEC 27000 Series at the time of this writing:

- **27000:2018:** Published overview of ISMSs and vocabulary
- **27001:2022:** Published ISMS requirements
- **27002:2022:** Published code of practice for information security controls
- **27003:2017:** Published guidance on the requirements for an ISMS
- **27004:2016:** Published ISMS monitoring, measurement, analysis, and evaluation guidelines
- **27005:2022:** Published information security risk management guidelines
- **27006:2015:** Published requirements for bodies providing audit and certification of ISMS
- **27007:2020:** Published ISMS auditing guidelines
- **27008:2019:** Published guidelines for the assessment of information security controls
- **27009:2020:** Published sector-specific application of ISO/IEC 27001 guidelines
- **27010:2015:** Published information security management for inter-sector and inter-organizational communications guidelines
- **27011:2016:** Published telecommunications organizations' information security management guidelines
- **27013:2021:** Published integrated implementation of ISO/IEC 27001 and ISO/IEC 20000-1 guidance
- **27014:2020:** Published information security governance guidelines
- **27016:2014:** Published ISMS organizational economics guidelines
- **27017:2015:** Published code of practice for information security controls based on ISO/IEC 27002 for cloud services
- **27018:2019:** Published code of practice for protection of personally identifiable information (PII) in public clouds acting as PII processors
- **27019:2017:** Published information security controls for the energy utility industry guidelines

- **27021:2017:** Published competence requirements for information security management systems professionals
- **27022:2021:** Published information security management system processes
- **27023:2015:** Published mapping of the revised editions of ISO/IEC 27001 and ISO/IEC 27002
- **27031:2011:** Published information and communication technology readiness for business continuity guidelines
- **27032:2023:** Published cybersecurity guidelines
- **27033-1:2015:** Published network security overview and concepts
- **27033-2:2012:** Published network security design and implementation guidelines
- **27033-3:2010:** Published network security threats, design techniques, and control issues guidelines
- **27033-4:2014:** Published securing communications between networks using security gateways
- **27033-5:2013:** Published securing communications across networks using virtual private networks (VPNs)
- **27033-6:2016:** Published securing wireless IP network access
- **27034-1:2011:** Published application security overview and concepts
- **27034-2:2015:** Published application security organization normative framework guidelines
- **27034-3:2018:** Published application security management process guidelines
- **27034-5:2018:** Published application security protocols and controls data structure guidelines
- **27034-6:2016:** Published case studies for application security
- **27034-7:2018:** Published assurance prediction framework
- **27035-1:2023:** Published information security incident management principles
- **27035-2:2016:** Published information security incident response readiness guidelines
- **27035-3:2020:** Published ICT incident response operations guidelines

- **27036-1:2021:** Published information security for supplier relationships overview and concepts
- **27036-2:2014:** Published information security for supplier relationships common requirements guidelines
- **27036-3:2023:** Published information and communication technology (ICT) supply chain security guidelines
- **27036-4:2016:** Published guidelines for security of cloud services
- **27037:2012:** Published digital evidence identification, collection, acquisition, and preservation guidelines
- **27038:2014:** Published information security digital redaction specification
- **27039:2015:** Published IDS selection, deployment, and operations guidelines
- **27040:2015:** Published storage security guidelines
- **27041:2015:** Published guidance on assuring suitability and adequacy of incident investigative method
- **27042:2015:** Published digital evidence analysis and interpretation guidelines
- **27043:2015:** Published incident investigation principles and processes
- **27050-1:2019:** Published electronic discovery (eDiscovery) overview and concepts
- **27050-2:2018:** Published guidance for governance and management of electronic discovery
- **27050-3:2020:** Published code of practice for electronic discovery
- **27050-4:2021:** Published technical readiness

These standards are developed by the ISO/IEC bodies, but certification or conformity assessment is provided by third parties.

NOTE The numbers after the colon for each standard stand for the year that the standard was published. You can find more information regarding ISO standards at www.iso.org. All ISO standards are copyrighted and must be purchased to obtain detailed information in the standards.

Zachman Framework

The ***Zachman Framework***, an enterprise architecture framework, is a two-dimensional classification system based on six communication questions (What, Where, When, Why, Who, and How) that intersect with different perspectives (Executive, Business Management, Architect, Engineer, Technician, and Enterprise). This system allows analysis of an organization to be presented to different groups in the organization in ways that relate to the groups' responsibilities. Although this framework is not security oriented, using this framework helps you relay information for personnel in a language and format that are most useful to them.

The Open Group Architecture Framework (TOGAF)

The Open Group Architecture Framework (TOGAF), another enterprise architecture framework, helps organizations design, plan, implement, and govern an enterprise information architecture. TOGAF is based on four interrelated domains: technology, applications, data, and business.

Department of Defense Architecture Framework (DoDAF)

The Department of Defense Architecture Framework (DoDAF) is an architecture framework that organizes a set of products under eight views: all viewpoint (required) (AV), capability viewpoint (CV), data and information viewpoint (DIV), operation viewpoint (OV), project viewpoint (PV), services viewpoint (SvcV), standards viewpoint (STDV), and systems viewpoint (SV). It is used to ensure that new DoD technologies integrate properly with the current infrastructures.

British Ministry of Defence Architecture Framework (MODAF)

The British Ministry of Defence Architecture Framework, or MODAF, is an architecture framework that divides information into seven viewpoints: strategic viewpoint (StV), operational viewpoint (OV), service-oriented viewpoint (SOV), systems viewpoint (SV), acquisition viewpoint (AcV), technical viewpoint (TV), and all viewpoint (AV).

Sherwood Applied Business Security Architecture (SABSA)

The Sherwood Applied Business Security Architecture (SABSA) is an enterprise security architecture framework that is similar to the Zachman Framework. It uses the six communication questions (What, Where, When, Why, Who, and How) that intersect with six layers (operational, component, physical, logical, conceptual, and contextual). It is a risk-driven architecture. See Table 1-1.

Table 1-1 SABSA Framework Matrix

Viewpoint	Layer	Assets (What)	Motivation (Why)	Process (How)	People (Who)	Location (Where)	Time (When)
Business	Contextual	Business	Risk model	Process model	Organizations and relationships	Geography	Time dependencies
Architect	Conceptual	Business attributes profile	Control objectives	Security strategies and architectural layering	Security entity model and trust framework	Security domain model	Security-related lifetimes and deadlines
Designer	Logical	Business information model	Security policies	Security services	Entity schema and privilege profiles	Security domain definitions and associations	Security processing cycle
Builder	Physical	Business data model	Security rules, practices, and procedures	Security mechanism	Users, applications, and interfaces	Platform and network infrastructure	Control structure execution
Tradesman	Component	Detailed data structures	Security standards	Security tools and products	Identities, functions, actions, and ACLs	Processes, nodes, addresses, and protocols	Security step timing and sequencing
Facilities Manager	Operational	Operational continuity assurance	Operation risk management	Security service management and support	Application and user management and support	Site, network, and platform security	Security operations schedule

Control Objectives for Information and Related Technology (COBIT)

Control Objectives for Information and Related Technology (COBIT) 5 is a security controls development framework that documents five principles:

- Meeting stakeholder needs
- Covering the enterprise end-to-end
- Applying a single integrated framework
- Enabling a holistic approach
- Separating governance from management

These five principles drive control objectives categorized into seven enablers:

- Principles, policies, and frameworks
- Processes
- Organizational structures
- Culture, ethics, and behavior
- Information
- Services, infrastructure, and applications
- People, skills, and competencies

It also covers the 37 governance and management processes that are needed for enterprise IT.

National Institute of Standards and Technology (NIST) Special Publication (SP) 800 Series

The National Institute of Standards and Technology (NIST) 800 Series is a set of documents that describe U.S. federal government computer security policies, procedures, and guidelines. Although NIST publications are written to provide guidance to U.S. government agencies, other organizations can and often do use them. Each Special Publication (SP) within the series defines a specific area. Some of the publications included as part of the NIST 800 Series at the time of this writing are as follows:

- **SP 800-12 Rev. 1:** Introduces information security principles.
- **SP 800-16 Rev. 1:** Describes information technology/cybersecurity role-based training for federal departments, agencies, and organizations.

- **SP 800-18 Rev. 1:** Provides guidelines for developing security plans for federal information systems.
- **SP 800-30 Rev. 1:** Provides guidance for conducting risk assessments of federal information systems and organizations, amplifying the guidance in SP 800-39.
- **SP 800-34 Rev. 1:** Provides guidelines on the purpose, process, and format of information system contingency planning development.
- **SP 800-35:** Provides assistance with selecting, implementing, and managing IT security services through the IT security services life cycle.
- **SP 800-37 Rev. 2:** Provides guidelines for applying the risk management framework to federal information systems.
- **SP 800-39:** Provides guidance for an integrated, organization-wide program for managing information security risk.
- **SP 800-50:** Identifies the four critical steps in the IT security awareness and training life cycle: (1) awareness and training program design; (2) awareness and training material development; (3) program implementation; and (4) post-implementation. It is a companion publication to NIST SP 800-16 Rev. 1.
- **SP 800-53 Rev. 5:** Provides a catalog of security and privacy controls for federal information systems and a process for selecting controls.
- **SP 800-53A Rev. 4:** Provides a set of procedures for conducting assessments of security controls and privacy controls employed within federal information systems.
- **SP 800-55 Rev. 1:** Provides guidance on how to use metrics to determine the adequacy of in-place security controls, policies, and procedures.
- **SP 800-60 Vol. 1 Rev. 1:** Provides guidelines for mapping types of information and information systems to security categories.
- **SP 800-61 Rev. 2:** Provides guidelines for incident handling.
- **SP 800-82 Rev. 2:** Provides guidance on how to secure Industrial Control Systems (ICS), including Supervisory Control and Data Acquisition (SCADA) systems, Distributed Control Systems (DCSs), and other control system configurations, such as Programmable Logic Controllers (PLCs) (Rev. 3 pending).
- **SP 800-84:** Provides guidance on designing, developing, conducting, and evaluating test, training, and exercise (TT&E) events.
- **SP 800-86:** Provides guidelines for integrating forensic techniques into incident response.

- **SP 800-88 Rev. 1:** Provides guidelines for media sanitization.
- **SP 800-92:** Provides guidelines for computer security log management.
- **SP 800-101 Rev. 1:** Provides guidelines on mobile device forensics.
- **SP 800-115:** Provides guidelines for information security testing and assessment.
- **SP 800-122:** Provides guidelines for protecting the confidentiality of PII.
- **SP 800-123:** Provides guidelines for general server security.
- **SP 800-124 Rev. 2:** Provides guidelines for securing mobile devices.
- **SP 800-137:** Provides guidelines for an Information Security Continuous Monitoring (ISCM) program.
- **SP 800-144:** Provides guidelines on security and privacy in public cloud computing.
- **SP 800-145:** Provides the NIST definition of cloud computing.
- **SP 800-146:** Describes cloud computing benefits and issues, presents an overview of major classes of cloud technology, and provides guidelines on how organizations should consider cloud computing.
- **SP 800-150:** Provides guidelines for establishing and participating in cyber threat information-sharing relationships.
- **SP 800-153:** Provides guidelines for securing wireless local-area networks (WLANs).
- **SP 800-154 (Draft):** Provides guidelines on data-centric system threat modeling.
- **SP 800-160 Vol. 1:** Provides guidelines on a multidisciplinary approach in the engineering of trustworthy secure systems.
- **SP 800-160 Vol. 2:** Provides guidelines on system security engineering.
- **SP 800-161 Rev. 1:** Provides guidance to federal agencies on identifying, assessing, and mitigating information and communication technology (ICT) supply chain risks at all levels of their organizations.
- **SP 800-162:** Defines attribute-based access control (ABAC) and its considerations.
- **SP 800-163 Rev. 1:** Provides guidelines on vetting the security of mobile applications.

- **SP 800-164:** Provides guidelines on hardware-rooted security in mobile devices.
- **SP 800-167:** Provides guidelines on application whitelisting.
- **SP 800-175A and 175B Rev. 1:** Provide guidelines for using cryptographic standards in the federal government.
- **SP 800-181 Rev. 1:** Describes the National Initiative for Cybersecurity Education (NICE) Cybersecurity Workforce Framework (NICE Framework).
- **SP 800-183:** Describes the Internet of Things (IoT).

NOTE For many of the SPs in the preceding list, you simply need to know that the SP exists. For some, you need to understand details about the SP. Those NIST SPs are covered in more detail later in this chapter or in other chapters. Refer to the index in this book to determine which SPs are covered in more detail.

HITRUST CSF

HITRUST is a privately held U.S. company that works with healthcare, technology, and information security leaders to establish the ***HITRUST Common Security Framework (CSF)*** that can be used by all organizations that create, access, store, or exchange sensitive and/or regulated data. It was written to address the requirements of multiple regulations and standards. Version 9.4.2 was released in December 2020. It is primarily used in the healthcare industry.

This framework has 14 control categories:

0.0: Information Security Management Program

1.0: Access Control

2.0: Human Resources Security

3.0: Risk Management

4.0: Security Policy

5.0: Organization of Information Security

6.0: Compliance

7.0: Asset Management

8.0: Physical and Environmental Security

9.0: Communications and Operations Management

10.0: Information Systems Acquisition, Development, and Maintenance

11.0: Information Security Incident Management

12.0: Business Continuity Management

13.0: Privacy Practices

Within each control category, objectives are defined and assigned levels based on their compliance with documented control standards.

CIS Critical Security Controls

The Center for Internet Security (CIS) released Critical Security Controls that lists 18 CIS controls. The first 5 controls eliminate the vast majority of an organization's vulnerabilities. Implementing all 20 controls will secure an entire organization against today's most pervasive threats. The 18 controls are as follows:

CIS Control 1: Inventory and Control of Enterprise Assets

CIS Control 2: Inventory and Control of Software Assets

CIS Control 3: Data Protection

CIS Control 4: Secure Configuration of Enterprise Assets and Software

CIS Control 5: Account Management

CIS Control 6: Access Control Management

CIS Control 7: Continuous Vulnerability Management

CIS Control 8: Audit Log Management

CIS Control 9: Email Web Browser and Protections

CIS Control 10: Malware Defenses

CIS Control 11: Data Recovery

CIS Control 12: Network Infrastructure Management

CIS Control 13: Network Monitoring and Defense

CIS Control 14: Security Awareness and Skills Training

CIS Control 15: Service Provider Management

CIS Control 16: Application Software Security

CIS Control 17: Incident Response Management

CIS Control 18: Penetration Testing

The CIS Critical Security Controls provide a mapping of these controls to known standards, frameworks, laws, and regulations.

Committee of Sponsoring Organizations (COSO) of the Treadway Commission Framework

Committee of Sponsoring Organizations (COSO) is a corporate governance framework that consists of five interrelated components: control environment, risk assessment, control activities, information and communication, and monitoring activities. COBIT was derived from the COSO framework. COSO is for corporate governance; COBIT is for IT governance.

Operationally Critical Threat, Asset, and Vulnerability Evaluation (OCTAVE)

Operationally Critical Threat, Asset, and Vulnerability Evaluation, or OCTAVE, which was developed by Carnegie Mellon University's Software Engineering Institute, provides a suite of tools, techniques, and methods for risk-based information security strategic assessment and planning. Using OCTAVE, an organization implements small teams across business units and IT to work together to address the organization's security needs. Figure 1-3 shows the phases and processes of OCTAVE Allegro.

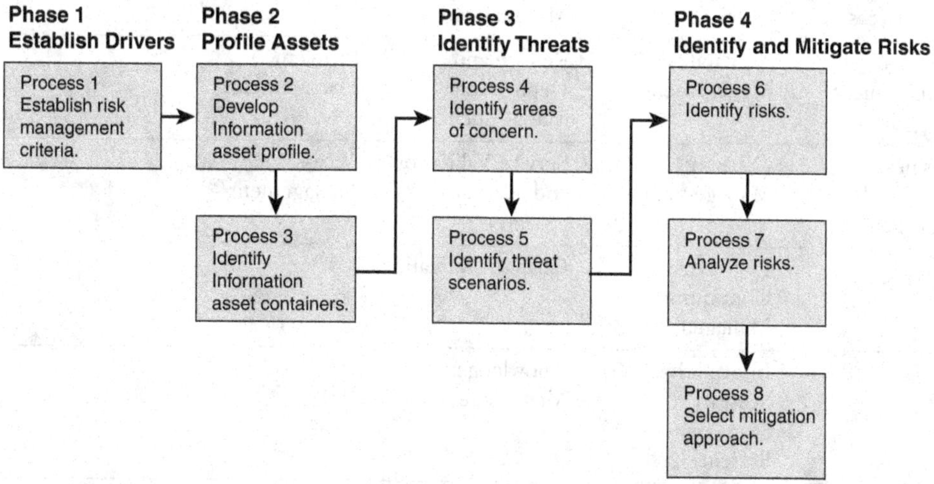

Figure 1-3 OCTAVE Allegro Phases and Processes

Information Technology Infrastructure Library (ITIL)

Information Technology Infrastructure Library (ITIL) is a set of best practices for the management of IT services, while aligning those services with business goals. ITIL has five core publications: ITIL Service Strategy, ITIL Service Design, ITIL Service Transition, ITIL Service Operation, and ITIL Continual Service Improvement. These five core publications contain 26 processes. Although ITIL has a security component, it is primarily concerned with managing the service-level agreements (SLAs) between an IT department or organization and its customers. As part of the OMB Circular A-130, an independent review of security controls should be performed every three years.

Table 1-2 lists the five ITIL version 3 core publications and the 26 processes within them.

Table 1-2 ITIL v3 Core Publications and Processes

ITIL Service Strategy	ITIL Service Design	ITIL Service Transition	ITIL Service Operation	ITIL Continual Service Improvement
Strategy Management	Design Coordination	Transition Planning and Support	Event Management	Continual Service Improvement
Service Portfolio Management	Service Catalogue	Change Management	Incident Management	
Financial Management for IT Services	Service-Level Management	Service Asset and Configuration Management	Request Fulfillment	
Demand Management	Availability Management	Release and Deployment Management	Problem Management	
Business Relationship Management	Capacity Management	Service Validation and Testing	Access Management	
	IT Service Continuity Management	Change Evaluation		
	Information Security Management System	Knowledge Management		
	Supplier Management			

Six Sigma

Six Sigma is a process improvement standard that includes two project methodologies that were inspired by Deming's Plan–Do–Check–Act cycle. The DMAIC methodology includes Define, Measure, Analyze, Improve, and Control. The DMADV methodology includes Define, Measure, Analyze, Design, and Verify. Six Sigma was designed to identify and remove defects in the manufacturing process but can be applied to many business functions, including security.

NOTE The Deming cycle is discussed in more detail later in this chapter.

Figures 1-4 and 1-5 show both of the Six Sigma methodologies.

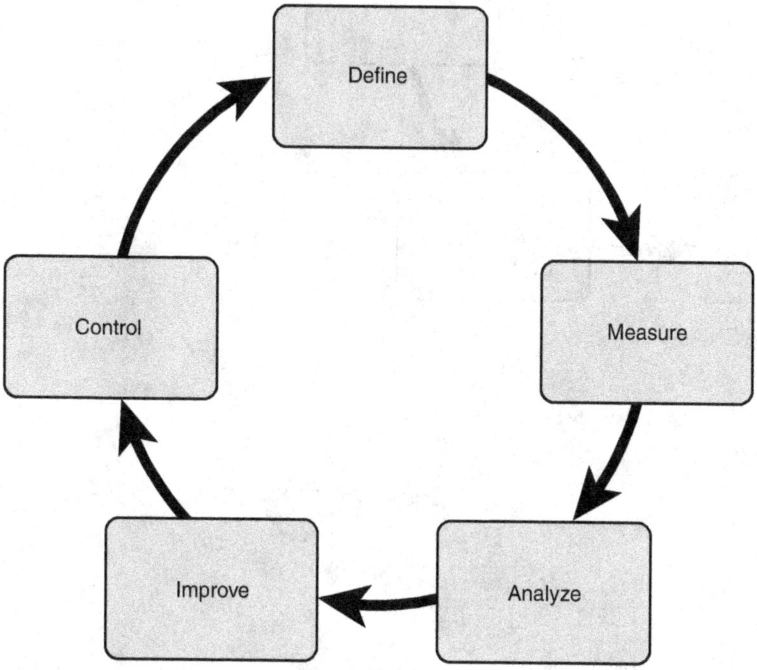

Figure 1-4 Six Sigma DMAIC

Capability Maturity Model Integration (CMMI)

Capability Maturity Model Integration (CMMI) is a process improvement approach that addresses three areas of interest: product and service development (CMMI for development), service establishment and management (CMMI for services), and product service and acquisition (CMMI for acquisitions). CMMI has five levels of maturity for processes: Level 1 Initial, Level 2 Managed, Level 3 Defined, Level 4 Quantitatively Managed, and Level 5 Optimizing. All processes within each level of interest are assigned one of the five levels of maturity. A graphic illustration of the model is displayed in Figure 1-6.

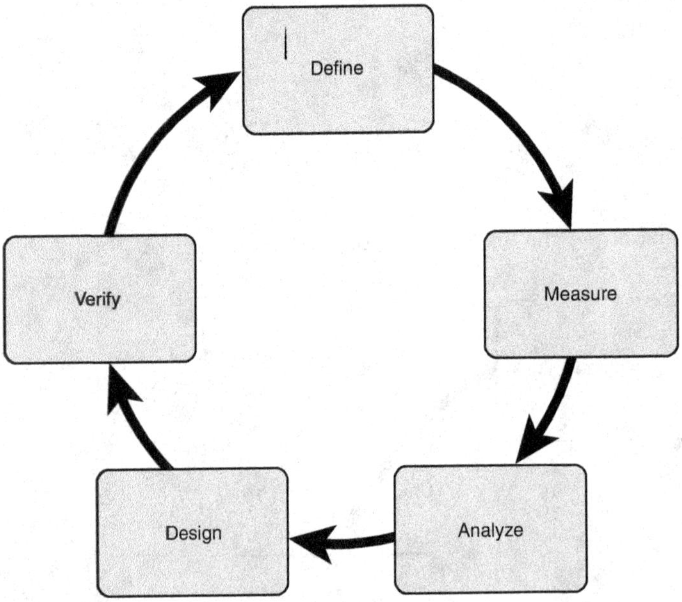

Figure 1-5 Six Sigma DMADV

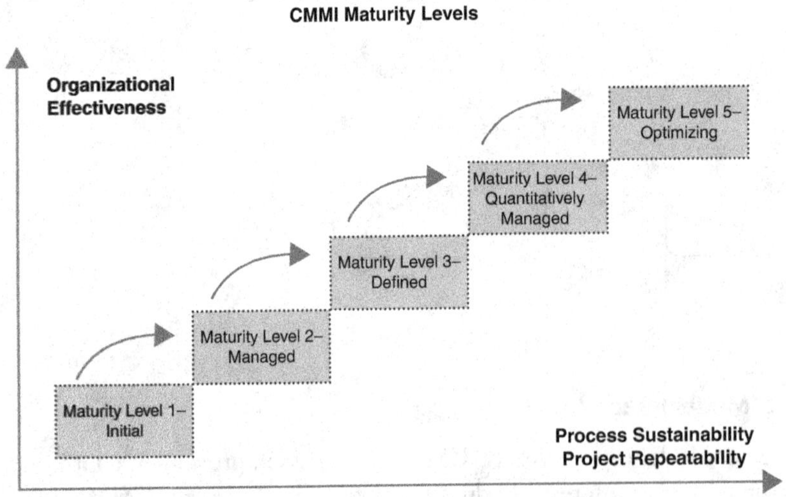

Figure 1-6 CMMI Model

CCTA Risk Analysis and Management Method (CRAMM)

CCTA Risk Analysis and Management Method, or CRAMM, is a qualitative risk analysis and management tool developed by the UK government's Central Computer and Telecommunications Agency (CCTA). A CRAMM review includes three steps:

1. Identify and value assets.
2. Identify threats and vulnerabilities and calculate risks.
3. Identify and prioritize countermeasures.

NOTE No organization will implement all of the aforementioned frameworks or methodologies. Security professionals should help their organization pick the framework that best fits the needs of the organization.

Federal Risk and Authorization Management Program (FedRAMP)

FedRAMP focuses on understanding the standards and processes for securing cloud services within the U.S. federal government context. FedRAMP is a government-wide program that standardizes the security assessment, authorization, and continuous monitoring for cloud products and services used by U.S. federal agencies. It ensures that cloud services and products meet consistent security requirements.

FedRAMP is built around a core set of security controls derived from NIST SP 800-53. CISSP professionals must be familiar with these standards and how they are applied in cloud security. FedRAMP has a detailed process for security assessment, authorization, and continuous monitoring. CISSP professionals working with cloud services in the federal space must understand these processes, including how to obtain and maintain FedRAMP authorization.

Security professionals must ensure that data handled by cloud service providers (CSPs) is protected according to FedRAMP standards, which is crucial for maintaining the confidentiality, integrity, and availability of government information stored in the cloud.

Payment Card Industry Data Security Standard (PCI DSS)

PCI DSS is a set of security standards designed to ensure that all companies that accept, process, store, or transmit credit card information maintain a secure environment. The standard is mandated by the card brands but administered by the

Payment Card Industry Security Standards Council (PCI SSC). Security professionals in companies that collect and store credit card data must understand this standard and ensure that it is implemented for the organization. It affects most of the domains of knowledge within the CISSP exam.

Security professionals must understand the principles of data privacy and protection, which are integral to PCI DSS. This includes securing cardholder data, both stored and transmitted, and ensuring that only authorized personnel have access to this sensitive information. Regular audits and assessments are key components of PCI DSS compliance. CISSP professionals are often involved in these activities to assess the security posture of their organization and to ensure adherence to PCI DSS requirements.

Top-Down Versus Bottom-Up Approach

In a top-down approach, management initiates, supports, and directs the security program. In a bottom-up approach, staff members develop a security program prior to receiving direction and support from management. A top-down approach is much more efficient than a bottom-up approach because management's support is one of the most important components of a security program.

Security Program Life Cycle

Any security program has a continuous life cycle and should be assessed and improved constantly. The security program life cycle includes the following steps:

1. **Plan and Organize:** Includes performing risk assessment, establishing management and steering committee, evaluating business drivers, and obtaining management approval.
2. **Implement:** Includes identifying and managing assets, managing risk, managing identity and access control, training on security and awareness, implementing solutions, assigning roles, and establishing goals.
3. **Operate and Maintain:** Includes performing audits, carrying out tasks, and managing SLAs.
4. **Monitor and Evaluate:** Includes reviewing auditing and logs, evaluating security goals, and developing improvement plans for integration into the Plan and Organize step (step 1).

Figure 1-7 shows a diagram of the security program life cycle.

Key Topic

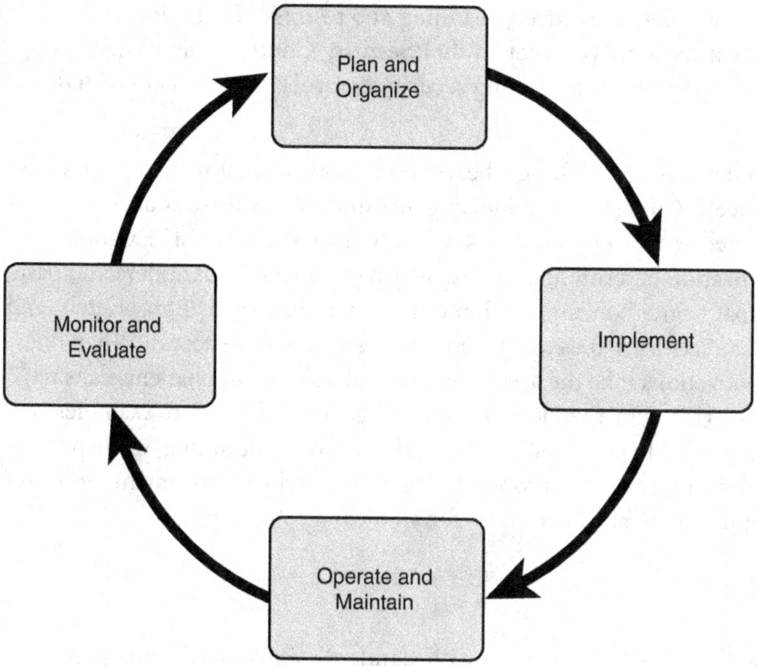

Figure 1-7 Security Program Life Cycle

Due Care and Due Diligence

Due care and *due diligence* are two related terms that organizations must understand as they relate to the security of the organization and its assets and data.

Due care is the standard of care that a prudent person would have exercised under normal conditions. In the context of security, due care means that an organization takes reasonable measures to protect its assets, systems, and supporting infrastructure. These measures include making sure that the correct policies, procedures, and standards are in place and are being followed.

Due care is all about action. Organizations must institute the appropriate protections and procedures for all organizational assets, especially intellectual property. In due care, failure to meet minimum standards and practices is considered negligent. If an organization does not take actions that a prudent person would have taken under similar circumstances, the organization is considered to have violated due care.

Due diligence is the act of investigation and assessment. Organizations must institute the appropriate procedures to determine any risks to organizational assets. Due diligence then provides the information necessary to ensure that the organization practices due care. Without adequate due diligence, due care cannot occur.

Due diligence is a process that includes but is not limited to employee background checks, business partner credit checks, system security assessments, risk assessments, penetration tests, and disaster recovery planning and testing. NIST SP 800-53 Rev. 5, discussed earlier in this chapter, in the "Security Control Frameworks" section, provides guidance for implementing security controls that will help with due diligence.

Both due care and due diligence have a bearing on the security governance and risk management process. Consequently, due diligence and due care are codependent. When due diligence occurs, organizations will recognize areas of risk. Examples include an organization determining that regular personnel do not understand basic security issues, that printed documentation is not being discarded appropriately, and that employees are accessing files to which they should not have access. When due care occurs, organizations take the areas of identified risk and implement plans to protect against the risks. For the identified due diligence and due care examples, an organization must provide personnel with security awareness training, while putting procedures into place for the proper destruction of printed documentation, and implementing appropriate access controls for all files.

Compliance

Compliance involves being in alignment with standards, guidelines, regulations, and/or legislation. An organization must comply with governmental, industrial, and applicable laws and regulations. However, compliance with standards bodies and industry associations can be considered optional in some cases although it is mandatory for contractual obligations (like Payment Card Industry Data Security Standard) and certification requirements (like ISO 27001).

All security professionals must understand security and privacy standards, guidelines, regulations, and laws. Usually, these are industry specific, meaning that the standards, guidelines, regulations, and laws are based on the type of business the organization is involved in. A great example is the healthcare industry. Due to the Health Insurance Portability and Accountability Act (HIPAA), healthcare organizations must follow regulations regarding how to collect, use, store, and protect PII. Often consideration must be given to local, regional, state, federal, and international governments and bodies.

Organizations and the security professionals that they employ must determine which rules they must comply with. An organization should adopt the strictest rules to which it must comply. If rules conflict with each other, organizations must take the time to determine which rule should take precedence. This decision could be based on data type, industry type, data collection method, data usage, or individual residence of those on whom they collect PII.

Any discussion of compliance would be incomplete without a discussion of a risk management approach, referred to as governance, risk management, and compliance (GRC). Governance covers core organizational activities, authority within the organization, organizational accountability, and performance measurement. Risk management identifies, analyzes, evaluates, and implements countermeasures and monitors risk. Compliance ensures that organizational activities comply with established rules. Each of the three separate objectives accepts input from and supplies input to the other objectives. The GRC relationship is shown in Figure 1-8.

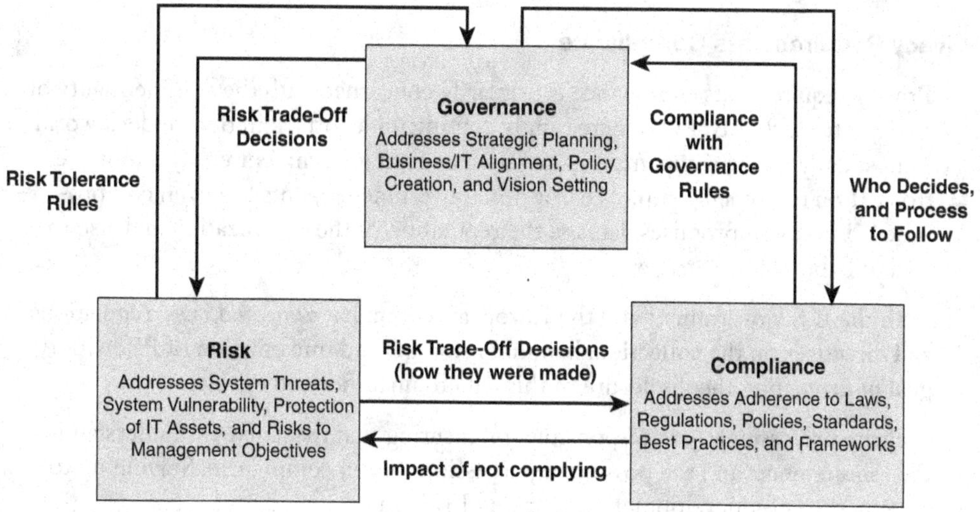

Figure 1-8 GRC Relationship

As part of the discussion of compliance, security professionals must understand legislative and regulatory compliance and privacy requirements.

Contractual, Legal, Industry Standards, and Regulatory Compliance

No organization operates within a bubble. All organizations are affected by laws, regulations, and compliance requirements. Organizations must ensure that they comply with all contracts, laws, industry standards, and regulations. Security professionals must understand the laws and regulations of the country or countries they are working in and the industry within which they operate. In many cases, laws and regulations are written in a manner whereby specific actions must be taken. However, there are cases where laws and regulations leave it up to the organization to determine how to comply.

The United States and European Union both have established laws and regulations that affect organizations that do business within their area of governance. Although security professionals should strive to understand laws and regulations, they might not have the level of knowledge and background to fully interpret these laws and regulations to protect their organization. In these cases, security professionals should work with legal representation regarding legislative or regulatory compliance.

NOTE Specific laws and regulations are discussed later, in the "Privacy" subsection of the "Legal and Regulatory Issues" section of this chapter.

Privacy Requirements Compliance

Privacy requirements compliance is primarily concerned with the confidentiality of data, particularly PII. PII is increasingly coming under attack in our modern world. Almost daily, a new company, organization, or even government entity announces that PII on customers, employees, or even government agents has been compromised. These compromises damage the reputation of the organization and also can lead to liability for damages.

Both the U.S. government and the European Union have enacted laws, regulations, and directives on the collection, handling, storage, and transmission of PII, with the goal of protecting the disclosure of this data to unauthorized entities.

Security professionals are responsible for ensuring that management understands the requirements and the possible repercussions of noncompliance. Staying up to date on the latest developments regarding PII is vital.

Legal and Regulatory Issues

The legal and regulatory issues that affect organizations today have vastly expanded with the usage of computers and networks. Gone are the days when physical security of data was the only worry. With technological advances come increasing avenues of attack. The following sections discuss computer crime concepts, major legal systems, licensing and intellectual property, cyber crimes and data breaches, import/export controls, trans-border data flow, and privacy.

Computer Crime Concepts

Computer crimes today are usually made possible by a victim's carelessness. If a computer crime has occurred, proving criminal intent and causation is often difficult. The ability to investigate and prosecute computer crimes is complicated by jurisdiction; many state-sponsored hackers reside in countries where the United States does not maintain a mutual legal assistance treaty (MLAT). An MLAT between two countries allows those countries to cooperate on law enforcement investigations, which may lead to the extradition of a criminal suspect.

Because of these computer crime issues, it is important that security professionals understand the following computer crime concepts:

Key Topic

- Computer-assisted crime
- Computer-targeted crime
- Incidental computer crime
- Computer prevalence crime
- Hackers versus crackers

Computer-Assisted Crime

A ***computer-assisted crime*** occurs when a computer is used as a tool to help commit a crime. Criminals can steal confidential organizational data in many different ways. This crime is possible without a computer. But when criminals use computers to help them steal confidential organizational data, then a computer-assisted crime has occurred.

Computer-Targeted Crime

A ***computer-targeted crime*** occurs when a computer is the victim of an attack that's sole purpose is to harm the computer and its owner. Computer crimes that fit into this category include denial-of-service (DoS) and buffer overflow attacks.

Incidental Computer Crime

An ***incidental computer crime*** occurs when a computer is involved in a computer crime without being the victim of the attack or the attacker. A computer being used as a zombie in a botnet is part of an incidental computer crime.

Computer Prevalence Crime

A ***computer prevalence crime*** occurs due to the fact that computers are so widely used in today's world. This type of crime occurs only because computers exist. Software piracy is an example of this type of crime.

Hackers Versus Crackers

Hacker and *cracker* are two terms that are often used interchangeably in media but do not actually have the same meaning. Hackers are individuals who attempt to break into secure systems to obtain knowledge about the systems and possibly use that knowledge to carry out pranks or commit crimes. Crackers, on the other hand, are individuals who attempt to break into secure systems without using the knowledge gained for any nefarious purposes.

In the security world, the terms *white hat*, *gray hat*, and *black hat* are more easily understood and less often confused than the terms *hackers* and *crackers*. A white hat does not have any malicious intent. A black hat has malicious intent. A gray hat is considered somewhere in the middle of the two. A gray hat will often try to break into a system, notify the administrator of the security hole, and may or may not offer to fix the security issues for a fee.

Computer Crime Examples

Now that you understand the different categories of computer crime and the individuals who perpetuate the crimes, it is appropriate to give some examples of computer crimes that are prevalent today.

Through social engineering tactics, hackers often scare users/victims into installing fake or rogue antivirus software on their computers. Pop-up boxes tell users that a virus infection has occurred and that by clicking the button in the pop-up box, the users can purchase and install the antivirus software to remove the virus. If users click the button, they unknowingly infect the computer with malware. Web browsers today deploy mechanisms that allow users to block pop-up messages. However, this type of mechanism has the drawback of sometimes preventing required pop-ups. Pop-ups should be disabled by default and exceptions made later when a pop-up is necessary.

Ransomware is a special category of malware that attempts to extort money out of possible victims. Ransomware generally encrypts the users' data until a payment is made to the attacker. One type of ransomware informs users that their computer or smartphone has been used for illegal activities and that a fine must be paid to prevent prosecution. In this case, the "fine" is paid to the attacker, posing as a government official or law enforcement agency. The more prevalent type of ransomware simply encrypts all files on an organization's network and demands that a ransom be paid—usually in cryptocurrency, such as Bitcoin. After the ransom has been paid, a key is sent to the organization to decrypt files on the computers. Ransomware has become so sophisticated that it can check for backups on a network and may also encrypt backed-up files.

Scareware is a category of software that attempts to scare users. Generally, this type of attack uses a banner on a website that warns users that their computer has been infected with malware. A false report showing that a scan has detected malware running on a computer may display, and the users are instructed to download a malware removal tool. The download can contain malware and subsequently lock the users' files or computer.

These are only a few examples of computer attacks, and attackers continue to innovate and come up with new methods every day. It is a security professional's responsibility to stay aware of the newest trends in this area. If a new method of attack is discovered, security professionals should take measures to make end users aware of the new attack as soon as possible. In addition, security professionals should ensure that security awareness training is updated to include any new attack methods. End-user education is one of the best ways to mitigate these attacks.

Major Legal Systems

Security professionals should have an understanding of different legal systems that are used in other countries, especially laws or regulations that impact security and privacy.

These systems include the following:

Key Topic

- Civil code law
- Common law
- Criminal law
- Civil/tort law
- Administrative/regulatory law
- Customary law
- Religious law
- Mixed law

Civil Law

Civil law, also sometimes known as ***civil code law***, developed in Europe, is based on written laws. It is a rule-based law and does not rely on precedence in any way. The most common legal system in the world, civil code law does not require lower courts to follow higher court decisions.

NOTE Do not confuse the civil code law of Europe with the United States civil/ tort laws. Civil laws are different from one country to the other and can vary widely and as such security professionals working in a country should be aware of that country's laws.

Common Law

Common law, developed in England, is based on customs and precedent because no written laws were available. Common law reflects on the morals of the people and relies heavily on precedence. In this system, the lower court must follow any precedents that exist due to higher court decisions. This type of law is still in use today in the United Kingdom, the United States, Ireland, India, New Zealand, Australia, Canada, and the West Indies.

Today, common law uses a jury-based system, which can be waived so that the case is decided by a judge. Common law is divided into three systems: criminal law, civil/tort law, and administrative/regulatory law.

Criminal Law

Criminal law covers any actions that are considered harmful to others. It deals with conduct that violates public protection laws. But the prosecution must prove guilt beyond a reasonable doubt. The plaintiff is usually the civil body, such as the state or federal government, that establishes the law that is violated. In criminal law, guilty parties might be imprisoned and/or fined. Criminal law is based on common law and statutory law. Statutory law is handed down by federal, state, or local legislative bodies.

Civil/Tort Law

Civil/tort law deals with wrongs that have been committed against an individual or organization. A defendant is liable for damages to the victim (plaintiff) if the defendant had a duty of care to the victim, breached that duty (was negligent), and was the actual cause of harm to the victim. Under civil law, the victim is entitled to seek compensatory, punitive, and statutory damages. Compensatory damages are those that compensate the victim for losses. Punitive damages are those that are handed down by juries to punish the liable party. Statutory damages are those that are based on damages established by laws.

In civil law, the liable party has caused injury to the victim. Civil laws include economic damages, liability, negligence, intentional damage, property damage, personal damage, nuisance, and dignitary torts.

In the United States, civil law allows senior officials of an organization to be held liable for any civil wrongdoing by the organization. So, if an organization is negligent, the senior officials can be pursued by any parties that were wronged.

Administrative/Regulatory Law

In ***administrative law***, standards of performance or conduct are set by government agencies for organizations and industries to follow. Common sectors that are covered by administrative or ***regulatory law*** include public utilities, communications, banking, safety and environmental protection regulations, and healthcare.

Customary Law

Customary law is based on the customs of a country or region. Customary law is not used in most systems in isolation, but rather incorporated into many mixed legal systems, such as those used in many African countries, China, and Japan. Monetary fines or public service is the most common form of restitution in this legal system.

Religious Law

Religious law is based on religious beliefs. Although most religious law will be based on a particular religion and its primary written rules, cultural differences can vary from country to country and will affect the laws that are enforced.

Mixed Law

Mixed law combines two or more of the other law types. The most often mixed law uses civil law and common law.

Licensing and Intellectual Property

Intellectual property law is a group of laws that recognize exclusive rights for creations of the mind. Intellectual property is a tangible or intangible asset to which the owner has exclusive rights.

The intellectual property covered by this type of law includes the following:

Key Topic

- Patent
- Trade secret
- Trademark
- Copyright

- Software piracy and licensing issues
- Digital rights management (DRM)

The following sections explain these types of intellectual properties and the internal protection of these properties.

Patent

A ***patent*** is granted to an individual or company to cover an invention that is described in the patent's application. When the patent is granted, only the patent owner can make, use, or sell the invention for a period of time, usually 20 years. Although the patent is considered one of the strongest intellectual property protections available, the invention becomes public domain after the patent expires, thereby allowing any entity to manufacture and sell the product.

Patent litigation is common in today's world. Technology companies, such as Apple, Microsoft, HP, and Google, commonly file lawsuits regarding infringement on patents (often against the other). For this reason, many companies involve a legal team in patent research before developing new technologies. Being the first to be issued a patent is crucial in today's highly competitive market.

Any product that is produced that is currently undergoing the patent application process will usually be identified with the Patent Pending seal, shown in Figure 1-9.

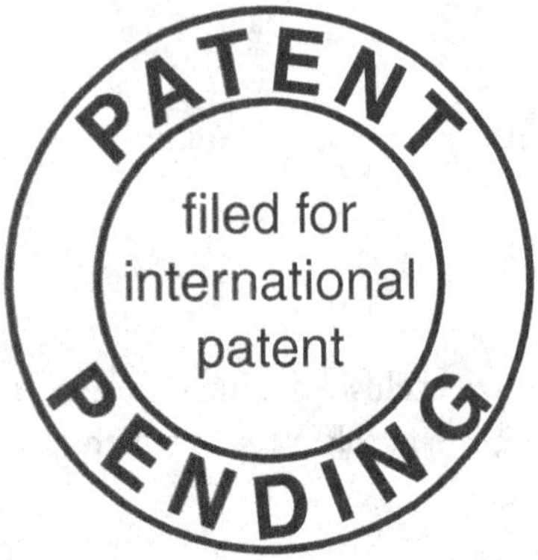

Figure 1-9 Patent Pending Seal

Trade Secret

A ***trade secret*** ensures that proprietary technical or business information remains confidential. A trade secret gives an organization a competitive edge. Trade secrets include recipes, formulas, ingredient listings, and so on that must be protected against disclosure. A trade secret can be kept indefinitely if confidentiality is maintained. After the trade secret is obtained by or disclosed to a competitor or the general public, it is no longer considered a trade secret.

Most organizations that have trade secrets attempt to protect these secrets using nondisclosure agreements (NDAs). These NDAs must be signed by any entity that has access to information that is part of the trade secret. Anyone who signs an NDA will suffer legal consequences if the organization is able to prove that the signer violated it.

Trademark

A ***trademark*** ensures that a symbol, sound, or expression that identifies a product or an organization is protected from being used by another organization. This trademark allows the product or organization to be recognized by the general public. Trademarks are valid for 10 years, at which point the organization should renew the registration.

Most trademarks are marked with one of the designations shown in Figure 1-10.

Figure 1-10 Trademark Designations

If the trademark is not registered, an organization should use a capital *TM*. If the trademark is registered, an organization should use a capital *R* that is encircled.

Copyright

A ***copyright*** ensures that a work that is authored is protected from any form of reproduction or use without the consent of the copyright holder, usually the author or artist who created the original work. A copyright lasts longer than a patent.

Although the U.S. Copyright Office has several guidelines to determine the amount of time a copyright lasts, the general rule for works created after January 1, 1978, is the life of the author plus 70 years.

In 1996, the World Intellectual Property Organization (WIPO) standardized the treatment of digital copyrights. Copyright management information (CMI) is licensing and ownership information that is added to any digital work. In this standardization, WIPO stipulated that CMI included in copyrighted material cannot be altered.

The symbol shown in Figure 1-11 denotes a work that is copyrighted.

Figure 1-11 Copyright Symbol

Software Piracy and Licensing Issues

To understand software piracy and licensing issues, professionals should understand the following terms that are used to differentiate between the types of software available:

- **Freeware:** Software available free of charge, including all rights to copy, distribute, and modify the software. Because the software is free, the user by default accepts the risks associated with the use of freeware.
- **Shareware:** Software that is shared for a limited time. After a certain amount of time (the trial period), the software requires that the user purchase the software to access all the software's features. This is also referred to as trialware.
- **Commercial software:** Software that is licensed by a commercial entity for purchase in a wholesale or retail market.

Software piracy is the unauthorized reproduction or distribution of copyrighted software. Although software piracy is a worldwide issue, it is much more prevalent in Asia, Europe, Latin America, and Africa/Middle East. Part of the problem with software piracy stems from the cross-jurisdictional issues that arise. Obtaining the cooperation of foreign law enforcement agencies and government is often difficult, time-consuming, and/or impossible. Combine this with the availability of the hardware needed to create pirated software and the speed with which it can be made, and you have a problem that will only increase over the coming years.

Security professionals and the organizations they work with must ensure that their organizations take measures to ensure that employees understand the implications of installing pirated software. In addition, large organizations might need to utilize an enterprise software inventory application that will provide administrators with a report on the software that is installed.

Internal Protection

As mentioned earlier in this chapter, employees are the greatest threat for any organization. For this reason, organizations should take measures to protect confidential resources from unauthorized internal access. Any information that is part of a patent, trade secret, trademark, or copyright should be marked and given the appropriate classification. Access controls should be customized for this information, and audit controls should be implemented that alert personnel should any access occur. Due care procedures and policies must be in place to ensure that any laws that protect these assets can be used to prosecute offenders.

Digital Rights Managements (DRM)

Hardware manufacturers, publishers, copyright holders, and individuals use ***Digital Rights Managements (DRM)*** to control the use of digital content. DRM often also involves device controls.

First-generation DRM software controls copying. Second-generation DRM controls executing, viewing, copying, printing, and altering works or devices.

The U.S. Digital Millennium Copyright Act (DMCA) of 1998 imposes criminal penalties on those who make available technologies whose primary purpose is to circumvent content protection technologies. DRM includes restrictive license agreements and encryption. DRM protects computer games and other software, documents, ebooks, films, music, and television.

In most enterprise implementations, the primary concern is the DRM control of documents by using open, edit, print, or copy access restrictions that are granted on a permanent or temporary basis. Solutions can be deployed to store the protected data in a central or decentralized model. Encryption is used in the DRM implementation to protect the data both at rest and in transit.

Cyber Crimes and Data Breaches

A ***data breach*** is any incident in which data or information that is considered private or confidential is released to unauthorized parties. Organizations must have a plan in place to detect and respond to these incidents in the correct manner. Simply having an incident response plan is not enough, though. An organization must also have an incident response plan in place, with trained personnel who are familiar with the incident response plan and the skills to respond to any incidents that occur.

A ***cyber crime*** is any criminal activity that is carried out by means of computers or the Internet. Computer crime concepts are covered earlier in this chapter. The U.S. Federal Bureau of Investigation (FBI) is the lead federal agency for investigating cyberattacks by criminals, overseas adversaries, and terrorists. Cyber crimes are becoming more commonplace, more dangerous, and more sophisticated. According to the FBI, the key priorities are computer and network intrusions, and the related priorities are going dark, identity theft, and online predators. The FBI has launched multiple initiatives and partnerships to help in their fight against cyber crime, including the Internet Crime Complaint Center (IC3), the Cyber Action Team (CAT), and the National Cyber-Forensics & Training Alliance (NCFTA).

NOTE *Going dark* means that those charged with protecting people are not always able to access the evidence needed to prosecute crime and prevent terrorism even with lawful authority. Although they have the legal authority to intercept and access communications and information pursuant to court order, law enforcement officials often lack the technical ability and required tools to do so.

Import/Export Controls

Many organizations today develop trade relationships with organizations that are located in other countries. Organizations must be aware of the export and import laws of both the source and destination countries. Encryption technologies are some of the most restricted technologies in regard to import and export laws. Although the United States does limit the export of encryption technologies for national security reasons, other countries, such as China and Russia, limit the import of these same technologies because the countries do not want their citizens to have access to them. Publicly available technology and software are exempt from most export laws, except for encryption technologies.

Any organization that engages in export and import activities with entities based in other countries should ensure that legal counsel is involved in the process so that all laws and regulations are followed. In addition, the organization should implement the appropriate controls to ensure that personnel do not inadvertently violate any import and export laws, regulations, or internal corporate policies.

Trans-Border Data Flow

In today's world, data is moved across national borders. Trans-border data transfers allow organizations and industries to digitally share information in a much quicker manner than in the past. As data moves from server to server and across networks, the data location and the location of the data host must be considered. Data is subject to the laws and legal systems of every jurisdiction along its route.

Jurisdiction is the power or right of a legal or political agency to exercise its authority over a person, subject matter, or territory. This issue gets even more complicated because jurisdiction can be affected when the organization that owns the data is in one country while the data itself is stored in a facility in another country. Security professionals must oversee the privacy and data protection laws of all jurisdictions that may affect the organization. For this reason, security professionals should develop a detailed data flow map for all organizational processes.

Cloud computing presents its own risks because often it is hard to determine exactly where the data is stored. Organizations that store data in the cloud should work with their cloud service providers to ensure that all application laws and regulations regarding the security and privacy of data are followed.

Privacy

Privacy is the right of individuals to control the use of their personal information. When considering technology and its use today, privacy is a major concern for users. This privacy concern usually covers three areas: what personal information can be shared with whom, whether messages can be exchanged confidentially, and whether and how messages can be sent anonymously. Privacy is an integral part of any security measures that an organization takes.

As part of the security measures that organizations must take to protect privacy, PII must be understood, identified, and protected. Organizations must also understand the privacy laws that governments have adopted. Finally, organizations must ensure that they comply with all laws and regulations regarding privacy.

Personally Identifiable Information (PII)

Personally identifiable information (PII) is any piece of data that can be used alone or with other information to identify a single person. Any PII that an organization collects must be protected in the strongest manner possible. PII includes full name, identification numbers (including driver's license number and Social Security number), date of birth, place of birth, biometric data, financial account numbers (both bank account and credit card numbers), and digital identities (including social media names and tags). With more people interested in their ancestry and subscribing to DNA testing, there have been more discussions about the privacy of DNA and genetic information.

Different countries and levels of government can have different qualifiers for identifying PII. Security professionals must ensure that they understand international, national, state, and local regulations and laws regarding PII. As the data items that can be called PII expand, and theft of this data becomes even more prevalent, you can expect more laws to be enacted that will affect your job.

A complex listing of PII is shown in Figure 1-12.

Key Topic

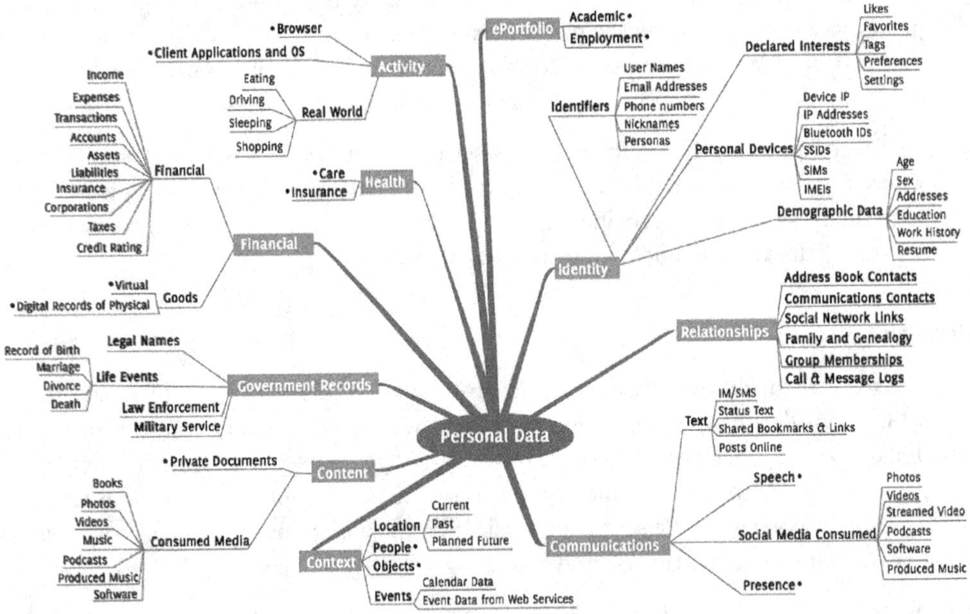

Figure 1-12 PII List

Laws and Regulations

Security professionals are usually not lawyers. As such, they are not expected to understand all the specifics of the laws that affect their organization. However, security professionals must be aware of the laws and at a minimum understand how those laws affect the operations of their organization. For example, a security professional at a healthcare facility in the United States would need to understand all security guidelines in the Health Insurance Portability and Accountability Act (HIPAA) as well as the Patient Protection and Affordable Care Act (PPACA) and Health Care and Education Reconciliation Act of 2010, commonly known as Obamacare.

Here, we discuss many of the laws that will affect security professionals. For testing purposes, you don't need to worry about all the details of the law. You simply need to understand the law's name(s), purpose, and the industry it affects (if applicable).

NOTE As a CISSP candidate, you should ensure that you understand privacy laws and import/export/trans-border data flow regulations.

Sarbanes-Oxley (SOX) Act

The Public Company Accounting Reform and Investor Protection Act of 2002, more commonly known as the ***Sarbanes-Oxley (SOX) Act***, affects any organization that is publicly traded in the United States. It controls the accounting methods and financial reporting for the organizations and stipulates penalties and even jail time for executive officers.

Health Insurance Portability and Accountability Act (HIPAA)

In the United States, the ***Health Insurance Portability and Accountability Act (HIPAA)***, also known as the ***Kennedy-Kassebaum Act***, affects all healthcare facilities, health insurance companies, and healthcare clearinghouses. It is enforced by the Office of Civil Rights of the Department of Health and Human Services. It provides standards and procedures for storing, using, and transmitting medical information and healthcare data. HIPAA overrides state laws unless the state laws are stricter. HIPAA was amended by the Health Care and Education Reconciliation Act of 2010. However, the majority of the amendments from the Health Care and Education Reconciliation Act of 2010 do not affect the rules for the security or privacy of healthcare data as set forth in HIPAA.

Gramm-Leach-Bliley Act (GLBA) of 1999

The ***Gramm-Leach-Bliley Act (GLBA) of 1999*** affects all financial institutions, including banks, loan companies, insurance companies, investment companies, and credit card providers. It provides guidelines for securing all financial information and limits the sharing of some consumer financial information with third parties. Financial institutions must disclose what information they share with third parties, must disclose changes to their information-sharing policies, and provide the ability for customers to opt out of PII sharing. The reality is that in most jurisdictions, consumers are limited in their ability to prevent much of their personal information from being shared.

Computer Fraud and Abuse Act (CFAA) of 1986

The ***Computer Fraud and Abuse Act (CFAA) of 1986*** affects any entities that might engage in hacking of "protected computers" as defined in the act. It was amended in 1989, 1994, 1996; in 2001 by the USA PATRIOT Act; in 2002; and in 2008 by the Identity Theft Enforcement and Restitution Act. A "protected computer" is a computer used exclusively by a financial institution or the U.S. government or used in or affecting interstate or foreign commerce or communication, including a computer located outside the United States that is used in a manner that affects interstate or foreign commerce or communication of the United States. Due to the interstate nature of most Internet communication, any ordinary computer has come under the jurisdiction of the law, including cellphones. The law includes several definitions of hacking, including knowingly accessing a computer without authorization; intentionally accessing a computer to obtain financial records, U.S. government information, or protected computer information; and transmitting fraudulent commerce communication with the intent to extort.

Federal Privacy Act of 1974

The ***Federal Privacy Act of 1974*** affects any computer that contains records used by a federal agency. It provides guidelines on collection, maintenance, use, and dissemination of PII about individuals that is maintained in systems of records by federal agencies on collecting, maintaining, using, and distributing PII.

Federal Intelligence Surveillance Act (FISA) of 1978

The ***Federal Intelligence Surveillance Act (FISA) of 1978*** affects law enforcement and intelligence agencies. It was the first act to give procedures for the physical and electronic surveillance and collection of "foreign intelligence information" between "foreign powers" and "agents of foreign powers" and only applied to traffic within the United States. It was amended by the USA PATRIOT Act of 2001, the FISA Amendments Act of 2008, and the USA Freedom Act of 2015.

Electronic Communications Privacy Act (ECPA) of 1986

The ***Electronic Communications Privacy Act (ECPA) of 1986*** affects law enforcement and intelligence agencies. It extended government restrictions on wiretaps from telephone calls to include transmissions of electronic data by computer and prohibited access to stored electronic communications. It was amended by the Communications Assistance to Law Enforcement Act (CALEA) of 1994, the USA PATRIOT Act of 2001, and the FISA Amendments Act of 2008.

Computer Security Act of 1987

The ***Computer Security Act of 1987*** was superseded by the Federal Information Security Management Act (FISMA) of 2002. This act was the first law written to require a formal computer security plan. It was written to protect and defend any of the sensitive information in the federal government systems and provide security for that information. It also placed requirements on government agencies to train employees and identify sensitive systems.

United States Federal Sentencing Guidelines of 1991

The ***United States Federal Sentencing Guidelines of 1991*** affects individuals and organizations convicted of felonies and serious (Class A) misdemeanors. It provides guidelines to prevent sentencing disparities that existed across the United States.

Communications Assistance for Law Enforcement Act (CALEA) of 1994

The ***Communications Assistance for Law Enforcement Act (CALEA) of 1994*** mandates that telecommunications companies, VoIP service providers, and Internet service providers (ISPs) facilitate the government with lawful intercept requests. A lawful intercept is a process that enables a law enforcement agency to conduct electronic surveillance on a target, when approved by the judicial system, and without the target being able to detect that intercept.

Personal Information Protection and Electronic Documents Act (PIPEDA)

The ***Personal Information Protection and Electronic Documents Act (PIPEDA)*** affects how private sector organizations collect, use, and disclose personal information in the course of commercial business in Canada. The act was written to address European Union (EU) concerns over the security of PII in Canada. The law requires organizations to obtain consent when they collect, use, or disclose personal information and to have personal information policies that are clear, understandable, and readily available.

California Consumer Privacy Act (CCPA)

The ***California Consumer Privacy Act (CCPA)*** was signed into law in June 2018 and then became effective January 1, 2020. The act was devised to provide citizens of California with greater protection of their personal data, in addition to providing greater control over their personal data. CCPA does not stipulate how a company must develop and maintain cybersecurity policies. Nevertheless, the act carries implications for cybersecurity personnel, cyber legal, and IT risk. Inferior security protocols and/or an improper incident response plan can result in hefty fines.

Internal Traffic in Arms Regulations (ITAR)

Internal Traffic in Arms Regulations (ITAR) controls the import and export of defense-related articles, services, or technical data. It is important to understand what type of information is subject to ITAR, especially when it comes to incident response and the loss (or potential loss) of data as a result of an incident.

NYS DFS Rule 500

NYS DFS Rule 500 was introduced by the New York State Department of Financial Services. This regulation became effective in March 2017. By August 28, 2017, financial institutions were required to have established a risk-based cybersecurity program and an incident response plan. According to then-governor Andrew Cuomo, this regulation was designed to "help guarantee the financial services industry upholds its obligation to protect consumers and ensure that its systems are sufficiently constructed to prevent cyber attacks to the fullest extent possible." This regulation impacts the banking industry, insurance, and money service businesses.

Investigatory Powers Act 2016

The ***Investigatory Powers Act 2016***, passed by both Houses of Parliament in 2016, details what digital data law enforcement and intelligence agencies in the United Kingdom may access and what they cannot access. The purpose of the act is to improve national security and intelligence, and the capabilities of law enforcement when investigating crime, by providing greater access to more electronic data. In particular, the act provides greater guidance about the lawful inception of communications data. The Investigatory Powers Commissioner's Office (IPCO) oversees the use of investigatory powers, by law enforcement, intelligence agencies, and other public authorities. IPCO's staff includes 15 Judicial Commissioners (current and retired judges) and a Technical Advisory Panel of scientific experts.

Information Technology (Reasonable Security Practices and Procedures and Sensitive Personal Data or Information) Rules 2011 (India)

In April 2011, India introduced new privacy legislation known as ***Information Technology (Reasonable Security Practices and Procedures and Sensitive Personal Data or Information) Rules 2011***. The legislation was introduced to protect the privacy of online consumers, and it is important to know that this legislation impacts U.S. companies that outsource services to India. This legislation contains five primary tenets:

1. **Privacy Policy:** All organizations must maintain a privacy policy of how they process and use personal data. This policy must be posted on their website. This information can be helpful for investigators who need to find out how much information may be available about customers that they are investigating.
2. **Consent:** Individuals need to provide an organization with consent before their information is shared with a third party.
3. **Consumer Access and Editing:** Individuals have the right to access personal information being collected about them and can dispute any erroneous data.
4. **Transfer of Personal Data:** Consent from customers must be obtained before sensitive information is transferred to another party, and the organization must ensure that recipients have similar standards for data privacy.
5. **Security:** An organization must maintain best practices in terms of security. However, the guidelines on what exemplifies best practices are not clearly outlined.

Personal Data Protection Act (PDPA) in Singapore

The ***Personal Data Protection Act (PDPA) in Singapore*** came into effect in 2014 and directs businesses on what personal data they can collect and what they can use. The act also established a "Do Not Call Registry" to help Singaporeans to opt out of telemarketing.

Basel II

Basel II affects financial institutions. It addresses minimum capital requirements, supervisory review, and market discipline. Its main purpose is to protect against risks that banks and other financial institutions face. It is an international accord, and compliance is not mandatory.

Federal Information Security Management Act (FISMA) of 2002

The ***Federal Information Security Management Act (FISMA) of 2002*** affects every federal agency and government contractor. It requires the federal agencies to develop, document, and implement an agencywide information security program. The Federal Information Security Modernization Act of 2014 amended FISMA 2002 to (1) reestablish the oversight authority of the Director of the Office of Management and Budget (OMB) with respect to agency information security policies and practices, and (2) set forth authority for the Secretary of Homeland Security (DHS) to administer the implementation of such policies and practices for information systems (see www.congress.gov/bill/113th-congress/senate-bill/2521).

Economic Espionage Act of 1996

The ***Economic Espionage Act of 1996*** covers a multitude of issues because of the way the act was structured. For the purposes of the CISSP exam, this act affects companies that have trade secrets and any individuals who plan to use encryption technology for criminal activities. A trade secret does not need to be tangible to be protected by this act. Per this law, theft of a trade secret is a federal crime, and the U.S. Sentencing Commission must provide specific information in its reports regarding encryption or scrambling technology that is used illegally.

USA PATRIOT Act of 2001

The ***Uniting and Strengthening America by Providing Appropriate Tools Required to Intercept and Obstruct Terrorism (USA PATRIOT) Act of 2001*** affects law enforcement and intelligence agencies in the United States. Its purpose is to enhance the investigatory tools that law enforcement can use, including email communications, telephone records, Internet communications, medical records, and financial records. When this law was enacted, it amended several other laws, including FISA and the ECPA of 1986.

Although the USA PATRIOT Act does not restrict private citizen use of investigatory tools, exceptions include if the private citizen is acting as a government agent (even if not formally employed), if the private citizen conducts a search that would require law enforcement to have a warrant, if the government is aware of the private citizen's search, or if the private citizen is performing a search to help the government.

Section 202 of the USA PATRIOT Act provides law enforcement with the authority to intercept voice communications in computer hacking investigations. Previously, law enforcement could not apply for a wiretap order or wire intercept for violations of the Computer Fraud and Abuse Act.

Health Care and Education Reconciliation Act of 2010

The ***Health Care and Education Reconciliation Act of 2010*** affects healthcare and educational organizations. For the CISSP exam, you need to understand that this act increased some of the security measures that must be taken to protect healthcare information.

USA Freedom Act of 2015

The ***USA Freedom Act of 2015*** was written into law in June 2015 to restore several provisions of the USA PATRIOT Act, which had just expired. The act imposed restrictions on the bulk collection of telecommunications metadata on U.S. citizens—metadata that was made available to intelligence agencies, including the National Security Agency (NSA). The act can be viewed as a response to the NSA bulk collection programs, which had been disclosed by Edward Snowden. What has changed is that the NSA is no longer responsible for bulk collection, but rather those bulk records now remain with the telecommunications providers; these records can subsequently be made available, with the approval of the Foreign Intelligence Surveillance Court (FISC), and in the interests of national security.

CLOUD (Clarifying Lawful Overseas Use of Data) Act

Enacted in 2018, the federal legislation known as ***CLOUD (Clarifying Lawful Overseas Use of Data) Act*** obliges U.S.-based technology corporations to provide data to federal law enforcement, which is stored on servers domestically and internationally, when in possession of a subpoena or a warrant.

Employee Privacy Issues and Expectation of Privacy

Employee privacy issues must be addressed by all organizations to ensure that these organizations are protected. However, organizations must give employees the proper notice of any monitoring that might be used. Organizations must also ensure that the monitoring of employees is applied in a consistent manner. Many organizations implement a no-expectation-of-privacy policy that employees must sign after receiving the appropriate training. Keep in mind that this policy should specifically describe any unacceptable behavior. Companies should also keep in mind that some actions are protected by the Fourth Amendment. Security professionals and senior management should consult with legal counsel when designing and implementing any monitoring solution.

European Union & General Data Protection Regulation (GDPR)

The EU has implemented several laws and regulations that affect security and privacy. The EU Principles on Privacy include strict laws to protect private data. The EU's Data Protection Directive provides direction on how to follow the laws set forth in the principles. The EU then created the Safe Harbor Privacy Principles to help guide U.S. organizations in compliance with the EU Principles on Privacy. Some of the guidelines include the following:

- Data should be collected in accordance with the law.
- Information collected about an individual cannot be shared with other organizations unless given explicit permission by the individual.
- Information transferred to other organizations can be transferred only if the sharing organization has adequate security in place.
- Data should be used only for the purpose for which it was collected.
- Data should be used only for a reasonable period of time.

NOTE Do not confuse the term *safe harbor* with *data haven*. According to the EU, a safe harbor is an entity that conforms to all the requirements of the EU Principles on Privacy. A data haven is a country that fails to legally protect personal data with the main aim being to attract companies engaged in the collection of the data.

The Safe Harbor Privacy Principles were replaced by the EU-U.S. Privacy Shield. It provided a framework for transatlantic personal data exchanges for commercial purposes between the European Union and the United States.

The EU Electronic Security Directive defines electronic signature principles. In this directive, a signature must be uniquely linked to the signer and to the data to which it relates so that any subsequent data change is detectable. The signature must be capable of identifying the signer.

Beginning on May 25, 2018, the members of the EU began applying the General Data Protection Regulation (GDPR). The GDPR applies to EU-based organizations that collect or process the personal data of EU residents and to organizations outside the EU that monitor behavior or offer goods and services to EU residents. It gives a wider definition of personal and sensitive data to include online identifiers and genetic and biometrics data, such as cookies, IP address, health information, biometric data, and genetic information. The GDPR affects service providers that process personal data on behalf of an organization, including cloud services, call centers, and payroll services. It strengthens individual privacy rights to include the following:

- **Valid consent:** Organizations must follow stricter rules for consent as a legal basis for processing.
- **Transparency:** Organizations must be transparent regarding what information is collected and how the information is processed.
- **Correction:** Organizations must allow individuals to correct inaccurate personal data.
- **Erasure:** Organizations must allow individuals to request that their personal data be erased under certain conditions.
- **Data portability:** Organizations must allow individuals to move personal data from one service provider to another.
- **Automated processing:** Organizations must not use automated processing as the sole decision maker.

Under GDPR, organizations are obligated to provide accountability by maintaining a record of all data processing activities. A Data Protection Impact Assessment (DPIA) is mandatory if processing activity is likely to result in a high risk to an individual's rights. Organizations must keep personal data secure through "appropriate technical and organizational measures." Organizations must report data breaches to the regulator within 72 hours of discovery. Organizations that are public authorities, monitoring individuals on a large scale, or processing sensitive data must name a data protection officer. For all other organizations, a data protection officer is recommended but not required. Finally, data transfer outside the EU is allowed only if appropriate safeguards are in place.

Organizations that do not comply with GDPR can be levied with fines up to €20 million or 4 percent of global annual turnover. In addition, they may have to compensate victims for damage claims. Finally, noncompliance may result in reputational damage and consumer loss of trust.

To learn more details regarding the GDPR, refer to www.itgovernance.co.uk/data-protection-dpa-and-eu-data-protection-regulation.

Personal Information Protection Law (PIPL)

The Personal Information Protection Law (PIPL) is a significant data protection law implemented by the Chinese government. The PIPL was enacted by the Standing Committee of the National People's Congress of China. It came into effect on November 1, 2021, marking China's first comprehensive law focused on data protection and privacy.

The law also applies to processing information outside of PRC if an organization will

- Provide products or services to individuals in China;
- Analyze individuals in China; or
- Circumstances are impacted by laws or administrative regulations.

PIPL is particularly relevant to security professionals working with data that falls under Chinese jurisdiction, requiring them to understand and comply with these regulations. The PIPL sets out rules for data processing activities and establishes rights for individuals regarding their personal data. It shares similarities with the European Union's General Data Protection Regulation (GDPR) in its approach to data protection and privacy.

For organizations operating in China or handling Chinese personal data, compliance with PIPL is crucial to avoid legal repercussions and fines. One of the critical aspects of PIPL that CISSP professionals should be aware of is the regulation around cross-border data transfer. The law places restrictions on transferring personal data out of China and requires specific conditions to be met, such as security assessments and certifications.

PIPL mandates organizations to implement necessary security measures to protect personal data, including encryption, access controls, and regular security audits. Under PIPL, there are requirements for breach notification and handling.

Protection of Personal Information Act (POPIA)

The Protection of Personal Information Act (POPIA) is a data protection law in South Africa. POPIA was enacted by the South African Parliament. The law came into effect on July 1, 2020, with certain sections phased in over time. It's overseen by the Information Regulator, an independent body established in accordance with POPIA.

Understanding POPIA is vital, especially for those working with data protection and privacy in a global context or within South Africa. POPIA sets forth principles for the lawful processing of personal information. These principles include accountability, processing limitation, purpose specification, further processing limitation, information quality, openness, security safeguards, and data subject participation.

Under POPIA, there's a strong emphasis on implementing appropriate security measures to protect personal data. This includes technical and organizational measures to prevent loss, damage, unauthorized destruction, or unlawful access to personal information. POPIA includes provisions on cross-border transfer of personal information.

The act mandates reporting of certain data breaches to the Information Regulator and, in some cases, to the data subjects. Effective incident response planning and management must align with these requirements.

Investigation Types

Security professionals are called on to investigate any incidents that occur. As a result of the different assets that are affected, security professionals must be able to perform different types of investigations, including operations/administrative, criminal, civil, regulatory, industry standard, and eDiscovery investigations. These investigation types are discussed in the following sections.

Operations/Administrative

Administrative investigations are investigations that do not result in any criminal, civil, or regulatory issue. Administrative investigations can also be referred to as ***operations investigations***. In most cases, this type of investigation is completed to determine the root cause of an incident so that steps can be taken to prevent this incident from occurring again in the future. This process is referred to as ***root-cause analysis (RCA)***. Because no criminal, civil, or regulatory law has been violated, it is not as important to document the evidence. However, security professionals should still take measures to document the lessons learned.

As an example of this type of investigation, a user is assigned permissions that were not based on the job role. If this was the result of criminal misconduct, then a criminal investigation should occur. However, this assignment of permissions could have occurred simply through mistakes made by personnel. Because a security professional would not know the cause of these unjustified permissions, they would need to conduct the investigation using community-accepted forensic protocols in case this evidence would need to be admissible in court one day. If determined that an incident was the result of an accident, forensic protocols would not need to be adhered to. Any individual who carries out this type of investigation must ensure that the appropriate changes are made to prevent such an incident from occurring again, including putting in place security controls. In the case of the inappropriate permissions example, the security professional might find that the user account template that was used to create the user account was assigned to an inappropriate group and must therefore ensure that the user account template is revised.

Criminal

Criminal investigations are investigations that are carried out because a federal, state, or local law has been violated. In this type of investigation, an organization should ensure that law enforcement is involved in the investigation as early as possible to ensure that the crime can be properly documented, investigated, and prosecuted. Criminal investigations result in a criminal trial. In a criminal trial, a jury must unanimously decide, beyond a reasonable doubt, whether the defendant is guilty. The judge will determine punishment and a date of sentencing if a jury's verdict is guilty.

Civil

In a civil trial, a case is brought by an individual or organization (including corporations and the government), referred to as the plaintiff, against an individual or organization.

Civil trials generally involve disputes over money. If successful, the plaintiff is awarded money by the jury. A civil trial identifies whether an entity failed to act reasonably and prudently under a certain set of circumstances. The standard that needs to be met to win a civil trial is referred to as preponderance of the evidence. This means that most of the evidence presented indicates which party was in the right and which party was in the wrong. In a criminal trial, the burden of proof is on the prosecution to prove that the defendant is guilty. In a civil trial, the burden of proof begins with the plaintiff.

Regulatory

Certain group of industries are controlled by regulations; for example, a chemical factory producing chemical products, such as lawn weed removers, are controlled by chemical regulations. These regulations are set by regulatory body for safety and usability of the product. A regulatory investigation occurs when a regulatory body investigates an organization for a regulatory infraction. In recent history, the

Securities and Exchange Commission (SEC) has carried out many regulatory investigations regarding organizations and their financial dealings. No matter which regulatory body is performing the investigation, the organization being investigated will be notified that an investigation is being carried out. The organization should have policies and guidelines in place to ensure full compliance with the investigation. Failure to comply with such an investigation can result in charges being filed against the organization and any personnel involved.

Industry Standards

As defined earlier, standards provide criteria within an industry relating to the standard functioning and carrying out of operations in their respective fields of production. In digital forensics, standards provide the generally accepted requirements followed by digital investigators.

Organizations should investigate the digital forensics standards available, including those from NIST and ISO/IEC. NIST SP 800-86 provides guidelines to integrating forensic techniques into incident response.

To establish an organizational forensic capability, NIST SP 800-86 provides the following guidelines:

- Organizations should have a capability to perform computer and network forensics.
- Organizations should determine which parties should handle each aspect of forensics.
- Incident handling teams should have robust forensic capabilities.
- Many teams within an organization should participate in forensics.
- Forensic considerations should be clearly addressed in policies.
- Organizations should create and maintain guidelines and procedures for performing forensic tasks.

According to NIST SP 800-86, the basic phases of the forensic process are collection, examination, analysis, and reporting. This process differs slightly from the one reported earlier. In some cases, the first two steps presented earlier (identification and preservation) are considered part of incident response but not part of the forensic process itself. However, the four phases in NIST SP 800-86 correspond to steps 3 to 7 of the earlier process. Figure 1-13 shows the forensic process as it transforms media into evidence, whether evidence is needed for law enforcement or for an organization's internal usage.

Key Topic

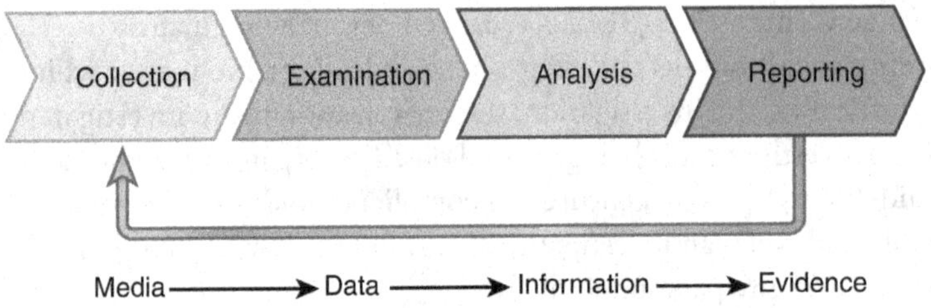

Figure 1-13 NIST SP 800-86 Forensic Process (Image Courtesy of NIST)

During collection, data related to a specific event is identified, labeled, recorded, and collected, and its integrity is preserved. In the second phase, examination, forensic tools and techniques appropriate to the types of data that were collected are executed to identify and extract the relevant information from the collected data while protecting its integrity. Examination may use a combination of automated tools and manual processes. The next phase, analysis, involves analyzing the results of the examination to derive useful information that addresses the questions that were the impetus for performing the collection and examination. The final phase involves reporting the results of the analysis, which may include describing the actions performed, determining what other actions need to be performed, and recommending improvements to policies, guidelines, procedures, tools, and other aspects of the forensic process.

The key recommendations for the forensic process are as follows:

- Organizations should perform forensics using a consistent process.
- Analysts should be aware of the range of possible data sources.
- Organizations should be proactive in collecting useful data.
- Analysts should perform data collection using a standard process.
- Analysts should use a methodical approach to studying the data.
- Analysts should review their processes and practices.

NIST SP 800-86 provides guidelines for using data from data files, operating systems, network traffic, and applications. The key recommendations presented for using data from data files are as follows:

- Analysts should examine copies of files, not the original files.
- Analysts should preserve and verify file integrity.

- Analysts should rely on file headers, not file extensions, to identify file content types.
- Analysts should have a forensic toolkit for data examination and analysis.

The key recommendations presented for using data from OSs are as follows:

- Analysts should act appropriately to preserve volatile OS data.
- Analysts should use a forensic toolkit for collecting volatile OS data.
- Analysts should choose the appropriate shutdown method for each system.

The key recommendations presented for using data from network traffic are as follows:

- Organizations should have policies regarding privacy and sensitive information.
- Organizations should provide adequate storage for network activity-related logs.
- Organizations should configure data sources to improve the collection of information.
- Analysts should have reasonably comprehensive technical knowledge.
- Analysts should consider the fidelity and value of each data source.
- Analysts should generally focus on the characteristics and impact of the event.

The key recommendations presented for using data from applications are as follows:

- Analysts should consider all possible application data sources.
- Analysts should bring together application data from various sources.

The key recommendations presented for using data from multiple sources are as follows:

- Analysts can handle many situations most effectively by analyzing several individual data sources and then correlating events among them.
- Organizations should be aware of the technical and logistical complexity of analysis.

eDiscovery

Electronic discovery (***eDiscovery***) refers to civil litigation or government investigations that deal with the exchange of information in electronic format as part of the discovery process. It involves electronically stored information (ESI) and includes emails, documents, presentations, databases, voicemail, audio and video files, social media, and websites. Security professionals should ensure that the original content and metadata of ESI are preserved to prevent claims of spoliation or tampering with evidence later in the litigation. After the appropriate ESI is collected, it must be held in a secure environment for review.

Professional Ethics

Ethics for any profession are the right and wrong actions that are the moral principle of that occupation. Security professionals, particularly those who hold the CISSP certification, should understand the ethics that are published by the International Information Systems Security Certification Consortium (ISC)^2, the Computer Ethics Institute, the Internet Architecture Board (IAB), and the organization they are employed by.

An organization and its employees must understand, adhere to, and promote professional ethics. The following sections provide ethics guidance for security professionals.

(ISC)^2 Code of Ethics

(ISC)^2 provides a strict Code of Ethics for its certificate holders. All certificate holders must follow the Code of Ethics. Any reported violations of the code are investigated. Certificate holders who are found to be guilty of violation will have their certification revoked.

The four mandatory canons for the Code of Ethics, also known as PAPA by their first letters, are as follows:

- Protect society, the common good, necessary public trust and confidence, and the infrastructure.
- Act honorably, honestly, justly, responsibly, and legally.
- Provide diligent and competent service to principals.
- Advance and protect the profession.

CISSP certificate holders are required to report any actions by other certificate holders that they feel are in violation of the Code. If a certificate holder is reported, a peer review committee will investigate the actions and make a decision as to the certificate holder's standing.

Certification is a privilege that must be earned and maintained. Certificate holders are expected to complete certain educational requirements to prove their continued competence in all aspects of security. They are also expected to promote the understanding and acceptance of prudent information security measures.

Computer Ethics Institute

The Computer Ethics Institute created the "Ten Commandments of Computer Ethics." The following list summarizes these 10 ethics:

1. Do not use a computer for harm.
2. Do not interfere with the computer work of other people.
3. Do not snoop around in the computer files of other people.
4. Do not use a computer to steal.
5. Do not use a computer to lie.
6. Do not install and use licensed software unless you have paid for it.
7. Do not use another person's computer unless you have permission or have paid the appropriate compensation for said usage.
8. Do not appropriate another person's intellectual output.
9. Consider the consequences of the program you are writing or the system you are designing.
10. Always use a computer in ways that ensure consideration and respect of other people and their property.

Internet Architecture Board

The Internet Architecture Board, or IAB, oversees the design, engineering, and management of the Internet. This board meets regularly to review Internet standardization recommendations. Internet ethics is just a small part of the area covered. Ethics statements issued by the IAB usually detail any acts that they deem irresponsible. These actions include wasting resources, destroying data integrity, compromising privacy, and accessing resources that users are not authorized to access.

Request for Comments (RFC) 1087, called "Ethics and the Internet," is the specific IAB document that outlines unethical Internet behavior. Refer to https://datatracker.ietf.org/doc/html/rfc1087 for more information.

Organizational Code of Ethics

Organizations should develop an internal ethics statement and ethics program. By adopting a formal statement and program, the organization is stressing to its employees that they are expected to act in an ethical manner in all business dealings.

Several laws in the United States can affect the development and adoption of an organizational ethics program. If an organization adopts an ethics program, the liability of the organization is often limited, even when the employees are guilty of wrongdoing, provided the organization ensures that personnel have been instructed on the organization's ethics.

Security Documentation

Within an organization, information security governance consists of several documents that are used to provide comprehensive security management. Data and other assets should be protected mainly based on their value and sensitivity. Strategic plans guide the long-term security activities (3–5 years or more). ***Tactical plans*** achieve the goals of the strategic plan and are shorter in length (6–18 months).

Because management is the most critical link in the computer security chain, management approval must be obtained as part of the first step in forming and adopting an information security policy. Senior management must complete the following steps prior to the development of any organizational security policy:

1. Define the scope of the security program.
2. Identify all assets that need protection.
3. Determine the level of protection that each asset needs.
4. Determine personnel responsibilities.
5. Develop consequences for noncompliance with the security policy.

By fully endorsing an organizational security policy, senior management accepts the ownership of an organization's security. High-level security policies are statements that indicate senior management's intention to support organizational security.

After senior management approval has been obtained, the first step in establishing an information security program is to adopt an organizational information security statement. The organization's security policy comes from this organizational information security statement. The security planning process must define how security will be managed, who will be responsible for setting up and monitoring compliance, how security measures will be tested for effectiveness, who is involved in establishing the security policy, and where the security policy is defined.

Security professionals must understand how information security documents work together to form a comprehensive security plan. Information security governance documents include

Key Topic

- Policies
- Processes
- Procedures
- Standards
- Guidelines
- Baselines

Policies

A security policy dictates the role of security as provided by senior management and is strategic in nature, meaning that it provides the end result of security. Policies are defined in two ways: the level in the organization at which they are enforced and the category to which they are applied. Policies must be general in nature, meaning they are independent of a specific technology or security solution. Policies outline goals but do not give any specific ways to accomplish the stated goals. All policies must contain an exception area to ensure that management will be able to deal with situations that might require exceptions.

Policies are broad and provide the foundation for development of processes, standards, baselines, guidelines, and procedures, all of which provide the security structure. Administrative, technical, and physical access controls fill in the security and structure needed to complete the security program.

The policy levels used in information security are organizational security policies, system-specific security policies, and issue-specific security policies. The policy categories used in information security are regulatory security policies, advisory security policies, and informative security policies. The policies are divided as shown in Figure 1-14.

Key Topic

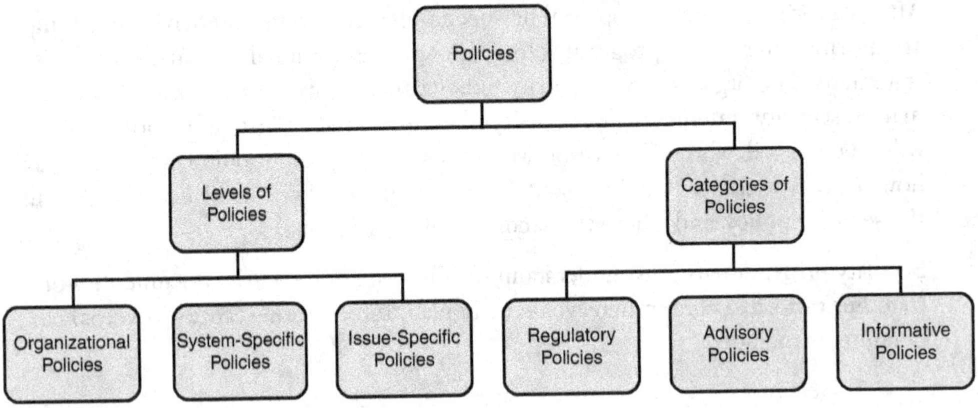

Figure 1-14 Levels and Categories of Security Policies

Organizational Security Policy

An ***organizational security policy*** is the highest-level security policy adopted by an organization. Business goals steer the organizational security policy. An organizational security policy contains general directions and should have the following components:

- Define overall goals of security policy.
- Define overall steps and importance of security.
- Define security framework to meet business goals.
- State management approval of policy, including support of security goals and principles.
- Define all relevant terms and acronyms used.
- Define security roles and responsibilities.
- Address all relevant laws and regulations.
- Identify major functional areas.
- Define compliance requirements and noncompliance consequences.

An organizational security policy must be supported by all stakeholders and should have high visibility for all personnel and be discussed regularly. In addition, it should be reviewed on a regular basis and revised based on the findings of the regular review. Each version of the policy should be maintained and documented in the document library with each new release.

System-Specific Security Policy

A ***system-specific security policy*** addresses security for a specific computer, network, technology, or application. This policy type is much more technically focused than an issue-specific security policy. It outlines how to protect the system or technology.

Issue-Specific Security Policy

An ***issue-specific security policy*** addresses specific security issues. Issue-specific policies include email privacy policies, virus checking policies, employee termination policies, no-expectation-of-privacy policies, and so on. Issue-specific policies support the organizational security policy.

Policy Categories

Regulatory security policies address specific industry regulations, including mandatory standards. Examples of industries that must consider regulatory security policies include healthcare facilities, public utilities, and financial institutions.

Advisory security policies provide instruction on acceptable and unacceptable activities. In most cases, this policy is considered to be strongly suggested, not compulsory. This type of policy usually gives examples of possible consequences if users engage in unacceptable activities.

Informative security policies provide information on certain topics and act as an educational tool. Nevertheless, policies are only as good as their implementation.

Processes

A ***process*** is a series of actions or steps taken in order to achieve a particular end. Organizations will define individual processes and their relationship to one another. For example, an organization may define a process for how customers enter an online order, how the payment is processed, and how the order is fulfilled after the payment is processed. Although each of these processes is separate and includes a list of unique tasks that must be completed, the processes all rely on each other for completion. The process lays out how the goal or task is completed. Processes then lead to procedures.

Procedures

Procedures embody all the detailed actions that personnel are required to follow and encompass the use of computers and other devices. Procedures often include step-by-step lists on how processes, policies, standards, and guidelines are implemented.

Standards

Standards describe how policies will be implemented within an organization. They are mandatory actions or rules that are tactical in nature, meaning they provide the steps necessary to achieve security. Just like policies, standards should be regularly reviewed and revised.

Guidelines

Guidelines are recommended actions that are much more flexible than standards, thereby providing allowance for circumstances that can occur. Guidelines provide guidance when standards do not apply.

Baselines

A ***baseline*** is a reference point that is defined and captured to be used as a future reference. Although capturing baselines is important, using those baselines to assess the security state is just as important. Even the most comprehensive baselines are useless if they are never used.

Capturing a baseline at the appropriate point in time is also important. Baselines should be captured when a system is properly configured and fully updated. When updates occur, new baselines should be captured and compared to the previous baselines. At that time, adopting new baselines based on the most recent data might be necessary.

Business Continuity

Business continuity is an organization's capability to continue delivery of products or services at acceptable predefined levels following a disruptive incident. As part of risk management, security professionals should ensure that the organization prepares appropriate business continuity plans. The following sections cover business continuity and disaster recovery concepts, business continuity scope and plan, and business impact analysis.

Business Continuity and Disaster Recovery Concepts

Security professionals must be involved in the development of any business continuity and disaster recovery processes.

As a result, security professionals must understand the basic concepts involved in business continuity and disaster recovery planning, including the following:

Key Topic

- Disruptions
- Disasters
  - Technological
  - Man-made
  - Natural
- Disaster recovery and the disaster recovery plan (DRP)
- Continuity planning and the business continuity plan (BCP)
- Business impact analysis (BIA)
- Contingency plan
- Availability
- Reliability
- External dependencies

Disruptions

A ***disruption*** is typically any unplanned event that results in the temporary interruption of any organizational asset, including processes, functions, and devices. Disruptions are grouped into three main categories: nondisaster, disaster, and catastrophe.

Nondisasters are temporary interruptions that occur due to malfunction or failure. Nondisasters might or might not require public notification and are much easier to recover from than disasters or catastrophes.

A disaster is a suddenly occurring event that has a long-term negative impact on life. Disasters require that the organization publicly acknowledge the event and provide the public with information on how the organization will recover. Disasters require more effort for recovery than nondisasters but less than catastrophes.

A catastrophe is a disaster that has a much wider and much longer impact. In most cases, a disaster is considered a catastrophe if facilities are destroyed, thereby resulting in the need for the rebuilding of the facilities and the use of a temporary offsite facility.

Disasters

A ***disaster*** is an emergency that goes beyond the normal response of resources. A disaster usually affects a wide geographical area and results in severe damage, injury, loss of life, and loss of property. Any disaster has negative financial and reputational effects on the organization. The severity of the financial and reputational damage is also affected by the amount of time the organization takes to recover from the disaster.

Key Topic

The causes of disasters are categorized into three main areas according to origin: technological disasters, man-made disasters, and natural disasters. A disaster is officially over when all business elements have returned to normal function at the original site. The primary concern during any disaster is personnel safety.

Technological Disasters

Technological disasters occur when a device fails. This failure can be the result of device defects, incorrect implementation, incorrect monitoring, or human error. Technological disasters are not always intentional. If a technological disaster is not recovered from in a timely manner, an organization might suffer a financial collapse.

If a disaster occurs because of a deliberate attack against an organization's infrastructure, the disaster is considered a man-made disaster even if the attack is against a specific device or technology. In the past, all technological disasters were actually considered man-made disasters because technological disasters are usually due to human error or negligence. However, in recent years, experts have started categorizing technological disasters separately from man-made disasters, although the two are closely related.

Man-Made Disasters

Man-made disasters occur through human intent or error. Man-made disasters include enemy attacks, bombings, sabotage, arson, terrorism, strikes or other job actions, infrastructure failures, personnel unavailability due to emergency evacuation, and mass hysteria. In most cases, man-made disasters are intentional.

Natural Disasters

Natural disasters occur because of a natural hazard. Natural disasters include flood, tsunami, earthquake, hurricane, tornado, and other such natural events. A fire that is not the result of arson is also considered a natural disaster.

Disaster Recovery and the Disaster Recovery Plan (DRP)

Disaster recovery minimizes the effect of a disaster and includes the steps necessary to resume normal operation. Disaster recovery must take into consideration all organizational resources, functions, and personnel. Effective disaster recovery will sustain an organization during and after a disruption due to a disaster.

Each organizational function or system will have its own disaster recovery plan (DRP). The DRP for each function or system is created as a direct result of that function or system being identified as part of the business continuity plan (BCP). The DRP is implemented when the emergency occurs and includes the steps to restore functions and systems. The goal of disaster recovery is to minimize or prevent property damage and prevent loss of life. More details on disaster recovery are given later in this chapter.

Continuity Planning and the Business Continuity Plan (BCP)

Continuity planning deals with identifying the impact of any disaster and ensuring that a viable recovery plan for each function and system is implemented. Its primary focus is how to carry out the organizational functions when a disruption occurs.

The BCP considers all areas of an organization that are affected by a disaster, including functions, systems, personnel, and facilities. It lists and prioritizes the services that are needed, particularly the telecommunications and IT functions. More details about continuity planning are detailed in the next few sections.

Business Impact Analysis (BIA)

A business impact analysis (BIA) is a functional analysis that occurs as part of business continuity and disaster recovery. Performing a thorough BIA will help business units understand the impact of a disaster. The resulting document that is produced from a BIA lists the critical and necessary business functions, their resource dependencies, and their level of criticality to the overall organization. More details on the BIA are given later in this chapter in the "BIA Development" section. The United States government website provides detailed information about creating a BIA (www.ready.gov/business-impact-analysis), in addition to resources related to risk assessments and disaster preparedness planning.

Contingency Plan

A contingency plan is sometimes referred to as "Plan B" because it can be also used as an alternative for action if expected results fail to materialize. Contingency planning is a component of business continuity, disaster recovery, and risk management.

Contingency planning is covered in more detail in the "Business Contingency Planning" section later in this chapter.

Availability

Availability is one of the key principles of the confidentiality, integrity, and availability (CIA) triad and will be discussed in almost every defined CISSP domain. Availability is a main consideration of business continuity planning. The organization must determine the acceptable level of availability for each function or system. If the availability of a resource falls below this defined level, then specific actions must be followed to ensure that availability is restored.

With regard to availability, most of the unplanned downtime of functions and systems is attributed to hardware failure. Availability places emphasis on technology.

Reliability

Reliability is the ability of a function or system to consistently perform according to specifications. It is vital in business continuity to ensure that the organization's processes can continue to operate. Reliability places emphasis on processes.

External Dependencies

External dependencies in the context of business continuity refer to the reliance of a business on third-party services, vendors, or infrastructure that are critical for its operations. Understanding and managing these dependencies is crucial for ensuring business continuity, especially in the face of disruptions or crises.

External dependencies can include a wide range of elements such as cloud service providers, supply chain partners, utility services, third-party software, hardware vendors, and outsourced services. These are external entities that a business relies on for its daily operations and strategic functions. BCP involves preparing for and ensuring continuous business operations during and after a disaster or disruption. Given that many critical business functions might depend on external entities, any disruption in these dependencies can significantly impact the business. Therefore, identifying and planning for risks associated with external dependencies is a crucial part of BCP.

Part of managing external dependencies involves conducting risk assessments to identify vulnerabilities and potential threats associated with these third-party services or vendors. This includes evaluating the likelihood of a disruption and its potential impact on business operations. Security professional should scrutinize the security and business continuity practices of third parties and ensure they align with the organization's standards and requirements.

Service-level agreements (SLAs) and other contractual terms with external parties should clearly define expectations regarding availability, performance, and response during disruptions. Regularly reviewing and updating these agreements is part of effective external dependency management.

Developing contingency plans for critical external dependencies is essential. This might involve having backup vendors, alternate resources, or plans for temporarily handling critical functions in-house.

Business continuity plans, including those involving external dependencies, should be regularly tested and reviewed. This ensures that they remain effective and current, and that the organization is prepared to respond to changes and potential disruptions.

Scope and Plan

Creating the BCP is vital to ensure that the organization can recover from a disaster or disruptive event. Several groups have established standards and best practices for business continuity. These standards and best practices include many common components and steps.

Next, we cover the personnel components, the scope, and the business continuity steps that must be completed.

Personnel Components

The most important personnel in the development of the BCP is senior management. Senior management support of business continuity and disaster recovery drives the overall organizational view of the process. Without senior management support, this process will fail.

Senior management sets the overall goals of business continuity and disaster recovery. A business continuity coordinator should be named by senior management and lead the BCP committee. The committee develops, implements, and tests the BCP and DRP. The BCP committee should contain a representative from each business unit. At least one member of senior management should be part of this committee. In addition, the organization should ensure that the IT, legal, security, and communications departments are represented because of the vital role that these departments play during and after a disaster.

With management direction, the BCP committee must work with business units to ultimately determine the business continuity and disaster recovery priorities. Senior business unit managers are responsible for identifying and prioritizing time-critical systems. After all aspects of the plans have been determined, the BCP committee should be tasked with regularly reviewing the plans to ensure they remain current and viable. Senior management should closely monitor and control all business continuity efforts.

Personnel from all other departments should be involved in the disaster recovery planning as needed. Personal safety is always the priority.

Scope

To ensure that the development of the BCP is successful, senior management must define the BCP scope. A business continuity project with an unlimited scope can often become too large for the BCP committee to handle correctly. For this reason, senior management might need to split the business continuity project into smaller, more manageable pieces.

When considering splitting the BCP into pieces, an organization might want to split the pieces based on geographic location or facility. However, an enterprisewide BCP should be developed that ensures compatibility of the individual plans.

Business Contingency Planning

Many organizations have developed standards and guidelines for performing business contingency planning. One of the most popular standards is Special Publication (SP) 800-34 Rev. 1 from NIST.

The steps of SP 800-34 Rev. 1 are as follows:

Key Topic

1. Develop a contingency planning policy.
2. Conduct a business impact analysis (BIA).
3. Identify preventive controls.
4. Create contingency strategies.
5. Develop a contingency plan.
6. Conduct contingency plan testing, training, and exercises.
7. Maintain the plan.

Figure 1-15 shows a more detailed listing of the tasks included in SP 800-34 R1.

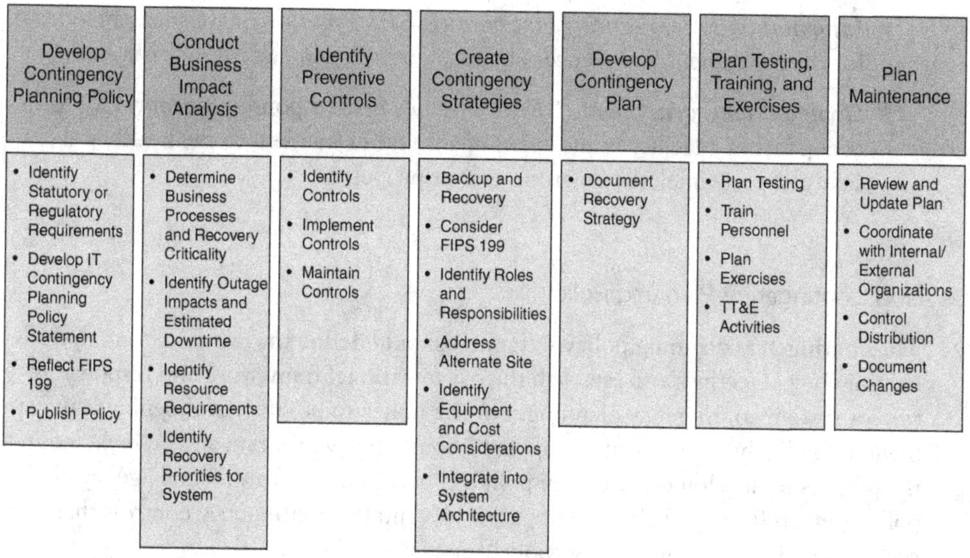

Figure 1-15 NIST Special Publication 800-34 Rev. 1

NIST 800-34 Rev. 1 includes the following types of plans that should be included during contingency planning:

- ***Business continuity plan (BCP)*:** Focuses on sustaining an organization's mission/business processes during and after a disruption.
- ***Continuity of operations plan (COOP)*:** Focuses on restoring an organization's mission-essential functions (MEFs) at an alternate site and performing those functions for up to 30 days before returning to normal operations.
- ***Crisis communications plan*:** Documents standard procedures for internal and external communications in the event of a disruption using a crisis communications plan. It also provides various formats for communications appropriate to the incident.
- ***Critical infrastructure protection (CIP) plan*:** Provides a set of policies and procedures that serve to protect and recover these assets and mitigate risks and vulnerabilities.
- ***Cyber incident response plan*:** Establishes procedures to address cyberattacks against an organization's information system(s).
- ***Disaster recovery plan (DRP)*:** Documents an information system–focused plan designed to restore operability of the target system, application, or computer facility infrastructure at an alternate site after an emergency.

- ***Information system contingency plan (ISCP)***: Provides established procedures for the assessment and recovery of a system following a system disruption.
- ***Occupant emergency plan (OEP)***: Outlines first-response procedures for occupants of a facility in the event of a threat or incident to the health and safety of personnel, the environment, or property.

Develop Contingency Planning Policy

The contingency planning policy statement should define the organization's overall contingency objectives and establish the organizational framework and responsibilities for system contingency planning. For the policy to be successful, senior management, most likely the CIO, must support a contingency program and be included in the process to develop the program policy. If being applied to a federal agency, the policy must reflect the FIPS 199 impact levels and the contingency controls that each impact level establishes. Key policy elements are as follows:

- Roles and responsibilities
- Scope as applies to common platform types and organization functions (i.e., telecommunications, legal, media relations) subject to contingency planning
- Resource requirements
- Training requirements
- Exercise and testing schedules
- Plan maintenance schedule
- Minimum frequency of backups and storage of backup media

NOTE FIPS 199 is discussed in more detail later in this chapter.

Conduct the BIA

The purpose of the BIA is to correlate the system with the critical mission/business processes and services provided and, based on that information, characterize the consequences of a disruption.

Identify Preventive Controls

The impact of an outage, identified in the BIA, may be mitigated or eliminated through preventive measures that deter, detect, and/or reduce impacts to the system. Where feasible and cost-effective, preventive methods are preferable to actions that may be necessary to recover the system after a disruption.

Create Contingency Strategies

Organizations are required to adequately mitigate the risk arising from use of information and information systems in the execution of mission/business processes. This includes backup methods, offsite storage, recovery, alternate sites, and equipment replacement.

Develop Contingency Plan

Using the information that has been obtained up to this point, an organization should develop the contingency plan, including backup and recovery solutions. This plan must document the roles and responsibilities of personnel in the organization as part of this plan.

Plan Testing, Training, and Exercises (TT&E)

Testing, training, and exercises for business continuity should be carried out regularly based on NIST SP 800-84. Organizations should conduct TT&E events periodically as regularly as possible or at least once a year, following organizational or system changes, or the issuance of new TT&E guidance, or as otherwise needed.

Maintain the Plan

To be effective, the plan must be maintained in a ready state that accurately reflects system requirements, procedures, organizational structure, and policies. As a general rule, the plan should be reviewed for accuracy and completeness at an organization-defined frequency (at least once a year) or whenever significant changes occur to any element of the plan.

BIA Development

The BCP development depends most on the development of the BIA. The BIA helps the organization to understand what impact a disruptive event would have on the organization. This management-level analysis identifies the impact of losing an organization's resources.

Key Topic

The four main steps of the BIA are as follows:

1. Identify critical processes and resources.
2. Identify outage impacts and estimate downtime.
3. Identify resource requirements.
4. Identify recovery priorities.

The BIA relies heavily on any vulnerability analysis and risk assessment that is completed. The vulnerability analysis and risk assessment may be performed by the BCP committee or by a separately appointed risk assessment team. The risk assessment process is discussed later in the NIST "SP 800-30 Rev. 1" section.

Identify Critical Processes and Resources

When identifying the critical processes and resources of an organization, the BCP committee must first identify all the business units or functional areas within the organization. After all units have been identified, the BCP team should select which individuals will be responsible for gathering all the needed data and select how to obtain the data.

These individuals will gather the data using a variety of techniques, including questionnaires, interviews, and surveys. They might also actually perform a vulnerability analysis and risk assessment or use the results of these tests as input for the BIA.

During the data gathering, the organization's business processes and functions, and the resources upon which these processes and functions depend, should be documented. This list should include all business assets, including physical and financial assets that are owned by the organization, and any assets that provide competitive advantage or credibility.

Identify Outage Impact and Estimate Downtime

After determining all of the business processes, functions, and resources, the organization should then determine the criticality level of each resource.

As part of determining how critical an asset is, you need to understand the following terms:

Key Topic

- ***Maximum tolerable downtime (MTD)***: The maximum amount of time that an organization can tolerate a single resource or function being down. This is also referred to as maximum period time of disruption (MPTD).

- ***Mean time to repair (MTTR):*** The average time required to repair a single failed component or device when a disaster or disruption occurs.
- ***Mean time between failure (MTBF):*** The estimated amount of time a device will operate before a failure occurs. This amount is calculated by the device vendor. System reliability is increased by a higher MTBF and lower MTTR.
- ***Recovery time objective (RTO):*** The time period after a disaster or disruptive event within which a resource or function must be restored to avoid unacceptable consequences. RTO assumes that an acceptable period of downtime exists. RTO should be smaller than MTD.
- **Work recovery time (WRT):** The amount of time that is needed to verify system and/or data integrity.
- ***Recovery point objective (RPO):*** The maximum targeted period in which data might be lost from an IT service due to a major incident.

Figure 1-16 provides a graphical representation of RPO and RTO. A data center can be impacted by a bad server upgrade, a cyberattack, a power outage, or another disaster. The organization is then reliant on a data backup. How quickly an organization can get back up and running depends on two factors: (1) recovery point objective (RPO), which is the amount of data loss since the last backup, and (2) recovery time objective (RTO), which is the amount of time required to recover the data since the last backup. To summarize, RTO is the amount of data that an organization can lose, whereas RPO is the length of time that a business can be inoperable.

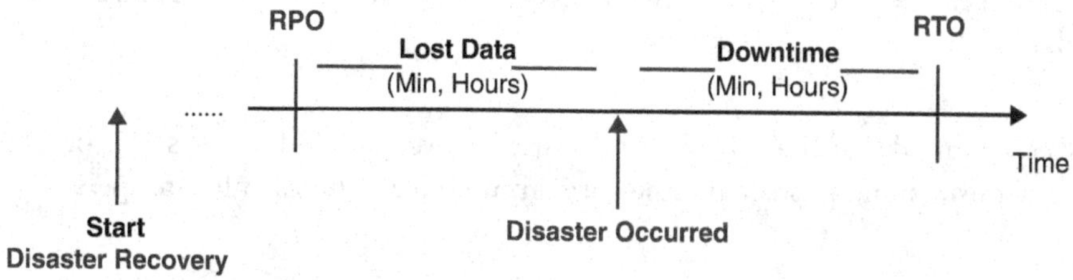

Figure 1-16 Recovery Point Objective (RPO) and Recovery Time Objective (RTO)

Each organization must develop its own documented criticality levels. A good example of organizational resource and function criticality levels includes critical, urgent, important, normal, and nonessential:

- Critical resources are those resources that are most vital to the organization's operation and should be restored within minutes or hours of the disaster or disruptive event.

- Urgent resources should be restored within 24 hours but are not considered as important as critical resources.
- Important resources should be restored within 72 hours but are not considered as important as critical or urgent resources.
- Normal resources should be restored within 7 days but are not considered as important as critical, urgent, or important resources.
- Nonessential resources should be restored within 30 days.

Each process, function, and resource must have its criticality level defined to act as an input into the DRP. If critical priority levels are not defined, a DRP might not be operational within the timeframe the organization needs to recover. Keep in mind that some resources rely on others to be fully functional. As such these relationships should be documented to ensure full functionality.

Identify Resource Requirements

After the criticality level of each function and resource is determined, you need to determine all the resource requirements for each function and resource. For example, an organization's accounting system might rely on a server that stores the accounting application, another server that holds the database, various client systems that perform the accounting tasks over the network, and the network devices and infrastructure that support the system. Resource requirements should also consider any human resources requirements. When human resources are unavailable, the organization can be just as negatively impacted as when technological resources are unavailable.

NOTE Keep in mind that the priority for disaster recovery should be the safety of human life. Consider and protect all other organizational resources only after personnel are safe.

The organization must document the resource requirements for every resource that would need to be restored when the disruptive event occurs. These requirements include device name, operating system or platform version, hardware requirements, and device interrelationships.

Identify Recovery Priorities

After all the resource requirements have been identified, the organization must identify the recovery priorities. The organization should establish recovery priorities by taking into consideration process criticality, outage impacts, tolerable downtime, and system resources. After all this information is compiled, the result is an information system recovery priority hierarchy.

Three main levels of recovery priorities should be used: high, medium, and low. The BIA stipulates the recovery priorities but does not provide the recovery solutions. Those solutions are explained in the DRP.

Recoverability

Recoverability is the ability of a function or system to be recovered in the event of a disaster or disruptive event. As part of recoverability, downtime must be minimized. Recoverability places an emphasis on the personnel and resources used for recovery.

Salvage

Salvage occurs when an asset is irreparably damaged. Often parts of the asset are recoverable. A salvage team works together to determine what parts of an asset can be salvaged and then actually cleans up and recovers them.

Fault Tolerance

Fault tolerance is provided when a backup component begins operation when the primary component fails. One of the key aspects of fault tolerance is the lack of service interruption.

Varying levels of fault tolerance can be achieved at most levels of the organization based on how much an organization is willing to spend. However, the backup component often does not provide the same level of service as the primary component. For example, an organization might implement a high-speed gigabit connection to the Internet. However, the backup connection to the Internet that is used in the event of the failure of the gigabit line might be much slower but at a much lower cost of implementation than the primary connection.

Personnel Security Policies and Procedures

Personnel are responsible for the vast majority of security issues within an organization, whether they realize it or not. For this reason, it is vital that an organization implement the appropriate personnel security policies. Organizations should have personnel security policies and procedures in place that address candidate screening and hiring; employment agreements and policies; onboarding and termination processes; vendor, consultant, and contractor agreements and controls; compliance policy requirements; privacy policy requirements; and job rotation and separation of duties. Security professionals should work with human resources personnel to ensure that the appropriate personnel security policies are in place.

Candidate Screening and Hiring

Personnel screening should occur prior to an offer of employment and might include a criminal history, work history, background investigations, credit history, driving records, substance-abuse testing, reference checks, education and licensing verification, Social Security number verification and validation, and a check for inclusion on a suspected terrorist watch list. Each organization should determine the screening needs based on the organization's needs and the prospective personnel's employment level. Some jobs now require certain vaccinations, which may include COVID-19 vaccinations. Job descriptions should contain the roles and responsibilities of the job role and any experience or education that is required. If skills must be maintained or upgraded, the job description should list the annual training requirements, especially if specialized security training is needed.

Criminal history checks are allowed under the United States Fair Credit Reporting Act (FCRA). Employers can request criminal records for most potential employees for the past seven years provided the applicant provides consent. If the applicant will be earning more than $75,000 annually, there are no time restrictions on criminal history. Employers need to search state and county criminal records, sex and violent offender records, and prison records. Many companies provide such services for a fee.

Work history should be verified. Former employers should be contacted to confirm dates employed, positions, performance, and reason for leaving. However, security professionals should keep in mind that some companies will verify only the employment term.

A background investigation should research any claim made on applicants' applications or resumes. Verification of the applicants' claims serves to protect the hiring organization by ensuring that the applicants hold the skills and experience that they claim to have. Employees should also be reinvestigated based on their employment level. For example, employees with access to financial data and transactions should undergo periodic credit checks.

Credit history ensures that personnel who are involved in financial transactions for the organization will not be risks for financial fraud. The FCRA and Equal Employment Opportunity Commission (EEOC) provide guidelines that can help human resources personnel in this area. Consent from the applicant should be obtained. In addition, it is a good idea to involve legal counsel.

Driving records are necessary if the applicant will be operating a motor vehicle as part of their job. Often this type of check for other applicants can help reveal lifestyle issues, such as driving under the influence or license suspension, that can cause employment problems later.

Substance-abuse testing will reveal to the employer any drug use. If substance-abuse testing is needed for any roles, it is recommended to require it for all personnel. Because a history of drug use can cause productivity issues and absenteeism, it is always best to perform such testing before offering employment. However, security professionals should ensure that any substance testing is clearly stated as part of the job posting.

Two types of reference checks are performed: work and personal. Work reference checks verify employment history. Personal reference checks contact individuals supplied by the applicants and ask questions regarding the applicants' capabilities, skills, and personality.

Education and licensing verification is usually fairly easy to complete. Employers can request transcripts from educational institutions. For any licensing or certification, the licensing or certification body can verify the license or certification held.

Social Security number verification and validation can be achieved by contacting the Social Security Administration. Such a check ensures that the Social Security information is accurate. The Social Security Administration will alert the organization if the Social Security number has been misused, including if the number belongs to a deceased person or a person in a detention facility.

Just as there are companies that can provide criminal history checks, companies, such as National Surveillance Agency Telephones and Terrorism (NSAT&T), have recently started providing services to search federal and international lists of suspected terrorists. Organizations involved in defense, aviation, technology, and biotechnology fields should consider performing such a check for all applicants.

As any security professional knows, the sensitivity of the information that applicants will have access to should be the biggest determining factor as to which checks to perform. Organizations should never get lax in their pre-employment applicant screening processes.

Employment Agreements and Policies

Personnel hiring procedures should include signing all the appropriate documents, including government-required documentation, a confidentiality agreement, a nondisclosure agreement (NDA), and the acceptable use policy (AUP). The objective of an NDA is to protect data from unauthorized disclosure. NDAs are generally used to establish data ownership, protect information from disclosure, prevent forfeiture of patent rights, and define handling standards including disposal. Annual participation in security awareness training and other compliance requirements should be included as part of the employment agreement. Training should also be provided at the point of hire and periodically throughout the employment term, usually annually.

An AUP details appropriate use of information systems, handling standards, monitoring, and privacy expectations.

- An AUP should be written in language that can be easily and unequivocally understood.
- By signing the associated agreement, the user acknowledges, understands, and agrees to the stated rules and obligations.

Organizations usually have a personnel handbook and other hiring information that must be communicated to the employee. The hiring process should include a formal verification that the employee has completed all the training. Employee IDs and passwords may be issued at this time.

Code of conduct, conflict of interest, and ethics agreements should also be signed at this time and will often be requested periodically while employed. Also, any noncompete agreements should be verified to ensure that employees do not leave the organization for a competitor if an employee ever signed such an agreement. Employees should be given guidelines for periodic performance reviews, compensation, and recognition of achievements.

Policy-driven requirements related to employee agreements play a crucial role and are integral to ensuring that the organization's security posture is maintained through the adherence of its staff to established security policies and practices. This includes the following points:

- Organizations must ensure that their employees are aware of and understand the company's security policies and procedures. This often includes regular training sessions on security best practices, emerging threats, and specific organizational protocols.
- Employees are typically required to sign agreements or acknowledgments stating that they have read, understood, and agreed to abide by the organization's security policies. This agreement might cover areas like acceptable use of IT resources, data confidentiality, and security protocols.
- Depending on their role, employees may need to agree to specific security policies tailored to their responsibilities. For example, IT staff might have different security obligations compared to other employees, especially regarding access to sensitive systems and data.

- Confidentiality agreements or NDAs are common in many organizations. These agreements bind employees to keep organizational information confidential and not disclose it to unauthorized parties.
- In regard to regulations like GDPR, HIPAA, and others, employees often need to understand and agree to specific data protection and privacy policies, especially if their role involves handling personal or sensitive data.
- Employees must be aware of and agree to follow incident reporting procedures. This is crucial for timely and effective response to security incidents, breaches, or any observed suspicious activities.
- The employee agreement should clearly articulate the consequences of violating security policies. This could range from disciplinary action to termination, depending on the severity of the violation.
- Security policies and procedures are dynamic and may change in response to new threats, technological advancements, or regulatory requirements. Employees should periodically review and re-acknowledge their understanding and agreement to these changes.
- Employment agreements might include clauses related to access control policies, such as the responsibility to protect credentials and report any suspected compromise of accounts.
- With the rise of remote work and Bring Your Own Device (BYOD) policies, employees often need to agree to specific guidelines governing the secure use of personal devices for work purposes and security measures for remote working environments.

Security professionals must ensure these policy-driven requirements are effectively communicated, understood, and agreed upon by employees. This not only helps in maintaining a secure environment but also inculcates a culture of security awareness and responsibility throughout the organization.

Employee Onboarding and Offboarding Policies

Onboarding is the process of integrating new employees with a company and culture as well as providing the tools and information they need to be successful. Onboarding includes the following:

- User *orientation* is the initial task of completing paperwork (including confidentiality and AUP agreements), introductions, and initial training.
- User *provisioning* is the process of creating user accounts and credentials, assigning access rights and permissions, and providing assets.

Each department should have documented procedures related to user onboarding.

Offboarding is the process for transitioning employees out of an organization and is also referred to as termination. Tasks include

- Documenting separation details
- Performing tasks and responsibilities prior to departure
- Ensuring knowledge transfer
- Completing an exit interview

Personnel termination must be handled differently based on whether the termination is friendly or unfriendly. Procedures defined by the human resources department can ensure that the organization's property is returned, user access is removed at the appropriate time, and exit interviews are completed. With unfriendly terminations, organizational procedures must be proactive to prevent damage to organizational assets. The security department should be notified early in the process of an unfriendly termination. Unfriendly termination procedures should include terminating or disabling all system and facility access prior to employee termination notification as well as security escort from the premises.

Vendor, Consultant, and Contractor Agreements and Controls

Organizations often work with vendors, consultants, and contractors. Any third party that is given access to an organization's facility should be given limited access to the facility and other organizational assets. An organization should implement appropriate controls to ensure that these third parties do not cause security issues. Third parties, even those that visit frequently, should be escorted within the organization's facility. If a third party needs more permanent access, a background investigation should be performed, and nondisclosure agreements should be implemented. Any access to the network and information assets should be monitored using virtual monitoring and audit logs.

Compliance Policy Requirements

Management must also ensure that appropriate security policies are in place during employment. These policies include separation of duties, job rotation, and least privilege. Another management control is mandatory vacations, which requires that employees take their vacations and that another employee performs the absent employee's job duties during that vacation time. Some positions might require employment agreements to protect the organization and its assets even after these employees are no longer with the organization. These agreements can include NDAs, noncompete clauses, AUPs, and code of conduct and ethics agreements.

Privacy Policy Requirements

Personnel expect a certain amount of privacy even in their workplace. Companies should implement a no-expectation-of-privacy policy that details what areas personnel should consider as not being private, including company email, Internet access, and access to high-security areas. Closed-circuit televisions (CCTVs) and other video recording equipment are becoming commonplace in the workplace. It is considered acceptable to conduct video monitoring of parking areas, work areas, and high-security areas. However, using video monitoring in bathrooms, locker rooms, or other areas considered private is never a good idea.

Security professionals should ensure that personnel are regularly reminded of the no-expectation-of-privacy policy of the organization, which is often accomplished using screen banners. In some cases, they may also want to place notification signs in areas where video monitoring occurs.

Job Rotation

Job rotation ensures that more than one person fulfills the job tasks of a single position within an organization. This job rotation ensures that more than one person is capable of performing those tasks, providing redundancy. It is also an important tool in helping an organization to recognize when fraudulent activities have occurred.

Separation of Duties

Separation of duties ensures that one person is not capable of compromising organizational security. Any activities that are identified as high risk should be divided into individual tasks, which can then be allocated to different personnel or departments. When an organization implements adequate separation of duties, collusion between two or more personnel would be required to carry out fraud against the organization. Split knowledge, a variation of separation of duties, ensures that no single employee knows all the details to perform a task. An example would be two individuals knowing parts of a combination for a safety lock or server room. Another variation is dual control, which requires that two employees must be available to complete a specific task to complete the job. An example is two managers being required to turn keys simultaneously in separate locations to launch a missile.

Key Topic

Risk Management Concepts

When implementing risk analysis and ***risk management***, it is important to understand the different concepts associated with this area. Next, we explain the following terms: *asset*, *asset valuation*, *vulnerability*, *threat*, *threat agent*, *exploit*, *risk*, *exposure*, *countermeasure*, *risk appetite*, *attack*, and *breach*.

We also discuss risk management policy; risk management team; risk analysis team; risk assessment; implementation; control categories; control types; control assessment, monitoring, and measurement; reporting and continuous improvement; and risk frameworks.

Asset and Asset Valuation

An ***asset*** is any resource, human, animal, product, process, system, or other thing that has value to an organization and must be protected. ***Physical assets*** or ***tangible assets***, including equipment or computers, are assets that can physically exist on or off property. ***Intangible assets***, including information or intellectual property, are assets that hold value to the organization but often may not physically exist. All organizational assets should be documented.

As part of risk management, all documented assets must be assessed for their value to the organization. Three basic elements are used to determine an asset's value:

- The initial and ongoing cost for purchasing, licensing, developing, and maintaining the physical or information asset
- The asset's value to the enterprise's operations
- The asset's value established on the external marketplace and estimated value of the intellectual property

Many organizations also factor in additional elements, including the following:

- Value of the asset to adversaries
- Cost to replace the asset if lost
- Operational and productivity costs incurred if the asset is unavailable
- Liability issues if the asset is compromised

No matter which elements are used to determine ***asset valuation***, it is important that this information is documented. When new assets are acquired, they should be documented and assessed to add to the risk management plan. In addition, organizations should reassess assets and their value to the organization at least annually.

Vulnerability

A ***vulnerability*** is a weakness. Vulnerabilities can occur in software, hardware, facilities, or personnel. An example of a vulnerability is unrestricted access to a folder on a computer shared by several people. Most organizations implement a vulnerability assessment to identify vulnerabilities.

Threat

A ***threat*** is the next logical progression in risk management. A threat occurs when a vulnerability is identified or exploited and is a potential danger. A threat would occur when an attacker identifies the folder on a shared computer that has an inappropriate or absent ACL.

Threat Agent

A threat is carried out by a ***threat agent***. Continuing with the example above, the attacker who takes advantage of the inappropriate or absent ACL is the threat agent. Keep in mind, though, that threat agents can discover and/or exploit vulnerabilities. Not all threat agents will actually exploit an identified vulnerability.

Exploit

An exploit occurs when a threat agent successfully takes advantage of a vulnerability.

Risk

A ***risk*** is the probability that a threat agent will exploit a vulnerability and the impact if the threat is successfully carried out. Risk is expressed in terms of the likelihood and impact of a threat event. The risk in the vulnerability example would be fairly high if the data residing in the folder is confidential. However, if the folder contains only public data, then the risk would be low. Identifying the potential impact of a risk often requires security professionals to enlist the help of subject matter experts.

Exposure

An ***exposure*** is an opening or an opportunity for an attacker. If the folder with the inappropriate or absent ACL exists, the organization is exposed to the possibility of data exposure and loss.

Countermeasure

A control (sometimes called a ***countermeasure*** or ***safeguard***) is a tactic, mechanism, or strategy that accomplishes one or more of the following:

- Reduces or eliminates a vulnerability
- Reduces or eliminates the likelihood that a threat agent will be able to exploit a vulnerability
- Reduces or eliminates the impact of an exploit

For our example, a good countermeasure would be to implement the appropriate ACL and to encrypt the data. The ACL protects the integrity of the data, and the encryption protects the confidentiality of the data.

Countermeasures or controls come in many categories and types. The categories and types of controls are discussed in the "Control Categories" and "Control Types" sections later in this chapter.

All the aforementioned security concepts work together in a relationship that is demonstrated in Figure 1-17.

Risk Appetite

Risk appetite is the level of risk an organization is prepared to withstand or absorb. The risk appetite for an organization can only be defined based on the organization's needs, and risk appetites will vary from organization to organization.

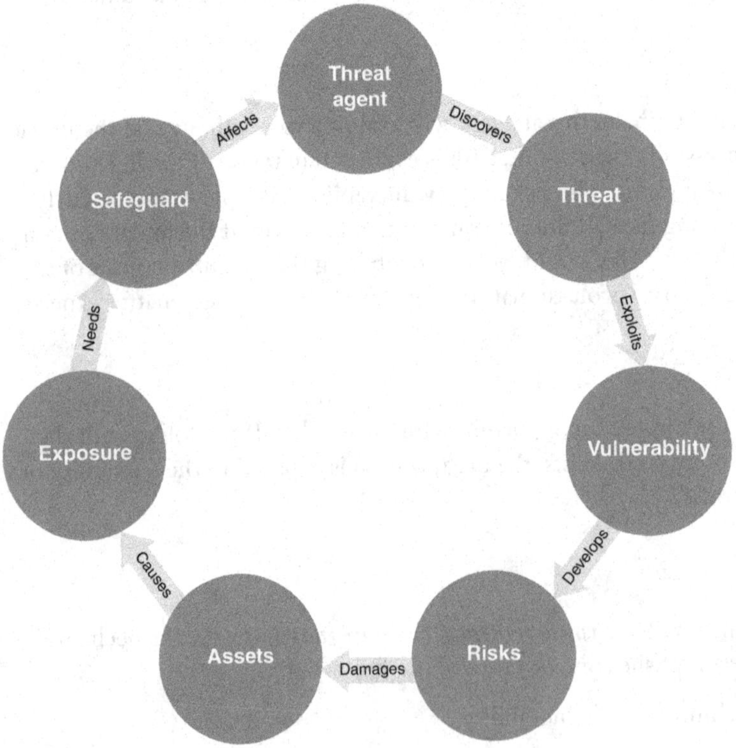

Figure 1-17 Security Concept Cycle

Incident

An ***incident*** is any event that violates an organization's security or privacy policies. It is important that all incidents are documented and fully analyzed so that the organization can take measures to prevent the incident from happening again. The measures that are taken can also prevent the incident from becoming an attack in the future.

Attack

An ***attack*** is an incident that attempts to compromise a device or the data stored on the device. Not all incidents become an attack, but all attacks are incidents.

Breach

A ***breach*** is an attack that has been successful in reaching its goal. Often, a breach of an organization's data constitutes a security incident that the organization is legally required to report to affected individuals, regulatory agencies, and sometimes credit reporting agencies and media. It is vital that an organization quickly and effectively responds when an incident does escalate into a data breach. When a data breach has occurred, security professionals should, at minimum, quantify the damage and follow the organizational policies and procedures to determine the response.

Risk Management Policy

Senior management has a responsibility for and must commit to the risk management process. The risk management policy is a formal statement of senior management's commitment to risk management. The policy also provides risk management direction.

A risk management policy must include the overall risk management plan and list the risk management team and must specifically list the risk management team's objectives, responsibilities and roles, acceptable level of risk, risk identification process, risk and safeguards mapping, safeguard effectiveness, monitoring process and targets, and future risk analysis plans and tasks.

Risk Management Team

Depending on the size of the organization, the risk management team might be an actual team of employees or might consist of only a single team member. For any organization, the team's goal is to protect the organization and its assets from risk in the most cost-effective way. Because in most cases the risk management team members are not dedicated solely to risk management, senior management must specifically put a resource allocation measure in place to ensure the success of the risk management process.

Management must also ensure that the members of the risk management team, particularly the team leader, be given the necessary training and tools for risk management. In larger organizations, the team leader should be able to dedicate the majority of their time to the risk management process.

Risk Analysis Team

To perform the most comprehensive risk analysis, the risk analysis team must consist of a representative from as many departments and as many employment levels as possible. Having a diverse risk analysis team ensures that risks from all areas of the organization can be determined.

If the risk analysis team cannot contain members from all departments, the members must interview each department to understand all the threats encountered by that department. During the risk analysis process, the risk analysis team should determine the threat events that could occur, the potential impact of the threats, the frequency of the threats, and the level of confidence in the information gathered.

Risk Assessment

A risk assessment is a tool used in risk management to identify vulnerabilities and threats, assess the impact of those vulnerabilities and threats, and determine which controls to implement. Risk assessment or analysis has four main goals:

- Identify assets and asset value.
- Identify vulnerabilities and threats.
- Calculate threat probability and business impact.
- Balance threat impact with countermeasure cost.

Prior to starting the risk assessment, management and the risk assessment team must determine which assets and threats to consider. This process determines the size of the project. The risk assessment team must then provide a report to management on the value of the assets considered. Management can then review and finalize the asset list, adding and removing assets as it sees fit, and then determine the budget of the risk assessment project.

If a risk assessment is not supported and directed by senior management, it will not be successful. Management must define the risk assessment's purpose and scope and allocate the personnel, time, and monetary resources for the project.

As you will later learn, the NIST Special Publication 800-30 Rev. 1 provides guidelines for conducting a risk assessment on federal information systems and organizations.

Information and Asset (Tangible/Intangible) Value and Costs

As stated earlier, the first step of any risk assessment is to identify the assets and determine the asset value. Assets are both tangible and intangible. Tangible assets include computers, facilities, supplies, and personnel. Intangible assets include intellectual property, data, computer software, and organizational reputation. The value of an asset should be considered in respect to the asset owner's view. The six following considerations can be used to determine the asset's value:

- Value to owner
- Work required to develop or obtain the asset
- Costs to maintain the asset
- Damage that would result if the asset were lost
- Cost that competitors would pay for asset
- Penalties that would result if the asset were lost

After determining the value of the assets, you should determine the vulnerabilities and threats to each asset.

Identity Threats and Vulnerabilities

When determining vulnerabilities and threats to an asset, considering the threat agents first is often easiest. Threat agents can be grouped into the following six categories:

- **Human:** Includes both malicious and nonmalicious insiders and outsiders, terrorists, spies, and terminated personnel.
- **Natural:** Includes floods, fires, tornadoes, hurricanes, earthquakes, or other natural disasters or weather events.
- **Technical:** Includes hardware and software failure, malicious code, and new technologies.
- **Physical:** Includes CCTV issues, perimeter measures failure, and biometric failure.

- **Environmental:** Includes power and other utility failure, traffic issues, biological warfare, and hazardous material issues (such as spillage).
- **Operational:** Includes any process or procedure that can affect CIA.

When the vulnerabilities and threats have been identified, the loss potential for each must be determined. This loss potential is determined by using the likelihood of the event combined with the impact that such an event would cause. An event with a high likelihood and a high impact would be given more importance than an event with a low likelihood and a low impact. Different types of risk analysis, including quantitative risk analysis and qualitative risk analysis, should be used to ensure that the data that is obtained is maximized.

Risk Assessment/Analysis

After the risk analysis team is formed, it is time to actually start the risk analysis or assessment process. Prior to performing a risk assessment or analysis, the scope of the risk assessment or analysis must be documented. This process includes two different types of risk analysis: quantitative risk analysis and qualitative risk analysis.

Risk Assessment/Analysis Scope

The scope of risk assessment/analysis defines the assets, processes, department, or other organizational aspect that will be assessed for risks during the current risk assessment or analysis. It is important that the scope of the risk assessment/analysis is documented to ensure that the team responsible will assess the correct components.

Risk assessment/analysis is a time-consuming process even with the smallest of scopes. The organization should document the scope prior to choosing the members of the team performing the assessment/analysis. This ensures that the team members chosen are the best ones for the job.

For example, if the organization is performing a risk assessment/analysis for a particular human resources server, members of the human resources department likely need to be involved. Without involving the right team members, risks may be missed or not properly valued during the risk assessment/analysis process.

Quantitative Risk Analysis

A ***quantitative risk analysis*** assigns monetary and numeric values to all facets of the risk analysis process, including asset value, threat frequency, vulnerability severity, impact, safeguard costs, and so on. Equations are used to determine total and residual risks. The most common equations are for single loss expectancy (SLE) and ***annual loss expectancy (ALE)***.

Key Topic

The SLE is the monetary impact of each threat occurrence. To determine the SLE, you must know the asset value (AV) and the ***exposure factor (EF)***. The EF is the percent value or functionality of an asset that will be lost when a threat event occurs. The calculation for obtaining the SLE is as follows:

$$SLE = AV \times EF$$

For example, an organization has a web server farm with an AV of $20,000. If the risk assessment has determined that a power failure could occur for the web server farm and the exposure factor for a power failure is 25 percent, the SLE for this event equals $20,000 × 0.25 = $5,000.

Key Topic

The ALE is a calculation of an annual threat event that demonstrates monetary loss should the risk materialize. To determine the ALE, you must know the SLE and the ***annualized rate of occurrence (ARO)***. The ARO is the estimate of how often a given threat might occur annually. The calculation for obtaining the ALE is as follows:

$$ALE = SLE \times ARO$$

Using the previously mentioned example, if the risk assessment has determined that the ARO for the power failure of the web server farm is two times (per year), the ALE for this event equals $5,000 × 2 = $10,000. Security professionals should keep in mind that this calculation can be adjusted for different geographical locations. For example, a DNS server located in a small town may have a higher risk of power outage than one in a large city.

Using the ALE, the organization can decide whether to implement controls or not. If the annual cost of the control to protect the web server farm is more than the ALE, the organization could easily choose to accept the risk by not implementing the control. If the annual cost of the control to protect the web server farm is less than the ALE, the organization should consider implementing the control.

Keep in mind that even though quantitative risk analysis uses numeric value, a purely quantitative analysis cannot be achieved because some level of subjectivity is always part of the data. In this example, how does the organization know that damage from the power failure will be 25 percent of the asset? This type of estimate should be based on historical data, industry experience, current and future conditions, and expert opinion.

An advantage of quantitative over qualitative risk analysis is that quantitative uses less guesswork than qualitative. Disadvantages of quantitative risk analysis include the difficulty of the equations, the time and effort needed to complete the analysis, and the level of data that must be gathered for the analysis.

Qualitative Risk Analysis

Qualitative risk analysis does not assign monetary and numeric values to all facets of the risk analysis process. Qualitative risk analysis techniques include intuition, experience, and best practice techniques, such as brainstorming, focus groups, surveys, questionnaires, meetings, and interviews. Although all of these techniques can be used, most organizations will determine the best technique(s) based on the threats to be assessed. Experience and education on the threats are needed.

All members of the group who have been chosen to participate in the qualitative risk analysis use their experience to rank the likelihood of each threat and the damage that might result. After each group member ranks the threat possibility, loss potential, and safeguard advantage, data is combined in a report to present to management. All levels of staff should be represented as part of the qualitative risk analysis, but it is vital that some participants in this process have some expertise in risk analysis.

Advantages of qualitative over quantitative risk analysis include the fact that qualitative analysis prioritizes the risks and identifies areas for immediate improvement in addressing the threats. Disadvantages of qualitative risk analysis include all results are subjective and a dollar value is not provided for cost-benefit analysis or for budget help.

Most risk analysis includes some hybrid use of both quantitative and qualitative risk analyses. Most organizations favor using quantitative risk analysis for tangible assets and qualitative risk analysis for intangible assets.

Countermeasure (Safeguard) Selection

Key Topic

The criteria for choosing a safeguard are the cost effectiveness of the safeguard or control, for compliance reasons, or to fulfill contractual obligations. Planning, designing, implementing, and maintenance costs need to be included in determining the total cost of a safeguard. To calculate a cost-benefit analysis, use the following equation:

> (ALE before safeguard) – (ALE after safeguard) – (Annual cost of safeguard) = Safeguard value

To complete this equation, you must know the revised ALE after the safeguard is implemented. Implementing a safeguard can improve the ARO but will not completely do away with it. In the example mentioned earlier in the "Quantitative Risk Analysis" section, the ALE for the given event is $5,000. Let's assume that implementing the safeguard reduces the ARO to one time per year, so the ALE after the safeguard is calculated is $5,000 × 1 or $5,000. You could then calculate the safeguard value for a control that costs $1,000 as follows:

$10,000 – $5,000 – $1,000 = $4,000

Knowing the corrected ARO after the safeguard is implemented is necessary for determining the safeguard value. A legal liability exists if the cost of the safeguard is less than the estimated loss that would occur if the threat were exploited.

Maintenance costs of safeguards are not often fully considered during this process. Organizations should fully research the costs of maintaining safeguards. New staff or extensive staff training often must occur to properly maintain a new safeguard. In addition, the cost of the labor involved must be determined. So, the cost of a safeguard must include the actual cost to implement plus any training costs, testing costs, labor costs, and so on. Some of these costs might be hard to identify, but a thorough risk analysis will account for these costs.

Inherent Risk Versus Residual Risk

Inherent risk is the risk that an organization could encounter if it decides not to implement any safeguards. No environment is ever fully secure, so you must always deal with residual risk. ***Residual risk*** is risk that is left over after safeguards have been implemented. Residual risk is represented using the following equation:

Residual risk = Inherent risk – Countermeasures

This equation is considered to be more conceptual than for actual calculation.

Handling Risk and Risk Response

Risk reduction is the process of altering a process, system, or device of the organization in response to risk analysis. After an organization understands its total and residual risk, it must determine how to handle the risk.

The following four basic risk response methods are used to handle risk:

Key Topic

- ***Risk avoidance***: Terminating the activity that causes a risk or choosing an alternative that is not as risky
- ***Risk transfer***: Passing some or all of the risk on to a third party, including insurance companies

- ***Risk mitigation*:** Defining the acceptable risk level the organization can tolerate and reducing the risk to that level
- ***Risk acceptance*:** Understanding and accepting the level of risk as well as the cost of damages that can occur

Organizations should document all the identified risks and the possible risk responses in a risk register. When an identified risk occurs, security professionals should consult the risk register to determine the steps that should be taken as documented in the risk register.

After selecting a risk response strategy, the next step is to develop and implement risk treatment plans. This involves:

- **Define actions:** Outline specific actions to be taken in line with the chosen risk response strategy. For mitigation, this could involve deploying new technologies or revising policies and procedures.
- **Allocate resources:** Determine and allocate the necessary resources, including budget, personnel, and technology, to implement the treatment plan.
- **Assign responsibility:** Assign individuals or teams responsible for implementing the risk treatment plan.
- **Set timelines:** Establish clear timelines for the implementation of risk treatment actions.
- **Monitor and review:** Continuous monitoring of risk treatment actions is essential to assess their effectiveness. This should be coupled with regular reviews to adjust the treatment plans as necessary, based on changes in the risk environment or the business itself.

For security professionals, understanding and effectively applying risk response and treatment strategies is essential. They are expected to guide the risk management process, ensuring that risks are appropriately addressed, resources are efficiently used, and the organization's information assets are adequately protected.

Implementation

Before implementing any controls that have been chosen as part of the risk analysis process, security professionals must consider the frameworks used for reference, tools deployed, and metrics for managing the controls. These three facets ensure the success of the security architecture. The goal of any risk countermeasure implementation is to improve the organization's security without negatively impacting performance.

All organizational personnel should be involved in the deployment of countermeasures and controls for risk management. Each individual involved in the implementation will have a unique perspective on the risks of that individual's position. Documentation and communication across all areas will ensure that each individual business unit's risk management implementation is as complete as possible.

Control Categories

You implement access controls as a countermeasure to identified vulnerabilities. Access control mechanisms that can be used are divided into seven main categories:

Key Topic

- Compensative
- Corrective
- Detective
- Deterrent
- Directive
- Preventive
- Recovery

Any access control that is implemented will fit into one or more access control categories.

NOTE Access controls are also defined by the type of protection they provide. Access control types are discussed later in the chapter.

Compensative

Compensative controls, also known as compensating controls, are in place to substitute for a primary access control and mainly act as a mitigation to risks. Using compensative controls, you can reduce the risk to a more manageable level. Examples of compensative controls include requiring two authorized signatures to release sensitive or confidential information and requiring two keys owned by different personnel to open a safety deposit box.

Corrective

Corrective controls, also known as correcting controls, are in place to reduce the effect of an attack or other undesirable event. Using corrective controls fixes or restores the entity that is attacked. Examples of corrective controls include installing fire extinguishers, isolating or terminating a connection, implementing new firewall rules, and using server images to restore to a previous state.

Detective

Detective controls, also known as detecting controls, are in place to detect a threat prior to is becoming an attack or while an attack is occurring to alert appropriate personnel. Examples of detective controls include motion detectors, intrusion detection systems (IDSs), logs, guards, investigations, and job rotation.

Deterrent

Deterrent controls, also known as deterring controls, deter or discourage an attacker. Via deterrent controls, attacks can be discovered early in the process. Deterrent controls often trigger preventive and corrective controls. Examples of deterrent controls include user identification and authentication, fences, lighting, and organizational security policies, such as an NDA.

Directive

Directive controls, also known as directing controls, specify acceptable practice within an organization. They are in place to formalize an organization's security directive mainly to its employees. The most popular directive control is an acceptable use policy (AUP) that lists proper (and often examples of improper) procedures and behaviors that personnel must follow. Any organizational security policies or procedures usually fall into this access control category. Directive controls are efficient only if there is a stated consequence for not following the organization's directions.

Preventive

Preventive controls, also known as preventing controls, prevent an attack from occurring. Examples of preventive controls include locks, badges, biometric systems, encryption, intrusion prevention systems (IPSs), antivirus software, personnel security, security guards, passwords, and security awareness training.

Recovery

Recovery controls, also known as recovering controls, recover a system or device after an attack or incident has occurred. The primary goal of recovery controls is restoring resources. Examples of recovery controls include disaster recovery plans, data backups, and offsite facilities.

Control Types

Whereas the access control categories classify the access controls based on where they fit in time, access control types divide access controls on their method of implementation. The three types of access controls are

Key Topic

- Administrative (management) controls
- Logical (technical) controls
- Physical controls

In any organization where defense in depth is a priority, access control requires the use of all three types of access controls. Even if you implement the strictest physical and administrative controls, you cannot fully protect the environment without logical controls.

Administrative (Management)

Administrative controls or ***management controls*** are implemented to administer the organization's assets and personnel and include security policies, procedures, standards, baselines, and guidelines that are established by management. These controls are commonly referred to as soft controls. Specific examples are personnel controls, data classification, data labeling, security awareness training, and supervision.

Security awareness training is a very important administrative control. Its purpose is to improve the organization's attitude about safeguarding data. The benefits of security awareness training include a reduction in the number and severity of errors and omissions, a better understanding of information value, and improved administrator recognition of unauthorized intrusion attempts. A cost-effective way to ensure that employees take security awareness seriously is to create an award or recognition program.

Table 1-3 lists many administrative controls and includes in which access control categories the controls fit.

Security professionals should help develop organization policies and procedures to ensure that personnel understand what is expected and how to properly carry out their duties. Applicant evaluation, prior to employment, is also important to protect the organization. Personnel security, evaluation, and clearances ensure that personnel are given access only to those resources or areas required by their specific roles within the organization. Monitoring and logs ensure that security professionals have a way to analyze behavior. User access should be managed, including user access approval, unique user IDs, periodic reviews of user access, user password processes, and access modification and revocation procedures.

Table 1-3 Administrative (Management) Controls

Administrative (Management) Controls	Compensative	Corrective	Detective	Deterrent	Directive	Preventive	Recovery
Personnel procedures						X	
Security policies				X	X	X	
Monitoring			X				
Separation of duties						X	
Job rotation	X		X				
Information classification						X	
Security awareness training						X	
Investigations			X				
Disaster recovery plan						X	X
Security reviews			X				
Background checks			X				
Termination		X					
Supervision	X						

Logical (Technical)

Logical controls or technical controls are software or hardware components used to restrict access. Specific examples of logical controls include firewalls, IDSs, IPSs, encryption, authentication systems, protocols, auditing and monitoring, biometrics, smart cards, and passwords.

Although auditing and monitoring are logical controls and are often listed together, they are actually two different controls. Auditing is a one-time or periodic event to evaluate the security posture of the organization or component. Monitoring is an ongoing activity that examines either the system or users.

Table 1-4 lists many logical controls and includes in which access control categories the controls fit.

Network access, remote access, application access, and computer or device access all fit into this category.

Physical

Physical controls are implemented to protect an organization's facilities and personnel. Personnel concerns should take priority over all other concerns. Specific examples of physical controls include perimeter security, badges, swipe cards, guards, dogs, man traps, biometrics, and cabling.

Table 1-5 lists many physical controls and includes in which access control categories the controls fit.

When controlling physical entry into a building, security professionals should ensure that the appropriate policies are in place for visitor control, including visitor logs, visitor escort, and limitations on visitor access to sensitive areas.

Table 1-4 Logical (Technical) Controls

Logical (Technical) Controls	Compensative	Corrective	Detective	Deterrent	Directive	Preventive	Recovery
Password						X	
Biometrics						X	
Smart cards						X	
Encryption						X	
Protocols						X	
Firewalls						X	
IDS			X				
IPS						X	
Access control lists						X	
Routers						X	
Auditing			X				
Monitoring			X				
Data backups							X
Antivirus software						X	
Configuration standards					X		
Warning banners				X			
Connection isolation and termination		X					

Table 1-5 Physical Controls

Physical (Technical) Controls	Compensative	Corrective	Detective	Deterrent	Directive	Preventive	Recovery
Fencing				X		X	
Locks						X	
Guards			X			X	
Fire extinguisher		X					
Badges						X	
Swipe cards						X	
Dogs			X			X	
Man traps						X	
Biometrics						X	
Lighting				X			
Motion detectors			X				
CCTV	X		X			X	
Data backups							X
Antivirus software						X	
Configuration standards					X		
Warning banner				X			
Hot, warm, and cold sites							X

Controls Assessment, Monitoring, and Measurement

Security control assessments (SCAs) should be used to verify that the security goals of an organization or a business unit are being met. Vulnerability assessments and penetration tests are considered part of this process and are covered in Chapter 6, "Security Assessment and Testing." If a security control is implemented that does not meet a security goal, this security control is ineffective. After the assessment has been conducted, security professionals should use the assessment results to determine which security controls have weaknesses or deficiencies. Security professionals should then work to eliminate the vulnerabilities or deficiencies.

Security controls should be monitored to ensure that they are always performing in the way expected. As part of this monitoring, security professionals should review all logs. In addition, performance reports should be run and compared with the performance baselines for all security devices and controls. This analysis allows security professionals to anticipate some issues and resolve them before they become critical. The performance measurements that are taken should be retained over time. New baselines need to be captured if significant events or changes occur. For example, if you add 200 new users who will need authentication, you need to capture new authentication baselines to ensure that authentication can still occur in a timely manner. In addition, if you change an authentication setting, such as implementing an account lockout policy, you should monitor the effect that the setting has on performance and security.

Reporting and Continuous Improvement

Security professionals can never just sit back, relax, and enjoy the ride. Security needs are always changing because the "bad guys" never take a day off. It is therefore vital that security professionals continuously work to improve their organization's security. Tied into this is the need to improve the quality of the security controls currently implemented.

Quality improvement commonly uses a four-step quality model, known as Deming's Plan–Do–Check–Act cycle. These are the steps in this cycle:

1. **Plan:** Identify an area for improvement and make a formal plan to implement it.
2. **Do:** Implement the plan on a small scale.
3. **Check:** Analyze the results of the implementation to determine whether it made a difference.
4. **Act:** If the implementation made a positive change, implement it on a wider scale. Continuously analyze the results.

Other similar guidelines include Six Sigma, Lean, and Total Quality Management. No matter which of these an organization uses, the result should be a continuous cycle of improvement organizationwide.

Internal Reporting

The primary goal of internal reporting is to inform the organization's management and relevant stakeholders about the current risk landscape, the effectiveness of risk mitigation strategies, and any need for adjustments in risk management policies. The audience of the internal report typically includes senior management, the board of directors, department heads, and other relevant internal stakeholders.

Internal reports may contain details about identified risks, the impact and likelihood of these risks, mitigation actions taken, and any residual risk. They also cover incidents that have occurred, lessons learned, and recommendations for future actions. Internal reporting is often conducted at regular intervals (e.g., monthly, quarterly, annually) and may be presented in various formats such as formal reports, dashboards, or briefings. Effective internal reporting ensures that risk management is integrated into the organization's decision-making process, aligning with business goals and objectives.

External Reporting

The primary goal of internal reporting is to inform entities outside the organization, often to meet regulatory requirements, compliance needs, or contractual obligations. The audience of the external report includes regulators, investors, customers, partners, and other external stakeholders.

Depending on the audience and purpose, external reports might include compliance status with specific regulations (like GDPR or HIPAA), details about security breaches (if disclosure is required), and general information about the organization's risk management practices. Many industries have specific reporting requirements. For instance, companies in the financial sector might have to report to regulatory bodies like the SEC or FINRA, detailing their risk management practices and compliance status.

External reporting can also be a tool for building transparency and trust with customers and partners, showcasing the organization's commitment to effective risk management.

CISSP professionals are expected to have a deep understanding of both internal and external reporting mechanisms as part of their risk management responsibilities. They should be skilled in identifying what needs to be reported, to whom, and in what format. This includes understanding legal and regulatory requirements for external reporting and the strategic needs of internal stakeholders.

CISSP professionals should be adept at communicating complex risk information in an accessible manner and ensuring that documentation meets the necessary standards of clarity, completeness, and accuracy.

Risk Frameworks

Risk frameworks can serve as guidelines to any organization that is involved in the risk analysis and management process. Organizations should use these frameworks as guides but should also feel free to customize any plans and procedures they implement to fit their needs.

NIST

To comply with the federal standard, organizations first determine the security category of their information system in accordance with Federal Information Processing Standard (FIPS) Publication 199, *Standards for Security Categorization of Federal Information and Information Systems*, derive the information system impact level from the security category in accordance with FIPS Publication 200, and then apply the appropriately tailored set of baseline security controls in NIST Special Publication 800-53 Rev. 5.

The NIST risk management framework includes the following steps:

Key Topic

1. Categorize information systems.
2. Select security controls.
3. Implement security controls.
4. Assess security controls.
5. Authorize information systems.
6. Monitor security controls.

These steps implement different NIST publications, including FIPS 199, SP 800-60, FIPS 200, SP 800-53 Rev. 5, SP 800-160 Vol. 2, SP 800-53A Rev. 4, SP 800-37 Rev. 2, and SP 800-137.

Figure 1-18 shows the NIST risk management framework.

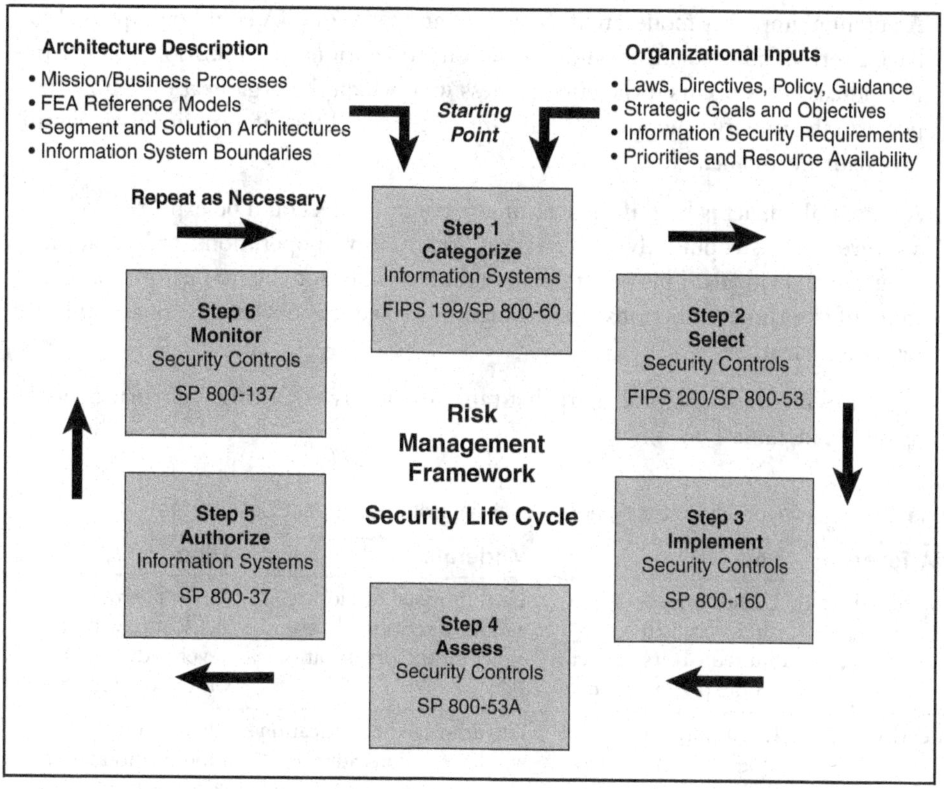

Figure 1-18 NIST Risk Management Framework (Image Courtesy of NIST)

FIPS 199

FIPS 199 defines standards for security categorization of federal information systems. The FIPS 199 nomenclature may be referred to as the *aggregate CIA score*. This U.S. government standard establishes security categories of information systems used by the federal government.

FIPS 199 requires federal agencies to assess their information systems in the categories of confidentiality, integrity, and availability and rate each system as low, moderate, or high impact in each category. An information system's overall security category is the highest rating from any category.

A potential impact is low if the loss of any tenet of CIA could be expected to have a limited adverse effect on organizational operations, organizational assets, or individuals. This occurs if the organization is able to perform its primary function but not as effectively as normal. This category involves only minor damage, financial loss, or harm.

A potential impact is moderate if the loss of any tenet of CIA could be expected to have a serious adverse effect on organizational operations, organizational assets, or individuals. This occurs if the effectiveness with which the organization is able to perform its primary function is significantly reduced. This category involves significant damage, financial loss, or harm.

A potential impact is high if the loss of any tenet of CIA could be expected to have a severe or catastrophic adverse effect on organizational operations, organizational assets, or individuals. This occurs if an organization is not able to perform one or more of its primary functions. This category involves major damage, financial loss, or severe harm.

FIPS 199 provides a helpful chart that ranks the levels of CIA for information assets, as shown in Table 1-6.

Key Topic

Table 1-6 Confidentiality, Integrity, and Availability Potential Impact Definitions

CIA Tenet	Low	Moderate	High
Confidentiality	Unauthorized disclosure will have limited adverse effect on the organization.	Unauthorized disclosure will have serious adverse effect on the organization.	Unauthorized disclosure will have severe adverse effect on the organization.
Integrity	Unauthorized modification will have limited adverse effect on the organization.	Unauthorized modification will have serious adverse effect on the organization.	Unauthorized modification will have severe adverse effect on the organization.
Availability	Unavailability will have limited adverse effect on the organization.	Unavailability will have serious adverse effect on the organization.	Unavailability will have severe adverse effect on the organization.

It is also important that security professionals and organizations understand the information classification and life cycle. Classification varies depending on whether the organization is a commercial business or a military/government entity.

According to Table 1-6, FIPS 199 defines three impacts (low, moderate, and high) for the three security tenets. But the levels that are assigned to organizational entities must be defined by the organization because only the organization can determine whether a particular loss is limited, serious, or severe.

Key Topic

According to FIPS 199, the security category (SC) of an identified entity expresses the three tenets with their values for an organizational entity. The values are then used to determine which security controls should be implemented. If a particular asset is made up of multiple entities, then you must calculate the SC for that asset based on the entities that make it up. FIPS 199 provides a nomenclature for expressing these values, as shown here:

$$SC_{\textit{information type}} = \{(\text{confidentiality, impact}), (\text{integrity, impact}), (\text{availability, impact})\}$$

Let's look at an example of this nomenclature in a real-world example:

$$SC_{\textit{public site}} = \{(\text{confidentiality, low}), (\text{integrity, moderate}), (\text{availability, high})\}$$

$$SC_{\textit{partner site}} = \{(\text{confidentiality, moderate}), (\text{integrity, high}), (\text{availability, moderate})\}$$

$$SC_{\textit{internal site}} = \{(\text{confidentiality, high}), (\text{integrity, moderate}), (\text{availability, moderate})\}$$

Now let's assume that all of the sites reside on the same web server. To determine the nomenclature for the web server, you need to use the highest values of each of the categories:

$$SC_{\textit{web server}} = \{(\text{confidentiality, high}), (\text{integrity, high}), (\text{availability, high})\}$$

Some organizations may decide to place the public site on a web server and isolate the partner site and internal site on another web server. In this case, the public web server would not need all of the same security controls and would be cheaper to implement than the partner/internal web server.

SP 800-60 Vol. 1 Rev. 1

Security categorization is the key first step in the NIST risk management framework. FIPS 199 works with NIST SP 800-60 to identify information types, establish security impact levels for loss, and assign security categorization for the information types and for the information systems as detailed in the following process:

1. Identify information types.
   a. Identify mission-based information types based on 26 mission areas, including defense and national security, homeland security, disaster management, natural resources, energy, transportation, education, health, and law enforcement.
   b. Identify management and support information based on 13 lines of business, including regulatory development, planning and budgeting, risk management and mitigation, and revenue collection.
2. Select provisional impact levels using FIPS 199.

3. Review provisional impact levels and finalize impact levels.

4. Assign system security category.

Let's look at an example: An information system used for acquisitions contains both sensitive, presolicitation phase contract information, and routine administrative information. The management within the contracting organization determines that

- For the sensitive contract information, the potential impact from a loss of confidentiality is moderate, the potential impact from a loss of integrity is moderate, and the potential impact from a loss of availability is low.
- For the routine administrative information (non-privacy-related information), the potential impact from a loss of confidentiality is low, the potential impact from a loss of integrity is low, and the potential impact from a loss of availability is low.

The resulting security categories, or SCs, of these information types are expressed as

$SC_{\textit{contract information}}$ = {(confidentiality, moderate), (integrity, moderate), (availability, low)}

$SC_{\textit{administrative information}}$ = {(confidentiality, low), (integrity, low), (availability, low)}

The resulting security category of the information system is expressed as

$SC_{\textit{acquisition system}}$ = {(confidentiality, moderate), (integrity, moderate), (availability, low)}

This represents the high-water mark or maximum potential impact values for each security objective from the information types on the acquisition system.

In some cases, the impact level for a system security category will be higher than any security objective impact level for any information type processed by the system.

The primary factors that most commonly raise the impact levels of the system security category above that of its constituent information types are aggregation and critical system functionality. Other factors that can affect the impact level include public information integrity, catastrophic loss of system availability, large interconnecting systems, critical infrastructures and key resources, privacy information, and trade secrets.

The end result of NIST SP 800-60 Vol. 1 Rev. 1 is security categorization documentation for every information system. These categories can then be used to complete the business impact analysis (BIA), design the enterprise architecture, design the disaster recovery plan (DRP), and select the appropriate security controls.

SP 800-53 Rev. 5

NIST SP 800-53 Rev. 5 is a security controls development framework developed by the NIST body of the U.S. Department of Commerce.

SP 800-53 Rev. 5 divides the controls into three classes: technical, operational, and management. Each class contains control families or categories.

Table 1-7 lists the NIST SP 800-53, Rev. 5 control families.

Key Topic

Table 1-7 NIST SP 800-53 Control Families

Family
Access Control (AC)
Awareness and Training (AT)
Audit and Accountability (AU)
Assessment, Authorization, and Monitoring (CA)
Configuration Management (CM)
Contingency Planning (CP)
Identification and Authentication (IA)
Incident Response (IR)
Maintenance (MA)
Media Protection (MP)
Physical and Environmental Protection (PE)
Planning (PL)
Program Management (PM)
Personnel Security (PS)
PII Processing and Transparency (PT)
Risk Assessment (RA)
System and Services Acquisition (SA)
System and Communications Protection (SC)
System and Information Integrity (SI)
Supply Chain Risk Management (SR)

To assist organizations in making the appropriate selection of security controls for information systems, this framework introduces the concept of baseline controls. Baseline controls are the starting point for the security control selection process described in SP 800-53 Rev. 5 and are chosen based on the security category and associated impact level of information systems determined in accordance with FIPS Publication 199 and FIPS Publication 200, respectively. This publication recommends that the organization assigns responsibility for common controls to appropriate organizational officials and coordinates the development, implementation, assessment, authorization, and monitoring of the controls.

The process in this NIST publication includes the following steps:

Key Topic

1. Select security control baselines.
2. Tailor baseline security controls.
3. Document the control selection process.
4. Apply the control selection process to new development and legacy systems.

Figure 1-19 shows the NIST security control selection process.

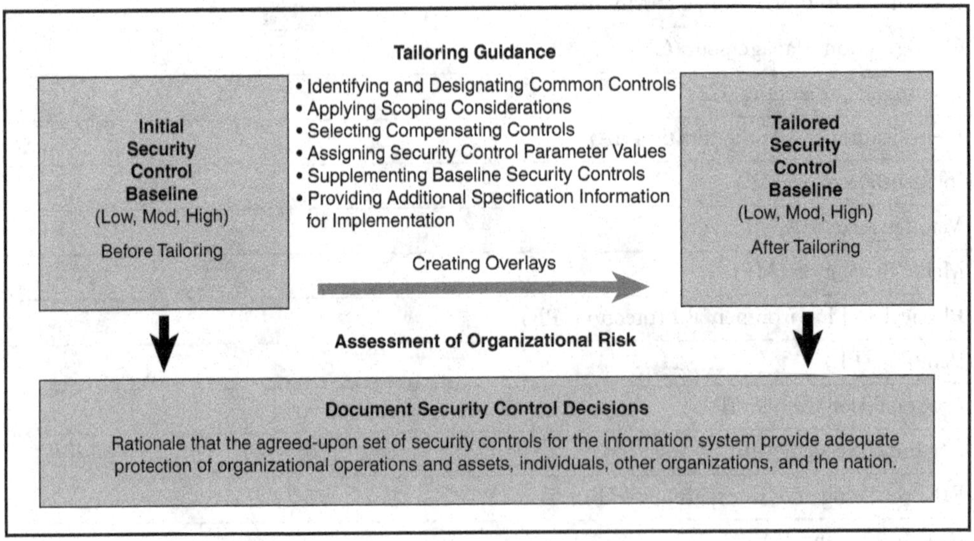

Figure 1-19 NIST Security Control Selection Process (Image Courtesy of NIST)

SP 800-160

NIST SP 800-160 defines the systems security engineering framework. It defines and focuses the systems security engineering activities, both technical and non-technical, toward the achievement of stakeholder security objectives and presents a coherent, well-formed, evidence-based case that those objectives have been achieved. It is shown in Figure 1-20.

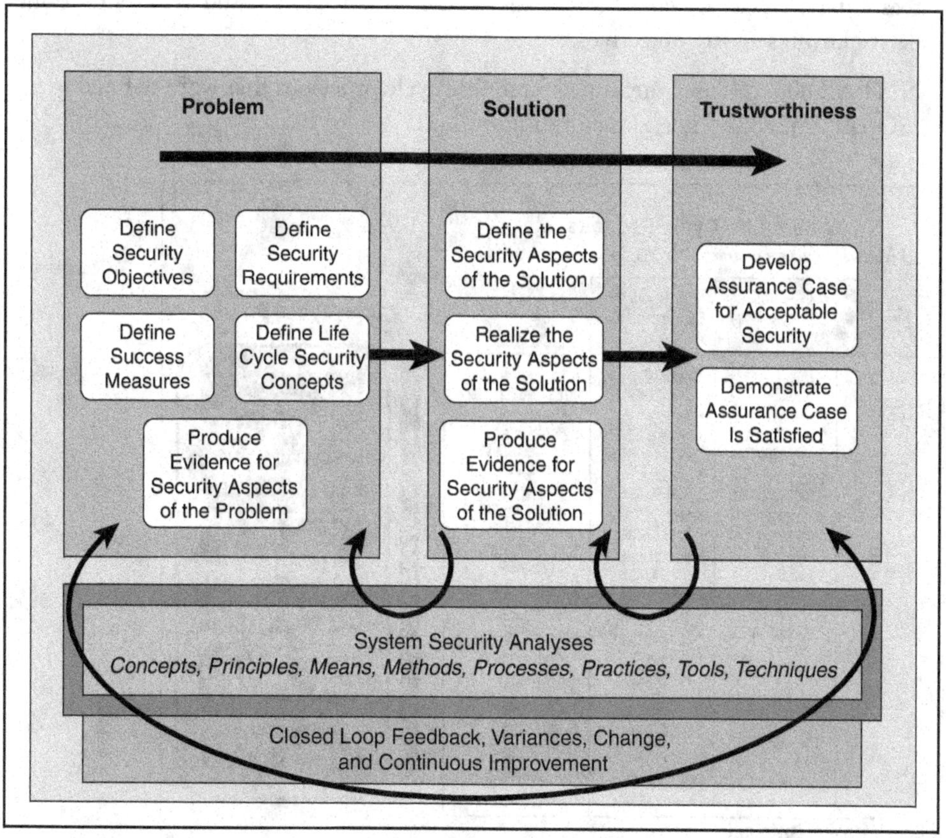

Figure 1-20 NIST Systems Security Engineering Framework (Image Courtesy of NIST)

The framework defines three contexts within which the systems security engineering activities are conducted. These are the problem context, the solution context, and the trustworthiness context.

The problem context defines the basis for a secure system given the stakeholder's mission, capability, performance needs, and concerns; the constraints imposed by stakeholder concerns related to cost, schedule, risk, and loss tolerance; and other constraints associated with life cycle concepts for the system. The solution context transforms the stakeholder security requirements into system design requirements; addresses all security architecture, design, and related aspects necessary to realize a system that satisfies those requirements; and produces sufficient evidence to demonstrate that those requirements have been satisfied. The trustworthiness context is a decision-making context that provides an evidence-based demonstration, through reasoning, that the system of interest is deemed trustworthy based on a set of claims derived from security objectives.

NIST SP 800-160 uses the same system life cycle processes that were defined in ISO/IEC 15288:2015, as shown in Figure 1-21.

Key Topic

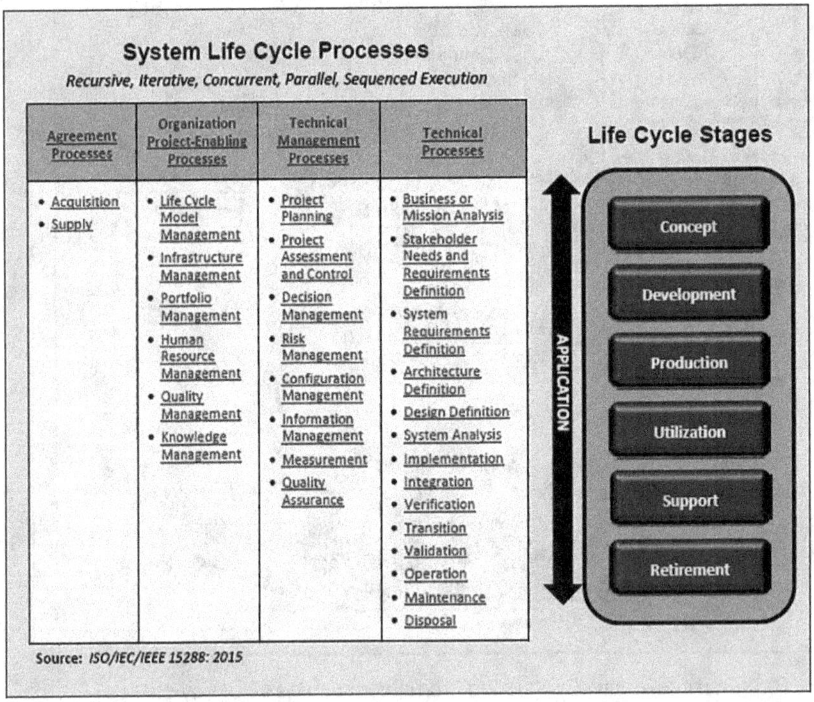

Figure 1-21 NIST System Life Cycle Processes and Stages (Image Courtesy of NIST)

The following naming convention is established for the system life cycle processes. Each process is identified by a two-character designation. Table 1-8 provides a listing of the system life cycle processes and their associated two-character designators.

Table 1-8 System Life Cycle Processes and Codes

ID	Process	ID	Process
AQ	Acquisition	MS	Measurement
AR	Architecture Definition	OP	Operation
BA	Business or Mission Analysis	PA	Project Assessment and Control
CM	Configuration Management	PL	Project Planning
DE	Design Definition	PM	Portfolio Management
DM	Decision Management	QA	Quality Assurance
DS	Disposal	QM	Quality Management
HR	Human Resource Management	RM	Risk Management
IF	Infrastructure Management	SA	System Analysis
IM	Information Management	SN	Stakeholder Needs and Requirements Definition
IN	Integration	SP	Supply
IP	Implementation	SR	System Requirements Definition
KM	Knowledge Management	TR	Transition
LM	Life Cycle Model Management	VA	Validation
MA	Maintenance	VE	Verification

Each process listed in Table 1-8 has a unique purpose within the life cycle. Each process has tasks associated with it.

SP 800-37 Rev. 2

NIST SP 800-37 Rev. 2 defines the tasks that should be carried out in each step of the risk management framework as follows (see also Figure 1-22):

Step 1. Prepare tasks.

Step 2. Categorize information system.

Step 3. Select security controls.

Step 4. Implement security controls.

Step 5. Assess security controls.

Step 6. Authorize the information system.

Step 7. Monitor security controls.

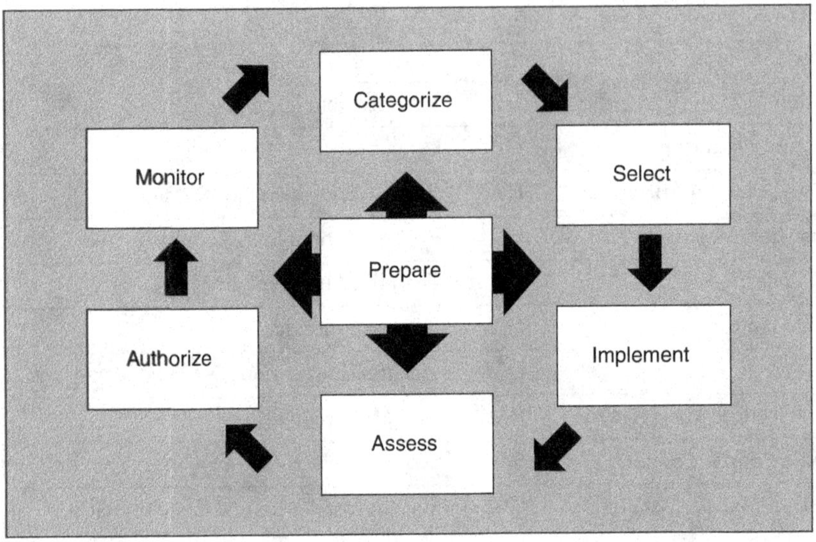

Figure 1-22 NIST SP 800-37 Rev. 2 Risk Management (Image Courtesy of NIST)

SP 800-30 Rev. 1

Key Topic

According to NIST SP 800-30 Rev. 1, common information-gathering techniques used in risk analysis include automated risk assessment tools, questionnaires, interviews, and policy document reviews. Multiple sources should be used to determine the risks to a single asset. NIST SP 800-30 identifies the following steps in the risk assessment process:

1. Prepare for the assessment.
2. Conduct the assessment.
   a. Identify threat sources and events.
   b. Identify vulnerabilities and predisposing conditions.
   c. Determine likelihood of occurrence.
   d. Determine magnitude of impact.
   e. Determine risk as a combination of likelihood and impact.
3. Communicate results.
4. Maintain the assessment.

Figure 1-23 shows the risk assessment process according to NIST SP 800-30.

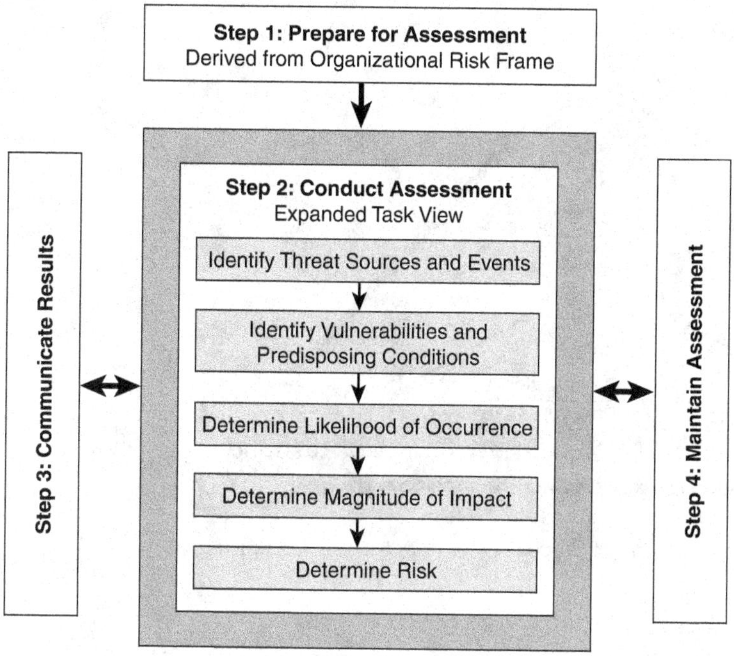

Figure 1-23 NIST SP 800-30 Risk Assessment Process (Image Courtesy of NIST)

SP 800-39

The purpose of NIST SP 800-39 is to provide guidance for an integrated, organizationwide program for managing information security risk to organizational operations (i.e., mission, functions, image, and reputation), organizational assets, individuals, other organizations, and the nation resulting from the operation and use of federal information systems. NIST SP 800-39 defines three tiers in an organization.

Tier 1 is the organization view, which addresses risk from an organizational perspective by establishing and implementing governance structures that are consistent with the strategic goals and objectives of organizations and the requirements defined by federal laws, directives, policies, regulations, standards, and missions/business functions. Tier 2 is the mission/business process view, which designs, develops, and implements mission/business processes that support the missions/business functions defined at Tier 1. Tier 3 is the information systems view, which includes operational systems, systems under development, systems undergoing modification, and systems in some phase of the system development life cycle.

Figure 1-24 shows the risk management process applied across all three tiers identified in NIST SP 800-39.

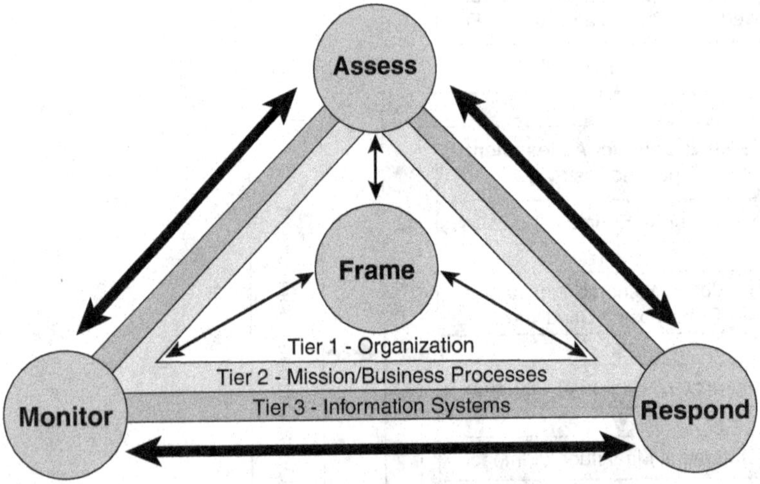

Figure 1-24 NIST Risk Management Process Applied Across All Three Tiers (Image Courtesy of NIST)

The risk management process involves the following steps:

1. Frame risk.
2. Assess risk.
3. Respond to risk.
4. Monitor risk.

NIST Framework for Improving Critical Infrastructure Cybersecurity

Key Topic

The NIST Framework for Improving Critical Infrastructure Cybersecurity provides a cybersecurity risk framework. The framework is based on five framework core functions:

1. **Identify (ID):** Develop the organizational understanding to manage cybersecurity risk to systems, assets, data, and capabilities.
2. **Protect (PR):** Develop and implement the appropriate safeguards to ensure delivery of critical infrastructure services.

3. **Detect (DE):** Develop and implement the appropriate activities to identify the occurrence of a cybersecurity event.
4. **Respond (RS):** Develop and implement the appropriate activities to take action regarding a detected cybersecurity event.
5. **Recover (RC):** Develop and implement the appropriate activities to maintain plans for resilience and to restore any capabilities or services that were impaired due to a cybersecurity event.

Within each of these functions, security professionals should define cybersecurity outcomes closely tied to organizational needs and particular activities. Each category is then divided into subcategories that further define specific outcomes of technical and/or management activities. The function and category unique identifiers are shown in Figure 1-25.

Framework implementation tiers describe the degree to which an organization's cybersecurity risk management practices exhibit the characteristics defined in the framework. The following four tiers are used:

- **Tier 1: Partial** means that risk management practices are not formalized, and risk is managed in an ad hoc and sometimes reactive manner.
- **Tier 2: Risk Informed** means that risk management practices are approved by management but may not be established as organizationwide policy.
- **Tier 3: Repeatable** means that the organization's risk management practices are formally approved and expressed as policy.
- **Tier 4: Adaptive** means that the organization adapts its cybersecurity practices based on lessons learned and predictive indicators derived from previous and current cybersecurity activities through a process of continuous improvement.

Finally, a framework profile is the alignment of the functions, categories, and subcategories with the business requirements, risk tolerance, and resources of the organization. A profile enables organizations to establish a roadmap for reducing cybersecurity risk that is well aligned with organizational and sector goals, considers legal/regulatory requirements and industry best practices, and reflects risk management priorities.

Function Unique Identifier	Function	Category Unique Identifier	Category
ID	Identify	ID.AM	Asset Management
		ID.BE	Business Environment
		ID.GV	Governance
		ID.RA	Risk Assessment
		ID.RM	Risk Management Strategy
		ID.SC	Supply Chain Risk Management
PR	Protect	PR.AC	Access Control
		PR.AT	Awareness and Training
		PR.DS	Data Security
		PR.IP	Information Protection Processes and Procedures
		PR.MA	Maintenance
		PR.PT	Protective Technology
DE	Detect	DE.AE	Anomalies and Events
		DE.CM	Security Continuous Monitoring
		DE.DP	Detection Processes
RS	Respond	RS.RP	Response Planning
		RS.CO	Communications
		RS.AN	Analysis
		RS.MI	Mitigation
		RS.IM	Improvements
RC	Recover	RC.RP	Recovery Planning
		RC.IM	Improvements
		RC.CO	Communications

Figure 1-25 NIST Cybersecurity Framework Function and Category Unique Identifiers (Image Courtesy of NIST)

The following steps illustrate how an organization could use the framework to create a new cybersecurity program or improve an existing program. These steps should be repeated as necessary to continuously improve cybersecurity:

1. Prioritize and scope.
2. Orient.
3. Create a current profile.
4. Conduct a risk assessment.
5. Create a target profile.

6. Determine, analyze, and prioritize gaps.
7. Implement the action plan.

An organization may repeat the steps as needed to continuously assess and improve its cybersecurity.

ISO/IEC 27005:2018

ISO/IEC 27005:2018 supports the concepts detailed in ISO/IEC 27001:2013. According to ISO/IEC 27005:2018, the risk management process consists of the following steps:

Key Topic

1. **Context Establishment:** Defines the risk management's boundary.
2. **Risk Analysis (Risk Identification & Estimation phases):** Evaluates the risk level.
3. **Risk Assessment (Risk Analysis & Evaluation phases):** Analyzes the identified risks and takes into account the objectives of the organization.
4. **Risk Treatment (Risk Treatment & Risk Acceptance phases):** Determines how to handle the identified risks.
5. **Risk Communication:** Shares information about risk between the decision makers and other stakeholders.
6. **Risk Monitoring and Review:** Detects any new risks and maintains the risk management plan.

Figure 1-26 shows the risk management process based on ISO/IEC 27005:2018.

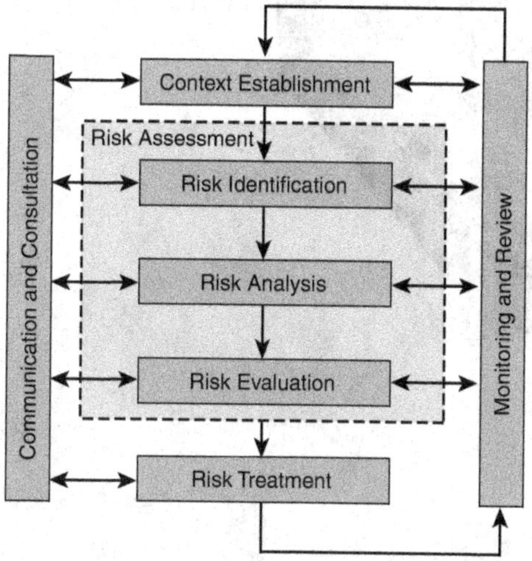

Figure 1-26 ISO/IEC 27005:2018 Risk Management Process

ISO/IEC 27005:2018 has been published. ISO/IEC FDIS 27005 is currently under development at time of writing.

COSO's Enterprise Risk Management (ERM) Integrated Framework

COSO broadly defines enterprise risk management, or ERM, as "the culture, capabilities and practices integrated with strategy-setting and its execution, that organizations rely on to manage risk in creating, preserving and realizing value." The ERM framework is presented in the form of a three-dimensional matrix. The matrix includes four categories of objectives across the top: strategic, operations, reporting, and compliance. There are eight components of enterprise risk management. Finally, the organization, its divisions, and business units are depicted as the third dimension of the matrix for applying the framework. The three-dimensional matrix of COSO's ERM is shown in Figure 1-27.

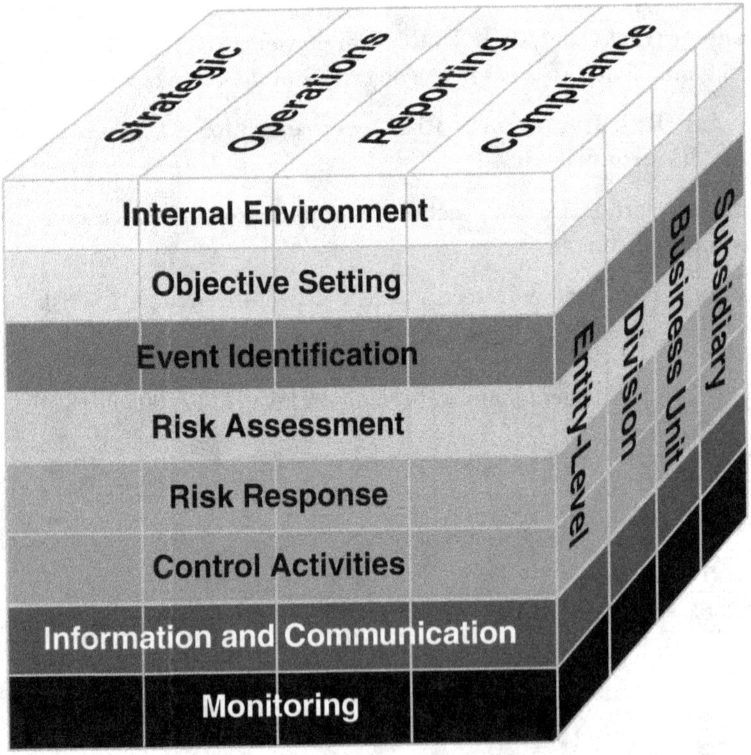

Figure 1-27 COSO's ERM Integrated Framework

A Risk Management Standard by the Federation of European Risk Management Associations (FERMA)

A Risk Management Standard by the Federation of European Risk Management Associations (FERMA) provides guidelines for managing risk in an organization. Figure 1-28 shows FERMA's risk management process as detailed in this standard.

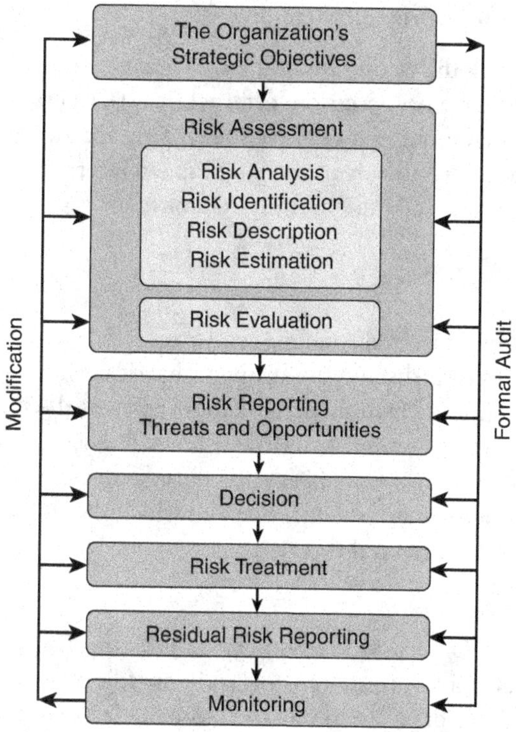

Figure 1-28 FERMA's Risk Management Process

Geographical Threats

Many threats are a function of the geographic location of the office or facility. The following sections discuss a wide variety of threats and issues, some of which apply to only certain areas. Security professionals must be prepared to anticipate and mitigate those issues.

Internal Versus External Threats

When talking about threats to the physical security of assets, we can frame the conversation by threats that appear from outside the organization and those that come from within the organization. Many of the mitigation techniques discussed in the following sections are designed to address maintaining perimeter security or access to the building or room, whereas other techniques are designed to address threats from those who might have some access to the room or building.

For example, an electric fence surrounding the facility is designed to prevent access to the building by those who should not have *any* access (an external threat), whereas a door lock system on the server room that requires a swipe of the employee card is designed to prevent access by those who are already in the building (an internal threat). Keep this distinction in mind as you read the following sections.

Natural Threats

Many of the physical threats that must be addressed and mitigated are caused by the forces of nature. Building all facilities to withstand the strongest hurricanes, tornadoes, and earthquakes is not economically feasible because in many areas these events happen infrequently, if ever. What *can* be done is to make a realistic assessment of the historical weather conditions of an area and perform a prudent cost/benefit analysis to determine which threats should be addressed and which should be accepted. Here, we discuss some of the major natural threats.

Hurricanes/Tropical Storms

In certain areas, hurricanes and tropical storms are so frequent and unpredictable that all buildings are required to be capable of withstanding the more moderate instances of these storms. In other areas, doing that makes no sense even though these storms do occur from time to time. The location of the facility should dictate how much is spent in mitigating possible damages from these events.

Tornadoes

Although events of the last few years might seem to contradict this statement, over the long haul certain areas are more prone to tornadoes than others. A study of the rate and severity of tornadoes in an area from a historical perspective can help to determine measures that make sense for a particular location.

NOTE In recent tornado outbreaks, many cellphone towers have been knocked out completely. In rural areas especially, communication with loved ones can be next to impossible. But the problem occurs not just in rural areas. In the Dallas–Fort Worth tornado outbreak in December 2015, it took many individuals up to 48 hours to locate loved ones because of lack of communications. You can imagine how this loss of communication would affect a company, school, or hospital. If an organization's systems relied on a failed communication network, this would affect availability of the systems to users.

Earthquakes

Earthquakes should be treated in the same way as hurricanes, tropical storms, and tornadoes; that is, the location of the specific facility should dictate the amount of preparation and the measures to take to address this risk. For example, facilities in California might give this issue more attention than those in the southeast of the United States where these events are extremely rare.

Floods

Flooding should always be a consideration because it is an event that can occur with the right circumstances just about anywhere. If at all possible, computing systems and equipment should be kept off the floor, and server rooms and wiring closets should be built on raised floors and away from windows and exit doors to help prevent damage that could occur in even a small flood.

Volcanoes

Volcanoes, like earthquakes, should be considered if the location warrants. For example, facilities in Hawaii might give this more consideration than facilities in the northeast United States.

System Threats

Some of the threats that exist are not from the forces of nature but from failures in systems that provide basic services, such as electricity and utilities. Although these ***system threats*** can sometimes arise from events of nature, here we discuss guidelines for preparing and dealing with these events, which can occur in any location and in any type of weather conditions.

Electrical

Electricity is the lifeline of the organization and especially in regard to computing systems; outages not only are an inconvenience but also can damage equipment and cause loss of data. Moreover, when the plug is pulled, to a large degree the enterprise grinds to a halt in today's world.

For this reason, all mission-critical systems should have uninterruptible power supplies (UPSs) that can provide power on a short-term basis until the system can be cleanly shut down. In cases where power must be maintained for longer than a matter of minutes, onsite generators should be available to provide the power to keep systems running on a longer-term basis until power is restored.

Noise, humidity, and brownouts are also issues that affect the electricity supply. The recommended optimal relative humidity range for computer operations is 40 to 60 percent. Critical systems must be protected from both power sags and surges. Neither is good for equipment. Line conditioners placed between the system and the power source can help to even out these fluctuations and prevent damage.

Finally, the most prevalent cause of computer center fires is electrical distribution systems. Checking these systems regularly can identify problems before they occur.

Communications

Protecting the physical security of communication, such as email, telephone, and fax systems, is a matter of preventing unauthorized access to the physical communication lines (cables and so on) and physical and logical access to equipment used to manage these systems.

For example, in the case of email, the email servers should be locked away, and access to them over the network must be tightly controlled with usernames and complex passwords.

In the case of fax machines, implementing policies and procedures can prevent sensitive faxes from becoming available to unauthorized persons. In some cases, preventing certain types of information from being transmitted with faxes might be necessary.

Many phone systems now have been merged into the data network using Voice over IP (VoIP). With these systems, routers and switches might be involved in managing the phone system and should be physically locked away and logically protected from network access in the same fashion as email servers. Because email and VoIP both use the data network, an organization should ensure that cabling is not exposed to tampering and malicious destruction. A plenum space is a pathway that can facilitate heating and cooling system airflow and should be considered when developing building or renovating server rooms.

NOTE The term *plenum* is also used in cabling technologies. Plenum cabling is any cabling that is run in the plenum space of a building. As such, this cabling must follow certain fire guidelines to obtain the plenum designation.

The following are some additional considerations that can impact disaster recovery:

- Maintain fault-tolerant connections to the Internet, such as gigabit as the primary connection and a backup fiber connection.
- Establish phone connections to employees besides primary organizational phone connections. Know cellphone and home numbers for employee notifications.
- Establish radio communications over the entire campus with repeater antennae to provide communication during emergencies. Many primary forms of communication (such as phone lines and cellphones) can go down.

Utilities

Some utilities systems, such as gas and water, can be routed into the facility through ducts and tunnels that might provide an unauthorized entry point to the building. These ducts and tunnels, which provide this opportunity, should be monitored with sensors and access control mechanisms.

Any critical parts of the systems where cut-off valves and emergency shutdown systems are located should be physically protected from malicious tampering. In some cases, covering and protecting these valves and controls using locking cages might be beneficial.

Human-Caused Threats

Although many of the physical threats organizations face are a function of natural occurrences and random events, some of them are purposeful. Next, we explore some of the physical threats faced from malicious and careless humans. These ***human-caused threats*** come from both external forces and internal forces.

Explosions

Explosions can be both intentional and accidental. Intentional explosions can occur as a result of political motivation (covered in more detail in the section "Politically Motivated Threats"), or they can simply be vandalism. Accidental explosions can be the result of a failure to follow procedures and the failure of physical components.

With regard to intentional explosions, the best defense is to prevent access to areas where explosions could do significant damage to the enterprise's operational components, such as server rooms, wiring closets, and areas where power and utilities enter the building. When an intentional explosion occurs, typically the perpetrator will consider locating the explosive where the most harm can be done, so those areas should get additional physical protection.

Fire

Fires can happen anywhere and thus are a consideration at all times. Chapter 3 covers both fire suppression and fire detection techniques. Organizations should address the threat of fire in the contexts of both an accident and an intentional attack. An *auxiliary station alarm* might be beneficial in many cases. This mechanism automatically causes an alarm originating in a data center to be transmitted over the local municipal fire or police alarm circuits for relaying to both the local police/fire station and the appropriate headquarters.

Fire extinguishers are classified using the standard system shown in Tables 1-9 and 1-10. In Chapter 3, we talk more about fire extinguishers and suppression systems for the various types.

Table 1-9 Fire Extinguisher Classes (USA)

Class	Type of Fire
Class A	Ordinary combustible, like paper or wood
Class B	Flammable liquids, flammable gases
Class C	Electrical equipment
Class D	Combustible metals
Class K	Cooking oil or fat

Table 1-10 Fire Extinguisher Classes (UK)

Class	Type of Fire
Class A	Ordinary combustibles
Class B	Flammable liquids
Class C	Flammable gases
Class D	Combustible metals
Electrical Fires	Electrical appliances
Class F	Cooking oil or fat

With respect to construction materials, according to (ISC)^2, all walls must have a two-hour minimum fire rating in an information processing facility. Knowing that the most prevalent cause of computer center fires is electrical distribution systems is also useful. Regardless of the fire source, the first action to take in the event of a fire is the evacuation of all personnel.

Vandalism

Vandalism is intentional destruction and can often result in defacement of walls, bathrooms, and such, but when critical components are accessible, this threat can impact operations. Cut cables and smashed devices are reasons stressed in preventing physical access to these components.

Even when all measures have been taken, vandalism can still cause problems. For example, a purposefully plugged toilet can flood a floor and damage equipment if the flooding is undetected and equipment is reached by the water.

Fraud

In the context of physical security, fraud involves gaining access to systems, equipment, or the facility through deception. For example, both someone who enters the facility posing as a service person and someone who tailgates and follows an employee through the card system use forms of fraudulent physical access. Physical access control systems become critical to preventing this type of fraud and the damage it can lead to.

Theft

Preventing physical theft of company assets depends on preventing physical access to the facility. Physical theft is the risk that will most likely affect CIA. For assets that leave the facility, such as laptops, you should think about protecting sensitive data that might exist on them through the use of encryption, preferably through encrypted drives. If a portable device never leaves the facility, using a cable lock would prevent device theft.

Collusion

Collusion occurs when two or more employees work together to accomplish a theft of some sort that could not be accomplished without their combined knowledge or responsibilities. Organizations should use proper separation of duties to prevent a single person from controlling enough of a process to hide their actions.

Limiting the specific accesses of operations personnel forces an operator into collusion with an operator of a different category to have access to unauthorized data. Collusion is much less likely to occur from a statistical standpoint than a single person operating alone. When you consider this fact, the trade-off in exchanging one danger for another is justified.

Politically Motivated Threats

Although it might seem at times like many more politically motivated threats exist today, these threats have always existed. The enterprise is often unwillingly dragged into these confrontations if they are seen as contributing to whatever the issue of the day might be. These threats can be costly in terms of lost productivity, destruction of company assets, and even physical danger to employees and officers of the company. Here, we cover some of the major ways these threats can manifest themselves along with measures to take that can lessen or mitigate the risk they present.

An advanced persistent threat (APT) uses a set of stealthy and continuous computer hacking processes, often orchestrated by a person or persons targeting a specific entity. An APT usually targets either private organizations, states, or both for business and political motives.

Strikes

Although strikes might be the least dangerous of the threats in this list, they can still damage the enterprise. In countries like the United States, basic rules of order have been established that prevent the worst of the possible outcomes, but even then an orderly strike can cost productivity and can hurt the image of the company. In other countries, strikes can be much more dangerous, especially when other political issues become intertwined with monetary issues.

Riots

Riots often occur seemingly out of nowhere, although typically an underlying issue causes the initial incident. These events can be very dangerous as large mobs will often participate in activities that none of the individuals would normally do on their own. Often the enterprise is seen as a willing participant in some perceived slight or wrong suffered by the rioters. In that case, the company and its assets become a large and somewhat easy target. At larger organizations, a threat intelligence group may be able to provide an alert about a potential riot in close proximity.

Civil Disobedience

Civil disobedience is the intentional refusal to obey certain laws, demands, and commands of a government and is commonly, though not always, defined as being nonviolent resistance. One of the typical by-products of this is a disruption of some process to bring attention to the perceived injustice of the law or a rule being broken.

This behavior might also manifest itself as an action against some practice by the enterprise that might not be illegal but might be seen by some groups as harmful in some way. When this is the case, the physical security of the facility becomes important because in some cases action might be taken by malicious actors to harm the facility.

Terrorist Acts

Increasingly, and more so after the 9/11 attacks, the threats of terrorist activity have caused a new focus on not only the security of facilities both at home and abroad but also of the physical safety of workers and officers. In many cases, certain industries have found it beneficial to include emergency planning designed to address terrorist acts. Reactions to common scenarios are rehearsed to ensure the best possible outcome in the case of an attack.

Active Shooter

Active shooter situations are becoming more common in today's world. Organizations should drill personnel on sheltering in place and defensive tactics. Often involving trained law enforcement will ensure that the organizational response is improved.

Bombing

Bombing of facilities or company assets, once a rare occurrence, is no longer so in many parts of the world today. Increasingly, the enterprise is driven to include such considerations as local disturbance levels and general political unrest in an area before company sites are chosen. In many cases the simple threat of a bomb is enough to engage evacuation plans that are both costly and disruptive. Despite this, evacuation plans that address terrorist threats and bombings have become an integral part of any security policy, especially in certain parts of the world.

Threat Modeling

Earlier in this chapter, in the "Risk Management Concepts" section, we defined vulnerabilities, threats, threat agents, and other concepts. Threat modeling allows an organization to use a structured approach to security and to address the top threats that have the greatest potential impact to the organization first. Threat modeling is used to identify and rate the threats that are most likely to impact an organization.

Threat modeling can be carried out using three different perspectives:

Key Topic

- **Application-centric threat modeling:** This perspective involves using application architecture diagrams to analyze threats.
- **Asset-centric threat modeling:** This perspective involves identifying the assets of an organization and classifying them according to data sensitivity and their intrinsic value to a potential attacker, in order to prioritize risk levels. This method uses attack trees, attack graphs, or displayed patterns to determine how an asset can be attacked.
- **Attacker-centric threat modeling:** This perspective involves profiling an attacker's characteristics, skills, and motivation to exploit vulnerabilities. Attacker profiles are then used to understand the type of attacker who would be most likely to execute specific types of exploits and implement a mitigation strategy accordingly. Tree diagrams are often used.

No matter which threat modeling method you decide to use, the basic steps in the threat modeling process are as follows:

Key Topic

1. Identify assets.
2. Identify threat agents and possible attacks.
3. Research existing countermeasures in use by the organization.
4. Identify any vulnerabilities that can be exploited.
5. Prioritize the identified risks.
6. Identify countermeasures to reduce the organization's risk.

Threat Modeling Concepts

When considering threat modeling, security professionals should understand both the attack side and the defense side of any threat. The basic concepts related to the attack side of threat modeling include vulnerability, exploit and attack, attack vector, and threat. The basic concepts related to the defense side of threat modeling include risk, security controls, and security objectives.

NOTE Vulnerability, attack, threat, and risk are covered earlier in this chapter in the "Risk Management Concepts" section.

To exploit a vulnerability is to use it to violate security objectives, such as confidentiality, integrity, and availability. The program code or other commands used to exploit a vulnerability are generically referred to as an exploit or an attack. Attacks are either intentional or inadvertent.

An ***attack vector*** is a segment of the communication path that an attack uses to access a vulnerability. Each attack vector can be thought of as comprising a source of malicious content, a potentially vulnerable processor of that malicious content, and the nature of the malicious content itself.

Security controls are the management, operational, and technical controls used by information systems to protect the confidentiality, integrity, and availability of the system and its information. All types of security controls are covered earlier in this chapter.

Organizations create security objectives to protect the confidentiality, integrity, and availability of assets. Security objectives vary based on the asset's value and importance to the organization.

Threat Modeling Methodologies

Threat modeling methodologies have been developed to help organizations to determine the threats that they face and how to best address these threats. Threat methodologies include STRIDE, PASTA, Trike, VAST, and NIST SP 800-154.

STRIDE Model

Developed by Microsoft, STRIDE is a threat classification model that is used to assess the threats in an application. It covers the following six categories:

- Spoofing of user identity
- Tampering
- Repudiation
- Information disclosure (privacy breach or data leak)
- Denial of service (DoS)
- Elevation of privilege

This method usually requires subject matter experts (SMEs) to determine the threats, threat classifications, and relevance of security properties to the elements of a threat model.

Process for Attack Simulation and Threat Analysis (PASTA) Methodology

The Process for Attack Simulation and Threat Analysis methodology, known as PASTA, provides a seven-step process for analyzing applications to align business objectives and technical requirements. The steps in the process are as follows:

1. Business objectives definition
2. Technical scope definition
3. Application decomposition
4. Threat analysis
5. Vulnerability detection
6. Attack enumeration
7. Risk and impact analysis

This method provides a threat identification, enumeration, and scoring process. It is intended to provide an attacker-centric view of the application and infrastructure from which defenders can develop an asset-centric mitigation strategy.

Trike Methodology

Trike is both a methodology and a tool with its basis in a requirements model designed to ensure the level of risk assigned to each asset is classified as acceptable by stakeholders. With this methodology, an implementation model is created and then analyzed to produce a threat model. Risk values are assigned to the identified threats. Mitigating controls are assigned to the vulnerabilities that lead to the identified threats.

The main difference between Trike and STRIDE is that Trike uses a risk-based approach.

Visual, Agile, and Simple Threat (VAST) Model

Visual, Agile, and Simple Threat, aka VAST, was created as a result of the shortcomings in the other models and methodologies. VAST threat modeling scales across the infrastructure and entire development portfolio. It is meant to work in an Agile environment and uses both application and operational threat models.

Table 1-11 compares the features of the four threat methodologies.

Table 1-11 Threat Modeling Methodology Comparison

What Users Want in a Threat Modeling Methodology				
	STRIDE	**PASTA**	**Trike**	**VAST**
Implements application security at design time	✓	✓	✓	✓
Identifies relevant mitigating controls	✓	✓	✓	✓
Directly contributes to risk management		✓	✓	✓
Prioritizes threat mitigation efforts		✓	✓	✓
Encourages collaboration among all stakeholders			✓	✓
Outputs for stakeholders across the organization				✓
Provides consistent repeatability			✓	✓
Automates the threat modeling process			✓	✓
Integrates into an Agile DevOps environment				✓
Able to scale across thousands of threat models				✓

NIST SP 800-154

NIST SP 800-154 is a draft publication for data-centric system threat modeling. It includes the following steps:

Key Topic

1. Identify and characterize the system and data of interest.
2. Identify and select the attack vectors to be included in the model.
3. Characterize the security controls for mitigating the attack vectors.
4. Analyze the threat model.

Most of the actions within the methodology can be addressed in a wide variety of ways in terms of both content (what information is captured) and format/structure (how that information is captured). Organizations should customize as they see fit.

Identifying Threats

Identifying threats and threat actors as part of threat modeling is not much different from identifying threats and vulnerabilities as discussed earlier in this chapter, in the "Risk Assessment" section. However, when carrying out threat modeling, you may decide to develop a more comprehensive list of threat actors to assist in scenario development.

Security professionals should analyze all the threats to identify all the actors who pose significant threats to the organization. Examples of threat actors include both internal and external actors, such as the following:

Key Topic

- Internal actors
  - Reckless employee
  - Untrained employee
  - Partner
  - Disgruntled employee
  - Internal spy
  - Government spy
  - Vendor
  - Thief
- External actors
  - Anarchist
  - Competitor
  - Corrupt government official
  - Data miner
  - Government cyber warrior
  - Irrational individual
  - Legal adversary
  - Mobster
  - Activist
  - Terrorist
  - Vandal

These actors can be subdivided into two categories: nonhostile and hostile. Of the actors listed, three are usually considered nonhostile: reckless employee, untrained employee, and partner. All the other actors should be considered hostile.

An organization needs to analyze each of these threat actors according to set criteria. The organization should give each threat actor a ranking to help determine which ones should be analyzed. Examples of some of the most commonly used criteria include the following:

- **Skill level:** None, minimal, operational, adept
- **Resources;** Individual, team, organization, government
- **Visibility:** Overt, covert, clandestine, don't care
- **Objective:** Copy, destroy, injure, take, don't care
- **Outcome:** Acquisition/theft, business advantage, damage, embarrassment, technical advantage

Based on these criteria, the organization must then determine which of the actors it wants to analyze. For example, the organization may choose to analyze all hostile actors who have a skill level of adept and resources of organization or government. Then the list is consolidated to include only the threat actors that fit all these criteria.

Next, the organization must determine what it really cares about protecting. Often this determination is made using some sort of business impact analysis. After the vital assets are determined, the organization should then select the scenarios that could have a catastrophic impact on the organization by using the objective and outcome values from the threat actor analysis and the asset value and business impact information from the impact analysis.

Potential Attacks

To identify the potential attacks that can occur, an organization must create scenarios that can be fully analyzed. For example, an organization may decide to analyze a situation in which a hacktivist group performs prolonged DoS attacks, causing sustained outages to damage an organization's reputation. Then a risk assessment should be made for each scenario. (Risk assessment is discussed earlier in this chapter.)

After all the scenarios are determined, the organization should develop an attack tree for each potential attack. The attack tree should include all the steps and/or conditions that must occur for the attack to be successful. The organization then needs to map security controls to the attack trees.

To determine what security controls can be used, an organization needs to look at industry standards, including NIST SP 800-53 Rev. 5 (discussed earlier in this chapter). Finally, the controls need to be mapped back to the attack tree to ensure that controls are implemented at as many levels of the attack as possible.

NOTE Specific attacks are discussed throughout this book. Cryptanalytic attacks are covered in Chapter 3, "Security Architecture and Engineering." Network attacks are covered in Chapter 4, "Communication and Network Security." Access control attacks are covered in Chapter 5, "Identity and Access Management (IAM)."

Remediation Technologies and Processes

Security professionals should be prepared as part of any threat modeling to analyze the threats, examine the security controls in place, and make recommendations on remediation technologies and processes. Remediation technologies may simply be used to provide additional protection against an identified threat. In developing remediation processes, however, security professionals or auditors need to analyze internal processes, identify the weakness(es) in the current processes, and revise the current processes or develop new ones that better protect against identified threats. For example, after analyzing the process for being issued a new password, a security professional might realize that it is possible for an attacker to have an internal user's password reset. The security professional might then establish a process whereby users must provide some identification factors prior to having their password reset.

Security Risks in the Supply Chain

Earlier we discussed corporate acquisitions. Here, we discuss the security risks in acquiring hardware, software, and services, which is often referred to as supply chain risk management (SCRM). As part of this discussion, the following sections cover third-party assessment and monitoring, minimum security requirements, and service-level agreements.

Risks Associated with Hardware, Software, and Services

Organizations acquire hardware, software, and services as part of day-to-day business. The supply chain for tangible property is vital to every organization. An organization should understand all risks for the supply chain and implement a risk management program that is appropriate for it. But the supply chain does not just involve tangible property, such as hardware. It also can include information, software, and services.

Some of these acquisitions have built-in security mechanisms. However, these security mechanisms are not enough to fully protect the acquisitions. In addition, any security mechanisms need to be regularly updated and perhaps even replaced with more recent, stronger security mechanisms.

Understanding the risks associated with the acquisition of products and services from suppliers and providers is crucial. Supply chain risks can significantly impact an organization's security posture and overall risk landscape. Some of these risks include:

- **Product Tampering:** Product tampering involves unauthorized alterations or modifications to products during the manufacturing or distribution process. Tampering can introduce vulnerabilities or backdoors into products, compromising their integrity and security. Security professionals must ensure mechanisms are in place to detect and prevent tampering. This includes vetting suppliers, conducting regular security audits, and implementing secure transportation and handling processes.
- **Counterfeit Products:** Counterfeit products are unauthorized replicas of the real product, often of lower quality and reliability. Using counterfeit products can lead to security breaches, system failures, and non-compliance with regulations. They may lack the necessary security features and can be more vulnerable to attacks. Security professionals need to establish processes for verifying the authenticity of products, such as checking certificates of authenticity or using trusted suppliers.
- **Implants (Hardware/Software):** Implants refer to unauthorized hardware or software embedded into products to conduct surveillance, gain unauthorized access, or cause harm. Implants can be used for espionage, data theft, or sabotage, posing significant security threats. Security professionals should implement strict inspection and testing processes for new products to detect any unauthorized implants. This includes conducting detailed security reviews and using trusted and verified suppliers.
- **Supply Chain Interdependencies:** Dependence on key suppliers or service providers creates vulnerabilities. A breach or failure at one point in the supply chain can have cascading effects. Risk assessments should consider the entire supply chain, identifying critical dependencies and developing contingency plans.
- **Compliance Risks:** Suppliers may not adhere to the necessary legal, regulatory, or security compliance standards, leading to potential legal issues and security breaches. Regular compliance audits and ensuring suppliers meet the required standards are key responsibilities.

- **Geopolitical Risks:** Political instability, trade restrictions, or conflicts in regions where suppliers are located can disrupt supply chains. SCRM must include assessments of geopolitical risks, and plans should be in place to mitigate these risks.
- **Third-Party Service Providers:** Outsourcing services can lead to loss of control over certain aspects of security. There's a risk that third-party providers may not have adequate security controls. Due diligence, regular security assessments, and contractual obligations are critical in managing these risks.
- **Quality Control Failures:** Poor quality control can lead to defective or insecure products entering the supply chain. Implementing and monitoring quality control measures with suppliers and throughout the supply chain is essential.
- **Logistics and Transportation Risks:** Products can be damaged, lost, or compromised during transportation. Secure logistics and tracking mechanisms should be in place to safeguard products during transit.

Security professionals should be involved in any hardware, software, and service acquisition to ensure that security is an integral part of the decision. If no security advocate is part of the acquisition process, acquisitions are often made that actually put the organization at risk.

As part of the related security considerations, security professionals should develop baseline requirements for acquisitions, train personnel to adapt to security changes with new acquisitions, use common security terms and definitions for acquisitions, and develop a strategy to ensure that acquisitions are minimized.

Third-Party Assessment and Monitoring

For many organizations, a third-party audit or assessment ensures that the organization complies with industry or governmental standards and regulations. This third party is an independent party that performs analysis of organizational operations and any other area dictated by the certifying or regulating organization. The third party reports all results of its findings to the certifying or regulating organization. The contract with the third party should stipulate that any findings or results should be communicated only with the organization that is being analyzed and with the regulating organization. A third party may also provide assessment and monitoring services as part of an organization's regular security policy.

A member of high-level management usually manages this process so that the third party is given access as needed after obtaining proper signatures on forms. As part of this analysis, the third party might need to perform an onsite assessment, a document exchange, or a process/policy review.

Onsite Assessment

An onsite assessment involves a team from the third party. This team needs access to all aspects of the organization under regulation. This assessment might include observing employees as they perform their day-to-day duties, reviewing records, reviewing documentation, and performing other tasks. Management should delegate a member of management to whom the team can make formal requests.

Document Exchange/Review

A document exchange/review involves transmitting a set of documents to the third party. The process used for the document exchange must be secure on both ends of the exchange.

Process/Policy Review

A process/policy review focuses on a single process or policy within the organization and ensures that the process or policy follows regulations.

Other Third-Party Governance Issues

Third-party governance may apply when an organization employs third parties to provide services to an organization. An example of this is using a public cloud solution, such as Infrastructure as a Service (IaaS), Platform as a Service (PaaS), or Software as a Service (SaaS). When using a third-party partner like this, security professionals must ensure that the organization obtains the appropriate SLA. In addition, security professionals must help the organization ensure that the third party implements appropriate due diligence in all aspects that affect the organization. This assurance can be provided only by inspection, review, and assessment of the third-party provider. Finally, security professionals should be aware of any countries or individuals that may have jurisdiction over the third party's systems.

Supply Chain Assessment and Monitoring

Supply chain assessment and monitoring involves evaluating and continuously monitoring the security posture of third-party vendors or suppliers. Security professionals should ensure regular security assessments of third parties are conducted. This includes audits, compliance checks, and reviews of security practices to ensure they meet the organization's standards.

Silicon Root of Trust

Silicon root of trust is a hardware-based approach to establish a secure foundation for cryptographic operations and secure boot processes. Using hardware that incorporates a silicon root of trust can provide a more secure foundation for critical systems, reducing the risk of tampering and ensuring the integrity of the supply chain.

Physically Unclonable Function (PUF)

Physically unclonable function (PUF) is a hardware function used to uniquely identify a semiconductor device based on its inherent physical variations. Implementing PUFs can help in authenticating hardware components, ensuring they are genuine and have not been tampered with or replaced with counterfeit parts.

Software Bill of Materials (SBOM)

A software bill of materials (SBOM) is a comprehensive inventory of all components in a piece of software, including open source and proprietary elements. Using SBOMs allows security professionals to understand and manage the risks associated with software components used in their organization, including vulnerabilities, licensing issues, and dependencies.

Minimum Service-Level and Security Requirements

Minimum service-level requirements document the minimum level of service that a provider must maintain. The minimum service-level requirements are usually spelled out in a service-level agreement. SLAs should include provisions that provide minimum performance metrics and noncompliance penalties.

Security professionals should also define the minimum security requirements for any acquisitions made by the organization. For computers, these requirements may be best enforced using network access control (NAC), which defines and implements policies that describe how to secure access to network nodes by devices when they initially attempt to access the network. If a device attempts to connect and does not meet the minimum requirements, it is either denied access or placed on a quarantined network to protect the internal organizational network.

For each different acquisition type, it may be necessary to define separate security policies. For example, mobile devices that are not used may need to be locked in a file cabinet or safe. Keys for company vehicles should not be kept out in the open where they are easy to obtain. Computers that are located in a high-traffic area may need some sort of mechanism that locks the devices to desks. The security controls vary just as much as the acquisition types.

Service-Level Agreements (SLAs)

SLAs are agreements about the ability of a support system to respond to problems within a certain timeframe while providing an agreed level of service. These agreements can be internal between departments or external with service providers. Agreeing on the speed at which various problems are addressed introduces some predictability to the response to problems; this ultimately supports the maintenance of access to resources. The following are some examples of what may be included in an SLA:

- Loss of connectivity to the DNS server must be restored within a reasonable timeframe.
- Loss of connectivity to Internet service must be restored within a five-hour period.
- Loss of connectivity of a host machine must be restored within an eight-hour period.

Key Topic

Before an SLA can be written and signed, organizations must negotiate the service-level requirements. If an organization does not have carefully documented requirements, it cannot be sure that the SLA from the vendor will fulfill its needs. Requirements that need to be documented include the following:

- Description of service
- Hours of service needed
- Service interruption process
- Availability requirements
- Maintenance requirements and allowed downtime
- Workload expected
- Performance expected

Security professionals need to work with business unit managers when services must be obtained from a third party to ensure that the service-level requirements are documented.

Security Education, Training, and Awareness

Security education, *security training*, and *security awareness training* are three terms that are often used interchangeably but are actually three different things. Awareness training reinforces the fact that valuable resources must be protected by implementing security measures.

Levels Required

Security training teaches personnel the skills to enable them to perform their jobs in a secure manner. Awareness training and security training are usually combined as security awareness training, which improves user awareness of security and ensures that users can be held accountable for their actions. Security education is more independent and is targeted at security professionals who require security expertise to act as in-house experts for managing the security programs. Awareness training is the what, security training is the how, and security education is the why.

Security awareness training should be developed based on the audience. In addition, trainers must understand the corporate culture and how it will affect security. The audiences to be considered when designing training include high-level management, middle management, technical personnel, and regular staff.

For high-level management, the security awareness training must provide a clear understanding of potential risks and threats, effects of security issues on organizational reputation and financial standing, and any applicable laws and regulations that pertain to the organization's security program. Middle management training should discuss policies, standards, baselines, guidelines, and procedures, particularly how these components map to the individual departments. Also, middle management must understand their responsibilities regarding security. Technical staff should receive technical training on configuring and maintaining security controls, including how to recognize an attack when it occurs. In addition, technical staff should be encouraged to pursue industry certifications and higher education degrees. Regular staff need to understand their responsibilities regarding security so that they perform their day-to-day tasks in a secure manner. With regular staff, providing real-world examples to emphasize proper security procedures is effective.

Personnel should sign a document or receive a certificate of completion that indicates they have completed the training and understand all the topics. Although the initial training should occur when personnel is hired, security awareness training should be considered a continuous process, with future training sessions occurring annually at a minimum.

Methods and Techniques

Security education and training can be delivered in a variety of ways. Most mandatory awareness training that must be delivered to all personnel would be best delivered over a digital medium. Many companies specialize in the delivery of security awareness training courses over the Internet, and often these courses can be customized to fit the needs and cover the specific policies of the organization.

Another common method of delivery is live or video-on-demand training. This method is particularly useful when providing specialized training to technical personnel. Organizations should ensure that the training they select for technical personnel is up to date with the latest security issues and vulnerability testing and penetration testing techniques. Technical personnel must receive training in the tools that they will regularly use.

No matter the medium selected, it is the responsibility of the organization to ensure that the training covers all of the organization's policies and any repercussions for noncompliance.

Periodic Content Reviews

New security issues and threats are always cropping up in today's society. As a result, security professionals should review all the security awareness training and ensure that it is updated to address new security issues and threats. This review should be scheduled to occur at regular intervals and should include emerging technologies and trends, like cryptocurrency, artificial intelligence (AI), and blockchain.

Exam Preparation Tasks

As mentioned in the section "About the *CISSP Cert Guide*, Fifth Edition" in the Introduction, you have a couple of choices for exam preparation: the exercises here, Chapter 9, "Final Preparation," and the exam simulation questions in the Pearson Test Prep practice test software.

Review All Key Topics

Review the most important topics in this chapter, noted with the Key Topic icon in the outer margin of the page. Table 1-12 lists a reference of these key topics and the page numbers on which each is found.

Key Topic

Table 1-12 Key Topics for Chapter 1

Key Topic Element	Description	Page Number
Paragraph	Security control frameworks	21
Figure 1-7	Security Program Life Cycle	39
List	Computer crime concepts	43
List	Major legal systems	45
List	Licensing and intellectual property	47
Figure 1-12	PII List	54
Figure 1-13	NIST SP 800-86 Forensic Process	68

Key Topic Element	Description	Page Number
List	Information security documents	73
Figure 1-14	Levels and Categories of Security Policies	74
List	Business continuity and disaster recovery concepts	77
Paragraph	Causes of disasters	78
List	NIST SP 800-34 Rev. 1 contingency planning steps	82
List	BIA steps	86
List	Critical asset terms	86
Section	Risk Management Concepts	95
Paragraph	SLE calculation	103
Paragraph	ALE calculation	103
Paragraph	Countermeasure selection	104
List	Risk handling methods	105
List	Access control categories	107
List	Access control types	109
List	NIST risk management framework steps	116
Table 1-6	Confidentiality, Integrity, and Availability Potential Impact Definitions	118
Paragraph	FIPS 199 security category (SC) of an identified entity explanation	118
Table 1-7	NIST SP 800-53 Control Families	121
List	NIST SP 800-53 baseline control process	122
Figure 1-21	NIST System Life Cycle Processes and Stages	124
Paragraph	NIST SP 800-30 risk assessment process	126
Paragraph	NIST Framework for Improving Critical Infrastructure Cybersecurity core functions	128
List	ISO/IEC 27005:2018 risk management process	131
List	Threat modeling perspectives	142
List	Threat modeling process	142
List	NIST SP 800-154 data-centric system threat modeling steps	145
List	Threat actors	146
Paragraph	SLA requirements documentation	153

Complete the Tables and Lists from Memory

Print a copy of Appendix A, "Memory Tables," or at least the section from this chapter, and complete the tables and lists from memory. Appendix B, "Memory Tables Answer Key," includes completed tables and lists to check your work.

Define Key Terms

Define the following key terms from this chapter and check your answers in the glossary:

abstraction; accounting; administrative control; administrative law; annualized loss expectancy (ALE); annualized rate of occurrence (ARO); asset valuation; asset; attack; attack vector; auditing; availability; Basel II; baseline; breach; business case; business continuity plan (BCP); California Consumer Privacy Act (CCPA); CIA triad; civil code law; civil/tort law; CLOUD (Clarifying Lawful Overseas Use of Data) Act; common law; Communications Assistance for Law Enforcement Act (CALEA) of 1994; compensative control; Computer Fraud and Abuse Act (CFAA) of 1986; computer prevalence crime; Computer Security Act of 1987; computer-assisted crime; computer-targeted crime; confidentiality; continuity of operations plan (COOP); copyright; corrective control; countermeasure; criminal law; criminal investigations; crisis communications plan; critical infrastructure protection (CIP) plan; customary law; cyber crime; cyber incident response plan; data breach; data hiding; default security posture; defense in depth; detective control; deterrent control; digital rights management (DRM); directive control; disaster; disaster recovery plan (DRP); disruption; due care; due diligence; Economic Espionage Act of 1996; eDiscovery; Electronic Communications Privacy Act (ECPA) of 1986; exposure; exposure factor (EF); fault tolerance; Federal Information Security Management Act (FISMA) of 2002; Federal Intelligence Surveillance Act (FISA) of 1978; Federal Privacy Act of 1974; Gramm-Leach-Bliley Act (GLBA) of 1999; guideline; Health Care and Education Reconciliation Act of 2010; Health Insurance Portability and Accountability Act (HIPAA); HITRUST Common Security Framework (CSF); human-caused threats; incidental computer crime; information system contingency plan (ISCP); Information Technology (Reasonable Security Practices and Procedures and Sensitive Personal Data or Information) Rules 2011 (India); intangible assets; integrity; issue-specific security policy; Internal Traffic in Arms Regulations (ITAR); Investigatory Powers Act 2016; job rotation; Kennedy-Kassebaum Act; logical control; management control; man-made disasters; maximum tolerable downtime (MTD); mean time between failure (MTBF); mean time to repair (MTTR); mixed law; non-repudiation; NYS DFS Rule 500; occupant emergency plan (OEP); operations investigations; organizational security policy; patent; Personal Data Protection Act (PDPA) in Singapore; Personal Information Protection and

Electronic Documents Act (PIPEDA); Personal Information Protection Law (PIPL) in China; personally identifiable information (PII); physical assets; physical control; preventive control; procedure; process; qualitative risk analysis; quantitative risk analysis; recovery control; recovery point objective (RPO); recovery time objective (RTO); regulatory law; regulatory security policy; reliability; religious law; residual risk; risk; risk acceptance; risk avoidance; risk management; risk mitigation; risk transfer; root cause analysis (RCA); safeguard; Sarbanes-Oxley (SOX) Act; separation of duties; software piracy; standard; system threats; system-specific security policy; tactical plans (or goals); tangible assets; technological disasters; The Open Group Architecture Framework (TOGAF); threat; threat agent; trade secret; trademark; United States Federal Sentencing Guidelines of 1991; Uniting and Strengthening America by Providing Appropriate Tools Required to Intercept and Obstruct Terrorism (USA PATRIOT) Act of 2001; USA Freedom Act of 2015; vulnerability; Zachman Framework

Answer Review Questions

1. Which is the opposite of disclosure?
   - a. Integrity
   - b. Availability
   - c. Confidentiality
   - d. Authorization
2. Which of the following controls is an administrative control?
   - a. Security policy
   - b. CCTV
   - c. Data backups
   - d. Locks
3. What is a vulnerability?
   - a. The entity that carries out a threat
   - b. The exposure of an organizational asset to losses
   - c. An absence or a system weakness that can be exploited
   - d. A control that reduces risk

4. Which framework uses the six communication questions (what, where, when, why, who, and how) that intersect with six layers (operational, component, physical, logical, conceptual, and contextual)?
   a. Six Sigma
   b. SABSA
   c. ITIL
   d. ISO/IEC 27000 series
5. Which group of threat agents includes hardware and software failure, malicious code, and new technologies?
   a. Human
   b. Natural
   c. Environmental
   d. Technical
6. Which term indicates the monetary impact of each threat occurrence?
   a. Annual Rate of Occurrence (ARO)
   b. Annual Loss Expectancy (ALE)
   c. Exposure Factor (EF)
   d. Single Loss Expectancy (SLE)
7. What is risk avoidance?
   a. Risk that is left over after safeguards have been implemented
   b. Terminating the activity that causes a risk or choosing an alternative that is not as risky
   c. Passing the risk on to a third party
   d. Defining the acceptable risk level the organization can tolerate and reducing the risk to that level
8. Which of the following security policies provides instruction on acceptable and unacceptable activities?
   a. Informative security policies
   b. Regulatory security policies
   c. System-specific security policies
   d. Advisory security policies

9. Which organization role determines the classification level of the information to protect the data for which that role is responsible?
   a. Data owner
   b. Data custodian
   c. Security administrator
   d. Security analyst

10. Which type of crime occurs when a computer is used as a tool to help commit a crime?
    a. Computer-assisted crime
    b. Incidental computer crime
    c. Computer-targeted crime
    d. Computer prevalence crime

11. Which access control type reduces the effect of an attack or another undesirable event?
    a. Compensative control
    b. Preventive control
    c. Detective control
    d. Corrective control

12. What is the first stage of the security program life cycle?
    a. Plan and Organize
    b. Implement
    c. Operate and Maintain
    d. Monitor and Evaluate

13. Which of the following frameworks is a two-dimensional model that intersects communication interrogatives (what, why, where, and so on) with various viewpoints (planner, owner, designer, and so on)?
    a. SABSA
    b. Zachman Framework
    c. TOGAF
    d. ITIL

14. Which management officer implements and manages all aspects of security, including risk analysis, security policies and procedures, training, and emerging technologies?
    a. Data protection officer (DPO)
    b. Chief financial officer (CFO)
    c. Chief security officer (CSO)
    d. Chief information officer (CIO)

15. Which of the following do organizations have employees sign to protect trade secrets?
    a. Trademark
    b. Patent
    c. Digital Rights Management (DRM)
    d. Nondisclosure agreement (NDA)

16. Which type of access control type is an acceptable use policy (AUP) most likely considered?
    a. Corrective
    b. Detective
    c. Compensative
    d. Directive

17. What is the legal term used to describe an organization taking all reasonable measures to prevent security breaches and also taking steps to mitigate damages caused by successful breaches?
    a. Due care
    b. Due diligence
    c. Default security posture
    d. Qualitative risk analysis

18. Which threat modeling perspective profiles malicious characteristics, skills, and motivation to exploit vulnerabilities?
    a. Application-centric
    b. Asset-centric
    c. Attacker-centric
    d. Hostile-centric

19. Which of the following is *not* a consideration for security professionals during mergers and acquisitions?
    a. New data types
    b. New technology types
    c. Cost of the merger or acquisition
    d. The other organization's security awareness training program

20. What is the first step of CRAMM (CCTA Risk Analysis and Management Method)?
    a. Identify threats and vulnerabilities.
    b. Identify and value assets.
    c. Identify countermeasures.
    d. Prioritize countermeasures.

21. Which of the following is the process of taking away or removing characteristics from something to reduce it to a set of essential characteristics?
    a. Auditing
    b. Accounting
    c. Non-repudiation
    d. Abstraction

22. Which specific plan focuses on restoring an organization's mission-essential functions (MEFs) at an alternate site and performing those functions for up to 30 days before returning to normal operations?
    a. Continuity of operations plan
    b. Business continuity plan
    c. Crisis communications plan
    d. Cyber incident response plan

23. Which of the following is an information system–focused plan designed to restore operability of the target system, application, or computer facility infrastructure at an alternate site after an emergency?
    a. Occupant emergency plan
    b. Disaster recovery plan
    c. Information system contingency plan
    d. Critical infrastructure protection plan

24. Which of the following is a segment of the communication path that an attack uses to access a vulnerability?
    a. Breach
    b. Threat agent
    c. Attack vector
    d. Countermeasure

25. Which of the following is a six-category threat classification model developed by Microsoft to assess the threats in an application?
    a. Visual, Agile, and Simple Threat (VAST)
    b. Trike
    c. Process for Attack Simulation and Threat Analysis (PASTA)
    d. STRIDE (Spoofing of user identity, Tampering, Repudiation, Information disclosure, Denial of service, Elevation of privilege)

26. What is the first step of the NIST SP 800-154 draft publication for data-centric system threat modeling?
    a. Identify and select the attack vectors to be included in the model.
    b. Identify and characterize the system and data of interest.
    c. Analyze the threat model.
    d. Characterize the security controls for mitigating the attack vectors.

27. What investigation type specifically refers to litigation or government investigations that deal with the exchange of information in electronic format as part of the discovery process?
    a. Data loss prevention (DLP)
    b. Regulatory
    c. eDiscovery
    d. Operations

28. What is the second step of the forensic investigations process?
    a. Identification
    b. Collection
    c. Preservation
    d. Examination

Answers and Explanations

1. **c.** The opposite of disclosure is confidentiality. The opposite of corruption is integrity. The opposite of destruction is availability. The opposite of disapproval is authorization.
2. **a.** A security policy is an administrative control. CCTV and locks are physical controls. Data backups are a technical control.
3. **c.** A vulnerability is an absence or a weakness of a countermeasure that is in place. A threat occurs when a vulnerability is identified or exploited. A threat agent is the entity that carries out a threat. Exposure occurs when an organizational asset is exposed to losses. A countermeasure or safeguard is a control that reduces risk.
4. **b.** SABSA uses the six communication questions (what, where, when, why, who, and how) that intersect with six layers (operational, component, physical, logical, conceptual, and contextual). Six Sigma is a process improvement standard that includes two project methodologies that were inspired by Deming's Plan–Do–Check–Act cycle. ITIL is a process management development standard that has five core publications: ITIL Service Strategy, ITIL Service Design, ITIL Service Transition, ITIL Service Operation, and ITIL Continual Service Improvement. The ISO/IEC 27000 Series includes a list of standards, each of which addresses a particular aspect of information security management.
5. **d.** Technical threat agents include hardware and software failure, malicious code, and new technologies. Human threat agents include both malicious and nonmalicious insiders and outsiders, terrorists, spies, and terminated personnel. Natural threat agents include floods, fires, tornadoes, hurricanes, earthquakes, or other natural disasters or weather events. Environmental threat agents include power and other utility failure, traffic issues, biological warfare, and hazardous material issues (such as spillage).
6. **d.** Single loss expectancy (SLE) indicates the monetary impact of each threat occurrence. Annualized rate of occurrence (ARO) is the estimate of how often a given threat might occur annually. Annual loss expectancy (ALE) is the expected risk factor of an annual threat event. Exposure factor (EF) is the percent value or functionality of an asset that will be lost when a threat event occurs.
7. **b.** Risk avoidance is terminating the activity that causes a risk or choosing an alternative that is not as risky. Residual risk is risk that is left over after safeguards have been implemented. Risk transfer is passing the risk on to a third party. Risk mitigation is defining the acceptable risk level the organization can tolerate and reducing the risk to that level.

8. **d.** Advisory security policies provide instruction on acceptable and unacceptable activities. Informative security policies provide information on certain topics and act as an educational tool. Regulatory security policies address specific industry regulations, including mandatory standards. System-specific security policies address security for a specific computer, network, technology, or application.

9. **a.** The data owner determines the classification level of the information to protect the data for which that role is responsible. The data custodian implements the information classification and controls after they are determined. The security administrator maintains security devices and software. The security analyst analyzes the security needs of the organizations and develops the internal information security governance documents.

10. **a.** A computer-assisted crime occurs when a computer is used as a tool to help commit a crime. An incidental computer crime occurs when a computer is involved in a computer crime without being the victim of the attack or the attacker. A computer-targeted crime occurs when a computer is the victim of an attack in which the sole purpose is to harm the computer and its owner. A computer prevalence crime occurs due to the fact that computers are so widely used in today's world.

11. **d.** A corrective control reduces the effect of an attack or other undesirable event. A compensative control substitutes for a primary access control and mainly acts as mitigation to risks. A preventive control prevents an attack from occurring. A detective control detects an attack while it is occurring to alert appropriate personnel.

12. **a.** The four stages of the security program life cycle, in order, are as follows:
    1. Plan and Organize
    2. Implement
    3. Operate and Maintain
    4. Monitor and Evaluate

13. **b.** The Zachman Framework is a two-dimensional model that intersects communication interrogatives (what, why, where, and so on) with various viewpoints (planner, owner, designer, and so on). It is designed to help optimize communication between the various viewpoints during the creation of the security architecture.

14. **c.** The chief security officer (CSO) is the officer that leads any security effort and reports directly to the chief executive officer (CEO). The chief privacy officer (CPO) is the officer responsible for private information and usually reports directly to the chief information officer (CIO). The chief financial

officer (CFO) is the officer responsible for all financial aspects of an organization. The CFO reports directly to the CEO and must also provide financial data for the shareholders and government entities. The CIO is the officer responsible for all information systems and technology used in the organization and reports directly to the CEO or CFO.

15. **d.** Most organizations that have trade secrets attempt to protect these secrets using nondisclosure agreements (NDAs). These NDAs must be signed by any entity that has access to information that is part of the trade secret. A trademark is an intellectual property type that ensures that the symbol, sound, or expression that identifies a product or an organization is protected from being used by another. A patent is an intellectual property type that covers an invention described in a patent application and is granted to an individual or company. Digital rights management (DRM) is used by hardware manufacturers, publishers, copyright holders, and individuals to control the use of digital content. This often also involves device controls.

16. **d.** The most popular directive control is an acceptable use policy (AUP) that lists proper (and often examples of improper) procedures and behaviors that personnel must follow. Corrective controls are in place to reduce the effect of an attack or other undesirable event. Examples of corrective controls include installing fire extinguishers and implementing new firewall rules. Detective controls are in place to detect an attack while it is occurring to alert appropriate personnel. Examples of detective controls include motion detectors, IDSs, or guards. Compensative controls are in place to substitute for a primary access control and mainly act as a mitigation to risks. Examples of compensative controls include requiring two authorized signatures to release sensitive or confidential information and requiring two keys owned by different personnel to open a safety deposit box.

17. **a.** Due care is a legal term that is used when an organization took all reasonable measures to prevent security breaches and also took steps to mitigate damages caused by successful breaches. Due diligence is a legal term that is used when an organization investigated all vulnerabilities. The default security posture is the default security posture used by the organization. An allow-by-default security posture permits access to any data unless a need exists to restrict access. A deny-by-default security posture is much stricter because it denies any access that is not explicitly permitted. Qualitative risk analysis is a method of analyzing risk whereby intuition, experience, and best practice techniques are used to determine risk.

18. **c.** Attacker-centric threat modeling profiles an attacker's characteristics, skills, and motivation to exploit vulnerabilities. Application-centric threat modeling uses application architecture diagrams to analyze threats. Asset-centric threat

modeling uses attack trees, attack graphs, or displaying patterns to determine how an asset can be attacked. Hostile describes one of two threat actor categories: nonhostile and hostile.

19. **c.** A security professional should not be concerned with the cost of a merger or an acquisition. A security professional should be concerned only with issues that affect security and leave financial issues to financial officers.
20. **b.** CRAMM review includes three steps:
    1. Identify and value assets.
    2. Identify threats and vulnerabilities and calculate risks.
    3. Identify and prioritize countermeasures.
21. **d.** Abstraction is the process of taking away or removing characteristics from something to reduce it to a set of essential characteristics. Auditing is the process of providing a manual or systematic measurable technical assessment of a system or application. Accounting is the process whereby auditing results are used to hold users and organizations accountable for their actions or inaction. Non-repudiation is the assurance that a user cannot deny an action.
22. **a.** A continuity of operations plan (COOP) is a plan that focuses on restoring an organization's mission-essential functions (MEFs) at an alternate site and performing those functions for up to 30 days before returning to normal operations. A business continuity plan (BCP) is a plan that focuses on sustaining an organization's mission/business processes during and after a disruption. A crisis communications plan is a plan that documents standard procedures for internal and external communications in the event of a disruption using a crisis communications plan. It also provides various formats for communications appropriate to the incident. A cyber incident response plan is a plan that establishes procedures to address cyberattacks against an organization's information system(s).
23. **b.** A disaster recovery plan (DRP) is an information system–focused plan designed to restore operability of the target system, application, or computer facility infrastructure at an alternate site after an emergency. An occupant emergency plan (OEP) is a plan that outlines first-response procedures for occupants of a facility in the event of a threat or incident to the health and safety of personnel, the environment, or property. An information system contingency plan (ISCP) provides established procedures for the assessment and recovery of a system following a system disruption. A critical infrastructure protection (CIP) plan is a set of policies and procedures that serve to protect and recover assets and mitigate risks and vulnerabilities.

24. **c.** An attack vector is a segment of the communication path that an attack uses to access a vulnerability. A breach is an attack that has been successful in reaching its goal. A threat is carried out by a threat agent. Not all threat agents will actually exploit an identified vulnerability. A countermeasure reduces the potential risk. Countermeasures are also referred to as safeguards or controls.

25. **d.** Developed by Microsoft, STRIDE is a threat classification model that is used to assess the threats in an application. It covers the following six categories:

    - Spoofing of user identity
    - Tampering
    - Repudiation
    - Information disclosure (privacy breach or data leak)
    - Denial of service (DoS)
    - Elevation of privilege

    The Visual, Agile, and Simple Threat (VAST) model was created as a result of the shortcomings in the other models and methodologies. VAST threat modeling scales across the infrastructure and entire development portfolio. Trike is both a methodology and a tool with its basis in a requirements model designed to ensure the level of risk assigned to each asset is classified as acceptable by stakeholders. The Process for Attack Simulation and Threat Analysis (PASTA) methodology provides a seven-step process for analyzing applications to align business objectives and technical requirements. It is intended to provide an attacker-centric view of the application and infrastructure from which defenders can develop an asset-centric mitigation strategy.

26. **b.** NIST SP 800-154 is a draft publication for data-centric system threat modeling. It includes the following steps:

    1. Identify and characterize the system and data of interest.
    2. Identify and select the attack vectors to be included in the model.
    3. Characterize the security controls for mitigating the attack vectors.
    4. Analyze the threat model.

    Most of the actions within the methodology can be addressed in a wide variety of ways in terms of both content (what information is captured) and format/structure (how that information is captured).

27. **c.** Electronic discovery (eDiscovery) refers to litigation or government investigations that deal with the exchange of information in electronic format as part of the discovery process. It involves electronically stored information (ESI) and includes emails, documents, presentations, databases, voicemail, audio and

video files, social media, and websites. Data loss prevention (DLP) software attempts to prevent data leakage. It does this by maintaining awareness of actions that can and cannot be taken with respect to a document. A regulatory investigation occurs when a regulatory body investigates an organization for a regulatory infraction. Operations investigations involve any investigations that do not result in any criminal, civil, or regulatory issue. In most cases, this type of investigation is completed to determine the root cause so that steps can be taken to prevent this incident in the future.

28. **c.** The steps of the forensic investigation process are as follows:

    1. Identification
    2. Preservation
    3. Collection
    4. Examination
    5. Analysis
    6. Presentation
    7. Decision

This chapter covers the following topics:

- **Asset Security Concepts:** Concepts discussed include asset and data policies, data quality, and data documentation and organization.
- **Identify and Classify Information and Assets:** Classification topics discussed include data and asset classification, sensitivity and criticality, private sector classifications, and military and government classifications.
- **Information and Asset Handling Requirements:** Topics include marking, labeling, storing, and destruction.
- **Provision Resources Securely:** Topics include how to determine and document information, asset ownership, asset inventory, and asset management.
- **Data Life Cycle:** Components include the data life cycle, databases, data audit, data roles, data collection, data location, data maintenance, data retention, data remanence, collection limitation, and data destruction.
- **Asset Retention:** Retention concepts discussed include media, hardware, and personnel retention and asset retention terms.
- **Data Security Controls:** Topics include data security, data states, data access and sharing, data storage and archiving, baselines, scoping and tailoring, standards selections, and data protection methods.

CHAPTER 2

Asset Security

Assets are any entities that are valuable to an organization and include ***tangible*** and ***intangible assets***. As mentioned in Chapter 1, "Security and Risk Management," tangible assets include computers, facilities, supplies, and personnel. Intangible assets include intellectual property, data, and organizational reputation. All assets in an organization must be protected to ensure the organization's future success. Although securing some assets is as easy as locking them in a safe, other assets require more advanced security measures. The most valuable asset of any organization is its data.

The Asset Security domain addresses a broad array of topics, including information and asset identification and classification, information and asset handling, information and asset ownership, asset inventory and asset management, data life cycle, asset retention, and data security controls and compliance requirements. Out of 100 percent of the exam, this domain carries an average weight of 10 percent, which is the lowest weight of the domains.

A security professional must be concerned with all aspects of asset security. The most important factor in determining the controls used to ensure asset security is an asset's value. Although some assets in the organization may be considered more important because they have greater value, you should ensure that no assets are forgotten. This chapter covers all the aspects of asset security that you, as an IT security professional, must understand.

NOTE Throughout this chapter, the terms *information* and *data* are used interchangeably, as commonly happens in the real world.

Foundation Topics

Asset Security Concepts

Asset security concepts that you must understand include

- Asset and data policies
- Data quality
- Data documentation and organization

Asset and Data Policies

As a security professional, you should ensure that your organization implements a data ***policy*** that defines long-term goals for data management and asset policies that define long-term goals for each asset type at a minimum. In some cases, each asset may need its own defined policy to ensure that it is properly administered. Business units will need to define asset policies and data policies for any assets and data owned by that business unit. Asset and data policies should be based on the organization's overall asset and data policies. Individual roles and responsibilities should be defined to ensure that personnel understand their job tasks as related to these policies.

After the overall policies are created, asset and data management practices and procedures should be documented to ensure that the day-to-day tasks related to assets and data are completed. In addition, the appropriate quality assurance and quality control procedures must be put into place for data quality to be ensured. Storage and backup procedures must be defined to ensure that assets and data can be restored.

As part of a data policy, any databases implemented within an organization should be carefully designed based on user requirements and the type of data to be stored. All databases should comply with the data policies that are approved, created, and implemented. Data policies should be strictly enforced.

Prior to establishing a data policy, you should consider several issues that can affect it. These issues include risks, cost, liability, legal and regulatory requirements, privacy, sensitivity, and ownership.

The cost of any data management mechanism is usually the primary consideration of any organization. Often organizations do not implement a data policy because they think it is easier to allow data to be stored in whatever way each business unit or user desires. However, if an organization does not adopt formal data policies and procedures, data security issues can arise because of the different storage methods used. For example, suppose an organization's research department decides to implement a Microsoft SQL Server database to store all research data, but the organization does not have a data policy. If the database is implemented without a thorough understanding of the types of data that will be stored and the users' needs, the research department may end up with a database that is difficult to navigate and manage. In addition, the proper access control mechanism may not be in place, resulting in users being able to edit the data that should only have view access.

Liability involves protecting the organization from legal issues. Liability is directly affected by legal and regulatory requirements that apply to the organization. Issues that can affect liability include asset or data misuse, data inaccuracy, data corruption, data breach, and data loss or a data leak.

Data privacy is determined as part of data analysis. Data classifications must be determined based on the value of the data to the organization. After the data classifications are determined, data controls should be implemented to ensure that the appropriate security controls are implemented based on data classifications. Privacy laws and regulations must also be considered.

Sensitive data is any data that could adversely affect an organization or individual if it were released to the public or obtained by attackers. When determining sensitivity, you should understand the types of threats that can occur, the vulnerability of the data, and the data type. For example, Social Security numbers are more sensitive than physical address data.

Data ownership is the final issue that you must consider as part of data policy design. This issue is particularly important if multiple organizations store their data within the same asset or database. One organization may want completely different security controls in place to protect its data. Understanding legal ownership of data is important to ensure that you design a data policy that takes into consideration the different requirements of multiple data owners. While this is most commonly a consideration when multiple organizations are involved, it can also be an issue with different business units in the same organization. For example, data from the human resources department has different owners and therefore different requirements than research department data.

Data Quality

Data quality is defined as data's fitness for use. The integrity factor of the security triad drives the data quality. Data quality must be maintained throughout the data life cycle, including during data capture, data modification, data storage, data distribution, data usage, and data archiving. These terms are also known as *data in use*, *data at rest*, and *data in transit*. Security professionals must ensure that their organization adopts the appropriate quality control and quality assurance measures so that data quality does not suffer. Data quality is most often safeguarded by ensuring data integrity, which protects data from unintentional, unauthorized, or accidental changes. With data integrity, data is known to be good, and information can be trusted as being complete, consistent, and accurate. System integrity ensures that a system will work as intended.

Security professionals should work to document data standards, processes, and procedures to monitor and control data quality. In addition, internal processes should be designed to periodically assess data quality. When data is stored in databases, quality control and assurance are easier to ensure using the internal data controls in the database. For example, you can configure a field to only a valid number. By doing this, you would ensure that only numbers could be input into the field. This is an example of input validation. Input validation can occur on both the client side (using regular expressions) and the server side (using code or in the database) to avoid SQL injection attacks.

Data ***contamination*** occurs when data errors occur. Data can be corrupt due to network or hash corruptions, lack of integrity policies, transmission errors, and bad encryption algorithms. Data errors can be reduced through implementation of the appropriate quality control and assurance mechanisms. Data verification, an important part of the process, evaluates how complete and correct the data is and whether it complies with standards. Data verification can be carried out by personnel who have the responsibility of entering the data. Data validation evaluates data after data verification has occurred and tests data to ensure that data quality standards have been met. Data validation must be carried out by personnel who have the most familiarity with the data.

Organizations should develop procedures and processes that keep two key data issues in the forefront: error prevention and correction. Error prevention is provided at data entry, whereas error correction usually occurs during data verification and validation.

Data Documentation and Organization

Data documentation ensures that data is understood at its most basic level and can be properly organized into data sets. Data sets ensure that data is arranged and stored in a relational way so that the data can be used for multiple purposes. Data sets should be given unique, descriptive names that indicate their contents.

By documenting the data and organizing data sets, organizations can also ensure that duplicate data is not retained in multiple locations. For example, the sales department may capture all demographic information for all customers. However, the shipping department may also need access to this same demographic information to ensure that products are shipped to the correct address. In addition, the accounts receivable department will need access to customer demographic information for billing purposes. There is no need for each business unit to have separate data sets for this information. Identifying the customer demographic data set as being needed by multiple business units prevents duplication of efforts across business units.

Within each data set, documentation must be created for each type of data. In the customer demographic data set example, customer name, address, and phone number are all collected. For each of the data types, the individual parameters for each data type must be created. Whereas an address may allow a mixture of numerals and characters, a phone number should allow only numerals. In addition, each data type may have a maximum length. Finally, it is important to document which data is required—meaning that it must be collected and entered. For example, an organization may decide that fax numbers are not required but phone numbers are required. Remember that each of these decisions is best made by the personnel working most closely with the data.

After all the documentation has been completed, the data organization must be mapped out. This organization will include all interrelationships between the data sets. It should also include information on which business units will need access to data sets or subsets of a data set.

NOTE *Big data* is a term for data sets that are so large or complex that they cannot be analyzed by traditional data processing applications. Specialized applications have been designed to help organizations with their big data. The big data challenges that may be encountered include data analysis, data capture, data search, data sharing, data storage, data mining, and data privacy.

Identify and Classify Information and Assets

Security professionals should ensure that the organizations they work for properly identify and classify all organizational information and assets. The first step in this process is to identify all information and assets the organization owns and uses. To perform information and asset identification, security professionals should work with the representatives from each department or functional area. After the information and assets are identified, security professionals should perform data and asset classification and document sensitivity and criticality of data.

Security professionals must understand private sector classifications, military and government classifications, the information life cycle, databases, and data audit.

Data and Asset Classification

Data and assets should be classified based on their value to the organization and their sensitivity to disclosure. Assigning a value to data and assets allows an organization to determine the resources that should be used to protect them. Resources that are used to protect data include personnel resources, monetary resources, access control resources, and so on. Classifying data and assets allows you to apply different protective measures. Data classification is critical to all systems to protect the ***confidentiality***, ***integrity***, and ***availability*** (CIA) of data.

After data is classified, the data can be segmented based on its level of protection needed. The classification levels ensure that data is handled and protected in the most cost-effective manner possible. The assets could then be configured to ensure that data is isolated or protected based on these classification levels. An organization should determine the classification levels it uses based on the needs of the organization. A number of private sector classifications and military and government information classifications are commonly used.

NOTE The common private sector classifications and military and government classifications are discussed in a later section.

The information life cycle, covered in more detail later in this chapter, should also be based on the classification of the data. Organizations are required to retain certain information, particularly financial data, based on local, state, or government laws and regulations.

Sensitivity and Criticality

Data sensitivity is a measure of how freely data can be handled. Some data requires special care and handling, especially when inappropriate handling could result in penalties, identity theft, financial loss, invasion of privacy, or unauthorized access by an individual or many individuals. Some data is also subject to regulation by state or federal laws and requires notification in the event of a disclosure.

Data is assigned a level of sensitivity based on who should have access to it and how much harm would be done if it were disclosed. This assignment of sensitivity is called data classification.

Data criticality is a measure of the importance of the data. Data that is considered sensitive may not necessarily be considered critical. Assigning a level of criticality to a particular data set requires considering the answers to a few questions:

- Will you be able to recover the data in case of disaster?
- How long will it take to recover the data?

- How safely, accurately and quickly can an organization recover the data in case of an incident or disaster?
- What is the effect of this downtime, including loss of public standing?

Data is considered essential when it is critical to the organization's business. When essential data is not available, even for a brief period of time, or when its integrity is questionable, the organization is unable to function at its optimal level. Data is considered required when it is important to the organization but organizational operations would continue for a predetermined period of time even if the data were not available. Data is nonessential if the organization is able to operate without it during extended periods of time.

When the sensitivity and criticality of data are understood and documented, the organization should then work to create a data classification system. Most organizations either use a private sector classification system or a military and government classification system.

PII

Personally identifiable information (PII) was defined and explained in Chapter 1. PII is considered information that should be classified and protected. National Institute of Standards and Technology (NIST) Special Publication (SP) 800-122 gives ***guidelines*** on protecting the confidentiality of PII.

According to SP 800-122, organizations should implement the following recommendations to effectively protect PII:

Key Topic

- Organizations should identify all PII residing in their environment.
- Organizations should minimize the use, collection, and retention of PII to what is strictly necessary to accomplish their business purpose and mission.
- Organizations should categorize their PII by the PII confidentiality impact level.
- Organizations should apply the appropriate safeguards for PII based on the PII confidentiality impact level.
- Organizations should develop an incident response plan to handle breaches involving PII.
- Organizations should encourage close coordination among their chief privacy officers, senior agency officials for privacy, chief information officers, chief information security officers, and legal counsel when addressing issues related to PII.

SP 800-122 defines PII as "any information about an individual maintained by an agency, including (1) any information that can be used to distinguish or trace an individual's identity, such as name, Social Security number, date and place of birth, mother's maiden name, or biometric records; and (2) any other information that is linked or linkable to an individual, such as medical, educational, financial, and employment information." To distinguish an individual is to identify an individual. To trace an individual is to process sufficient information to make a determination about a specific aspect of an individual's activities or status. Linked information is information about or related to an individual that is logically associated with other information about the individual. In contrast, linkable information is information about or related to an individual for which there is a possibility of logical association with other information about the individual.

All PII should be assigned confidentiality impact levels based on the FIPS 199 designations. Those designations are

- LOW if the loss of confidentiality, integrity, or availability could be expected to have a limited adverse effect on organizational operations, organizational assets, or individuals.
- MODERATE if the loss of confidentiality, integrity, or availability could be expected to have a serious adverse effect on organizational operations, organizational assets, or individuals.
- HIGH if the loss of confidentiality, integrity, or availability could be expected to have a severe or catastrophic adverse effect on organizational operations, organizational assets, or individuals.

Determining the impact from a loss of confidentiality of PII should take into account relevant factors. Several important factors that organizations should consider are as follows:

- **Identifiability:** How easily PII can be used to identify specific individuals
- **Quantity of PII:** How many individuals are identified in the information
- **Data field sensitivity:** The sensitivity of each individual PII data field, as well as the sensitivity of the PII data fields together
- **Context of use:** The purpose for which PII is collected, stored, used, processed, disclosed, or disseminated
- **Obligation to protect confidentiality:** The laws, regulations, standards, and operating practices that dictate an organization's responsibility for protecting PII
- **Access to and location of PII:** The nature of authorized access to PII

PII should be protected through a combination of measures, including operational safeguards, privacy-specific safeguards, and security controls. Operational safeguards should include policy and procedure creation and awareness, training, and education programs. Privacy-specific safeguards help organizations collect, maintain, use, and disseminate data in ways that protect the confidentiality of the data and include minimizing the use, collection, and retention of PII; conducting privacy impact assessments; de-identifying information; and anonymizing information. Security controls include separation of duties, least privilege, auditing, identification and authorization, and others from NIST SP 800-53.

NOTE NIST SP 800-53 is covered in more detail in Chapter 1.

Organizations that collect, use, and retain PII should use NIST SP 800-122 to help guide the organization's efforts to protect the confidentiality of PII.

PHI

Protected health information (PHI), also referred to as electronic protected health information (***EPHI*** or ePHI), is any individually identifiable health information. PHI is treated as a special case of PII with different standards and frameworks. NIST SP 800-66 provides guidelines for implementing the Health Insurance Portability and Accountability Act (HIPAA) Security Rule. The Security Rule applies to the following covered entities:

- **Covered healthcare providers:** Any provider of medical or other health services, or supplies, who transmits any health information in electronic form in connection with a transaction for which HHS (U.S. Department of Health and Human Services) has adopted a standard.
- **Health plans:** Any individual or group plan that provides or pays the cost of medical care (e.g., a health insurance issuer and the Medicare and Medicaid programs).
- **Healthcare clearinghouses:** A public or private entity that processes another entity's healthcare transactions from a standard format to a nonstandard format, or vice versa.
- **Medicare prescription drug card sponsors:** A nongovernmental entity that offers an endorsed discount drug program under the Medicare Modernization Act.

Each covered entity must ensure the confidentiality, integrity, and availability of PHI that it creates, receives, maintains, or transmits; protect against any reasonably anticipated threats and hazards to the security or integrity of EPHI; and protect against reasonably anticipated uses or disclosures of such information that are not permitted by the Privacy Rule.

The Security Rule is separated into six main sections as follows:

- **Security Standards General Rules:** Includes the general requirements all covered entities must meet; establishes flexibility of approach; identifies standards and implementation specifications (both required and addressable); outlines decisions a covered entity must make regarding addressable implementation specifications; and requires maintenance of security measures to continue reasonable and appropriate protection of PHI.
- **Administrative Safeguards:** Defined in the Security Rule as the "administrative actions and policies, and procedures to manage the selection, development, implementation, and maintenance of security measures to protect electronic protected health information and to manage the conduct of the covered entity's workforce in relation to the protection of that information."
- **Physical Safeguards:** Defined as the "physical measures, policies, and procedures to protect a covered entity's electronic information systems and related buildings and equipment, from natural and environmental hazards, and unauthorized intrusion."
- **Technical Safeguards:** Defined as the "the technology and the policy and procedures for its use that protect electronic protected health information and control access to it."
- **Organizational Requirements:** Includes standards for business associate contracts and other arrangements, including memoranda of understanding between a covered entity and a business associate when both entities are government organizations; and requirements for group health plans.
- **Policies and Procedures and Documentation Requirements:** Requires implementation of reasonable and appropriate policies and procedures to comply with the standards, implementation specifications, and other requirements of the Security Rule; maintenance of written documentation (which may be also in electronic form such as email) and/or records that include policies, procedures, actions, activities, or assessments required by the Security Rule; and retention, availability, and update requirements related to the documentation.

NIST SP 800-66 includes a relationship linking the NIST Risk Management Framework (RMF) and the Security Rule. It also includes key activities that should be carried out for each of the preceding six main sections of the Security Rule. Organizations that collect, use, and retain PHI should use NIST SP 800-66 to help guide the organization's efforts to provide confidentiality, integrity, and availability for PHI.

Proprietary Data

Proprietary data is defined as internally generated data or documents that contain technical or other types of information controlled by an organization to safeguard its competitive edge. Proprietary data may be protected under copyright, patent, or trade secret laws. While there are no specific and different standards or frameworks to govern the protection of proprietary data, organizations must ensure that the confidentiality, integrity, and availability of proprietary data are protected. Because of this, many organizations protect proprietary data with the same types of controls that are used for PII and PHI.

Security professionals should ensure that proprietary data is identified and properly categorized to ensure that the appropriate controls are put into place.

Private Sector Data Classifications

Organizations in the private sector can generally classify their data using four main classification levels, listed from highest sensitivity level (1) to lowest (4):

Key Topic

1. Confidential
2. Private
3. Sensitive
4. Public

NOTE It is up to each organization to determine the number and type of classifications. Other classification options that an organization can choose to use include "protected" to indicate legally protected data and "proprietary" to indicate company-owned data (in a legal sense).

Data that is confidential includes trade secrets, intellectual data, application programming code, and other data that could seriously affect the organization if unauthorized disclosure occurred. Data at this level would be available only to personnel in the organization whose work needs, or is directly related to, the accessed data.

Access to confidential data usually requires authorization for each access. In most cases, the only way for external entities to have authorized access to confidential data is as follows:

- After signing a confidentiality agreement
- When complying with a court order
- As part of a government project or contract procurement agreement

Data that is private includes any information related to personnel, including human resources records, medical records, and salary information, that is used only within the organization. Data that is sensitive includes organizational financial information and requires extra measures to ensure its CIA and accuracy. Public data is data that is generally shared with the public and would not cause a negative impact on the organization. Examples of public data include how many people work in the organization and what products an organization manufactures or sells.

Military and Government Data Classifications

Military and governmental entities usually classify data using five main classification levels, listed from highest sensitivity level to lowest:

Key Topic

1. **Top Secret:** Disclosure would cause exceptionally grave danger to national security.
2. **Secret:** Disclosure would cause serious damage to national security.
3. **Confidential:** Disclosure would cause damage to national security.
4. **Sensitive but Unclassified:** Disclosure might harm national security.
5. **Unclassified:** Any information that can generally be distributed to the public without any threat to national interest.

U.S. federal agencies use the Sensitive but Unclassified (SBU) designation when information is not classified but still needs to be protected and requires strict controls over its distribution. There are over 100 different labels for SBU, including

- For official use only (FOUO)
- Limited official use
- Sensitive security information
- Critical infrastructure information

Executive order 13556 created a standard designation Controlled Unclassified Information (CUI). Implementation is in progress.

Data that is top secret includes weapon blueprints, technology specifications, spy satellite information, and other military information that could gravely damage national security if disclosed. Data that is secret includes deployment plans, missile placement, and other information that could seriously damage national security if disclosed. Data that is confidential includes strength of forces in the United States and overseas, technical information used for training and maintenance, and other information that could seriously affect the government if unauthorized disclosure occurred. Data that is sensitive but unclassified includes medical or other personal data that might not cause serious damage to national security if disclosed but could cause citizens to question the reputation of the government and may even lead to legal battles with lawsuits. Military and government information that does not fall into any of the four other categories is considered unclassified and usually available to the public based on the Freedom of Information Act.

NOTE Enacted on July 4, 1966, and taking effect one year later, the Freedom of Information Act (FOIA) provides a powerful tool to advocates for access to information. Under the FOIA, anyone may request and receive any records from federal agencies unless the documents are officially declared exempt based upon specific categories, such as top secret, secret, and confidential. To learn more about how to explore for FOIA data or make a FOIA request, visit www.foia.gov.

Information and Asset Handling Requirements

Organizations should establish the appropriate information and asset handling requirements to protect their assets. As part of these handling requirements, personnel should be instructed on how to mark, label, store, and destroy or dispose of media.

Handling requirements are spelled out in organizational standards and other documentation. Organizational standards and documentations must be enforced to ensure proper asset handling. Handling requirements inform custodians and users how to protect the information they use and systems with which they interact. Handling requirements dictate by classification level how information must be stored, transmitted, communicated, accessed, retained, and destroyed. Handling requirements can extend to incident management and breach notification. Handling requirements extend to automated tools, such as data loss prevention (DLP) solutions. Handling requirements should be succinctly documented in a usable format. Handling requirements compliance should be referenced in the acceptable use policy (AUP). Users should be introduced to handling requirements during the onboarding process. Handling requirements should be reinforced throughout the user life cycle.

Marking, Labeling, and Storing

Plainly label all forms of storage media (tapes, optical drives, and so on) and store them safely. Some guidelines in the area of media control are to

- Accurately and promptly mark all data storage media.
- Ensure proper environmental storage of the media.
- Ensure the safe and clean handling of the media.
- Log data media to provide a physical inventory control.

The environment where the media will be stored is also important. For example, damage could occur to magnetic media above 100 degrees Fahrenheit (38 degrees Celsius).

Media marking refers to the use of human-readable information about the media, while *media labeling* refers to the use of security attributes in internal ***data structures***. Marking is usually written on the media itself so the correct media can be easily identified. Labeling is internal to the media itself. A backup tape may be marked with a server name or other identifier of the asset to which the backup belongs. If an administrator accesses the backups on the backup tape, each backup will be labeled with a descriptive name that usually includes the date, time, and type of backup. In addition, ACLs may be configured on the different backup files to limit the users who can access the backup files.

Labeling is the vehicle for communicating the assigned classification to custodians, users, and applications (for example, access control and DLP). Labels make it easy to identify the data classification. Labels can take many forms: electronic, print, audio, or visual. Labeling recommendations are tied to media type. In electronic form, the classification label should be a part of the document name (for example, Customer Transaction History_Protected). On written or printed documents, the classification label should be clearly watermarked, as well as in either the document header or footer. For physical media, the classification label should be clearly marked on the case using words or symbols.

Destruction

During media disposal, you must ensure no data remains on the media. The most reliable, secure means of removing data from magnetic storage media, such as a magnetic tape cassette, is through *degaussing*, which exposes the media to a powerful, alternating magnetic field. It removes any previously written data, leaving the media in a magnetically randomized (blank) state. More information on the destruction of media is given earlier in this chapter, later in the "Data Remanence and Destruction" section, and in Chapter 7, "Security Operations."

Provision Resources Securely

While information and assets within an organization are ultimately owned by the organization, it is usually understood that information and assets within the organization are owned and managed by different business units. These business units must work together to ensure that the organizational mission is achieved and that the information and assets are protected.

For this reason, security professionals must understand where the different information and assets are located and work with the various owners to ensure that the information and assets are protected. The owners that security professionals need to work with include data owners, system owners, and business/mission owners. As part of asset ownership, security professionals should ensure that appropriate asset management procedures are developed and followed, as described in Chapter 7.

Asset Inventory and Asset Management

To properly secure organizational assets, security professionals must ensure that an accurate inventory of all assets is obtained. After all assets are inventoried, assets must be managed by the asset owners. To fully understand asset inventory and management, security professionals must understand the asset life cycle. According to the National Institute of Standards (NIST), the asset life cycle is an eight-phase process, as shown in Figure 2-1.

Key Topic

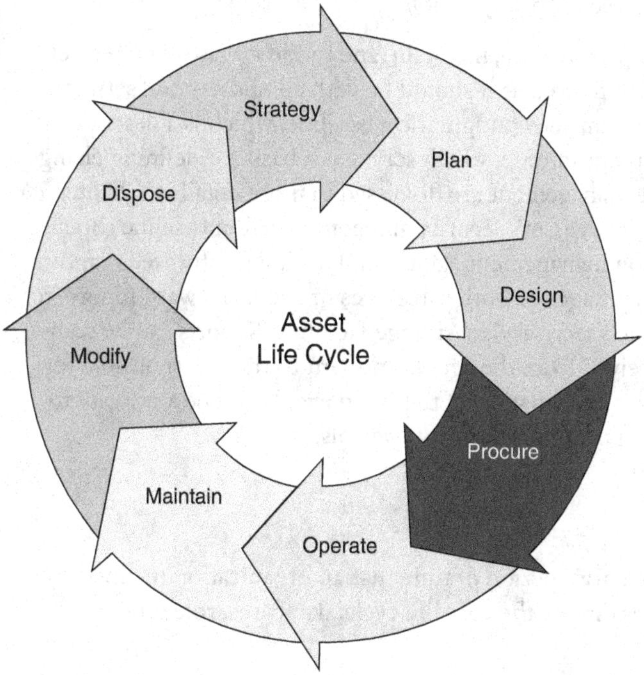

Figure 2-1 Asset Life Cycle

In a typical life cycle, an asset goes through the enrollment, operation, and end-of-life phases. The enrollment process involves manual IT staff activities, such as assigning and tagging the asset with a serial number and barcode, loading a baseline IT image, assigning the asset to an owner, and, finally, recording the serial number as well as other attributes into a database. The attributes might also include primary location, hardware model, baseline IT image, and owner. This process can also be referred to as the inventory phase.

As the asset goes through the operations phase, changes can occur. Such changes could include introduction of new or unauthorized software, the removal of certain critical software, or the removal of the physical asset itself from the enterprise. These changes need to be tracked and recorded. As a consequence, asset monitoring, anomaly detection, reporting, and policy enforcement are the primary activities in this phase.

The assets within the enterprise are monitored using installed agents that reside on the asset, as well as network-based monitoring systems that scan and capture network traffic. These monitoring systems collect data from and about the assets and send periodic reports to the analytics engine.

As an asset reaches the end of its operational life, it goes through activities within the end-of-life phase that include returning the asset to IT support for data removal and removing the serial number (or other organization labeling information) from the registration database and other associated databases. Finally, the asset is prepared for physical removal from the enterprise facility.

Asset management includes the operate, maintain, and modify phases of the asset life cycle. After an asset is configured as it should be with all updates and settings, administrators should document the configuration baseline, which is a description of an asset's attributes at a point in time, which serves as a basis for defining change. (Configuration and change management are discussed in more detail in Chapter 7.) As part of asset management, an asset's security and configuration baseline should be enforced by configuration management agents, and installed software is captured by software asset management agents. Both categories of agents forward reports to their respective servers, which serve as data storage facilities. Reports can be compiled based on the data received from the agents and sent to those responsible for managing the assets. Regular examination of these reports should be a priority to ensure that assets have the appropriate security controls.

Data Life Cycle

A *data life cycle* refers to the entire period of time that an organization retains data. The following sections discuss the data life cycle, databases, roles and responsibilities, data collection and limitation, data location, data maintenance, data retention, data remanence and destruction, and data audit.

Organizations should ensure that any information they collect and store is managed throughout the life cycle of that information. If no information life cycle is followed, the data would be retained indefinitely, never discarded, and rarely, if ever, updated. Security professionals must therefore ensure that data owners and custodians understand the information life cycle.

For most organizations, the five phases of the information life cycle are as follows:

Key Topic

1. Create/receive
2. Distribute
3. Use
4. Maintain
5. Dispose/store

During the create/receive phase, data is either created by organizational personnel or received by the organization via the data entry portal. If the data is created by organizational personnel, it is usually placed in the location from which it will be distributed, used, and maintained. However, if the data is received via some other mechanism, you might need to copy or import the data to an appropriate location. In this case, the data will not be available for distribution, usage, and maintenance until after the copy or import. Not all data is used by all users. As such, data needs to be sorted, stored, and distributed in various ways as the needs arise from each user or business unit. This phase also must contain data classification after receiving and creating. Received or created data must be given a classification and sensitivity before it can be distributed or data will be going everywhere.

After the create/receive phase, organizational personnel must ensure that the data is properly distributed. In most cases, this step involves placing the data in the appropriate location and possibly configuring the access permissions as defined by the data owner. Keep in mind, however, that in many cases the storage location and appropriate user and group permissions may already be configured. In such a case, it is just a matter of ensuring that the data is in the correct distribution location. Distribution locations include databases, shared folders, ***network-attached storage (NAS)***, storage-area networks (SANs), and data libraries.

After data has been distributed, personnel within the organization can use the data in their day-to-day operations. Whereas some personnel will have only read access to data, others may have write or full control permissions. Remember that the permissions allowed or denied are designated by the data owner but configured by the data custodian.

Now that data is being used in day-to-day operations, data maintenance is key to ensuring that data remains accessible and secure. Maintenance includes auditing, performing backups, performing data integrity checks, and managing data leaks and loss.

When data becomes old, invalid, and not fit for any further use, it is considered to be in the disposition stage. You should either properly dispose of it or ensure that it is securely stored. Some organizations must maintain data records for a certain number of years per local, state, or federal laws or regulations. This type of data should be archived for the required period. In addition, any data that is part of litigation should be retained as requested by the court of law, and organizations should follow appropriate chain of custody and evidence documentation processes. Data archival and destruction procedures should be clearly defined by the organization.

All organizations need policies in place for the retention and destruction of data. Data retention and destruction must follow all local, state, and government regulations and laws. Documenting proper procedures ensures that information is maintained for the required time to prevent financial fines and possible incarceration of high-level organizational officers. These procedures must include both the retention period and destruction process.

Figure 2-2 shows the information life cycle.

Figure 2-2 Information Life Cycle

A discussion of data would be incomplete without a discussion of databases.

Databases

Databases have become the technology of choice for storing, organizing, and analyzing large sets of data. End users who use data from databases generally access a database though a client interface. As the need arises to provide access to entities outside the enterprise, the opportunities for misuse increase. In the following sections, concepts necessary to discuss database security are covered as well as the security concerns surrounding database management and maintenance.

DBMS Architecture and Models

Databases contain data, and the main difference in database models is how that information is stored and organized. The model describes the relationships among the data elements, how the data is accessed, how integrity is ensured, and acceptable operations. The five models or architectures we discuss are

- Relational
- Hierarchical
- Network
- Object-oriented
- Object-relational

The *relational* model uses *attributes* (columns) and *tuples* (rows) to organize the data in two-dimensional tables. Each cell in the table represents the intersection of an attribute, and a tuple represents a record.

When working with relational database management systems (RDBMSs), you should understand the following terms:

- ***Relation***: A connection between one or more tables. One column in a table is a primary key that relates to another table as a foreign key.
- **Tuple:** A ***row*** in a table.
- **Attribute:** A column in a table.
- ***Schema***: Description of a ***relational database***.
- ***Record***: A collection of related data items.
- ***Base relation***: In SQL, a relation that is actually existent in the database.
- ***View***: The set of data derived from one or more tables or views available to a given user. Security is enforced through the use of views for users needing read-only access to the data.
- ***Degree***: The number of columns in a table.
- ***Cardinality***: The number of rows in a relation.
- ***Domain***: The set of allowable values that an attribute can take.
- **Primary key:** One or more columns that identify each row of a table unique.
- ***Foreign key***: An attribute in one relation that has values matching the primary key in another relation. Matches between the foreign key and the primary key

are important because they represent references from one relation to another and establish the connection among these relations.

- ***Candidate key***: An attribute in a row that uniquely identifies that row.
- ***Referential integrity***: A requirement that for any foreign key attribute, the referenced relation must have a tuple with the same value for its primary key.

An important element of database design that ensures that the attributes in a table depend only on the primary key is a process called *normalization*. Normalization includes

- Eliminating repeating groups by putting them into separate tables
- Eliminating redundant data (occurring in more than one table)
- Eliminating attributes in a table that are not dependent on the primary key of that table

In the ***hierarchical database*** model, data is organized into a hierarchy. An object can have one child (an object that is a subset of the parent object), multiple children, or no children. To navigate this hierarchy, you must know the branch in which the object is located. An example of the use of this system is the Windows Registry and a Lightweight Directory Access Protocol (LDAP) directory.

In the *network* model, as in the hierarchical model, data is organized into a hierarchy, but unlike the hierarchical model, objects can have multiple parents. Because of this, knowing which branch to find a data element in is not necessary because there will typically be multiple paths to it.

The *object-oriented* model can handle a variety of data types and is more dynamic than a relational database. ***Object-oriented database (OODB)*** systems are useful in storing and manipulating complex data, such as images and graphics. Consequently, complex applications involving multimedia, computer-aided design (CAD), video, graphics, and expert systems are more suited to the object-oriented model. It also has the characteristics of ease of reusing code and analysis and reduced maintenance.

Objects can be created as needed, and the data and the procedures (or methods) go with the object when it is requested. A *method* is the code defining the actions that the object performs in response to a message. This model uses some of the same concepts of a relational model. In the object-oriented model, the relation, column, and tuple (relational terms) are referred to as class, attribute, and instance objects.

The *object-relational* model is the marriage of object-oriented and relational technologies, combining the attributes of both. This is a relational database with a software interface that is written in an ***object-oriented programming (OOP)*** language. The logic and procedures are derived from the front-end software rather than the database. This means each front-end application can have its own specific procedures.

Database Interface Languages

Access to information in a database is facilitated by an application that allows you to obtain and interact with data. These interfaces can be written in several different languages. This section discusses some of the more important data programming languages:

- **ODBC:** ***Open Database Connectivity (ODBC)*** is an application programming interface (API) that allows communication with databases either locally or remotely. An API on the client sends requests to the ODBC API. The ODBC API locates the database, and a specific driver converts the request into a database command that the specific database will understand.
- **JDBC:** As you might expect from the title, ***Java Database Connectivity (JDBC)*** makes it possible for Java applications to communicate with a database. A Java API is what allows Java programs to execute SQL statements. It is database agnostic and allows communication with various types of databases. It provides the same functionality as the ODBC.
- **XML:** Data can be created in Extensible Markup Language (XML) format, but the XML:DB API allows XML applications to interact with more traditional databases, such as relational databases. It requires that the database have a database-specific driver that encapsulates all the database access logic.
- **OLE DB:** ***Object Linking and Embedding Database (OLE DB)*** is a replacement for ODBC, extending its functionality to nonrelational databases. Although it is COM-based and limited to Microsoft Windows–based tools, it provides applications with uniform access to a variety of data sources, including service through ActiveX objects.

Data Warehouses and Data Mining

Data warehousing is the process of combining data from multiple databases or data sources in a central location called a ***data warehouse***. The warehouse is used to carry out analysis. The data is not simply combined but is processed and presented in a more useful and understandable way. Data warehouses require stringent security because the data is not dispersed but located in a central location. Within data warehouses, organizations may also designate a data mart, which is a subset of data from the data warehouse that is used for analytics and business intelligence users.

Data mining is the process of using special tools to organize the data into a format that makes it easier to make business decisions based on the content. It analyzes large data sets in a data warehouse to find nonobvious patterns. These tools locate associations between data and correlate these associations into metadata, which is data about data. It allows for more sophisticated inferences (sometimes called business intelligence [BI]) to be made about the data. Three measures should be taken when using data warehousing applications:

- Control metadata from being used interactively.
- Monitor the ***data purging*** plan.
- Reconcile data moved between the operations environment and data warehouse.

Database Maintenance

Database administrators must regularly conduct database maintenance. Databases must be backed up regularly. All security patches and updates for the hardware and software, including the database software, must be kept up to date. Hardware and software upgrades are necessary as organizational needs increase and as technology advances.

Security professionals should work with database administrators to ensure that threat analysis for databases is performed at least annually. They should also work to develop the appropriate mitigations and controls to protect against the identified threats.

Database Threats

Security threats to databases usually revolve around unwanted access to data. Two security threats that exist in managing databases involve the processes of ***aggregation*** and ***inference***. Aggregation is the act of combining information from various sources. It can become a security issue with databases when users do not have access to a given set of data objects but do have access to them individually, or at least some of them, and are able to piece together the information to which they should *not* have access. On the other hand, an inference occurs when the attacker uses several pieces of generic nonsensitive information to determine or learn specific sensitive data.

Two types of access measures can be put in place to help prevent access to inferable information:

- *Content-dependent access control* bases access on the sensitivity of the data. For example, a department's manager might have access to the salaries of the employees in that department but not to the salaries of employees in other departments. The cost of this measure is an increased processing overhead.

- *Context-dependent access control* bases the access to data on multiple factors to help prevent inference. Access control can be a function of factors such as location, time of day, and previous access history.

Database Views

Access to the information in a database is usually controlled through the use of ***database views***. A view refers to the given set of data that a user or group of users can see when they access the database. Before a user is able to use a view, that user must have permission on both the view and all dependent objects. Views can be used to enforce the concept of least privilege.

Database Locks

Database locks are used when one user is accessing a record that prevents another user from accessing the record at the same time to prevent edits until the first user is finished. Locking not only provides exclusivity to writes but also controls reading of unfinished modifications or uncommitted data.

Polyinstantiation

Polyinstantiation is a process used to prevent data inference violations like the database threats previously covered. It does this by enabling a relation to contain multiple tuples with the same primary keys, with each instance distinguished by a security level. It prevents low-level database users from inferring the existence of higher-level data.

Database ACID Test

Every database should adhere to the rules of ACID. An ACID test ensures that each transaction has the following properties before it is committed:

- ***Atomicity***: Either all command operations are complete, or the database changes are rolled back.
- ***Consistency***: The transaction follows an integrity process that ensures that data is consistent in all places where it exists.
- ***Isolation***: A transaction does not interact with other transactions until completion.
- ***Durability***: After it's verified, the transaction is committed and cannot be rolled back.

Roles and Responsibilities

Many roles are tied to asset security. The three most important are data owners, data controllers, and data custodians. Data owners are the personnel who actually own a given set of data. These data owners determine the level of access that any users are given to their data. Data controllers are those who either alone or jointly with other persons determine the purposes for which and the manner in which any personal data is processed. Data custodians are the personnel who actually manage the access to a given set of data. While data owners determine the level of access given, it is the data custodians who actually configure the appropriate controls to grant or deny the user's access, based on the data owner's approval.

Other roles within an organization affect data but do not necessarily affect the data as much as data owners, controllers, and custodians. In the following sections, we discuss these roles and their effect on data.

Data Owner

Data owners must understand the way in which the data they are responsible for is used and when that data should be released. They must also determine the data's value to and impact on the organization. A data owner should understand what it will take to restore or replace data and the cost that will be incurred during this process. Finally, data owners must understand when data is inaccurate or no longer needed by the organization.

In most cases, each business unit within an organization designates a data owner, who must be given the appropriate level of authority for the data for which that owner is responsible. Data owners must understand any intellectual property rights and copyright issues for the data. Data owners are responsible for ensuring that the appropriate agreements are in place if third parties are granted access to the data.

Security professionals must work with the owners of information and assets to determine who should have access to the information and assets, the value of the information and assets, and the controls that should be implemented to protect the privacy of information and assets. As a result, security professionals must understand the role of data owners, system owners, and business/mission owners.

Unfortunately, in most cases, data owners do not own the systems on which their data resides. Therefore, it is important that the data owner work closely with the system owner. Even if the appropriate ACLs are configured for the data, the data can still be compromised if the system on which the data resides is not properly secured.

Data Controller

Data controllers determine the "why" and "how" personal data is processed. In some cases, the data controller role and the data owner role are the same. However, organizations should separate these roles when the data being stored and managed has special protections or laws that affect it. The data controller can focus on maintaining the privacy and confidentiality of the data.

In the European Union's General Data Protection Regulation (GDPR) and other privacy laws, the data controller has the most responsibility when it comes to protecting the privacy and rights of the data's subject, such as the user of a website. Simply put, the data controller controls the procedures and purpose of data usage. Data controllers should ensure that any data collected adheres to the applicable laws and regulations. The data controller is responsible for documenting how the data will be used.

Data Custodian

Data custodians must understand the levels of data access that can be given to users. Data custodians work with data owners to determine the level of access that should be given and implement the policies. This is an excellent example of separations. By having separate roles such as data owners and data custodians, an organization can ensure that no single role is responsible for data access. This setup prevents fraudulent creation of user accounts and assignment of rights.

Data custodians should understand data policies and guidelines. They should document the data structures in the organization and the levels of access given. They are also responsible for data storage, archiving, and backups. Finally, they should be concerned with data quality and should therefore implement the appropriate audit controls.

Centralized data custodians are common. Data owners give the data custodians the permission level that users and groups should be given. Data custodians actually implement the ***access control lists (ACLs)*** for the devices, databases, folders, and files.

System Owners

System owners are responsible for the systems on which data resides. While the data owner owns the data and the data custodian configures the appropriate permissions for user access to the data, the system owner must determine the parameters that govern the system, such as what types of data and applications can be stored on the system, who owns the data and applications, and who determines the users who can access the data and applications.

System Custodians

System custodians are responsible for administering the systems on which data resides based on the parameters set forth by the system owner.

Business/Mission Owners

Business or mission owners must ensure that all operations fit within the business goals and mission. This task includes ensuring that collected data is necessary for the business to function. Collecting unnecessary data wastes time and resources. Because the business/mission owner is primarily concerned with the overall business, conflicts between data owners, data custodians, and system owners may need to be resolved by the business/mission owner, who will need to make the best decision for the organization. For example, say that a data owner requests more room on a system for the storage of data. The data owner strongly believes that the new data being collected will help the sales team be more efficient. However, storage on the system owner's asset is at a premium. The system owner is unwilling to allow the data owner to use the amount of space requested. In this case, the business/mission owner would need to review both sides and decide whether collecting and storing the new data would result in enough increased revenue to justify the cost of allowing the data owner more storage space. If so, it may also be necessary to invest in more storage media for the system or to move the data to another system that has more resources available. But keep in mind that moving the data would possibly involve another system owner.

Security professionals should always be part of these decisions because they understand the security controls in place for any systems involved and the security controls needed to protect the data. Moving the data to a system that does not have the appropriate controls may cause more issues than just simply upgrading the system on which the data currently resides. Only a security professional is able to objectively assess the security needs of the data and ensure that they are met.

Data Processors

Data processors are any personnel within an organization who process the data that has been collected throughout the entire life cycle of the data. If any individual accesses the data in any way, that individual can be considered a data processor. However, in some organizations, data processors are only those individuals who can enter or change data.

No matter which definition an organization uses, it is important that security professionals work to provide training to all data processors on the importance of asset privacy, especially data privacy. This training is usually included as part of the security awareness training. It is also important to include any privacy standards or policies that are based on laws and regulations. After personnel have received the appropriate training, they should sign a statement saying that they will abide by the organization's privacy policy.

Data Users and Subjects

Data users are any individuals who are granted access to some or all data after proper forms are signed. These entities do not necessarily have any editing rights on the data. They often simply view and use the data as part of their day-to-day duties. In some cases, the terms *data users* and *data processors* are used synonymously. However, security professionals should keep in mind that processors can edit the data, whereas data users generally cannot.

Data subjects are any end users whose personal data can be collected. A data subject is any individual person who can be directly or indirectly identified via an identifier, including name, ID number, location data, or via factors specific to the person's physical, physiological, genetic, mental, economic, cultural, or social identity. Many laws and regulations now include rights for the data subjects so that they can request that data be modified or deleted.

Data Collection and Limitation

For any organization, a data collection limitation exists based on what is needed. System owners and data custodians should monitor the amount of free storage space so that they understand trends and can anticipate future needs before space becomes critical. Without appropriate monitoring, data can grow to the point where system performance is affected. No organization wants to have a vital data storage system shut down because there is no available free space. Disk quotas allow administrators to set disk space limits for users and then automatically monitor disk space usage. In most cases, the quotas can be configured to notify users when they are nearing space limits.

Collection of data is also limited based on laws and regulations and, in some cases, on gaining the consent of the subject of the data. Organizations should ensure that they fully document any laws and regulations that affect the collection of private data and adjust any private data collection policies accordingly. Organizations should document and archive the consent of the data subject. In addition, this consent should be renewed periodically, especially if the collection policy changes in any way.

Security professionals should work with system owners and data custodians to ensure that the appropriate monitoring and alert mechanisms are configured. System owners and data custodians can then be proactive when it comes to data storage needs.

Data Location

Data location is the physical location of the data when it is being stored, transmitted, and accessed. Many laws and regulations affect what kinds of data can be stored and how that data must be protected based on the citizenship of the data subject. But there are also laws and regulations that can affect data based on where it is stored. This issue is complicated by the fact that so many organizations are implementing cloud solutions for data storage.

Security professionals should ensure that organizations keep backup copies on site and another backup copy off site. If a disaster, such as a tornado, destroys the primary location, the organization would still have a backup copy stored off site.

The decision of how far off site to store the backup needs to be considered. If the backup is stored at the same location, it could be destroyed in the same tornado. Even if the backup was stored three miles away, it is possible a tornado could destroy both locations.

Some organizations maintain data in data centers. The organization may replicate this data to one or more other data centers to maintain critical data availability. These data centers are typically located in separate geographical locations. Organizations should verify the cloud storage locations to ensure they are in a separate geographical location.

Organizations such as Google, Amazon, and Netflix store data in content data servers around the country for easy access. Content servers store the content of data at various locations for users to connect quickly and play the video or order an item seamlessly.

Data Maintenance

Data maintenance includes efforts to organize and care for data throughout its lifetime. Maintenance includes updating the data on a regular schedule or when requested to do so by the data subject. If the data is stored on a single server, updating the data is easy. If data is stored on multiple servers and other devices, protecting the data and ensuring it is maintained are much more complicated.

Depending on whether the organization can truly isolate the classified or private data from unclassified data using separate networks, air gaps or unidirectional network bridges could be implemented to provide data protection. If an air gap is implemented, personnel would need to manually add data to the classified data network. If network bridges are used, personnel could copy data from the unclassified data network to the classified data network, provided the policies were appropriately configured.

Organizations should routinely review data policies to ensure that policies are updated and being followed. Security professionals should review recent data breaches and determine the root cause so that controls can be installed or updated.

Data Retention

Data retention involves retaining and maintaining important data as long as it is needed or required by law and destroying it when it is no longer needed. An organization's data policy typically identifies retention time frames for data based on data types. Some laws and regulations dictate the time that an organization should retain data, such as three years, seven years, or even indefinitely. Data can even be placed on legal hold based on pending litigation. Organizations have the responsibility of complying with all laws, regulations, and legal holds. However, even in the absence of external requirements, an organization should establish policies on the length for data retention of the different types of data.

For example, organizations may retain financial data for a different period of time than it retains PII. Audit logs may need different and longer or shorter retention periods than financial data or PII because audit logs allow security professionals to reconstruct actions that occurred during a breach. If appropriate retention policies are not in place, valuable data can be lost earlier than expected. A longer retention period means that the organization will need more backup media.

Data Remanence and Destruction

Whenever data is erased or removed from a storage media, residual data can be left behind. These remnants can allow data to be reconstructed when the organization disposes of the media, resulting in unauthorized individuals or groups gaining access to private data. Media that security professionals must consider include magnetic hard disk drives, solid-state drives, magnetic tapes, and optical media, such as CDs and DVDs. When considering data ***remanence***, security professionals must understand three countermeasures:

- **Clearing:** This countermeasure includes removing data from the media so that it cannot be reconstructed using normal file recovery techniques and tools. With this method, the data is only recoverable using special forensic techniques. Overwriting is a clearing technique that writes data patterns over the entire media, thereby eliminating any trace data. Another clearing technique is disk wiping. For clearing and wiping to work well, data must be cleared or wiped at least seven times.
- **Purging:** Also referred to as *sanitization*, purging makes the data unreadable even with advanced forensic techniques. With this technique, data should be

unrecoverable. Degaussing, a purging technique, exposes the media to a powerful, alternating magnetic field, removing any previously written data and leaving the media in a magnetically randomized (blank) state.

- **Destruction:** Destruction involves destroying the media on which the data resides. Encryption scrambles the data on the media, thereby rendering it unreadable without the encryption key. Destruction is the physical act of destroying media in such a way that it cannot be reconstructed. Shredding involves physically breaking media to pieces. Pulverizing involves reducing media to dust. Pulping chemically destroys the media and makes it unusable in any way. Finally, burning incinerates the media.

The majority of these countermeasures work for magnetic media. However, solid-state drives present unique challenges because they cannot be overwritten. Most solid-state drive vendors provide sanitization commands that can be used to erase the data on the drive. Security professionals should research these commands to ensure that they are effective. Another option for these drives is to erase the cryptographic key. Often a combination of these methods must be used to fully ensure that the data is removed.

Data remanence is also a consideration when using any cloud-based solution for an organization. Security professionals should be involved in negotiating any contract with a cloud-based provider to ensure that the contract covers data remanence issues, although it is difficult to determine that the data is properly removed. Using data encryption is a great way to ensure that data remanence is not a concern when dealing with the cloud.

Data Audit

While an organization may have the most up-to-date data management plan in place, data management alone is not enough to fully protect data. Organizations must also put into place a data auditing mechanism that will help administrators identify vulnerabilities before attacks occur. Auditing mechanisms can be configured to monitor almost any level of access to data. However, auditing mechanisms affect the performance of the systems being audited. Always carefully consider any performance impact that may occur as a result of the auditing mechanism. Although auditing is necessary, it is important not to audit so many events that the auditing logs are littered with useless or unused information.

Confidential or sensitive data should be more carefully audited than public information. As a matter of fact, it may not even be necessary to audit access to public information. But when considering auditing for confidential data, an organization may decide to audit all access to that data or just attempts to change the data. Only the organization and its personnel are able to develop the best auditing plan.

Finally, auditing is good only if there is a regular review of the logs produced. Administrators or security professionals should obtain appropriate training on reviewing audit logs. In addition, appropriate alerts should be configured if certain critical events occur. For example, if multiple user accounts are locked out due to invalid login attempts over a short period of time, this lockout may be an indication that systems are experiencing a dictionary or other password attack. If an alert were scheduled to notify administrators when a certain number of lockouts occur over a period of time, administrators may be able to curtail the issue before successful access is achieved by the attacker.

Asset Retention

Asset and data retention requirements vary based on several factors, including asset or data type, asset or data age, and legal and regulatory requirements. Security professionals must understand where data is stored and the type of data stored. In addition, security professionals should provide guidance on managing and archiving data. Therefore, data retention policies must be established with the help of organizational personnel. The assets that store data will use the data retention policies to help guide the asset retention guidelines. If a storage asset needs to be replaced, a thorough understanding of the data that resides on the asset is essential to ensure that data is still retained for the required period.

A retention policy usually contains the purpose of the policy, the portion of the organization affected by the policy, any exclusions to the policy, the personnel responsible for overseeing the policy, the personnel responsible for data, the data types covered by the policy, and the retention schedule. Security professionals should work with data owners to develop the appropriate data retention policy for each type of data the organization owns. Examples of data types include, but are not limited to, human resources data, accounts payable/receivable data, sales data, customer data, and email.

Security professionals should ensure that asset retention policies also are created and enforced. While asset retention policies are often governed by the data retention policies, organizations may find it necessary to replace physical assets while needing to retain the data stored on the asset. Security professionals should ensure that the data residing on an asset that will be retired is fully documented and properly retained as detailed by the data retention policy. Doing so will usually require that the data is moved to another asset. For example, suppose an organization stores all the PII data it retains on a SQL server located on the organization's demilitarized zone (DMZ). If the organization decides to replace the SQL server with a new Windows Server computer, it will be necessary to back up the PII from the old server and restore it to the new server. In addition, the organization may want to retain the backup of the PII and store it in a safe or other secured location, in case the organization should ever need it. Then the organization must ensure that the PII cannot be retrieved from the hard drive on the old server. Doing so may require physical destruction of the hard drive.

To design asset and data retention policies, the organization should answer the following questions:

- What are the legal/regulatory requirements and business needs for the assets/data?
- What are the types of assets/data?
- What are the retention periods and destruction needs for the assets/data?

The personnel who are most familiar with each asset and data type should work with security professionals to determine the asset and data retention policies. For example, human resources personnel should help design the data retention policies for all human resources assets and data. While designing asset and data retention policies, an organization must consider the media and hardware that will be used to retain the data. Then, with this information in hand, the organization and/or business unit should draft and formally adopt the asset and data retention policies.

As part of asset retention, security professionals need to understand two terms: ***end of life (EOL)*** and ***end of support (EOS)***. These terms apply to any software or hardware asset. *EOL* is the date when a vendor stops offering a product for sale. However, the product is still supported (such as warranties, updates, and repairs) by the vendor, at least for a while. This support usually includes deploying security updates for the product. *EOS*, also referred to as ***end-of-service life (EOSL)***, is the date when all vendor support ends. Organizations sometimes retain legacy hardware to access older data, such as data on tape drives. Legacy applications can also be retained if the application provides a particular function and a replacement application has not been selected. If legacy hardware or applications need to be retained, security professionals should take measures to ensure that they are deployed in a manner that prevents remote access, including deploying them on an isolated network.

After the asset and data retention policies have been created, personnel must be trained to comply with these policies. Auditing and monitoring should be configured to ensure data retention policy compliance. Periodically, data owners and processors should review the data retention policies to determine whether any changes need to be made. All data retention policies, implementation plans, training, and auditing should be fully documented. In addition, IT support staff should work to ensure that the assets on which the data is stored are kept up to date with the latest security patches and updates.

Remember that it is not possible to find a one-size-fits-all solution for all organizations because of the different types of information, assets, or data. Only those most familiar with each asset or data type can determine the best retention policy for that asset or data. Although a security professional should be involved in the design of the retention policies, the security professional is there to ensure that security is always considered and that retention policies satisfy organizational needs. The security professional should act only in an advisory role and should provide expertise when needed.

Data Security Controls

Now it is time to discuss the data security controls that organizations must consider as part of a comprehensive security plan. Security professionals must understand the following as part of data security controls: data security, data states (data at rest, data in transit, and data in use), data access and sharing, data storage and archiving, baselines, scoping and tailoring, standards selection, and cryptography.

Data Security

Data security includes the procedures, processes, and systems that protect data from unauthorized access. Unauthorized access includes unauthorized digital and physical access. Data security also protects data against any threats that can affect data confidentiality, integrity, or availability.

To provide data security, an organization should implement security using a ***defense-in-depth*** strategy, as discussed in Chapter 1. If a single layer of access is not analyzed, then data is at risk. For example, you can implement ***authentication*** mechanisms to ensure that users must authenticate before digitally accessing the network. But if you do not have the appropriate physical security controls in place to prevent unauthorized access to your facility, an attacker can easily gain access to your network just by connecting an unauthorized device to the network.

Security professionals should make sure their organization implements measures and safeguards for any threats that have been identified. In addition, security professionals must remain vigilant and constantly be on the lookout for new threats.

Data States

Three basic data states must be considered as part of asset security. These three states are data at rest, data in transit, and data in use. Security professionals must ensure that controls are implemented to protect data in all three of these states.

Data at Rest

Data at rest is data that is being stored and not being actively used at a certain point in time. While data is at rest, security professionals must ensure that the confidentiality, integrity, and availability of the data are ensured. Confidentiality can be provided by implementing data encryption. Integrity can be provided by implementing the appropriate authentication mechanisms and ACLs so that only authenticated, authorized users can edit data. Availability can be provided by implementing a fault-tolerant storage solution, such as RAID.

Data in Transit

Data in transit is data that is being transmitted over a network or sent via a physical medium, like a DVD or flash drive. While data is being transmitted, security professionals must ensure that the confidentiality, integrity, and availability of the data are ensured. Confidentiality can be provided by implementing link encryption or end-to-end encryption. As with data at rest, authentication and ACLs can help with data integrity of data in transit. Availability can be provided by implementing server farms and dual backbones.

Data in Use

Data in use is data that is being accessed or manipulated in some way. Data manipulation includes editing the data and compiling the data into reports. The main issues with data in use are to ensure that only authorized individuals have access to or can read the data and that only authorized changes are allowed to the data. Confidentiality can be provided by using privacy or screen filters to prevent unauthorized individuals from reading data on a screen. It can also be provided by implementing a document shredding policy for all reports that contain PII, PHI, proprietary data, or other confidential information. Data integrity can be provided by implementing the appropriate controls on the data. Data locks can prevent data from being changed, and data rules can ensure that changes occur only within defined parameters. For certain data types, organizations may decide to implement two-person controls to ensure that data changes are entered and verified. Availability can be provided by using the same strategies as used for data at rest and data in transit. In addition, organizations may wish to implement locks and views to ensure that users needing access to data obtain the most up-to-date version of that data. Data in use is the most difficult data to protect.

Data Access and Sharing

Personnel must be able to access and share data in their day-to-day duties. This data usage starts when the data owner approves access for a user. The data custodian then gives the user the appropriate permissions for the data. But these two steps are an oversimplification of the process. Security professionals must ensure that the organization understands issues such as the following:

- Are the appropriate data policies in place to control the access and use of data?
- Do the data owners understand the access needs of the users?
- What are the different levels of access needed by the users?
- Which data formats do the users need?
- Are there subsets of data that should have only restricted access for users?
- Of the data being collected, is there clearly identified private versus public data?
- Is data being protected both when it is at rest and when it is in transit?
- Are there any legal or jurisdictional issues related to data storage location, data transmission, or data processing?

While the data owners and data custodians work together to answer many of these questions, security professionals should be involved in guiding them through this process. If a decision is made to withhold data, the decision must be made based on privacy, confidentiality, security, or legal/regulatory restrictions. The criteria by which these decisions are made must be recorded as part of an official organizational data policy.

Data Storage and Archiving

Data storage and archiving are related to how an organization stores data—both digital data and physical data in the form of hard copies. It is very easy for data to become outdated. Once data is outdated, it is no longer useful to the organization.

Although data storage used to be quite expensive, it has become cheaper in recent years. Security professionals should work with data owners and data custodians to help establish a data review policy to ensure that data is periodically reviewed to determine whether it is needed and useful for the organization. Data should be archived in accordance with data retention policies and schedules. Data that is no longer needed or useful for the organization should be properly destroyed. The exception is data that has been archived and must be kept for a certain duration based on a set retention policy period, especially data that may be on legal hold.

NOTE Data retention is a set of rules within an organization that dictates types of unaltered data that must be kept and for how long. Archiving is the process of securely storing unaltered data for later potential retrieval. Data should be retained in accordance with a documented schedule, stored securely in accordance with its classification, and securely disposed of at the end of the retention period.

When considering data storage and archiving, security professionals need to ensure that the different aspects of storage are properly analyzed to ensure appropriate deployment. This includes analyzing server hardware and software, database maintenance, data backups, and network infrastructure. Each part of the digital trail that the data will travel must be understood so that the appropriate policies and procedures can be put into place to ensure asset privacy.

Data that is still needed and useful to the organization should remain in primary storage for easy access by users. Data marked for archiving must be moved to some sort of backup media or secondary storage. Organizations must determine the form of data archive storage that will best suit their needs. For some business units in the organization, it may be adequate to archive the data to magnetic tape or optical media, such as DVDs. With these forms of storage, restoring the data from the archive can be a laborious process. For business units that need an easier way to access the archived data, some sort of solid-state or hot-pluggable drive technology may be a better way to go.

No matter which media your organization chooses for archival purposes, security professionals must consider the costs of the mechanisms used and the security of the archive. Storing archived data that has been backed up to DVD in an unlocked file cabinet may be more convenient for a business unit, but it does not provide any protection of the data on the DVD. In this case, the security professional may need to work with the business unit to come up with a more secure storage mechanism for data archives. When data is managed centrally by the IT or data center staff, personnel usually better understand security issues related to data storage and may therefore not need as much guidance from security professionals.

Baselines

One practice that can make maintaining security simpler is to create and deploy standard images that have been secured with security baselines. A ***baseline*** is a set of configuration settings that provides a floor of minimum security in the image being deployed. Organizations should capture baselines for all devices, including network devices, computers, host computers, and virtual machines.

Baselines can be controlled through the use of Group Policy in Windows. These policy settings can be made in the image and applied to both users and computers. These settings are refreshed periodically through a connection to a domain controller and cannot be altered by the user. It is also quite common for the deployment image to include all of the most current operating system updates and patches.

When a network makes use of these types of technologies, the administrators have created a standard operating environment. The advantages of such an environment are more consistent behavior of the network and simpler support issues. System scans should be performed weekly to detect changes from the baseline.

Security professionals should help guide their organization through the process of establishing baselines. If an organization implements very strict baselines, it will provide a higher level of security that may actually be too restrictive. If an organization implements a very lax baseline, it will provide a lower level of security that will likely result in security breaches. Security professionals should understand the balance between protecting organizational assets and allowing users access, and they should work to ensure that both ends of this spectrum are understood.

Scoping and Tailoring

Scoping and tailoring are closely tied to the baselines. These processes allow an organization to narrow its focus to identify and address the appropriate risks.

Scoping instructs an organization on how to apply and implement security controls. Baseline security controls are the minimums that are acceptable to the organization. When security controls are selected based on scoping, documentation should be created that includes the security controls that were considered, whether the security controls were adopted, and how the considerations were made.

Tailoring allows an organization to more closely match security controls to the needs of the organization. When security controls are selected based on tailoring, documentation should be created that includes the security controls that were considered, whether the security controls were adopted, and how the considerations were made.

NIST SP 800-53, which is covered extensively in Chapter 1, provides some guidance on tailoring.

Standards Selection

Because organizations need guidance on protecting their assets, security professionals must be familiar with the ***standards*** that have been established. Many standards organizations have been formed, including NIST, the U.S. Department of Defense (DoD), and the ***International Organization for Standardization (ISO)***.

NOTE Standards are covered extensively in Chapter 1. To locate information on a particular NIST or ISO standard, refer to the index.

The U.S. DoD Instruction 8510.01 establishes a certification and accreditation process for DoD information systems.

The ISO organization works with the ***International Electrotechnical Commission (IEC)*** to establish many standards regarding information security. The ISO/IEC standards that security professionals need to understand are covered in Chapter 1.

Security professionals may also need to research other standards, including standards from the European Network and Information Security Agency (ENISA), European Union (EU), and U.S. National Security Agency (NSA). It is important that the organization researches the many standards available and apply the most beneficial guidelines based on the organization's needs.

Data Protection Methods

Data is protected in a variety of ways. Security professionals must understand the different data protection methods and know how to implement them. Data protection methods should include administrative (managerial), logical (technical), and physical controls. All types of controls are covered extensively in Chapter 1.

The most popular method of protecting data and ensuring data integrity is by using cryptography. However, security professionals should also understand Digital Rights Management (DRM), Data Loss Prevention (DLP), and ***Cloud Access Security Broker (CASB)***.

Cryptography

Cryptography, also referred to as encryption, can provide different protection based on which level of communication is being used. The two types of encryption communication levels are link encryption and end-to-end encryption.

NOTE Cryptography is discussed in greater detail in Chapter 3, "Security Architecture and Engineering."

Link Encryption

Link encryption encrypts all the data that is transmitted over a link. In this type of communication, the only portion of the packet that is not encrypted is the data-link control information, which is needed to ensure that devices transmit the data properly. All the information is encrypted, with each router or other device decrypting its header information so that routing can occur and then re-encrypting before sending the information to the next device.

If the sending party needs to ensure that data security and privacy are maintained over a public communication link, then link encryption should be used. This is often the method used to protect email communication or when banks or other institutions that have confidential data must send that data over the Internet.

Link encryption protects against packet sniffers and other forms of eavesdropping and occurs at the data link and physical layers of the OSI model. Advantages of link encryption include: All the data is encrypted, and no user interaction is needed for it to be used. Disadvantages of link encryption include: Each device that the data must be transmitted through must receive the key, key changes must be transmitted to each device on the route, and packets are decrypted at each device.

End-to-End Encryption

End-to-end encryption encrypts less of the packet information than link encryption. In end-to-end encryption, packet routing information and packet headers and addresses are not encrypted. As a result, potential hackers can obtain more information if a packet is acquired through packet sniffing or eavesdropping.

End-to-end encryption has several advantages. A user usually initiates end-to-end encryption, which allows the user to select exactly what gets encrypted and how. It affects the performance of each device along the route less than link encryption because every device does not have to perform encryption/decryption to determine how to route the packet.

Digital Rights Management (DRM)

Digital rights management (DRM) is a mechanism that provides copyright protection for copyrighted works. Using DRM, an organization or individual controls the use, modification, and distribution of copyrighted material.

When DRM is deployed, a DRM license is issued to grant access to the copyrighted material. The license defines the user's terms and usually includes a decryption key for the copyrighted material. DRM has an always-on requirement, also referred to as persistent online authentication, that requires an Internet connection to access the copyrighted material. This authentication mechanism will periodically check the connection to the authentication server and will block the use of the copyrighted material if the connection fails. DRM also provides an audit trail that tracks copyrighted material usage and detects concurrent usages of copyrighted material.

Finally, automatic expiration can be used so that copyrighted material can be shared as a subscription that blocks access after a certain date.

Pirating is any method of duplicating and distributing copyrighted works and is used for written material, videos, games, software, and more. DRM can be used to prevent the copying, printing, and forwarding of protected works.

Digital watermarking can be used to detect, but not prevent, copying of protected material. In addition, vendors sometimes insert metadata in the file that helps to identify the original purchaser of the protected content.

Each feature in DRM has advantages and disadvantages. Security professionals should work with management to perform a full risk analysis prior to deploying a DRM solution and include only those features that are needed.

Data Loss Prevention (DLP)

Data loss prevention (DLP) software scans communication to determine whether protected or confidential data is being exfiltrated. If the data being sent violates the DLP allowed rules, then the communication is blocked. The DLP system will look for data patterns or keywords based on the rules that a security administrator configures.

Two types of DLP systems are used: network-based and endpoint-based DLP. Network-based systems exist on a network edge and scan all data leaving the organization's network. An endpoint-based system exists on an endpoint device, such as a file server, and can be configured to scan all data stored on the endpoint or leaving the endpoint in any manner, including printing and copying to a USB flash drive. Administrators can configure alerts so that any violation results in immediate notification of appropriate personnel.

DLP systems can examine zipped files but cannot decrypt or examine encrypted data. They can, however, scan an internal or cloud network and perform data discovery, which scans all data and reports the location of the data back to administrators. This report can then be used to configure the appropriate DLP rules to protect any newly discovered data. Data discovery scans should be performed on a regular basis.

Cloud Access Security Broker (CASB)

A *cloud access security broker (CASB)* is an application that monitors activity between users and cloud-based resources to apply the organization's security policies, including policies that control authentication, authorize access, encrypt stored data, log all access, and alert appropriate personnel on suspicious activity. It can also provide authentication controls, authorization controls, activity alerts, and DLP services.

Exam Preparation Tasks

As mentioned in the section "About the *CISSP Cert Guide*, Fifth Edition" in the Introduction, you have a couple of choices for exam preparation: the exercises here, Chapter 9, "Final Preparation," and the exam simulation questions in the Pearson Test Prep practice test software.

Review All Key Topics

Review the most important topics in this chapter, noted with the Key Topic icon in the outer margin of the page. Table 2-1 lists a reference of these key topics and the page numbers on which each is found.

Key Topic

Table 2-1 Key Topics for Chapter 2

Key Topic Element	Description	Page Number
List	NIST SP 800-122 recommendations to effectively protect PII	177
List	Private sector classifications	181
List	Military and government classifications	182
Figure 2-1	Asset Life Cycle	185
List	Information life cycle	187

Define Key Terms

Define the following key terms from this chapter and check your answers in the glossary:

access control list (ACL); aggregation; atomicity; authentication; availability; base relation; baseline; candidate key; cardinality; certification; column or attribute; Cloud Access Security Broker (CASB); confidentiality; consistency; contamination; criticality; cryptography; data criticality; data custodian; data loss prevention (DLP); data mining; data owner; data processors; data purging; data quality; data sensitivity; data structure; data warehouse; data warehousing; database locks; database views; defense in depth; degree; Digital Rights Management (DRM); domain; durability; EPHI; end of life (EOL); end of support (EOS); end-of-service life (EOSL); foreign key; guideline; hierarchical database; inference; intangible assets; integrity; International Electrotechnical Commission (IEC); International Organization for Standardization (ISO); isolation; Java Database Connectivity (JDBC); liability; network-attached storage (NAS); Object Linking and Embedding Database (OLE DB); object-oriented programming (OOP); object-oriented database (OODB); Open Database Connectivity (ODBC); personally identifiable information (PII); policy; polyinstantiation; protected health information (PHI); record; referential integrity; relation; relational database; remanence; row; schema; standard; system owner; tangible assets; view

Answer Review Questions

1. What is the highest classification level for data in the U.S. military?
   a. Confidential
   b. Top Secret
   c. Private
   d. Sensitive
2. Who is responsible for deciding which users have access to data?
   a. Business owner
   b. System owner
   c. Data owner
   d. Data custodian
3. Which term is used for the fitness of data for use?
   a. Data sensitivity
   b. Data criticality
   c. Data quality
   d. Data classification
4. What is the highest level of data classification for private sector systems?
   a. Public
   b. Sensitive
   c. Private
   d. Confidential
5. What is the first phase of the information life cycle?
   a. Maintain
   b. Use

c. Distribute
d. Create/receive

6. Which organizational role owns a system and must work with other users to ensure that data is secure?
    a. Business owner
    b. Data custodian
    c. Data owner
    d. System owner

7. What is the last phase of the information life cycle?
    a. Distribute
    b. Maintain
    c. Dispose/store
    d. Use

Answers and Explanations

1. **b.** Military and governmental entities classify data using five main classification levels, listed from highest sensitivity level to lowest:
    1. Top Secret
    2. Secret
    3. Confidential
    4. Sensitive but unclassified
    5. Unclassified
2. **c.** The data owner is responsible for deciding which users have access to data.
3. **c.** Data quality is the fitness of data for use.
4. **d.** Private sector systems usually use the following classifications, from highest to lowest:
    1. Confidential
    2. Private
    3. Sensitive
    4. Public

5. **d.** The phases of the information life cycle are as follows:
    1. Create/receive
    2. Distribute
    3. Use
    4. Maintain
    5. Dispose/store
6. **d.** The system owner owns a system and must work with other users to ensure that data is secure.
7. **c.** The phases of the information life cycle are as follows:
    1. Create/receive
    2. Distribute
    3. Use
    4. Maintain
    5. Dispose/store

This chapter covers the following topics:

- **Information Systems Life Cycle:** Phases discussed include stakeholders' needs and requirements; requirements analysis; architectural design; development /implementation; integration; verification and validation; transition/ deployment; operations and maintenance/sustainment, and retirement/ disposal.
- **Engineering Processes Using Secure Design Principles:** Concepts discussed include the ISO/IEC 15288:2015 and NIST SP 800-160 systems engineering standards, objects and subjects, closed versus open systems, threat modeling, least privilege, defense in depth, secure defaults, fail securely, separation of duties (SoD), keep it simple and small, Zero Trust, Privacy by design, Trust but verify, shared responsibility, and secure access service edge (SASE).
- **Security Model Concepts:** Concepts discussed include confidentiality, integrity, and availability; security modes; security model types; security models; system architecture steps; ISO/IEC 42010:2011; computing platforms; security services; and system components.
- **System Security Evaluation Models:** Concepts discussed include TCSEC, ITSEC, Common Criteria, security implementation standards, and controls and countermeasures.
- **Certification and Accreditation:** Concepts discussed include certification, accreditation, and the phases of accreditation.
- **Control Selection Based on Systems Security Requirements:** Concepts discussed include selecting controls for systems based on security requirements.
- **Security Capabilities of Information Systems:** Concepts discussed include memory protection, virtualization, Trusted Platform Module, interfaces, fault tolerance, policy mechanisms, and encryption/decryption.
- **Security Architecture Maintenance:** Concepts discussed include maintaining security architecture.

- **Vulnerabilities of Security Architectures, Designs, and Solution Elements:** Concepts discussed include client-based systems, server-based systems, database systems, cryptographic systems, operational technology/industrial control systems, cloud-based systems, large-scale parallel data systems, distributed systems, Internet of Things, microservices, containerization, serverless, high-performance computing (HPC) systems, edge computing systems, and virtualized systems.
- **Vulnerabilities in Web-Based Systems:** Concepts discussed include maintenance hooks, time-of-check/time-of-use attacks, web-based attacks, XML, SAML, and OWASP.
- **Vulnerabilities in Mobile Systems:** Concepts discussed include the vulnerabilities encountered when using mobile systems, such as device security, application security, and mobile device concerns.
- **Vulnerabilities in Embedded Systems:** Concepts discussed include the issues that are currently being seen with the advent of machine-to-machine communication and the Internet of Things.
- **Cryptographic Solutions:** Topics discussed include cryptographic concepts, cryptography history, cryptosystem features, cryptographic mathematics, and cryptographic life cycle.
- **Cryptographic Types:** Concepts discussed include running key and concealment ciphers, substitution ciphers, transposition ciphers, symmetric algorithms, asymmetric algorithms, hybrid ciphers, elliptic curves, and quantum cryptography.
- **Symmetric Algorithms:** Algorithms discussed include Digital Encryption Standard and Triple Data Encryption Standard, Advanced Encryption Standard, IDEA, Skipjack, Blowfish, Twofish, RC4/RC5/RC6/RC7, and CAST.
- **Asymmetric Algorithms:** Algorithms discussed include Diffie-Hellman, RSA, El Gamal, ECC, Knapsack, and zero-knowledge proof.
- **Public Key Infrastructure and Digital Certificates:** Concepts discussed include CAs and RAs, certificates, certificate life cycle, CRLs, OCSP, PKI steps, and cross-certification.
- **Key Management Practices:** Concepts discussed include the key management practices that organizations should understand, including symmetric key management and asymmetric key management.
- **Message Integrity:** Concepts discussed include hashing, one-way hash, message authentication code, and salting.

- **Digital Signatures and Non-repudiation:** This section covers the use of digital signatures, including DSS and non-repudiation.
- **Applied Cryptography:** This section covers link encryption, end-to-end encryption, email security, and Internet security.
- **Cryptanalytic Attacks:** Attacks discussed include ciphertext-only attack, known plaintext attack, chosen plaintext attack, chosen ciphertext attack, social engineering, brute force, differential cryptanalysis, linear cryptanalysis, algebraic attack, frequency analysis, birthday attack, dictionary attack, replay attack, analytic attack, statistical attack, factoring attack, reverse engineering, meet-in-the-middle attack, ransomware attack, side-channel attack, implementation attacks, fault injection, timing attack, pass-the-hash attack, and Kerberos exploitation.
- **Digital Rights Management:** This section explains digital rights management, including document, music, movie, video game, and e-book DRM.
- **Site and Facility Design:** Concepts discussed include a layered defense model, CPTED, physical security plan, and facility selection issues.
- **Site and Facility Security Controls:** Controls discussed include doors, locks, biometrics, glass entries, visitor control, wiring closets/intermediate distribution facilities, restricted and work areas (secure data center, restricted work area, server room, media storage facilities, and evidence storage), environmental security and issues, and equipment security.

CHAPTER 3

Security Architecture and Engineering

The Security Architecture and Engineering domain addresses a broad array of topics including security engineering processes, security models, security controls, assessing and mitigating vulnerabilities, cryptography, and site and facility security controls. Out of 100 percent of the exam, this domain carries an average weight of 13 percent, which ties with two other domains for the third highest weight.

Security architecture and engineering are mainly concerned with the design, implementation, monitoring, and securing of information security assets. These assets include computers, equipment, networks, and applications. Within this area, a security professional must understand security models, system vulnerabilities, cryptography, and physical security. But simply understanding security architecture and engineering is not enough. A security professional must also know how to implement security architecture engineering to ensure that assets are protected. Organizations must understand what assets they need to secure, why they need to secure the assets, and how the assets will be secured.

Foundation Topics

Information Systems Life Cycle

Managing the information systems life cycle is a comprehensive process that encompasses the entire period from the initial conception of a system to its retirement and disposal. This life cycle management ensures that the system meets the stakeholders' needs and requirements effectively throughout its operational life.

The phases of the information systems life cycle are:

1. Stakeholders' Needs and Requirements
2. Requirements Analysis
3. Architectural Design
4. Development/Implementation
5. Integration
6. Verification and Validation
7. Transition/Deployment
8. Operations and Maintenance/Sustainment
9. Retirement/Disposal

The information systems life cycle is shown in Figure 3-1.

For security professionals, managing the information systems life cycle involves a strategic approach to integrating security throughout all phases. This ensures that the system not only meets the initial requirements but also remains secure, reliable, and compliant throughout its operational life, until its eventual decommissioning. The information life cycle will involve non-security professionals as well so it is important that security professionals are involved to ensure that security is always part of the process.

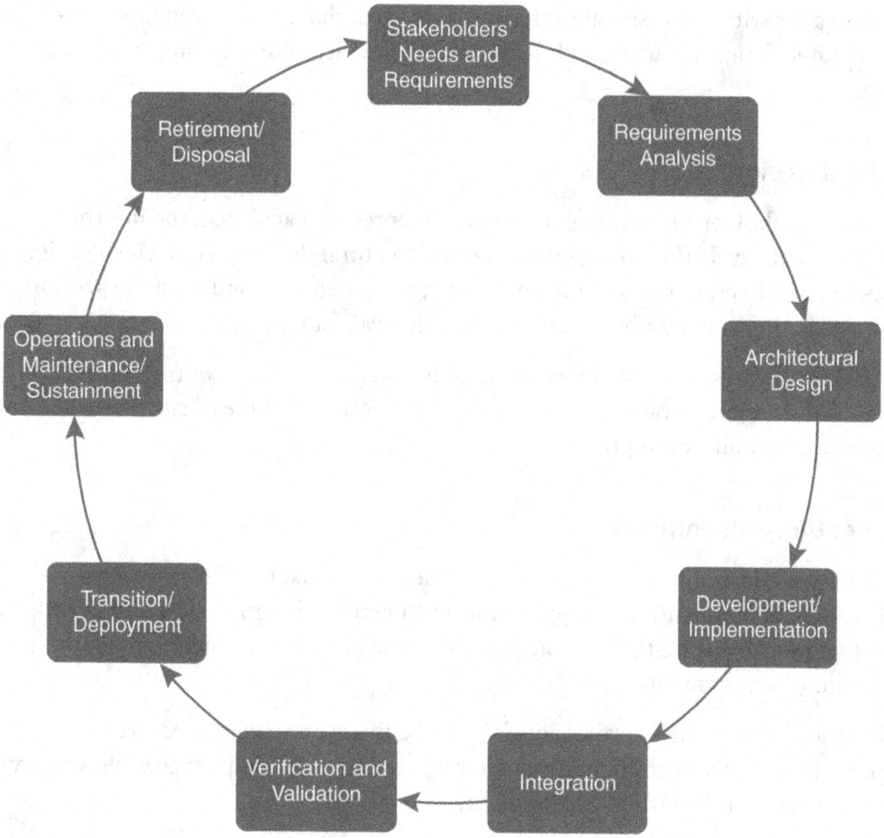

Figure 3-1 Information Systems Life Cycle

Stakeholders' Needs and Requirements

The first phase of the information systems life cycle includes identifying and documenting what stakeholders expect from the system in terms of functionality, security, performance, and compliance. It is important that a representatives of all stakeholder types are included as part of this phase in the life cycle. Leaving out an important stakeholder group can result in missing or inaccurate requirements documentation.

A security professional should help in this phase to fully understand the security expectations and regulatory requirements that the system must meet.

Requirements Analysis

The second phase of the information systems life cycle analyzes stakeholders' needs to create a detailed set of requirements, including security, functional, and non-functional requirements.

Involving a security professional in this phase ensures that security requirements are integrated from the outset, addressing confidentiality, integrity, and availability aspects.

Architectural Design

Once the stakeholders' requirements are documented and analyzed, the information systems life cycle then proceeds to the architectural design phase, which designs the system architecture to meet the analyzed requirements by outlining the system's components, their interactions, and the technological framework.

The security professional should work on incorporating security controls and measures into the architectural design, including segregation of duties, least privilege, and secure communication protocols.

Development/Implementation

The development/implementation phase is when the actual building or configuring of the system components according to the architectural design occurs. The team works together to ensure that all components are deployed as needed to meet the stakeholders' requirements.

During this phase, security professionals must be involved to ensure secure coding practices, secure system configuration, security testing, and compliance with security policies and standards during development.

Integration

The integration phase combines and configures system components to work together as a whole, ensuring compatibility and interoperability. The team works to ensure that all components perform the tasks for which they are responsible. In addition, each component should be tested to ensure that it does not negatively impact other components.

Security professionals should verify the security posture and data flows between integrated components, ensuring no new vulnerabilities are introduced.

Verification and Validation

This phase of the information systems life cycle tests the complete system to ensure it meets all requirements and specifications, including performance, reliability, and security testing.

A security professional should be engaged in conducting thorough security testing and audits to validate the effectiveness of security controls and to verify that the system meets security requirements.

Transition/Deployment

Now that the information system is verified and validated, the system should be transitioned and deployed so that the system is moved from development to production. This includes ensuring it is deployed securely and efficiently into the operational environment.

A security professional should ensure that secure deployment strategies, including secure data migration and access controls, are implemented. In addition, the security professional should ensure that there is minimal operational disruption.

Operations and Maintenance/Sustainment

Now that the information system is deployed, focus moves to the ongoing management of the system to ensure it continues to meet user needs and operates effectively. During this phase, updates, patches, and security monitoring must be regularly performed.

Security professionals should be involved to continuously assess and improve the system's security posture, respond to new threats and vulnerabilities, and ensure compliance with security policies.

Retirement/Disposal

The final phase of the information systems life cycle includes phasing out the system when it is no longer needed or can no longer be supported, ensuring that data is securely archived or destroyed and that system components are disposed of properly.

During this phase, ensuring secure data deletion or migration is the responsibility of security professionals. This includes ensuring that any sensitive information is properly handled to prevent data leaks or breaches.

Engineering Processes Using Secure Design Principles

Systems engineering is an approach for the design, realization, technical management, operations, and retirement of a system. In general, a *system* is a collection of elements that together produce results not obtainable by the individual elements alone. In IT specifically, a system may involve single or multiple computers or devices working together to achieve a particular result. For example, an online ordering system may involve a web server, an e-commerce server, and a database server. However, these systems alone cannot provide adequate security to online transactions. An organization may need to include security mechanisms to ensure that security is integrated into the total design solutions.

Organizations must implement and manage systems engineering processes using secure design principles. Systems engineering is usually modeled based on a life cycle. Chapter 1, "Security and Risk Management," discusses groups that establish standards, including the International Organization for Standardization (ISO)/International Electrotechnical Commission (IEC) and the National Institute of Standards and Technology (NIST). These groups both have established standards for systems engineering: ISO/IEC 15288:2015 and NIST Special Publication (SP) 800-160, which supersedes NIST SP 800-27.

ISO/IEC 15288:2015 establishes four categories of processes:

Key Topic

- **Agreement processes:** This category includes acquisition and supply.
- **Organizational project-enabling processes:** This category includes life cycle model management, infrastructure management, portfolio management, human resource management, quality management, and knowledge management.
- **Technical management processes:** This category includes project planning, project assessment and control, decision management, risk management, configuration management, information management, measurement, and quality assurance.
- **Technical processes:** This category includes business or mission analysis, stakeholder needs and requirements definition, system requirements definition, architecture definition, design definition, system analysis, implementation, integration, verification, transition, validation, operation, maintenance, and disposal.

The systems life cycle stages of this standard include concept, development, production, utilization, support, and retirement. While this standard defines systems life cycle processes, it does not by itself address security during systems engineering.

NIST SP 800-160 is based on ISO/IEC 15288:2015 and discussed in Chapter 1.

To understand engineering using secure design principles, organizations must understand the difference between objects and subjects and closed versus open systems.

Objects and Subjects

Objects are resources that a user or process wants to access, and ***subjects*** are the users or processes requesting access. If the resource is requesting access, it is a subject. If a resource is being accessed, it is an object. Many resources can be both objects and subjects.

Let's look at an example. Suppose Jim, a user, wants to access an application. In this case, Jim is a subject, and the application is an object. If the application Jim uses needs to access a database, then the application is the subject, and the database is the object.

Closed Versus Open Systems

A ***closed system*** is a proprietary system that is designed to work with a limited range of other systems. ***Open systems*** conform to industry standards and can work with systems that support the same standard. When an organization is integrating these systems, closed systems are harder to integrate, whereas open systems are much easier to integrate.

NOTE Do not confuse *closed versus open system* with *closed versus open source*. An open-source solution uses source code or a design model that is known to the public. A closed-source solution is known only to the manufacturer. Both open-source and closed-source solutions can be open or closed systems.

Threat Modeling

Threat modeling is the process of identifying potential threats and determining possible mitigations and countermeasures, if any, for the threats. The process can provide an organization with an attacker's profile, likely attack vectors, targeted asset, and an analysis of the controls or defenses that should be implemented for the identified threats.

NOTE Threat modeling is covered in more detail in Chapter 1.

Least Privilege

The principle of least privilege is important in the design of systems. *Least privilege* means that users are granted access only to the information and resources that are minimally necessary for them to do their jobs. If the principle of least privilege is strictly enforced across an organization and the appropriate procedures are in place, privilege creep, wherein user privileges accumulate over time, will be prevented so that systems are as secure as possible.

When designing operating system processes, security professionals should ensure that system processes run in user mode when possible. When a process executes in privileged mode, the potential for vulnerabilities greatly increases. If a process needs access to privileged services, it is best to use an application programming interface (API) to ask for supervisory-mode services.

Related to the principle of least privilege, the principle of least functionality is that systems and devices should be configured to provide only essential or minimally required capabilities and specifically prohibit or restrict the use of functions, ports, protocols, and services.

NOTE The principle of least privilege is also discussed in Chapter 5, "Identity and Access Management (IAM)," and Chapter 7, "Security Operations."

Defense in Depth

Communications security management and techniques are designed to prevent, detect, and correct errors so that the CIA of transactions over networks might be maintained. Most computer attacks result in a violation of one of the security properties: confidentiality, integrity, or availability. A defense-in-depth approach refers to deploying layers of protection. For example, even when you are deploying firewalls, access control lists (ACLs) should still be applied to resources to help prevent access to sensitive data in case the firewall is breached.

NOTE *Defense in depth* is covered in more detail in Chapter 1.

Secure Defaults

Secure defaults, also referred to as *secure by default*, is a term used to describe a condition wherein an application's or device's default settings are set to the most secure settings possible. If the application or device is reset, these secure defaults should be maintained. Security professionals should keep in mind that the most secure settings are not often the most user-friendly settings.

If a technology follows secure defaults principles, the technology will have embedded, built-in cybersecurity principles. Depending on the technology, device, or application, best practices in secure defaults should include password prompts, history, length and strength, the closing of unused ports or services, encryption, and remote access disablement.

Fail Securely

To understand the concept of fail securely, security professionals must understand two related terms: *fail safe* and *fail secure*. Most often these terms are used in conjunction with physical controls, particularly door locks.

A product that is fail safe is unlocked when power is removed. Personnel therefore can enter or leave the area. A product that is fail secure is locked when power is removed. In this case, personnel can leave the area, but they must use a key to enter the area. These terms refer to the status of the secure side of the door. Most products provide free egress or exit whether they are fail safe or fail secure.

NOTE Fail safe can also apply to database applications. A database that is fail safe will complete all transactions or safely roll back to the previous state.

Fail-safe products should never be used for areas of high security. Simply cutting the power would give a threat actor access to the security area. Security professionals should ensure that public or general areas use fail-safe products, whereas secure areas, such as data centers, use fail-secure products.

Separation of Duties (SoD)

Separation of duties (SoD) is an internal personnel control that distributes the tasks and associated privileges for a security process among multiple personnel. It is most often associated with an organization's financial accounting policies whereby controls are put into place for issuing checks. The person inputting the payment information is usually a separate person than the one who signs or otherwise authorizes the checks after printing. In addition, organizations often implement policies whereby checks above a certain amount require two signatures.

SoD, as it relates to security, has two primary objectives: (1) to prevent conflict of interest, fraud, abuse, or errors and (2) to detect control failures, including breaches, data theft, and circumvention of security controls.

SoD restricts the power or influence held by any one person. It also ensures that personnel do not have conflicting responsibilities and are not responsible for reporting on themselves or their superiors. For example, in an IT department, the person who creates the user accounts can only do so with the proper request made by a department head or asset owner, and the person who assigns the appropriate permissions can only do so with the proper request made by the data or asset owner.

Keep It Simple and Small

Keep it simple and small is a design principle that states a design and/or system should be as simple and small as possible and avoid unneeded complexity. Simplicity guarantees the greatest levels of user acceptance and interaction. Small guarantees that the design components require fewer resources to deploy.

Security professionals should ensure that organizations focus on implementing simple and small controls to provide security for confidentiality, integrity, and availability. To offset the need for controls to be simple and small, organizations should deploy a layered security model.

Zero Trust

Zero trust is a security model based on the principle of maintaining strict access controls and not trusting anyone or anything by default. Zero trust requires strict identity verification for every person and device trying to access resources on a private network, regardless of whether they are sitting within or outside of the network perimeter.

In a zero trust environment, each access request is fully identified, authenticated, authorized, and encrypted before granting access. A zero trust environment is built upon five fundamental elements:

- The person or device is assumed to be disgruntled or hostile.
- External and internal threats exist at all times.
- Location is not sufficient for deciding trust in a person or device.
- Every device, user, and communication is identified, authenticated, and authorized.
- Policies must be dynamic and calculated from as many sources of data as possible.

To fully implement zero trust, organizations must deploy multifactor authentication (MFA), the principle of least privilege, and endpoint validation.

Privacy by Design

Privacy by design is a term that implies data protection through technology design. Behind this is the thought that data protection in data processing procedures is best adhered to when it is already integrated in the technology at creation. It is a concept in the General Data Protection Regulation (GDPR).

In new systems, security professionals should implement privacy by design by emphasizing privacy and security throughout the design process. Privacy should be integrated into a system from day one. Security professionals should implement privacy by design in an existing system by deconstructing and analyzing the system. This is more difficult and time-consuming. A privacy audit should be performed on the existing system to examine how privacy has been embedded into the system, identify weak points and create new user-friendly solutions.

Trust but Verify

Trust but verify is a principle that is used when communicating entities trust each other but verify that such trust should be provided through the verification of an established relationship. When implementing trust but verify, security professionals should ensure their organizations

- Use multiple asset inventory tools for verification and validation.
- Use vulnerability management scanning tools to verify patching and hardening settings.
- Use account reviews to verify that the principle of least privilege is enforced.
- Use penetration tests and security posture testing in production environments.
- Document supporting artifacts and evidence for audits and reviews.

Using a trust but verify approach ensures that checks and balances are implemented and that the appropriate controls are deployed to meet the expectations of the organization.

Shared Responsibility

Shared responsibility is a principle that requires that each user is accountable for different aspects of security and all must work together to ensure full coverage. All personnel within an organization must be aware of their responsibilities regarding security. During annual security and awareness training, personnel should be given scenarios wherein they see when and how to report security issues they may encounter.

All organizations should implement a security issues reporting portal or process so that it becomes part of organizational culture. This portal should include a feature that allows personnel to anonymously report security issues or violations that they observe to the appropriate management. Personnel can choose to remain anonymous or to disclose their identity.

Secure Access Service Edge (SASE)

Secure Access Service Edge (SASE), often pronounced "sassy," is a network architecture that combines cloud-native security functions with wide-area network (WAN) capabilities to support the dynamic, secure access needs of organizations' mobile workforces and cloud applications. It represents a shift in enterprise networking and security from traditional data center-centric models to a model that is distributed, cloud-centric, and flexible.

SASE embodies the application of secure design principles to network architecture and access management in several key ways:

- Integration of security and networking: SASE converges networking and security services, such as software-defined WAN (SD-WAN), secure web gateway (SWG), Cloud Access Security Broker (CASB), Firewall as a Service (FWaaS), and Zero Trust Network Access (ZTNA), into a single, cloud-delivered service model. This integration facilitates a unified approach to secure and efficient data access and protection.
- Zero trust principles: SASE architectures are inherently aligned with zero trust security principles, which dictate that trust is never assumed and verification is required from everyone trying to access resources in the network, regardless of their location. Implementing SASE helps organizations apply zero trust principles by dynamically creating secure access based on the user's identity, context, and organizational policies, thereby enhancing security.
- Scalability and flexibility: SASE supports the dynamic nature of modern businesses, including remote work, mobile access, and cloud-based resources. It allows security policies to be applied consistently across all users and locations, which is crucial for managing access in distributed environments. This scalability and flexibility are core to secure design principles, emphasizing adaptability to changing threats and business needs.
- Simplification of security infrastructure: By consolidating multiple security functions into a single, cloud-delivered platform, SASE reduces the complexity of the security infrastructure. This simplification helps in managing and maintaining security controls, making it easier to apply comprehensive security measures consistently, which is a practice advocated by secure design principles.
- Privacy and compliance: SASE facilitates compliance with various regulatory requirements by providing centralized control over data and access policies. The ability to enforce data protection and privacy measures across all traffic, users, and applications supports security professionals in ensuring that engineering processes comply with legal and regulatory standards.

- Enhanced performance and user experience: SASE's cloud-native design optimizes access and security processes to improve the overall user experience and performance. By applying secure design principles that do not compromise performance for security, SASE ensures that security measures are user-friendly and efficient.

Security Model Concepts

Security measures must have a defined goal to ensure that the measure is successful. All measures are designed to provide one of a core set of protections. In the following sections, the three fundamental principles of security are discussed. Also, an approach to delivering these goals is covered. In addition, these sections cover the security modes, security model types, security models, and system architecture. Finally, it covers ISO/IEC 42010:2011, computing platforms, security services, and system components.

Confidentiality, Integrity, and Availability

The essential security principles of ***confidentiality***, ***integrity***, and ***availability*** are referred to as the CIA triad. Confidentiality is provided if the data cannot be read either through access controls and encryption for data as it exists on a hard drive or through encryption as the data is in transit. With respect to information security, confidentiality is the opposite of disclosure.

Integrity is provided if you can be assured that the data has not changed in any way. This is typically provided with a hashing algorithm or a checksum of some kind. Both methods create a number that is sent along with the data. When the data gets to the destination, this number can be used to determine whether even a single bit has changed in the data by calculating the hash value from the data that was received. This approach helps to protect data against undetected corruption.

Some additional integrity goals are to

- Prevent unauthorized users from making modifications.
- Maintain internal and external consistency.
- Prevent authorized users from making improper modifications.

Availability describes what percentage of the time the resource or the data is available. This is usually measured as a percentage of "up" time, with 99.9 percent up time representing more availability than 99 percent up time. Making sure that the data is accessible when and where it is needed is a prime goal of security.

NOTE CIA is discussed in more detail in Chapter 1, "Security and Risk Management."

Confinement

Confinement is a term used to describe isolating processes or machines/subsystems in a larger system. When a process is confined, the process is only allowed to read from and write to certain memory locations and resources. Confinement is usually carried out using the operating system, through a confinement service, or using a hypervisor.

Bounds

On a system, processes run at an assigned authority level, which defines what the process can do. Two common authority levels are user and kernel. The bounds of a process set limits on the memory addresses and resources the process can access. The bounds logically segment memory areas for each process to use. Highly secure systems will physically bound the processes, meaning that the processes run in memory areas that are physically separated from each other. Logically bounded memory is cheaper than but not as secure as physically bounded memory.

Isolation

A process runs in isolation when it is confined using bounds. Process isolation ensures that any actions taken by the process will only affect the memory and resources used by the isolated process. Isolation prevents other processes, applications, or resources from accessing the memory or resources of another.

Security Modes

A mandatory access control (MAC) system operates in different security modes at various times, based on variables such as sensitivity of data, the clearance level of the user, and the actions users are authorized to take. The following sections provide descriptions of these modes.

Dedicated Security Mode

A system is operating in dedicated security mode if it employs a single classification level. In this system, all users can access all data, but they must sign a nondisclosure agreement (NDA) and be formally approved for access on a need-to-know basis.

System High Security Mode

In a system operating in system high security mode, all users have the same security clearance (as in the dedicated security model), but they do not all possess a need- to-know clearance for all the information in the system. Consequently, although users might have clearance to access an object, they still might be restricted if they do not have need-to-know clearance pertaining to the object.

Compartmented Security Mode

In the compartmented security mode system, all users must possess the highest security clearance (as in both dedicated and system high security), but they must also have valid need-to-know clearance, a signed NDA, and formal approval for all information to which they have access. The objective is to ensure that the minimum number of people possible have access to information at each level or compartment.

Multilevel Security Mode

When a system allows two or more classification levels of information to be processed at the same time, it is said to be operating in multilevel security mode. Users must have a signed NDA for all the information in the system and will have access to subsets based on their clearance level, need-to-know, and formal access approval. These systems involve the highest risk because information is processed at more than one level of security, even when all system users do not have appropriate clearances or a need to know for all information processed by the system. This is also sometimes called controlled security mode. Table 3-1 compares the four security modes and their requirements.

Key Topic

Table 3-1 Security Modes Summary

	Signed NDA	Proper Clearance	Formal Approval	Valid Need to Know
Dedicated	All information	All information	All information	All information
System high	All information	All information	All information	Some information
Compartmented	All information	All information	Some information	Some information
Multilevel	All information	Some information	Some information	Some information

Assurance and Trust

Whereas a trust level describes the protections that can be expected from a system, assurance refers to the level of confidence that the protections will operate as planned. Typically, higher levels of assurance are achieved by dedicating more scrutiny to security in the design process. The section "System Security Evaluation Models," later in this chapter, discusses various methods of rating systems for trust levels and assurance.

Security Model Types

A security model describes the theory of security that is designed into a system from the outset. Formal models have been developed to approach the design of the security operations of a system. In the real world, the use of formal models is often skipped because it delays the design process somewhat (although the cost might be a lesser system). This section discusses some basic model types along with some formal models derived from the various approaches available.

A security model maps the desires of the security policy makers to the rules that a computer system must follow. Different model types exhibit various approaches to achieving this goal. The specific models that are contained in the section "Security Models" incorporate various combinations of these model types.

State Machine Models

The state of a system is its posture at any specific point in time. Activities that occur in the process of the system operating alter the state of the system. After the security professional examines every possible state the system could be in and ensures that the system maintains the proper security relationship between objects and subjects in each state, the system is said to be secure. The Bell-LaPadula model discussed in the later section "Security Models" is an example of a ***state machine model***.

Multilevel Lattice Models

The lattice-based access control model or ***multilevel lattice model*** was developed mainly to deal with confidentiality issues and focuses itself mainly on information flow. Each security subject is assigned a security label that defines the upper and lower bounds of the subject's access to the system. Controls are then applied to all objects by organizing them into levels or lattices. Objects are containers of information in some format. These pairs of elements (object and subject) are assigned a least upper bound of values and a greatest lower bound of values that define what can be done by that subject with that object.

A subject's label (remember a subject can be a person, but it can also be a process) defines what level someone can access and what actions can be performed at that level. With the lattice-based access control model, a security label is also called a security class. This model associates every resource and every user of a resource with one of an ordered set of classes. The lattice-based model aims at protecting against illegal information flow among the entities.

Matrix-Based Models

A ***matrix-based model*** organizes tables of subjects and objects indicating what actions individual subjects can take upon individual objects. This concept is found in other model types as well, such as the lattice model discussed in the previous section. Access control to objects is often implemented as a control matrix. It is a straightforward approach that defines access rights to subjects for objects. The two most common implementations of this concept are ACLs and capabilities. In its table structure, a row would indicate the access one subject has to an array of objects. Therefore, a row could be seen as a capability list for a specific subject. It consists of the following parts:

- A list of objects
- A list of subjects
- A function that returns an object's type
- The matrix itself, with the objects making the columns and the subjects making the rows

Noninterference Models

In multilevel security models, the concept of noninterference prescribes those actions that take place at a higher security level but do not affect or influence those that occur at a lower security level. Because this model is less concerned with the flow of information and more concerned with a subject's knowledge of the state of the system at a point in time, it concentrates on preventing the actions that take place at one level from altering the state presented.

Information Flow Models

Any of the models discussed in the next section that attempt to prevent the flow of information from one entity to another that violates or negates the security policy is called an ***information flow model***. In the information flow model, what relates two versions of the same object is called the flow. A flow is a type of dependency that relates two versions of the same object, and thus the transformation of one state of that object into another, at successive points in time. In a multilevel security (MLS) system, a one-way information flow device called a pump prevents the flow of information from a lower level of security classification or sensitivity to a higher level.

For example, the Bell-LaPadula model (discussed in the section "Security Models") concerns itself with the flow of information in the following three cases:

- When a subject alters an object
- When a subject accesses an object
- When a subject observes an object

The prevention of illegal information flow among the entities is the aim of an information flow model.

Take-Grant Model

A system in the Take-Grant model is represented as a directed graph, called a *protection graph*. The subjects and objects of the computer system are the vertices, and the access rights of subjects to objects are represented by arcs. Although the Take-Grant model uses standard access rights like read and write, the Take-Grant model includes two additional access rights:

- Take (t) is the right to take any access rights from the subject.
- Grant (g) is the right to assign its access rights to any subject.

Figure 3-2 shows a graph of the Take-Grant model's Take and Grant access rights.

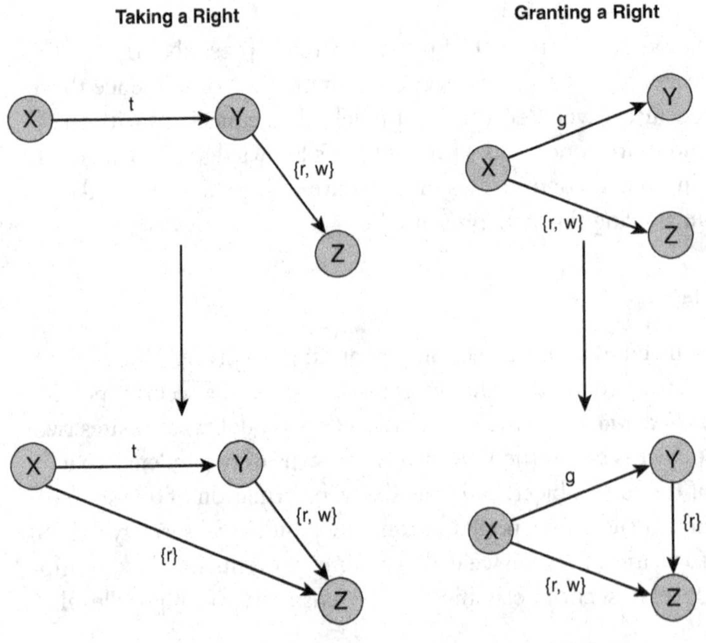

Figure 3-2 Take-Grant Model's Example of Take and Grant

Security Models

A number of formal models incorporating the concepts discussed in the previous section have been developed and used to guide the security design of systems. The following sections discuss some of the more widely used or important security models, including the following:

- Bell-LaPadula model
- Biba model
- Clark-Wilson integrity model
- Lipner model
- Brewer-Nash (Chinese Wall) model
- Graham-Denning model
- Harrison-Ruzzo-Ullman model
- Goguen-Meseguer model
- Sutherland model

Bell-LaPadula Model

The ***Bell-LaPadula model*** was the first mathematical model of a multilevel system that used both the concepts of a state machine and those of controlling information flow. It formalizes the U.S. DoD multilevel security policy. It is a state machine model capturing confidentiality aspects of access control. Any movement of information from a higher level to a lower level in the system must be performed by a trusted subject.

Bell-LaPadula, known as "no read up and no write down," incorporates three basic rules with respect to the flow of information in a system:

Key Topic

- **The simple security rule:** A subject cannot read data located at a higher security level than that possessed by the subject (also called no read up).
- **The star (*)-property rule:** A subject cannot write to a lower level than that possessed by the subject (also called no write down or the confinement rule).
- **The strong star property rule:** A subject can perform both read and write functions only at the same level granted to the subject.

The *-property rule is depicted in Figure 3-3.

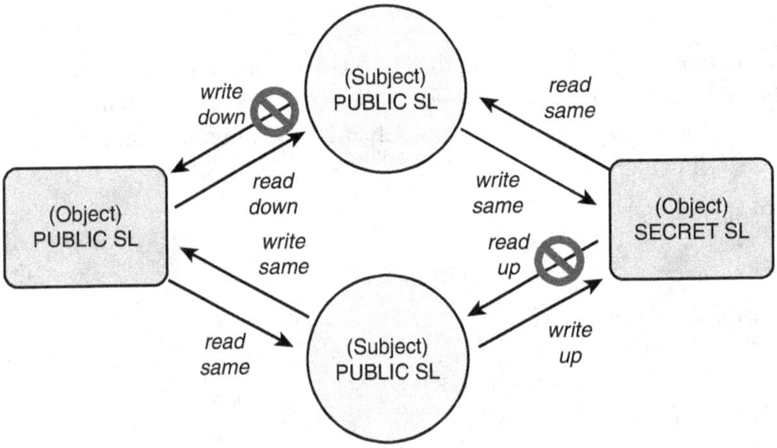

Figure 3-3 The *-Property Rule

The main concern of the Bell-LaPadula security model and its use of these rules is confidentiality. Although its basic model is a MAC system, another property rule called the discretionary security property (ds-property) makes a mixture of mandatory and discretionary controls possible. This property allows a subject to pass along permissions at its own discretion. In the discretionary portion of the model, access permissions are defined through an access control matrix using a process called ***authorization***, and security policies prevent information flowing downward from a high security level to a low security level.

The Bell-LaPadula security model does have limitations. Among those are

- It contains no provision or policy for changing data access control. Therefore, it works well only with access systems that are static in nature.
- It does not address what are called covert channels. A low-level subject can sometimes detect the existence of a high-level object when it is denied access. Sometimes it is not enough to hide the content of an object; also, their visibility might have to be hidden.
- Its main contribution at the expense of other concepts is confidentiality.

This security policy model was the basis for the Orange Book, discussed in the later section "TCSEC."

Biba Model

The ***Biba model*** came after the Bell-LaPadula model and shares many characteristics with that model. These two models are the most well known of the models discussed here. It is also a state machine model that uses a series of lattices or security levels, but the Biba model concerns itself more with the integrity of information rather than the confidentiality of that information. It does this by relying on a data classification system to prevent unauthorized modification of data. Subjects are assigned classes according to their trustworthiness; objects are assigned integrity labels according to the harm that would be done if the data were modified improperly.

Like the Bell-LaPadula model, the Biba model applies a series of properties or axioms to guide the protection of integrity. Its effect is that data must not flow from a receptacle of given integrity to a receptacle of higher integrity:

Key Topic

- **Integrity axiom:** Subjects cannot write to a higher integrity level than that to which they have access (no write up).
- **Simple integrity axiom:** Subjects cannot read to a lower integrity level than that to which they have access (no read down).
- **Invocation property:** Subjects cannot invoke (request service of) higher integrity.

Clark-Wilson Integrity Model

Developed after the Biba model, the ***Clark-Wilson integrity model*** also concerns itself with data integrity. The model describes a series of elements that are used to control the integrity of data as listed here:

Key Topic

- **User:** An active user's agent
- **Transformation procedure (TP):** An abstract operation, such as read, write, and modify, implemented through programming
- **Constrained data item (CDI):** An item that can be manipulated only through a TP
- **Unconstrained data item (UDI):** An item that can be manipulated by a user via read and write operations
- **Integrity verification procedure (IVP):** A check of the consistency of data with the real world

This model enforces these elements by allowing data to be altered only through programs and not directly by users. Rather than employing a lattice structure, it uses a three-part relationship of subject/program/object known as a triple. It also sets as its goal the concepts of separation of duties and well-formed transactions:

- **Separation of duties:** This concept ensures that certain operations require additional verification or that all personnel do their part.
- **Well-formed transaction:** This concept ensures that all values are checked before and after the transaction by carrying out particular operations to complete the change of data from one state to another.

To ensure that integrity is attained and preserved, the Clark-Wilson model asserts, integrity-monitoring and integrity-preserving rules are needed. Integrity-monitoring rules are called certification rules, and integrity-preserving rules are called enforcement rules.

Lipner Model

The ***Lipner model*** is an implementation that combines elements of the Bell-LaPadula model and the Biba model. The first way of implementing integrity with the Lipner model uses Bell-LaPadula and assigns subjects to one of two sensitivity levels—system manager and anyone else—and to one of four job categories. Objects are assigned specific levels and categories. Categories become the most significant integrity (such as access control) mechanism. The second implementation uses both Bell-LaPadula and Biba. This method prevents unauthorized users from modifying data and prevents authorized users from making improper data modifications. The implementations also share characteristics with the Clark-Wilson model in that it separates objects into data and programs.

Brewer-Nash (Chinese Wall) Model

The ***Brewer-Nash (Chinese Wall) model*** introduced the concept of allowing access controls to change dynamically based on a user's previous actions. One of its goals is to do this while protecting against conflicts of interest. This model is also based on an information flow model. Implementation involves grouping data sets into discrete classes, each class representing a different conflict of interest. Isolating data sets within a class provides the capability to keep one department's data separate from another in an integrated database.

> **NOTE** Similar to the UK brokerage system, the Chinese Wall model assumes impenetrable Chinese walls among company data sets, so that no conflict of interest occurs on the same side of the wall. According to the model, subjects are only granted access to data that is not in conflict with other data they possess.

Graham-Denning Model

The ***Graham-Denning model*** addresses an issue ignored by the Bell-LaPadula (with the exception of the ds-property) and Biba models. It deals with the delegate and transfer rights. It focuses on issues such as

- Securely creating and deleting objects and subjects
- Securely providing or transferring access rights

Harrison-Ruzzo-Ullman Model

The ***Harrison-Ruzzo-Ullman model*** also deals with access rights. It restricts the set of operations that can be performed on an object to a finite set to ensure integrity. It is used by software engineers to prevent unforeseen vulnerabilities from being introduced by overly complex operations.

Goguen-Meseguer Model

Although not as well known as Biba and other integrity models, the Goguen-Meseguer model is the foundation of the ***noninterference model***. With this model, the list of objects that a subject can access is predetermined. Subjects can then perform these predetermined actions only against the predetermined objects. Subjects are unable to interfere with each other's activities.

Sutherland Model

The Sutherland model focuses on preventing interference in support of integrity. Based on the state machine and information flow models, this model defines a set of system states, initial states, and state transitions. Using these predetermined secure states, the Sutherland model maintains integrity and prohibits interference.

System Architecture Steps

Various models and frameworks discussed in this chapter might differ in the exact steps toward developing a system ***architecture*** but do follow a basic pattern. The main steps include

1. **Design phase:** In this phase system requirements are gathered and the manner in which the requirements will be met is mapped out using modeling techniques that usually graphically depict the components that satisfy each requirement and the interrelationships of these components. At this phase many of the frameworks and security models discussed later in this chapter are used to help meet the architectural goals.

NOTE In some models, the requirements gathering occurs separately and prior to the design phase.

2. **Development phase:** In this phase hardware and software components are assigned to individual teams for development. At this phase the work done in the first phase can help to ensure these independent teams are working toward components that will fit together to satisfy requirements.

3. **Maintenance phase:** In this phase the system and security architecture are evaluated to ensure that the system operates properly and that security of the systems is maintained. The system and security should be periodically reviewed and tested.
4. **Retirement phase:** In this phase the system is retired from use in the live environment. Security professionals must ensure that the organization follows proper disposal procedures and ensure that data cannot be obtained from disposed assets.

ISO/IEC 42010:2011

ISO/IEC 42010:2011 uses specific terminology when discussing architectural frameworks. The following is a review of some of the most important terms:

- **Architecture:** The organization of the system, including its components and their interrelationships, along with the principles that guide its design and evolution
- **Architectural description (AD):** The set of documents that conveys the architecture in a formal manner
- **Stakeholders:** Individuals, teams, and departments, including groups outside the organization with interests or concerns to consider
- **View:** The representation of the system from the perspective of a stakeholder or a set of stakeholders
- **Viewpoint:** A template used to develop individual views that establish the audience, techniques, and assumptions made

Computing Platforms

A computing platform is composed of the hardware and software components that allow software to run. This typically includes the physical components, the operating systems, and the programming languages used. From a physical and logical perspective, a number of possible frameworks or platforms are in use. The following sections discuss some of the most common.

Mainframe/Thin Clients

When a mainframe/thin client platform is used, a client/server architecture exists. The server holds the application and performs all the processing. The client software runs on the user machines and simply sends requests for operations and displays the results. When a true thin client is used, very little exists on the user machine other than the software that connects to the server and renders the result.

Distributed Systems

The distributed platform also uses a client/server architecture, but the division of labor between the server portion and the client portion of the solution might not be quite as one-sided as you would find in a mainframe/thin client scenario. In many cases multiple locations or systems in the network might be part of the solution. Also, sensitive data may be more likely to be located on the user's machine, and therefore the users play a bigger role in protecting it with best practices.

Another characteristic of a distributed environment is multiple processing locations that can provide alternatives for computing in the event a site becomes unavailable.

Data is stored at multiple, geographically separate locations. Users can access the data stored at any location with the users' distance from those resources transparent to the users.

Distributed systems can introduce security weaknesses into the network that must be considered. The following are some examples:

- Desktop systems can contain sensitive information that might be at risk of being exposed.
- Users might generally lack security awareness.
- Lack of proper backup might exist.

Middleware

In a distributed environment, middleware is software that ties the client and server software together. It is neither a part of the operating system nor a part of the server software. It is the code that lies between the operating system and applications on each side of a distributed computing system in a network. It might be generic enough to operate between several types of client/server systems of a particular type.

Embedded Systems

An ***embedded system*** is a piece of software built into a larger piece of software that is in charge of performing some specific function on behalf of the larger system. The embedded part of the solution might address specific hardware communications and might require drivers to talk between the larger system and some specific hardware.

Mobile Computing

Mobile code is instructions passed across the network and executed on a remote system. An example of mobile code is Java and ActiveX code downloaded into a web browser from the World Wide Web. Any introduction of code from one system to another is a security concern but is required in some situations. An active content module that attempts to monopolize and exploit system resources is called a hostile applet. The main objective of the Java Security Model (JSM) is to protect the user from hostile, network mobile code. It does this by placing the code in a sandbox, which restricts its operations.

Virtual Computing

Virtual environments are increasingly being used as the computing platform for solutions. Most of the same security issues that must be mitigated in the physical environment must also be addressed in the virtual network.

In a virtual environment, instances of an operating system are called virtual machines (VMs). A host system can contain many VMs. Software called a hypervisor manages the distribution of resources (CPU, memory, and disk) to the VMs. Figure 3-4 shows the relationship between the host machine, its physical resources, the resident VMs, and the virtual resources assigned to them.

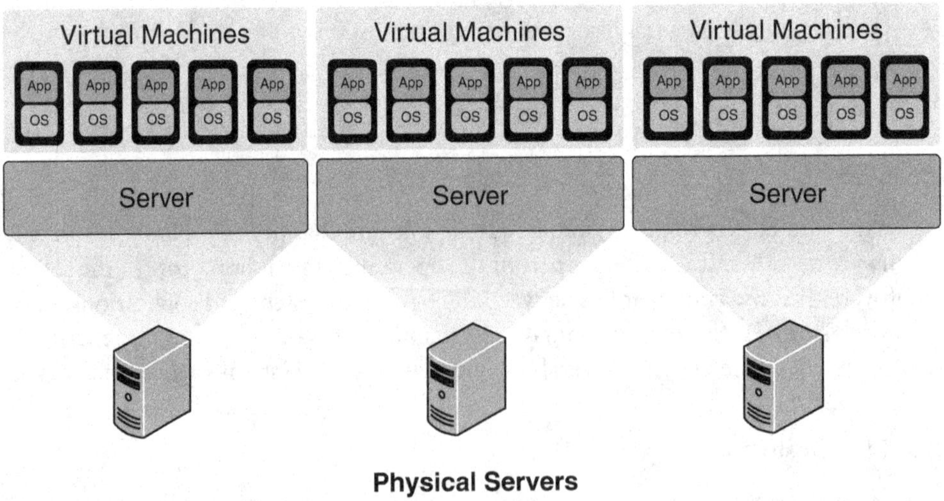

Figure 3-4 Virtualization

Security Services

The process of creating system architecture also includes design of the security that will be provided. These services can be classified into several categories depending on the protections they are designed to provide. The following sections briefly examine and compare types of security services.

Boundary Control Services

These services are responsible for placing various components in security zones and maintaining boundary control among them. Generally, this task is accomplished by indicating components and services as trusted or not trusted. As an example, memory space insulated from other running processes in a multiprocessing system is part of a protection boundary.

Access Control Services

In Chapter 5, you will learn about various methods of access control and how they can be deployed. An appropriate method should be deployed to control access to sensitive material and to give users the minimum required access they need to do their jobs.

Integrity Services

As you might recall, integrity implies that data has not been changed. When integrity services are present, they ensure that data moving through the operating system or application can be verified to not have been damaged or corrupted in the transfer.

Cryptography Services

If the system is capable of scrambling or encrypting information in transit, it is said to provide cryptography services. In some cases, this service is not natively provided by a system and if desired must be provided in some other fashion, but if the capability is present, it is valuable, especially in instances where systems are distributed and talk across the network.

Auditing and Monitoring Services

If the system has a method of tracking the activities of the users and of the operations of the system processes, it is said to provide auditing and monitoring services.

Although our focus here is on security, the value of this service goes beyond security because it also allows for monitoring what the system itself is actually doing.

System Components

When discussing the way security is provided in an architecture, having a basic grasp of the components in computing equipment is helpful. The following sections discuss those components and some of the functions they provide.

CPU

The central processing unit (CPU), also called the processor, is the hardware in the system that executes all the instructions. The CPU is the heart of a computer or IT systems. It has its own set of instructions for its internal operation, and those instructions define its architecture. The software that runs on the system must be compatible with this architecture, which really means the CPU and the software can communicate.

When more than one processor is present and available, the system becomes capable of multiprocessing. This capability allows the computer to execute multiple instructions in parallel. It can be done with separate physical processors or with a single processor with multiple cores. When multiple cores are used, each core operates as a separate CPU.

CPUs have a small amount of internal memory, and the CPU is able to access this memory faster than any other memory location. It also typically has cache memory where the most recently executed instructions are kept in case they are needed again. When a CPU gets an instruction from memory, the process is called ***fetching***. In the decode cycle, the CPU converts the instruction and determines what operation needs to be performed. In the execute cycle, the CPU performs the operation specified by the instruction.

An arithmetic logic unit (ALU) in the CPU performs the actual execution of the instructions. The control unit acts as the system manager while instructions from applications and operating systems are executed. CPU registers contain the instruction set information and data to be executed and include general registers, special registers, and a program counter register.

CPUs can work in user mode or privileged mode. When applications are communicating with the CPU, it is in user mode. If an instruction that is sent to the CPU is marked to be performed in privileged mode, also referred to as supervisor mode, it must be a trusted operating system process and is given functionality not available in user mode.

The CPU is connected to an address bus. Memory and I/O devices recognize this address bus. These devices can then communicate with the CPU, read requested data, and send it to the data bus.

When microcomputers were first developed, the instruction fetch time was much longer than the instruction execution time because of the relatively slow speed of memory access. This situation led to the design of the Complex Instruction Set Computer (CISC) CPU. In this arrangement, the set of instructions was reduced (while made more complex) to help mitigate the relatively slow memory access.

After memory access was improved to the point where not much difference existed in memory access times and processor execution times, the Reduced Instruction Set Computer (RISC) architecture was introduced. The objective of the RISC architecture was to reduce the number of cycles required to execute an instruction, which was accomplished by making the instructions less complex.

Multitasking and Multiprocessing

Multitasking is the process of carrying out more than one task at a time. Multitasking can be done in two different ways. When the computer has a single processor with one core, it is not really doing multiple tasks at once. It is dividing its CPU cycles between tasks at such a high rate of speed that it appears to be doing multiple tasks at once. However, when a computer has more than one processor or has a processor with multiple cores, then it is capable of actually performing two tasks at the same time. It can do this in two different ways:

- ***Symmetric mode***: In this mode the processors or cores are handed work on a round-robin basis, thread by thread.
- ***Asymmetric mode***: In this mode a processor is dedicated to a specific process or application; when work needs to be done for that process, it always is done by the same processor. Figure 3-5 shows the relationship between these two modes.

Preemptive multitasking means that task switches can be initiated directly out of interrupt handlers. With cooperative (nonpreemptive) multitasking, a task switch is only performed when a task calls the kernel and allows the kernel a chance to perform a task switch.

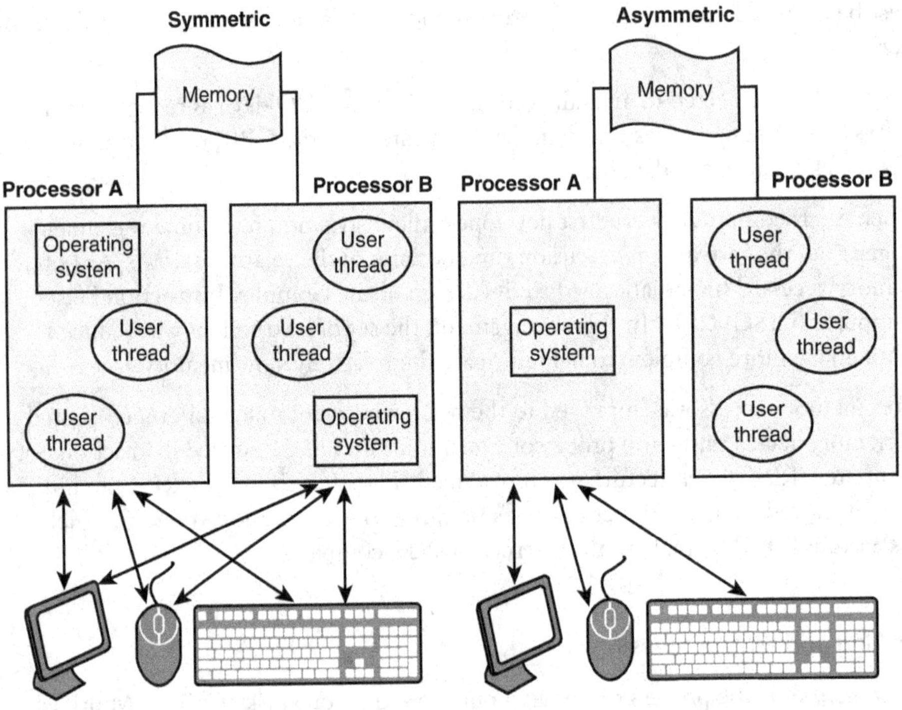

Figure 3-5 Types of Multiprocessing

Multithreading

Multithreading allows multiple tasks to be performed within a single process. A thread is a self-contained sequence of instruction that can execute in parallel with other threads that are part of the same process. Multithreading is often used in applications to reduce overhead and increase efficiency. An example of multithreading is having multiple Microsoft Excel spreadsheets open at the same time. In this situation, the computer does not run multiple instances of Microsoft Excel. Each spreadsheet is treated as a single thread within the single Microsoft Excel process with the software managing which thread is being accessed.

Single-State Versus Multistate Systems

Single-state systems manage information at different levels using policy mechanisms approved by security administrators. These systems handle one security level at a time. Multistate systems manage multiple security levels at the same time using the protection mechanisms described in the next section. Multistate systems are uncommon because they are so expensive to implement.

Process States

Process states are the different modes in which a process may run. A process can operate in one of several states:

- **Ready:** The process is ready to start processing when needed.
- **Waiting:** The process is ready for execution but is waiting for access to an object.
- **Running:** The process is being executed until the process is finished, the time expires, or the process is blocked or aborted.
- **Supervisory:** The process is performing an action that requires higher privileges.
- **Stopped:** The process is finished or terminated.

Memory and Storage

A computing system needs somewhere to store information, both on a long-term basis and a short-term basis. There are two types of storage locations: memory, for temporary storage needs, and long-term storage media. Information can be accessed much faster from memory than from long-term storage, which is why the most recently used instructions or information is typically kept in cache memory for a short period of time, which ensures the second and subsequent accesses will be faster than returning to long-term memory.

Computers can have both random-access memory (RAM) and read-only memory (ROM). RAM is volatile, meaning the information must continually be refreshed while the computer is powered on and will be lost if the system shuts down. Table 3-2 contains some types of RAM used in laptops and desktops.

Table 3-2 Memory Types

Desktop Memory	Description
SDRAM—synchronous dynamic random-access memory	Synchronizes itself with the CPU's bus.
DDR SDRAM—double data rate synchronous dynamic random-access memory	Supports data transfers on both edges of each clock cycle (the rising and falling edges), effectively doubling the memory chip's data throughput.
DDR2 SDRAM—double data rate two (2) synchronous dynamic random-access memory	Transfers 64 bits of data twice every clock cycle and is not compatible with current DDR SDRAM memory slots.

Desktop Memory	Description
DDR3-SDRAM—double data rate three (3) synchronous dynamic random-access memory	Offers reduced power consumption, a doubled pre-fetch buffer, and more bandwidth because of its increased clock rate. Allows for DIMMs of up to 16 GB in capacity.
DDR4-SDRAM—double data rate four (4) synchronous dynamic random-access memory	Includes higher module density and lower voltage requirements. Theoretically allows for DIMMs of up to 512 GB in capacity.
Laptop Memory	**Description**
SODIMM—small outline DIMM	Differs from desktop RAM in physical size and pin configuration. A full-size DIMM has 100, 168, 184, 240, or 288 pins and is usually 4.5 to 5 inches in length. In contrast, a SODIMM has 72, 100, 144, 200, 204, or 260 pins and is smaller—2.5 to 3 inches.

ROM, on the other hand, is not volatile and also cannot be overwritten without executing a series of operations that depend on the type of ROM. It usually contains low-level instructions of some sort that make the device on which it is installed operational. Some examples of ROM are

- ***Flash memory***: A type of electrically programmable ROM
- **Programmable logic device (PLD):** An integrated circuit with connections or internal logic gates that can be changed through a programming process
- ***Field-programmable gate array (FPGA)***: A type of PLD that is programmed by blowing fuse connections on the chip or using an antifuse that makes a connection when a high voltage is applied to the junction
- ***Firmware***: A type of ROM where a program or low-level instructions are installed

Memory directly addressable by the CPU, which is for the storage of instructions and data that are associated with the program being executed, is called *primary* memory. Regardless of which type of memory in which the information is located, in most cases the CPU must get involved in fetching the information on behalf of other components. *Direct memory access (DMA)* is a state of CPU wherein the CPU backs off when a device requests direct access to memory. The CPU grants the device's access and transfers the bus to the device. Memory access and transfer then lie with the device. The CPU stands back after granting the access. DMA is used for large data transfers and is very fast.

Some additional terms you should be familiar with in regard to memory include the following:

- ***Associative memory***: The type of memory that searches for a specific data value in memory rather than using a specific memory address.
- ***Implied addressing***: The type of memory addressing that refers to registers usually contained inside the CPU.
- ***Absolute addressing***: The type of memory addressing that addresses the entire physical memory space. The CPU uses the physical memory addresses that are called absolute addresses.
- ***Cache***: A relatively small amount (when compared to primary memory) of very high speed RAM buffer that holds the instructions and data from primary memory and that has a high probability of being accessed during the currently executing portion of a program.
- ***Indirect addressing***: The type of memory addressing where the address location that is specified in the program instruction contains the address of the final desired location.
- **Logical address:** The address at which a memory cell or storage element appears to reside from the perspective of an executing application program.
- **Relative address:** The address that specifies its location by indicating its distance from another physical memory address.
- **Virtual memory:** A location on the hard drive used temporarily for storage when memory space is low.
- **Memory leak:** A failure that occurs when a computer program incorrectly manages memory allocations, which can exhaust or corrupt available system memory as an application runs.
- ***Secondary memory***: Magnetic, optical, or flash-based media or other storage devices that contain data that must first be read by the operating system and stored into memory. This memory is less expensive than primary memory.
- ***Volatile memory***: Memory that is erased or lost when the device shuts down or when an application cleans up.
- ***Nonvolatile memory***: Long-term persistent storage that remains even when the device shuts down.

Random Versus Sequential Access

Random access devices read data immediately from any point on the drive. Sequential access devices read data as it is stored on the drive in the order in which it is stored. RAM, magnetic hard drives, and USB flash drives are random access devices, while magnetic tapes are sequential access devices because the tape must advance to the point where the data is stored.

Input/Output Devices

Input/output (I/O) devices are used to send and receive information to the system. Examples are the keyboard, mouse, displays, and printers. The operating system controls the interaction between the I/O devices and the system. In cases where the I/O device requires the CPU to perform some action, it may signal the CPU with a message called an ***interrupt***. Not all devices require an interrupt to communicate with the CPU.

Input/Output Structures

Some computer activities are general I/O operations that require manual configuration of devices. The I/O structures used by those activities utilize memory-mapped I/O, interrupt requests (IRQs), and direct memory access (DMA).

With memory-mapped I/O, the CPU manages access to a series of mapped memory addresses or locations. Using these memory-mapped locations, the user actually obtains input from the corresponding device. The input is copied to those memory locations when the device signals that it is ready. When the user writes to the memory-mapped locations, the output to the device is copied from the memory location to the device when the CPU indicates that the output is ready. When memory-mapped I/O is used, a single device or piece of hardware should map to a specific memory address. That address should be used by no other device or hardware. The operating system manages access to mapped-memory locations.

An IRQ assigns specific signal lines to a device through an interrupt controller. IRQs are mapped to specific CPU-addressed memory locations. When a device wants to communicate, it sends a signal to the CPU through its assigned IRQ. Older devices must have exclusive use of an IRQ, while newer plug-and-play (PnP) devices can share an IRQ. Older computers had IRQs 0–15, while newer computers have IRQs 0–23. If an IRQ conflict occurs, none of the devices sharing the IRQ will be available. The operating system manages access to IRQs.

DMA access uses a channel with two signal lines, one of which is the DMA request (DMQ) line and the other of which is the DMA acknowledgment (DACK) line. This I/O structure type allows devices to work directly with memory without waiting on the CPU. The CPU simply authorizes the access and then lets the device communicate with memory directly. A DACK signal is used to release the memory location back to the CPU. DMA is much faster than the other two methods. The operating system manages DMA assignments.

Firmware

Firmware is software that is stored on an EPROM or EEPROM chip within a device. While updates to firmware may become necessary, they are infrequent. Firmware can exist as the basic input/output system (BIOS) on a computer or device firmware.

BIOS/UEFI

A computer's BIOS contains the basic instruction that a computer needs to boot and load the operating system from a drive. The process of updating the BIOS with the latest software is referred to as flashing the BIOS. Security professionals should ensure that any BIOS updates are obtained from the BIOS vendor and have not been tampered with in any way.

The traditional BIOS has been replaced with the Unified Extensible Firmware Interface (UEFI). UEFI maintains support for legacy BIOS devices but is considered a more advanced interface than traditional BIOS. BIOS uses the master boot record (MBR) to save information about the hard drive data, while UEFI uses the GUID partition table (GPT). BIOS partitions were a maximum of 4 partitions, each being only 2 terabytes (TB). UEFI allows up to 128 partitions, with the total disk limit being 9.4 zettabytes (ZB) or 9.4 billion terabytes. UEFI is also faster and more secure than traditional BIOS. UEFI Secure Boot requires boot loaders to have a verifiable digital signature.

UEFI is an open standard interface layer between the firmware and the operating system that requires firmware updates to be digitally signed. Security professionals should understand the following points regarding UEFI:

- It was designed as a replacement for traditional PC BIOS.
- Additional functionality includes support for Secure Boot, network authentication, and universal graphics drivers.
- It protects against BIOS malware attacks including rootkits.

Secure Boot requires that all boot loader components (e.g., OS kernel, drivers) attest to their identity (digital signature) and the attestation is compared to the trusted list.

- When a computer is manufactured, a list of keys that identify trusted hardware, firmware, and operating system loader code (and in some instances, known malware) is embedded in the UEFI.
- It ensures the integrity and security of the firmware.
- It prevents malicious files from being loaded.
- Can be disabled for backward compatibility.

Device Firmware

Hardware devices, such as routers and printers, require some processing power to complete their tasks. This firmware is contained in the firmware chips located within the devices. Like with computers, this firmware is often installed on its own EEPROM to allow it to be updated. Again, security professionals should ensure that updates are obtained only from the device vendor and that the updates have not been changed in any manner, including modified by a third party.

Operating Systems

The operating system is the software that enables a human to interact with the hardware that comprises the computer. Without the operating system, the computer would be useless. Operating systems perform a number of noteworthy and interesting functions as part of the interfacing between the human and the hardware. In this section, we look at some of these activities.

A ***thread*** is an individual unit of an application for a specific process. A ***process*** is a set of threads that are part of the same larger application. An application's instructions are not considered processes until they have been loaded into memory where all instructions must first be copied to be processed by the CPU. A process can be in a running state, ready state, or blocked state. When a process is blocked, it is simply waiting for data to be transmitted to it, usually through user data entry. A group of processes that share access to the same resources is called a protection domain.

CPUs can be categorized according to the way in which they handle processes. A ***superscalar*** computer architecture is characterized by a processor that enables concurrent execution of multiple instructions in the same pipeline stage. A processor in which a single instruction specifies more than one concurrent operation is called a Very Long Instruction Word (VLIW) processor. A ***pipelined processor*** overlaps the steps of different instructions, whereas a scalar processor executes one instruction at a time, consequently increasing pipelining.

From a security perspective, processes are placed in a ring structure according to the concept of least privilege, meaning they are only allowed to access resources and components required to perform the task. A common visualization of this structure is shown in Figure 3-6.

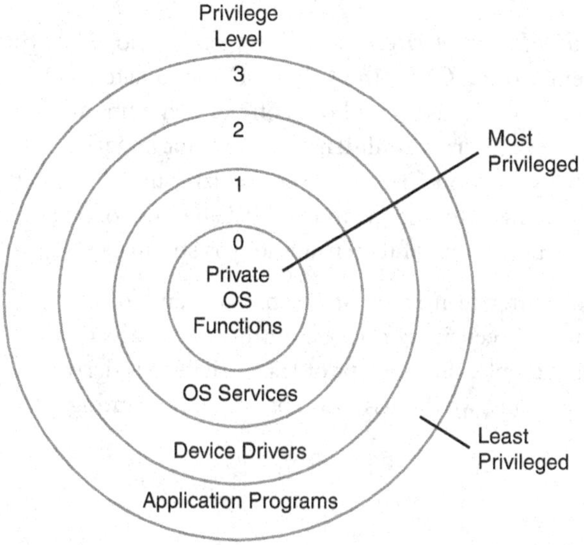

Figure 3-6 Ring Structure

When a computer system processes I/O instructions, it is operating in supervisor mode. The termination of selected, noncritical processing when a hardware or software failure occurs and is detected is referred to as a ***fail soft state***. It is in a ***fail safe state*** if the system automatically leaves system processes and components in a secure state when a failure occurs or is detected in the system.

Memory Management

Because all information goes to memory before it can be processed, secure management of memory is critical. Memory space insulated from other running processes in a multiprocessing system is part of a protection domain.

System Security Evaluation Models

In an attempt to bring order to the unexpected security threats that happen, several evaluation models have been created to assess and rate the security of these products. An assurance level examination attempts to examine the security-related components of a system and assign a level of confidence that the system can provide a particular level of security. In the following sections, we discuss organizations that have created such evaluation systems.

TCSEC

The ***Trusted Computer System Evaluation Criteria (TCSEC)*** was developed by the National Computer Security Center (NCSC) for the U.S. DoD to evaluate products. NCSC has issued a series of books focusing on both computer systems and the networks in which they operate. They address confidentiality, but not integrity. In 2005, TCSEC was replaced by the Common Criteria, discussed later in the chapter. However, security professionals still need to understand TCSEC because of its effect on security practices today and because some of its terminology is still in use.

With TCSEC, functionality and assurance are evaluated separately and form a basis for assessing the effectiveness of security controls built into automatic data-processing system products. For example, the concept of least privilege is derived from TCSEC. In the following sections, we discuss those books and the ratings they derive.

Rainbow Series

The original publication created by the TCSEC was the Orange Book, but as time went by, other books were also created that focused on additional aspects of the security of computer systems. Collectively, this set of more than 20 books is now referred to as the Rainbow Series, alluding to the fact that each book is a different color. For example, the Green Book focuses solely on password management. Next, we cover the most important books: the Red Book, Orange Book, and Green Book.

Red Book

The Trusted Network Interpretation (TNI) extends the evaluation classes of the TCSEC (DOD 5200.28-STD) to trusted network systems and components in the ***Red Book***. So where the Orange Book focuses on security for a single system, the Red Book addresses network security.

Orange Book

The ***Orange Book*** is a collection of criteria based on the Bell-LaPadula model that is used to grade or rate the security offered by a computer system product. Covert channel analysis, trusted facility management, and trusted recoveries are concepts discussed in this book.

The goals of this system can be divided into two categories, operational assurance requirements and life cycle assurance requirements, the details of which are defined next.

The operational assurance requirements specified in the Orange Book are as follows:

- System architecture
- System integrity
- Covert channel analysis
- Trusted facility management
- Trusted recovery

The life cycle assurance requirements specified in the Orange Book are as follows:

- Security testing
- Design specification and testing
- Configuration management
- Trusted distribution

TCSEC uses a classification system that assigns an alphabetic letter and a number to describe systems' security effectiveness. The assigned letter refers to a security assurance level or division as A, B, C, D, and the number refers to gradients within that security assurance level or class. Each division and class incorporates all the required elements of the ones below it.

In order of least secure to most secure, the four classes and their constituent divisions and requirements are as follows:

Key Topic

- **D—Minimal Protection**

  Reserved for systems that have been evaluated but that fail to meet the requirements for a higher division.

- **C—Discretionary Protection**
  - *C1—Discretionary Security Protection*
    - Requires identification and authentication.
    - Requires separation of users and data.
    - Uses discretionary access control (DAC) capable of enforcing access limitations on an individual or group basis.
    - Requires system documentation and user manuals.

- *C2—Controlled Access Protection*
  - Uses a more finely grained DAC.
  - Provides individual accountability through login procedures.
  - Requires protected audit trails.
  - Invokes object reuse theory.
  - Requires resource isolation.

- **B—Mandatory Protection**
  - *B1—Labeled Security Protection*
    - Uses an informal statement of the security policy.
    - Requires data sensitivity or classification labels.
    - Uses MAC over selected subjects and objects.
    - Capable of label exportation.
    - Requires removal or mitigation of discovered flaws.
    - Uses design specifications and verification.
  - *B2—Structured Protection*
    - Requires a clearly defined and formally documented security policy.
    - Uses DAC and MAC enforcement extended to all subjects and objects.
    - Analyzes and prevents covert storage channels for occurrence and bandwidth.
    - Structures elements into protection-critical and non-protection-critical categories.
    - Enables more comprehensive testing and review through design and implementation.
    - Strengthens authentication mechanisms.
    - Provides trusted facility management with administrator and operator segregation.
    - Imposes strict configuration management controls.
  - *B3—Security Domains*
    - Satisfies ***reference monitor*** requirements.
    - Excludes code not essential to security policy enforcement.
    - Minimizes complexity through significant systems engineering.
    - Defines the security administrator role.
    - Requires an audit of security-relevant events.
    - Automatically detects and responds to imminent intrusion detection, including personnel notification.
    - Requires trusted system recovery procedures.

   - Analyzes and prevents covert timing channels for occurrence and bandwidth.
   - An example of such a system is the XTS-300, a precursor to the XTS-400.

- **A—Verified Protection**
  - *A1—Verified Design*
    - Provides higher assurance than B3, but is functionally identical to B3.
    - Uses formal design and verification techniques, including a formal top-level specification.
    - Requires that formal techniques are used to prove the equivalence between the ***Trusted Computer Base (TCB)*** specifications and the security policy model.
    - Provides formal management and distribution procedures.
    - An example of such a system is Honeywell's Secure Communications Processor (SCOMP), a precursor to the XTS-400.

Green Book

The Green Book provides guidance on password creation and management. It includes single sign-on (SSO) responsibilities, user responsibilities, ***authentication*** mechanisms, and password protection. The following major features are advocated in this guideline:

- Users should be able to change their own passwords.
- Passwords should be machine-generated rather than user-created.
- Certain audit reports (e.g., date and time of last login) should be provided by the system directly to the user.

ITSEC

TCSEC addresses confidentiality only and bundles functionality and assurance. In contrast to TCSEC, the ***Information Technology Security Evaluation Criteria (ITSEC)*** addresses integrity and availability as well as confidentiality. Another difference is that the ITSEC was mainly a set of guidelines used in Europe, whereas the TCSEC was relied on more in the United States.

ITSEC has a rating system in many ways similar to that of TCSEC. ITSEC has 10 classes, F1 to F10, to evaluate the functional requirements and 7 TCSEC classes, E0 to E6, to evaluate the assurance requirements.

Security functional requirements include the following:

- **F00:** Identification and authentication
- **F01:** Audit
- **F02:** Resource utilization
- **F03:** Trusted paths/channels
- **F04:** User data protection
- **F05:** Security management
- **F06:** Product access
- **F07:** Communications
- **F08:** Privacy
- **F09:** Protection of the product's security functions
- **F10:** Cryptographic support

Security assurance requirements include the following:

- **E00:** Guidance documents and manuals
- **E01:** Configuration management
- **E02:** Vulnerability assessment
- **E03:** Delivery and operation
- **E04:** Life cycle support
- **E05:** Assurance maintenance
- **E06:** Development
- **E07:** Testing

The TCSEC and ITSEC systems can be mapped to one another, but the ITSEC provides a number of ratings that have no corresponding concept in the TCSEC ratings. Table 3-3 shows a mapping of the two systems.

Key Topic

Table 3-3 Mapping of ITSEC and TCSEC

ITSEC	TCSEC
E0	D
F1+E1	C1
F2+E2	C2

ITSEC	TCSEC
F3+E3	B1
F4+E4	B2
F5+E5	B3
F6+E6	A1
F6	Systems that provide high integrity
F7	Systems that provide high availability
F8	Systems that provide high data integrity during communication
F9	Systems that provide high confidentiality (using cryptography)
F10	Networks with high demands on confidentiality and integrity

The ITSEC has been largely replaced by Common Criteria, discussed in the next section.

Common Criteria

In 1990 the ISO identified the need for a standardized rating system that could be used globally. The ***Common Criteria (CC)*** for Information Technology Security Evaluation was the result of a cooperative effort to establish this system. This system uses Evaluation Assurance Levels (EALs) to rate systems, with each EAL representing a successively higher level of security testing and design in a system. The resulting rating represents the potential the system has to provide security. It assumes that the customer will properly configure all available security solutions, so it is required that the vendor always provide proper documentation to allow the customer to fully achieve the rating. ISO/IEC 15408-1:2009 is the ISO version of the CC.

The CC represents requirements for IT security of a product or system in two categories: functionality and assurance. This means that the rating should describe what the system does (functionality), and the degree of certainty the raters have that the functionality can be provided (assurance).

The CC has seven assurance levels, which range from EAL1 (lowest), where functionality testing takes place, through EAL7 (highest), where thorough testing is performed and the system design is verified.

The assurance designators used in the CC are as follows:

Key Topic

- **EAL1:** Functionally tested
- **EAL2:** Structurally tested

- **EAL3:** Methodically tested and checked
- **EAL4:** Methodically designed, tested, and reviewed
- **EAL5:** Semi-formally designed and tested
- **EAL6:** Semi-formally verified design and tested
- **EAL7:** Formally verified design and tested

The CC uses a concept called a protection profile during the evaluation process. The protection profile describes a set of security requirements or goals along with functional assumptions about the environment. Therefore, if someone identified a security need not currently addressed by any products, that person could write a protection profile that describes the need and the solution and all issues that could go wrong during the development of the system. This would be used to guide the development of a new product. A protection profile contains the following elements:

- **Descriptive elements:** The name of the profile and a description of the security problem that is to be solved.
- **Rationale:** Justification of the profile and a more detailed description of the real-world problem to be solved. The environment, usage assumptions, and threats are given along with security policy guidance that can be supported by products and systems that conform to this profile.
- **Functional requirements:** Establishment of a protection boundary, meaning the threats or compromises that are within this boundary to be countered. The product or system must enforce the boundary.
- **Development assurance requirements:** Identification of the specific requirements that the product or system must meet during the development phases, from design to implementation.
- **Evaluation assurance requirements:** Establishment of the type and intensity of the evaluation.

The result of following this process will be a security target. This is the vendor's explanation of what the product brings to the table from a security standpoint. Intermediate groupings of security requirements developed along the way to a security target are called packages.

While it is important to understand the EAL levels of the CC, the CC has been redesigned. Common Criteria Version 3.1, Revision 5, uses the term *Target of Evaluation (TOE)*. A TOE is defined as a set of software, firmware, and/or hardware possibly accompanied by guidance. The TOE consists of a specific version and a specific representation of the TOE. For example, the Windows 10 Enterprise OS is a specific version, and its configuration on a computer based on the organization's security policies is the specific representation.

The CC includes two types of evaluations: Security Target (ST)/TOE evaluation and Protection Profile (PP) evaluation. In an ST evaluation, the sufficiency of the TOE and the operational environment are determined. In a TOE evaluation, the correctness of the TOE is determined. The PP evaluation is a document, typically created by a user or user community, which identifies security requirements for a class of security devices relevant to that user for a particular purpose.

The Common Criteria has categorized PPs into 14 categories:

- Access control devices and systems
- Biometric systems and devices
- Boundary protection devices and systems
- Data protection
- Databases
- ICs, smart cards, and smart card–related devices and systems
- Key management systems
- Mobility
- Multifunction devices
- Network and network-related devices and systems
- Operating systems
- Other devices and systems
- Products for digital signatures
- Trusted computing

Protection profiles are assigned an EAL after analysis by a member organization in the Common Criteria Recognition Arrangement (CCRA). For more information on the latest Common Criteria implementation, go to www.commoncriteriaportal.org/. Click the Protection Profiles tab to see the available PPs.

Security Implementation Standards

It is important for a security professional to understand security implementation standards that have been published by international bodies. In addition, security professionals should examine standards in the industry that apply to their organizations and align the practices in their organization to these implementation standards. These standards include ISO/IEC 27001 and 27002 and PCI DSS.

NOTE COBIT 5 could also be discussed in this section. However, it is adequately covered in Chapter 1. ISO/IEC 27001 and 27002 are briefly mentioned in that chapter as well but are covered more in depth here.

ISO/IEC 27001

ISO/IEC 27001:2018 is the latest version of the 27001 standard and is one of the most popular standards by which organizations obtain certification for information security. It provides guidance on how to ensure that an organization's information security management system (ISMS) is properly built, administered, and maintained. It includes the following components:

- ISMS scope
- Information security policy
- Risk assessment process and its results
- Risk treatment process and its decisions
- Information security objectives
- Information security personnel competence
- ISMS-related documents that are necessary
- Operational planning and control documents
- Information security monitoring and measurement evidence
- ISMS internal audit program and its results
- Top management ISMS review evidence
- Identified nonconformities evidence and corrective actions

When an organization decides to obtain ISO/IEC 27001 certification, a project manager should be selected to ensure that all the components are properly completed.

To implement ISO/IEC 27001:2018, the selected project manager should complete the following steps:

Key Topic

1. Obtain management support.
2. Determine whether to use consultants or to complete the implementation in-house, and if the latter, purchase the 27001 standard, write the project plan, define the stakeholders, and organize the project kickoff.

3. Identify the requirements.
4. Define the ISMS scope, information security policy, and information security objectives.
5. Develop document control, internal audit, and corrective action procedures.
6. Perform risk assessment and risk treatment.
7. Develop a statement of applicability and risk treatment plan and accept all residual risks.
8. Implement controls defined in the risk treatment plan and maintain implementation records.
9. Develop and implement security training and awareness programs.
10. Implement the ISMS, maintain policies and procedures, and perform corrective actions.
11. Maintain and monitor the ISMS.
12. Perform an internal audit and write an audit report.
13. Perform management review and maintain management review records.
14. Select a certification body and complete certification.
15. Maintain records for surveillance visits.

ISO/IEC 27002

ISO/IEC 27002:2013 is the latest version of the 27002 standard and provides a code of practice for information security management.

It includes the following 14 content areas:

- Information security policy
- Organization of information security
- Human resources security
- Asset management
- Access control
- Cryptography
- Physical and environmental security

- Operations security
- Communications security
- Information systems acquisition, development, and maintenance
- Supplier relationships
- Information security incident management
- Information security aspects of business continuity
- Compliance

Payment Card Industry Data Security Standard (PCI DSS)

Payment Card Industry Data Security Standard (PCI DSS) Version 3.2 is for merchants and other entities involved in payment card processing, which includes storing, using, or transmitting payment card data. Compliance with the PCI DSS helps to alleviate vulnerabilities and protect cardholder data. There are three ongoing steps for adhering to PCI DSS:

- **Assess:** Identify all locations of cardholder data, take an inventory of your IT assets and business processes for payment card processing, and analyze them for vulnerabilities that could expose cardholder data.
- **Repair:** Fix identified vulnerabilities, securely remove any unnecessary cardholder data storage, and implement secure business processes.
- **Report:** Document assessment and remediation details, and submit compliance reports to the acquiring bank and card brands or other requesting entity.

PCI DSS applies to all entities that store, process, and/or transmit cardholder data. It covers technical and operational system components included in or connected to cardholder data. If an organization accepts or processes payment cards, then PCI DSS applies to that organization. If there is a breach or possibility of breach (even without harming cardholders in anyway) for an entity that follows PCI DSS, the entity should immediately be reported to customers.

For more information on PCI DSS, you can download the PCI DSS Quick Reference Guide at https://www.pcisecuritystandards.org/documents/ PCI_DSS-QRG-v3_2_1.pdf.

Controls and Countermeasures

After an organization implements a system security evaluation model and security implementation standard, the organization must ensure that the appropriate controls and countermeasures are implemented, based on the most recent vulnerability and risk assessments performed by security professionals. Understanding the different categories and types of access controls is vital to ensure that an organization implements a comprehensive security program. Information security should always be something that the organization assesses and pursues.

NOTE Access control categories and types are discussed in depth in Chapter 1.

Certification and Accreditation

Although the terms are used as synonyms in casual conversation, ***accreditation*** and ***certification*** are two different concepts in the context of assurance levels and ratings, although they are closely related. Certification evaluates the security features of system components, whereas accreditation occurs when the adequacy of a system's overall security is assessed by an approval authority as to the system's purpose.

The National Information Assurance Certification and Accreditation Process (NIACAP) provides a standard set of activities, general tasks, and a management structure to certify and accredit systems that will maintain the information assurance and security posture of a system or site.

The accreditation process developed by NIACAP has four phases:

Key Topic

- Phase 1: Definition
- Phase 2: Verification
- Phase 3: Validation
- Phase 4: Post Accreditation

NIACAP defines the following three types of accreditation:

- Type accreditation evaluates an application or system that is distributed to a number of different locations.
- System accreditation evaluates an application or support system.
- Site accreditation evaluates the application or system at a specific self-contained location.

Control Selection Based on Systems Security Requirements

Although controls should be selected based on systems security evaluation models, they also need to be selected based on the systems security requirements. Security controls include the management, operational, and technical countermeasures used within an organizational information system to protect the CIA of the system and its information.

Selecting and implementing the appropriate security controls for an information system are important tasks that can have major implications on the operations and assets of an organization. According to the NIST Risk Management Framework, organizations are required to adequately mitigate risk arising from use of information and information systems in the execution of missions and business functions. A significant challenge for organizations is to determine the appropriate set of security controls that, if implemented and determined to be effective, would most cost-effectively mitigate risk while complying with the security requirements defined by applicable federal laws, directives, policies, standards, or regulations.

The security control selection process includes, as appropriate:

Key Topic

- Choosing a set of baseline security controls
- Tailoring the baseline security controls by applying scoping, parameterization, and compensating control guidance
- Supplementing the tailored baseline security controls, if necessary, with additional controls or control enhancements to address unique organizational needs based on a risk assessment and local conditions, including environment of operation, organization-specific security requirements, specific threat information, cost-benefit analysis, or special circumstances
- Specifying minimum assurance requirements

The information system owner and information security architect are responsible for selecting the security controls for the information system and documenting the controls in the security plan.

NOTE The NIST Risk Management Framework is covered in more detail in Chapter 1.

Security Capabilities of Information Systems

Organizations must understand the security capabilities of any information systems that they implement. The following sections discuss memory protection, Trusted Platform Module, interfaces, and fault tolerance.

Memory Protection

In an information system, memory and storage are the most important resources. Damaged or corrupt data in memory can cause the system to stop functioning. Data in memory can be disclosed and therefore must be protected. Memory does not isolate running processes and threads from data. Security professionals must use processor states, layering, process isolation, abstraction, hardware segmentation, and data hiding to help keep data isolated.

Most processors support two processor states: supervisor state (or kernel mode) and problem state (or user mode). In supervisor state, the highest privilege level on the system is used so that the processor can access all the system hardware and data. In problem state, the processor limits access to system hardware and data. Processes running in supervisor state are isolated from the processes that are not running in that state; supervisor-state processes should be limited to only core operating system functions.

A security professional can use layering to organize programming into separate functions that interact in a hierarchical manner. In most cases, each layer has access only to the layers directly above and below it. Ring protection is the most common implementation of layering, with the inner ring (ring 0) being the most privileged ring and the outer ring (ring 3) being the lowest privileged. The OS kernel usually runs on ring 0, and user applications usually run on ring 3.

A security professional can isolate processes by providing memory address spaces for each process. Other processes are unable to access address spaces allotted to another process. Naming distinctions and virtual mapping are used as part of process isolation.

Hardware segmentation works like process isolation. It prevents access to information that belongs to a higher security level. However, hardware segmentation enforces the policies using physical hardware controls rather than the operating system's logical process isolation. Hardware segmentation is rare and is usually restructured to governmental use, although some organizations may choose to use this method to protect private or confidential data.

Data hiding prevents data at one security level from being seen by processes operating at other security levels.

Trusted Platform Module

Trusted Platform Module (TPM) is a security chip installed on computer motherboards that is responsible for managing symmetric and asymmetric keys, hashes, and digital certificates. This chip provides service to protect passwords, encrypt drives, and manage digital rights, making it much harder for attackers to gain access to the computers that have a TPM-chip enabled.

Two particularly popular uses of TPM are binding and sealing. Binding actually "binds" the hard drive through encryption to a particular computer. Because the decryption key is stored in the TPM chip, the hard drive's contents are available only when connected to the original computer. But keep in mind that all the contents are at risk if the TPM chip fails and a backup of the key does not exist.

Sealing, on the other hand, "seals" the system state to a particular hardware and software configuration. This technology prevents attackers from making any changes to the system. However, it can also make installing a new piece of hardware or a new operating system much harder. The system can only boot after the TPM verifies system integrity by comparing the original computed hash value of the system's configuration to the hash value of its configuration at boot time.

The TPM consists of both static memory and dynamic memory that are used to retain the important information when the computer is turned off.

The memory used in a TPM chip is as follows:

Key Topic

- **Endorsement Key (EK):** Persistent memory installed by the manufacturer that contains a public/private key pair
- **Storage Root Key (SRK):** Persistent memory that secures the keys stored in the TPM
- **Attestation Identity Key (AIK):** Dynamic memory that ensures the integrity of the EK
- **Platform Configuration Register (PCR) hashes:** Dynamic memory that stores data hashes for the sealing function
- **Storage keys:** Dynamic memory that contains the keys used to encrypt the computer's storage, including hard drives, USB flash drives, and so on

Interfaces

An interface is a mechanism that a user employs to access a system, an application, a device, or another entity. Most users assume that the interfaces they use are secure. Organizations are responsible for ensuring that secure interfaces are implemented across the network. If an entity has multiple user interfaces—such as a graphical user interface, a command-line interface, and a remote access interface—all these interfaces should require secure authentication. It is a security professional's job to understand the difference between secure and insecure interfaces and to ensure that interfaces without adequate security measures are replaced with interfaces that have security measures. If an interface does not have security features, the interfaces should be removed, discontinued, or replaced with interfaces that have adequate security measures.

Fault Tolerance

Fault tolerance allows a system to continue operating properly in the event that components within the system fail. For example, providing fault tolerance for a hard drive system involves using fault-tolerant drives and fault-tolerant drive adapters. However, the cost of any fault tolerance must be weighed against the cost of the redundant device or hardware. If security capabilities of information systems are not fault tolerant, attackers may be able to access systems if the security mechanisms fail. Organizations should weigh the cost of deploying a fault-tolerant system against the cost of any attack against the system being secured. It may not be vital to provide a fault-tolerant security mechanism to protect data that is classified as public, but it is very important to provide a fault-tolerant security mechanism to protect confidential data.

Policy Mechanisms

Organizations can implement different policy mechanisms to increase the security of information systems. The policy mechanisms include separation of privilege and accountability.

Separation of Privilege

The principle of separation of privilege is tied to the principle of least privilege. Separation of privilege requires that security professionals implement different permissions for each type of privileged operation. This principle ensures that the principle of least privilege is applied to administrative-level users. Very few administrative-level users need full administrative-level access to all systems. Separation of privilege ensures that administrative-level access is granted to users for only those resources or privileges that the administrative users need to perform their work.

For example, credit card service representatives on the phone cannot grant additional credit. However, they can view the credit limit or take your financial details and send a credit limit request application to their managers for processing.

NOTE Do not confuse separation of privilege with separation of duties, which is discussed in Chapter 1.

Accountability

Accountability ensures that users are held accountable for the actions that they take. However, accountability relies heavily on the system's ability to monitor activity. Accountability is usually provided using auditing functions. When auditing is enabled, it is also important to ensure that the auditing logs are preserved and cannot be edited. Finally, keep in mind that accounting also relies heavily on the authorization and authentication systems. Organizations can track user activities in a variety of ways.

Encryption/Decryption

Information systems use encryption and decryption to provide confidentiality of data. Encryption is the process of translating plaintext data (plaintext) into unreadable data (ciphertext), and decryption is the process of translating ciphertext back into plaintext. Encryption and decryption are covered later in this chapter in the "Cryptography" section.

Security Architecture Maintenance

After a product has been evaluated, certified, and accredited, the story is not over. The product typically evolves over time as updates and patches are developed to either address new security issues that arise or to add functionality or fix bugs that surface occasionally. When these changes occur, as ongoing maintenance, the security architecture must be maintained.

Ideally, solutions should undergo additional evaluations, certification, and accreditation as these changes occur, but in many cases the pressures of the real world prevent this time-consuming step. This situation is unfortunate because as developers fix and patch things, they often drift further and further from the original security design as they attempt to put out time-sensitive fires. In addition, developers may assume the fixes conform to the security guidelines or standards and may not verify. Unless disgruntled, a coder will not purposefully drift from security guidelines or standards, new or old, unless the coder is not fluent or knowledgeable about security in coding.

Maturity modeling becomes important at this point. Most maturity models are based on the Software Engineer Institute's CMMI, which is discussed in Chapter 1.

It has five levels: Initial, Managed, Defined, Quantitatively Managed, and Optimizing.

The U.S. Department of Defense (DoD) Software Engineering Institute's (SEI's) Capability Maturity Model (CMM) ranks organizations against industry best practices and international guidelines. It includes six rating levels, numbered from zero to five: nonexistent, initial, repeatable, defined, managed, and optimized. The nonexistent level does not correspond to any CMMI level, but all the other levels do.

Vulnerabilities of Security Architectures, Designs, and Solution Elements

Organizations must assess and mitigate the vulnerabilities of security architectures, designs, and solution elements. Insecure systems are exposed to many common vulnerabilities and threats. The following sections discuss the vulnerabilities of client-based systems, server-based systems, database systems, cryptographic systems, industrial control systems, cloud-based systems, large-scale parallel data systems, distributed systems, and the Internet of Things.

Client-Based Systems

In most networks, client systems are the most widely used because they are the systems that users most rely on to access resources. Client systems range from desktop systems to laptops to mobile devices of all types. This section focuses mainly on the vulnerabilities of desktops and laptops.

NOTE Security vulnerabilities of mobile devices are discussed later in this chapter.

Because client systems are so prolific, new attacks against these systems seem to crop up every day. Security practitioners must ensure that they know which client systems attach to the network so they can ensure that the appropriate controls are implemented to protect them.

Traditional client-side threats usually target web browsers, browser plug-ins, and email clients. But threats also exploit the applications and operating systems that are deployed. Client systems also tend to have exposed services deployed that are not needed. Often client systems are exposed to hostile servers. Added to these issues is the fact that most normal users are not security savvy and often inadvertently cause security issues on client systems.

Security architecture for client systems should include policies and controls that cover the following areas:

- Deploying only licensed, supported operating systems. These operating systems should be regularly updated with all vendor patches, security updates, and service packs as they are released.
- Deploying anti-malware and antivirus software on every client system. Updates to this software should also be configured as automatic to ensure that the most recently detected vulnerabilities are covered.
- Deploying a firewall with a well-configured access control list (ACL) and host-based intrusion detection system on the client systems.
- Using drive encryption such as BitLocker to protect the data on the hard drives.
- Issuing user accounts with the minimum permissions the users require to do their jobs. Users who need administrative access should have both an administrative account and a regular account and should use the administrative account only when performing administrative duties.
- Testing all updates and patches, including those to both the operating systems and applications, prior to deployment at the client level.

An applet is a small application that performs a specific task. It runs within a dedicated widget engine or a larger program, often as a plug-in. Java applets and ActiveX applets are examples. Malicious applets are often deployed by attackers and appear to come from legitimate sources. These applets can then be used to compromise a client system. A security professional should ensure that clients download applets only from valid vendors. In addition, a security professional should ensure that any application that includes applets is kept up to date with the latest patches.

A client system contains several types of local caches. The DNS cache holds the results of DNS queries on the Internet and is the cache that is most often attacked. Attackers may attempt to poison the DNS cache with false IP addresses for valid domains. They do this by sending a malicious DNS reply to an affected system. As with many other issues, you should ensure that the operating system and all applications are kept up to date. In addition, users should be trained to never click unverified or unknown links in email or on websites. They are not always pointing to the site shown in the visible link. The link may show a valid website, while the underlaying link may point to a malicious site.

Server-Based Systems

In some cases, an attack can focus on the operations of the server operating system itself rather than the web applications running on top of it. Later, we look at the way in which these attacks are implemented, focusing mainly on the issue of data flow manipulation.

Data Flow Control

Software attacks often subvert the intended data flow of a vulnerable program. For example, attackers exploit buffer overflows and format string vulnerabilities to write data to unintended locations. The ultimate aim is either to read data from prohibited locations or write data to memory locations for the purpose of executing malicious commands, crashing the system, or making malicious changes to the system. The proper mitigation for these types of attacks is proper input validation and data flow controls that are built into the system.

With respect to databases in particular, a data flow architecture is one that delivers the instruction tokens to the execution units and returns the data tokens to the content-addressable memory (CAM). (CAM is hardware memory, not the same as RAM.) In contrast to the conventional architecture, data tokens are not permanently stored in memory; rather, they are transient messages that exist only when in transit to the instruction storage. This makes them less likely to be compromised.

Database Systems

In many ways, a database is the Holy Grail for the attacker. It is typically where sensitive information resides. When considering database security, you need to understand the following terms: inference, aggregation, contamination, and data mining warehouse.

Inference

Inference occurs when someone has access to information at one level that allows them to infer information about another level. The main mitigation technique for inference is ***polyinstantiation***, which is the development of a detailed version of an object from another object using different values in the new object.

Polyinstantiation creates multiple instances of a shared resource to prevent a single user or process from contaminating the data required by others. In an operating system, it creates multiple instances of virtual memory or a temporary directory to maintain system security when the resource is accessed by multiple users.

Polyinstantiation in relational database management systems creates a single relation that is mapped to multiple instances of a row of data to assist users with different security levels.

Aggregation

Aggregation is defined as assembling or compiling units of information at one sensitivity level and having the resultant totality of data being of a higher sensitivity level than the individual components. So, you might think of aggregation as a different way of achieving the same goal as inference, which is to learn information about data on a level to which you do not have access.

Contamination

Contamination is the intermingling or mixing of data of one sensitivity or need-to-know level with that of another. Proper implementation of security levels is the best defense against these problems.

Data Mining Warehouse

A ***data warehouse*** is a repository of information from heterogeneous databases. It allows for multiple sources of data to not only be stored in one place but also to be organized in such a way that redundancy of data is reduced (called data normalizing), and more sophisticated data mining tools are used to manipulate the data to discover relationships that may not have been apparent before. Along with the benefits they provide, they also offer more security challenges.

The following control steps should be performed in data warehousing applications:

- Monitor summary tables for regular use.
- Monitor the data purging plan.
- Reconcile data moved between the operations environment and data warehouse.

Cryptographic Systems

By design, cryptographic systems are responsible for encrypting data to prevent data disclosure. Security professionals must ensure that their organization's software and IT systems are using the latest version of a cryptographic algorithm, if possible. Once a compromise of a cryptographic algorithm is known that algorithm should no longer be used.

NOTE Cryptography is discussed in greater detail later in this chapter.

Operational Technology/Industrial Control Systems

Operational Technology (OT) and Industrial Control Systems (ICS) are critical components of modern industrial operations and infrastructure. While they are closely related and often overlap in practice, there are distinct aspects to each. Understanding these differences is essential for effectively securing these systems against potential vulnerabilities and threats.

OT refers to the hardware and software systems designed to monitor and control physical processes, devices, and infrastructure. OT is prevalent in sectors like manufacturing, utilities, transportation, and energy. The primary focus of OT is on maintaining the availability and reliability of the system to ensure continuous operation and physical safety.

OT systems were traditionally isolated and relied on security through obscurity. However, with increased connectivity, OT systems are now exposed to cyber threats that were once exclusive to IT environments. Protecting OT systems involves implementing network segmentation, strict access control, and monitoring of physical access. The use of firewalls, intrusion detection systems (IDSs), and rigorous patch management processes is also critical.

ICS is a subset of OT and specifically focuses on the systems, networks, and devices used to operate and/or automate industrial processes. Examples include Supervisory Control and Data Acquisition (SCADA) systems, Distributed Control Systems (DCS), and Programmable Logic Controllers (PLC). ICS focuses on the direct control and automation of industrial processes. Like OT, the emphasis is on availability, reliability, and safety, but with a strong emphasis on precise control over industrial operations.

ICS includes the following components:

Key Topic

- **Sensors:** Sensors typically have digital or analog I/O and are not in a form that can be easily communicated over long distances.
- **Remote terminal units (RTUs):** RTUs connect to the sensors and convert sensor data to digital data, including telemetry hardware.
- **Programmable logic controllers (PLCs):** PLCs connect to the sensors and convert sensor data to digital data; they do not include telemetry hardware.
- **Telemetry system:** Such a system connects RTUs and PLCs to control centers and the enterprise and are generally used over short distances.
- **Human interface:** Such an interface presents data to the operator.

ICSs should be securely segregated from other networks as a security layer. The Stuxnet virus hit the SCADA used for the control and monitoring of industrial processes. SCADA components are considered privileged targets for cyberattacks. Through the use of cybertools, it is possible to destroy an industrial process. This was the idea used on the attack on the nuclear plant in Natanz in order to interfere with the Iranian nuclear program.

ICS systems can be vulnerable to cyber-physical attacks that not only threaten data integrity and confidentiality but also can cause physical harm or disrupt critical infrastructure. Security measures for ICS include network segmentation, application whitelisting, and the implementation of security protocols that can operate effectively in environments where legacy systems are prevalent. Ensuring secure communication between ICS components and employing real-time monitoring for unusual activities are also key.

When designing security solutions for ICS devices, security professionals should include the following considerations: timeliness and performance requirements, availability requirements, risk management requirements, physical effects, system operation, resource constraints, communications, change management, managed support, component lifetime, and component location.

Considering the criticality of the systems, physical access to SCADA-based systems must be strictly controlled. Systems that integrate IT security with physical access controls like badging systems and video surveillance should be deployed. In addition, the solution should be integrated with existing information security tools such as log management and IPS/IDS. A helpful publication by NIST, SP 800-82, provides recommendations on ICS security. Issues with these emerging systems include

- Required changes to the system may void the warranty.
- Products may be rushed to market, with security an afterthought.
- The return on investment may take decades.
- There is insufficient regulation regarding these systems.

NIST SP 800-82, Rev. 2 provides a guide to ICS security.

According to this publication, the major security objectives for an ICS implementation should include the following:

Key Topic

- Restricting logical access to the ICS network and network activity
- Restricting physical access to the ICS network and devices
- Protecting individual ICS components from exploitation

- Restricting unauthorized modification of data
- Detecting security events and incidents
- Maintaining functionality during adverse conditions
- Restoring the system after an incident

In a typical ICS, this means a defense-in-depth strategy that includes the following:

- Develop security policies, procedures, training, and educational material that apply specifically to the ICS.
- Address security throughout the life cycle of the ICS.
- Implement a network topology for the ICS that has multiple layers, with the most critical communications occurring in the most secure and reliable layer.
- Provide logical separation between the corporate and ICS networks.
- Employ a DMZ network architecture.
- Ensure that critical components are redundant and are on redundant networks.
- Design critical systems for graceful degradation (fault tolerant) to prevent catastrophic cascading events.
- Disable unused ports and services on ICS devices after testing to assure this will not impact ICS operation.
- Restrict physical access to the ICS network and devices.
- Restrict ICS user privileges to only those that are required to perform each person's job.
- Use separate authentication mechanisms and credentials for users of the ICS network and the corporate network.
- Use modern technology, such as smart cards, for Personal Identity Verification (PIV).
- Implement security controls such as intrusion detection software, antivirus software, and file integrity checking software, where technically feasible, to prevent, deter, detect, and mitigate the introduction, exposure, and propagation of malicious software to, within, and from the ICS.
- Apply security techniques such as encryption and/or cryptographic hashes to ICS data storage and communications were determined appropriate.
- Expeditiously deploy security patches after testing all patches under field conditions on a test system if possible, before installation on the ICS.

- Track and monitor audit trails on critical areas of the ICS.
- Employ reliable and secure network protocols and services where feasible.

ICS implementations use a variety of protocols and services, including

- ***Modbus*:** A master/slave protocol that uses port 50
- ***BACnet2*:** A master/slave protocol that uses port 47808
- ***LonWorks/LonTalk3*:** A peer-to-peer protocol that uses port 1679
- ***DNP3*:** A master/slave protocol that uses port 19999 when using Transport Layer Security (TLS) and port 20000 when not using TLS

They can also use IEEE 802.1X, Zigbee, and Bluetooth for communication.

The basic process for developing an ICS security program includes the following:

Key Topic

1. Develop a business case for security.
2. Build and train a cross-functional team.
3. Define charter and scope.
4. Define specific ICS policies and procedures.
5. Implement an ICS Security Risk Management Framework.
   a. Define and inventory ICS assets.
   b. Develop a security plan for ICS systems.
   c. Perform a risk assessment.
   d. Define the mitigation controls.
6. Provide training and raise security awareness for ICS staff.

The ICS security architecture should include network segregation and segmentation, boundary protection, firewalls, a logically separated control network, and dual network interface cards (NICs) and should focus mainly on suitable isolation between control networks and corporate networks.

Both OT and ICS require a security approach that goes beyond traditional IT security practices, emphasizing the protection of physical processes and safety. Assessing and mitigating vulnerabilities in these systems often involves a deep understanding of the specific technologies and processes in use, as well as the potential impacts of cyber threats on physical operations.

While OT encompasses the broader category of technologies managing and controlling physical devices, ICS refers more specifically to the systems controlling industrial processes. The security strategies, therefore, while overlapping, may differ in their application and emphasis, with ICS security measures often requiring more granular control over process execution and data flow.

For security professionals, assessing vulnerabilities in OT and ICS involves understanding the unique operational environments and the integration between IT and OT/ICS networks. The design and architectural vulnerabilities specific to OT/ICS, such as legacy systems that cannot be easily updated or patched, require tailored mitigation strategies that consider both cyber and physical security aspects. Security professionals should also understand that many ISC/SCADA systems use weak or no authentication and outdated operating systems. The inability to patch these systems (and even the lack of available patches) means that the vendor is usually not proactively addressing any identified or newly found security issues. Finally, many authentication systems may have never addressed unauthorized remote access, thereby making it easy for an attacker to breach the system with little effort.

In summary, while OT and ICS share common security concerns due to their focus on controlling and monitoring physical processes, the specific vulnerabilities and mitigation strategies can differ based on the operational context, system complexity, and the nature of the industrial processes controlled. Security professionals should apply a comprehensive and nuanced approach to secure these critical systems, balancing the need for operational continuity, safety, and cybersecurity.

Cloud-Based Systems

Cloud computing is the centralization of data, software, or the computing environment itself that can be accessed using an Internet connection. An organization can create a private cloud environment, or it can pay a vendor to provide this service. A private cloud is considered more secure than a public cloud. Using a public cloud introduces all sorts of security concerns. How do you know your data is kept separate from other customers? How do you know your data is safe? Outsourcing the security of their data makes many organizations uncomfortable.

Cloud computing is all the rage these days, and it comes in many forms. The basic idea of cloud computing is to make resources available via the Internet so the resources can be accessed from anywhere. A company can pay another company to host and manage the cloud environment, or a company can host the environment. Before a cloud deployment model is chosen, the organization must determine the needs of the organization and the security requirements for any data that will be stored in the cloud.

There is a trade-off when a decision must be made between the two architectures. A solution deployed on organizational resources provides the most control over the safety of your data but also requires the staff and the knowledge to deploy, manage, and secure the solution. A cloud solution deployed on a provider's resources puts your data's safety in the hands of a third party, but the third party is often more capable and knowledgeable about protecting data in this environment and managing the cloud environment. The third party's capabilities to protect data should be verified.

Cloud storage locates the data on a central server, but the key difference is that the data is accessible from anywhere and, in many cases, from a variety of device types.

NIST SP 800-145 gives definitions for cloud deployments that IT professionals should understand. Security professionals should be familiar with four cloud deployments:

Key Topic

- ***Private cloud*:** This is a solution owned and managed by one company solely for that company's use. This type of cloud provides the most control and security but also requires the biggest investment in both hardware and expertise.
- ***Public cloud*:** This is a solution provided by a third party. It offloads the details to that third party but gives up some control and can introduce security issues. Typically, you are a tenant sharing space with others, and in many cases you don't know where your data is being kept physically.
- ***Hybrid cloud*:** This is some combination of private and public. For example, perhaps you only use the facilities of the provider but still manage the data yourself.
- ***Community cloud*:** This is a solution owned and managed by a group of organizations that creates the cloud for a common purpose, perhaps to address a common concern such as regularity compliance.

When a public solution is selected, various levels of service can be purchased. Some of these levels include

Key Topic

- ***Infrastructure as a Service (IaaS)*:** Involves the vendor providing the hardware platform or data center and the company installing and managing its own operating systems and application systems. The vendor simply provides access to the data center and maintains that access.
- ***Platform as a Service (PaaS)*:** Involves the vendor providing the hardware platform or data center and the software running on the platform. This includes the operating systems and infrastructure software. The company is still involved in managing the system.

- ***Software as a Service (SaaS)***: Involves the vendor providing the entire solution. This includes the applications and data. This software includes the user-facing software, not just the infrastructure software. It might provide you with an email system, for example, whereby the vendor hosts and manages everything for you.

Figure 3-7 shows the relationships of these services to one another.

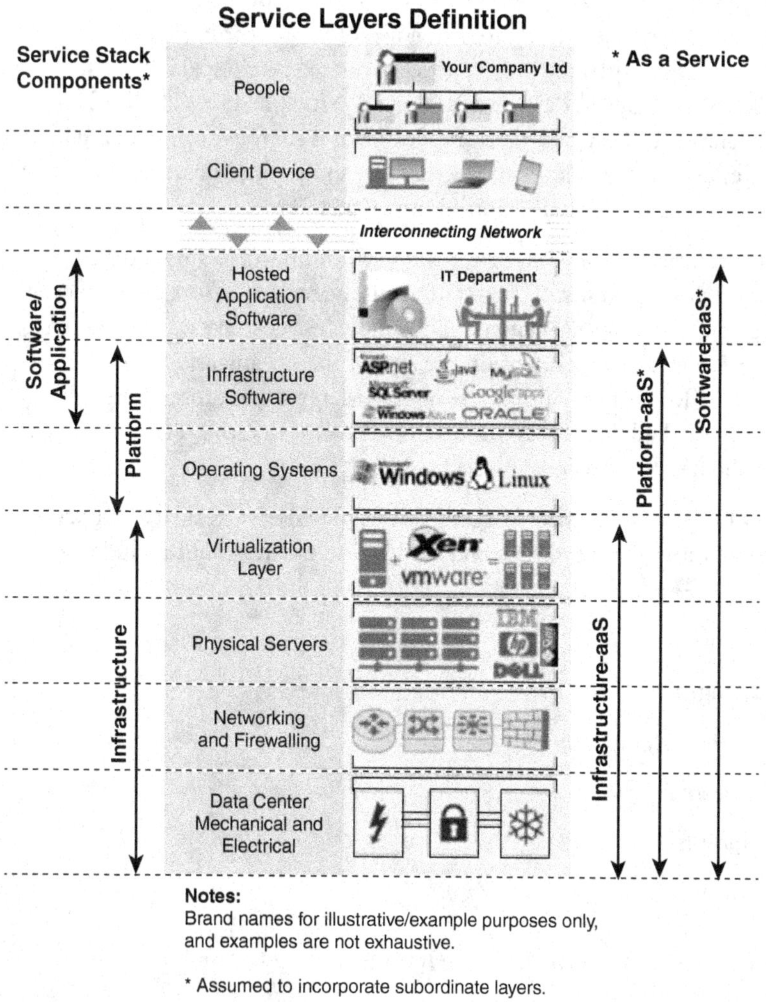

Figure 3-7 Cloud Computing

NIST SP 800-144 gives guidelines on security and privacy in public cloud computing. This publication defines two types of cloud computing service contracts: predefined non-negotiable agreements and negotiated agreements. Non-negotiable agreements are in many ways the basis for the economies of scale enjoyed by public cloud computing. The terms of service are prescribed completely by the cloud provider. They are typically not written with attention to federal privacy and security requirements. Furthermore, with some offerings, the provider can make modifications to the terms of service unilaterally (e.g., by posting an updated version online) without giving any direct notification to the cloud consumer. However, the service provider usually provides notification via an email and posted online.

Negotiated service agreements are more like traditional outsourcing contracts for information technology services. They are often used to address an organization's concerns about security and privacy policy, procedures, and technical controls, such as the vetting of employees, data ownership and exit rights, breach notification, isolation of tenant applications, data encryption and segregation, tracking and reporting service effectiveness, compliance with laws and regulations, and the use of validated products meeting national or international standards.

Critical data and applications may require an agency to undertake a negotiated service agreement. Because points of negotiation can negatively affect the service agreement, a negotiated service agreement is normally less cost effective. The outcome of a negotiation is also dependent on the size of the organization and the influence it can exert. Regardless of the type of service agreement, obtaining adequate legal and technical advice is recommended to ensure that the terms of service adequately meet the needs of the organization.

Potential areas of improvement where organizations may derive security and privacy benefits from transitioning to a public cloud computing environment include the following:

- Staff specialization
- Platform strength
- Resource availability
- Backup and recovery
- Mobile endpoints
- Data concentration

Some of the more fundamental concerns when transitioning to a public cloud include the following:

- System complexity
- Shared multitenant environment

- Internet-facing
- Loss of control

Table 3-4 provides a list of security and privacy issues and recommendations for public cloud deployments from NIST SP 800-144.

Key Topic

Table 3-4 NIST SP 800-144 Cloud Security and Privacy Issues and Recommendations

Areas	Recommendations
Governance	Extend organizational practices pertaining to the policies, procedures, and standards used for application development and service provisioning in the cloud, as well as the design, implementation, testing, use, and monitoring of deployed or engaged services. Put in place audit mechanisms and tools to ensure organizational practices are followed throughout the system life cycle.
Compliance	Understand the various types of laws and regulations that impose security and privacy obligations on the organization and potentially impact cloud computing initiatives, particularly those involving data location, privacy and security controls, records management, and electronic discovery requirements. Review and assess the cloud provider's offerings with respect to the organizational requirements to be met and ensure that the contract terms adequately meet the requirements. Ensure that the cloud provider's electronic discovery capabilities and processes do not compromise the privacy or security of data and applications.
Trust	Ensure that service arrangements have sufficient means to allow visibility into the security and privacy controls and processes employed by the cloud provider, and their performance over time. Establish clear, exclusive ownership rights over data. Institute a risk management program that is flexible enough to adapt to the constantly evolving and shifting risk landscape for the life cycle of the system. Continuously monitor the security state of the information system to support ongoing risk management decisions.
Architecture	Understand the underlying technologies that the cloud provider uses to provision services, including the implications that the technical controls involved have on the security and privacy of the system, over the full system life cycle and across all system components.

Areas	Recommendations
Identity and Access Management	Ensure that adequate safeguards are in place to secure authentication, authorization, and other identity and access management functions, and are suitable for the organization.
Software Isolation	Understand virtualization and other logical isolation techniques that the cloud provider employs in its multitenant software architecture, and assess the risks involved for the organization.
Data Protection	Evaluate the suitability of the cloud provider's data management solutions for the organizational data concerned and the ability to control access to data, to secure data while at rest, in transit, and in use, and to sanitize data. Take into consideration the risk of collating organizational data with that of other organizations whose threat profiles are high or whose data collectively represent significant concentrated value. Fully understand and weigh the risks involved in cryptographic key management with the facilities available in the cloud environment and the processes established by the cloud provider.
Availability	Understand the contract provisions and procedures for availability, data backup and recovery, and disaster recovery, and ensure that they meet the organization's continuity and contingency planning requirements. Ensure that during an intermediate or prolonged disruption or a serious disaster, critical operations can be immediately resumed, and that all operations can be eventually reinstituted in a timely and organized manner.
Incident Response	Understand the contract provisions and procedures for incident response and ensure that they meet the requirements of the organization. Ensure that the cloud provider has a transparent response process in place and sufficient mechanisms to share information during and after an incident. Ensure that the organization can respond to incidents in a coordinated fashion with the cloud provider in accordance with their respective roles and responsibilities for the computing environment.

Another NIST publication, NIST SP 800-146, gives a cloud computing synopsis and recommendations.

NIST SP 800-146 lists the following benefits of SaaS deployments:

Key Topic

- Very modest software tool footprint
- Efficient use of software licenses
- Centralized management and data
- Platform responsibilities managed by providers
- Savings in up-front costs

NIST SP 800-146 lists the following issues and concerns of SaaS deployments:

- Browser-based risks and risk remediation
- Network dependence
- Lack of portability between SaaS clouds
- Isolation vs. efficiency (security vs. cost trade-offs)

NIST SP 800-146 gives a single benefit of PaaS deployments:

- Facilitated scalable application development and deployment

The issues and concerns of PaaS deployments are as follows:

- Lack of portability between PaaS clouds
- Event-based processor scheduling
- Security engineering of PaaS applications

NIST SP 800-146 lists the following benefits of IaaS deployments:

- Full control of the computing resource through administrative access to VMs
- Flexible, efficient renting of computing hardware
- Portability and interoperability with legacy applications

The issues and concerns of IaaS deployments are as follows:

- Compatibility with legacy security vulnerabilities
- Virtual machine sprawl
- Verifying authenticity of an IaaS cloud provider website
- Robustness of VM-level isolation
- Features for dynamic network configuration for providing isolation
- Data erase practices

Large-Scale Parallel Data Systems

Most large-scale parallel data systems have been designed to handle scientific and industrial problems, such as air traffic control, ballistic missile defense, satellite-collected image analysis, missile guidance, and weather forecasting. They require enormous processing power. Because data in these systems is being analyzed so quickly, it is often difficult to detect and prevent an attempted intrusion. These types of systems must find a way to split the queries across multiple parallel nodes so the queries can be processed in parallel.

Because these parallel data systems often span multiple organizations, security professionals must consider the areas of trust, privacy, and general security any time their organizations operate within large-scale parallel data systems. Trust-related issues such as the following need to be considered in trusted networks:

- Cryptographic key verification
- Trust-based denial-of-service (DoS) and distributed DoS (DDoS) attack mitigation
- Data leakage detection

Privacy-related issues that need to be considered include the following:

- Remote authentication
- Decentralized access control
- Traffic masking
- Large-scale dataset cryptography

Other general security issues that need to be considered include inconsistent user credentials and authorization and data sharing issues related to using cryptography.

Distributed Systems

Distributed systems are discussed in the "Computing Platforms" section earlier in this chapter.

Grid Computing

Grid computing is the process of harnessing the CPU power of multiple physical machines to perform a job. In some cases, individual systems might be allowed to leave and rejoin the grid. Although the advantage of additional processing power is great, there has to be concern for the security of data that could be present on machines that are entering and leaving the grid without proper authentication and authorization. Therefore, grid computing is not necessarily a safe implementation when secrecy of the data is a key issue.

Peer-to-Peer Computing

Any client/server solution in which any platform/system may act as a client or server or both is called ***peer-to-peer computing***. A widely used example of this is instant messaging (IM). These implementations present security issues that do not present themselves in a standard client/server arrangement. In many cases these systems operate outside the normal control of the network administrators.

This situation can present problems such as the following:

- Viruses, worms, and Trojan horses can be transmitted through this entry point to the network.
- In many cases, lack of strong authentication allows for account spoofing.
- Buffer overflow attacks and attacks using malformed packets can sometimes be successful.

If these systems must be tolerated in the environment, security professionals should follow these guidelines:

- Security policies should address the proper use of these applications.
- All systems should have a firewall and antivirus products installed.
- Configure firewalls to block unwanted IM traffic.
- If possible, allow only products that provide encryption.

Internet of Things

The ***Internet of Things (IoT)*** refers to a system of interrelated computing devices, mechanical and digital machines, and objects that are provided with unique identifiers and the ability to transfer data over a network without requiring human-to-human or human-to-computer interaction. The IoT has presented attackers with a new medium through which to carry out an attack. Often the developers of the IoT devices add the IoT functionality without thoroughly considering the security implications of such functionality or without building in any security controls to protect the IoT devices.

NOTE *IoT* is a term for all physical objects, or "things," that are now embedded with electronics, software, and network connectivity. Thanks to the IoT, these objects—including automobiles, kitchen appliances, and heating and air-conditioning controllers—can collect and exchange data. Unfortunately, engineers give most of these objects this ability just for convenience and without any real consideration of the security impacts. When these objects are then deployed, consumers do not think of security either. The result is consumer convenience but also risk. As the IoT evolves, security professionals must be increasingly involved in the IoT evolution to help ensure that security controls are designed to protect these objects and the data they collect and transmit.

IoT Examples

IoT deployments include a wide variety of devices but are broadly categorized into five groups:

- **Smart home:** Includes products that are used in the home. They range from personal assistance devices, such as Amazon's Alexa, to HVAC components, such as the Nest Thermostat. The goals of these devices are home management and automation.
- **Wearables:** Includes products that are worn by users. They range from watches, such as the Apple Watch, to personal fitness devices, like the Fitbit.
- **Smart cities:** Includes devices that help resolve traffic congestion issues and reduce noise, crime, and pollution. They include smart energy, smart transportation, smart data, smart infrastructure, and smart mobility.
- **Connected cars:** Includes vehicles that have Internet access and data-sharing capabilities. They include GPS devices, OnStar, and AT&T-connected cars.
- **Business automation:** Includes devices that automate HVAC, lighting, access control, and fire detection for organizations.

Methods of Securing IoT Devices

Security professionals must understand the different methods of securing IoT devices. The following are some recommendations:

- Secure and centralize the access logs of IoT devices.
- Use encrypted protocols to secure communication.
- Create and implement secure password policies.
- Implement restrictive network communications policies, and set up virtual LANs.
- Regularly update device firmware based on vendor recommendations.

When selecting IoT devices, particularly those that are implemented at the organizational level, security professionals need to look into the following:

- Does the vendor design explicitly for privacy and security?
- Does the vendor have a bug bounty program and vulnerability reporting system?
- Does the device have default or manual overrides or special functions for disconnected operations?

NIST Framework for Cyber-Physical Systems

Cyber-physical systems (CPS) are smart systems that include engineered interacting networks of physical and computational components. These highly interconnected and integrated systems provide new functionalities to improve quality of life and enable technological advances in critical areas, such as personalized healthcare, emergency response, traffic flow management, smart manufacturing, defense and homeland security, and energy supply and use. In addition to CPS, there are many words and phrases (Industrial Internet, IoT, machine-to-machine [M2M], smart cities, and others) that describe similar or related systems and concepts. There is significant overlap between these concepts, in particular CPS and IoT, such that CPS and IoT are sometimes used interchangeably; therefore, the approach described in NIST's CPS Framework should be considered to be equally applicable to IoT.

The CPS Framework includes domains, aspects, and facets, as shown in Figure 3-8.

Key Topic

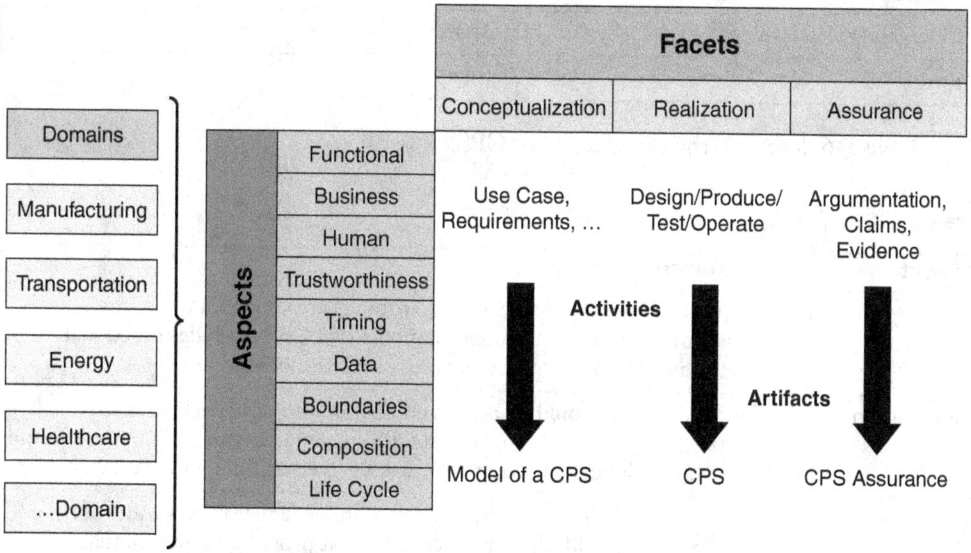

Figure 3-8 NIST CPS Framework (Image Courtesy of NIST)

Domains represent the different application areas of CPS and include all those listed in Table 3-5. This list is expected to expand as new CPS and IoT devices are launched.

Table 3-5 CPS Domains

Domains	
Advertising	Entertainment/sports
Aerospace	Environmental monitoring
Agriculture	Financial services
Buildings	Healthcare
Cities	Infrastructure (communications, power, water)
Communities	Leisure
Consumer	Manufacturing
Defense	Science
Disaster resilience	Social networks
Education	Supply chain/retail
Emergency response	Transportation
Energy	Weather

Table 3-6 describes the three facets of CPS.

Table 3-6 CPS Facets

Facet	**Description**
Conceptualization	What things should be and what things are supposed to do: the set of activities that produce a model of a CPS (includes functional decomposition, requirements, and logical models).
Realization	How things should be made and operate: the set of activities that produce, deploy, and operate a CPS (includes engineering trade-offs and detailed designs in the critical path to the creation of a CPS instance).
Assurance	How to achieve a desired level of confidence that things will work the way they should: the set of activities that provide confidence that a CPS performs as specified (includes claims, evidence, and argumentation).

Table 3-7 lists the different aspects of the CPS Framework.

Table 3-7 CPS Framework Aspects

Aspect	**Description**
Functional	Concerns about function including sensing, actuation, control, communications, physicality, and so on.
Business	Concerns about enterprise, time to market, environment, regulation, cost, and so on.

Aspect	Description
Human	Concerns about human interaction with and as part of a CPS.
Trustworthiness	Concerns about trustworthiness of CPS including security, privacy, safety, reliability, and resilience.
Timing	Concerns about time and frequency in CPS, including the generation and transport of time and frequency signals, timestamping, managing latency, timing composability, and so on.
Data	Concerns about data interoperability including fusion, metadata, type, identity, and so on.
Boundaries	Concerns related to demarcations of topological, functional, organizational, or other forms of interactions.
Composition	Concerns related to the ability to compute selected properties of a component assembly from the properties of its components. Compositionality requires components that are composable: they do not change their properties in an assembly. Timing composability is particularly difficult.
Life cycle	Concerns about the life cycle of CPS including its components.

To learn more about the CPS Framework and other IoT initiatives from NIST, go to https://www.nist.gov/itl/applied-cybersecurity/nist-cybersecurity-iot-program/related-initiatives-nist.

Microservices

Microservices is a term for an application design technique whereby developers design highly scalable, flexible applications by decomposing the application into discrete services that implement specific business functions. These services, often referred to as "loosely coupled," can then be built, deployed, and scaled independently.

Microservices are based on container technology. Security professionals should ensure that security is deployed at the container level. Containers are based on baseline images, which may contain vulnerabilities. Organizations should perform regular scans of container images to ensure the images do not contain security issues. To protect containers at runtime, organizations should adopt the principle of least privilege.

Microservices should also be secured by creating one entry point, which all clients and systems access, and which can easily be secured. This entry point is called an API gateway. The API gateway performs authentication and authorization, and filters requests to sensitive resources.

Using microservices, each service is a separate, isolated application and remains an isolated application by itself. Programmers should be able to implement, maintain, modify, extend, and update microservices without affecting other microservices. Isolation should also be performed at other layers of the infrastructure, such as the database.

Containerization

Containerization is the use of containers to isolate and maintain an application. All resources that the application requires to run are placed inside that container. When an application is contained, you can pick it up and move it around regardless of the host operating system if a virtualization host is deployed.

Organizations can run software without worrying about operating systems or dependencies. Because an operating system runs underneath the containerization platform, developers do not have to build a production environment with the right settings and libraries. These are built into the container. Containers are not dependent on the underlying OS and are more portable than virtual machines.

Container isolation provides security benefits. However, isolation does not make a container safe by default. If attackers can find a container escape flaw, this flaw can be used to gain access to sensitive data in other containers. Also, container platforms often do not take advantage of network segmentation. Without network segmentation, an attacker can more easily cross from one compromised container to other vulnerable ones on the same network.

Because containers are portable and easy to set up, attackers can create their own malware-laden containers and upload them to public resources. Before running containers, security professionals should understand the source and assess the container's security to ensure it is trustworthy and not opening the organization's network for attackers.

Security professionals must update and securely configure the host OS, harden the containerization layers and any orchestration software, and configure accounts based on the principle of least privilege. Otherwise, attackers will focus on insecurely configured containerization layers. In addition, security professionals should ensure protections are in place for all sensitive information, such as credentials, API keys, and tokens at every level: the containerization platform, orchestration platforms, and the individual containers.

Serverless Systems

Serverless is a term used for a model wherein applications rely on managed services that do away with the need to manage, patch, and secure infrastructure and virtual machines. This is most commonly seen deployed in the cloud. Serverless systems have many vulnerabilities of which security professionals must be aware.

Any misconfigurations may open an unexpected vulnerability for attacks against serverless architectures. With many independent functions and services, security professionals should ensure that the principle of least privilege is followed for all user accounts. In addition, the privileges of functions should be properly configured because privilege escalation is considered a potential security threat.

Injection flaws in applications are one of the most common security risks. They include untrusted inputs in application calls, cloud storage event triggers, NoSQL databases, and code changes.

Monitoring and logging in serverless systems must be properly configured as if these systems were physical systems. In addition, any third-party dependencies must be documented and the security of them verified.

Developers should implement meaningful error messages and enable the debugging mode. But these should be disabled when the application is moved to production because they may reveal information about serverless functions and the logic used. These meaningful error messages should not show any configuration, setup, or file location information.

High-Performance Computing Systems

High-Performance Computing (HPC) systems process data and perform complex calculations at high speeds. One of the best-known types of HPC solutions is the supercomputer. Another example of an HPC is a cluster.

By definition, clusters are closely-coupled machines that are centrally administered and share common resources, such as storage. Security professionals should secure these internal distributed resources against unauthorized access, while at the same time allowing easy access by legitimate users.

It can often be difficult to differentiate legitimate versus illegitimate use unless there are obvious malicious process signatures. In addition, security must be coordinated across different node platforms and different specialized function nodes in an HPC system. Tools to automate security management need to be aware of the similarities and differences present among HPC system resources.

The security of the resources in an HPC system is dependent on the integrity of all nodes. A single compromised node represents a dramatic risk increase to the rest of the nodes due to the fact that many nodes share identical configurations.

Edge Computing Systems

Edge computing systems are part of a distributed computing topology that brings computation and data storage closer to the devices where it's being gathered, primarily on the edge of the network perimeter, rather than relying on a central location far away. Edge computing devices are often small, lacking built-in security, and without automatic updates. They are often an easy entry point into the network, which can then be used to access main systems.

Security professionals should ensure that edge computing systems are protected against digital and physical attacks. Employing security by design is basic to securing edge computing systems. Poorly configured and poorly secured edge computing systems provide attackers more opportunities to disrupt operations or to gain access to the broader enterprise network. If the edge computing systems interact with the service provider edge, organizations should examine the service provider's security processes, service-level agreements (SLAs), and architecture alignment. Employing zero trust will ensure that untrusted devices will be more easily detectable.

Virtualized Systems

Today physical servers are increasingly being consolidated as virtual servers on the same physical box. Virtual networks using virtual switches even exist in the physical devices that host these virtual servers. These virtual network systems and their traffic can be segregated in all the same ways as in a physical network using subnets, VLANs, and of course, virtual firewalls. Virtual firewalls are software that has been specifically written to operate in the virtual environment. Increasingly, virtualization vendors such as VMware are making part of their code available to security vendors to create firewalls (and antivirus products) that integrate closely with the product.

Keep in mind that in any virtual environment each virtual server that is hosted on the physical server must be configured with its own security mechanisms. These mechanisms include antivirus and anti-malware software and all the latest service packs and security updates for *all* the software hosted on the virtual machine. Also, remember that all the virtual servers share the resources of the physical device.

Vulnerabilities in Web-Based Systems

Despite all efforts to design a secure web architecture, attacks to a web-based system still occur and still succeed. In the following sections, we examine some of the more common types of attacks, including maintenance hooks, time-of-check/time-of-use attacks, and web-based attacks. We also explore XML and SAML vulnerabilities and OWASP, a resource dedicated to defending against web-based attacks.

Maintenance Hooks

From the perspective of software development, a ***maintenance hook*** is a set of instructions built into the code that allows someone who knows about the so-called backdoor to use the instructions to connect to view and edit the code without using the normal access controls. In many cases, maintenance hooks are placed in an application to make it easier for the vendor to load patches, fix bugs, and/or otherwise provide software support to the customer. In other cases, maintenance hooks can be used in testing and tracking the activities of the product and not removed when the application is deployed.

NOTE A maintenance account is often confused with a maintenance hook. A maintenance account is an account created by programmers to give an administrator or developer full permissions in a particular application or operating system. A maintenance account can usually be deleted or disabled easily, but a true maintenance hook is often a hidden part of the programming and needs a program revision to disable it. Both of these are considered potential security issues because many attackers try the documented maintenance hooks and maintenance accounts first to gain access to a program. You would be surprised at the number of computers attacked on a daily basis because these two security issues are left unaddressed.

Regardless of how the maintenance hooks got into the code, they can present a major security issue if they become known to hackers who can use them to access the system. It is also a vulnerability if the original coder of the maintenance hook becomes a disgruntled employee. Hooks should be regularly monitored, updated, and removed as employees move into and out of the projects and organizations. Countermeasures on the part of the customer to mitigate the danger are

- Use a host-based IDS to record any attempts to access the system using one of these hooks.
- Encrypt all sensitive information contained in the system.
- Implement auditing to supplement the IDS.

The best solution is for the vendor to remove all maintenance hooks before the product goes into production. Code reviews should be performed as one method to identify and remove these hooks.

Time-of-Check/Time-of-Use Attacks

Time-of-check/time-of-use attacks attempt to take advantage of the sequence of events that occurs as the system completes common tasks. It relies on knowledge of the dependencies present when a specific series of events occurs in multiprocessing systems. By attempting to insert themselves between events and introduce changes, hackers can gain control of the result.

A term often used as a synonym for a time-of-check/time-of-use attack is *race condition*, which is actually a different attack. In this attack, hackers insert themselves between instructions, introduce changes, and alter the order of execution of the instructions, thereby altering the outcome.

Countermeasures to these attacks are to make critical sets of instructions atomic, known as all or nothing. This means that they either execute in order and in entirety, or the changes they make are rolled back or prevented. It is also best for the system to lock access to certain items it will use or touch when carrying out these sets of instructions.

Web-Based Attacks

Attacks upon information security infrastructures have continued to evolve steadily over time, and the latest attacks use largely more sophisticated web application–based attacks. These attacks have proven more difficult to defend with traditional approaches using perimeter firewalls.

XML

Extensible Markup Language (XML) is the most widely used web language now and has come under some criticism. The method currently used to sign data to verify its authenticity has been described as inadequate by some, and the other criticisms have been directed at the architecture of XML security in general. Next, we discuss an extension of this language that attempts to address some of these concerns.

SAML

Security Assertion Markup Language (SAML) is an XML-based open standard data format for exchanging authentication and authorization data between parties, in particular between an identity provider and a service provider. SAML allows the user to have a portable identity for authentication and authorization on the Internet. The major issue on which it focuses is called the web browser single sign-on (SSO) problem.

SSO is the ability to authenticate once to access multiple sets of data. SSO at the Internet level is usually accomplished with cookies, but extending the concept beyond the Internet has resulted in many propriety approaches that are not interoperable. SAML's goal is to create a standard for this process.

OWASP

The ***Open Web Application Security Project (OWASP)*** is an open-source application security project. This group creates guidelines, testing procedures, and tools to assist with web security. They are also known for maintaining a top-10 list of web application security risks. Information on OWASP can be obtained from www.owasp.org.

Vulnerabilities in Mobile Systems

As mobile devices have become more popular, security issues related to those devices have increased. Security professionals face unique challenges due to the increasing use of mobile devices combined with the fact that many of these devices connect using public networks with little or no security.

Educating users on the risks related to mobile devices and ensuring that they implement appropriate security measures can help protect against threats involved with these devices. Some of the guidelines that should be provided to mobile device users include implementing a device-locking PIN, using device encryption, implementing GPS location services, and implementing remote wiping. Also, users should be cautioned about downloading apps without ensuring that they are coming from a reputable source. In recent years, mobile device management (MDM) and mobile application management (MAM) systems have become popular in enterprises. These systems are implemented to ensure that an organization can control mobile device settings, applications, and other parameters when those devices are attached to the enterprise.

The threats presented by the introduction of personal mobile devices (smartphones and tablets) to an organization's network include

- Insecure web browsing
- Insecure Wi-Fi connectivity
- Lost or stolen devices holding company data
- Corrupt application downloads and installations
- Missing security patches
- Constant upgrading of personal devices
- Use of location services

While the most common types of corporate information stored on personal devices are corporate emails and company contact information, it is alarming to note that almost half of these devices also contain customer data, network login credentials, and corporate data accessed through business applications.

The main issues regarding mobile systems are device security, application security, and mobile device concerns. Also, we cover NIST SP 800-164, which provides guidelines for mobile devices.

Device Security

Device security involves the physical security of the mobile device. In the event that a device is lost or stolen, users also need the capability to remotely track and lock the device. Some of the recommendations for device security include

- Locking your phone with a password or biometric detection
- Encrypting your data
- Setting up remote wipe
- Backing up phone, credit card, pictures, and other personal data
- Avoiding jail-breaking your iPhone or rooting your Android
- Updating the operating system as updates are available
- Being aware of social engineering scams
- Using public Wi-Fi with added caution

Application Security

Although device security is important for mobile devices, application security is just as important. Users should download approved apps only from the vendor application stores. Some of the recommendations for application security include

- Avoiding untested, unapproved, unknown, or vulnerable third-party apps
- Being aware of social engineering scams
- Downloading reputable and proven-to-work anti-malware for your mobile device

Mobile Device Concerns

To address these issues and to meet the rising demand to bring and use personal devices, many organizations have created bring-your-own-device (BYOD) policies. In supporting a BYOD initiative, a security professional should consider that careless users are a greater threat than hackers. Not only are users less than diligent in maintaining security updates and patches on devices, but they also buy new devices as often as they change clothes. These factors make it difficult to maintain control over the security of the networks in which these devices are allowed to operate.

Other initiatives today include company-owned, business only (COBO), company-owned, personally enabled (COPE), and choose-your-own-device (CYOD) deployments. No matter which deployment an organization uses, security professionals must ensure that the risks of each model are understood and that the appropriate policies are in place to protect company data and assets. Security professionals are responsible for ensuring that management understands these risks and implements the appropriate tools to control access to the enterprise.

Centralized mobile device management tools are a fast-growing solution. Some of these tools leverage the messaging server's management capabilities, and others are third-party tools that can manage multiple brands of devices. Systems Manager by Cisco is one example that integrates with the Cisco Meraki cloud services. Another example for iOS devices is the Apple Configurator. One of the challenges with implementing such a system is that not all personal devices may support native encryption and/or the management process.

Typically, centralized mobile device management tools handle company-issued and personal mobile devices differently. For organization-issued devices, a mobile device management application typically manages the configuration and security of the mobile device.

Regardless of whether a centralized mobile device management tool is in use, a BYOD policy should include the following in the organization's security policy:

- Identify the allowed uses of personal devices on the corporate network.
- Create a list of allowed applications on the devices and design a method of preventing the installation of applications not on the list (for example, software restriction policies).
- Ensure that high levels of management are on board and supportive.
- Train and regularly enforce policies for user devices. Noncompliance should result in eviction of the personal device from the enterprise network.

In the process of deploying and supporting a mobile solution, follow these guidelines:

- Ensure that the selected solution supports applying security controls remotely.
- Ensure that the selected vendor has a good track record of publicizing and correcting security flaws.
- Make the deployment of an MDM tool a top priority.

- In the absence of an MDM system, design a process to ensure that all devices are kept up to date on security patches.
- Update the policy as technology and behaviors change.
- Require all employees to agree to allow remote wiping of any stolen or lost devices.
- Strictly forbid rooted (Android) or jail-broken (iOS) devices from accessing the network.
- If possible, choose a product that supports:
    - Encrypting the solid state drive (SSD) and nonvolatile RAM
    - Requiring a PIN to access the device
    - Locking the device when a specific number of incorrect PINs are attempted

As with many of the other security issues discussed in this book, user education is key. A security professional must ensure that users understand the importance of mobile device security.

If an organization does not implement an MDM or MAM solution, the mobile device security policy should include, at minimum, the following policies:

- Implement anti-malware/antivirus software on all mobile devices.
- Use only secure communications.
- Use strong authentication.
- Require a PIN or some other login mechanism with each use of the device after a certain idle period (no more than 10 minutes of inactivity).
- Limit third-party software.
- Implement GPS and other location services.
- Enable remote locking and remote wiping features.
- Never leave the device unattended.
- Immediately report any missing or stolen device.
- Disable all unnecessary options, applications, and services, including Bluetooth.
- Regularly back up data.
- Install all updates from the device manufacturer.

NIST SP 800-164

NIST SP 800-164 is a draft Special Publication that gives guidelines on hardware-rooted security in mobile devices. It defines three required security components for mobile devices: Roots of Trust (RoTs), an application programming interface (API) to expose the RoTs to the platform, and a Policy Enforcement Engine (PEnE).

Roots of Trust are the foundation of assurance of the trustworthiness of a mobile device. RoTs must always behave in an expected manner because their misbehavior cannot be detected. Hardware RoTs are preferred over software RoTs due to their immutability, smaller attack surfaces, and more reliable behavior. They can provide a higher degree of assurance that they can be relied upon to perform their trusted function or functions. Software RoTs could provide the benefit of quick deployment to different platforms. To support device integrity, isolation, and protected storage, devices should implement the following RoTs:

- Root of Trust for Storage (RTS)
- Root of Trust for Verification (RTV)
- Root of Trust for Integrity (RTI)
- Root of Trust for Reporting (RTR)
- Root of Trust for Measurement (RTM)

The RoTs need to be exposed by the operating system to applications through an open API. This exposure will provide application developers a set of security services and capabilities they can use to secure their applications and protect the data they process. By providing an abstracted layer of security services and capabilities, these APIs can reduce the burden on application developers to implement low-level security features, and instead allow them to reuse trusted components provided in the RoTs and the OS. The APIs should be standardized within a given mobile platform and, to the extent possible, across platforms. Applications can use the APIs, and the associated RoTs, to request device integrity reports, protect data through encryption services provided by the RTS, and store and retrieve authentication credentials and other sensitive data.

The PEnE enforces policies on the device with the help of other device components and enables the processing, maintenance, and management of policies on both the device and in the information owners' environments. The PEnE provides information owners with the ability to express the control they require over their information. The PEnE needs to be trusted to implement the information owner's requirements correctly and to prevent one information owner's requirements from adversely affecting another's. To perform key functions, the PEnE needs to be able to query the device's configuration and state.

Mobile devices should implement the following three mobile security capabilities to address the challenges with mobile device security:

- **Device integrity:** Device integrity is the absence of corruption in the hardware, firmware, and software of a device. A mobile device can provide evidence that it has maintained device integrity if its software, firmware, and hardware configurations can be shown to be in a state that is trusted by a relying party.
- **Isolation:** Isolation prevents unintended interaction between applications and information contexts on the same device.
- **Protected storage:** Protected storage preserves the confidentiality and integrity of data on the device while at rest, while in use (in the event an unauthorized application attempts to access an item in protected storage), and upon revocation of access.

Vulnerabilities in Embedded Systems

An embedded system is a computer system with a dedicated function within a larger system, often with real-time computing constraints. It is embedded as part of the device, often including hardware and mechanical parts. Embedded systems control many devices in common use today and include systems embedded in cars, HVAC systems, security alarms, and even lighting systems. Machine-to-machine (M2M) communication, the Internet of Things (IoT), and remotely controlled industrial systems have increased the number of connected devices and simultaneously made these devices targets.

Because embedded systems are usually placed within another device without input from a security professional, security is not even built into the device. So while allowing the device to communicate over the Internet with a diagnostic system provides a great service to the consumer, oftentimes the manufacturer has not considered that a hacker can then reverse communication and take over the device with the embedded system. As of this writing, reports have surfaced of individuals being able to take control of vehicles using their embedded systems. Manufacturers have released patches that address such issues, but not all vehicle owners have applied or even know about the patches.

As M2M and IoT increase in popularity, security professionals can expect to see a rise in incidents like this. A security professional is expected to understand the vulnerabilities these systems present and how to put controls in place to reduce an organization's risk.

Cryptographic Solutions

While security architecture and engineering involves securing all the devices that an organization implements, it is not enough just to secure the devices. Organizations must also secure the data as it resides on the devices and as it is transmitted over the network. Cryptography involves using algorithms to protect data. The following sections discuss cryptography concepts, cryptography history, cryptosystem features, cryptographic mathematics, and cryptographic life cycle.

Cryptography Concepts

A security professional should understand many terms and concepts related to cryptography.

These terms are often used when discussing cryptography:

Key Topic

- ***Encryption***: The process of converting data from plaintext to ciphertext. Also referred to as enciphering.
- ***Decryption***: The process of converting data from ciphertext to plaintext. Also referred to as deciphering.
- ***Key***: A parameter that controls the transformation of plaintext into ciphertext or vice versa. Determining the original plaintext data without the key is impossible. Keys can be both public and private. Also referred to as a ***cryptovariable***.
- ***Synchronous***: When encryption or decryption occurs immediately.
- ***Asynchronous***: When encryption or decryption requests are processed from a queue. This method utilizes hardware and multiple processors in the process.
- ***Symmetric***: An encryption method whereby the same private key both encrypts and decrypts the data. Also referred to as ***private*** or ***secret key encryption***.
- ***Asymmetric***: An encryption method whereby a key pair, one private key and one public key, performs encryption and decryption. One key performs the encryption, whereas the other key performs the decryption. Also referred to as ***public key encryption***.
- ***Digital signature***: A method of providing sender authentication and message integrity. The message acts as an input to a hash function, and the sender's private key encrypts the hash value. The receiver can perform a hash computation on the received message to determine the validity of the message.
- ***Hash***: A one-way function that reduces a message to a hash value. A comparison of the sender's hash value to the receiver's hash value determines message integrity. If the resultant hash values are different, then the message has been

altered in some way, provided that both the sender and receiver used the same hash function.

- ***Digital certificate***: An electronic document that identifies the certificate holder.
- ***Plaintext***: A message in its original format. Also referred to as ***cleartext***.
- ***Ciphertext***: An altered form of a message that is unreadable without knowing the key and the encryption system used. Also referred to as a ***cryptogram***.
- ***Cryptosystem***: The entire cryptographic process, including the algorithm, key, and key management functions. The security of a cryptosystem is measured by the size of the keyspace and available computational power.
- ***Cryptanalysis***: The science of decrypting ciphertext without prior knowledge of the key or cryptosystem used. The purpose of cryptanalysis is to forge coded signals or messages that will be accepted as authentic signals or messages.
- ***Key clustering***: The grouping that occurs when different encryption keys generate the same ciphertext from the same plaintext message.
- ***Keyspace***: All the possible key values when using a particular algorithm or other security measure. A 40-bit key would have 2^{40} possible values, whereas a 128-bit key would have 2^{128} possible values.
- ***Collision***: An event that occurs when a hash function produces the same hash value on different messages.
- ***Algorithm***: A mathematical function that encrypts and decrypts data. Also referred to as a ***cipher***.
- ***Cryptology***: The science that studies encrypted communication and data.
- ***Encoding***: The process of changing data into another form using code.
- ***Decoding***: The process of changing an encoded message back into its original format.
- ***Transposition***: The process of shuffling or reordering the plaintext to hide the original message. Also referred to as ***permutation***. For example, AEEGMSS is a transposed version of MESSAGE.
- ***Substitution***: The process of exchanging one byte in a message for another. For example, ABCCDEB is a substituted version of MESSAGE.
- ***Confusion***: The process of changing a key value during each round of encryption. Confusion is often carried out by substitution. Confusion conceals a

statistical connection between the plaintext and ciphertext. Claude Shannon first discussed confusion.

- ***Diffusion*:** The process of changing the location of the plaintext within the ciphertext. Diffusion is often carried out using transposition. Claude Shannon first introduced diffusion.
- ***Avalanche effect*:** The condition where any change in the key or plaintext, no matter how minor, will significantly change the ciphertext. Horst Feistel first introduced avalanche effect.
- ***Work factor* or work function:** The amount of time and resources that would be needed to break the encryption.
- ***Trapdoor*:** A secret mechanism that allows the implementation of the reverse function in a one-way function.
- ***One-way function*:** A mathematical function that can be more easily performed in one direction than in the other.

Cryptography History

Cryptography has its roots in ancient civilizations. Although early cryptography solutions were simplistic in nature, they were able to provide leaders with a means of hiding messages from enemies.

In their earliest forms, most cryptographic methods implemented some sort of substitution cipher, where each character in the alphabet was replaced with another. A ***mono-alphabetic substitution cipher*** uses only one alphabet, and a ***polyalphabetic substitution cipher*** uses multiple alphabets. As with all other cryptography methods, the early substitution ciphers had to be replaced by more complex methods.

The Spartans created the scytale cipher, which used a sheet of papyrus wrapped around a wooden rod. The encrypted message had to be wrapped around a rod of the correct size to be deciphered, as shown in Figure 3-9.

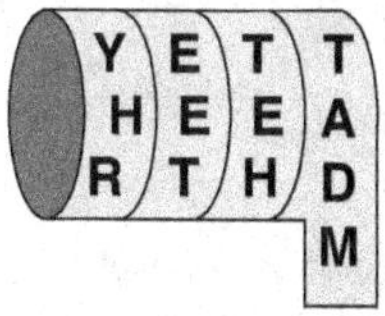

Figure 3-9 Scytale Cipher

Other notable advances in cryptography history include the following:

- Caesar cipher
- Vigenere cipher
- Kerckhoff's principle
- World War II Enigma
- Lucifer by IBM

Julius Caesar and the Caesar Cipher

Julius Caesar developed a mono-alphabetic cipher that shifts the letters of the alphabet three places. Although this technique is very simplistic, variations of it were very easy to develop because the key (the number of locations that the alphabet shifted) can be changed. Because it was so simple, it is easy to reverse engineer and led to the development of polyalphabetic ciphers.

An example of a Caesar cipher–encrypted message is shown in Figure 3-10. In this example, the letters of the alphabet are applied to a three-letter substitution shift, meaning the letters were shifted by three letters. When the end of the alphabet is reached with a cipher, it resumes at the beginning. As you can see, the standard English alphabet is listed first. Underneath it, the substitution letters are listed.

Standard Alphabet
ABCDEFGHIJKLMNOPQRSTUVWXYZ
DEFGHIJKLMNOPQRSTUVWXYZABC
Caesar Cipher

Plaintext – PEARSON EDUCATION
Ciphertext – SHDUVRQ HGXFDWLRQ

Figure 3-10 Caesar Cipher

Vigenere Cipher

In the sixteenth century, Blaise de Vigenere of France developed one of the first polyalphabetic substitution ciphers, today known as the Vigenere cipher. Although it is based on the Caesar cipher, the Vigenere cipher is considerably more complicated because it uses 27 shifted alphabets (see the Vigenere table in Figure 3-11). To encrypt a message, you must know the security key and use it in conjunction with the plaintext message to determine the ciphertext.

	A	B	C	D	E	F	G	H	I	J	K	L	M	N	O	P	Q	R	S	T	U	V	W	X	Y	Z
A	A	B	C	D	E	F	G	H	I	J	K	L	M	N	O	P	Q	S	S	T	U	V	W	X	Y	Z
B	B	C	D	E	F	G	H	I	J	K	L	M	N	O	P	Q	R	S	T	U	V	W	X	Y	Z	A
C	C	D	E	F	G	H	I	J	K	L	M	N	O	P	Q	R	S	T	U	V	W	X	Y	Z	A	B
D	D	E	F	G	H	I	J	K	L	M	N	O	P	Q	R	S	T	U	V	W	X	Y	Z	A	B	C
E	E	F	G	H	I	J	K	L	M	N	O	P	Q	R	S	T	U	V	W	X	Y	Z	A	B	C	D
F	F	G	H	I	J	K	L	M	N	O	P	Q	R	S	T	U	V	W	X	Y	Z	A	B	C	D	E
G	G	H	I	J	K	L	M	N	O	P	Q	R	S	T	U	V	W	X	Y	Z	A	B	C	D	E	F
H	H	I	J	K	L	M	N	O	P	Q	R	S	T	U	V	W	X	Y	Z	A	B	C	D	E	F	G
I	I	J	K	L	M	N	O	P	Q	R	S	T	U	V	W	X	Y	Z	A	B	C	D	E	F	G	H
J	J	K	L	M	N	O	P	Q	R	S	T	U	V	W	X	Y	Z	A	B	C	D	E	F	G	H	I
K	K	L	M	N	O	P	Q	R	S	T	U	V	W	X	Y	Z	A	B	C	D	E	F	G	H	I	J
L	L	M	N	O	P	Q	R	S	T	U	V	W	X	Y	Z	A	B	C	D	E	F	G	H	I	J	K
M	M	N	O	P	Q	R	S	T	U	V	W	X	Y	Z	A	B	C	D	E	F	G	H	I	J	K	L
N	N	O	P	Q	R	S	T	U	V	W	X	Y	Z	A	B	C	D	E	F	G	H	I	J	K	L	M
O	O	P	Q	R	S	T	U	V	W	X	Y	Z	A	B	C	D	E	F	G	H	I	J	K	L	M	N
P	P	Q	R	S	T	U	V	W	X	Y	Z	A	B	C	D	E	F	G	H	I	J	K	L	M	N	O
Q	Q	R	S	T	U	V	W	X	Y	Z	A	B	C	D	E	F	G	H	I	J	K	L	M	N	O	P
R	R	S	T	U	V	W	X	Y	Z	A	B	C	D	E	F	G	H	I	J	K	L	M	N	O	P	Q
S	S	T	U	V	W	X	Y	Z	A	B	C	D	E	F	G	H	I	J	K	L	M	N	O	P	Q	R
T	T	U	V	W	X	Y	Z	A	B	C	D	E	F	G	H	I	J	K	L	M	N	O	P	Q	R	S
U	U	V	W	X	Y	Z	A	B	C	D	E	F	G	H	I	J	K	L	M	N	O	P	Q	R	S	T
V	V	W	X	Y	Z	A	B	C	D	E	F	G	H	I	J	K	L	M	N	O	P	Q	R	S	T	U
W	W	X	Y	Z	A	B	C	D	E	F	G	H	I	J	K	L	M	N	O	P	Q	R	S	T	U	V
X	X	Y	Z	A	B	C	D	E	F	G	H	I	J	K	L	M	N	O	P	Q	R	S	T	U	V	W
Y	Y	Z	A	B	C	D	E	F	G	H	I	J	K	L	M	N	O	P	Q	R	S	T	U	V	W	X
Z	Z	A	B	C	D	E	F	G	H	I	J	K	L	M	N	O	P	Q	R	S	T	U	V	W	X	Y

Figure 3-11 Vigenere Table

As an example of a message on which the Vigenere cipher is applied, let's use the security key PEARSON and the plaintext message of MEETING IN CONFERENCE ROOM. The first letter in the plaintext message is M, and the first letter in the key is P. We should locate the letter M across the headings for the columns. We follow that column down until it intersects with the row that starts with the letter P, resulting in the letter B. The second letter of the plaintext message is E, and the second letter in the key is E. Using the same method, we obtain the letter I. We continue in this same manner until we run out of key letters, and then we start over with the key, which would result in the second letter I in the plaintext message working with the letter P of the key.

So applying this technique to the entire message, the MEETING IN CONFERENCE ROOM plaintext message converts to BIEKABT XR CFFTRGINTW FBDQ ciphertext message.

Kerckhoffs's Principle

In the nineteenth century, Auguste Kerckhoffs developed six design principles for the military use of ciphers. The six principles are as follows:

- The system must be practically, if not mathematically, indecipherable.
- The system must not be required to be secret, and it must be able to fall into the hands of the enemy without inconvenience.
- Its key must be communicable and retainable without the help of written notes, and changeable or modifiable at the will of the correspondents.
- It must be applicable to telegraphic correspondence.
- It must be portable, and its usage and function must not require the concourse of several people.
- Finally, given the circumstances that command its application, the system needs to be easy to use, requiring neither mental strain nor the knowledge of a long series of rules to observe.

In Kerckhoffs's principle, remember that the key is secret, and the algorithm is known.

World War II Enigma

During World War II, most of the major military powers developed encryption machines. The most famous of the machines used during the war was the Enigma machine, developed by Germany. The Enigma machine consisted of rotors and a plug board.

To convert a plaintext message to ciphertext, the machine operator would first configure its initial settings. Then the operator would type each letter of the original plaintext message into the machine one at a time. The machine would display a different letter for each letter entered. After the operator wrote down the ciphertext letter, the operator would advance the rotors to the new setting. So with each letter entered, the operator had to change the machine setting. The key of this process was the initial machine setting and the series of increments used to advance the rotor, both of which had to be known by the receiver to properly convert the ciphertext back to plaintext.

As complicated as the system was, a group of Polish cryptographers were able to break the code, thereby being credited with shortening World War II by two years.

Lucifer by IBM

The Lucifer project, developed by IBM, developed complex mathematical equations. These equations later were used by the U.S. National Security Agency in the development of the U.S. ***Digital Encryption Standard (DES)***, which is still used today in some form. Lucifer used a Feistel cipher, an iterated block cipher that encrypts the plaintext by breaking the block into two halves. The cipher then applies a round of transformation to one of the halves using a subkey. The output of this transformation is Exclusive ORed (XORed) with the other block half. Finally, the two halves are swapped to complete the round.

Cryptosystem Features

A cryptosystem consists of software, protocols, algorithms, and keys. The strength of any cryptosystem comes from the algorithm and the length and secrecy of the key. For example, one method of making a cryptographic key more resistant to exhaustive attacks is to increase the key length. If the cryptosystem uses a weak key, it facilitates attacks against the algorithm.

While a cryptosystem supports the three core principles of the CIA triad, cryptosystems directly provide authentication, confidentiality, integrity, authorization, and non-repudiation. The availability tenet of the CIA triad is supported by cryptosystems, meaning that implementing cryptography will help to ensure that an organization's data remains available. However, cryptography does not directly ensure data availability although it can be used to protect the data.

Authentication

Cryptosystems provide authentication by being able to determine the sender's identity and validity. Digital signatures verify the sender's identity. Protecting the key ensures that only valid users can properly encrypt and decrypt the message.

Confidentiality

Cryptosystems provide confidentiality by altering the original data in such a way as to ensure that the data cannot be read except by the valid recipient. Without the proper key, unauthorized users are unable to read the message.

Integrity

Cryptosystems provide integrity by allowing valid recipients to verify that data has not been altered. Hash functions do not prevent data alteration but provide a means to determine whether data alteration has occurred.

Authorization

Cryptosystems provide authorization by providing the key to valid users after those users prove their identity through authentication. The key given to a user will allow the user to access a resource.

Non-repudiation

Non-repudiation in cryptosystems provides proof of the origin of data, thereby preventing senders from denying that they sent a message and supporting data integrity. However, it can only verify the source as accurate but cannot prevent corrupted data from being purposefully sent. Public key cryptography and digital signatures provide non-repudiation.

NIST SP 800-175A and B

NIST SP 800-175A and B are two Special Publications that provide guidelines for using cryptographic standards in the federal government. SP 800-175A lists all the directives, mandates, and policies that affect the selection of cryptographic standards for the federal government, while SP 800-175B discusses the cryptographic standards that are available and how they should be used.

NIST SP 800-175A lists the following laws as affecting cryptographic standards:

- Federal Information Security Management Act (FISMA)
- Health Information Technology for Economic and Clinical Health (HITECH) Act
- Federal Information Systems Modernization Act of 2014
- Cybersecurity Enhancement Act of 2014

The executive actions and the Office of Management and Budget (OMB) circulars and memorandums that affect U.S. government systems cryptography standards are also listed in NIST SP 800-175A. It also gives the definitions for the following policies:

- **Information management policy:** Specifies what information is to be collected or created, and how it is to be managed
- **Information security policy:** Supports and enforces portions of the organization's information management policy by specifying in more detail what information is to be protected from anticipated threats and how that protection is to be attained

- **Key management policy:** Includes descriptions of the authorization and protection objectives and constraints that apply to the generation, distribution, accounting, storage, use, recovery, and destruction of cryptographic keying material, and the cryptographic services to be provided

Finally, NIST SP 800-175A lists the Risk Management Framework steps from NIST SP 800-37 that affect cryptography selection: categorization of information and information systems and selection of security controls.

NOTE The laws and NIST SP 800-37 are covered in Chapter 1.

NIST SP 800-175B covers the following cryptographic algorithms:

- Cryptographic hash functions
- Symmetric key algorithms
- Asymmetric key algorithms

It also discusses algorithm security strength, algorithm lifetime, and key management.

Security professionals who need help in selecting the appropriate cryptographic algorithms should refer to these SPs.

Cryptographic Mathematics

All cryptographic algorithms involve the use of mathematics. The fundamental mathematical concepts for cryptography are discussed in the following sections.

Boolean

The rules used for the bits and bytes that form a computer are established by Boolean mathematics. In a Boolean system, the values of each circuit are either true or false, usually denoted by 1 and 0, respectively.

Logical Operations (And, Or, Not, Exclusive Or)

When you are dealing with Boolean mathematics, four basic logical operators are used: AND, OR, NOT, and EXCLUSIVE OR. The AND, OR, and EXCLUSIVE OR operators take in two values and output one value. The NOT operator takes in one value and outputs one value.

An AND operation, also referred to as conjunction, checks to see whether two values are both true. Table 3-8 shows the result of an AND operation.

Table 3-8 AND Operation Results

X Value	Y Value	AND Operation Result
0	0	0
0	1	0
1	0	0
1	1	1

An OR operation, also referred to as disjunction, checks to see whether at least one of the values is true. Table 3-9 shows the result of an OR operation.

Table 3-9 OR Operation Results

X Value	Y Value	OR Operation Result
0	0	0
0	1	1
1	0	1
1	1	1

A NOT operation, also referred to as negation, reverses the value of a variable. Table 3-10 shows the result of a NOT operation.

Table 3-10 NOT Operation Results

X Value	NOT Operation Result
0	1
1	0

An EXCLUSIVE OR operation, also referred to as XOR, returns a true value when only one of the input values is true. If both values are true or both values are false, the output is always false. Table 3-11 shows the result of an XOR operation.

Table 3-11 XOR Operation Results

X Value	Y Value	XOR Operation Result
0	0	0
0	1	1
1	0	1
1	1	0

Modulo Function

Used in cryptography, a modulo function is the value that is left over/remainder after a division operation is performed. For example, 32 divided by 8 would have a remainder of 0 because 8 goes into 32 an even number of times (4); modulo in this case is 0. The number 10 divided by 3 would have a remainder of 1 because 10 divided by 3 equals 3 with a remainder of 1. Therefore, modulo of 10 divided by 3 is 1.

One-Way Function

A one-way function produces output values for each possible combination of inputs. This makes it impossible to retrieve the input values of a one-way function. Public key algorithms are based on one-way functions. The inputs used are prime numbers. For example, suppose an input contains only prime numbers with three digits. The output or result of those three prime numbers could be determined using a good calculator. However, if someone obtains the result of 19,786,001, it would be hard to determine which three three-digit prime numbers were used. (By the way, 101, 227, and 863 are the three prime numbers used.)

Nonce

A ***nonce*** is a random number that is used only once and acts as a placeholder variable in functions. When the function is actually executed, the nonce is replaced with a random number generated at the time of processing. A common example of a nonce is an initialization vector (IV). IVs are values that are used to create a unique ciphertext every time the same message is encrypted using the same key.

Split Knowledge

Split knowledge is the term used when information or privilege is divided between multiple users or entities so that no single user has sufficient privileges to compromise security. An example of split knowledge in cryptography is key escrow. With key escrow, the key is held by a third party to ensure that the key could be retrieved if the issuing party ceases to exist or has a catastrophic event.

Cryptographic Life Cycle

When considering implementing cryptography or encryption techniques in an organization, security professionals must fully analyze the needs of the organization. Each technique has strengths and weaknesses. In addition, they each have specific purposes. Analyzing the needs of the organization will ensure that you identify the best algorithm to implement.

Professional organizations manage algorithms to ensure that they provide the protection needed. It is essential that security professionals research the algorithms they implement and understand any announcements from the governing organization regarding updates, retirements, or replacements to the implemented algorithms. The life cycle of any cryptographic algorithm involves implementation, maintenance, and retirement or replacement. Security professionals who fail to obtain up-to-date information regarding the algorithms implemented might find the organization's reputation and their own personal reputation damaged as the result of this negligence.

Key Management

Key management in cryptography is essential to ensure that the cryptography provides confidentiality, integrity, and authentication. If a key is compromised, it can have serious consequences throughout an organization.

Key management involves the entire process of ensuring that keys are protected during creation, distribution, transmission, storage, and disposal. As part of this process, keys must also be destroyed properly. When you consider the vast number of networks over which the key is transmitted and the different types of systems on which a key is stored, the enormity of this issue really comes to light.

As the most demanding and critical aspect of cryptography, it is important that security professionals understand key management principles.

Keys should always be stored in ciphertext when stored on a noncryptographic device. Key distribution, storage, and maintenance should be automatic by integrating the processes into the application.

Because keys can be lost, backup copies should be made and stored in a secure location. A designated individual should have control of the backup copies with other designated individuals serving as emergency backups. The key recovery process should also require more than one operator to ensure that only valid key recovery requests are completed. In some cases, keys are even broken into parts and deposited with trusted agents, who provide their part of the key to a central authority when authorized to do so. Although other methods of distributing parts of a key are used, all the solutions involve the use of trustee agents entrusted with part of the key and a central authority tasked with assembling the key from its parts. Also, key recovery personnel should span across the entire organization and not just be members of the IT department.

Organizations should also limit the number of keys that are used. The more keys that you have, the more keys you must worry about and ensure are protected. Although a valid reason for issuing a key should never be ignored, limiting the number of keys issued and used reduces the potential damage.

When designing the key management process, security professionals should consider how to do the following:

Key Topic

- Securely store and transmit the keys.
- Use random keys.
- Issue keys of sufficient length to ensure protection.
- Properly destroy keys when no longer needed.
- Back up the keys to ensure that they can be recovered.

Algorithm Selection

When selecting an algorithm, organizations need to understand the data that needs protecting and the organizational environment, including any regulations and standards with which they must comply. Organizations should answer the following questions when selecting the algorithm to use:

- **What is the encryption timeframe?** Use encryption that can survive a brute-force attack at least long enough that the data is no longer important to keep secret.
- **What data types need to be encrypted?** Data at rest, data in use, and data in motion need different types of encryption for protection.
- **What system restrictions exist?** Considerations include budget, operating system restrictions, infrastructure restrictions, and so on.
- **Who will be exchanging the encrypted data?** Legacy systems may cause restrictions on the encryption that can be used when data is exchanged.

Cryptographic Types

Algorithms that are used in computer systems implement complex mathematical formulas when converting plaintext to ciphertext. The two main components to any encryption system are the key and the algorithm. In some encryption systems, the two communicating parties use the same key. In other encryption systems, the two communicating parties use different keys in the process, but the keys are related.

In the following sections, we discuss the following:

- Running key and concealment ciphers
- Substitution ciphers

- Transposition ciphers
- Symmetric algorithms
- Asymmetric algorithms
- Hybrid ciphers

Running Key and Concealment Ciphers

Running key ciphers and ***concealment ciphers*** are considered classical methods of producing ciphertext. The running key cipher uses a physical component, usually a book, to provide the polyalphabetic characters. An indicator block must be included somewhere within the text so that the receiver knows where in the book the originator started. Therefore, the two parties must agree upon which book to use and where the indicator block will be included in the cipher message. Running key ciphers are also referred to as key ciphers and running ciphers.

A ***concealment cipher***, also referred to as a ***null cipher***, occurs when plaintext is interspersed somewhere within other written material. The two parties must agree on the key value, which defines which letters are part of the actual message. For example, every third letter or the first letter of each word is part of the real message. A concealment cipher belongs in the steganography realm.

NOTE Steganography is discussed shortly.

Substitution Ciphers

A ***substitution cipher*** uses a key to substitute characters or character blocks with different characters or character blocks. The Caesar cipher and Vigenere cipher are two of the earliest forms of substitution ciphers.

Another example of a substitution cipher is a modulo 26 substitution cipher. With this cipher, the 26 letters of the alphabet are numbered in order starting at zero. The sender takes the original message and determines the number of each letter in the original message. Then the letter values for the keys are added to the original letter values. The value result is then converted back to text.

Figure 3-12 shows an example of a modulo 26 substitution cipher encryption. With this example, the original message is PEARSON, and the key is KEY. The ciphertext message is ZIYBSMX.

Modulo 26 Letter Chart

a	0	h	7	o	14	v	21
b	1	i	8	p	15	w	22
c	2	j	9	q	16	x	23
d	3	k	10	r	17	y	24
e	4	l	11	s	18	z	25
f	5	m	12	t	19		
g	6	n	13	u	20		

Orginal Message	Orginal Value	Key	Key Value	Result	Mod 26	Cipher Message
P	15	K	10	25	25	Z
E	4	E	4	8	8	I
A	0	Y	24	24	24	Y
R	17	K	10	27	1	B
S	18	E	0	18	18	S
O	14	Y	24	38	12	M
N	13	K	10	23	23	X

Figure 3-12 Modulo 26 Substitution Cipher Example

Substitution ciphers explained here include the following:

- One-time pads
- Steganography

One-Time Pads

A ***one-time pad***, invented by Gilbert Vernam, is the most secure encryption scheme that can be used. If it's used properly, an attacker cannot break a one-time pad. A one-time pad works like a running cipher in that the key value is added to the value of the letters. However, a one-time pad uses a key that is the same length as the plaintext message, whereas the running cipher uses a smaller key that is repeatedly applied to the plaintext message.

Figure 3-13 shows an example of a one-time pad encryption. With this example, the original message is PEARSON, and the key is JOHNSON. The ciphertext message is YSHEKCA.

Modulo 26 Letter Chart

a	0	h	7	o	14	v	21
b	1	i	8	p	15	w	22
c	2	j	9	q	16	x	23
d	3	k	10	r	17	y	24
e	4	l	11	s	18	z	25
f	5	m	12	t	19		
g	6	n	13	u	20		

Orginal Message	Orginal Value	Key	Key Value	Result	Mod 26	Cipher Message
P	15	J	9	24	24	Y
E	4	O	14	18	18	S
A	0	H	7	7	7	H
R	17	N	13	30	4	E
S	18	S	18	36	10	K
O	14	O	14	28	2	C
N	13	N	13	26	0	A

Figure 3-13 One-Time Pad Example

To ensure that the one-time pad is secure, the following conditions must exist:

- Must be used only one time
- Must be as long as (or longer than) the message

- Must consist of random values
- Must be securely distributed
- Must be protected at its source and destination

Although the earlier example uses a one-time pad in a modulo 26 scheme, one-time pads can also be used at the bit level. When the bit level is used, the message is converted into binary, and an XOR operation occurs two bits at a time. The bits from the original message are combined with the key values to obtain the encrypted message. When you combine the values, the result is 0 if both values are the same and 1 if both values are different. An example of an XOR operation is as follows:

Original message 0 1 1 0 1 1 0 0

Key 1 1 0 1 1 1 0 0

Cipher message 1 0 1 1 0 0 0 0

Steganography

Steganography occurs when a message is hidden inside another object, such as a picture, audio file, video file, or a document. In steganography, it is crucial that only those who are expecting the message know that the message exists.

A concealment cipher, discussed earlier, is one method of steganography. Another method of steganography is digital watermarking, which is a logo or trademark that is embedded in documents, pictures, or other objects. The watermarks deter people from using the materials in an unauthorized manner.

Transposition Ciphers

A ***transposition cipher*** scrambles the letters of the original message in a different order. The key determines the positions to which the letters are moved.

Figure 3-14 shows an example of a simple transposition cipher. With this example, the original message is PEARSON EDUCATION, and the key is 4231 2314. The ciphertext message is REAP ONSE AUCD IOTN. So you take the first four letters of the plaintext message (PEAR) and use the first four numbers (4231) as the key for transposition. In the new ciphertext, the letters would be REAP. Then you take the next four letters of the plaintext message (SONE) and use the next four numbers (2314) as the key for transposition. In the new ciphertext, the letters would be ONSE. Then you take the next four letters of the original message and apply the first four numbers of the key because you do not have any more numbers in the key. Continue this pattern until complete.

Original message:	PEARSON EDUCATION			
Broken into groups:	PEAR	SONE	DUCA	TION
Key:	4231	2314	4231	2314
Ciphertext message:	REAP	ONSE	AUCD	IOTN

Figure 3-14 Transposition Example

Symmetric Algorithms

Symmetric algorithms use a private or secret key that must remain secret between the two parties. Each party pair requires a separate private key. Therefore, a single user would need a unique secret key for every user with whom they communicate.

Consider an example where there are 10 unique users. Each user needs a separate private key to communicate with the other users. To calculate the number of keys that would be needed in this example, you would use the following formula:

# of users × (# of users – 1) / 2

Using this example, you would calculate 10 × (10 – 1) / 2, or 45 needed keys.

With symmetric algorithms, the encryption key must remain secure. To obtain the secret key, the users must find a secure out-of-band method for communicating the secret key, including courier or direct physical contact between the users.

A special type of symmetric key called a session key encrypts messages between two users during one communication session.

Symmetric algorithms can be referred to as single-key, secret-key, private-key, or shared-key cryptography.

Symmetric systems provide confidentiality but not authentication or non-repudiation. If both users use the same key, determining where the message originated is impossible.

Symmetric algorithms include DES, AES, IDEA, Skipjack, Blowfish, Twofish, RC4/RC5/RC6/RC7, and CAST. All these algorithms are discussed later in this chapter.

Table 3-12 lists the strengths and weaknesses of symmetric algorithms.

Key Topic

Table 3-12 Symmetric Algorithm Strengths and Weaknesses

Strengths	Weaknesses
1,000 to 10,000 times faster than asymmetric algorithms	Remembering or maintaining the number of unique keys needed can cause key management issues.
Hard to break	Secure key distribution is critical.
Cheaper to implement than asymmetric	Key compromise occurs if one party is compromised, thereby allowing impersonation.

The two broad types of symmetric algorithms are stream-based ciphers and block ciphers. Initialization vectors (IVs) are an important part of block ciphers. These three components are discussed next.

Stream-Based Ciphers

Stream-based ciphers perform encryption on a bit-by-bit basis and use keystream generators. The keystream generators create a bit stream that is XORed with the plaintext bits. The result of this XOR operation is the ciphertext.

A synchronous stream-based cipher depends only on the key, and an asynchronous stream cipher depends on the key and plaintext. The key ensures that the bit stream that is XORed to the plaintext is random.

An example of a stream-based cipher is RC4, which is discussed later in this chapter.

Advantages of stream-based ciphers include the following:

Key Topic

- Generally have lower error propagation because encryption occurs on each bit
- Generally used more in hardware implementation
- Use the same key for encryption and decryption
- Generally cheaper to implement than block ciphers
- Employ only confusion concept

NOTE *Confusion* is defined in the "Cryptography Concepts" section, earlier in this chapter. Remember to refer to that list anytime you encounter terms in this chapter with which you are unfamiliar.

Block Ciphers

Block ciphers perform encryption by breaking the message into fixed-length units, called blocks. A message of 1,024 bits could be divided into 16 blocks of 64 bits each.

Each of those 16 blocks is processed by the algorithm formulas, resulting in a single block of ciphertext.

Examples of block ciphers include IDEA, Blowfish, RC5, and RC6, which are discussed later in this chapter.

Advantages of block ciphers include the following:

Key Topic

- Implementation is easier than stream-based cipher implementation.
- Generally less susceptible to security issues.
- Generally used more in software implementations.

Block ciphers employ both confusion and diffusion. Block ciphers often use different modes: ECB, CBC, CFB, and CTR. These modes are discussed in detail later in this chapter.

Initialization Vectors (IVs)

The modes mentioned earlier use IVs to ensure that patterns are not produced during encryption. These IVs provide this service by using random values with the algorithms. Without using IVs, a repeated phrase within a plaintext message could result in the same ciphertext. Attackers, when they obtain IVs, can possibly use these patterns to break the encryption.

Asymmetric Algorithms

Asymmetric algorithms use both a public key and a private or secret key. The public key is known by all parties, and the private key is known only by its owner. One of these keys encrypts the message, and the other decrypts the message.

In asymmetric cryptography, determining a user's private key is virtually impossible even if the public key is known, although both keys are mathematically related. However, if a user's private key is discovered, the encryption system can be compromised.

Asymmetric algorithms can be referred to as dual-key or public key cryptography.

Asymmetric systems provide confidentiality, integrity, authentication, and non-repudiation. Because both users have one unique key that is part of the process, determining where the message originated is possible.

If confidentiality is the primary concern for an organization, a message should be encrypted with the receiver's public key, which is referred to as the secure message format. If authentication is the primary concern for an organization, a message should be encrypted with the sender's private key, which is referred to as the open message format. When the open message format is used, the message can be decrypted by anyone with the sender's public key.

Asymmetric algorithms include Diffie-Hellman, RSA, El Gamal, ECC, Knapsack, DSA, and zero-knowledge proof. All of these algorithms are discussed later in this chapter.

Table 3-13 lists the strengths and weaknesses of asymmetric algorithms.

Key Topic

Table 3-13 Asymmetric Algorithm Strengths and Weaknesses

Strengths	Weaknesses
Key distribution is easier and more manageable than with symmetric algorithms.	More expensive to implement than symmetric algorithms.
Key management is easier because the same public key is used by all parties.	1,000 to 10,000 times slower than symmetric algorithms.

Hybrid Ciphers

Because both symmetric and asymmetric algorithms have weaknesses, solutions have been developed that use both types of algorithms in a hybrid cipher. By using both algorithm types, the cipher provides confidentiality, authentication, and non-repudiation.

The process for hybrid encryption is as follows:

1. The symmetric algorithm provides the keys used for encryption.
2. The symmetric keys are then passed to the asymmetric algorithm, which encrypts the symmetric keys and automatically distributes them.
3. The message is then encrypted with the symmetric key.
4. Both the message and the key are sent to the receiver.
5. The receiver decrypts the symmetric key and uses the symmetric key to decrypt the message.

An organization should use hybrid encryption if the parties do not have a shared secret key and large quantities of sensitive data must be transmitted.

Elliptic Curves

Elliptic curves are public key algorithms that use mathematical functions to create faster, smaller, and more efficient cryptographic keys based on the elliptic curve theory. The algebraic structure of the elliptic curves over infinite fields provides a more difficult to break mechanism.

NOTE Elliptic Curve Cryptosystem (ECC) is discussed in detail later in this chapter.

Quantum Cryptography

Quantum cryptography, also called quantum encryption, uses quantum mechanics principles to encrypt messages. Quantum's multiple states, coupled with its "no change theory," are used as part of the process. Quantum cryptography requires a quantum computer, which has the immense computing power to encrypt and decrypt data. A quantum computer could quickly crack current public key (asymmetric) cryptography.

Longer keys are a good defense against quantum computers breaking public key cryptography. Another good defense is to use symmetric encryption for the messages themselves and then use asymmetric encryption just for the keys.

Symmetric Algorithms

Symmetric algorithms were explained earlier in this chapter. In the following sections, we discuss some of the most popular symmetric algorithms. Some of these might no longer be commonly used because there are more secure alternatives.

Security professionals should be familiar with the following symmetric algorithms:

- DES/3DES
- AES
- IDEA
- Skipjack
- Blowfish
- Twofish
- RC4/RC5/RC6/RC7
- CAST

DES and 3DES

Digital Encryption Standard (DES) is a symmetric encryption system created by the U.S. National Security Agency (NSA) but based on the 128-bit Lucifer algorithm by IBM. Originally, the algorithm was named Data Encryption Algorithm (DEA), and the DES acronym was used to refer to the standard. But in today's world, DES is the more common term for both.

DES uses a 64-bit key, 8 bits of which are used for parity. Therefore, the effective key length for DES is 56 bits. DES divides the message into 64-bit blocks. Sixteen rounds of transposition and substitution are performed on each block, resulting in a 64-bit block of ciphertext.

DES has mostly been replaced by 3DES and AES (which is discussed later).

DES-X is a variant of DES that uses multiple 64-bit keys in addition to the 56-bit DES key. The first 64-bit key is XORed to the plaintext, which is then encrypted with DES. The second 64-bit key is XORed to the resulting cipher.

Double-DES, a DES version that uses a 112-bit key length, is no longer used. After it was released, a security attack occurred that reduced Double-DES security to the same level as DES.

DES Modes

DES comes in the following five modes:

Key Topic

- ***Electronic Code Book (ECB)***
- ***Cipher Block Chaining (CBC)***
- ***Cipher Feedback (CFB)***
- ***Output Feedback (OFB)***
- ***Counter Mode (CTR)***

In ECB, 64-bit blocks of data are processed by the algorithm using the key. The ciphertext produced can be padded to ensure that the result is a 64-bit block. If an encryption error occurs, only one block of the message is affected. ECB operations run in parallel, making it a fast method.

Although ECB is the easiest and fastest mode to use, it has security issues because every 64-bit block is encrypted with the same key. If an attacker discovers the key, all the blocks of data can be read. If an attacker discovers both versions of the 64-bit block (plaintext and ciphertext), the key can be determined. For these reasons, the mode should not be used when encrypting a large amount of data because patterns would emerge.

ECB is a good choice if an organization needs encryption for its databases because ECB works well with the encryption of short messages. Figure 3-15 shows the ECB encryption process.

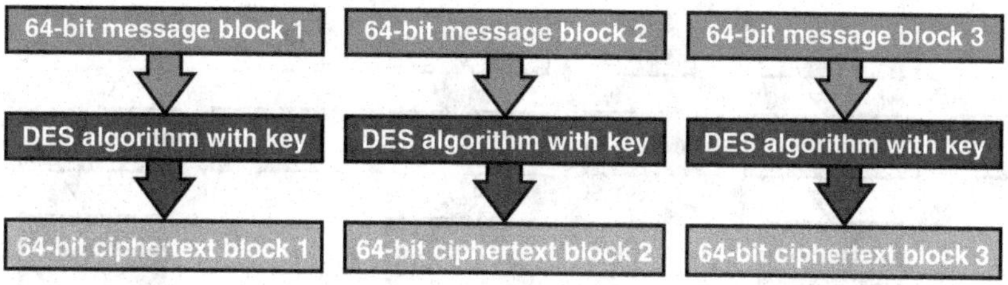

Figure 3-15 ECB Mode of DES

In CBC, each 64-bit block is chained together because each resultant 64-bit ciphertext block is applied to the next block. So plaintext message block 1 is processed by the algorithm using an IV (discussed earlier in this chapter). The resultant ciphertext message block 1 is XORed with plaintext message block 2, resulting in ciphertext message 2. This process continues until the message is complete.

Unlike ECB, CBC encrypts large files without having any patterns within the resulting ciphertext. If a unique IV is used with each message encryption, the resultant ciphertext will be different every time, even in cases where the same plaintext message is used. Figure 3-16 shows the CBC encryption process.

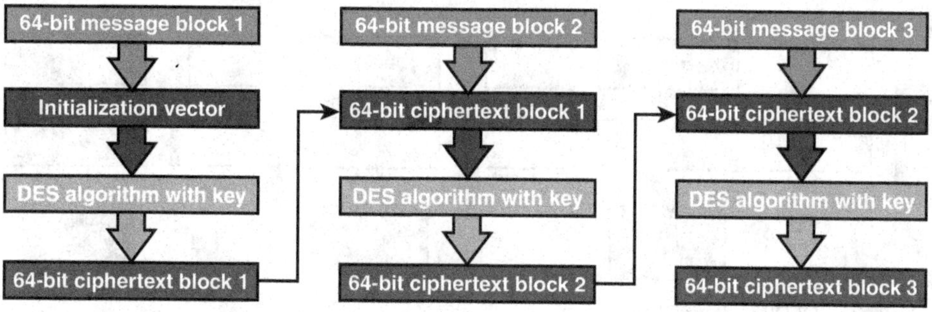

Figure 3-16 CBC Mode of DES

Whereas CBC and ECB require 64-bit blocks, CFB works with 8-bit (or smaller) blocks and uses a combination of stream ciphering and block ciphering. Like CBC, the first 8-bit block of the plaintext message is XORed by the algorithm using a keystream, which is the result of an IV and the key. The resultant ciphertext message is applied to the next plaintext message block. Figure 3-17 shows the CFB encryption process.

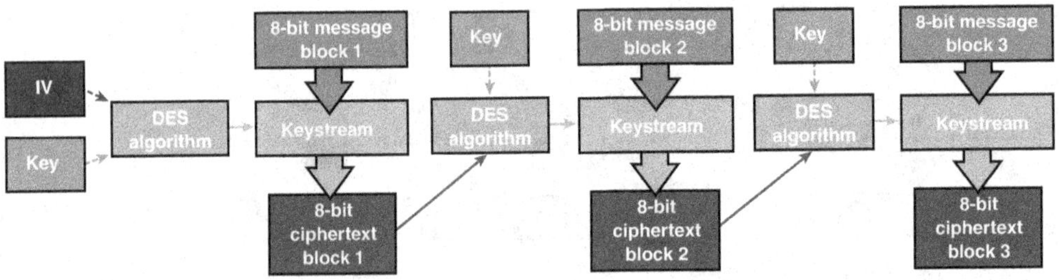

Figure 3-17 CFB Mode of DES

The size of the ciphertext block must be the same size as the plaintext block. The method that CFB uses can have issues if any ciphertext result has errors because those errors will affect any future block encryption. For this reason, CFB should not be used to encrypt data that can be affected by this problem, particularly video or voice signals. This problem led to the need for DES OFB mode.

Similar to CFB, OFB works with 8-bit (or smaller) blocks and uses a combination of stream ciphering and block ciphering. However, OFB uses the previous keystream with the key to create the next keystream. Figure 3-18 shows the OFB encryption process.

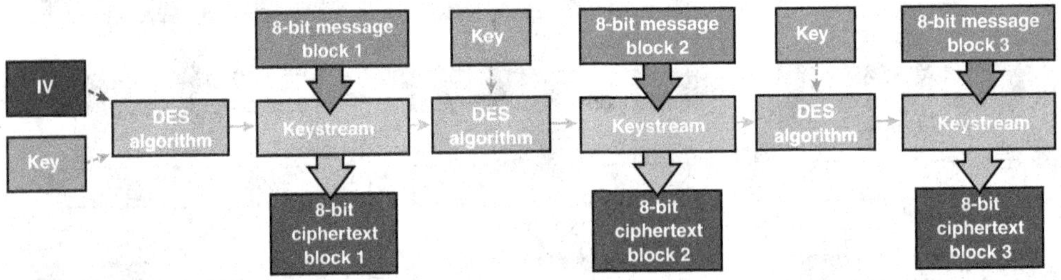

Figure 3-18 OFB Mode of DES

With OFB, the size of the keystream value must be the same size as the plaintext block. Because of the way in which OFB is implemented, OFB is less susceptible to the error type that CFB has.

CTR mode is similar to OFB mode. The main difference is that CTR mode uses an incrementing IV counter to ensure that each block is encrypted with a unique keystream. Also, the ciphertext is not chaining into the encryption process. Because this chaining does not occur, CTR performance is much better than the other modes. Figure 3-19 shows the CTR encryption process.

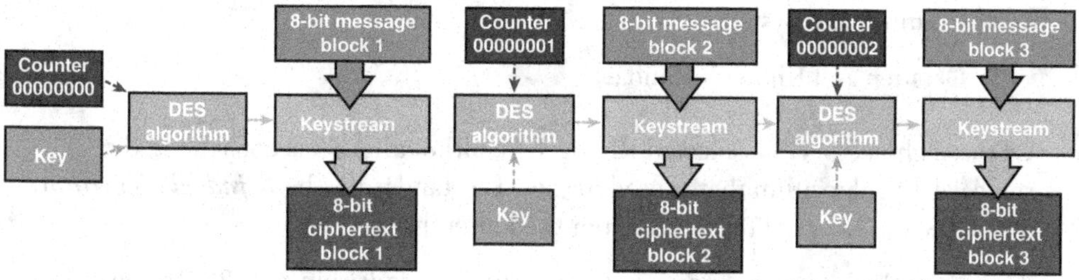

Figure 3-19 CTR Mode of DES

3DES and Modes

Because of the need to quickly replace DES, ***Triple DES (3DES)***, a version of DES that increases security by using three 56-bit keys, was developed. Although 3DES is resistant to attacks, it is up to three times slower than DES. 3DES did serve as a temporary replacement to DES. However, NIST has actually designated the Advanced Encryption Standard (AES) as the replacement for DES. Even though 3DES was an improvement over DES, modern applications should not use 3DES.

3DES comes in the following four modes:

Key Topic

- **3DES-EEE3:** Each block of data is encrypted three times, each time with a different key.
- **3DES-EDE3:** Each block of data is encrypted with the first key, decrypted with the second key, and encrypted with the third key.
- **3DES-EEE2:** Each block of data is encrypted with the first key, encrypted with the second key, and finally encrypted again with the first key.
- **3DES-EDE2:** Each block of data is encrypted with the first key, decrypted with the second key, and finally encrypted again with the first key.

AES

Advanced Encryption Standard (AES) is the replacement algorithm for DES. When NIST decided a new standard was needed because DES had been cracked, NIST was presented with five industry options:

- IBM's MARS
- RSA Laboratories' RC6
- Anderson, Biham, and Knudsen's Serpent

- Counterpane Systems' Twofish
- Daemen and Rijmen's Rijndael

Of these choices, NIST selected Rijndael. So although AES is considered the standard, the algorithm that is used in the AES standard is the ***Rijndael algorithm***. The AES and Rijndael terms are often used interchangeably.

The three block sizes that are used in the Rijndael algorithm are 128, 192, and 256 bits. A 128-bit key with a 128-bit block size undergoes 10 transformation rounds. A 192-bit key with a 192-bit block size undergoes 12 transformation rounds. Finally, a 256-bit key with a 256-bit block size undergoes 14 transformation rounds.

Rijndael employs transformations composed of three layers: the nonlinear layer, key addition layer, and linear-maxing layer. The Rijndael design is very simple, and its code is compact, which allows it to be used on a variety of platforms. It is the required algorithm for sensitive but unclassified U.S. government data.

IDEA

International Data Encryption Algorithm (IDEA) is a block cipher that uses 64-bit blocks. Each 64-bit block is divided into 16 smaller blocks. IDEA uses a 128-bit key and performs eight rounds of transformations on each of the 16 smaller blocks.

IDEA is faster and harder to break than DES. However, IDEA is not as widely used as DES or AES because it was patented, and licensing fees had to be paid to IDEA's owner, a Swiss company named Ascom. However, the patent expired in 2012. IDEA is used in PGP, which is discussed later in this chapter.

Skipjack

Skipjack is a block-cipher, symmetric algorithm developed by the U.S. NSA. It uses an 80-bit key to encrypt 64-bit blocks. This is the algorithm that is used in the Clipper chip. Algorithm details are classified.

Blowfish

Blowfish is a block cipher that uses 64-bit data blocks using anywhere from 32- to 448-bit encryption keys. Blowfish performs 16 rounds of transformation. Initially developed with the intention of serving as a replacement to DES, Blowfish is one of the few algorithms that are not patented.

Twofish

Twofish is a version of Blowfish that uses 128-bit data blocks using 128-, 192-, and 256-bit keys. It uses 16 rounds of transformation. Like Blowfish, Twofish is not patented.

RC4/RC5/RC6/RC7

A total of seven RC algorithms have been developed by Ron Rivest. RC1 was never published, RC2 was a 64-bit block cipher, and RC3 was broken before release. So the main RC implementations that a security professional needs to understand are RC4, RC5, RC6, and RC7.

RC4, also called ARC4, is one of the most popular stream ciphers. It is used in SSL and WEP (both of which are discussed in more detail in Chapter 4, "Communication and Network Security"). RC4 uses a variable key size of 40 to 2,048 bits and up to 256 rounds of transformation.

RC5 is a block cipher that uses a key size of up to 2,048 bits and up to 255 rounds of transformation. Block sizes supported are 32, 64, or 128 bits. Because of all the possible variables in RC5, the industry often uses an RC5=*w*/*r*/*b* designation, where *w* is the block size, *r* is the number of rounds, and *b* is the number of 8-bit bytes in the key. For example, RC5-64/16/16 denotes a 64-bit word (or 128-bit data blocks), 16 rounds of transformation, and a 16-byte (128-bit) key.

RC6 is a block cipher based on RC5, and it uses the same key size, rounds, and block size. RC6 was originally developed as an AES solution, but lost the contest to Rijndael. RC6 is faster than RC5.

RC7 is a block cipher based on RC6. Although it uses the same key size and rounds, it has a block size of 256 bits. In addition, it uses six working registers instead of four. As a result, it is much faster than RC6.

CAST

CAST, invented by Carlisle Adams and Stafford Tavares, has two versions: ***CAST-128*** and ***CAST-256***. CAST-128 is a block cipher that uses a 40- to 128-bit key that will perform 12 or 16 rounds of transformation on 64-bit blocks. CAST-256 is a block cipher that uses a 128-, 160-, 192-, 224-, or 256-bit key that will perform 48 rounds of transformation on 128-bit blocks.

Table 3-14 lists the key facts about each symmetric algorithm.

Key Topic

Table 3-14 Symmetric Algorithms Key Facts

Algorithm Name	Block or Stream Cipher?	Key Size	Number of Rounds	Block Size
DES	Block	64 bits (effective length 56 bits)	16	64 bits
3DES	Block	56, 112, or 168 bits	48	64 bits
AES	Block	128, 192, or 256 bits	10, 12, or 14 (depending on block/key size)	128, 192, or 256 bits
IDEA	Block	128 bits	8	64 bits
Skipjack	Block	80 bits	32	64 bits
Blowfish	Block	32–448 bits	16	64 bits
Twofish	Block	128, 192, or 256 bits	16	128 bits
RC4	Stream	40–2,048 bits	Up to 256	N/A
RC5	Block	Up to 2,048	Up to 255	32, 64, or 128 bits
RC6	Block	Up to 2,048	Up to 255	32, 64, or 128 bits
RC7	Block	Up to 2,048	Up to 255	256 bits
CAST-128	Block	Up to 128	12–16	64 bits
CAST-256	Block	128–256 bits	48	128 bits

Asymmetric Algorithms

Asymmetric algorithms were explained earlier in this chapter. In the following sections, we discuss some of the most popular asymmetric algorithms. Some of them might no longer be commonly used because more secure alternatives are available.

Security professionals should be familiar with the following symmetric algorithms:

- Diffie-Hellman
- RSA
- El Gamal
- ECC
- Knapsack
- Zero-knowledge proof

Diffie-Hellman

Diffie-Hellman is an asymmetric key agreement algorithm created by Whitfield Diffie and Martin Hellman. Diffie-Hellman is responsible for the key agreement process. The key agreement process includes the following steps:

1. John and Sally need to communicate over an encrypted channel and decide to use Diffie-Hellman.
2. John is given a private and public key, and Sally is given a private and a public key.
3. John and Sally share their public keys with each other.
4. An application on John's computer uses John's private key and Sally's public key and applies the Diffie-Hellman algorithm, and an application on Sally's computer uses Sally's private key and John's public key and applies the Diffie-Hellman algorithm.
5. Through this application, the same shared value is created for John and Sally, which in turn creates the same symmetric key on each system using the asymmetric key agreement algorithm.

Through this process, Diffie-Hellman provides secure key distribution, but not confidentiality, authentication, or non-repudiation. The key to this algorithm is dealing with discrete logarithms. Diffie-Hellman is susceptible to man-in-the-middle (or on-path) attacks unless an organization implements digital signatures or digital certificates for authentication at the beginning of the Diffie-Hellman process.

NOTE Meet-in-the-middle attacks are discussed later in this chapter.

RSA

RSA is the most popular asymmetric algorithm and was invented by Ron Rivest, Adi Shamir, and Leonard Adleman. RSA can provide key exchange, encryption, and digital signatures. The strength of the RSA algorithm is the difficulty of finding the prime factors of very large numbers. RSA uses a 1,024- to 4,096-bit key and performs one round of transformation.

RSA-768 and RSA-704 have been factored. If factorization of the prime numbers used by an RSA implementation occurs, then the implementation is considered breakable and should not be used. RSA-2048 is the largest RSA number. RSA-4096 is also available and has not been broken either. While RSA-4096 is considered stronger, organizations may be unable to deploy RSA-4096 because an application may limit them to 2048.

As a key exchange protocol, RSA encrypts a DES or an AES symmetric key for secure distribution. RSA uses a one-way function to provide encryption/decryption and digital signature verification/generation. The public key works with the one-way function to perform encryption and digital signature verification. The private key works with the one-way function to perform decryption and signature generation.

In RSA, the one-way function is a trapdoor. The private key knows the one-way function. The private key is capable of determining the original prime numbers. Finally, the private key knows how to use the one-way function to decrypt the encrypted message.

Attackers can use Number Field Sieve (NFS), a factoring algorithm, to attack RSA.

El Gamal

El Gamal is an asymmetric key algorithm based on the Diffie-Hellman algorithm. Like Diffie-Hellman, El Gamal deals with discrete logarithms. However, whereas Diffie-Hellman can be used only for key agreement, El Gamal can provide key exchange, encryption, and digital signatures.

With El Gamal, any key size can be used. However, a larger key size negatively affects performance. Because El Gamal is the slowest asymmetric algorithm, using a key size of 1,024 bits or less would be wise.

ECC

Elliptic Curve Cryptosystem (ECC) provides secure key distribution, encryption, and digital signatures. The elliptic curve's size defines the difficulty of the problem.

Although ECC can use a key of any size, it can use a much smaller key than RSA or any other asymmetric algorithm and still provide comparable security. Therefore, the primary benefit promised by ECC is a smaller key size, reducing storage and transmission requirements. ECC is more efficient and provides better security than RSA keys of the same size.

Figure 3-20 shows an elliptic curve example with the elliptic curve equation.

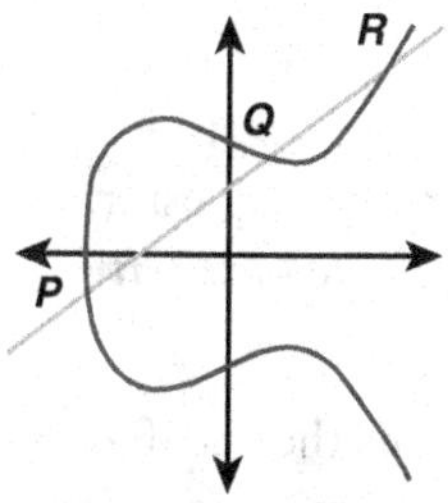

$y^2 = x^3 + ax + b$

Figure 3-20 Elliptic Curve Example with Equation

Knapsack

Knapsack is a series of asymmetric algorithms that provide encryption and digital signatures. This algorithm family is no longer used due to security issues.

Zero-Knowledge Proof

A zero-knowledge proof is a technique used to ensure that only the minimum needed information is disclosed without giving all the details. An example of this technique occurs when one user encrypts data with a private key and the receiver decrypts with the originator's public key. The originator has not given the private key to the receiver. But the originator is proving that they have their private key simply because the receiver can read the message.

Public Key Infrastructure and Digital Certificates

A public key infrastructure (PKI) includes systems, software, and communication protocols that distribute, manage, and control public key cryptography. A PKI publishes digital certificates. Because a PKI establishes trust within an environment, a PKI can certify that a public key is tied to an entity and verify that a public key is valid. Public keys are published through digital certificates.

The X.509 standard is a framework that enables authentication between networks and over the Internet. A PKI includes timestamping and certificate revocation to ensure that certificates are managed properly. A PKI provides confidentiality, message integrity, authentication, and non-repudiation.

The structure of a PKI includes certification authorities, certificates, registration authorities, certificate revocation lists, cross-certification, and the Online Certificate Status Protocol (OCSP). In the following sections, we discuss these PKI components as well as a few other PKI concepts.

Certificate Authority and Registration Authority

Any participant that requests a certificate must first go through the ***registration authority (RA)***, which verifies the requestor's identity and registers the requestor. After the identity is verified, the RA passes the request to the ***certificate authority (CA)***.

A CA is the entity that creates and signs digital certificates, maintains the certificates, and revokes them when necessary. Every entity that wants to participate in the PKI must contact the CA and request a digital certificate. The CA is the ultimate authority for the authenticity for every participant in the PKI and signs each digital certificate. The certificate binds the identity of the participant to the public key.

There are different types of CAs. Some existing organizations provide a PKI as a payable service to companies that need them. An example is Symantec. Some organizations implement their own private CAs so that the organization can control all aspects of the PKI process. If an organization is large enough, it might need to provide a structure of CAs, with the root CA being the highest in the hierarchy.

Because more than one entity is often involved in the PKI certification process, certification path validation allows the participants to check the legitimacy of the certificates in the certification path.

Certificates

A digital certificate provides an entity, usually a user, with the credentials to prove its identity and associates that identity with a public key. At a minimum, a digital certificate must provide the serial number, the issuer, the subject (owner), and the public key.

An X.509 certificate complies with the X.509 standard. An X.509 certificate contains the following fields (but can be programmed to include more if the organization needs them):

- Version
- Serial Number
- Algorithm ID
- Issuer
- Validity
- Subject
- Subject Public Key Info
- Public Key Algorithm

- Subject Public Key
- Issuer Unique Identifier (optional)
- Subject Unique Identifier (optional)
- Extensions (optional)

Symantec first introduced the following digital certificate classes:

- **Class 1:** For individuals; used to protect email. These certificates get saved by web browsers.
- **Class 2:** For organizations that must provide proof of identity.
- **Class 3:** For servers and software signing in which independent verification and identity and authority checking are done by the issuing CA.

Certificate Life Cycle

Security professionals should understand the certificate life cycle. According to Microsoft, the certificate life cycle includes the following events:

- CAs are installed, and the CA certificates are issued.
- Certificates are issued by CAs to entities.
- Certificates are revoked (as necessary), renewed, or allowed to expire.
- The CAs' certificates are renewed before they expire, are revoked, or retired.

NIST Interagency Report (NISTIR) 7924, titled "Reference Certificate Policy," identifies a baseline set of security controls and practices to support the secure issuance of certificates. This report is in its second draft and can be found at https://csrc.nist.gov/CSRC/media/Publications/nistir/7924/draft/documents/nistir_7924_2nd_draft.pdf.

According to NISTIR 7924, the certificate application process must provide sufficient information to

- Establish the applicant's authorization (by the employing or sponsoring organization) to obtain a certificate.
- Establish and record the identity of the applicant.
- Obtain the applicant's public key and verify the applicant's possession of the private key for each certificate required.
- Verify any role or authorization information requested for inclusion in the certificate.

In this document, the steps of the certificate process are as follows:

1. Certificate application
2. Certificate application processing
3. Certificate issuance
4. Certificate acceptance
5. Key pair and certificate usage
6. Certificate renewal
7. Certificate re-key
8. Certificate modification
9. Certificate revocation and suspension
10. End of subscription
11. Key escrow and recovery

These steps may be performed in any order that is convenient for the CA and applicants that does not compromise security, but all must be completed before certificate issuance.

For the CISSP exam, you should know the four main steps that involve how a certificate is issued to an entity: enrollment, verification, revocation, and renewal and modification.

Enrollment

Enrollment is the process of requesting a certificate from the CA. According to NISTIR 7924, a certificate application shall be submitted to the CA by the subscriber, an authorized organizational representative (AOR), or an RA on behalf of the subscriber. Multiple certificate requests from one RA or AOR may be submitted as a batch.

When a subscriber is enrolled, all communications among PKI authorities supporting the certificate application and issuance process will be authenticated and protected from modification; any electronic transmission of shared secrets and personally identifiable information will be protected. Communications may be electronic or out-of-band. Where electronic communications are used, cryptographic mechanisms commensurate with the strength of the public/private key pair will be used. Out-of-band communications will protect the confidentiality and integrity of the data.

Verification

Verification is the process whereby an application verifies that a certificate is valid. Applications use two types of verification methods to check the validity of a digital certificate: certificate revocation lists (CRLs) and Online Certificate Status Protocol (OCSP), both of which are discussed in the sections that follow.

To issue a certificate, the CA must verify that the identity and authorization of the applicant have been verified. If this information cannot be verified, upon receiving the request, the CAs/RAs will

- Verify the identity of the requester.
- Verify the authority of the requester and the integrity of the information in the certificate request.
- Build and sign a certificate if all certificate requirements have been met (in the case of an RA, have the CA sign the certificate).
- Make the certificate available to the subscriber after confirming that the subscriber has formally acknowledged their obligations.

The certificate request may already contain a to-be-signed certificate built by either the RA or the subscriber. This certificate will not be signed until all verifications and modifications, if any, have been completed to the CA's satisfaction. All authorization and other attribute information received from a prospective subscriber will be verified before inclusion in a certificate. Failure to object to the certificate or its contents will constitute acceptance of the certificate.

Revocation

Revocation is the process whereby a certificate is revoked. CAs operating under NISTIR 7924 will make public a description of how to obtain revocation information for the certificates they publish, and an explanation of the consequences of using dated revocation information. This information will be given to subscribers during certificate request or issuance, and will be readily available to any potential relying party. Revocation requests must be authenticated.

A certificate will be revoked when the binding between the subject and the subject's public key defined within the certificate is no longer considered valid. When this situation occurs, the associated certificate will be revoked and placed on the CRL and/or added to the OCSP responder. (Both CRL and OCSP are explained in the following sections.) Revoked certificates will be included on all new publications of the certificate status information until the certificates expire.

CAs should revoke certificates as quickly as practical upon receipt of a proper revocation request and by the requested revocation time.

Renewal and Modification

Any certificate may be renewed if the public key has not reached the end of its validity period, the associated private key has not been revoked or compromised, and the Subscriber name and attributes are unchanged. In addition, the validity period of the certificate must not exceed the remaining lifetime of the private key.

CA certificates and OCSP responder certificates may be renewed as long as the aggregated lifetime of the public key does not exceed the certificate lifetime. The CA may renew previously issued certificates during recovery from CA key compromise without subject request or approval as long as the CA is confident of the accuracy of information to be included in the certificates.

A CA may perform certificate modification for a subscriber whose characteristics have changed (e.g., name change due to marriage). If the subscriber name has changed, the subscriber will undergo the initial registration process.

Certificate Revocation List

A ***certificate revocation list (CRL)*** is a list of digital certificates that a CA has irreversibly revoked. To find out whether a digital certificate has been revoked, the browser must either check the CRL or receive the CRL values pushed out from the CA. This process can become quite daunting when you consider that the CRL contains every certificate that has ever been revoked.

One concept to keep in mind is the revocation request grace period. This period is the maximum amount of time between when the revocation request is received by the CA and when the revocation actually occurs. A shorter revocation period provides better security but often results in a higher implementation cost.

OCSP

Online Certificate Status Protocol (OCSP) is an Internet protocol that obtains the revocation status of an X.509 digital certificate. OCSP is an alternative to the standard CRL that is used by many PKIs. OCSP automatically validates the certificates and reports back the status of the digital certificate by accessing the CRL on the CA.

PKI Steps

The steps involved in requesting a digital certificate are as follows:

Key Topic

1. A user requests a digital certificate, and the RA receives the request.
2. The RA requests identifying information from the requestor.
3. After the required information is received, the RA forwards the certificate request to the CA.
4. The CA creates a digital certificate for the requestor. The requestor's public key and identity information are included as part of the certificate.
5. The user receives the certificate.

After the user has a certificate, that user is considered a trusted entity and is ready to communicate with other trusted entities. The process for communication between entities is as follows:

1. User 1 requests User 2's public key from the certificate repository.
2. The repository sends User 2's digital certificate to User 1.
3. User 1 verifies the certificate and extracts User 2's public key from the Global Address List (GAL).
4. User 1 encrypts the session key with User 2's public key and sends the encrypted session key and User 1's certificate to User 2.
5. User 2 receives User 1's certificate and verifies the certificate with a trusted CA.

After this certificate exchange and verification process occurs, the two entities are able to communicate using encryption.

Cross-Certification

Cross-certification establishes trust relationships between CAs so that the participating CAs can rely on the other participants' digital certificates and public keys. It enables users to validate each other's certificates when they are actually certified under different certification hierarchies. A CA for one organization can validate digital certificates from another organization's CA when a cross-certification trust relationship exists.

Quantum Key Distribution

Quantum Key Distribution (QKD) represents a significant advancement in the field of secure communications, leveraging the principles of quantum mechanics to achieve secure key exchange. When discussing QKD in the context of PKI, it is essential to understand both the potential enhancements QKD offers to traditional cryptographic systems and the challenges it presents.

QKD is a method for secure communication that uses quantum mechanics to securely distribute encryption keys between two parties, ensuring that any attempt at eavesdropping or intercepting the key can be detected. The security of QKD stems from the fundamental principles of quantum mechanics, such as the no-cloning theorem and the observer effect, which states that measuring a quantum system's state inherently alters that state. This means that any attempt to intercept or measure the quantum keys being exchanged would be detectable as it would change the state of the quantum bits (qubits) used in the key.

QKD enhances PKI security by ensuring the secure exchange of keys used for encryption and decryption. Because PKI security relies heavily on the key secrecy and integrity, integrating QKD could potentially offer a method to distribute keys with a theoretically unbreakable level of security. Traditional cryptographic algorithms used in PKI, especially public key cryptography algorithms like RSA and ECC, are at risk due to quantum computers' potential to efficiently break these algorithms. QKD presents a solution to this vulnerability, offering a secure method of key exchange that is not susceptible to quantum computing attacks.

Integrating QKD with existing PKI systems poses significant technical and infrastructural challenges. QKD requires a direct quantum communication channel between the parties, which is difficult and expensive to implement over long distances with current technology. Additionally, QKD addresses only the key distribution aspect, not the encryption/decryption processes, which would still need to be secure against quantum attacks.

For security professionals focused on selecting and determining cryptographic solutions, understanding QKD's potential and limitations is crucial. They must evaluate:

- The current technological landscape and the practicality of implementing QKD within their organization's infrastructure.
- The balance between the theoretical security benefits of QKD and the operational challenges it presents.
- The ability to integrate QKD into existing PKI systems to enhance security, especially in preparation for the era of quantum computing.

While QKD offers a promising solution to secure key distribution, potentially enhancing the security foundations of PKI, its practical application requires careful consideration of current technological limitations and future advancements. Security professionals must stay informed about quantum cryptography developments and assess how these innovations can be adopted within their PKI to ensure robust security in the quantum computing age.

Key Management Practices

A discussion of cryptography would be incomplete without coverage of key management practices. NIST SP 800-57 contains recommendations for key management in three parts:

- **Part 1:** This publication covers general recommendations for key management.
- **Part 2:** This publication covers the best practices for a key management organization.
- **Part 3:** This publication covers the application-specific key management guidance.

Security professionals should at least understand the key management principles in Part 1 of SP 800-57 Revision 1. If security professionals are involved in organizations that provide key management services to other organizations, understanding Part 2 is a necessity. Part 3 is needed when an organization implements applications that use keys. In this section, we cover the recommendations in Part 1.

Part 1 defines the different types of keys. The keys are identified according to their classification as public, private, or symmetric keys, as well as according to their use. For public and private key agreement keys, status as static or ephemeral keys is also specified.

In general, a single key is used for only one purpose (e.g., encryption, integrity, authentication, key wrapping, random bit generation, or digital signatures). A *cryptoperiod* is the time span during which a specific key is authorized for use by legitimate entities, or the time that the keys for a given system will remain in effect. Among the factors affecting the length of a cryptoperiod are

- The cryptographic strength (e.g., the algorithm, key length, block size, and mode of operation)
- The embodiment of the mechanisms (e.g., a FIPS 140 Level 4 implementation or a software implementation on a personal computer)

- The operating environment (e.g., a secure limited-access facility, open office environment, or publicly accessible terminal)
- The volume of information flow or the number of transactions
- The security life of the data
- The security function (e.g., data encryption, digital signature, key derivation, or key protection)
- The rekeying method (e.g., keyboard entry, rekeying using a key loading device where humans have no direct access to key information, or remote rekeying within a PKI)
- The key update or key-derivation process
- The number of nodes in a network that share a common key
- The number of copies of a key and the distribution of those copies
- Personnel turnover (e.g., CA system personnel)
- The threat to the information from adversaries (e.g., from whom the information is protected and their perceived technical capabilities and financial resources to mount an attack)
- The threat to the information from new and disruptive technologies (e.g., quantum computers)

A key is used differently, depending on its state in the key's life cycle. Key states are defined from a system point of view, as opposed to the point of view of a single cryptographic module. The states that an operational or backed-up key may assume are as follows:

- **Pre-activation state:** The key has been generated but has not been authorized for use. In this state, the key may be used to perform only proof-of-possession or key confirmation.
- **Active state:** The key may be used to cryptographically protect information (e.g., encrypt plaintext or generate a digital signature), to cryptographically process previously protected information (e.g., decrypt ciphertext or verify a digital signature), or both. When a key is active, it may be designated for protection only, processing only, or both protection and processing, depending on its type.
- **Suspended state:** The use of a key or key pair may be suspended for several possible reasons; in the case of asymmetric key pairs, both the public and private keys are suspended at the same time. One reason for a suspension might be a possible key compromise, and the suspension has been issued to allow

time to investigate the situation. Another reason might be that the entity that owns a digital signature key pair is not available (e.g., is on an extended leave of absence); signatures purportedly signed during the suspension time would be invalid. A suspended key or key pair may be restored to an active state at a later time or may be deactivated or destroyed, or may transition to the compromised state.

- **Deactivated state:** Keys in the deactivated state are not used to apply cryptographic protection, but in some cases, they may be used to process cryptographically protected information. If a key has been revoked (for reasons other than a compromise), then the key may continue to be used for processing. Note that keys retrieved from an archive can be considered to be in the deactivated state unless they are compromised.
- **Compromised state:** Generally, keys are compromised when they are released to or determined by an unauthorized entity. A compromised key shall not be used to apply cryptographic protection to information. However, in some cases, a compromised key or a public key that corresponds to a compromised private key of a key pair may be used to process cryptographically protected information. For example, a signature may be verified to determine the integrity of signed data if its signature has been physically protected since a time before the compromise occurred. This processing shall be done only under very highly controlled conditions, where the users of the information are fully aware of the possible consequences.
- **Destroyed state:** The key has been destroyed as specified in the destroyed phase, discussed shortly. Even though the key no longer exists when in this state, certain key metadata (e.g., key state transition history, key name, type, cryptoperiod) may be retained.

The cryptographic key management life cycle can be divided into the following four phases:

1. **Pre-operational phase:** The keying material is not yet available for normal cryptographic operations. Keys may not yet be generated or are in the pre-activation state. System or enterprise attributes are also established during this phase. During this phase, the following functions occur:
    a. User registration
    b. System initialization
    c. User initialization
    d. Key establishment
    e. Key registration

2. **Operational phase:** The keying material is available and in normal use. Keys are in the active or suspended state. Keys in the active state may be designated as protect only, process only, or protect and process; keys in the suspended state can be used for processing only. During this phase, the following functions occur:
    a. Normal operational storage
    b. Continuity of operations
    c. Key change
    d. Key derivation
3. **Post-operational phase:** The keying material is no longer in normal use, but access to the keying material is possible, and the keying material may be used for processing only in certain circumstances. Keys are in the deactivated or compromised states. Keys in the post-operational phase may be in an archive when not processing data. During this phase the following functions occur:
    a. Archive storage and key recovery
    b. Entity (user or device) deregistration
    c. Key deregistration
    d. Key destruction
    e. Key revocation
4. **Destroyed phase:** Keys are no longer available. Records of their existence may or may not have been deleted. Keys are in the destroyed states. Although the keys themselves are destroyed, the key metadata (e.g., key name, type, cryptoperiod, usage period) may be retained.

Systems that process valuable information require controls in order to protect the information from unauthorized disclosure and modification. Cryptographic systems that contain keys and other cryptographic information are especially critical. Security professionals should work to ensure that the protection of keying material provides accountability, audit, and survivability.

Accountability involves the identification of entities and the work they perform (via logs) that have access to, or control of, cryptographic keys throughout their life cycles. Accountability can be an effective tool to help prevent key compromises and to reduce the impact of compromises when they are detected. Although it is preferred that no humans be able to view keys, as a minimum, the key management system should account for all individuals who are able to view plaintext cryptographic keys. In addition, more sophisticated key management systems may account for all individuals authorized to access or control any cryptographic keys, whether in plaintext or ciphertext form.

Two types of audits should be performed on key management systems:

- **Security:** The security plan and the procedures that are developed to support the plan should be periodically audited to ensure that they continue to support the key management policy.
- **Protective:** The protective mechanisms employed should be periodically reassessed with respect to the level of security they currently provide and are expected to provide in the future. They should also be assessed to determine whether the mechanisms correctly and effectively support the appropriate policies. New technology developments and attacks should be considered as part of a protective audit.

Key management survivability entails backing up or archiving copies of all keys used. Key backup and recovery procedures must be established to ensure that keys are not lost. System redundancy and contingency planning should also be properly assessed to ensure that all the systems involved in key management are fault tolerant.

Message Integrity

Integrity is one of the three basic tenets of security. Message integrity ensures that a message has not been altered by using parity bits, cyclic redundancy checks (CRCs), or checksums.

The parity bit method adds an extra bit to the data. The parity bit simply indicates the number of 1s in a digital bit stream. Parity is either odd or even parity. The parity bit is set before the data is transmitted. When the data arrives, the parity bit is checked against the other data. If the parity bit doesn't match the data sent, then an error is sent to the originator.

The CRC method uses polynomial division to determine the CRC value for a file. The CRC value is usually 16 or 32 bits long. Because CRC is very accurate, the CRC value will not match up if a single bit is incorrect.

The checksum method adds up the bytes of data being sent and then transmits that number to be checked later using the same method. The source adds up the values of the bytes and sends the data and its checksum. The receiving end receives the information, adds up the bytes in the same way the source did, and gets the checksum. The receiver then compares their checksum with the source's checksum. If the values match, message integrity is intact. If the values do not match, the data should be re-sent or replaced. Checksums are also referred to as hash sums because they typically use hash functions for the computation.

Message integrity is provided by hash functions and message authentication code.

Hashing

Hash functions were explained earlier in this chapter. In the following sections, we discuss some of the most popular hash functions. Some of them might no longer be commonly used because more secure alternatives are available.

Security professionals should be familiar with the following hash functions:

- One-way hash
- MD2/MD4/MD5/MD6
- SHA/SHA-2/SHA-3
- HAVAL
- RIPEMD-160
- Tiger

One-Way Hash

A hash function takes a message of variable length and produces a fixed-length hash value. Hash values, also referred to as message digests, are calculated using the original message. If the receiver calculates a hash value that is the same, then the original message is intact. If the receiver calculates a hash value that is different, then the original message has been altered.

Using a given function H, the following equation must be true to ensure that the original message, M1, has not been altered or replaced with a new message, M2:

H(M1) < > H(M2)

For a one-way hash to be effective, creating two different messages with the same hash value must be mathematically impossible. Given a hash value, discovering the original message from which the hash value was obtained must be mathematically impossible. A one-way hash algorithm is collision free if it provides protection against creating the same hash value from different messages.

Unlike symmetric and asymmetric algorithms, the hashing algorithm is publicly known. Hash functions are always performed in one direction. Using it in reverse is unnecessary.

However, one-way hash functions do have limitations. If an attacker intercepts a message that contains a hash value, the attacker can alter the original message to create a second invalid message with a new hash value. If the attacker then sends the second invalid message with the newly generated hash value to the intended recipient, the intended recipient will have no way of knowing that they received an incorrect message. When the receiver performs a hash value calculation, the invalid message will look valid because the invalid message was appended with the attacker's new hash value, not the original message's hash value. To prevent this from occurring, the sender should use message authentication code (MAC).

Encrypting the hash function with a symmetric key algorithm generates a keyed MAC. The symmetric key does not encrypt the original message. It is used only to protect the hash value.

NOTE The basic types of MAC are discussed later in this chapter.

Figure 3-21 illustrates the basic steps of a hash function.

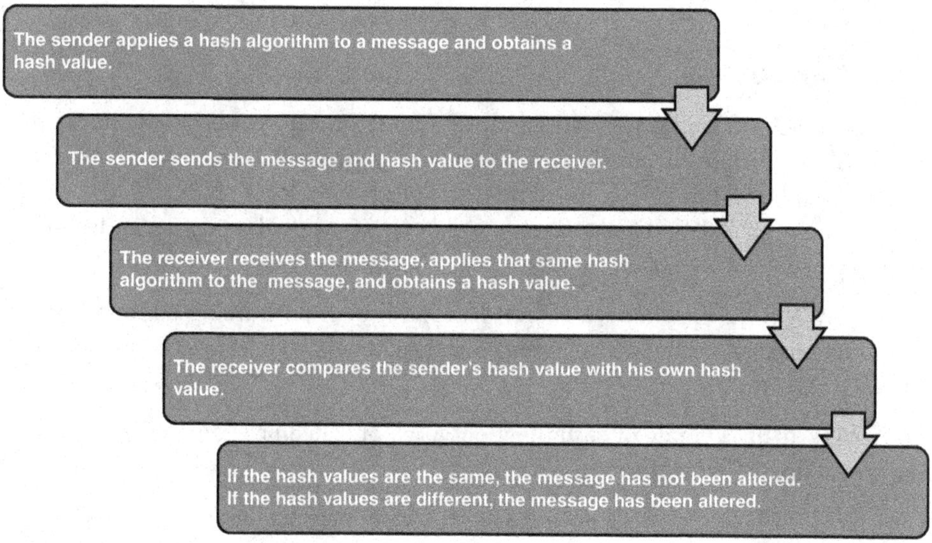

Figure 3-21 Hash Function Process

MD2/MD4/MD5/MD6

The ***MD2*** message digest algorithm produces a 128-bit hash value. It performs 18 rounds of computations. Although MD2 is still in use today, it is much slower than MD4, MD5, and MD6.

The ***MD4*** algorithm also produces a 128-bit hash value. However, it performs only three rounds of computations. Although MD4 is faster than MD2, its use has significantly declined because attacks against it have been so successful.

Like the other MD algorithms, the ***MD5*** algorithm produces a 128-bit hash value. It performs four rounds of computations. It was originally created because of the issues with MD4, and it is more complex than MD4. However, MD5 is not collision free. For this reason, it should not be used for SSL certificates or digital signatures. The U.S. government requires the usage of SHA-2 instead of MD5. However, in commercial usage, many software vendors publish the MD5 hash value when they release software patches so customers can verify the software's integrity after download.

The ***MD6*** algorithm produces a variable hash value, performing a variable number of computations. Although it was originally introduced as a candidate for SHA-3, it was withdrawn because of early issues the algorithm had with differential attacks. MD6 has since been re-released with this issue fixed. However, that release was too late to be accepted as the NIST SHA-3 standard.

SHA/SHA-2/SHA-3

Secure Hash Algorithm (SHA) is a family of four algorithms published by the U.S. NIST. SHA-0, originally referred to as simply SHA because there were no other "family members," produces a 160-bit hash value after performing 80 rounds of computations on 512-bit blocks. SHA-0 was never very popular because collisions were discovered.

Like SHA-0, SHA-1 produces a 160-bit hash value after performing 80 rounds of computations on 512-bit blocks. SHA-1 corrected the flaw in SHA-0 that made it susceptible to attacks.

SHA-2 is actually a family of hash functions, each of which provides different functional limits. The SHA-2 family is as follows:

- **SHA-224:** Produces a 224-bit hash value after performing 64 rounds of computations on 512-bit blocks.
- **SHA-256:** Produces a 256-bit hash value after performing 64 rounds of computations on 512-bit blocks.
- **SHA-384:** Produces a 384-bit hash value after performing 80 rounds of computations on 1,024-bit blocks.
- **SHA-512:** Produces a 512-bit hash value after performing 80 rounds of computations on 1,024-bit blocks.
- **SHA-512/224:** Produces a 224-bit hash value after performing 80 rounds of computations on 1,024-bit blocks. The 512 designation here indicates the internal state size.

- **SHA-512/256:** Produces a 256-bit hash value after performing 80 rounds of computations on 1,024-bit blocks. Once again, the 512 designation indicates the internal state size.

SHA-3, like SHA-2, is a family of hash functions. SHA-2 has not yet been broken. The hash value sizes for SHA-3 range from 224 to 512 bits. The block sizes range from 576 to 1,152 bits. SHA-3 performs 120 rounds of computations, by default.

Keep in mind that SHA-1 and SHA-2 are still widely used today. SHA-3 was not developed because of some security flaw with the two previous standards but was instead proposed as an alternative hash function to the others.

HAVAL

HAVAL is a one-way function that produces variable-length hash values, including 128 bits, 160 bits, 192 bits, 224 bits, and 256 bits, and uses 1,024-bit blocks. The number of rounds of computations can be three, four, or five. Collision issues have been discovered if producing a 128-bit hash value with three rounds of computations.

RIPEMD-160

Although several variations of the RIPEMD hash function exist, security professionals should only worry about ***RIPEMD-160*** for exam purposes. RIPEMD-160 produces a 160-bit hash value after performing 160 rounds of computations on 512-bit blocks.

Tiger

Tiger is a hash function that produces 128-, 160-, or 192-bit hash values after performing 24 rounds of computations on 512-bit blocks, with the most popular version being the one that produces 192-bit hash values. Unlike MD5, RIPEMD, SHA-0, and SHA-1, Tiger is not built on the MD4 architecture.

Message Authentication Code

MAC was explained earlier in this chapter. Here, we discuss the three types of MACs with which security professionals should be familiar:

- HMAC
- CBC-MAC
- CMAC

HMAC

A ***hash MAC (HMAC)*** is a keyed-hash MAC that involves a hash function with symmetric key. HMAC provides data integrity and authentication. Any of the previously listed hash functions can be used with HMAC, with the HMAC name being appended with the hash function name, as in HMAC-SHA-1. The strength of HMAC depends on the strength of the hash function, including the hash value size and the key size.

HMAC's hash value output size will be the same as the underlying hash function. HMAC can help to reduce the collision rate of the hash function.

The basic steps of an HMAC process are as follows:

Key Topic

1. The sender and receiver agree on which symmetric key to use.
2. The sender joins the symmetric key to the message.
3. The sender applies a hash algorithm to the message and obtains a hash value.
4. The sender adds a hash value to the original message, and the sender sends the new message to the receiver.
5. The receiver receives the message and joins the symmetric key to the message.
6. The receiver applies the hash algorithm to the message and obtains a hash value.
7. If the hash values are the same, the message has not been altered. If the hash values are different, the message has been altered.

CBC-MAC

Cipher Block Chaining MAC (CBC-MAC) is a block-cipher MAC that operates in CBC mode. CBC-MAC provides data integrity and authentication.

The basic steps of a CBC-MAC process are as follows:

Key Topic

1. The sender and receiver agree on which symmetric block cipher to use.
2. The sender encrypts the message with the symmetric block cipher in CBC mode. The last block is the MAC.
3. The sender adds the MAC to the original message, and the sender sends the new message to the receiver.
4. The receiver receives the message and encrypts the message with the symmetric block cipher in CBC mode.

5. The receiver obtains the MAC and compares it to the sender's MAC.
6. If the values are the same, the message has not been altered. If the values are different, the message has been altered.

CMAC

Cipher-Based MAC (CMAC) operates in the same manner as CBC-MAC but with much better mathematical functions. CMAC addresses some security issues with CBC-MAC and is approved to work with AES and 3DES.

Salting

Lookup tables and rainbow tables work because each password is hashed exactly the same way. If two users have the same password, they have the same hashed password if random hashes are not used. To prevent attack, security professionals should ensure that each hash is randomized. Then, when the same password is hashed twice, the hashes are not the same.

Salting means randomly adding data to a one-way function that "hashes" a password or passphrase. The primary function of salting is to defend against dictionary attacks versus a list of password hashes and against precomputed rainbow table attacks.

A security professional should randomize the hashes by appending or prepending a random string, called a salt, to the password before hashing. To check whether a password is correct, the attacker needs to know the value of the salt added. The salt usually can be stored in the user account database, or another secure location, along with the hash, or as part of the hash string itself.

Attackers do not know in advance what the salt will be, so they cannot precompute a lookup table or rainbow table. If each user's password is hashed with a different salt, a reverse lookup table attack doesn't work either.

If salts are used, security professionals must ensure that they are not reused and are not too short. A new random salt must be generated each time an administrator creates a user account or a user changes their password. A good rule of thumb is to use a salt that is the same size as the output of the hash function. For example, the output of SHA-256 is 256 bits (32 bytes), so the salt should be at least 32 random bytes.

Salts should be generated using a cryptographically secure pseudo-random number generator (CSPRNG). As the name suggests, a CSPRNG is designed to provide a high level of randomness and is completely unpredictable.

Digital Signatures and Non-repudiation

A digital signature is a hash value encrypted with the sender's private key. A digital signature provides authentication, non-repudiation, and integrity. A blind signature is a form of digital signature where the contents of the message are masked before it is signed.

Public key cryptography, which is discussed later, is used to create digital signatures. Users register their public keys with a CA, which distributes a certificate containing the user's public key and the CA's digital signature. The digital signature is computed by the user's public key and validity period being combined with the certificate issuer and digital signature algorithm identifier.

When considering cryptography, keep the following facts in mind:

- Encryption provides confidentiality.
- Hashing provides integrity.
- Digital signatures provide authentication, non-repudiation, and integrity.

DSS

The ***Digital Signature Standard (DSS)*** is a federal digital security standard that governs the Digital Security Algorithm (DSA). DSA generates a message digest of 160 bits. The U.S. federal government requires the use of DSA, RSA (discussed earlier in this chapter), or Elliptic Curve DSA (ECDSA) and SHA for digital signatures. DSA is slower than RSA and provides only digital signatures. RSA provides digital signatures, encryption, and secure symmetric key distribution.

Non-repudiation

Non-repudiation occurs when a sender is provided with proof of delivery to a receiver, and a receiver is provided with proof of the sender's identity. If non-repudiation is implemented correctly, the sender cannot later deny having sent the information.

In addition to digital signatures, non-repudiation is also used in digital contracts and email. Email non-repudiation involves methods such as email tracking.

Applied Cryptography

Encryption can provide different protection based on which level of communication is being used. The two types of encryption communication levels are link encryption and end-to-end encryption. In addition, cryptography is used for email and Internet security. These topics are discussed in detail in the "Communications Cryptography" section in Chapter 4.

Link Encryption Versus End-to-End Encryption

Link encryption encrypts all the data that is transmitted over a link. End-to-end encryption encrypts less of the packet information than link encryption.

Email Security

Email security methods include the PGP, MIME, and S/MIME email standards that are popular in today's world.

Internet Security

Internet security includes remote access; SSL/TLS; HTTP, HTTPS, and S-HTTP; SET; cookies; SSH; and IPsec and ISAKMP.

Cryptanalytic Attacks

Cryptography attacks are categorized as either passive or active attacks. A passive attack is usually implemented just to discover information and is much harder to detect because it is usually carried out by eavesdropping or packet sniffing. Active attacks involve an attacker actually carrying out steps, like message alteration or file modification. Cryptography is usually attacked by exploiting the key, algorithm, execution, data, or people. But most of these attacks are attempting to discover the key used.

Cryptography attacks that are discussed include the following:

- Ciphertext-only attack
- Known plaintext attack
- Chosen plaintext attack
- Chosen ciphertext attack
- Social engineering
- Brute force
- Differential cryptanalysis
- Linear cryptanalysis
- Algebraic attack

- Frequency analysis
- Birthday attack
- Dictionary attack
- Replay attack
- Analytic attack
- Statistical attack
- Factoring attack
- Reverse engineering
- Meet-in-the-middle attack
- Ransomware attack
- Side-channel attack
- Implementation attack
- Fault injection
- Timing attack
- Pass-the-hash attack

Ciphertext-Only Attack

In a ***ciphertext-only attack***, an attacker uses several encrypted messages (ciphertext) to figure out the key used in the encryption process. Although it is a very common type of attack, it is usually not successful because so little is known about the encryption used.

Known Plaintext Attack

In a ***known plaintext attack***, an attacker uses various plaintext and ciphertext versions of a message or more messages to discover the key used. This type of attack implements reverse engineering, frequency analysis, or brute force to determine the key so that all messages can be deciphered.

Chosen Plaintext Attack

In a ***chosen plaintext attack***, an attacker chooses the plaintext to get encrypted to obtain the ciphertext. The attacker sends a message hoping that the user will forward that message as ciphertext to another user. The attacker captures the ciphertext version of the message and tries to determine the key by comparing the plaintext version that was originated with the captured ciphertext version. Once again, key discovery is the goal of this attack.

Chosen Ciphertext Attack

A ***chosen ciphertext attack*** is the opposite of a chosen plaintext attack. In a chosen ciphertext attack, an attacker chooses the ciphertext to be decrypted to obtain the plaintext. This attack is more difficult because control of the system that implements the algorithm is needed.

Social Engineering

Social engineering attacks against cryptographic algorithms do not differ greatly from social engineering attacks against any other security area. Attackers attempt to trick users into giving the attacker the cryptographic key used. Common social engineering methods include intimidation, enticement, or inducement.

Brute Force

As with a *brute-force attack* against passwords, a brute-force attack executed against a cryptographic algorithm uses all possible keys until a key is discovered that successfully decrypts the ciphertext. This attack requires considerable time and processing power and is very difficult to complete.

Differential Cryptanalysis

Differential cryptanalysis measures the execution times and power required by the cryptographic device. The measurements help to detect the key and algorithm used.

Linear Cryptanalysis

Linear cryptanalysis is a known plaintext attack that uses linear approximation, which describes the behavior of the block cipher. An attacker is more successful with this type of attack when more plaintext and matching ciphertext messages are obtained.

Algebraic Attack

Algebraic attacks rely on the algebra used by cryptographic algorithms. If an attacker exploits known vulnerabilities of the algebra used, looking for those vulnerabilities can help the attacker to determine the key and algorithm used.

Frequency Analysis

Frequency analysis is an attack that relies on the fact that substitution and transposition ciphers will result in repeated patterns in ciphertext. Recognizing the patterns of 8 bits and counting them can allow an attacker to use reverse substitution to obtain the plaintext message.

Frequency analysis usually involves the creation of a chart that lists all the letters of the alphabet alongside the number of times that letter occurs. So if the letter Q in the frequency lists has the highest value, a good possibility exists that this letter is actually E in the plaintext message because E is the most used letter in the English language. The ciphertext letter is then replaced in the ciphertext with the plaintext letter.

Today's algorithms are considered too complex to be susceptible to this type of attack.

Birthday Attack

A birthday attack uses the premise that finding two messages that result in the same hash value is easier than matching a message and its hash value. Most hash algorithms can resist simple birthday attacks.

Dictionary Attack

Similar to a brute-force attack, a dictionary attack uses all the words in a dictionary until a key is discovered that successfully decrypts the ciphertext. This attack requires considerable time and processing power and is very difficult to complete. It also requires a comprehensive dictionary of words.

Replay Attack

In a replay attack, an attacker sends the same data repeatedly in an attempt to trick the receiving device. This data is most commonly authentication information. The best countermeasures against this type of attack are timestamps and sequence numbers.

Analytic Attack

In analytic attacks, attackers use known structural weaknesses or flaws to determine the algorithm used. If a particular weakness or flaw can be exploited, then the possibility of a particular algorithm being used is more likely.

Statistical Attack

Whereas analytic attacks look for structural weaknesses or flaws, statistical attacks use known statistical weaknesses of an algorithm to aid in the attack.

Factoring Attack

A factoring attack is carried out against the RSA algorithm by using the solutions of factoring large numbers.

Reverse Engineering

One of the most popular cryptographic attacks, reverse engineering occurs when an attacker purchases a particular cryptographic product to attempt to reverse engineer the product to discover any information about the cryptographic algorithm used, whether the information is the key or the algorithm itself.

Meet-in-the-Middle Attack

In a meet-in-the middle attack, an attacker tries to break the algorithm by encrypting from one end and decrypting from the other to determine the mathematical problem used.

Ransomware Attack

In a ransomware attack, a user accidentally installs a program that allows an attacker to encrypt files or folders on the user's computer. To obtain access to the files and folders that are encrypted, the victim must pay a fine to obtain access to their data. Two of the more recent variants of this type of attack are the CryptoLocker, which targeted Windows computers and infected email attachments using a Trojan, and WannaCry, which also targeted Windows computers and demanded payment in Bitcoin.

Side-Channel Attack

In a side-channel attack, information from the implementation of a computer system is obtained, rather than exploiting a weakness in the algorithm itself. Areas that are exploited include the computer's cache, timing, acoustics, and data remanence. It usually involves monitoring communication within the different components of the computer to determine the secret key.

Implementation Attack

An implementation attack, a specific type of side-channel attack, exploits implementation weaknesses in algorithms, focusing on software code, errors, and other flaws. This type of attack can be carried out in a physical or logical manner. Physical attacks target physical leakage of a device, meaning the attacker attempts to obtain the data from the hard drive or the hard drive itself. Logical attacks try to observe some parameters of the algorithm.

Fault Injection

Fault injection attacks, which are a type of side-channel attack, are carried out on crypto-devices. A single fault injected during encryption can reveal the cipher's secret key. Fault injection attacks on crypto-devices include power supply voltage variations, clock signal irregularity injections, electro-magnetics disturbances, overheating, and light exposure.

Timing Attack

A timing attack is a type of side-channel attack wherein an attacker attempts to compromise an algorithm by analyzing the time taken to encrypt or decrypt data. Timing attacks are easier to carry out if the attacker knows hardware implementation details and the cryptographic system used.

Pass-the-Hash Attack

A pass-the-hash attack allows an attacker to authenticate to a remote server or service by using the underlying hash of a user's password, instead of the plaintext password itself. This attack requires that an attacker steal the password's hash, rather than the plaintext password, and use it for authentication.

Digital Rights Management

Digital rights management (DRM) is covered in Chapter 1. For security architecture and engineering, security professionals must ensure that organizations employ DRM policies and procedures to protect intellectual property, including documents, music, movies, video games, and e-books.

Today's DRM implementations include the following:

- Directories:
  - Lightweight Directory Access Protocol (LDAP)
  - Active Directory (AD)
  - Custom

- Permissions:
  - Open
  - Print
  - Modify
  - Clipboard
- Additional controls:
  - Expiration (absolute, relative, immediate revocation)
  - Version control
  - Change policy on existing documents
  - Watermarking
  - Online/offline
  - Auditing
- Ad hoc and structured processes:
  - User initiated on desktop
  - Mapped to system
  - Built into workflow process

Document DRM

Organizations implement DRM to protect confidential or sensitive documents and data. Commercial DRM products allow organizations to protect documents and include the capability to restrict and audit access to documents. Some of the permissions that can be restricted using DRM products include reading and modifying a file, removing and adding watermarks, downloading and saving a file, printing a file, or even taking screenshots. If a DRM product is implemented, the organization should ensure that the administrator is properly trained and that policies are in place to ensure that rights are appropriately granted and revoked.

Music DRM

DRM has been used in the music industry for some time now. Subscription-based music services, such as Napster, use DRM to revoke a user's access to downloaded music after their subscription expires. Although technology companies have petitioned the music industry to allow them to sell music without DRMs, the industry has been reluctant to do so.

Movie DRM

Although the movie industry has used a variety of DRM schemes over the years, two main technologies are used for the mass distribution of media:

- **Content Scrambling System (CSS):** Uses encryption to enforce playback and region restrictions on DVDs. This system can be broken using Linux's DeCSS tool.
- **Advanced Access Content System (AACS):** Protects Blu-ray and HD DVD content. Hackers have been able to obtain the encryption keys to this system.

This industry continues to make advances to prevent hackers from creating unencrypted copies of copyrighted material.

Video Game DRM

Most video game DRM implementations rely on proprietary consoles that use Internet connections to verify video game licenses. Most consoles today verify the license upon installation and allow unrestricted use from that point. However, to obtain updates, the license will again be verified prior to download and installation of the update.

E-book DRM

E-book DRM is considered to be the most successful DRM deployment. Both Amazon's Kindle and Barnes and Noble's Nook devices implement DRM to protect electronic forms of books. Both of these companies have released mobile apps that function like the physical e-book devices.

Today's implementation uses a decryption key that is installed on the device. This means that the e-books cannot be easily copied between e-book devices or applications. Adobe created the Adobe Digital Experience Protection Technology (ADEPT) that is used by most e-book readers except Amazon's Kindle. With ADEPT, AES is used to encrypt the media content, and RSA encrypts the AES key.

Site and Facility Design

For many forward-thinking organizations, physical security considerations begin during physical site selection and design, such as a building and location. These companies have learned that building in security is easier than patching the security after the fact. In the following sections, we cover physical site selection and site building practices that can lead to increased physical security.

Layered Defense Model

All physical security should be based in a ***layered defense model***. In such a model, reliance should not be based on any single physical security concept but on the use of multiple approaches that support one another. The theory is that if one tier of defense (say, for example, perimeter security) fails, another layer will serve as a backup (such as locks on the server room door). Layering the concepts discussed in this chapter can strengthen the overall physical security.

CPTED

Crime Prevention Through Environmental Design (CPTED) refers to designing a facility from the ground up to support physical security. It is actually a broad concept that can be applied to any project (housing developments, office buildings, and retail establishments). It addresses the building entrance, landscaping, and interior design. It aims to create behavioral effects that reduce crime. The three main strategies that guide CPTED are covered here.

Natural Access Control

The ***natural access control*** concept applies to the entrances of the facility. It encompasses the placement of the doors, lights, fences, and even landscaping. It aims to satisfy security goals in the least obtrusive and most aesthetically appealing manner. A single object can be designed in many cases to fulfill multiple security objectives.

For example, many buildings have ***bollards*** or large posts in the front of the buildings with lights on them. These objects serve a number of purposes. They protect the building entrance from vehicular traffic being driven into it. The lights also brighten the entrance to discourage crime, and can help show a clear way to the entrance.

Natural access control also encourages the idea of creating security zones in the building. These areas can be labeled, and then card systems can be used to prevent access to more sensitive areas. This concept also encourages a minimization of entry points and a tight control over those entry points. It also encourages designing and designating a separate entrance for suppliers that is not accessible or highly visible to the public eye.

Natural Surveillance

Natural surveillance is the use of physical environmental features to promote visibility of all areas and thus discourage crime in those areas. The idea is to encourage the flow of people such that the largest possible percentage of the building is always populated, because people in an area discourage crime. It also attempts to maximize the visibility of all areas.

Natural Territorials Reinforcement

The goal of ***natural territorials reinforcement*** is to create a feeling of community in the area. It attempts to extend the sense of ownership to the employees. It also attempts to make potential offenders feel that their activities are at risk of being discovered. This is often implemented in the form of walls, fences, landscaping, and lighting design.

Physical Security Plan

Another important aspect of site and facility design is the proper convergence between the physical layout and the physical security plan. Achieving all the goals of CPTED may not be always possible, and in cases where gaps exist, the physical security plan should include policies and/or procedures designed to close any gaps. The plan should address the following issues.

Deter Criminal Activity

Both the layout and supporting policies should deter criminal activity. For example, as many areas as possible should be open and clearly seen. There should be a minimum of isolated and darkened areas. Signage that indicates cameras or onsite monitoring and the presence of guards can also serve as deterrents.

Delay Intruders

Another beneficial characteristic of the physical security plan is to add impediments to entry, such as locks, fences, and barriers. Any procedures that slow, deter, and monitor the entry of people into the facility can also help. The more delay intruders encounter, the less likely they are to choose the facility and the more likely they are to be caught.

Detect Intruders

Systems and procedures should be in place that allow for criminal activity to be detected. Motion sensors, cameras, and the like are all forms of intruder detection. Logging all visitors could also be a form of deterrence.

Assess Situation

The plan should identify specific personnel and actions to be taken when an event occurs. Compiling a list of incident types that indicate an acceptable response, response time, and contact names might be beneficial. Written plans developed ahead of time provide a much more effective and consistent response.

Respond to Intrusions and Disruptions

The plan should also attempt to anticipate and develop appropriate responses to intruders and to common disruptions (power outages, utility problems, and so on). Although anticipating every potential event is impossible, creating a list covering possible intrusions and disruptions should be doable. Scripted responses can then be developed to ensure a consistent and predictable response to these events from all personnel.

Facility Selection Issues

When an organization moves to a new facility or enlarges an existing one, it is a great opportunity to include physical security issues in the site selection process or in the expansion plan. Next, we look at some critical items to consider if this opportunity presents itself.

Visibility

The amount of visibility desired depends on the organization and the processes being carried out at the facility. In some cases having high visibility of the location to help promote the brand or for the convenience of customers is beneficial. In other cases a lower profile is desired when sensitive operations are taking place. When this is the case, the likelihood of eavesdropping from outside the facility through windows should be considered. Considering common areas is also important. If possible, these areas should not be isolated or darkened. Place them in visible areas with lighting to discourage crime. Such areas include hallways, parking lots, and other shared spaces.

NOTE Perimeter security controls, including lighting, fencing, and perimeter intrusion detection, are covered in more depth in Chapter 7.

Surrounding Area and External Entities

Considering the environment in which the facility is located is also important. What type of neighborhood is it? Is it an area that has a high crime rate, or is it isolated?

Isolation can be good, but it also invites crime that might go undetected for a longer period of time. Also consider the distance to law enforcement, medical facilities, and fire stations. Finally, consider the nature of the operations of the surrounding businesses. Do they pose any sort of threat to your operations?

Accessibility

The ease with which employees and officers can access the facility is a consideration. What are the traffic conditions that the employees will encounter? If this is a new facility replacing an old one, is it inconvenient for the bulk of the employees? Do you risk losing employees over the commute? Is this location convenient to transportation options, such as train stations and airports? If a lot of travel is required of your employees, accessibility could be important. If you often host employees from other locations on a temporary basis or host business partners, are safe accommodations nearby?

Construction

The materials used to construct a facility are another critical issue. But the issues to consider here do not stop at simply the makeup of the walls and ceilings, although that is crucial. The support systems built into the building are also important and include the following:

- Walls
- Doors
- Ceilings
- Windows
- Flooring
- HVAC
- Power source
- Utilities
- Fire detection and suppression

Some special considerations include the following:

- All external walls must have a two-hour minimum fire-resistant rating.
- Doors must resist forcible entry.

- Location and type of fire suppression systems should be known.
- Flooring in server rooms and wiring closets should be raised to help mitigate flooding damage.
- Backup and alternate power sources should exist.
- Separate AC units must be dedicated, and air quality/humidity should be controlled for data centers and computer rooms.

Internal Compartments

In many areas of a facility, partitions are used to separate work areas. These partitions, although appearing to be walls, are not full walls in that they do not extend all the way to the ceiling. When this construction approach is combined with a drop ceiling, also common in many buildings, an opportunity exists for someone to gain access to an adjoining room through the drop ceiling. All rooms that need to be secured, such as server rooms and wiring closets, should not have these types of walls.

Computer and Equipment Rooms

While we are on the subject of rooms that contain equipment to which physical access should be controlled, such as those that contain sensitive servers and crucial network gear, computer and equipment rooms should be locked at all times and secured and fitted with the following safeguards:

- Locate computer and equipment rooms in the center of the building, when possible.
- Computer and equipment rooms should have a single access door or point of entry.
- Avoid the top floors of buildings for computer and equipment rooms.
- Install and frequently test fire detection and suppression systems.
- Install raised flooring.
- Install separate power supplies for computer and equipment rooms when possible.
- Use only solid doors.

Site and Facility Security Controls

Although perimeter security is important, security within the building is also important as prescribed in the concentric circle model. The following sections cover issues affecting the interior of the facility.

Doors

A variety of door types and door materials can be used in buildings. They can either be hollow, which are used inside the building, or solid, typically used at the edge of the building and in places where additional security is required. Some door types with which a security professional should be familiar and prepared to select for protection are

- **Vault doors:** Leading into walk-in safes or security rooms
- **Personnel doors:** Used by humans to enter the facility
- **Industrial doors:** Large doors that allow access to larger vehicles
- **Vehicle access doors:** Doors to parking building or lots
- **Bullet-resistant doors:** Doors designed to withstand firearms

Door Lock Types

Door locks can either be mechanical or electronic. Electric locks or ***cipher locks*** use a key pad that requires the correct code to open the lock. These locks are programmable, and organizations that use them should change the password frequently. Another type of door security system is a ***proximity authentication device***, with which a programmable card is used to deliver an access code to the device either by swiping the card or in some cases just being in the vicinity of the reader. These devices typically contain the following Electronic Access Control (EAC) components:

- An electromagnetic lock
- A credential reader
- A closed-door sensor

Turnstiles and Mantraps

Two special types of physical access control devices, turnstiles and mantraps, also require mention. Although you might be familiar with a turnstile, which can be opened by scanning or swiping an access card, a mantrap is an unusual system with which you might not be familiar.

A ***mantrap*** is a series of two doors with a small room between them. The user is authenticated at the first door and then allowed into the room. At that point, additional verification occurs (such as a guard visually identifying the person), and then the person is allowed through the second door. These doors are typically used only in very high security situations. Mantraps also typically require that the first door is closed prior to enabling the second door to open. Figure 3-22 shows a mantrap design.

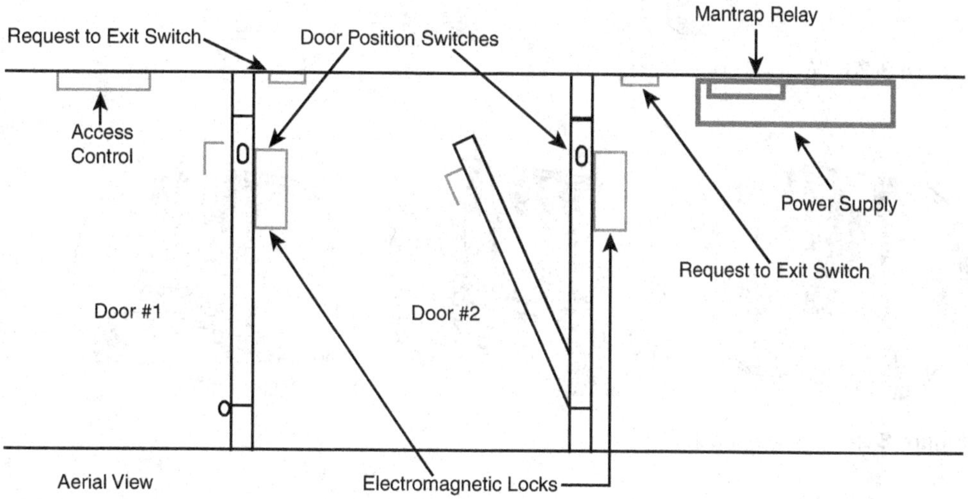

Figure 3-22 Mantrap

Locks

Locks are also used in places other than doors, such as protecting cabinets and securing devices. Types of mechanical locks with which you should be familiar are

- ***Warded locks***: These have a spring-loaded bolt with a notch in it. The lock has wards or metal projections inside the lock with which the key will match and enable opening the lock. A warded lock design is shown in Figure 3-23.
- ***Tumbler locks***: These have more moving parts than the warded locks, and the key raises the lock metal piece to the correct height. A tumbler lock design is shown in Figure 3-24.

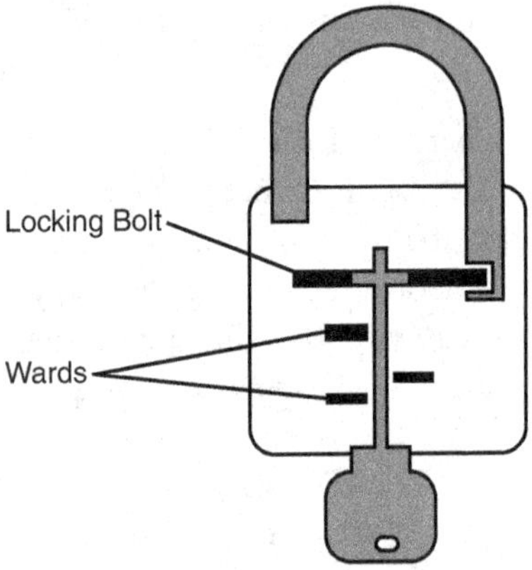

Figure 3-23 Warded Lock

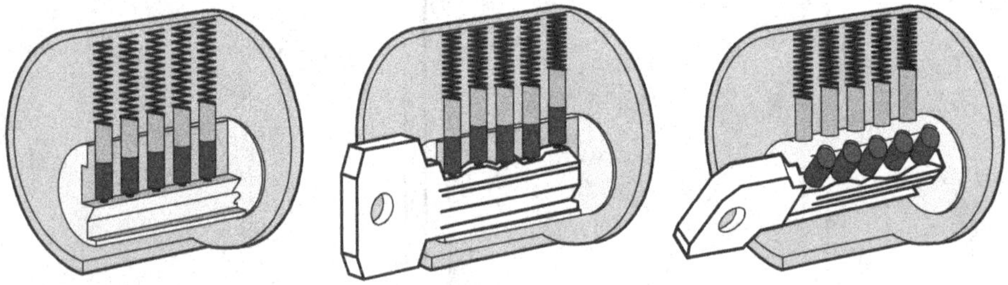

Figure 3-24 Tumbler Lock

- ***Combination locks*:** These require rotating the lock in a pattern that, if correct, lines up the tumblers, opening the lock. A combination lock design is shown in Figure 3-25.

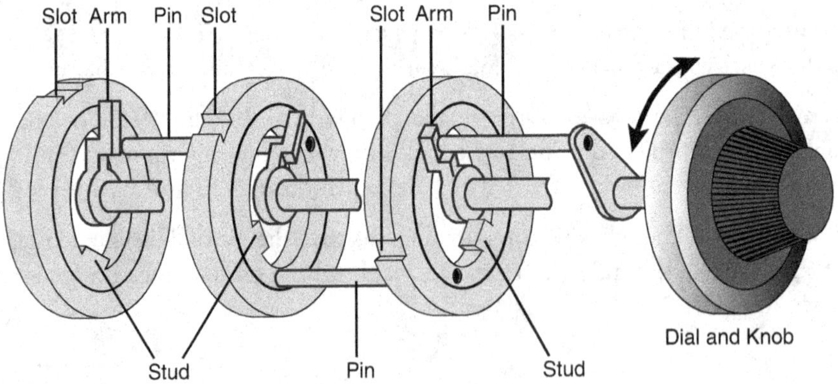

Figure 3-25 Combination Lock

In the case of device locks, laptops are the main item that must be protected because they are so easy to steal. Laptops should never be left in the open without being secured to something solid with a ***cable lock***. These are vinyl-coated steel cables that connect to the laptop and then lock around a hard-to-move object, such as a table or desk leg.

Biometrics

The most expensive physical access control to deploy is a biometric device. Biometric devices rely on human interaction and are covered extensively in Chapter 5.

Type of Glass Used for Entrances

Glass entryways, which have become common in many facilities, include windows, glass doors, and glass walls. The proper glass must be selected for the situation. A security professional should be familiar with the following types of glass:

- ***Standard glass***: Used in residential areas and is easily broken
- ***Tempered glass***: Created by heating the glass, which gives it extra strength
- ***Acrylic glass***: Made of polycarbonate acrylic; is much stronger than regular glass but produces toxic fumes when burned
- ***Laminated glass***: Made of two sheets of glass with a plastic film between, which makes breaking it more difficult

In areas where regular glass must be used but security is a concern, glass that is embedded with wire to reduce the likelihood of breaking and entering can be used. An even stronger option is to supplement the windows with steel bars.

Visitor Control

Some system of identifying visitors and controlling their access to the facility must be in place. The best system is to have a human present to require all visitors to sign in before entering. If that option is unfeasible, another option is to provide an entry point at which visitors are presented with a locked door and a phone that can be used to call and request access. Either of these methods helps to prevent unauthorized persons from simply entering the building and going where they please.

Another best practice with regard to visitors is to have personnel always accompany a contractor or visitor to their destination to help ensure they are not going where they shouldn't. In low security situations, this practice might not be necessary but is recommended in high security areas. Finally, log all visitors.

Wiring Closets/Intermediate Distribution Facilities

Lock any areas where equipment is stored, and control access to them. Having a strict inventory of all equipment so theft can be discovered is also important. For data centers and server rooms, the bar is raised even higher. There is more on this topic later.

Restricted and Work Areas

Some system should be in place to separate areas by security. Some specific places where additional security measures might be required are discussed here. Most of these measures apply to both visitors and employees. Following the least privilege policies and prohibiting some employees from certain areas might be beneficial.

Secure Data Center

Data centers must be physically secured with lock systems and should not have drop ceilings. The following are some additional considerations for rooms that contain lots of expensive equipment:

- They should not be located on top floors or in basements.
- An off switch should be located near the door for easy access.
- Separate HVAC for these rooms is recommended.
- Environmental monitoring should be deployed to be alert to temperature or humidity problems.
- Floors should be raised to help prevent water damage.
- All systems should have a UPS with the entire room connected to a generator.

Restricted Work Area

The facility might have areas that must be restricted to only the workers involved, even from other employees. In these cases, physical access systems must be deployed using smart cards, proximity readers, keypads, or any of the other physical access mechanisms described in this book.

Server Room

Some smaller companies implement a server room instead of a secure data center. The physical security controls needed for a server room are similar to those deployed in a secure data center or restricted work area.

Media Storage Facilities

A media storage facility is a building or a secured area within a building where media is stored. Because media can come in a variety of forms, organizations must determine which storage media they will use before selecting a media storage facility. If only one media is being stored, it might suffice to just install a fireproof safe in an organization's existing data center and to store a backup copy at a remote location. However, in some cases, a much larger solution is necessary because of the amount of data that is being protected. If a separate media storage facility is needed, then the organization must ensure that the facility provides the appropriate physical security to protect the media stored there and the organization follows the storage/backup/recovery policies.

Evidence Storage

If an organization has collected evidence that is crucial to an investigation, the organization must ensure that the evidence is protected from being accessed by unauthorized users. Only personnel involved in the investigation should have access to evidence that is stored. Evidence should be stored in a locked room, and access to the evidence should be logged. When required, evidence should be turned over to law enforcement at the appropriate time. If backup copies of digital evidence are retained during the investigation, the backup copies should also be in a secure storage area with limited personnel access.

Environmental Security and Issues

Although most considerations concerning security revolve around preventing mischief, preventing damage to data and equipment from environmental conditions is also the responsibility of the security team because it addresses the availability part of the CIA triad. In the following sections, we cover some of the most important considerations.

NOTE Environmental security and issues are directly affected by disruptions and disasters, including natural and man-made disasters. These concepts were discussed in Chapter 1, "Security and Risk Management" in the "Business Continuity" section.

Fire Protection

Fire protection has a longer history than many of the topics discussed in this book, and although the traditional considerations concerning preventing fires and fire damage still hold true, the presence of sensitive computing equipment requires different approaches to detection and prevention, which we discuss next.

Fire Detection

Several options are available for fire detection.

Security professionals should be familiar with the following basic types of fire detection systems:

Key Topic

- ***Smoke-activated sensor*:** Operates using a photoelectric device to detect variations in light caused by smoke particles.
- ***Heat-activated sensor* (also called heat-sensing sensor):** Operates by detecting temperature changes. These systems can either alert when a predefined temperature is met or alert when the rate of rise is a certain value.
- ***Flame-actuated sensor*:** Operates by "looking at" the protected area with optical devices. They generally react faster to a fire than nonoptical devices do.

Fire Suppression

Although fire extinguishers (covered in Chapter 1) are a manual form of fire suppression, other more automated systems also exist.

Security professionals should be familiar with the following sprinkler system types:

Key Topic

- ***Wet pipe extinguisher*:** This system uses water contained in pipes to extinguish the fire. In some areas, the water might freeze and burst the pipes, causing damage. These extinguishers are also not recommended for rooms where equipment will be damaged by the water.
- ***Dry pipe extinguisher*:** In this system, the water is not held in the pipes but in a holding tank. The pipes hold pressurized air, which is reduced when fire is detected, allowing the water to enter the pipe and the sprinklers. This structure minimizes the chance of an accidental discharge.
- ***Preaction extinguisher*:** This system operates like a dry pipe system except that the sprinkler head holds a thermal-fusible link that must be melted before the water is released. This is currently the recommended system for a computer room.
- ***Deluge extinguisher*:** This system allows large amounts of water to be released into the room, which obviously makes this not a good choice where computing equipment will be located.

At one time, fire suppression systems used Halon gas, which works well by suppressing combustion through a chemical reaction. However, these systems are no longer used because they have been found to damage the ozone layer.

Current EPA-approved replacements for Halon include

- Water
- Argon
- NAF-S-III

Another fire suppression system that can be used in computer rooms that will not damage computers and is safe for humans is FM-200.

Power Supply

The power supply is the lifeblood of the enterprise, its IT systems, and all of its equipment. Here, we look at common power issues and some of the prevention mechanisms and mitigation techniques that will allow the company to continue to operate when power problems arise.

Types of Outages

When discussing power issues, security professionals should be familiar with the following terms:

Key Topic

- ***Surge***: A prolonged high voltage
- ***Brownout***: A prolonged drop in power that is below normal voltage
- ***Fault***: A momentary power outage
- ***Blackout***: A prolonged power outage
- ***Sag***: A momentary reduction in the level of power

However, possible power problems go beyond partial or total loss of power. Power lines can introduce noise and interfere with communications in the network. In any case where large electric motors or sources of certain types of light, such as fluorescent lighting, are present, shielded cabling should be used to help prevent radio frequency interference (RFI) and electromagnetic interference (EMI).

Preventive Measures

Procedures to prevent static electricity from damaging components should be observed. Some precautions to take are

- Use antistatic sprays.
- Maintain proper humidity levels.
- Use antistatic mats and wrist bands.

To protect against dirty power (sags and surges) and both partial and total power outages, the following devices can be deployed:

- ***Power conditioners***: Go between the wall outlet and the device and smooth out the fluctuations of power delivered to the device, protecting against sags and surges.
- ***Uninterruptible power supplies (UPSs)***: Go between the wall outlet and the device and use a battery to provide power if the source from the wall is lost. UPSs also exist that can provide power to a server room.

HVAC

Heating, ventilation, and air-conditioning systems are not just in place for the comfort of the employees. The massive amounts of computing equipment deployed by most enterprises are even more dependent on these systems than humans. Without the proper environmental conditions, computing equipment won't complain; it will just stop working. Computing equipment and infrastructure devices, like routers and switches, must be protected from the following conditions:

- **Heat:** Excessive heat causes reboots and crashes.
- **Humidity:** Humidity causes corrosion problems with connections.
- **Low humidity:** Dry conditions encourage static electricity, which can damage equipment.

With respect to temperature, some important facts to know are

- At 100 degrees Fahrenheit, damage starts occurring to magnetic media.
- At 175 degrees Fahrenheit, damage starts occurring to computers and peripherals.
- At 350 degrees Fahrenheit, damage starts occurring to paper products.

In summary, the conditions need to be perfect for these devices. It is for this reason that AC units should be dedicated to the information processing facilities and on a separate power source than the other HVAC systems.

Water Leakage and Flooding

As much as computing systems dislike heat, they dislike water even more. It also can cause extensive damage to flooring, walls, and the facility foundation. Water detectors should be placed under raised floors and over dropped ceilings so that leaks in the ceiling and water under the floors are detected before they cause a problem.

Speaking of raised floors, in areas such as wiring closets, data centers, and server rooms, all floors should be raised to provide additional margin for error in the case of rising water.

Environmental Alarms

An error that causes a system to be vulnerable because of the environment in which it is installed is called an ***environmental error***. Considering the various challenges presented by the environmental demands placed on the facility by the computing equipment and the costs of failing to address these needs, it behooves the enterprise to have some system that alerts when environmental conditions are less than desirable. An alert system such as a ***hygrometer***, which monitors humidity, should be in place in areas where sensitive equipment resides. The system should also monitor temperature. These types of controls are considered physical controls.

Equipment Physical Security

The physical security of the equipment is stressed throughout this book. Here, we discuss corporate procedures concerning equipment and media and the use of safes and vaults for protecting other valuable physical assets. IT systems are not the only physical assets.

Corporate Procedures

Physical security of equipment and media should be designed into the security policies and procedures of the company. These procedures should address the issues covered in the sections that follow.

Tamper Protection

Unauthorized persons should not be able to access and change the configuration of any devices. Ensuring device safety means taking additional measures, such as the ones in the following sections, to prevent such access. Tampering includes defacing, damaging, or changing the configuration of a device. Applications should use integrity verification programs to look for evidence of data tampering, errors, and omissions.

Data Encryption

Encrypting sensitive data stored on devices can help to prevent the exposure of data in the event of a theft or in the event of inappropriate access of the device. Cryptography and encryption concepts are covered extensively earlier in this chapter. While not considered a physical security control, implementing data encryption protects the data on the physical device even if the physical device is stolen.

Inventory

Recognizing when items are stolen is impossible if no item count or inventory system exists. All equipment should be inventoried, and all relevant information about each device should be maintained and kept up to date. Maintain this information both electronically and in hard copy.

Physical Protection of Security Devices

Security devices, such as firewalls, NAT devices, and intrusion detection and prevention systems, should receive the most attention because they relate to physical and logical security.

Beyond these devices, devices that can be easily stolen, such as laptops, tablets, and smartphones, should be locked away. If locking devices away is not practical, then lock these types of devices to a stationary object. A good example is the cable locks used with laptops.

Tracking Devices

When the technology is available, small devices can be tracked to help mitigate loss of both devices and their data, as previously covered. Most smartphones now include tracking software that allows you to locate these devices after they have been stolen or lost by using either cell tower tracking or GPS. Deploy this technology when available and affordable.

Another useful feature available on these same types of devices is a remote wipe feature. This feature allows sending a signal to a stolen device instructing it to wipe out the data contained on the device. Finally, these devices typically also come with the ability to remotely lock the device when misplaced.

Portable Media Procedures

As previously covered, strict control of the use of portable media devices can help prevent sensitive information from leaving the network. These devices include CDs,

DVDs, flash drives, thumb drives, and external hard drives. Although written rules should be in effect about the use of these devices, using security policies to prevent the copying of data to these media types is also possible. Allowing the copying of data to these drive types as long as the data is encrypted is also possible. If the operating system allows administrators to prevent the use of these drives or require encryption, administrators should ensure that such functions are enabled.

Safes, Vaults, and Locking

With respect to protecting physical assets such as laptops, smartphones, tablets, and so on, nothing beats physically locking the devices away. In cases where it is possible to do so, lockable cabinets are a good solution for storing these devices. In addition to selecting the proper locks (locks are discussed earlier in this chapter), all equipment should be inventoried, and a system devised for maintaining these counts as the devices come and go.

Some items require even more protection than a locked cabinet. Keep important legal documents and any other items of extreme value in a safe or a vault for the added protection these items require. Fireproof safes and vaults can provide protection for contents even during a fire.

Exam Preparation Tasks

As mentioned in the section "About the *CISSP Cert Guide*, Fifth Edition" in the Introduction, you have a couple of choices for exam preparation: the exercises here, Chapter 9, "Final Preparation," and the exam simulation questions in the Pearson Test Prep practice test software.

Review All Key Topics

Review the most important topics in this chapter, noted with the Key Topic icon in the outer margin of the page. Table 3-15 lists a reference of these key topics and the page numbers on which each is found.

Key Topic

Table 3-15 Key Topics for Chapter 3

Key Topic Element	Description	Page Number
List	ISO/IEC 15288:2015 categories of processes	224
Table 3-1	Security Modes Summary	233
List	Bell-LaPadula rules	237
List	Biba axioms	239

Key Topic Element	Description	Page Number
List	Clark-Wilson elements	239
List	TCSEC classification system	257
Table 3-3	Mapping of ITSEC and TCSEC	260
List	Common Criteria assurance levels	261
List	ISO/IEC 27001:2018 steps	264
List	NIACAP phases	267
List	Security control selection process	268
List	TPM chip memory	270
List	Industrial control systems components	277
List	NIST SP 800-82, Rev. 2 ICS security objectives	278
List	ICS security program steps	280
List	NIST SP 800-145 cloud deployments	282
List	Cloud levels	282
Table 3-4	NIST SP 800-144 Cloud Security and Privacy Issues and Recommendations	285
List	NIST SP 800-146 benefits of SaaS	286
List	NIST SP 800-146 issues and concerns of SaaS	287
List	NIST SP 800-146 benefits of PaaS	287
List	NIST SP 800-146 issues and concerns of PaaS	287
List	NIST SP 800-146 benefits of IaaS	287
List	NIST SP 800-146 issues and concerns of IaaS	287
Figure 3-8	NIST CPS Framework	291
List	Cryptography concepts	305
List	Key management process elements	317
Table 3-12	Symmetric Algorithm Strengths and Weaknesses	322
List	Advantages of stream-based ciphers	322
List	Advantages of block ciphers	323
Table 3-13	Asymmetric Algorithm Strengths and Weaknesses	324
List	DES modes	326
List	3DES modes	329
Table 3-14	Symmetric Algorithms Key Facts	332

Key Topic Element	Description	Page Number
List	PKI steps	341
List	Basic steps of an HMAC process	352
List	Basic steps of a CBC-MAC process	352
List	Basic types of fire detection systems	374
List	Sprinkler system types	374
List	Power issue terms	375

Complete the Tables and Lists from Memory

Print a copy of Appendix A, "Memory Tables," or at least the section from this chapter, and complete the tables and lists from memory. Appendix B, "Memory Tables Answer Key," includes completed tables and lists to check your work.

Define Key Terms

Define the following key terms from this chapter and check your answers in the glossary:

absolute addressing; accreditation; acrylic glass; aggregation; algorithm; architecture; associative memory; asymmetric encryption; asymmetric mode; asynchronous encryption; authentication; authorization; availability; avalanche effect; BACnet2; Bell-LaPadula model; Biba model; blackout; block cipher; Blowfish; bollards; Brewer-Nash (Chinese Wall) model; brownout; cable lock; cache; CAST-128; CAST-256; certificate authority (CA); certificate revocation list (CRL); certification; chosen ciphertext attack; chosen plaintext attack; cipher; Cipher Block Chaining (CBC); Cipher Block Chaining MAC (CBC-MAC); Cipher Feedback (CFB); cipher locks; ciphertext; ciphertext-only attack; Clark-Wilson integrity model; cleartext; closed system; cloud computing; collision; combination lock; Common Criteria (CC); community cloud; concealment cipher; concentric circle; confidentiality; confinement; confusion; contamination; Counter Mode (CTR); Crime Prevention Through Environmental Design (CPTED); cryptanalysis; cryptogram; cryptography; cryptology; cryptosystem; cryptovariable; data warehouse; decoding; decryption; defense in depth; deluge extinguisher; DES-X; diffusion; digital certificate; Digital Encryption Standard (DES); digital signature; Digital Signature Standard (DSS); DNP3; Double-DES; dry pipe extinguisher; Electronic Code Book (ECB); embedded system; encoding; encryption; enrollment; environmental error; Extensible Markup Language (XML); fail safe state; fail soft state; fault; fetching; field-programmable gate array (FPGA); firmware; flame-actuated sensor; flash memory; Graham-Denning model; grid computing; Harrison-Ruzzo-Ullman model; hash; hash

MAC (HMAC); HAVAL; heat-activated sensor; hybrid cloud; hygrometer; implied addressing; indirect addressing; inference; information flow model; Information Technology Security Evaluation Criteria (ITSEC); Infrastructure as a Service (IaaS); integrity; International Data Encryption Algorithm (IDEA); Internet of Things (IoT); interrupt; key; key clustering; keyspace; known plain-text attack; laminated glass; layered defense model; Lipner model; LonWorks/LonTalk3; maintenance hook; mantrap; matrix-based model; MD2; MD4; MD5; MD6; mobile code; Modbus; mono-alphabetic substitution cipher; multilevel lattice model; multitasking; multithreading; natural access control; natural surveillance; natural territorials reinforcement; nonce; noninterference model; non-repudiation; nonvolatile memory; null cipher; object; one-time pad; one-way function; Online Certificate Status Protocol (OCSP); open systems; Open Web Application Security Project (OWASP); Orange Book; Output Feedback (OFB); Payment Card Industry Data Security Standard (PCI DSS); peer-to-peer computing; permutation; pipelined processor; plaintext; Platform as a Service (PaaS); polyalphabetic substitution cipher; polyinstantiation; power conditioner; preaction extinguisher; private cloud; private key encryption; process; proximity authentication device; public cloud; public key encryption; RC4; RC5; RC6; RC7; Red Book; reference monitor; registration authority (RA); revocation; Rijndael algorithm; RIPEMD-160; running key cipher; salting; secondary memory; secret key encryption; Security Assertion Markup Language (SAML); Skipjack; smoke-activated sensor; Software as a Service (SaaS); standard glass; state machine models; steganography; stream-based cipher; subject; substitution; substitution cipher; superscalar; supervisor mode; surge; symmetric encryption; symmetric mode; synchronous encryption; tempered glass; thread; Tiger; time-of-check/time-of-use attack; transposition; transposition cipher; trapdoor (encryption); Triple DES (3DES); Trusted Computer Base (TCB); Trusted Computer System Evaluation Criteria (TCSEC); Trusted Platform Module (TPM); tumbler lock; Twofish; uninterruptible power supply (UPS); verification; volatile memory; warded lock; wet pipe extinguisher; work factor (encryption)

Answer Review Questions

1. Which of the following is provided if data cannot be read?
   a. Integrity
   b. Confidentiality
   c. Availability
   d. Defense in depth

2. In a distributed environment, which of the following is software that ties the client and server software together?
   a. Embedded system
   b. Mobile code
   c. Virtual computing
   d. Middleware

3. Which of the following is composed of the components (hardware, firmware, and/or software) that are expected to enforce the security policy of the system?
   a. Security perimeter
   b. Reference monitor
   c. Trusted Computer Base (TCB)
   d. Security kernel

4. Which process converts plaintext into ciphertext?
   a. Hashing
   b. Decryption
   c. Encryption
   d. Digital signature

5. Which type of cipher is the Caesar cipher?
   a. Polyalphabetic substitution
   b. Mono-alphabetic substitution
   c. Polyalphabetic transposition
   d. Mono-alphabetic transposition

6. Which of the following is the most secure encryption scheme?
   a. Concealment cipher
   b. Symmetric algorithm
   c. One-time pad
   d. Asymmetric algorithm

7. Which 3DES implementation encrypts each block of data three times, each time with a different key?
   a. 3DES-EDE3
   b. 3DES-EEE3

   c. 3DES-EDE2
   d. 3DES-EEE2

8. Which of the following is NOT a hash function?
   a. ECC
   b. MD6
   c. SHA-2
   d. RIPEMD-160

9. Which of the following is an example of a preventive control?
   a. A door lock system on a server room
   b. An electric fence surrounding a facility
   c. Armed guards outside a facility
   d. Parking lot cameras

10. Which of the following is NOT one of the three main strategies that guide CPTED?
    a. Natural access control
    b. Natural surveillance reinforcement
    c. Natural territorials reinforcement
    d. Natural surveillance

11. What occurs when different encryption keys generate the same ciphertext from the same plaintext message?
    a. Key clustering
    b. Cryptanalysis
    c. Keyspace
    d. Confusion

12. Which encryption system uses a private or secret key that must remain secret between the two parties?
    a. Running key cipher
    b. Concealment cipher
    c. Asymmetric algorithm
    d. Symmetric algorithm

13. Which of the following is an asymmetric algorithm?
    a. IDEA
    b. Twofish
    c. RC6
    d. RSA

14. Which PKI component contains a list of all the certificates that have been revoked?
    a. CA
    b. RA
    c. CRL
    d. OCSP

15. Which attack executed against a cryptographic algorithm uses all possible keys until a key is discovered that successfully decrypts the ciphertext?
    a. Frequency analysis
    b. Reverse engineering
    c. Ciphertext-only attack
    d. Brute force

16. In ISO/IEC 15288:2015, which process category includes acquisition and supply?
    a. Technical management processes
    b. Technical processes
    c. Agreement processes
    d. Organizational project-enabling processes

17. Which statement is true of dedicated security mode?
    a. It employs a single classification level.
    b. All users have the same security clearance, but they do not all possess a need-to-know clearance for all the information in the system.
    c. All users must possess the highest security clearance, but they must also have valid need-to-know clearance, a signed NDA, and formal approval for all information to which they have access.
    d. Systems allow two or more classification levels of information to be processed at the same time.

18. What is the first step in ISO/IEC 27001:2013?
    a. Identify the requirements.
    b. Perform risk assessment and risk treatment.
    c. Maintain and monitor the ISMS.
    d. Obtain management support.

19. Which two states are supported by most processors in a computer system?
    a. Supervisor state and problem state
    b. Supervisor state and kernel state
    c. Problem state and user state
    d. Supervisor state and elevated state

20. When supporting a BYOD initiative, from which group do you probably have most to fear?
    a. Hacktivists
    b. Careless users
    c. Software vendors
    d. Mobile device vendors

21. Which term applies to embedded devices that bring with them security concerns because engineers that design these devices do not always worry about security?
    a. BYOD
    b. NDA
    c. IoT
    d. ITSEC

22. Which option best describes the primary concern of NIST SP 800-57?
    a. Asymmetric encryption
    b. Symmetric encryption
    c. Message integrity
    d. Key management

23. Which of the following key types requires only integrity security protection?
    a. Public signature verification key
    b. Private signature key
    c. Symmetric authentication key
    d. Private authentication key

24. What is the final phase of the cryptographic key management life cycle, according to NIST SP 800-57?
    a. Operational phase
    b. Destroyed phase
    c. Pre-operational phase
    d. Post-operational phase

Answers and Explanations

1. **b.** Confidentiality is provided if the data cannot be read. It can be provided either through access controls and encryption for data as it exists on a hard drive or through encryption as the data is in transit.
2. **d.** In a distributed environment, middleware is software that ties the client and server software together. It is neither a part of the operating system nor a part of the server software. It is the code that lies between the operating system and applications on each side of a distributed computing system in a network.
3. **c.** The Trusted Computer Base (TCB) is composed of the components (hardware, firmware, and/or software) that are trusted to enforce the security policy of the system and that if compromised jeopardize the security properties of the entire system.
4. **c.** Encryption converts plaintext into ciphertext. Hashing reduces a message to a hash value. Decryption converts ciphertext into plaintext. A digital signature is an object that provides sender authentication and message integrity by including a digital signature with the original message.
5. **b.** The Caesar cipher is a mono-alphabetic substitution cipher. The Vigenere substitution is a polyalphabetic substitution.
6. **c.** A one-time pad is the most secure encryption scheme because it is used only once.
7. **b.** The 3DES-EEE3 implementation encrypts each block of data three times, each time with a different key. The 3DES-EDE3 implementation encrypts each block of data with the first key, decrypts each block with the second key,

and encrypts each block with the third key. The 3DES-EDE2 implementation encrypts each block of data with the first key, decrypts each block with the second key, and then encrypts each block with the first key. The 3DES-EEE2 implementation encrypts each block of data with the first key, encrypts each block with the second key, and then encrypts each block with the third key.

8. **a.** Elliptic Curve Cryptosystem (ECC) is NOT a hash function. It is an asymmetric algorithm. All the other options are hash functions.
9. **a.** An electric fence surrounding a facility is designed to prevent access to the building by those who should not have any access (an external threat), whereas a door lock system on the server room that requires a swipe of the employee card is designed to prevent access by those who are already in the building (an internal threat).
10. **b.** The three strategies are natural access control, natural territorials reinforcement, and natural surveillance.
11. **a.** Key clustering occurs when different encryption keys generate the same ciphertext from the same plaintext message. Cryptanalysis is the science of decrypting ciphertext without prior knowledge of the key or cryptosystem used. A keyspace is all the possible key values when using a particular algorithm or other security measure. Confusion is the process of changing a key value during each round of encryption.
12. **d.** A symmetric algorithm uses a private or secret key that must remain secret between the two parties. A running key cipher uses a physical component, usually a book, to provide the polyalphabetic characters. A concealment cipher occurs when plaintext is interspersed somewhere within other written material. An asymmetric algorithm uses both a public key and a private or secret key.
13. **d.** RSA is an asymmetric algorithm. All the other algorithms are symmetric algorithms.
14. **c.** A certificate revocation list (CRL) contains a list of all the certificates that have been revoked. A certificate authority (CA) is the entity that creates and signs digital certificates, maintains the certificates, and revokes them when necessary. A registration authority (RA) verifies the requestor's identity, registers the requestor, and passes the request to the CA. Online Certificate Status Protocol (OCSP) is an Internet protocol that obtains the revocation status of an X.509 digital certificate.
15. **d.** A brute-force attack executed against a cryptographic algorithm uses all possible keys until a key is discovered that successfully decrypts the ciphertext. A frequency analysis attack relies on the fact that substitution and transposition ciphers will result in repeated patterns in ciphertext. A reverse engineering attack occurs when an attacker purchases a particular cryptographic product to

attempt to reverse engineer the product to discover confidential information about the cryptographic algorithm used. A ciphertext-only attack uses several encrypted messages (ciphertext) to figure out the key used in the encryption process.

16. **c.** ISO/IEC 15288:2015 establishes four categories of processes:
    - Agreement processes, including acquisition and supply
    - Organizational project-enabling processes, including infrastructure management, quality management, and knowledge management
    - Technical management processes, including project planning, risk management, configuration management, and quality assurance
    - Technical processes, including system requirements definition, system analysis, implementation, integration, operation, maintenance, and disposal
17. **a.** Dedicated security mode employs a single classification level.
18. **d.** The first step in ISO/IEC 27001:2013 is to obtain management support.
19. **a.** Two processor states are supported by most processors: supervisor state (or kernel mode) and problem state (or user mode).
20. **b.** As a security professional, when supporting a BYOD initiative, you should take into consideration that you probably have more to fear from the carelessness of the users than you do from hackers.
21. **c.** Internet of Things (IoT) is the term used for embedded devices and their security concerns because engineers that design these devices do not always worry about security.
22. **d.** Key management is the primary concern of NIST SP 800-57.
23. **a.** Public signature verification keys require only integrity security protection.
24. **b.** The destroyed phase is the final phase of the cryptographic key management life cycle, according to NIST SP 800-57.

This chapter covers the following topics:

- **Secure Network Design Principles:** Concepts covered include the OSI and TCP/IP models.
- **IP Networking:** Concepts discussed include common TCP/UDP ports, logical and physical addressing, network transmission, and network types.
- **Protocols and Services:** Protocols and services discussed include ARP, DHCP, DNS, FTP, HTTP, ICMP, IMAP, LDAP, NAT, NetBIOS, NFS, PAT, POP, CIFS/SMB, SMTP, SNMP, and multilayer protocols.
- **Converged Protocols:** Protocols discussed include FCoE, InfiniBand, CXL, MPLS, VoIP, and iSCSI.
- **Wireless Networks:** Concepts covered include wireless techniques, WLAN structure, WLAN standards, and WLAN security.
- **Communications Cryptography:** Concepts discussed include link encryption, end-to-end encryption, email security, and Internet security.
- **Secure Network Components:** Concepts covered include operation of hardware, transmission media, network access control devices, endpoint security, and content-distribution networks.
- **Secure Communication Channels:** Topics discussed include voice, multimedia collaboration, remote access, data communications, and virtualized networks.
- **Network Attacks:** Concepts discussed include cabling attacks, network component attacks, ICMP attacks, DNS attacks, email attacks, wireless attacks, remote attacks, and other attacks.

CHAPTER 4

Communication and Network Security

Sensitive data must be protected from unauthorized access when the data is at rest (on a hard drive or on a backup) and in transit (moving through a network). Moreover, sensitive communications of other types such as emails, instant messages, and phone conversations must also be protected from prying eyes and ears. Many communication processes send information in a form that can be read and understood if captured with a protocol analyzer or sniffer.

The Communication and Network Security domain addresses a broad array of topics including network architecture, components, and secure communication channels. Out of 100 percent of the exam, this domain carries an average weight of 13 percent, which is the second highest weight of all the eight domains. So, pay close attention to the many details in this chapter!

In the world of communication today, you should assume that your communications are being closely monitored and may be captured without your knowledge regardless of how unlikely you think that might be. You should also take steps to protect or encrypt the transmissions so they will be useless to anyone capturing them. This chapter covers the protection of wired and wireless transmissions and of the network devices that perform the transmissions, as well as some networking fundamentals required to understand transmission security.

Foundation Topics

Secure Network Design Principles

To properly configure communication and network security, security professionals must understand secure network design principles. They need to know how to ensure that a network is set up properly and will need minimal reconfiguration in the future. To use secure network design principles, security professionals must understand the OSI and TCP/IP models.

OSI Model

A complete understanding of networking requires an understanding of the ***Open Systems Interconnection (OSI) model***. Created in the 1980s by the International Organization for Standardization (ISO), as a part of its mission to create a protocol set to be used as a standard for all vendors, the OSI model breaks the communication process into layers. Although the ensuing protocol set did not catch on as a standard (Transmission Control Protocol/Internet Protocol [TCP/IP] was adopted), the model has guided the development of technology since its creation. It also has helped generations of students understand the network communication process between two systems. Finally, it is important to understand that this is a conceptual model, and therefore, not all technologies fit nicely into just one layer of the OSI model.

The OSI model breaks up the process into seven layers, or modules. The benefits of doing this are

- It breaks up the communication process into layers with standardized interfaces between the layers, allowing for changes and improvements on one layer without necessitating changes on other layers.
- It provides a common framework for hardware and software developers, fostering interoperability.

This open systems architecture can act as a blueprint or model for developers to work with. Various protocols operate at different layers of this model. A *protocol* is a set of rules; in this case, these are rules for communication between two systems. Some protocols depend on other protocols for services, and as such, these protocols operate in concert and allow transmissions to occur, much like the team at the post office that gets letters delivered. Some people sort, others deliver, and still others track lost shipments.

The OSI model and the TCP/IP model, explained later, are often both used to describe the process called *packet creation*, or ***encapsulation***. Until a packet is created to hold the data, it cannot be sent on the transmission medium.

With a modular approach, it is possible for a change in a protocol or the addition of a new protocol to be accomplished without having to rewrite the entire protocol *stack* (a term for all the protocols that work together at all layers). The OSI model has seven layers. The following sections discuss each layer's function and its relationship to the layer above and below it in the model. The layers are often referred to by their number with the numbering starting at the bottom of the model at Layer 1, the Physical layer.

The process of creating a packet or encapsulation begins at Layer 7, the Application layer rather than Layer 1, so we discuss the process starting at Layer 7 and work down the model to Layer 1, the Physical layer, where the packet is sent out on the transmission medium.

Application Layer

The ***Application layer (Layer 7)*** is where the encapsulation process begins. This layer receives the raw data from the application in use and provides services, such as file transfer and message exchange to the application (and thus the user). An example of a protocol that operates at this layer is ***Hypertext Transfer Protocol (HTTP)***, which is used to transfer web pages across the network. Other examples of protocols that operate at this layer are DNS, FTP, and SMTP. The Dynamic Host Configuration Protocol (DHCP) and DHCP for IPv6 (DHCPv6) also operate at this layer. There are many other protocols found at this layer, which we will briefly explain. Network News Transfer Protocol (NNTP) is a protocol for Usenet, which is for news groups. Session Initiation Protocol (SIP) is used with Internet telephone, such as LTE. Domain Name System (DNS) translates easily readable domains to a numeric IP address. This means that people do not need to remember a numeric address but can use words instead, such as whitehouse.gov.

The user application interfaces with these application protocols through a standard interface called an application programming interface (API). The Application layer protocol receives the raw data and places it in a container called a protocol data unit (PDU). When the process gets down to Layer 4, these PDUs have standard names, but at Layers 5–7, the PDU is simply referred to as "data."

Presentation Layer

The information that is developed at Layer 7 is then handed to the ***Presentation layer (Layer 6)***. Each layer makes no changes to the data received from the layer above it. It simply adds information to the developing packet. In the case of the Presentation layer, information is added that standardizes the formatting of the information if required.

Layer 6 is responsible for the manner in which the data from the Application layer is represented (or presented) to the Application layer on the destination device (explained more fully in the section "Encapsulation and De-encapsulation"). If any translation between formats is required, this layer will take care of the translation. Layer 6 also communicates the type of data within the packet and the application that might be required to read it on the destination device.

This layer consists of two sublayers: the common application service element (CASE) sublayer and the specific application service element (SASE) sublayer. CASE provides services to the Application layer and requests services from the Session layer. SASE supports application-specific services.

Session Layer

As its name suggests, the ***Session layer (Layer 5)*** is responsible for initiating, maintaining, and terminating processes on different systems. The Session layer is responsible for adding information to the packet that makes a communication session between a service or application on the source device possible with the same service or application on the destination device. Do not confuse this process with the one that establishes a session between the two physical devices. That occurs not at this layer but at Layers 3 and 4. This session is built and closed after the physical session between the computers has taken place.

The application or service in use is communicated between the two systems with an identifier called a port number. This information is passed on to the Transport layer, which also makes use of these port numbers.

Transport Layer

The protocols that operate at the ***Transport layer (Layer 4)*** work to establish a session between the two physical systems. The service provided can be either connection-oriented or connectionless, depending on the transport protocol in use. The "TCP/IP Model" section (TCP/IP being the most common standard networking protocol suite in use) discusses the specific transport protocols used by TCP/IP in detail.

The Transport layer receives all the information from Layers 7, 6, and 5 and adds information that identifies the transport protocol in use and the specific port number that identifies the required Layer 7 protocol. At this layer, the PDU is called a segment because this layer takes a large transmission and segments it into smaller pieces for more efficient transmission on the medium. Transport Control Protocol (TCP) is a connection-oriented protocol, which includes error checking and is used with HTTP. User Datagram Protocol (UDP) is a connectionless protocol, which does not include error checking and therefore is faster than TCP. Voice over Internet Protocol (VoIP) uses UDP. We will also discuss these protocols later in this chapter.

Network Layer

At the ***Network layer (Layer 3)***, information required to route the packet is added. This information is in the form of a source and destination logical address (meaning one that is assigned to a device in some manner and can be changed). In TCP/IP, this is in terms of a source and destination IP address. An IP address is a number that uniquely differentiates a host from all other devices on the network. It is based on a numbering system that makes it possible for computers (and ***routers***) to identify whether the destination device is on the local network or on a remote network. Any time a packet needs to be sent to a different network or subnet (IP addressing is covered later in the chapter), it must be routed and the information required to do that is added here. At this layer, the PDU is called a packet. Address Resolution Protocol (ARP) is an important protocol at this layer since it binds a logical IP address to a physical MAC address. We will discuss this protocol later in this chapter.

Data Link Layer

The ***Data Link layer (Layer 2)*** is responsible for determining the destination physical address. Network devices have logical addresses (IP addresses) and the network interfaces they possess have a physical address (a ***media access control [MAC] address***), which is permanent in nature. When the transmission is handed off from routing device to routing device, at each stop this source and destination address pair changes, whereas the source and destination logical addresses (in most cases IP addresses) do not. This layer is responsible for determining what those MAC addresses should be at each hop (router interface) and adding them to this part of the packet. The later section "TCP/IP Model" covers how this resolution is performed in TCP/IP. After this is done, the PDU is called a frame.

In some networks, the Data Link layer is discussed as including the media access control (MAC) and logical link control (LLC) sublayers. In the Data Link layer, the IEEE 802.2 LLC protocol can be used with all of the IEEE 802 MAC layers.

Something else happens that is unique to this layer. Not only is a Layer 2 header placed on the packet but also a trailer at the "end" of the frame. Information contained in the trailer is used to verify that none of the data contained has been altered or damaged during transmission.

Physical Layer

Finally, the packet (or frame, as it is called at Layer 2) is received by the ***Physical layer (Layer 1)***. Layer 1 is responsible for turning the information into bits (ones and zeros) and sending it out on the medium. The way in which this is accomplished can vary according to the media in use. For example, in a wired network, the ones and zeros are represented as electrical charges. In wireless, they are represented by altering the radio waves. In an optical network, they are represented with light.

The ability of the same packet to be routed through various media types is a good example of the independence of the layers. As a PDU travels through different media types, the physical layer will change, but all the information in Layers 2–7 will not. Similarly, when a frame crosses routers or hops, the MAC addresses change, but none of the information in Layers 3–7 changes. The upper layers depend on the lower layers for various services, but the lower layers leave the upper layer information unchanged.

Figure 4-1 shows common protocols mapped to the OSI model. The next section covers another model that perhaps more accurately depicts what happens in a TCP/IP network. Because TCP/IP is the standard now for transmission, comparing these two models is useful. Although they have a different number of layers and some of the layer names are different, they describe the same process of packet creation or encapsulation.

Key Topic

OSI model
7. Application layer
NNTP • SIP • DNS • FTP • HTTP • NFS • NTP • SMPP • SMTP * SNMP • Telnet • DHCP
6. Presentation layer
MIME • TLS • SSL
5. Session layer
Named pipes • NetBIOS • SAP • PPTP • RTP • SOCKS • TLS/SSL
4. Transport layer
TCP • UDP • SCTP • DCCP
3. Network layer
IP • (IPv4 • IPV6) • ARP • ICMP • IPsec • IGMP
2. Data Link layer
ATM • SDLC • HDLC • IEEE 802.2 • L2TP • IEEE 802.3 • Frame Relay • PPP • X.25
1. Physical layer
SONET • DSL • IEEE 802.3 - IEEE 802.11 • USB • Bluetooth • RS-232 •

Figure 4-1 Protocol Mappings

TCP/IP Model

The protocols developed when the OSI model was developed (sometimes referred to as OSI protocols) did not become the standard for the Internet. The Internet as we know it today has its roots in a wide area network (WAN) developed by the Department of Defense (DoD), with TCP/IP being the protocol developed for that network. The Internet is a global network of public networks and Internet service providers (ISPs) throughout the world.

This model bears many similarities to the OSI model, which is not unexpected because they both describe the process of packet creation or encapsulation. The difference is that the OSI model breaks the process into seven layers, whereas the TCP/IP model breaks it into four. If you examine them side by side, however, it becomes apparent that many of the same functions occur at the same layers, while the TCP/IP model combines the top three layers of the OSI model into one and the bottom two layers of the OSI model into one. Figure 4-2 shows the two models next to one another.

Key Topic

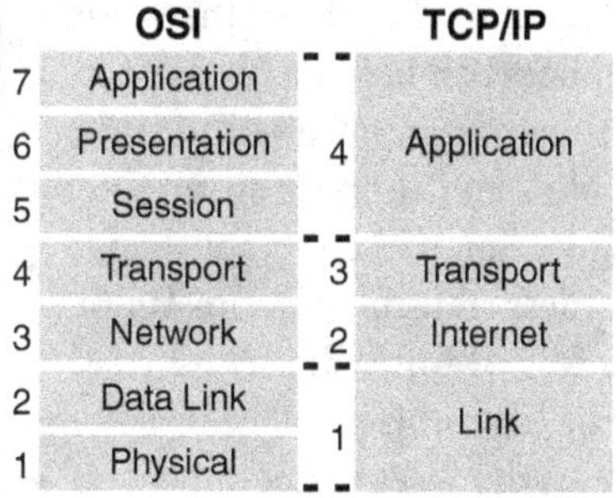

Figure 4-2 OSI and TCP/IP Models

The TCP/IP model has only four layers and is useful to study because it focuses its attention on TCP/IP. Next, we explore those four layers and their functions and relationships to one another and to layers in the OSI model.

Application Layer

Although the Application layer in the TCP/IP model has the same name as the top layer in the OSI model, the Application layer in the TCP/IP model encompasses all the functions performed in Layers 5–7 in the OSI model. Not all functions map perfectly because both are simply conceptual models. Within the Application layer, applications create user data and communicate this data to other processes or applications on another host. For this reason, it is sometimes also referred to as the process-to-process layer.

Examples of protocols that operate at this layer are SMTP, FTP, SSH, and HTTP. These protocols are discussed in the section "Protocols and Services," later in this chapter. In general, however, these are usually referred to as higher layer protocols that perform some specific function, whereas protocols in the TCP/IP suite that operate at the Transport and Internet layers perform location and delivery service on behalf of these higher layer protocols.

A port number identifies to the receiving device these upper layer protocols and the programs on whose behalf they function. The number identifies the protocol or service. Many port numbers have been standardized. For example, Domain Name System (DNS) is identified with the standard port number 53. The "Common TCP/UDP Ports" section covers these port numbers in more detail.

Transport Layer

The Transport layers of the OSI model and the TCP/IP model perform the same function, which is to open and maintain a connection between hosts. This connection must be established before the session between the processes can occur, and can be performed in TCP/IP in two ways: connectionless and connection-oriented. A connection-oriented transmission means that a connection will be established before any data is transferred, whereas in a connectionless transmission this is not done. One of two different Transport layer protocols is used for each process. If a connection-oriented transport protocol is required, the Transmission Control Protocol (TCP) is used. If the process is connectionless, the User Datagram Protocol (UDP) is used.

Application developers can choose to use either TCP or UDP as the Transport layer protocol used with the application. Regardless of which transport protocol is used, the application or service will be identified to the receiving device by its port number and the transport protocol (UDP or TCP).

Although TCP provides more functionality and reliability, the overhead required by this protocol is substantial when compared to UDP. Consequently, a much higher percentage of the packet consists of the header when using TCP than when using UDP. This configuration is necessary to provide the required fields that contain the information needed to provide the additional checks. Figure 4-3 shows a comparison of the sizes of the two respective headers.

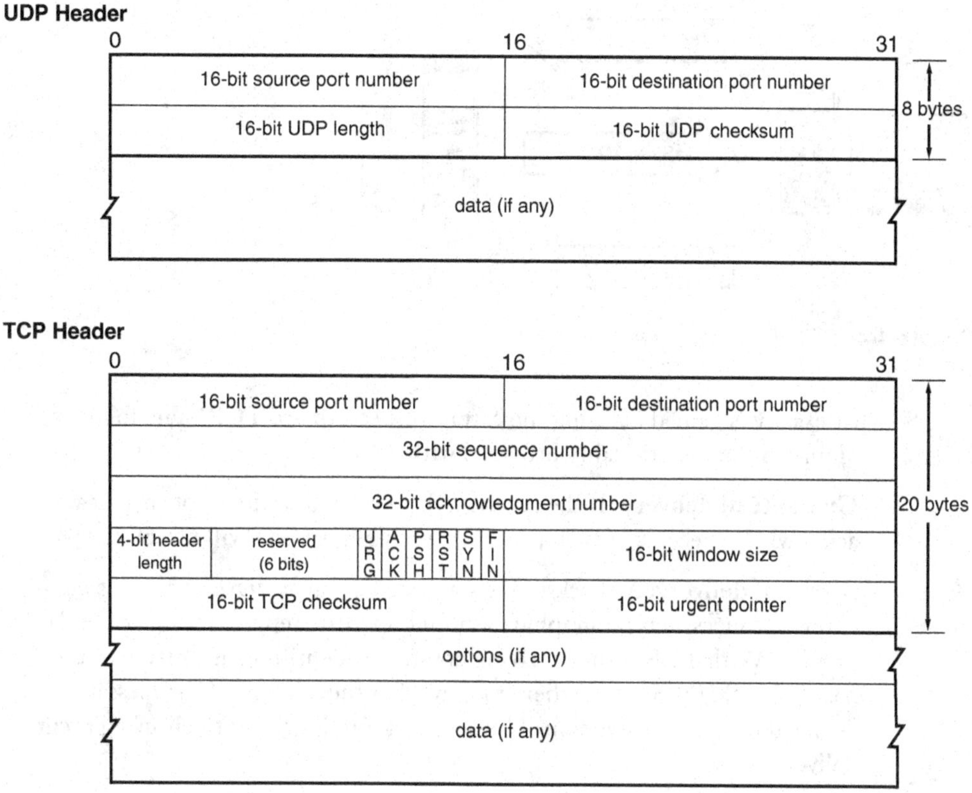

Figure 4-3 TCP and UDP Headers

When an application is written and uses TCP, a state of connection is established between two hosts before any data is transferred. This connection is established using a process known as the ***TCP three-way handshake***. This process is followed exactly, and no data is transferred until it is complete. Figure 4-4 shows the steps in this process. The steps are as follows:

1. The initiating computer sends a packet with the SYN flag set (one of the fields in the TCP header), which indicates a desire to create a connection.
2. The receiving host acknowledges receiving this packet and indicates a willingness to create a state of connection by sending back a packet with both the SYN and ACK flags set.
3. The first host acknowledges completion of the connection process by sending a final packet back with only the ACK flag set.

Key Topic

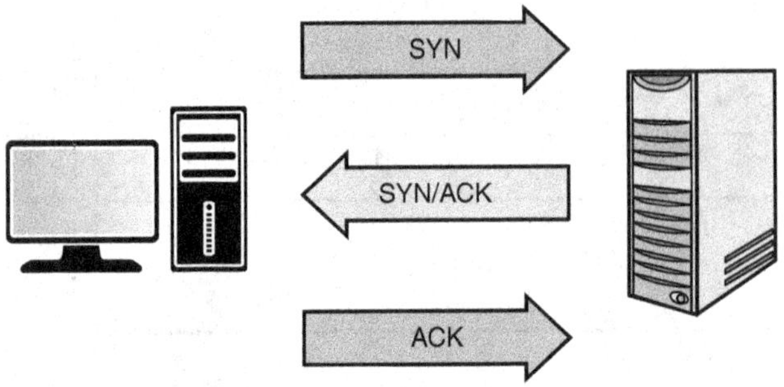

Figure 4-4 TCP Three-Way Handshake

So what exactly is gained by using the extra overhead to use TCP? The following are examples of the functionality provided with TCP:

- **Guaranteed delivery:** If the receiving host computer does not specifically acknowledge receipt of each packet, the sending system will resend the packet.
- **Accurate delivery:** A checksum is generated using an algorithm. This algorithm produces a cryptographic hash function that represents a piece of data or a file. With TCP, if the receiving computer identifies a mismatch in the hash value that it receives, then it knows that the content of the message has changed during transmission. Thus, a checksum is critical to ensuring accurate delivery.
- **Sequencing:** In today's routed networks, the packets might take many different routes to arrive and might not arrive in the order in which they were sent. A sequence number added to each packet allows the receiving host to reassemble the entire transmission using these numbers.
- **Flow control:** The receiving host has the capability of sending the acknowledgment packets back to signal the sender to slow the transmission if it cannot process the packets as fast as they are arriving.

Many applications do not require the services provided by TCP or cannot tolerate the overhead required by TCP. In these cases, the process will use UDP, which transmits data on a "best effort" basis with no guarantee of delivery or retransmission of missing packets. In many cases, some of these functions are provided by the Application layer protocol itself rather than relying on the Transport layer protocol.

Internet Layer

The Transport layer can neither create a state of connection nor transmit using UDP until the location and route to the destination are determined, which occurs on the Internet layer. The four protocols in the TCP/IP suite that operate at this layer are

- **Internet Protocol (IP):** The protocol responsible for putting the source and destination IP addresses in the packet and for routing the packet to its destination.
- **Internet Control Message Protocol (ICMP):** The protocol used by the network devices to send messages regarding the success or failure of communications and used by humans for troubleshooting. When you use the **ping** or **traceroute/tracert** commands, you are using ICMP.
- **Internet Group Management Protocol (IGMP):** The protocol used when multicasting, which is a form of communication whereby one host sends to a group of destination hosts rather than a single host (called a unicast transmission) or to all hosts (called a broadcast transmission). There are three versions of IGMP. Version 2 adds two query types: general query and group-specific query. Version 3 adds a membership query.
- **Address Resolution Protocol (ARP):** The protocol that resolves the IP address placed in the packet to a physical address (called a MAC address in Ethernet).

The relationship between IP and ARP is worthy of more discussion. IP places the source and destination IP addresses in the header of the packet. As described earlier, when a packet is being routed across a network, the source and destination IP addresses never change, but the Layer 2 or MAC address pairs change at every router hop. ARP uses a process called the ARP broadcast to learn the MAC address of the interface that matches the IP address of the next hop. After it has learned the address, a new header for data to be processed, under Layer 2, is created. Again, nothing else in the upper layer changes in this process, just Layer 2. An IP address is a logical address, whereas a MAC address is a physical address.

This description raises an important point: mapping ARP to the TCP/IP model. Although ARP is generally placed on the Internet layer, the information it derives from this process is placed in the Link layer or Layer 2, the next layer in our discussion.

Just as the Transport layer added a header to the packet, so does the Internet layer. One of the improvements made by IPv6 is the streamlining of the IP header. Although the same information is contained in the header and the header is larger, it has a much simpler structure. Figure 4-5 shows a comparison of the two.

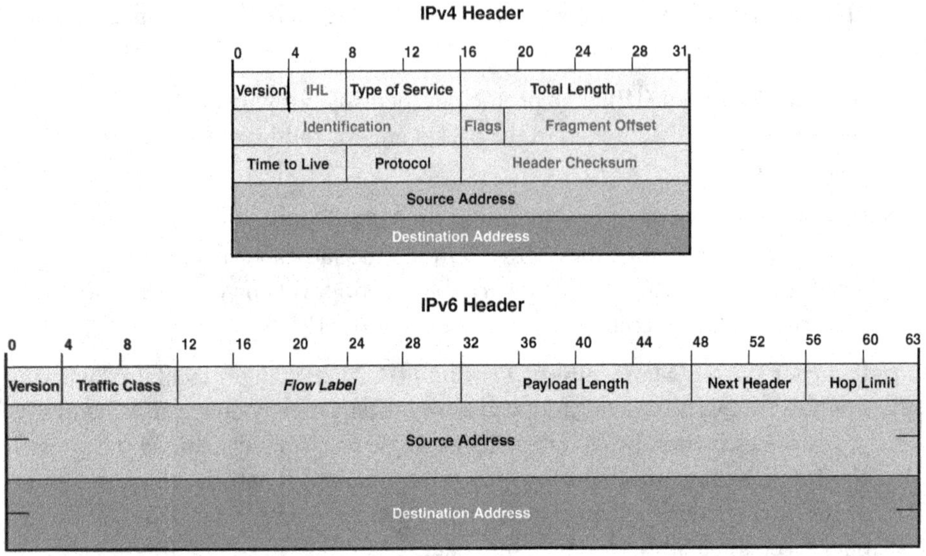

Figure 4-5 IPv6 and IPv4 Headers

Link Layer

The Link layer, also called Network Access layer, of the TCP/IP model displays the services provided by both the Data Link and the Physical layers in the OSI model. The source and destination MAC addresses are placed in this layer's header. A trailer is also placed on the packet at this layer, with information in the trailer that can be used to verify the integrity of the data.

This layer is also concerned with placing the bits on the medium, as discussed in the "OSI Model" section, earlier in this chapter. Again, the exact method of implementation varies with the physical transmission medium. It might be in terms of electrical impulses, light waves, or radio waves.

Encapsulation and De-encapsulation

The beginning of a packet is called the *header*, and the end of the packet is called the *trailer*. The data between the header and the trailer is commonly referred to as the *payload*. In either model, as the packet is created, information is added to the header at each layer, and then a trailer is placed on the packet before transmission. This process is called *encapsulation*. Intermediate devices, such as routers and switches, read only the layers of concern to that device (for a switch, Layer 2, and for a router, Layer 3). The ultimate receiver strips off the entire header with each layer, making use of the information placed in the header by the corresponding layer on the sending device. This process is called *de-encapsulation*. In fact, de-encapsulation is just the opposite process of unpacking the data from the capsule. Figure 4-6 shows how encapsulation works. If the arrows are reversed, the process can closely resemble de-encapsulation.

Key Topic

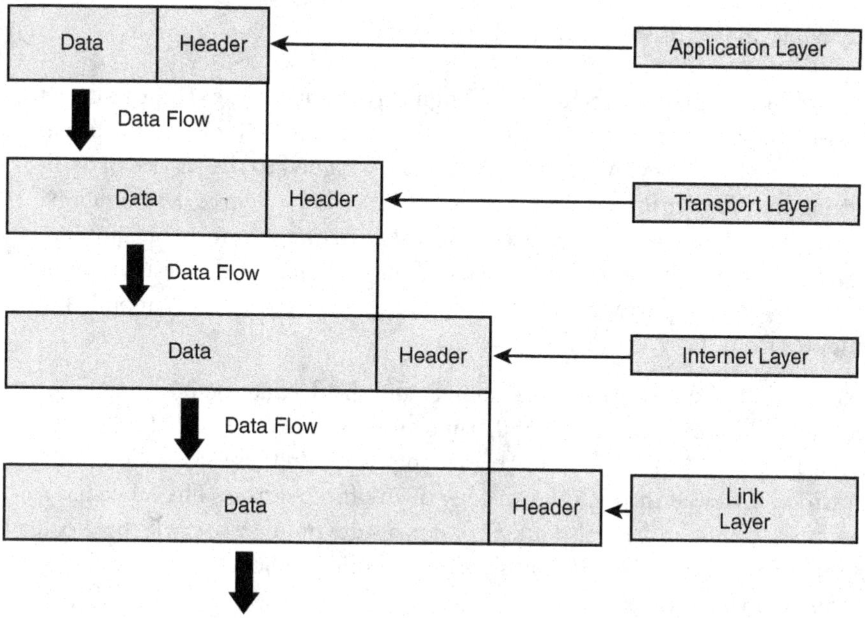

Figure 4-6 Encapsulation

IP Networking

Now that you understand secure design principles and the OSI and TCP/IP models, it is time to delve more deeply into IP networking. The ***Internet Protocol (IP)*** is the main communications protocol in the TCP/IP suite and is responsible for relaying datagrams across network boundaries. The following sections cover common TCP/UDP ports, logical and physical addressing, network transmission, and network types.

Common TCP/UDP Ports

When the Transport layer learns the required port number for the service or application required on the destination device from the Application layer, it is recorded in the header as either a TCP or UDP port number. Both UDP and TCP use 16 bits in the header to identify these ports. There are 65,536 possible numbers for ports, ranging from 0 to 65,535. Port numbers are assigned in various ways, based on three ranges:

- System, or well-known, ports (0–1023)
- User ports (1024–49151)
- Dynamic and/or private ports (49152–65535)

System ports are assigned by the Internet Engineering Task Force (IETF) for standards-track protocols, as per RFC 6335. User ports can be registered with the Internet Assigned Numbers Authority (IANA) and assigned to the service or application using the "Expert Review" process, as per RFC 6335. Source devices use dynamic ports as source ports when accessing a service or application on another machine. For example, if computer A is sending an FTP packet, the destination port will be the well-known port for FTP, and the source will be selected randomly by the computer from the dynamic range.

The combination of the destination IP address and the destination port number is called a *socket*. For example, port 1580, using an IP address of 172.28.90.123 has a socket of 172.28.90.123 : 1580. The relationship between these two values can be understood if viewed through the analogy of an office address. The office has a street address, but the address also must contain a suite number because there could be thousands (in this case, 65,535) of suites in the building. Both are required to get the information where it should go.

As a security professional, you should be aware of well-known port numbers of common services. In many instances, firewall rules and access control lists (ACLs) are written or configured in terms of the port number of what is being allowed or denied rather than the name of the service or application. Table 4-1 lists some of the more important port numbers. Some use more than one port.

Key Topic

Table 4-1 Common TCP/UDP Port Numbers

Application Protocol	Transport Protocol	Port Number
Telnet	TCP	23
SMTP	UDP	25
HTTP	TCP	80
SNMP	TCP and UDP	161 and 162
FTP	TCP and UDP	20 and 21
FTPS	TCP	989 and 990
SFTP	TCP	22
TFTP	UDP	69

Application Protocol	Transport Protocol	Port Number
POP3	TCP and UDP	110
DNS	TCP and UDP	53
DHCP	UDP	67 and 68
SSH	TCP	22
LDAP	TCP and UDP	389
NetBIOS	TCP and UDP	137 (TCP), 138 (TCP), and 139 (UDP)
CIFS/SMB	TCP	445
NFSv4	TCP	2049
SIP	TCP and UDP	5060
XMPP	TCP	5222
IRC	TCP and UDP	194
RADIUS	TCP and UDP	1812 and 1813
rlogin	TCP	513
rsh and RCP	TCP	514
IMAP	TCP	143
HTTPS	TCP and UDP	443
RDP	TCP and UDP	3389
AFP over TCP	TCP	548

Logical and Physical Addressing

During the process of encapsulation at Layer 3 of the OSI model, IP places source and destination IP addresses in the packet. Then at Layer 2, the matching source and destination MAC addresses that have been determined by ARP are placed in the packet. IP addresses are examples of logical addressing, and MAC addresses are examples of physical addressing. IP addresses are considered logical because these addresses are administered by humans and can be changed at any time. MAC addresses, on the other hand, are permanently assigned to the network interface controller of Ethernet and Wi-Fi–enabled devices during the manufacturing process. It is important to note, however, that although these addresses are permanent, they can be spoofed. When this is done, however, the hacker is not actually changing the physical address but rather telling the interface to place a different MAC address in the Layer 2 headers.

Here, we discuss both address types, with a particular focus on how IP addresses are used to create separate networks or subnets in the larger network. We also discuss how IP addresses and MAC addresses are related and used during a network transmission.

IPv4

IPv4 addresses are 32 bits in length and can be represented in either binary or in decimal, as a dotted-decimal format. The number of possible IP addresses using 32 bits can be calculated by raising the number 2 (the number of possible values in the binary number system) to the 32nd power. The result is 4,294,967,296, which on the surface appears to be enough IP addresses. But with the explosion of the Internet and the increasing number of devices that require an IP address, this number has proven to be insufficient.

Due to the eventual exhaustion of the IPv4 address space, several methods of preserving public IP addresses (more on that in a bit, but for now these are addresses that are legal to use on the Internet) have been implemented, including the use of private addresses and Network Address Translation (NAT), both discussed in following sections. The ultimate solution lies in the adoption of IPv6, a newer system that uses 128 bits and allows for enough IP addresses for every device in the world today and in the future. We discuss IPv6 later in this chapter.

IP addresses that are written in dotted-decimal format, the format in which humans usually work with them, have four fields, called octets, separated by dot characters or by period characters. Each field is called an octet because, with addresses in binary format, 8 bits in binary represent each decimal number that appears in the octet when it is viewed in dotted-decimal format. Therefore, in the address 216.5.41.3, four decimal numbers are separated by dots, where each would be represented by 8 bits if viewed in binary. The following is the binary version of this same address:

11011000.00000101.00101001.00000011

There are 32 bits in the address, with 8 bits in each of the four octets.

The structure of IPv4 addressing lends itself to dividing the network into subdivisions called subnets. Each IP address also has a required companion value called a subnet mask. The subnet mask is used to specify which part of the address is the *network* part and which part is the *host*. The network part, on the left side of the address, determines on which network the device resides, whereas the host portion on the right identifies the device on that network. Figure 4-7 shows the network and host portions of the three default classes of IP address.

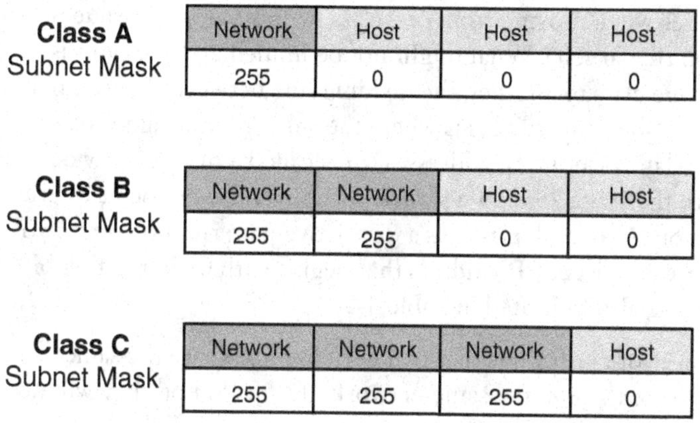

Figure 4-7 Network and Host Bits

When the IPv4 system was first created, there were only three default subnet masks. They yielded only three classes of networks, which later proved to be inconvenient and wasteful of public IP addresses. Eventually, a system called Classless Inter-Domain Routing (CIDR) was adopted; it uses subnet masks that allow subnets or subdivisions to be created from the major classful networks possible before CIDR. CIDR is beyond the scope of the CISSP exam, but it is worth knowing about. You can find more information about how CIDR works at https://searchnetworking.techtarget.com/definition/CIDR.

IP Classes

Classful subnetting (pre-CIDR) created five classes of networks. Each class represented a range of IP addresses. Table 4-2 shows the five classes. Only the first three (A, B, and C) are used for individual network devices. The other ranges are for special use.

Key Topic

Table 4-2 Classful IP Addressing

Class	Range	Mask	Initial Bit Pattern of First Octet	Network/Host Division
Class A	0.0.0.0–127.255.255.255	255.0.0.0	01	net.host.host.host
Class B	128.0.0.0–191.255.255.255	255.255.0.0	10	net.net.host.host
Class C	192.0.0.0–223.255.255.255	255.255.255.0	11	net.net.net.host
Class D	224.0.0.0–239.255.255.255	Used for multicasting		
Class E	240.0.0.0–255.255.255.255	Reserved for research		

The key value that changes when moving from one class to another is the value of the first octet (the one on the far left). What might not be immediately obvious is that when moving from one class to another, the dividing line between the host portion and network portion also changes. This is where the subnet mask value comes in. When the mask is overlaid with the IP addresses (thus called a mask), every octet in the subnet mask where there is a 255 is a network portion, and every octet where there is a 0 is a host portion. Also, each class has a distinctive pattern in the first two bits of the first octet. For example, *any* IP address that begins with 01 in the first bit positions *must* be in Class A, also indicated in Table 4-2.

The significance of the network portion is that two devices must share the same values in the network portion to be in the same network. If they do not, they will not be able to communicate.

Public Versus Private IP Addresses

The initial solution used (and still in use) to address the exhaustion of the IPv4 address space involved the use of private addresses and NAT. Three ranges of IP addresses were set aside to be used *only* within private networks and are *not* routable on the Internet. RFC 1918 set aside the ***private IP address*** ranges in Table 4-3 to be used for this purpose. Because these addresses are not routable on the public network, they must be translated to public addresses before being sent to the Internet. This process, called Network Address Translation, is discussed in the next section.

Key Topic

Table 4-3 Private IP Address Ranges

Class	IP Address Range
Class A	10.0.0.0–10.255.255.255
Class B	172.16.0.0–172.31.255.255
Class C	192.168.0.0–192.168.255.255

NAT

Network Address Translation (NAT) is a service that can be supplied by a router or by a server. The device that provides the service stands between the local-area network (LAN) and the Internet. When packets need to go to the Internet, the packets go through the NAT service first. The NAT service changes the private IP address to a public address that is routable on the Internet. When the response is returned from the Web, the NAT service receives it, translates the address back to the original private IP address, and sends it back to the originator.

To overcome the shortage of public IP addresses, private IP addresses are used on local-area networks. Figure 4-8 shows four computing devices: two desktop computers, a laptop, and a smartphone, each of which is assigned a private IP address. A router has both a public IP address and a private IP address. Communication between hosts on the LAN and the router occurs using a private IP address. The public IP address, or static IP address, is what is used to communicate with servers on the Internet. Therefore, a web server will respond to a request from a router based on its public IP address.

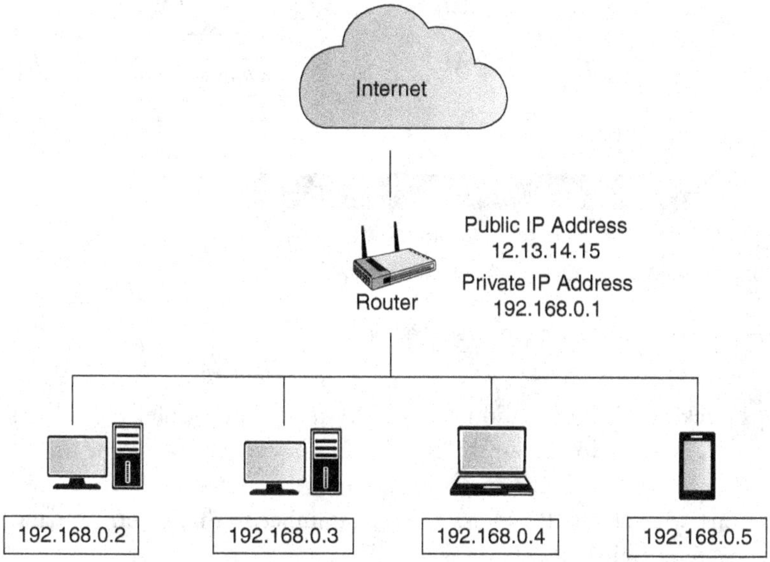

Figure 4-8 Private IP Addresses on a Local-Area Network (LAN)

Figure 4-9 shows an example of how NAT works. Here, a computer on a LAN wants to request information about the weather forecast for Dublin, Ireland, and obtain that information from weather.com. The private IP address for the requesting computer is 192.168.0.3. The request is sent through the router, and the router converts the client source IP address with its own IP address.

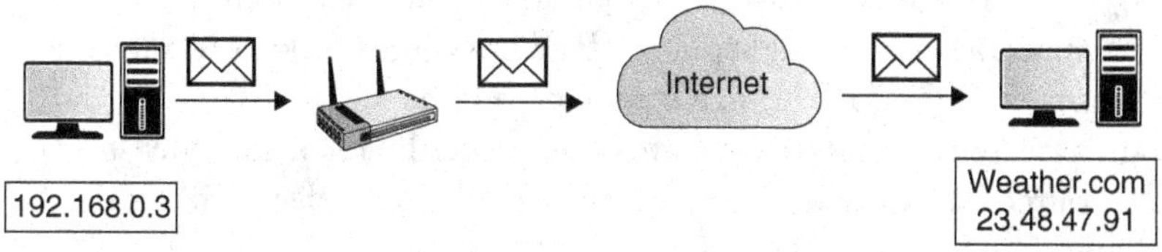

Figure 4-9 Computer with a Private IP Address Makes a Request to a Web Server

Figure 4-10 shows that the request from the client computer to weather.com is received by the router. Again, the router replaces the client source IP address with its own IP address of 12.13.14.15. The router also generates a source port number and replaces the source port in the package with the generated one, which in this case is 24603.

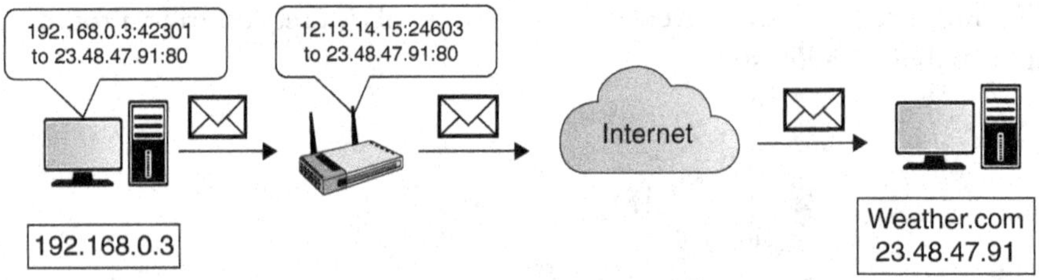

NAT Forwarding Table	
Private Side	**Public Side**
192.168.0.3:42301	12.13.14.15:24603

Figure 4-10 Client Computer Makes a Request to Weather.com

The router keeps track of this information in the NAT forwarding table. This means that the router stores information about the client computer request and how that request was made on the public-facing Internet. Again, the router maintains a table of active connections, with client IP address and port number so that incoming data can be redirected to the original client.

The web server for weather.com receives the request and does not see the IP address for the host on the network but sees only the static IP address for the router. The HTML file is then sent to the router (see Figure 4-11). When the router receives the file, it examines the destination port and looks up the NAT forwarding table to identify established connections. The router then replaces the IP address and port number so that the packet can be sent to the requesting client computer.

Translation can be done on a one-to-one basis (one private address to one public address), but to save IP addresses, usually the NAT service will represent the entire private network with a single public IP address. This process is called ***Port Address Translation (PAT)***. This name comes from the fact that the NAT service keeps the private clients separate from one another by recording their private address and the source port number (usually a unique number) selected when the packets were built.

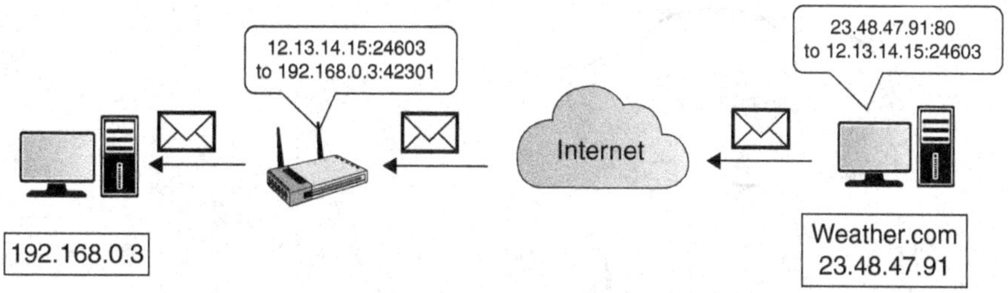

NAT Forwarding Table	
Private Side	**Public Side**
192.168.0.3:42301	12.13.14.15:24603

Figure 4-11 Router Receives File(s) from Weather.com Web Server

Allowing NAT to represent an entire network (perhaps thousands of computers) with a single public address has been quite effective in saving public IP addresses. However, many applications do not function properly through NAT, and thus it has never been seen as a permanent solution to resolving the lack of IP addresses. That solution is IPv6.

NAT is not compatible with IP Security (IPsec, discussed later in this chapter) because NAT modifies packet headers. Some versions of NAT are designed to support IPsec.

Security professionals need to understand stateful NAT, static versus dynamic NAT, and APIPA.

Stateful NAT

Stateful NAT (SNAT) implements two or more NAT devices to work together as a translation group. One member provides network translation of IP address information. The other member uses that information to create duplicate translation table entries. If the primary member that provides network translation fails, the backup member can then become the primary translator. It is called *stateful* NAT because it maintains a table about the communication sessions between internal and external systems. Figure 4-12 illustrates an example of a SNAT deployment.

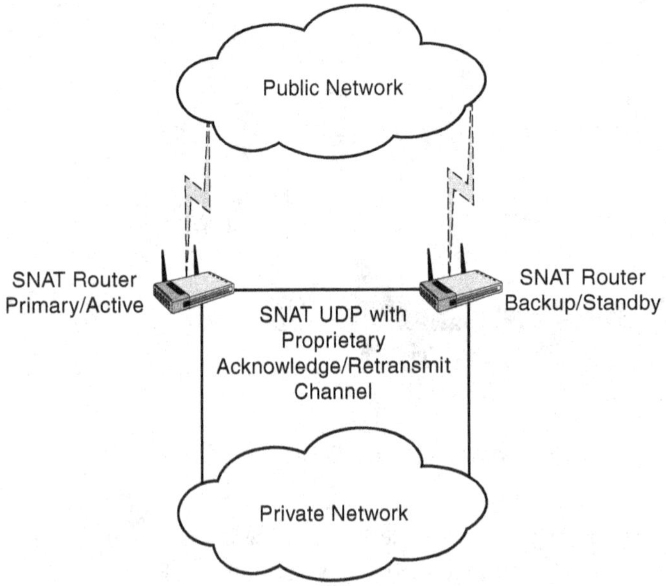

Figure 4-12 Stateful NAT

Static Versus Dynamic NAT

NAT operates in two modes: static and dynamic. With ***static NAT***, an internal private IP address is mapped to a specific external public IP address. This is a one-to-one-mapping. With ***dynamic NAT***, multiple internal private IP addresses are given access to multiple external public IP addresses. This is a many-to-many mapping.

APIPA

Automatic Private IP Addressing (APIPA) assigns an IP address to a device if the device is unable to communicate with the DHCP server and is primarily implemented in Windows. The range of IP addresses assigned is 169.254.0.1 to 169.254.255.254 with a subnet mask of 255.255.0.0.

When a device is configured with an APIPA address, it is able to communicate only with other APIPA-configured devices on the same subnet. It is unable to communicate with non-APIPA devices on the same subnet or with devices on a different subnet. If a technician notices that a device is configured with an APIPA address, a communication problem exists between the device and DHCP, which could range from a bad network interface card or controller (NIC) or cable to DHCP router or server failure.

Media Access Control (MAC) Addressing

All the discussion about addressing thus far has been addressing that is applied at Layer 3, which is IP addressing. Physical addresses reside at Layer 2. In Ethernet, these are also called MAC addresses. They are physical addresses because these 48-bit (6 bytes) addresses expressed in hexadecimal are permanently assigned to the network interfaces of devices. Here is an example of a MAC address:

01:23:45:67:89:AB

As a packet is transferred across a network, at every router hop and then again when it arrives at the destination network, the source and destination MAC addresses change. ARP resolves the next hop address to a MAC address using a process called the ARP broadcast. MAC addresses are unique; at the beginning of the address, each manufacturer has a different set of values assigned to it, called the organizationally unique identifier (OUI). Each manufacturer ensures that it assigns no duplicate within its OUI. The OUI is the first three bytes of the MAC address.

Network Transmission

Data can be communicated across a variety of media types, using several possible processes. These communications can also have a number of characteristics that you need to understand. Next, we discuss some of the most common methods and their characteristics.

Analog Versus Digital

Data can be represented in various ways on a medium. On a wired medium, the data can be transmitted in either analog or digital format. For example, analog signals can represent data as sound that is used in analog telephony. Analog signals differ from digital in that there is an infinite possible number of values. An analog signal on a graph looks like a wave going up and down. Figure 4-13 shows an analog waveform compared to a digital one.

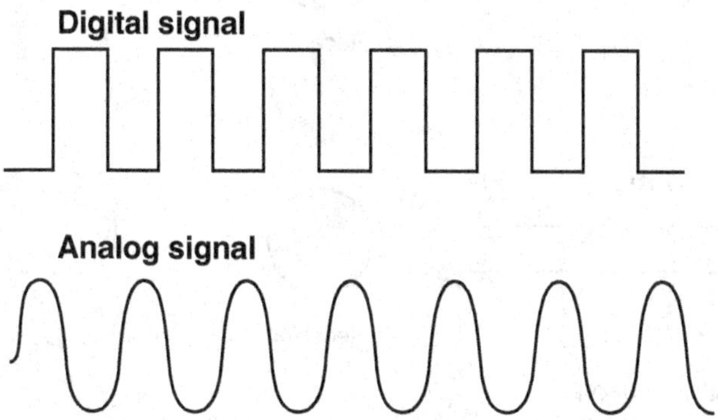

Figure 4-13 Digital and Analog Signals

Digital signaling, on the other hand, which is the type used in most computer transmissions, does not have an infinite number of possible values; it has only two: on and off. A digital signal shown on a graph exhibits a sawtooth pattern, as shown in Figure 4-13. Digital signals are usually preferable to analog because they are more reliable and less susceptible to noise on the line. Transporting more information on the same line at a higher quality over a longer distance than with analog is also possible.

Asynchronous Versus Synchronous

When two systems are communicating, they not only need to represent the data in the same format (analog/digital) but must also use the same synchronization technique. This process tells the receiver when a specific communication begins and ends so that two-way conversations can happen without talking over one another. The two types of techniques are asynchronous transmission and synchronous transmission.

With ***asynchronous transmissions***, the systems use *start* and *stop* bits to communicate when each byte is starting and stopping. This method also uses *parity bits* for the purpose of ensuring that each byte has not changed or been corrupted en route. This method introduces additional overhead to the transmission.

Synchronous transmission uses a clocking mechanism to sync up the sender and receiver. Data is transferred in a stream of bits with no start, stop, or parity bits. This clocking mechanism is embedded into the Layer 2 protocol. It uses a different form of error checking such as cyclic redundancy check (or CRC) and is preferable for high-speed, high-volume transmissions. Figure 4-14 shows a visual comparison of the two techniques.

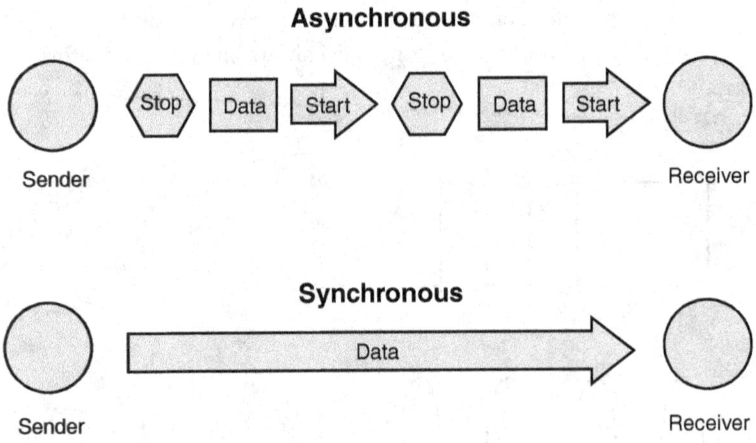

Figure 4-14 Asynchronous Versus Synchronous

Broadband Versus Baseband

All data transfers use a communication channel. Multiple transmissions might need to use the same channel. This medium can be shared in two different ways: using broadband or baseband. The difference is in how the medium is shared.

In ***baseband***, the entire medium is used for a single transmission, and then multiple transmission types are assigned time slots to use this single circuit. This process is called ***time-division multiplexing (TDM)***. Multiplexing is the process of using the same medium for multiple transmissions. The transmissions take turns rather than send at the same time.

Broadband, on the other hand, divides the medium into different frequencies, a process called ***frequency-division multiplexing (FDM)***. This process has the benefit of allowing true simultaneous use of the medium.

An example of broadband transmission is Digital Subscriber Line (DSL), where the phone signals are sent at one frequency and the computer data at another. This is why you can talk on the phone and use the Web at the same time. Figure 4-15 illustrates these two processes.

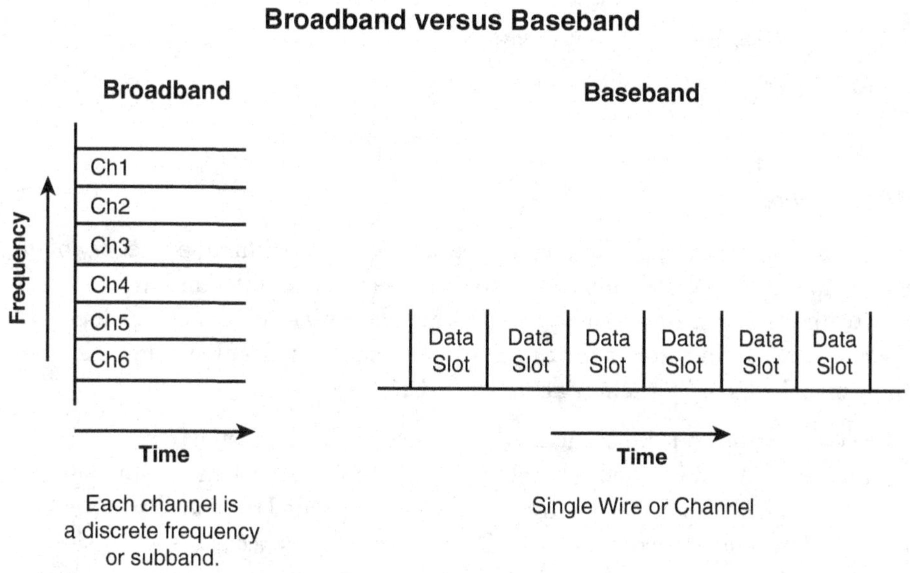

Figure 4-15 Broadband Versus Baseband

Unicast, Multicast, and Broadcast

When systems are communicating in a network, they might send out three types of transmissions. These methods differ in the scope of their reception as follows:

- ***Unicast*:** Transmission from a single system to another single system. It is considered one-to-one.
- ***Multicast*:** A signal is received by all others in a group called a multicast group. It is considered one-to-many.
- ***Broadcast*:** A transmission sent by a single system to all systems in the network. It is considered one-to-all.

Figure 4-16 illustrates the three methods.

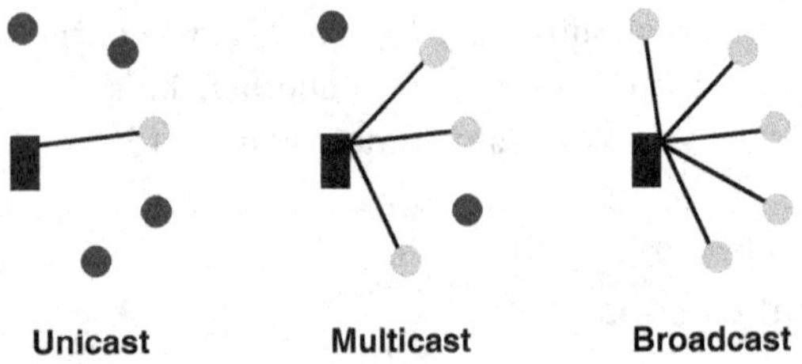

Figure 4-16 Unicast, Multicast, and Broadcast

Wired Versus Wireless

Not all transmissions occur over a wired connection. Even within the category of wired connections, the ones and zeros can be represented in different ways. In a copper wire, the ones and zeros (binary) are represented with changes in the voltage of the signal, whereas in a fiber optic cable, they are represented with manipulation of a light source (lasers or light-emitting diodes [LEDs]).

In wireless transmission, radio waves or light waves are manipulated to represent the ones and zeros. When infrared technology is used, this is done with infrared light. With wireless LANs (WLANs), radio waves are manipulated to represent the ones and zeros. These differences in how the bits are represented occur at the Physical and Data Link layers of the OSI model. When a packet goes from a wireless section of the network to a wired section, these two layers are the only layers that change.

When a different physical medium is used, typically a different Layer 2 (Data Link) protocol is called for. For example, while the data is traveling over the wired Ethernet network, the 802.3 standard is used. However, when the data gets to a wireless section of the network, it needs a different Layer 2 protocol. Depending on the technology in use, it could be either 802.11 (WLAN) or 802.16 (WiMAX).

The packet's capability to traverse various media types is just another indication of the independence of the OSI layers because the information in OSI Layers 3–7 remains unchanged regardless of how many Layer 2 transitions must be made to get the data to its final destination.

IPv6

IPv6 was developed to address the issue of the exhaustion of the IPv4 address space that had only 32 bits. Although private addressing and the use of NAT have helped to delay the inevitable address exhaustion, the use of NAT introduces its own set of problems, such as some applications will not work if NAT is enabled. The IPv6 system uses 128 bits to generate a large number of possible addresses, measured in undecillions, which should suffice for many years to come.

IPv6 addresses look different than IPv4 addresses because they use a different format and use the hexadecimal number system, so there are letters and numbers in them, similar to what you would see in a MAC address. There are eight fields, containing 16 bits, with a hexadecimal format, separated by colons, not dots.

Here is a sample IPv6 address:

2001:00000:4137:9e76:30ab:3035:b541:9693

Many of the security features that were add-ons to IPv4 (such as IPsec) have been built into IPv6, providing better security. Moreover, while DHCP can be used with IPv6, IPv6 enables a host to locate its local router, configure itself, and discover the IP addresses of its neighbors. Finally, broadcast traffic is completely eliminated in IPv6 and replaced by multicast communications.

Table 4-4 shows the differences between IPv4 and IPv6.

Key Topic

Table 4-4 Differences Between IPv4 and IPv6 (Adapted from NIST SP 800-119)

Property	IPv4	IPv6
Address size and network size	32 bits, network size 8–30 bits	128 bits, network size 64 bits
Packet header size	20–60 bytes	40-byte fixed header
Header-level extension	Limited number of small IP options	Unlimited number of IPv6 extension headers
Fragmentation	Sender or any intermediate router allowed to fragment	Only sender may fragment
Control protocols	Mixture of non-IP (ARP), ICMP, and other protocols	All control protocols based on ICMPv6

Property	IPv4	IPv6
Minimum allowed MTU (max transition unit)	576 bytes	1280 bytes
Path MTU discovery	Optional, not widely used	Strongly recommended
Address assignment	Usually one address per host	Usually multiple addresses per interface
Address types	Use of unicast, multicast, and broadcast address types	Broadcast addressing no longer used; use of unicast, multicast, and anycast address types
Address configuration	Devices configured manually or with host configuration protocols like DHCP	Devices configure themselves independently using stateless address autoconfiguration (SLAAC) or use DHCP

NIST SP 800-119

NIST Special Publication (SP) 800-119 provides guidelines for the secure deployment of IPv6. According to this SP, organizations planning the deployment of IPv6 should consider the following during the planning process:

- IPv6 is a protocol that is not backward compatible with IPv4.
- In most cases, IPv4 will still be a component of an IT infrastructure. As such, even after the deployment of IPv6, organizations will require mechanisms for IPv6 and IPv4 coexistence.
- IPv6 can be deployed just as securely as IPv4, although it should be expected that vulnerabilities within the protocol, as well as with implementation errors, will lead to an initial increase in IPv6-based vulnerabilities. As a successor to IPv4, IPv6 does incorporate many of the lessons learned by the IETF for IPv4.
- IPv6 has already been deployed and is currently in operation in large networks globally.

To overcome possible obstacles associated with deploying IPv6, organizations should consider the following recommendations:

- Encourage staff to increase their knowledge of IPv6 to a level comparable with their current understanding of IPv4.
- Plan a phased IPv6 deployment utilizing appropriate transition mechanisms to support business needs; don't deploy more transition mechanisms than necessary.
- Plan for a long transition period with dual IPv4/IPv6 coexistence.

Organizations that have not deployed IPv6 globally should implement the following recommendations:

- Disable all IPv6-compatible ports, protocols, and services on all software and hardware.
- Begin to acquire familiarity and expertise with IPv6, through laboratory experimentation and/or limited pilot deployments.
- Make organization web servers, located outside of the organizational firewall, accessible via IPv6 connections. This will enable IPv6-only users to access the servers and aid the organization in acquiring familiarity with some aspects of IPv6 deployment.

Organizations that are deploying IPv6 should implement the following recommendations to mitigate IPv6 threats:

- Apply an appropriate mix of different types of IPv6 addressing (privacy addressing, unique local addressing, sparse allocation, and so on) to limit access and knowledge of IPv6-addressed environments.
- Use automated address management tools to avoid manual entry of IPv6 addresses, which is prone to error because of their length.
- Develop a granular ICMPv6 (ICMP for IPv6) filtering policy for the enterprise. Ensure that ICMPv6 messages that are essential to IPv6 operation are allowed but others are blocked.
- Use IPsec to authenticate and provide confidentiality to assets that can be tied to a scalable trust model (an example is access to Human Resources assets by internal employees who make use of an organization's public key infrastructure [PKI] to establish trust).
- Identify capabilities and weaknesses of network protection devices in an IPv6 environment.
- Enable controls that might not have been used in IPv4 due to a lower threat level during initial deployment (implementing default deny access control policies, implementing routing protocol security, and so on).
- Pay close attention to the security aspects of transition mechanisms such as tunneling protocols.
- Ensure that IPv6 routers, packet filters, firewalls, and tunnel endpoints enforce multicast scope boundaries and make sure that Multicast Listener Discovery (MLD) packets are not inappropriately routable.

- Be aware that switching from an environment in which NAT provides IP addresses to unique global IPv6 addresses could trigger a change in the Federal Information Security Management Act (FISMA) system boundaries.

The following sections on IPv6 are adapted from NIST SP 800-119. For more information on IPv6 beyond what is provided here, please refer to NIST SP 800-119.

IPv6 Major Features

According to NIST SP 800-119, IPv6 has many features that make it significantly different from its predecessor, IPv4. These features include extended address space, autoconfiguration, header structure, extension headers, IPsec, mobility, quality of service, route aggregation, and efficient transmission.

Extended Address Space

Each IPv4 address is typically 32 bits long and is written as four decimal numbers representing 8-bit octets and separated by decimal points or periods. A sample IPv4 address is 172.30.128.97. Each IPv6 address is 128 bits long (as defined in RFC 4291) and is written as eight 16-bit fields in colon-delimited hexadecimal notation (an example is fe80:43e3:9095:02e5:0216:cbff:feb2:7474). This 128-bit address space provides an enormous number of unique addresses, 2^{128} (or 3.4×10^{38}) addresses, compared with IPv4's 2^{32} (or 4.3×10^{9}) addresses.

Autoconfiguration

Essentially plug-and-play networking, IPv6 Stateless Address Auto-Configuration (SLAAC) is one of the most interesting and potentially valuable addressing features in IPv6. This feature allows devices on an IPv6 network to configure themselves independently using a stateless protocol. In IPv4, hosts are configured manually or with host configuration protocols like DHCP; with IPv6, autoconfiguration takes this a step further by defining a method for some devices to configure their IP addresses and other parameters without the need for a server. Moreover, it also defines a method, renumbering, whereby the time and effort required to renumber a network by replacing an old prefix with a new prefix are vastly reduced.

Header Structure

The IPv6 header is much simpler than the IPv4 header and has a fixed length of 40 bytes (as defined in RFC 2460). Even though this header is almost twice as long as the minimum IPv4 header, much of the header is taken up by two 16-byte IPv6 addresses, leaving only 8 bytes for other header information. This simplified header allows for improved fast processing of packets and protocol flexibility.

Extension Headers

An IPv4 header can be extended from 20 bytes to a maximum of 60 bytes, but this option is rarely used because it impedes performance and is often administratively prohibited for security reasons. IPv6 has a method to handle options, which allows substantially improved processing and avoids some of the security problems that IPv4 options generated. IPv6 RFC 2460 defines six extension headers: hop-by-hop option header, routing header, fragment header, destination options header, authentication header (AH), and encapsulating security payload (ESP) header. Each extension header is identified by the Next Header field in the preceding header.

Mandatory IPsec Support

Internet Protocol Security (IPsec) is a suite of protocols for securing IP communications by authenticating the sender and providing integrity protection plus, optionally, confidentiality for the transmitted data. The negotiation and management of IPsec security protections and the associated secret keys are handled by the Internet Key Exchange (IKE) protocol. IPsec is a mandatory part of an IPv6 implementation; however, its use is not required. IPsec is also specified for securing particular IPv6 protocols (e.g., Mobile IPv6 and OSPFv3 [Open Shortest Path First version 3]).

Mobile Compatibility

Mobile IPv6 (MIPv6) is an enhanced protocol supporting roaming for a mobile node so that it can move from one network to another without losing IP-layer connectivity (as defined in RFC 3775). Mobile IPv6 uses IPv6's vast address space and Neighbor Discovery (RFC 4861) to solve the handover problem at the network layer and maintain connections to applications and services if a device changes its temporary IP address. Mobile IPv6 also introduced security concerns, such as route optimization (RFC 4449), where data flow between the home agent and mobile node will need to be appropriately secured.

Quality of Service

IP (for the most part) treats all packets alike because they are forwarded with best-effort treatment and no guarantee for delivery through the network. TCP adds delivery confirmations but has no options to control parameters such as delay or bandwidth allocation. Quality of service (QoS) offers enhanced policy-based networking options to prioritize the delivery of information. Existing IPv4 and IPv6 implementations use similar QoS capabilities, such as Differentiated Services and Integrated Services, to identify and prioritize IP-based communications during periods of network congestion. Within the IPv6 header, two fields can be used for QoS: the Traffic Class and Flow Label fields. The Flow Label field and enlarged Traffic Class field in the main IPv6 header allow more efficient and finer-grained differentiation of various types of traffic. The Flow Label field can contain a label identifying or prioritizing a certain packet flow, such as Voice over IP (VoIP) or videoconferencing, both of which are sensitive to timely delivery. IPv6 QoS was developed to help with traffic shaping, weighted random early detection (WRED), and policing of IPv6 packets.

Route Aggregation

IPv6 incorporates a hierarchical addressing structure and has a simplified header allowing for improved routing of information from a source to a destination. The large amount of address space allows organizations with large numbers of connections to obtain blocks of contiguous address space.

Contiguous address space allows organizations to aggregate addresses under one prefix for identification on the Internet. This structured approach to addressing reduces the amount of information Internet routers must maintain and store and promotes faster routing of data. This will allow for ISPs to summarize route advertisements to minimize the size of the IPv6 Internet routing tables.

Efficient Transmission

IPv6 packet fragmentation control occurs at the IPv6 source host, not at an intermediate IPv6 router. With IPv4, a router can fragment a packet when the maximum transmission unit (MTU) of the next link is smaller than the packet it has to send. The router does this by slicing a packet to fit into the smaller MTU and sends it out as a set of fragments. The destination host collects the fragments and reassembles them. All fragments must arrive for the higher-level protocol to receive the complete packet. Therefore, when one fragment is missing or an error occurs, the entire transmission has to be redone.

In IPv6, a host uses a procedure called Path Maximum Transmission Unit Discovery (PMTUD) to learn the path MTU size and eliminate the need for routers to perform fragmentation. The IPv6 Fragment Extension Header is used when an IPv6 host wants to fragment a packet, so fragmentation occurs at the source host, not the router, which allows efficient transmission.

IPv4 Versus IPv6 Threat Comparison

Based on the threat comparison between IPv4 and IPv6, the following actions are recommended to mitigate IPv6 threats during the deployment process:

- Apply different types of IPv6 addressing (privacy addressing, unique local addressing, sparse allocation, etc.) to limit access and knowledge of IPv6-addressed environments.
- Assign subnet and interface identifiers randomly to increase the difficulty of network scanning.
- Develop a granular ICMPv6 filtering policy for the enterprise. Ensure that ICMPv6 messages that are essential to IPv6 operation are allowed but others are blocked.
- Use IPsec to authenticate and provide confidentiality to assets that can be tied to a scalable trust model (an example is access to Human Resources assets by internal employees that make use of an organization's PKI to establish trust).
- Identify capabilities and weaknesses of network protection devices in an IPv6 environment.
- Enable controls that might not have been used in IPv4 due to a lower threat level during initial deployment (implementing default deny access control policies, implementing routing protocol security, etc.).
- Pay close attention to the security aspects of transition mechanisms such as tunneling protocols.

IPv6 Addressing

According to NIST SP 800-119, IPv6 addresses are 128 bits long and are written in what is called colon-delimited hexadecimal notation. An IPv6 address is composed of eight distinct numbers representing 16 bits each and written in base-16 (hexadecimal or hex) notation. The valid hex digits are 0 through 9 and A through F and together with the colon separator are the only characters that can be used for writing an IPv6 address. A comparison of IPv4 and IPv6 addressing conventions is illustrated in Figure 4-17.

Key Topic

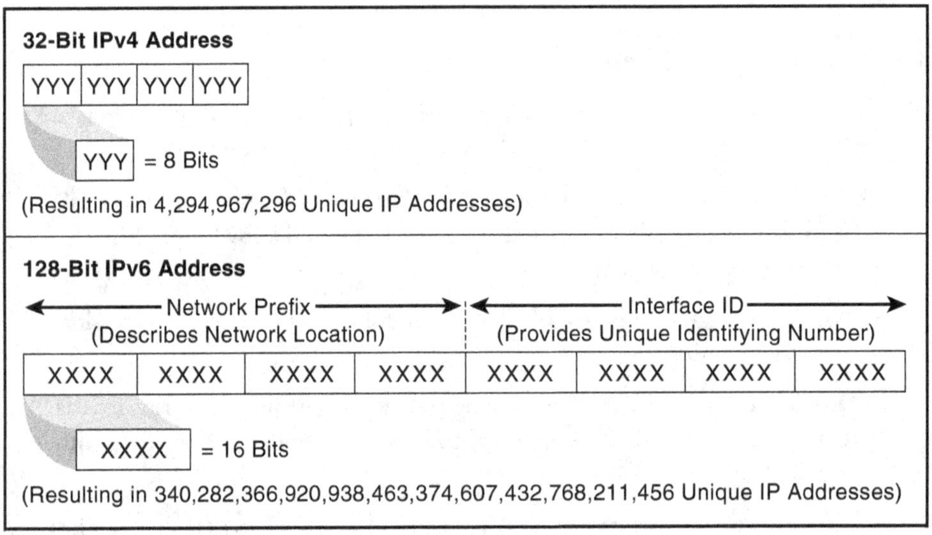

Figure 4-17 Comparison of IPv4 and IPv6 Addressing

As a reminder, an example of an IPv6 address is

2001:0db8:9095:02e5:0216:cbff:feb2:7474

Note that the address contains eight distinct hextets, separated by colons. Each of these values represents 16 bits, for a total of 128 bits in the entire address. IPv6 addresses are not case sensitive.

IPv6 addresses are divided among the network prefix, the subnet identifier, and the host identifier portions of the address (see Figure 4-18). The network prefix is the high-order bits of an IP address, used to identify a specific network and, in some cases, a specific type of address. The subnet identifier (subnet ID) identifies a link within a site. The subnet ID is assigned by the local administrator of the site; a single site can have multiple subnet IDs. This is used as a designator for the network upon which the host bearing the address is resident. The subnet ID should not be confused with the subnet mask, which only exists in IPv4. The host identifier (host ID) of the address is a unique identifier for the node within the network upon which it resides. It is identified with a specific interface of the host.

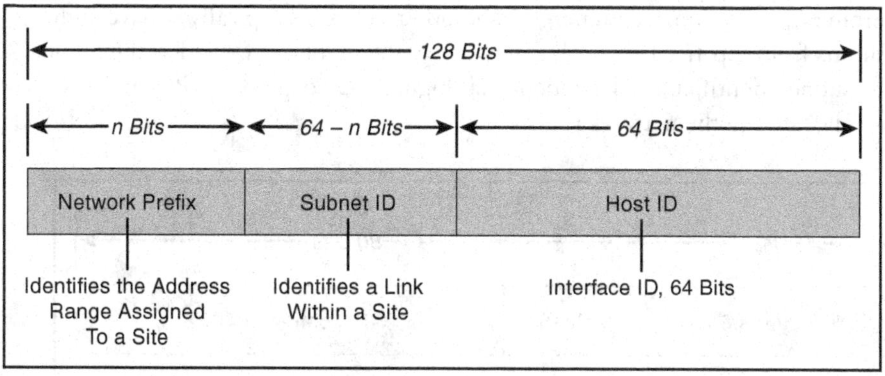

Figure 4-18 IPv6 Address Format

Although there is no subnet mask in IPv6, the slash notation used to identify the network address bits is similar to IPv4's subnet mask notation. The IPv6 notation appends the prefix length and is written as a number of bits with a slash, which leads to the following format: IPv6 address/prefix length. The prefix length specifies how many of the address's leftmost bits comprise the network prefix. A sample address with a 32-bit network prefix is

2001:0db8:9095:02e5:0216:cbff:feb2:7474/32

Quantities of IPv6 addresses are assigned by the international registry services and ISPs based in part on the size of the entity receiving the addresses. Large, top-tier networks may receive IPv6 address allocations with a network prefix of 32 bits as long as the need is justified (see Figure 4-19). In this case, the first two groupings of hexadecimal values (hextets), separated by colons, comprise the network prefix for the assignee of the addresses. The remaining 96 bits are available to the local administrator primarily for reallocation of the subnet ID and the host ID. The subnet ID identifies a link within a site, which can have multiple subnet IDs. The host ID within a network must be unique and identifies an interface on a subnet for the organization, similar to an assigned IPv4 address.

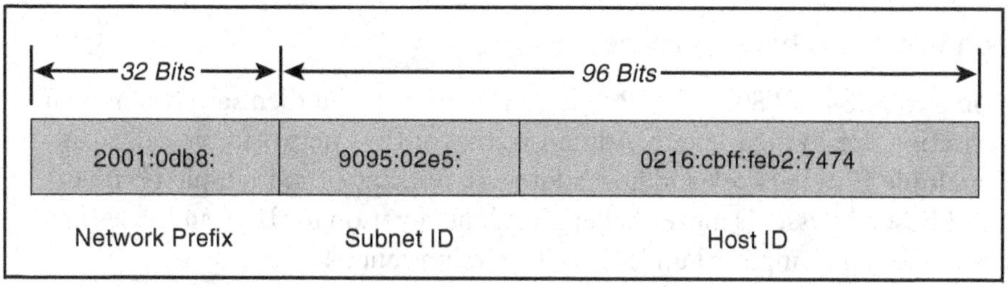

Figure 4-19 IPv6 32-bit Network Prefix

Government, educational, commercial, and other networks typically receive address allocations from top-tier ISPs with a network prefix of 48 bits (/48), leaving 80 bits for the subnet identifier and host identifier. Figure 4-20 depicts an IPv6 address with 48 bits allocated to the network prefix.

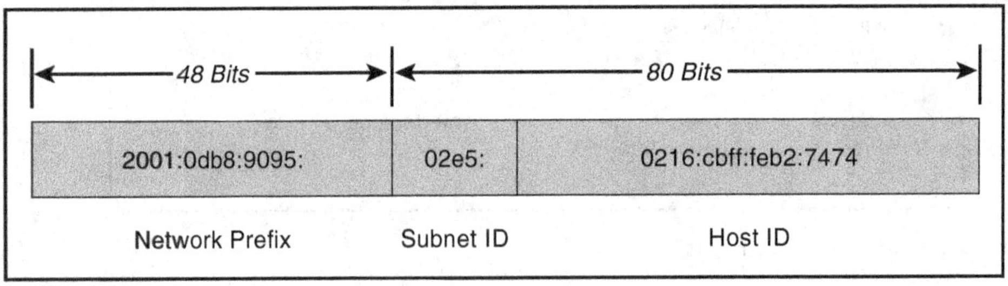

Figure 4-20 IPv6 48-bit Network Prefix

Subnets within an organization often have network prefixes of 64 bits (/64), leaving 64 bits for allocation to hosts' interfaces. The host ID should use a 64-bit interface identifier that follows EUI-64 (Extended Unique Identifier) format when a global network prefix is used (001 to 111), except in the case when multicast addresses (1111 1111) are used. Figure 4-21 depicts an IPv6 address with 64 bits allocated to the network prefix.

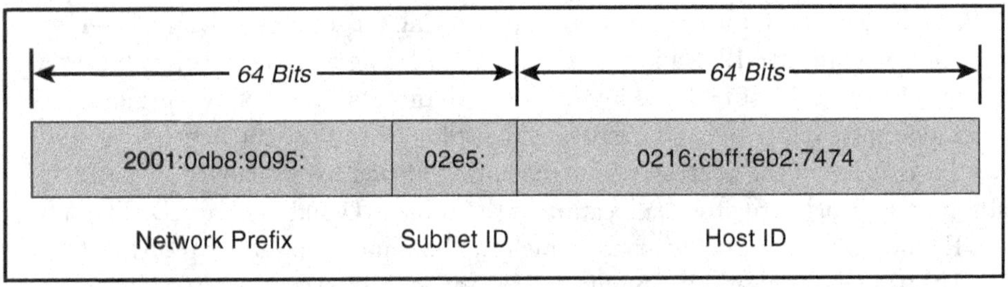

Figure 4-21 IPv6 64-bit Network Prefix

Shorthand for Writing IPv6 Addresses

According to NIST SP 800-119, IPv6 addresses do not lend themselves to human memorization due to their length. Administrators of IPv4 networks typically can recall multiple IPv4 network and host addresses; remembering multiple IPv6 network and host addresses is more challenging. The notation for IPv6 addresses may be compressed and simplified under specific circumstances.

One to three zeros that appear as the leading digits in any colon-delimited hexadecimal grouping may be dropped. This simplifies the address and makes it easier to read and to write. For example,

2001:0db8:0aba:02e5:0000:0ee9:0000:0444/48

becomes

2001:db8:aba:2e5:0:ee9:0:444/48

It is important to note that trailing zeros may not be dropped because they have intrinsic place value in the address format.

Further efficiency is gained by combining all-zero portions of the address. Any colon-delimited portion of an address containing all zeros may be compressed so that nothing appears between the leading and trailing colons. For example,

2001:0db8:0055:0000:cd23:0000:0000:0205/48

becomes

2001:db8:55:0:cd23::205/48

In this example, the sixth and seventh hextet contain all zeros; they were compressed by eliminating the zeros completely, as well as the colon that divided the two groupings. Nevertheless, compressing an address by removing one or more consecutive colons between groups of zeros may be done only once per address. The fourth 16-bit grouping in the example also contains all zeros, but in the condensed form of the address, it is represented with a single zero. A choice had to be made as to which group of zeros was to be compressed. The sample address could be written

2001:db8:55::cd23:0:0:205/48

but this is not as efficient as

2001:db8:55:0:cd23::205/48

It is important to note that both of the preceding addresses are properly formatted, but the latter address is shorter. Compression is just a convention for writing addresses; *it does not affect* how an address is used, and it makes no difference whether compression falls within the network prefix, host identifier, or across both portions of the address.

IPv6 Address Types

According to NIST SP 800-119, IPv6 addressing differs from IPv4 addressing in several ways aside from the address size. In both IPv4 and IPv6, addresses specifically belong to interfaces, not to nodes. However, because IPv6 addresses are not in short supply, interfaces often have multiple addresses. IPv6 addresses consist of a network prefix in the higher order bits and an interface identifier in the lower order bits. Moreover, the prefix indicates a subnet or link within a site, and a link can be assigned multiple subnet IDs.

Many IPv6 address ranges are reserved or defined for special purposes by the IETF's IPv6 standards and by IANA. Table 4-5 lists the major assignments and how to identify the different types of IPv6 addresses from the high-order bits.

Table 4-5 IPv6 Address Types (Copied from NIST SP 800-119)

Address Type	IPv6 Notation	Uses
Embedded IPv4 address	::FFFF/96	Prefix for embedding IPv4 address in an IPv6 address
Loopback	::1/128	Loopback address on every interface
Global unicast	2000::/3	Global unicast and anycast (allocated)
Global unicast	4000::/2–FC00::/9	Global unicast and anycast (unallocated)
Teredo	2001:0000::/32	Teredo
Non-routable	2001:DB8::/32	Non-routable. Documentation purposes only
6to4	2002::/16	6to4
6Bone	3FFE::/16	Deprecated. 6Bone testing assignment, 1996 through mid-2006
Link-local unicast	FE80::/10	Link-local unicast
Reserved	FEC0::/10	Deprecated. Formerly Site-local address space, unicast and anycast
Local IPv6 address	FC00::/7	Unicast unique local address space, unicast and anycast
Multicast	FF00::/8	Multicast address space

IPv6 uses the notion of address types for different situations. These different address types are defined in the following list and can also be referred to in RFC 4291:

- **Unicast address:** An address that identifies one interface on a single node; a packet with a unicast destination address is delivered to that interface.
- **Multicast address:** RFC 4291 defines a multicast address as "An identifier for a set of interfaces (typically belonging to different nodes). A packet sent to a multicast address is delivered to all interfaces identified by that address." Although multicast addresses are common in both IPv4 and IPv6, in IPv6

multicasting has additional applications. The single most important aspect of multicast addressing under IPv6 is that it enables fundamental IPv6 functionality, including neighbor discovery (ND) and router discovery. Multicast addresses begin with FF00::/8. They are intended for efficient one-to-many and many-to-many communication. The IPv6 standards prohibit sending packets from a multicast address; multicast addresses are valid only as destinations.

- **Anycast address:** An address that can identify more than one interface; a packet with an anycast destination address is delivered to one of the interfaces bearing the address, usually the closest one as determined by routing protocols. Anycast addressing was introduced as an add-on for IPv4, but it was designed as a basic component of IPv6.

The format of anycast addresses is indistinguishable from unicast addresses.

Broadcast addressing is a common attribute of IPv4, but is not defined or implemented in IPv6. Multicast addressing in IPv6 meets the requirements of broadcast addressing.

IPv6 Address Scope

According to NIST SP 800-119, in the original design for IPv6, link-local, site-local, and global addresses were defined; later, it was realized that site-local addresses were not defined well enough to be useful. Site-local addresses were abandoned and replaced with unique local addresses. Older implementations of IPv6 may still use site-local addresses, so IPv6 firewalls need to recognize and handle site-local addresses correctly.

The IPv6 standards define several scopes for meaningful IPv6 addresses:

- **Interface-local:** This applies only to a single interface; the loopback address has this scope.
- **Link-local:** This applies to a particular LAN or network link; every IPv6 interface on a LAN must have an address with this scope. Link-local addresses start with FE80::/10. Packets with link-local destination addresses are not routable and must not be forwarded off the local link. Link-local addresses are used for administrative purposes, such as neighbor and router discovery.
- **Site-local:** This scope was intended to apply to all IPv6 networks or a single logical entity, such as the network within an organization. Addresses with this scope start with FEC0::/10. They were intended not to be globally routable but potentially routed between subnets within an organization. Site-local addresses have been deprecated and replaced with unique local addresses.

- **Unique local unicast:** This scope is meant for a site, campus, or enterprise's internal addressing. It replaces the deprecated site-local concept. Unique local addresses (ULAs) may be routable within an enterprise. Use of unique local addresses is not yet widespread.
- **Global:** The global scope applies to the entire Internet. These globally unique addresses are routable across all publicly connected networks.
- **Embedded IPv4 unicast:** The IPv6 specification has the ability to leverage existing IPv4 addressing schemes. The transition to IPv6 has been gradual, so two special types of addresses have been defined for backward compatibility with IPv4: IPv4-compatible IPv6 addresses (rarely used and deprecated in RFC 4291) and IPv4-mapped IPv6 addresses. Both allow the protocol to derive addresses by embedding IPv4 addresses in the body of an IPv6 address. An IPv4-mapped IPv6 address is used to represent the addresses of IPv4-only nodes as an IPv6 address, which allows an IPv6 node to use this address to send a packet to an IPv4-only node.

IPv6 makes use of addresses other than those shown previously. The unspecified address consists of all zeros (0:0:0:0:0:0:0:0 or simply ::) and may be the source address of a node soliciting its own IP address from an address assignment authority (such as a DHCPv6 server). IPv6-compliant routers never forward a packet with an unspecified address. The loopback address is used by a node to send a packet to itself. The loopback address, 0:0:0:0:0:0:0:1 (or simply ::1), is defined as being interface local.

IPv6-compliant hosts and routers never forward packets with a loopback destination.

Network Types

So far we have discussed network topologies and technologies, so now let's look at a third way to describe networks: *network type*. Network type refers to the scope of the network. Is it a LAN or a WAN? Is it a part of the internal network, or is it an extranet? In the following sections, we discuss and differentiate all these network types.

LAN

First, let's talk about what makes a ***local-area network (LAN)*** local (see Figure 4-22). Although classically a LAN is thought of as a network located in one location, such as a single office, referring to a LAN as a group of systems that are connected with a *fast* connection is more correct. For purposes of this discussion, that is any connection over 10 Mbps.

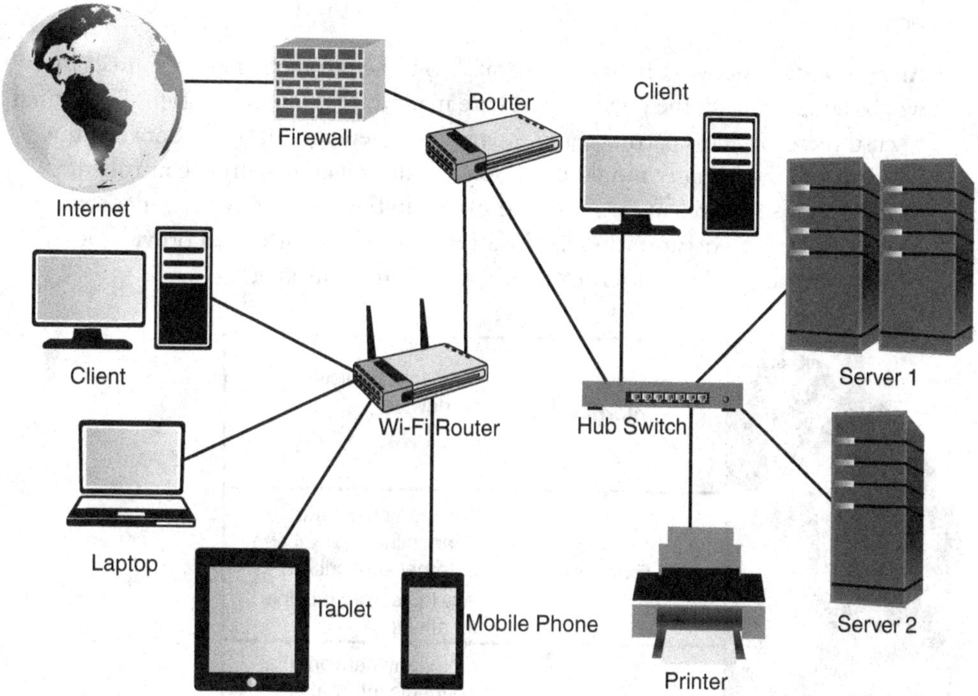

Figure 4-22 Local-Area Network (LAN)

A 10 Mbps connection might not seem very fast to you, but it is when compared to a WAN. Even a T1 connection is only 1.544 Mbps. Using this connection as a yardstick, if a single campus network has a WAN connection between two buildings, then the two networks are considered two LANs rather than a single LAN. In most cases, however, networks in a single campus are typically *not* connected with a WAN connection, which is why a LAN is usually defined as a network in a single location.

Intranet

Within the boundaries of a single LAN, there can be subdivisions for security purposes. The LAN might be divided into an intranet and an extranet. The ***intranet*** is the internal network of the enterprise. It would be considered a trusted network and typically houses any sensitive information and systems and should receive maximum protection with firewalls and strong authentication mechanisms.

Extranet

An ***extranet*** is a network logically separate from the intranet where resources that will be accessed from the outside world are made available. Access might be granted to customers, business partners, and the public in general. All traffic between this network and the intranet should be closely monitored and securely controlled. Nothing of a sensitive nature should be placed in the extranet. An extranet can be worldwide if an organization has locations globally. Figure 4-23 provides a comparison between the Internet, an extranet, and an intranet.

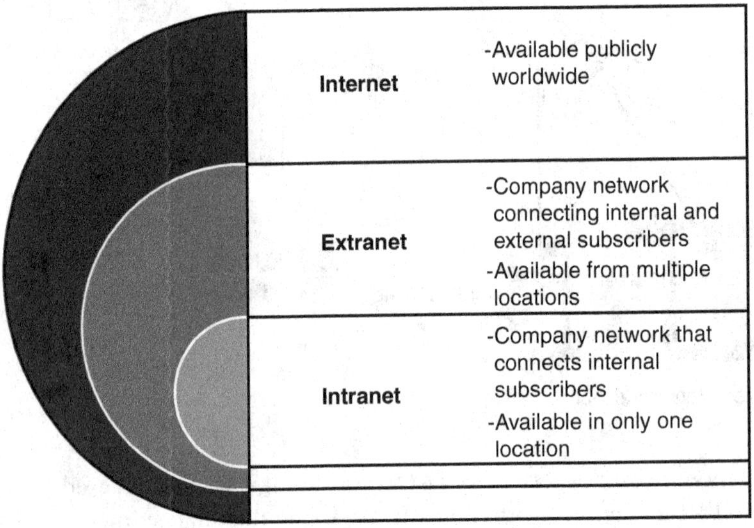

Figure 4-23 Comparison of the Internet, an Extranet, and an Intranet

MAN

A ***metropolitan-area network (MAN)*** is a type of LAN that encompasses a large area such as the downtown of a city (see Figure 4-24). In many cases, it is a backbone that is provided for LANs to hook into. Three technologies are usually used in a MAN:

- Fiber Distributed Data Interface (FDDI)
- Synchronous Optical Networking (SONET)
- Metro Ethernet

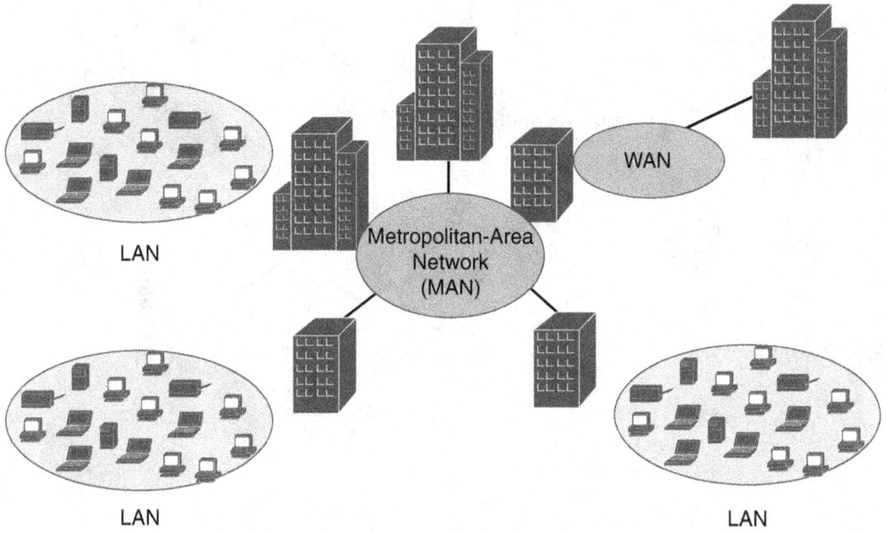

Figure 4-24 Metropolitan-Area Network (MAN)

FDDI and SONET rings, which both rely on fiber cabling, can span large areas, and businesses can connect to the rings using T1, fractional T1, or T3 connections. FDDI rings are a double ring with fault tolerance built in. SONET is also *self-healing*, meaning it has a double ring with a backup line if a line goes bad.

Metro Ethernet is the use of Ethernet technology over a wide area. It can be pure Ethernet or a combination of Ethernet and other technologies such as the ones mentioned in this section. Traditional Ethernet (the type used on a LAN) is less scalable. It is often combined with Multiprotocol Label Switching (MPLS) technology, which is capable of carrying packets of various types, including Ethernet.

Less capable MANs often feed into MANs of higher capacity. Conceptually, the MAN architecture can be divided into three sections: customer, aggregation, and core layer. The customer section is the local loop that connects from the customer to the aggregation network, which then feeds into the high-speed core. The high-speed core connects the aggregation networks to one another.

WAN

Wide-area networks (WANs) are used to connect LANs and MANs together (see Figure 4-25). Many technologies can be used for these connections. They vary in capacity and cost, and access to these networks is purchased from a telecommunications company. The ultimate WAN is the Internet, the global backbone to which all MANs and LANs are connected. However, not all WANs connect to the Internet because some are private, dedicated links to which only the company paying for them has access.

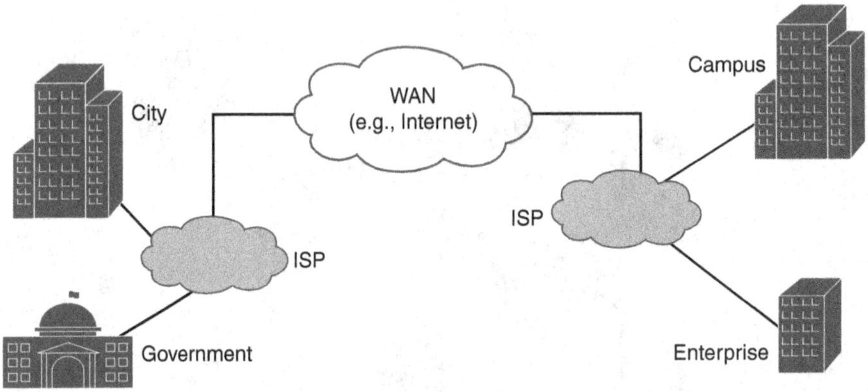

Figure 4-25 Wide-Area Network (WAN)

WLAN

A ***wireless local-area network (WLAN)*** allows devices to connect wirelessly to each other via a wireless access point (WAP). Multiple WAPs can work together to extend the range of the WLAN. WLAN technologies are discussed in more detail later in this chapter. Figure 4-26 displays a WLAN in which a variety of computing devices and a network printer are connected to an access point in the center of the figure.

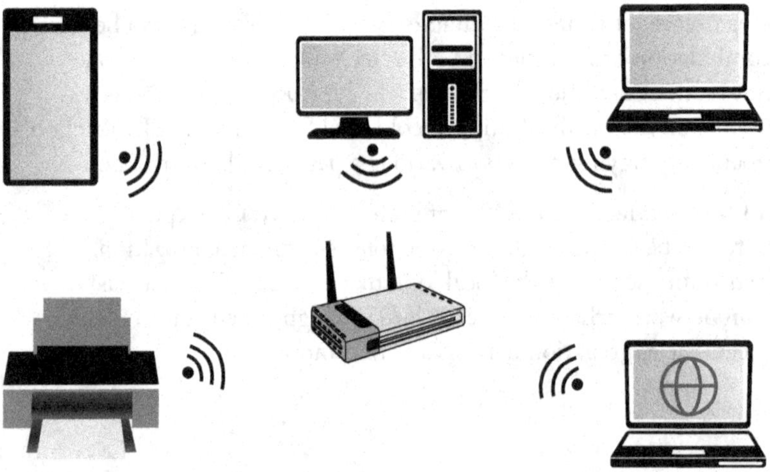

Figure 4-26 Wireless Local-Area Network (WLAN)

SAN

A ***storage-area network (SAN)*** provides a connection to data storage devices through a technology like Fibre Channel or iSCSI, both of which are discussed in more detail later in this chapter.

CAN

A ***campus-area network (CAN)*** includes multiple LANs but is smaller than a MAN. A CAN is typically implemented on the campus of a large hospital complex, university, or corporation.

PAN

A ***personal-area network (PAN)*** includes devices, such as computers, telephones, tablets, and mobile phones, that are in close proximity with one another (see Figure 4-27). PANs are usually implemented using Bluetooth, Z-Wave, Zigbee, and Infrared Data Association (IrDA).

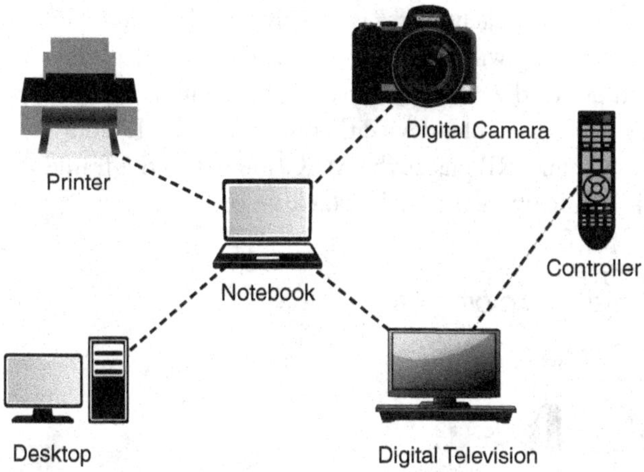

Figure 4-27 Personal-Area Network (PAN)

Protocols and Services

Many protocols and services have been developed over the years to add functionality to networks. In many cases, these protocols reside at the Application layer of the OSI model. These Application layer protocols usually perform a specific function and rely on the lower layer protocols in the TCP/IP suite and protocols at Layer 2 (like Ethernet) to perform routing and delivery services.

The following sections cover some of the most important of these protocols and services, including some that do *not* operate at the Application layer, focusing on the function and port number of each. Port numbers are important to be aware of from a security standpoint because in many cases port numbers are referenced when configuring firewall rules. In cases where a port or protocol number is relevant, it will be given as well.

ARP/RARP

Address Resolution Protocol (ARP), one of the protocols in the TCP/IP suite, operates at Layer 3 of the OSI model. The information it derives is utilized at Layer 2, however. ARP's job is to resolve the destination IP address placed in the header by IP to a Layer 2 or MAC address. Remember, when frames are transmitted on a local segment, the transfer is done in terms of MAC addresses, not IP addresses, so this information must be known.

Whenever a packet is sent across the network, at every router hop and again at the destination subnet, the source and destination MAC address pairs change, but the source and destination IP addresses do not. The process that ARP uses to perform this resolution is called an ARP broadcast.

First, an area of memory called the ARP cache is consulted. If the MAC address has been recently resolved, the mapping will be in the cache, and a broadcast is not required. If the record has aged out of the cache, ARP sends a broadcast frame to the local network that all devices will receive. The device that possesses the IP address responds with its MAC address. Then ARP places the MAC address in the frame and sends the frame. Figure 4-28 illustrates the ARP broadcast process.

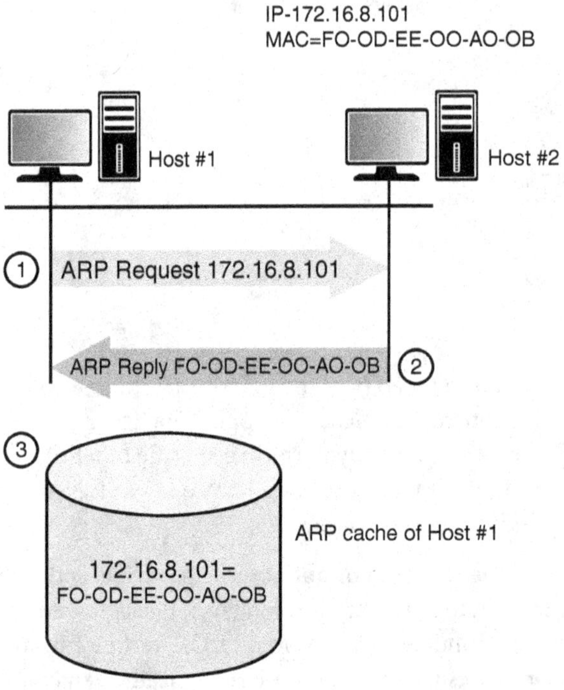

Figure 4-28 ARP Broadcast

You can view the ARP cache on your computer by following the following steps:

- **Windows users:** To view the ARP cache (table) on your Windows PC, enter **cmd** in the Search bar and then press **Enter**. At the command line prompt, type **arp -a** and then press **Enter**.
- **macOS users:** To view the ARP cache (table) on your MacBook, go to **Applications > Utilities**, and then open the Terminal. At the $ or # prompt, type **arp -a** and then press **Return**.

You should see some results similar to those displayed in Example 4-1.

Example 4-1 ARP Cache

```
Dad's iPhone (192.168.1.175) at 6a:e:7a:52:22:ca on en0 ifscope
[ethernet]
Fiona Samsung (192.168.1.152) at a6:2b:9d:de:f0:ea on en0 ifscope
[ethernet]
f9fcmc36mf3m (192.168.1.163) at 31:d9:6b:1b:87:91 on en0 ifscope
[ethernet]
Sean-iphone (192.168.1.161) at 8a:14:61:f0:21:82 on en0 ifscope
[ethernet]
```

Reverse ARP (RARP) resolves MAC addresses to IP addresses.

In IPv6 networks, the functionality of ARP is provided by the Neighbor Discovery Protocol (NDP).

DHCP/BOOTP

Dynamic Host Configuration Protocol (DHCP) is a service that can be used to automate the process of assigning an IP configuration to the devices in the network. A DHCP server uses the bootstrap protocol (BOOTP) to perform its functions. Manual configuration of an IP address, subnet mask, default gateway, and DNS server is not only time-consuming but fraught with opportunity for human error. Using DHCP can not only automate this but can also eliminate network problems from this human error.

DHCP is a client/server program. All modern operating systems contain a DHCP client, and the server component can be implemented either on a server or on a router. When a computer that is configured to be a DHCP client starts, it performs a precise four-step process to obtain its configuration. Conceptually, the client broadcasts for the IP address of the DHCP server. All devices receive this broadcast, but only DHCP servers respond. The device accepts the configuration offered by the first DHCP server from which it hears. The process uses four packets with distinctive names (see Figure 4-29). DHCP uses UDP ports 67 and 68. Port 67 sends data to the server, and port 68 sends data to the client.

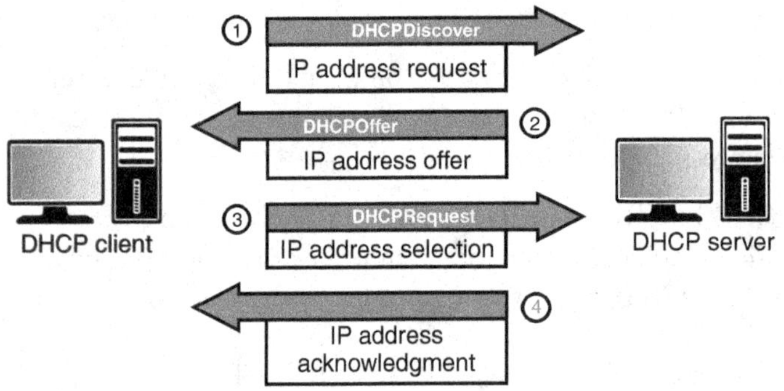

Figure 4-29 DHCP

DNS

Just as DHCP relieves us from having to manually construct the IP configuration of each system, ***Domain Name System (DNS)*** relieves all humans from having to know the IP address of every computer with which they want to communicate. Ultimately, an IP address must be known to connect to another computer. DNS resolves a computer name (or in the case of the Web, a domain name) to an IP address.

DNS is another client/server program with the client included in all modern operating systems. The server part resides on a series of DNS servers located both in the local network and on the Internet. When a DNS client needs to know the IP address that goes with a particular computer name or domain name, it queries the local DNS server. If the local DNS server does not have the resolution, it contacts other DNS servers on the client's behalf, learns the IP address, and relays that information to the DNS client. DNS uses UDP port 53 and TCP port 53. The DNS servers use TCP port 53 to exchange information, and the DNS clients use UDP port 53 for queries.

FTP, FTPS, SFTP, and TFTP

File Transfer Protocol (FTP) and the more secure versions FTPS and SFTP transfer files from one system to another. FTP is insecure in that the username and password are transmitted in cleartext. The original cleartext version uses TCP port 20 for data and TCP port 21 as the control channel. For this reason, using the original cleartext version of FTP is not recommended when security is a prime consideration.

FTPS is a variation of FTP that adds support for the Transport Layer Security (TLS) and the Secure Sockets Layer (SSL) cryptographic protocols. FTPS uses TCP ports 989 and 990.

FTPS is not the same as and should not be confused with another secure version of FTP, ***SSH File Transfer Protocol (SFTP)***. This is an extension of the Secure Shell (SSH) protocol. There have been a number of different SFTP versions, with version 6 being the latest. Because it uses SSH for the file transfer, it uses TCP port 22.

Trivial FTP (TFTP) does not use authentication and runs over UDP port 69.

HTTP, HTTPS, and S-HTTP

One of the most frequently used protocols today is Hypertext Transfer Protocol (HTTP) and its secure versions, HTTPS. This protocol is used to view and transfer web pages or web content between a web server and a web client. With each new address that is entered into the web browser, whether from initial user entry or by clicking a link on the page displayed, a new connection is established because HTTP is a stateless protocol. The original version (HTTP) has no encryption, so when security is a concern, one of the two secure versions should be used. HTTP uses TCP port 80.

Hypertext Transfer Protocol Secure (HTTPS) layers HTTP on top of the SSL/TLS protocol, thus adding the security capabilities of SSL/TLS to standard HTTP communications. SSL/TLS keeps the session open using a secure channel. HTTPS websites will *always* include the https:// designation at the beginning. It is often used for secure websites because it requires no software or configuration changes on the web client to function securely. When HTTPS is used, port 80 is not used. Rather, it uses port 443.

Unlike HTTPS, which encrypts the entire communication, ***secure HTTP (S-HTTP)*** encrypts only the served page data and submitted data such as POST fields, leaving the initiation of the protocol unchanged. Secure-HTTP and HTTP processing can operate on the same TCP port, port 80. This version is now obsolete.

ICMP

Internet Control Message Protocol (ICMP) operates at Layer 3 (Network layer) of the OSI model and is used by devices to transmit error messages regarding problems with transmissions. It also is the protocol used when the **ping** and **traceroute** commands are used to troubleshoot network connectivity problems.

ICMP announces network errors and network congestion. It also assists in troubleshooting and announces timeouts.

ICMP is a protocol that can be leveraged to mount several network attacks based on its operation, and for this reason many networks choose to block ICMP.

IGMP

Internet Group Management Protocol (IGMP) provides multicasting capabilities to devices. Multicasting allows devices to transmit data to multiple recipients. Many gaming platforms use IGMP.

IMAP

Internet Message Access Protocol (IMAP) is an Application layer protocol for email retrieval. Its latest version is IMAP4. It is a client email protocol used to access email from a server. Unlike POP3, another email client that can only download messages from the server, IMAP4 allows a user to download a copy and leave a copy on the server. IMAP4 uses port 143. A secure version also exists, IMAPS (IMAP over SSL), that uses port 993.

LDAP

Lightweight Directory Access Protocol (LDAP) is a directory query protocol that is based on the X.500 series of computer networking standards. Vendor implementations of LDAP include Microsoft's Active Directory Services, NetIQ's eDirectory, and Network Information Service (NIS). By default, LDAP uses TCP/UDP port 389.

LDP

Label Distribution Protocol (LDP) allows routers capable of MPLS to exchange label mapping information. Two routers with an established session are called LDP peers, and the exchange of information is bidirectional. For inner label distribution, targeted LDP (tLDP) is used. LDP and tLDP discovery runs on UDP port 646, and the session is built on TCP port 646.

NAT

Network Address Translation (NAT) is a service that maps private IP addresses to public IP addresses. NAT is discussed as a subtopic in the section "IPv4" earlier in this chapter.

NetBIOS

Network Basic Input/Output System (NetBIOS) is an API. NetBIOS over TCP/IP (NetBT) runs on TCP ports 137, 138, and 139. An application programming interface enables a company to allow third-party companies or individuals to have access to their application data and functionality.

NFS

Developed by Sun Microsystems, Network File System (NFS) is a client/server file-sharing protocol used in Unix/Linux. Version 4 is the most current version of NFS. It operates over TCP port 2049. Secure NFS (SNFS) offers confidentiality using the Digital Encryption Standard (DES).

PAT

Port Address Translation (PAT) is a specific version of NAT that uses a single public IP address to represent multiple private IP addresses. Its operation is discussed below the section "Logical and Physical Addressing," earlier in this chapter.

POP

Post Office Protocol (POP) is an Application layer email retrieval protocol. POP3 is the latest version. It allows for downloading messages only and does not allow the additional functionality provided by IMAP4. POP3 uses port 110. A version that runs over SSL is also available; it uses port 995.

CIFS/SMB

Common Internet File System (CIFS)/Server Message Block (SMB) is a file-sharing protocol. It uses TCP port 445.

SMTP

POP and IMAP are client email protocols used for retrieving email, but when email servers are talking to each other, they use a protocol called ***Simple Mail Transfer Protocol (SMTP)***, a standard Application layer protocol. This is also the protocol used by clients to send email. SMTP uses port 25, and when it is run over SSL, it uses port 465.

Enhanced SMTP (ESMTP) allows larger field sizes and extension of existing SMTP commands.

SNMP

Simple Network Management Protocol (SNMP) is an Application layer (OSI model) protocol that is used to retrieve information from network devices and to send configuration changes to those devices. SNMP uses TCP port 162 and UDP ports 161 and 162.

SNMP devices are organized into communities, and the community name must be known to either access information from or send a change to a device. The community name also can be used with a password. SNMP versions 1 and 2 are susceptible to packet sniffing, and all versions are susceptible to brute-force attacks on the community strings and password used. The defaults of community string names, which are widely known, are often left in place. The latest version, SNMPv3, is the most secure.

SSL/TLS

Secure Sockets Layer (SSL) is a Transport layer protocol that provides encryption, server and client authentication, and message integrity. Netscape developed SSL to transmit private documents over the Internet. Although SSL implements either 40-bit (SSL 2.0) or 128-bit (SSL 3.0) encryption, the 40-bit version is susceptible to attacks because of its limited key size. SSL allows an application to have encrypted, authenticated communication across a network. SSL has been deprecated and replaced by TLS.

Transport Layer Security (TLS) is an open-community standard that provides many of the same services as SSL. TLS 1.0 is based on SSL 3.0 but is more extensible. The main goal of TLS is privacy and data integrity between two communicating applications.

TLS 1.1 was an update to TLS 1.0 that provides protection against cipher-block chaining (CBC) attacks. TLS 1.2 used MDS-SHA-1 with pseudorandom functions (PRFs).

TLS 1.2 provides access to advanced cipher suites that support elliptic curve cryptography (ECC) and block cipher modes. TLS 1.3 is the latest version. TLS 1.3 is enabled on Windows 10 and Windows 11. TLS 1.3 removes support for weaker elliptic curves. TLS 1.3 is also faster and provides better encryption.

SSL and TLS are most commonly used when data needs to be encrypted while it is being transmitted (in transit) over a medium from one system to another. When other protocols include SSL/TLS in their implementation to improve security, the protocols usually operate over a different port than the standard, unsecured version.

Multilayer Protocols

Key Topic

Many protocols, such as FTP and DNS, operate on a single layer of the OSI model. However, many protocols operate at multiple layers of the OSI model. The best example is TCP/IP, the networking protocol used on the Internet and on the vast majority of LANs.

Many of the multilayer protocols were designed as part of proprietary protocols and have evolved into what they are today. Today multilayer protocols are being used to control critical infrastructure components, such as power grids and industrial control systems (ICSs). Because these critical infrastructure components were not originally designed for deployment over the Internet, unique challenges have arisen. It is virtually impossible to deploy antivirus software on an ICS. Many ICSs were installed without any thought to the physical security of the control system itself. Unlike in IT systems, delays in ICSs are unacceptable because of the time criticality of responding to emergencies. ICSs often have a lifetime much longer than the average IT system. Availability of ICSs is usually 24/7/365, whereas an IT system can tolerate short periods of unavailability in some industries and areas. When you consider this and other issues, you can easily see why an organization should fully consider the security implications when deploying an ICS that uses multilayer protocols. Deploying a vendor-developed protocol is not always the answer because the protocols developed by the vendor are concerned only with uptime and device control, without any consideration of security.

Distributed Network Protocol version 3 (DNP3) is a multilayer protocol that is used between components in process automation systems in electric and water companies. It was developed for communications between various types of data acquisition and control equipment. It plays a crucial role in supervisory control and data acquisition (SCADA) systems.

Converged Protocols

Key Topic

IP convergence involves carrying different types of traffic over one network. The traffic includes voice, video, data, and images. It is based on the Internet Protocol.

When IP convergence is deployed, a single platform is used for all types of traffic, involving all devices. It supports multimedia applications. Management and flexibility of the network are greatly improved because there is uniform setup and the ability to mold communication patterns. QoS can be deployed to allow administrators to ensure that certain services have a higher priority than others.

Implementation of IP convergence includes FCoE, InfiniBand, CXL, MPLS, VoIP, and iSCSI.

FCoE

Fibre Channel over Ethernet (FCoE) is a protocol that encapsulates Fibre Channel frames over Ethernet networks, thereby allowing Fibre Channel to use 10-Gigabit Ethernet networks or higher while preserving the Fibre Channel protocol. FCoE uses the following ports to communicate among the FCoE devices:

- **Network (N) port:** Connects a node to a Fibre Channel switch from the node. Also referred to as a node port.
- **Fabric (F) port:** Connects the Fibre Channel fabric to a node from the switch.

- **Loop (L) port:** Connects a node to a Fibre Channel loop from the node.
- **Network + loop (NL) port:** Connects to both loops and switches from the node.
- **Fabric + loop (FL) port:** Connects to both loops and switches from the switch.
- **Extender (E) port:** Cascades Fibre Channel switches together, thereby extending the fabric.
- **General (G) port:** Emulates other port types.
- **External (EX) port:** Connects a Fibre Channel router and a Fibre Channel switch. The EX port is on the router side, and the E port is on the switch side.
- **Trunking E (TE) port:** Allows multiple virtual SAN (VSAN) routing and provides standard E port functions.

FCoE has a number of benefits, including the following: Technicians need to wire the server only once; fewer cables and adapters are needed; the I/O uses software provisioning; interoperation with existing Fibre Channel SANs is possible; and gateways are not used.

InfiniBand

InfiniBand is a communications standard that has been developed by the InfiniBand Trade Association (IBTA). The IBTA steering committee is comprised of representatives from Intel, IBM, HPE, and NVIDIA, who ensure compliance interoperability for InfiniBand products.

InfiniBand defines high-speed, low-latency networking communications that are used in high-performance computing (HPC) environments. InfiniBand defines input/output architecture that links servers, storage, and other network communications infrastructure. InfiniBand uses a switched fabric network topology instead of Ethernet. InfiniBand transfer data rates can reach 200 gigabits per second (Gbps), which is greatly superior to the transfer data rates associated with Ethernet. The fastest Ethernet speed is 100 Gbps. InfiniBand also supports Remote Direct Memory Access (RDMA), whereby data can be transferred between servers without involving the CPU, which increases data transfer rates. Ethernet does not support RDMA.

Specialized InfiniBand hardware is used to facilitate high-speed transfer data rates. For example, InfiniBand switches, which are used in data centers, support high throughput and low latency. There are InfiniBand cables and connectors, which are critical to supporting the InfiniBand network infrastructure. Their active copper technology allows signals to be amplified over long distances, while reducing signal loss. InfiniBand adapters are network interface cards and range from single-port adapters to quad-port adapters. These adapters support different speeds, from

10 Gbps to 200 Gbps. InfiniBand is also more scalable than Ethernet, and its switch-based fabric architecture can support literally millions of nodes on a network.

InfiniBand operates in the same manner as Ethernet—just faster. Therefore, the security approach to InfiniBand is similar to Ethernet. InfiniBand uses similar protocols to Ethernet, such as Secure Shell (SSH). Consequently, the inherent security built into SSH is used, including strong encryption and protection against man-in-the-middle attacks.

Compute Express Link (CXL)

Compute Express Link (CXL) is an open standard for high-speed CPU-to-device and CPU-to-memory interconnect. This standard accelerates data center performance. CXL is aimed at maintaining memory coherency between the CPU memory space and memory on attached devices, allowing for efficient sharing of resources and improving performance in high-bandwidth, low-latency computing environments, as shown in Figure 4-30.

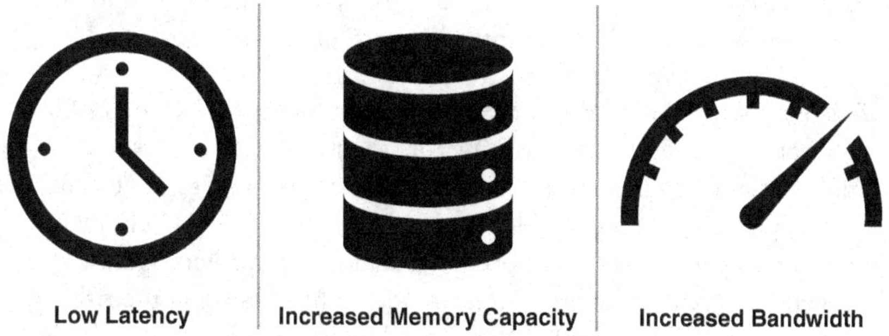

Figure 4-30 Benefits of Compute Express Link

This technology supports various types of high-speed data processing and storage devices, such as GPUs, FPGAs, and other accelerators, making it particularly relevant for applications in artificial intelligence, machine learning, and big data analytics. Understanding CXL involves recognizing its role in creating efficient and secure network architectures that support a wide range of services and applications.

Some important points about CXL that security professionals should know include the following:

- **High-speed, efficient connectivity:** CXL provides a means to securely connect CPUs to high-speed, low-latency devices and memory systems. It enables better performance for data-intensive applications, which is crucial for maintaining operational efficiency and security in environments where rapid data processing and analysis are required.

- **Resource sharing and coherency:** CXL's support for coherent memory access between the CPU and connected devices allows for more efficient resource utilization. This coherency is vital for ensuring that data is consistently and accurately shared across different components, which reduces the risk of data corruption or loss and enhances the overall integrity of the system.
- **Convergence of protocols:** Just like iSCSI allows SCSI commands to be transmitted over IP networks, and InfiniBand over Ethernet provides high-throughput, low-latency networking, CXL represents another step toward the convergence of high-performance computing and networking technologies. This convergence requires a deep understanding of how to secure mixed environments where traditional network traffic and high-performance interconnects coexist.
- **Security considerations:** While CXL focuses on performance and efficiency, integrating it into network architectures requires careful consideration of security implications, such as protecting against unauthorized access to shared memory resources and ensuring the integrity of data in transit between the CPU and CXL-enabled devices. Security controls and protocols need to be adapted to address these high-speed interconnects' unique characteristics.

Security professionals must consider how CXL and other converged protocols fit into the broader network architecture, ensuring that their integration does not introduce vulnerabilities or compromise the network's security posture. It's essential to implement appropriate security controls for environments utilizing CXL, including access controls, encryption, and monitoring mechanisms, to protect against potential threats and ensure data integrity and confidentiality. Assessing the risks associated with deploying CXL and other high-speed interconnect technologies is critical. Security professionals should evaluate potential vulnerabilities, assess the impact of security breaches, and develop strategies to mitigate these risks.

MPLS

Multiprotocol Label Switching (MPLS) routes data from one node to the next based on short path labels rather than long network addresses, avoiding complex lookups in a routing table. It includes the ability to control how and where traffic is routed, delivers data transport services across the same network, and improves network resiliency through MPLS Fast Reroute.

MPLS uses Label Switched Path (LSP), which is a unidirectional tunnel between routers. An MPLS network may use the following roles:

- **Label edge router (LER):** The first router that encapsulates a packet inside LSP and makes the path selection. This is commonly referred to as the ingress node.

- **Label switching router (LSR):** A router that performs MPLS switching somewhere along the LSP. This is also referred to as the transit node.
- **Egress node:** The last router at the end of an LSP.
- **Ingress node:** The starting point of an LSP.
- **Demarkation point:** Often referred to as a demarc, a physical boundary where the telecommunications cabling connects with an internal network.

When an LSP is terminated, an implicit or explicit null can be used. Implicit nulls remove the label when it reaches the next-to-last hop. Explicit nulls keep the label to the last router.

When MPLS is deployed as part of a virtual private network (VPN), the following router roles can be used:

- **Provider (P) router:** A backbone router that performs only label switching.
- **Provider edge (PE) router:** A router that faces the customer and performs label popping and imposition. It can terminate multiple services.
- **Customer edge (CE) router:** The customer router with which the PE router communicates.

MPLS uses two command routing protocols: Label Distribution Protocol (LDP) and ReSerVation Protocol with Traffic Engineering (RSVP-TE). RSVP-TE is much more complex than LDP. LDP is used more on MPLS VPN, whereas RSVP-TE is required for traffic engineering.

VoIP

Voice over Internet Protocol (VoIP) includes technologies that deliver voice communications and multimedia sessions over IP networks, such as the Internet. VoIP is also referred to as IP telephony, Internet telephony, broadband telephony, and broadband phone service. VoIP can be implemented using a variety of protocols, including H.323, Session Initiation Protocol (SIP), Media Gateway Control Protocol (MGCP), and Real-time Transport Protocol (RTP). NIST SP 800-58 contains detailed information on the implementation of VoIP.

NOTE VoIP is discussed in more detail later in this chapter.

iSCSI

Internet Small Computer System Interface (iSCSI) allows SCSI commands to be sent end-to-end over LANs, WANs, or the Internet over TCP. It provides storage consolidation and disaster recovery. iSCSI has a number of benefits, including the following: Technicians need to wire the server only once; fewer cables and adapters are needed; a new operational model is used; and there is broad industry support, including vendor iSCSI drivers, gateways, and native iSCSI storage arrays.

Wireless Networks

Perhaps the area of the network that keeps network and system administrators awake at night more than any other is the wireless portion of the network. In the early days of 802.11 WLAN deployments, many administrators simply chose not to implement wireless for fear of the security holes it created. However, it became apparent that not only did users demand this implementation, but in some cases users were bringing their own APs (access points) to work and hooking them up, and suddenly there was a wireless network!

Today WLAN security has evolved to the point that security is no longer a valid reason to avoid wireless. The following sections offer a look at the protocols used in wireless, the methods used to convert the data into radio waves, the various topologies in which WLANs can be deployed, and security measures that should be taken.

FHSS, DSSS, OFDM, VOFDM, FDMA, TDMA, CDMA, OFDMA, GSM, and Massive MIMO

When data leaves an Ethernet NIC and is sent out on the network, the ones and zeros that constitute the data are represented with different electric voltages. In wireless, this information must be represented in radio waves. A number of different methods exist for performing this operation, which is called modulation. You should also understand some additional terms to talk intelligently about wireless. We define a number of terms to provide a background for the discussion found in the following sections. In particular, we cover techniques used in WLANs and techniques used in cellular networking.

802.11 Techniques

The following techniques are used in WLANs:

- ***Frequency-hopping spread spectrum (FHSS)***: FHSS and DSSS were a part of the original 802.11 standard. FHSS is unique in that it changes frequencies or channels every few seconds in a set pattern that both transmitter and receiver know. This is not a security measure because the patterns are well known, although it does make capturing the traffic difficult. It helps avoid interference by only occasionally using a frequency where the interference is present. Later amendments to the 802.11 standard did not include this technology. It can attain up to 2 Mbps.

- ***Direct-sequence spread spectrum (DSSS)*:** DSSS and FHSS were a part of the original 802.11 standard. DSSS is the modulation technique used in 802.11b. The modulation technique used in wireless had a huge impact on throughput. In the case of DSSS, it spreads the transmission across the spectrum at the same time as opposed to hopping from one frequency to another as in FHSS. This allows it to attain up to 11 Mbps.
- ***Orthogonal frequency-division multiplexing (OFDM)*:** OFDM is a more advanced technique of modulation where a large number of closely spaced orthogonal subcarrier signals are used to carry the data on several parallel data streams. It is used in 802.11a, 802.11ac, 802.11ax, 802.11g, and 802.11n. It makes speed up to 54 Mbps possible. Wi-Fi 6 routers use OFDM. OFDM enables an 802.11ax router to send data to and receive data from multiple devices simultaneously by splitting a transmission channel into several transmission subchannels.
- **Vectored orthogonal frequency-division multiplexing (VOFDM):** Developed by Cisco, VOFDM uses special diversity to increase noise, interference, and multipath tolerance.

Cellular or Mobile Wireless Techniques

The following techniques are used in cellular networking:

- ***Frequency-division multiple access (FDMA)*:** FDMA is one of the modulation techniques used in cellular wireless networks. It divides the frequency range into bands and assigns a band to each subscriber. This was used in 1G cellular networks.
- ***Time-division multiple access (TDMA)*:** TDMA increases the speed over FDMA by dividing the channels into time slots and assigning slots to calls. It also helps to prevent eavesdropping in calls.
- ***Code-division multiple access (CDMA)*:** CDMA assigns a unique code to each call or transmission and spreads the data across the spectrum, allowing a call to make use of all frequencies.
- ***Orthogonal frequency-division multiple access (OFDMA)*:** OFDMA takes FDMA a step further by subdividing the frequencies into subchannels. This is the technique required by 4G devices.
- ***Global System for Mobile communications (GSM)*:** GSM is an international standard for signal communications, which uses TDMA and FDD (frequency-division duplex) communication methods. It is a standard created by the European Telecommunications Standards Institute (ETSI), which was primarily

designed by Nokia and Ericsson. GSM mobile devices contain a subscriber identity module (SIM) card. The two primary functions of a SIM card are to identify the subscriber to a cellular network and to store data. GSM devices are susceptible to SIM card cloning—a process whereby the SIM card is fraudulently copied. Some devices contain an embedded SIM (eSIM), where the SIM is not removable and is a part of the printed circuit board (PCB). Another alternative is an iSIM, which has grown in popularity. GSM is the default global standard for mobile communication.

- ***Massive multiple input, multiple output (MIMO)***: MIMO refers to a wireless network that allows the transmission and reception of multiple data signals simultaneously on the same radio channel. MIMO generally uses two or four antennae, whereas Massive MIMO uses tens or hundreds of antennae.

5G

The 1G cellular service allowed people to talk, and then 2G provided the ability to text (SMS). With the advent of 3G, people could access the Web on mobile devices. Then came 4G LTE (Long Term Evolution), which increased data speed by about tenfold. Speed has increased exponentially with the introduction of 5G. The introduction of 5G is dramatically changing society and communications, especially for those who live and work in major cities. 5G will make smart cities, which will be heavily dependent on the Internet of Things (IoT), a reality. ***5G*** is the fifth generation of cellular technologies. With 5G, latency (the delay between sending and receiving data) has been dramatically reduced. Although 5G-ready mobile devices are prohibitively expensive for many, 5G will certainly grow in popularity when the carriers make 5G more pervasive.

5G is not just about improving cellular communications. It will also impact many other technologies. IoT devices will benefit greatly from the change. 5G will be integrated into vehicles, thereby making self-driving vehicles more of a reality. 5G will be important for industrial robotics, where robots will communicate with one another and drones will be able to coordinate their activities in groups. The technology still has obstacles that need to be overcome, such as walls and bad weather. 5G uses millimeter waves, and therefore, a new infrastructure—with new transmitters in closer proximity—will need to be built. Thus, major cities will see 5G well before suburban and rural areas. Hundreds of thousands of new towers will need to be constructed.

The costs of implementing 5G are huge, and therefore, it is possible that there will be changes to the structure of the mobile network operators (MNOs). The path that traffic takes in a network will change with 5G. Two key concepts associated with 5G are MEC and CUPS. ***Multi-access Edge Computing (MEC)*** is a networking protocol that enables mobile users to establish direct connections, using available network infrastructure, at the edge of the network, rather than being routed through the mobile network operator's core network. ***Control and User Plane Separation (CUPS)*** is a 3GPP specification that facilitates MEC, whereby control functions, like establishing a connection with another device, take a different route through a network. The goal of MEC and CUPS is to create more bandwidth for users and significantly reduce latency by facilitating connections at the network edge, while moving away from a centralized network. MEC will also benefit virtual reality gaming and self-driving cars.

Another element of 5G is D2D. ***Device-to-device (D2D) communication*** is technology that enables user equipment (UE) to communicate with one another, with or without a network infrastructure. Examples of UE can be a mobile device or can be vehicle-to-vehicle communication. The primary benefit of D2D communication is ultra-low latency. Another benefit of D2D is the reduction of network capacity issues, thereby enabling devices to communicate with each other without the need to connect with a network.

IEEE 802.11p is part of the ***dedicated short-range communications (DSRC)*** system and is a standard for adding ***wireless access in vehicle environments (WAVE)***. With the proliferation of 5G, more vehicles will be able to communicate with one another, especially in corporate fleets. Vehicle-to-vehicle communication is already available with Tesla cars, for example.

The GSMA represents the telecommunications industry, and it has developed a digital authentication standard called Mobile Connect. This standard will allow a subscriber to create a universal digital identity with a single sign-on (SSO). Mobile Connect is a 5G technology that matches a user's mobile number to an account, thereby allowing the user to log in to websites and applications, without remembering the login and password.

Voice over 5G (Vo5G) is a standard for voice/video on the fifth generation of mobile technologies and is approved by 3GPP. Vo5G will use ***Voice over New Radio (VoNR)*** for calls on a 5G network. VoNR will use a 5G network and replace ***Voice over LTE (VoLTE)***.

Telecommunications and Hardware Support

Third-party connectivity involves the integration of external services, such as telecom providers and hardware support, into an organization's network infrastructure. These connections are essential for enabling various business operations, including Internet access, cloud services, voice communications, and technical support for critical hardware components. However, integrating third-party services also introduces potential security risks and vulnerabilities that must be managed effectively.

Key considerations for securing third-party connectivity include

- **Risk assessment:** Before establishing connectivity with a third party, conduct a comprehensive risk assessment to identify potential security risks associated with the connection. This assessment should consider the nature of the data being transmitted, the security posture of the third party, and any regulatory compliance requirements.
- **Encryption:** Use encryption to protect data in transit between the organization and third-party services. Encryption ensures that data is unreadable to unauthorized parties, protecting against interception and eavesdropping. Protocols such as Transport Layer Security (TLS) are commonly used for this purpose.
- **Virtual private networks (VPNs):** Implement VPNs to create secure, encrypted communication channels for transmitting sensitive information to and from third-party providers. VPNs provide a secure tunnel through which data can travel, isolating it from other traffic on shared or public networks.
- **Access controls:** Define strict access controls to limit third-party access to only the necessary systems and data. Implement the principle of least privilege, ensuring that third-party providers have only the minimum level of access required to perform their services.
- **Service level agreements (SLAs):** Negotiate SLAs with third-party providers that specify security requirements and expectations. SLAs should cover aspects such as data protection measures, incident response times, customer support, and compliance with security standards.
- **Monitoring and auditing:** Continuously monitor and audit the connections to third-party services for any suspicious activities or security breaches. Implement intrusion detection systems (IDSs) and regular security audits to ensure that the security measures are effective and that third parties are adhering to agreed-upon security practices.
- **Compliance and regulatory requirements:** Ensure that third-party connectivity complies with relevant legal and regulatory requirements, especially those related to data protection and privacy. This may involve verifying that third-party providers have certifications or attestations that demonstrate compliance with industry standards.

Telecom Providers

In the United States, there are three major mobile network operators (MNOs): Verizon, T-Mobile, and AT&T; U.S. Cellular and Dish Wireless are also MNOs with a smaller market share. These (MNO) telecom providers own and operate the telecommunications infrastructure. Mobile virtual network operators (MVNOs), such as Consumer Cellular, do not own telecom infrastructure, but purchase minutes of use (MOU) from MNOs and operate over their telecommunications infrastructure.

Telecom providers play a crucial role in facilitating the external communication channels organizations rely on for voice, data, and Internet services. The security of these channels is paramount, as they often serve as the backbone for business operations, including the transfer of sensitive or proprietary information, and are potential vectors for cybersecurity threats.

The key considerations for both telecom providers and security professionals include

- **Data encryption:** Data transmitted over the networks provided by telecom providers should be encrypted both in transit and at rest. Encryption ensures that even if data is intercepted, it remains unreadable and secure from unauthorized access. Common encryption protocols include TLS for Internet traffic and Secure Real-time Transport Protocol (SRTP) for VoIP.
- **VPN use:** VPNs are essential when using telecom services for transmitting sensitive information. VPNs create a secure, encrypted tunnel for data traffic, which is particularly important for remote access and mobile communications that rely on public networks.
- **SLAs:** Organizations should negotiate SLAs with telecom providers that include specific security requirements and protocols. SLAs should cover aspects such as uptime guarantees, data protection measures, and the provider's responsibilities in the event of a security breach.
- **Compliance and regulatory requirements:** Telecom providers must comply with various legal and regulatory frameworks that govern data protection and privacy (e.g., GDPR, HIPAA). Organizations need to ensure that their chosen providers adhere to these regulations to avoid legal and financial penalties.
- **Network segmentation and access controls:** Implementing network segmentation can help isolate sensitive data and systems from the broader network used for external communications. Access controls should be employed to limit who can communicate through the telecom provider's services, preventing unauthorized access or data exfiltration.
- **Monitoring and incident response:** Continuous monitoring of communication channels is necessary to detect potential security threats or breaches quickly. Organizations should work with telecom providers to ensure that adequate monitoring tools are in place and that there are clear procedures for incident response and notification.

- **Redundancy and resilience:** Telecom services should be designed for redundancy and resilience to ensure continuous operation during outages or attacks. This may involve using multiple providers or diverse routing paths to reduce the risk of a single point of failure.

For security professionals, understanding the nuances of securing third-party connectivity via telecom providers involves

- Assessing the security measures and capabilities of potential telecom providers as part of the vendor selection process.
- Integrating secure communication practices, such as encryption and VPN use, into the organization's overall security strategy.
- Collaborating with telecom providers to ensure alignment with security, compliance, and operational requirements.
- Educating stakeholders within the organization on the risks associated with telecom services and the importance of following secure communication practices.

Ensuring the security of third-party connectivity through telecom providers is critical for protecting organizational data and maintaining trust with clients and partners. Security professionals play a vital role in designing, implementing, and managing secure communication channels that align with organizational security policies and industry best practices.

Satellites

Satellites can be used to provide TV service—and have for some time—but now they can also be used to deliver Internet access to homes and businesses. The connection is two-way rather than one-way as is done with TV service. In most cases, the downloads come from the satellite signals, whereas the uploads occur through a ground line. Microwave technology can also be used for *terrestrial transmission*, which means ground station to ground station rather than satellite to ground. Satellite is being used more and more to facilitate 4G and 5G communications, especially in rural areas. Satellite now facilitates high-speed Internet access for many people. This is now possible with the introduction of large satellite constellations in low Earth orbit. An increasing reliance on satellite communications, coupled with more state-sponsored attacks on the critical infrastructure, means that satellite communications security becomes even more imperative. The 2022 attack against the Viasat KA-SAT (satellite) network, which was attributed to Russian state actors, caused service interruptions.

Backhaul Networks

Backhaul networks play a pivotal role in the realm of data communications. *Backhaul* refers to the intermediate links between the core network, or backbone network, and the small subnetworks at the edge of the entire network. In telecommunications, this often involves the connections between cell sites and the network's backbone, but the concept also applies more broadly to any part of a network that carries data between different network nodes.

Backhaul networks provide the following roles in data communications:

- **Connectivity:** Backhaul networks provide the crucial connectivity that allows data to travel from local networks or individual service points (like cell towers in a mobile network) to central nodes of the broader network, where it can be routed to its ultimate destination. This connectivity is essential for ensuring that users have access to network services and resources.
- **Capacity and speed:** The capacity and speed of the backhaul network directly impact the performance and reliability of the overall network. High-capacity, high-speed backhaul links are necessary to handle the volume of data traffic generated by users and to meet performance expectations.
- **Evolution toward high-bandwidth requirements:** With the increasing demand for high-bandwidth applications (such as video streaming, cloud computing, and large-scale data transfers), backhaul networks have evolved to support greater data throughput. Technologies like fiber optics, microwave links, and, more recently, 5G wireless technology are commonly used to meet these demands.

Implementing secure communication channels within backhaul networks is critical, given their role in transmitting sensitive and potentially high volumes of data. This involves the following key considerations:

- **Encryption:** Data transmitted over backhaul networks should be encrypted to ensure its confidentiality and integrity. Encryption prevents unauthorized access and protects against eavesdropping and interception attacks.
- **Virtual private networks:** VPNs can be used over backhaul links to create secure, encrypted tunnels for data transmission. This is especially important when backhaul connections pass through potentially unsecured or shared networks.
- **Authentication and access control:** Proper authentication mechanisms should be in place to verify the identity of devices and nodes communicating over the backhaul network. Access control ensures that only authorized entities can initiate or participate in data transmissions.

- **Monitoring and detection:** Continuous monitoring of backhaul network traffic helps in detecting anomalies or signs of unauthorized access. IDSs and network monitoring tools are essential for identifying potential security threats and responding appropriately.
- **Resilience and redundancy:** Designing backhaul networks with resilience and redundancy in mind ensures that data communication can continue securely even in the event of failures or attacks. This might involve using multiple backhaul links or alternative routes to provide backup paths for data transmission.

Hardware Support

Third-party hardware support involves the maintenance, management, and security of physical devices that facilitate data communication within an organization. These devices can include routers, switches, firewalls, servers, and other network appliances provided by external vendors or service providers. The security of these hardware components is critical, as they often serve as the backbone of an organization's network infrastructure, directly impacting the security of communication channels.

The key considerations for secure hardware support include

- **Secure configuration:** Hardware devices should be securely configured according to industry best practices and organizational security policies. This includes changing default passwords, disabling unnecessary services, configuring firewalls, and setting up VPNs for secure remote management.
- **Patch management:** Regularly updating and patching hardware devices to address known vulnerabilities is crucial. Organizations should have a process in place for monitoring vendor releases of firmware and software updates and applying these patches in a timely manner to mitigate potential security risks.
- **Physical security:** Physical access to network and server hardware should be strictly controlled to prevent unauthorized access, tampering, or theft. This may involve secure data center practices, such as access control systems, surveillance cameras, and environmental controls to protect against damage.
- **Vendor support and SLAs:** SLAs with hardware vendors or support providers should explicitly cover security aspects, including response times for addressing hardware failures, availability of security updates, and procedures for handling end-of-life (EOL) equipment.
- **Secure disposal:** When hardware devices reach their end of life or are replaced, secure disposal practices must be followed to ensure that sensitive data cannot be recovered from discarded devices. This might involve data wiping, physical destruction, or using certified disposal services.

- **Access controls and authentication:** Implementing robust access controls and authentication mechanisms for managing hardware devices is essential. This includes using multi-factor authentication (MFA) for administrative access and tracking who has access to configure or manage the devices.
- **Monitoring and logging:** Continuous monitoring and logging of hardware device activity can help detect unauthorized access attempts, configuration changes, or other suspicious activities. These logs should be regularly reviewed and protected against tampering.

For security professionals, ensuring the security of third-party hardware support involves

- Conducting risk assessments to identify potential security vulnerabilities associated with hardware devices and their support mechanisms.
- Collaborating with vendors to understand their security practices and ensure they align with the organization's security requirements.
- Designing and implementing a secure infrastructure that includes encrypted communication channels, resilient network architectures, and secure remote access solutions.
- Developing policies and procedures for hardware lifecycle management, from acquisition and deployment to maintenance, updating, and eventual disposal.
- Training IT staff and relevant personnel on secure hardware management practices, including the secure configuration, patch management, and physical security measures.

Securing hardware support is a critical component of maintaining secure communication channels and overall network security. Security professionals must be proactive in managing the security risks associated with third-party hardware to protect organizational assets and data effectively.

WLAN Structure

Before we can discuss 802.11 wireless, which has come to be known as WLAN, we need to discuss the components and the structure of a WLAN. The following sections cover basic terms and concepts.

Access Point

An ***access point (AP)*** is a wireless transmitter and receiver that hooks into the wired portion of the network and provides an access point to this network for wireless devices. It can also be referred to as a wireless access point (WAP). In some cases, APs are simply wireless switches, and in other cases, they are also routers. Early APs were devices with all the functionality built into each device, but increasingly these "fat" or intelligent APs are being replaced with "thin" APs that are really only antennas that hook back into a central system called a controller.

Service Set Identifier (SSID)

The ***Service Set Identifier (SSID)*** is a name or value assigned to identify the WLAN from other WLANs. The SSID either can be broadcast by the AP, as is done in a free mobile hotspot, or can be hidden. When it is hidden, a wireless station will have to be configured with a profile that includes the SSID to connect. Although some view hiding the SSID as a security measure, it is not an effective measure because hiding the SSID removes only one type of frame, the beacon frame, while it still exists in other frame types and can be easily learned by sniffing the wireless network.

Infrastructure Mode Versus Ad Hoc Mode

When an access point (AP) is present in a WLAN, the WLAN is said to be operating in ***Infrastructure mode***. In this mode, all transmissions between stations or devices go through the AP, and no direct communication between stations occurs. When the WLAN is in ***Ad Hoc mode***, there is no AP, and the stations or devices communicate directly with one another.

WLAN Standards

Since its original invention, the 802.11 wireless standard has been amended a number of times to add features and functionality. Here, we discuss these amendments, which are sometimes referred to as standards although they really are amendments to the original standard.

802.11

The original 802.11 standard specified the use of either FHSS or DSSS and supported operations in the 2.4 GHz frequency range at speeds of 1 Mbps and 2 Mbps.

802.11a (Wi-Fi 2)

The first amendment to the standard was ***802.11a***. This standard called for the use of orthogonal frequency-division multiplexing (OFDM). Because that would require hardware upgrades to existing equipment, this standard saw limited adoption for some time. It operates in a different frequency than 802.11 (5 GHz) and by using OFDM supports speeds up to 54 Mbps.

802.11b (Wi-Fi 1)

The ***802.11b*** amendment dropped support for FHSS and enabled an increase of speed to 11 Mbps. It was widely adopted because it both operates on the same frequency as 802.11 and is backward compatible with it and can coexist in the same WLAN.

802.11g (Wi-Fi 3)

The ***802.11g*** amendment added support for OFDM, which made it capable of 54 Mbps. It also operates in the 2.4 GHz frequency, so it is backward compatible with both 802.11 and 802.11b. Although it is just as fast as 802.11a, one reason many switched to 802.11a over 802.11g is that the 5 GHz band is much less crowded than the 2.4 GHz band.

802.11n (Wi-Fi 4)

The ***802.11n*** standard uses several newer concepts to achieve up to 650 Mbps. It does this using channels that are 40 MHz wide, using multiple antennas that allow for up to four spatial streams at a time (a feature called multiple input, multiple output [MIMO]). It can be used in both the 2.4 GHz and 5.0 GHz bands but performs best in a pure 5.0 GHz network because in that case it does not need to implement mechanisms that allow it to coexist with 802.11b and 802.11g devices. These mechanisms slow the performance. This standard was retroactively named ***Wi-Fi 4***.

802.11ac (Wi-Fi 5)

The ***802.11ac*** standard, like the 802.11a standard, operates on the 5 GHz frequency (***Wi-Fi 5***). The most important feature of this standard is its multi-station WLAN throughput of at least 1 Gbps and single-link throughput of 500 Mbps. It provides this by implementing ***multi-user multiple-input, multiple-output (MU MIMO)*** technologies in which the wireless access points have multiple antennae. The 802.11ac standard is faster and more scalable than 802.11n. Advantages of 802.11ac include

- Increased speed
- Higher speeds over longer distances
- Less interference
- Increased number of clients supported by an access point
- Extended battery life
- Extended Wi-Fi coverage
- Reduction of dead spots

802.11ax (Wi-Fi 6)

Wi-Fi 6 (***802.11ax***) is a standard developed by the Wi-Fi Alliance. Because so many devices are Internet-enabled today, we need to ensure that Wi-Fi can handle all of these additional devices. It is not just the addition of more devices that needs to be considered but also the increase in data with advances in technology. For example, 4K video has double the bit rate of high definition (HD) video. Wi-Fi 6 was a much-needed upgrade to handle the billions of new mobile and IoT devices—especially on public networks, where a lot of devices are serviced on a single network.

Wi-Fi 6 operates on 2.4 GHz or 5 GHz and has a theoretical maximum throughput of 10.53 Gbps, but in reality there is about a 30 percent increase in speed. Quadrature amplitude modulation (QAM) is a modulation scheme in digital telecommunication systems, like Wi-Fi. Data is transmitted wirelessly by modulating radio waves. Wi-Fi 6 is 1024-QAM and can transmit 10 bits at a time, which is 2 bits more than Wi-Fi 5. Thus, QAM increases the performance associated with Wi-Fi 6 by pushing out more bits in each transmission.

Wi-Fi 6 routers have a label with "Wi-Fi 6 Certified" on them. Wi-Fi 6 routers can deliver up to 12 simultaneous Wi-Fi streams, which reduces latency. Wi-Fi 6 routers use orthogonal frequency-division multiple access (OFDMA) technology. OFDMA enables an 802.11ax router to send and receive data to multiple devices simultaneously by splitting a transmission channel into a number of transmission subchannels.

802.11be (Wi-Fi 7)

Wi-Fi 7 (***802.11be***) will have throughput greater than 30 Gbps and have low latency. This protocol will support ***Extremely High Throughput (EHT)*** devices, while targeting newer technologies, such as augmented reality (AR), virtual reality, and ***cloud computing***. Wi-Fi 7 will work on three frequency bands—2.4 GHz, 5 GHz, and 6 GHz—to take advantage of an additional 1200 MHz of spectrum in countries where it is allowed. Wi-Fi 7 will increase the QAM modulation order to 4096 QAM to reach the highest data rate.

802.11bn (Wi-Fi 8)

Wi-Fi 8 (***802.11bn***) will support Ultra High Reliability (UHR); it is at the early stages of development and is likely to be released in 2028. It is anticipated that this protocol will provide greater reliability and ultra-low latency. The primary features of Wi-Fi 8 include the following:

- Multiple access point coordination and transmission
- Millimeter wave frequencies
- Low latency

Multiple AP coordination and transmission in Wi-Fi refers to improved coordination of access points in a wireless network, such as an office complex, whereby access points are configured to avoid overlapping channels and better coordinate transmissions.

Table 4-6 provides a comparison of the Wi-Fi standards that we have just covered in detail.

Table 4-6 Wi-Fi Standards Comparison

New Official Name	IEEE Standard Name	Introduced	Radio Frequency
Wi-Fi 1	802.11b	1999	2.4
Wi-Fi 2	802.11a	1999	5
Wi-Fi 3	802.11g	2003	2.4
Wi-Fi 4	802.11n	2009	2.4, 5
Wi-Fi 5	802.11ac	2014	5
Wi-Fi 6	802.11ax	2019	2.4, 5
Wi-Fi 7	802.11be	2024	2.4, 5, 6
Wi-Fi 8	802.11bn	2028 (expected)	2.4, 5, 6, 7, 42.5, 71

Bluetooth

Bluetooth is developed and maintained by the Bluetooth Special Interest Group (Bluetooth.com). This wireless technology is used to create personal-area networks (PANs); these are simply short-range connections that are between devices and peripherals, such as headphones. Bluetooth versions 1.0 and 2.0 operate in the 2.4 GHz frequency at speeds of 1 Mbps to 3 Mbps at a distance of up to 10 meters. Bluetooth 3.0 and 4.0 can operate at speeds of 24 Mbps. In January 2020, Bluetooth 5.2 was announced. This version introduced a feature called ***Isochronous Channels (ISOC)***, which supports both connectionless and connection-oriented communication.

Several attacks can take advantage of Bluetooth technology. ***Bluejacking*** occurs when an unsolicited message is sent to a Bluetooth-enabled device, often for the purpose of adding a business card to the victim's contact list. This type of attack can be prevented by placing the device in non-discoverable mode.

Bluesnarfing is the unauthorized access to a device using the Bluetooth connection. In this case the attacker is trying to access information on the device rather than send messages to the device.

Infrared

Infrared is a short-distance wireless process that uses light rather than radio waves—in this case, infrared light. It is used for short connections between devices that both have an infrared port. It operates up to 5 meters at speeds up to 4 Mbps and requires a direct line of sight between the devices. There is one infrared mode or protocol that can introduce security issues. The Infrared Transfer Picture (IrTran-P) protocol is used in digital cameras and other digital image capture devices. All incoming files sent over IrTran-P are automatically accepted. Because incoming files might contain harmful programs, users should ensure that the files originate from a trustworthy source.

Near Field Communication (NFC)

Near Field Communication (NFC) is a set of communication protocols that allow two electronic devices, one of which is usually a mobile device, to establish communication by bringing them within 2 inches of each other. NFC-enabled devices can be provided with apps to read electronic tags or make payments when connected to an NFC-compliant apparatus.

Zigbee

Zigbee is an IEEE 802.15.4-based specification that is used to create personal-area networks with small, low-power digital radios, such as for home automation, medical device data collection, and other low-power, low-bandwidth needs. Zigbee is capable of up to 250 Kbps and operates in the 2.4 GHz band.

WLAN Security

To safely implement 802.11 wireless technologies, you must understand all the methods used to secure a WLAN. Here, we discuss the most important measures, including some measures that, although they are often referred to as security measures, provide no real security whatsoever.

Open System Authentication

Open System Authentication is the original default authentication used in 802.11. The authentication request contains only the station ID and authentication response. Although it can be used with WEP, authentication management frames are sent in cleartext because WEP only encrypts data.

Shared Key Authentication

Shared Key Authentication uses WEP and a shared secret key for authentication. The challenge text is encrypted with WEP using the shared secret key. The client returns the encrypted challenge text to the wireless access point.

WEP

Wired Equivalent Privacy (WEP) was the first security measure used with 802.11. It was specified as the algorithm in the original specification. It can be used to both authenticate a device and encrypt the information between the AP and the device. The problem with WEP is that it implements the RC4 encryption algorithm in a way that allows hackers to crack the encryption. It also was found that the mechanism designed to guarantee the integrity of data (that the data has not changed) was inadequate and that it was possible for the data to be changed and for these changes to go undetected.

When WEP is implemented with a secret key or password that is configured on the AP, any station will need that password to connect. Above and beyond the problem with the implementation of the RC4 algorithm, it is never good security for all devices to share the same password.

WPA

To address the widespread concern with the vulnerabilities of WEP, the Wi-Fi Alliance, a group of manufacturers that promotes interoperability, created an alternative mechanism called ***Wi-Fi Protected Access (WPA)*** that was designed to improve on WEP. There are four types of WPA, but first let's talk about how the original version improves over WEP.

First, WPA uses the Temporal Key Integrity Protocol (TKIP) for encryption, which generates a new key for each packet. Second, the integrity check used with WEP can detect any changes to the data. WPA uses a message integrity check algorithm called Michael to verify the integrity of the packets. There are two versions of WPA (covered in the upcoming section "Personal Versus Enterprise").

Some legacy devices might support only WPA. You should always check with a device's manufacturer to find out whether a security patch has been released that allows for WPA2 support.

WPA2

WPA2 is an improvement over WPA. ***WPA2*** uses Counter Cipher Mode with Block Chaining Message Authentication Code Protocol (CCMP) based on Advanced Encryption Standard (AES), rather than TKIP. AES is a much stronger method and is required for Federal Information Processing Standards (FIPS)-compliant transmissions. There are also two versions of WPA2 (covered in the next section).

Personal Versus Enterprise

Both WPA and WPA2 come in Enterprise and Personal versions. The Enterprise versions require the use of an authentication server, typically a RADIUS server. The Personal versions do not and use passwords configured on the AP and the stations. Table 4-7 provides a quick overview of WPA and WPA2.

Key Topic

Table 4-7 WPA and WPA2

Variant	Access Control	Encryption	Integrity
WPA Personal	Pre-shared key	TKIP	Michael
WPA Enterprise	802.1X (RADIUS)	TKIP	Michael
WPA2 Personal	Pre-shared key	CCMP, AES	CCMP
WPA2 Enterprise	802.1X (RADIUS)	CCMP, AES	CCMP

WPA3

WPA3 was introduced in 2018 to address security deficiencies associated with WPA2. One of the security enhancements with WPA3 was to reduce the risks associated with brute-force attacks. Previously, WEP and WPA/WPA2 allowed for continuous password attempts. This protocol also facilitates encryption on a per-user basis so that the encryption protocol varies for each connection. WPA3 uses 128-bit encryption for WPA3 Personal and 192-bit encryption for WPA3 Enterprise.

Like previous protocols, WPA3 has been hacked. WPA3 relies on a more secure handshake than its predecessors, a handshake protocol that is known as Dragonfly. Dragonfly protects Wi-Fi networks against offline dictionary attacks.

The Dragonblood vulnerability was discovered by security researchers Mathy Vanhoef and Eyal Ronen. WPA3 devices are backward-compatible to accept connections to WPA2 devices, using a "transitional mode of operation." This "transitional mode of operation" is susceptible to a downgrade attack, which an attacker can use to set up a rogue access point that supports only WPA2, thereby forcing WPA3 devices to connect using WPA2's four-way handshake. Attackers therefore only need to know the SSID of the WPA3-SAE network.

802.1X

802.1X is a port access protocol that protects networks via authentication. It is used widely in wireless environments. When 802.1X authentication is used, the access point opens a virtual port for communication. If authorization is unsuccessful, the virtual port is unavailable, and communication is blocked.

There are three basic entities during 802.1X authentication:

- ***Supplicant*:** A software client running on the Wi-Fi workstation
- ***Authenticator*:** The wireless access point
- **Authentication server (AS):** A server that contains an authentication database, usually a RADIUS server

Extensible Authentication Protocol (EAP) passes the authentication information between the supplicant and the AS. The actual authentication is defined and handled by the EAP type. The access point acts as a communication bridge to allow the supplicant and the authentication server to communicate.

Multiple types of EAP can be used, depending on how much security the organization needs, the administrative overhead, and the features needed. The different types of EAP authentication are as follows:

- **EAP-Message Digest 5 (EAP-MD5):** Provides base-level EAP support using one-way authentication. This method is not recommended for WLAN implementations because it may allow the user's password to be derived.
- **EAP-Transport Layer Security (EAP-TLS):** Uses certificates to provide mutual authentication of the client and the network. The certificates must be managed on both the client side and server side.
- **EAP-Tunneled TLS (EAP-TTLS):** Provides for certificate-based, mutual authentication of the client and network through an encrypted channel (or tunnel). It requires only server-side certificates.
- **EAP-Flexible Authentication via Secure Tunneling (EAP-FAST):** Uses Protected Access Credential (PAC) for authentication. The PAC can be manually or automatically distributed to the client. Manual provisioning is delivery to the client via disk or a secured network distribution method. Automatic provisioning is an in-band, over-the-air distribution.
- **Lightweight EAP (LEAP):** Used primarily in Cisco Aironet WLANs. It encrypts data transmissions using dynamically generated WEP keys and supports mutual authentication.
- **Protected EAP (PEAP):** Securely transports authentication data, including legacy password-based protocols, via 802.11 Wi-Fi networks using tunneling between PEAP clients and an AS. It uses only server-side certificates.

Table 4-8 compares the different EAP types.

Key Topic

Table 4-8 EAP Type Comparison

802.1X EAP Types Feature/Benefit	MD5	TLS	TTLS	FAST	LEAP	PEAP
Client-side certificate required	No	Yes	No	No (PAC)	No	No
Server-side certificate required	No	Yes	No	No (PAC)	No	Yes
WEP key management	No	Yes	Yes	Yes	Yes	Yes
Rogue AP detection	No	No	No	Yes	Yes	No
Provider	MS	MS	Funk	Cisco	Cisco	MS
Authentication attributes	One way	Mutual	Mutual	Mutual	Mutual	Mutual
Deployment difficulty	Easy	Difficult (because of client certificate deployment)	Moderate	Moderate	Moderate	Moderate
Wi-Fi security	Poor	Very high	High	High	High when strong protocols are used	High

SSID Broadcast

Issues related to the SSID broadcast are covered in the section "WLAN Structure," earlier in this chapter.

MAC Filter

Another commonly discussed security measure is to create a list of allowed MAC addresses on the AP. When this is done, only the devices with MAC addresses on the list can make a connection to the AP. Although, on the surface, this approach might seem like a good security measure, in fact hackers can easily use a sniffer to learn the MAC addresses of devices that have successfully authenticated. Then, by changing the MAC address on their devices to one that is on the list, they can gain entry.

MAC filters can also be configured to deny access to certain devices. The limiting factor of this configuration is that only the devices with the denied MAC addresses are specifically denied access. All other connections will be allowed.

Wireless Site Surveys

A wireless site survey allows administrators to determine the wireless networks in range. Wireless site surveys are used for many purposes. Often administrators perform a site survey prior to deploying a new wireless network to determine the standard and possible channels deployed. After a wireless network is deployed, site surveys are used to determine whether rogue access points have been deployed or to determine where new access points should be deployed to increase the range of the wireless network.

Security professionals should periodically perform wireless site surveys as part of regular maintenance.

Antenna Placement and Signal Power Levels

When deploying wireless networks, administrators should ensure that the WAPs are deployed in an appropriate location based on the results of the site survey. The WAP should be placed in a possible location, and then the functionality of the WAP should be tested in that location. The WAP should be moved to several different locations to determine the location where the best signal strength and connection quality occur.

The power level of the WAP also affects the signal transmission. If a site survey shows that the signal extends well beyond the range that needs coverage, administrators should lower the power level of the WAP. This is especially true if the signal extends outside the building if all users will be accessing it from within the building. By lowering the power level, the administrator will be decreasing the radius of the coverage area and thereby possibly mitigating attacks.

When deploying a new WAP, an administrator should keep the following guidelines in mind:

- Deploy in a central location to all the devices that need wireless access.
- Avoid deploying a WAP near a solid obstruction.
- Avoid deploying a WAP near a reflective or metal surface.
- Avoid deploying a WAP near electrical equipment.
- Adjust the WAP's power level to decrease the coverage radius. (Why is this important? To avoid attackers recognizing the network, attackers creating a possible rogue AP, and so on.)

Antenna Types

Wireless antennas in WAPs come in two main types: omnidirectional and directional. Omnidirectional antennas can send data in all directions that are perpendicular to the line of the antenna. Directional antennas can send data in one primary direction. Yagi, parabolic, and backfire antennas are all directional antennas.

Administrators need to understand the type of antenna included in a WAP to ensure that it is deployed in such a manner as to optimize the signal and coverage radius.

Communications Cryptography

Encryption can provide different protection based on which level of communication is being used. The two types of encryption communication levels are link encryption and end-to-end encryption.

NOTE Cryptography, including encryption mechanisms and public key infrastructure, is covered in more depth in Chapter 3, "Security Architecture and Engineering."

Link Encryption

Link encryption encrypts all the data that is transmitted over a link. In this type of communication, the only portion of the packet that is not encrypted is the data-link control information, which is needed to ensure that devices transmit the data properly. All the information is encrypted, with each router or other device decrypting its header information so that routing can occur and then re-encrypting before sending the information to the next device.

If the sending party needs to ensure that data security and privacy are maintained over a public communication link, then link encryption should be used. This method is often used to protect email communication or when banks or other institutions that have confidential data must send that data over the Internet.

Link encryption protects against packet sniffers and other forms of eavesdropping and occurs at the Data Link and Physical layers of the OSI model. Advantages of link encryption include: All the data is encrypted, and no user interaction is needed for it to be used. Disadvantages of link encryption include: Each device that the data must be transmitted through must receive the key, key changes must be transmitted to each device on the route, and packets are decrypted at each device.

End-to-End Encryption

End-to-end encryption encrypts less of the packet information than link encryption. In end-to-end encryption, packet routing information, as well as packet headers and addresses, are not encrypted. When there is no encryption for routing, headers, or addresses, it allows potential hackers to intercept communications and obtain more information through packet sniffing.

But end-to-end encryption has several advantages. A user usually initiates end-to-end encryption, which allows the user to select exactly what gets encrypted and how. This type of encryption affects the performance of each device along the route less than link encryption because not every device has to perform encryption/decryption to determine how to route the packet. An example of end-to-end encryption is IPsec.

Email Security

Email has become an integral part of almost everyone's life, particularly as it relates to their business communication. But many email implementations provide very little security natively without the incorporation of encryption, digital signatures, or keys. For example, email authenticity and confidentiality are provided by signing the message using the sender's private key and encrypting the message with the receiver's public key.

In the following sections, we briefly discuss the PGP, MIME, and S/MIME email standards that are popular in today's world and also give a brief description of quantum cryptography.

PGP

Pretty Good Privacy (PGP) provides email encryption over the Internet and uses different encryption technologies based on the needs of the organization. PGP can provide confidentiality, integrity, and authenticity based on which encryption methods are used.

PGP provides key management using RSA. PGP uses a web of trust to manage the keys. By sharing public keys, users create this web of trust, instead of relying on a certificate authority (CA). The public keys of all the users are stored on each user's computer in a key ring file. Within that file, each user is assigned a level of trust. The users within the web vouch for each other. So if User 1 and User 2 have a trust relationship and User 1 and User 3 have a trust relationship, User 1 can recommend the other two users to each other. Users can choose the level of trust initially assigned to a user but can change that level later if circumstances warrant a change. But compromise of a user's public key in the PGP system means that the user must contact everyone with whom they have shared their key to ensure that this key is removed from the key ring file.

PGP provides data encryption for confidentiality using the International Data Encryption Algorithm (IDEA). However, other encryption algorithms can be used.

Implementing PGP with MD5 provides data integrity. Public certificates with PGP provide authentication.

MIME and S/MIME

Multipurpose Internet Mail Extensions (MIME) is an Internet standard that allows email to include non-text attachments, non-ASCII character sets, multiple-part message bodies, and non-ASCII header information. In today's world, SMTP in MIME format transmits a majority of email.

MIME allows the email client to send an attachment with a header describing the file type. The receiving system uses this header and the file extension listed in it to identify the attachment type and open the associated application. Consequently, the computer can automatically launch the appropriate application when the user double-clicks the attachment. If no application is associated with that file type, the user is able to choose the application using the Open With option, or a website might offer the necessary application.

Secure MIME (S/MIME) allows MIME to encrypt and digitally sign email messages and encrypt attachments. It adheres to the Public Key Cryptography Standards (PKCS), which is a set of public key cryptography standards designed by the owners of the RSA algorithm.

S/MIME uses encryption to provide confidentiality, hashing to provide integrity, public key certificates to provide authentication, and message digests to provide nonrepudiation.

Quantum Cryptography

Quantum cryptography is a method of encryption that combines quantum physics and cryptography and offers the possibility of factoring the products of large prime numbers. Quantum cryptography provides strong encryption and eavesdropping detection.

This type of encryption would be an excellent choice for any organization that transmits top-secret data, including the U.S. government.

Internet Security

The World Wide Web is a collection of HTTP servers that manage websites and their services. The Internet is a network that includes all the physical devices and protocols over which web traffic is transmitted. The web browser that is used allows users to read web pages via HTTP. Browsers can natively read many protocols. Any protocols not natively supported by the web browser can only be read by installing a plug-in or application viewer, thereby expanding the browser's role.

In our discussion of Internet security, we cover the following topics:

- Remote access
- HTTP, HTTPS, and S-HTTP
- SET
- Cookies
- SSH
- IPsec

Remote Access

Remote access applications allow users to access an organization's resources from a remote connection. These remote connections can be direct dial-in connections but more commonly use the Internet as the network over which the data is transmitted. If an organization allows remote access to internal resources, the organization must ensure that the data is protected using encryption when the data is being transmitted between the remote access client and remote access server. Remote access servers can require encrypted connections with remote access clients, which means that any connection attempt that does not use encryption will be denied.

Remote Desktop Connection (RDC), also referred to as Remote Desktop, is Microsoft's implementation that allows a user with proper identification to log in to a remote computer. RDC operates using the Remote Desktop Protocol (RDP), which operates over port 3389. RDP became even more popular during the COVID-19 pandemic, as the protocol allowed employees to remotely connect to their office computers without physically being in the office. However, RDP inherently creates a security risk for organizations because when it is enabled it creates an additional vector for an unauthorized user to access a specific host on a network. In fact, it is frequently an indicator of compromise (IoC) that incident responders look for on a compromised host Windows PC. If RDP has not been enabled, then during a network breach a hacker will often enable RDP to facilitate remote access.

HTTP, HTTPS, and S-HTTP

HTTP, HTTPS, and S-HTTP are discussed in detail earlier in this chapter.

Secure Electronic Transaction (SET)

Secure Electronic Transaction (SET), proposed by Visa and MasterCard, secured credit card transaction information over the Internet. It was based on X.509 certificates and asymmetric keys. It used an electronic wallet on a user's computer to send encrypted credit card information. But to be fully implemented, SET would have required the full cooperation of financial institutions, credit card users, wholesale and retail establishments, and payment gateways. It was never fully adopted.

Visa now promotes the 3-D Secure protocol. 3-D Secure, which uses XML, provides an additional layer of security for online credit card transactions, and is implemented under the names Verified by Visa, MasterCard SecureCode, American Express SafeKey, and J/Secure. It transmits the XML messages over SSL. It links the financial authorization process with the online authentication. Three domains, which is where the 3-D part of the name comes from, that are used include the acquirer domain, issuer domain, and interoperability domain. The acquirer domain is the bank and the merchant receiving the payment, the issuer domain is the bank issuing the card, and the interoperability domain is the infrastructure that supports the 3-D protocol.

In recent years, mobile device credit/debit card processing technology, including Apple Pay, Google Pay, Venmo, and Zelle, have become popular alternatives.

Cookies

Cookies are small text files that are stored on a user's hard drive or memory. These files usually store information about the user's Internet browsing or shopping habits. Because a website's servers actually determine how cookies are used, malicious sites can use cookies to discover a large amount of private information about a user.

Although the information retained in cookies on the hard drive usually does not include any confidential information, attackers can still use it to obtain information about a user that can help the attackers develop a better targeted attack. For example, if the cookies reveal to an attacker that a user accesses a particular bank's public website on a daily basis, that action may indicate that a user has an account at that bank, resulting in the attacker attempting a ***phishing*** attack using an email that looks to come from the user's legitimate bank.

Many antivirus or anti-malware applications include functionality that allows you to limit the type of cookies downloaded and to hide personally identifiable information (PII), such as email addresses. In most locations today, websites must notify users about cookies and PII or user data collection.

SSH

Secure Shell (SSH) is an application and protocol that is used to remotely log in to another computer using a secure tunnel. After the secure channel is established after a session key is exchanged, all communication between the two computers is encrypted over the secure channel. Although SSH and Telnet provide much of the same functionalities, SSH is considered the secure alternative to Telnet. By default, SSH uses port 22.

IPsec

IPsec is covered in detail earlier in this chapter.

Secure Network Components

An organization can secure network components to ensure that its network assets are protected. If an organization fails to properly secure these components, all traffic on the network can be compromised. The network components include operation of hardware, transmission media, network access control devices, endpoint security, and content-distribution networks.

Network Monitoring and Management

Network observability is an important concept today, whereby several different data sources provide a holistic view of the network's functionality and health, which includes the end-user's perspective. This contrasts with traditional ***network monitoring***, where a narrower focus on metrics and predetermined thresholds has been the norm. The disadvantage of network monitoring has been data overload and network monitoring fatigue.

Network observability tools provide recommendations about how to improve performance and address network problems, often using a global enterprise dashboard. This dashboard displays data from the user's perspective. Consequently, this new approach provides a real-time, full-stack, network intelligence approach to monitoring and managing the enterprise's network. To summarize, observability tools look at device connections and issues from a user perspective, while network monitoring tools show devices, their connections, and network metrics, without focusing on the user experience.

Network observability relies on telemetry, which gathers data from a variety of sources, thereby providing information about the current state and health of the network; this can include application latency, flow logs, and test data, for example. Artificial intelligence and deep packet inspection may also be integrated into telemetry. A data platform then ingests this telemetry data and provides information about the network's performance and issues in an intuitive way, thereby making it easier to understand the user's experience and to resolve network problems faster. Finally, taking action is an important concept in network observability, whereby network performance issues are addressed through employee collaboration.

Traffic shaping, sometimes referred to as *packet shaping*, is a QoS process that focuses on reducing network congestion by regulating data transfers across a network. This may be accomplished by prioritizing the transfer of packets and subsequently delaying the transmission of lower prioritized data. For example, an Internet service provider many limit bandwidth for certain applications or even certain customers. The goal of this congestion management process is to optimize use of bandwidth while also reducing latency, jitter, and loss.

Capacity management of a network is critical to an enterprise, its customers, and its vendors. However, maintaining the necessary capacity is a challenge for IT administrators because network requirements continually change, which can be due to the transmission of more data over time, changes in applications (used by the network and the user), new computing devices, such as IoT devices, new protocols, such as 5G, and perhaps changes in business requirements. Frequently, performance is impacted by capacity issues—applications may be slower to respond because of inadequate bandwidth.

Capacity and performance management are not only requirements for normal business operations but planning is essential in case of network outages that can result from a power outage, a natural disaster, or a cyberattack. Unfortunately, many organizations plan to manage network capacity based on a baseline during normal business operations but fail to consider capacity requirements for an unforeseen event, including a disaster. Additional capacity, as a result of a natural disaster or cyberattack, for example, can be provided internally or by using a third-party contingency partner. This capacity should be located in a different geographic area and on a different power grid to mitigate the risks associated with a natural disaster that impacts a particular region. Nevertheless, baselining and trending on a network are integral to effective capacity management. Of course, the reality is that network managers face problems associated with hiring trained staff and contending with constraints on fiscal budgets. Capacity management can benefit from effective service level agreements that enable the owner of a network to hold third parties accountable for issues related to network capacity and other QoS problems.

When discussing capacity management, two terms are frequently mentioned: data plane and control plane. The ***data plane*** refers to capacity and performance issues related to the data that is transmitted across the network. The ***control plane*** refers to the resources required to maintain an effective data plane. CPU and memory are just two considerations to ensuring an effective data plane and control plane.

Fault detection and handling refers to identifying, isolating, and rectifying problems on a network. There are fault management systems that facilitate this process. A fault occurs when a device does not function properly—possibly because of a hardware problem, an issue with connectivity, or a change in protocol. Moreover, a fault may occur as a result of malware. Ideally, the fault management system should quickly alert a network administrator about a network issue via an SMS text message or email alert. In the process of restoring the network to normal service, the system should log all network faults and events, quarantine issues such as malware, and fix malfunctions or correct conditions leading to faults.

Operation of Infrastructure

Network resiliency is critical to the success of an organization. Data redundancy is an important part of this process, in case of a disaster, a cyber attack, or any other unforeseen event. Maintaining a redundant power supply is vital to ensuring an uninterrupted power supply to critical systems and equipment in an effort to reduce downtime and disruption. More specifically, organizations need to maintain redundant power supplies for telecommunication, data centers, and other critical infrastructure. Redundant power can be supplied via backup batteries, uninterruptible power supplies (UPSs), or generators, which seamlessly take over during a power outage. In parallel, an organization should mitigate the risk of power surges by using surge protectors. Regular testing of backup power supplies is very important to ensuring that power is available when needed. Data redundancy and power redundancy are also important concepts for disaster recovery planning and business continuity planning.

Finally, an enterprise should also consider purchasing warranty coverage for network equipment and critical systems, in addition to reviewing third-party support for these systems.

Hardware

When securing network components, security professionals must consider all network devices as part of a comprehensive security solution. The devices include patch panels, multiplexers, hubs, switches and VLANs, routers, gateways, firewalls, proxy servers, PBXs, honeypots, IDSs, and IPSs. An understanding of network routing, including all routing protocols, is also vital. The following sections discuss all these components.

Network Devices

Network devices operate at all layers of the OSI model. The layer at which they operate reveals quite a bit of information about their level of intelligence and about the type of information used by each device. Here, we cover common devices and their respective roles in the overall picture.

Patch Panel

Patch panels operate at the Physical layer (Layer 1) of the OSI model and simply function as a central termination point for all the cables running through the walls from wall outlets, which in turn are connected to computers with cables. The cables running through the walls to the patch panel are permanently connected to the panel. Short cables called patch cables are then used to connect each panel port to a switch or hub. The main thing to be concerned with regarding patch panels is their physical security. They should be placed in a locked room or closet.

Multiplexer

A ***multiplexer*** is a Physical layer (Layer 1 of OSI) device that combines several input information signals into one output signal, which carries several communication channels, by means of some multiplexing technique. Conversely, a ***demultiplexer*** takes a single input signal that carries many channels and separates those over multiple output signals. The same physical medium can be shared in a number of different ways: on the basis of frequencies used (frequency-division multiplexing or FDM) or by using time slots (time-division multiplexing or TDM).

Telco Concentrator

A telco concentrator is a type of multiplexer that combines multiple channels onto a single transmission medium so that all the individual channels are active simultaneously. For example, ISPs use concentrators to combine their multiple dial-up connections into faster T-1 lines. Concentrators are also used in LANs to combine network transmissions from a cluster of nodes. Telco concentrators are Layer 1 devices.

VPN Concentrator

A virtual private network (VPN) concentrator provides secure creation of VPN connections and delivery of messages between VPN nodes. It is a type of router device built specifically for creating and managing VPN communication infrastructures. It works at the Network layer (Layer 3).

Hub

A ***hub*** is a Physical layer (Layer 1) device that functions as a junction point for devices in a star topology. It is considered a Physical layer device because it has no intelligence. When a hub receives traffic, it broadcasts that traffic out of every port because it lacks intelligence to make any decisions about where the destination is located or what is included in the traffic.

Although this broadcast results in more collisions and poor performance, from a security standpoint, the problem is that the hub broadcasts all traffic to all ports. A sniffer connected to any port will be able to sniff all traffic. The operation of a hub is shown in Figure 4-31. When a switch is used, that is not the case (switches are covered shortly).

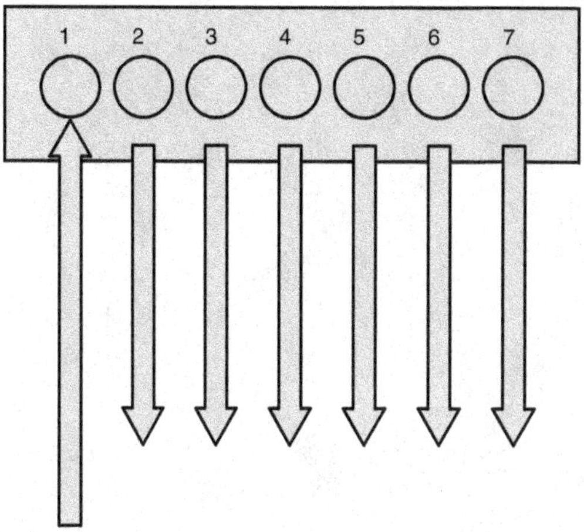

Figure 4-31 Hub

Repeater

A repeater is a device that extends the range of a network. Because the signal strength is reduced over distance due to various electrical and physical interferences, a repeater is recommended if you need to extend a network over a distance or area that is more than the recommended maximum for the cable type.

Bridge

Bridges are Layer 2 devices that filter traffic between network segments based on MAC addresses. Bridges prevent frames that go only to the local network from being transmitted outside the local network. But they forward all network broadcasts. They can connect LANs that use different media, such as connecting a twisted pair (TP) network to a fiber optic network. To provide security, bridges should implement some form of Link layer encryption.

Switch

Switches are similar to bridges; they are intelligent and operate at Layer 2 of the OSI model. They map to Layer 2 because they make switching decisions based on MAC addresses, which reside at Layer 2. This process is called *transparent bridging*. Figure 4-32 shows this process.

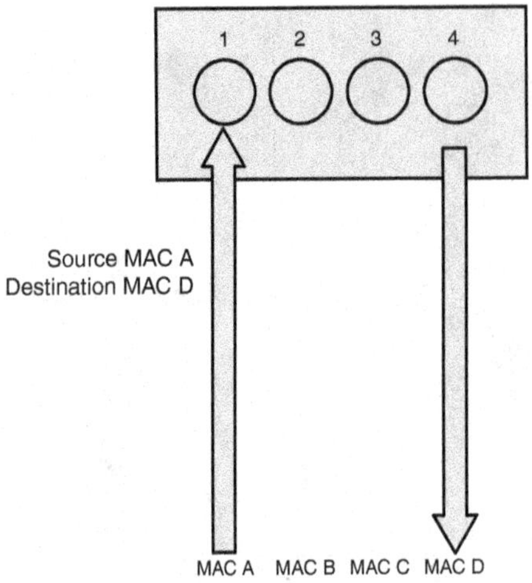

Figure 4-32 Transparent Bridging

Switches improve performance over hubs because they eliminate collisions. Each switch port is in its own collision domain, whereas all ports of a hub are in the same collision domain. From a security standpoint, switches are more secure in that a sniffer connected to any single port will be able to capture only traffic destined for or originating from that port.

Switches are more expensive, faster, and harder to implement than bridges and hubs. Both bridges and switches provide better performance than hubs.

Some switches, however, can act as both routers and switches, and in that case they are called Layer 3 switches because they route and switch.

Layer 3 Versus Layer 4 Switching

Typically, the switching process is mapped to Layer 2 of the OSI model because Layer 2 addresses are used to make frame-forwarding decisions. This doesn't mean that a single physical device cannot be capable of both functions. A ***Layer 3 switch*** is such a device. It is a switch with the routing function also built in. It can both route and switch and can combine the two functions in an integrated way such that a single data stream can be routed when the first packet arrives, and then the rest of the packets in the stream can be fast switched, resulting in better performance.

Layer 4 switches go a step further by providing additional routing above Layer 3 by using the port numbers found in the Transport layer header to make routing decisions. The largest benefit of Layer 4 switching is the ability to prioritize data traffic by application, which means QoS can be defined for each user.

VLANs

Enterprise-level switches can be used to create ***virtual local-area networks (VLANs)***. These are logical subdivisions of a switch that segregate ports from one another as if they were in different LANs. These VLANs can also span multiple switches, meaning that devices connected to switches in different parts of a network can be placed in the same VLAN regardless of physical location.

VLANs offer another way to add a layer of separation between sensitive devices and the rest of the network. For example, if only two devices should be able to connect to the HR server, the two devices and the HR server could be placed in a VLAN separate from the other VLANs. Traffic between VLANs can occur only through a router. Routers can be used to implement ACLs that control the traffic allowed between VLANs.

Router

Routers operate at Layer 3 (Network layer) when we are discussing the routing function in isolation. As previously discussed, certain devices can combine routing functionality with switching and Layer 4 filtering. However, because routing uses Layer 3 information (IP addresses) to make decisions, it is a Layer 3 function.

Routers use a routing table that tells them in which direction to send traffic destined for a particular network. Although routers can be configured with routes to individual computers, typically they route toward networks, not individual computers. When the packet arrives at a particular router that is directly connected to the destination network, that router performs an ARP broadcast to learn the MAC address of the computer and send the packets as frames at Layer 2.

Routers also perform an important security function because ACLs are typically configured on routers. ACLs are ordered sets of rules that control the traffic that is permitted or denied the use of a path through the router. These access rules can operate at Layer 3 of the OSI, where decisions on the basis of IP addresses are made, or else at Layer 4, where only certain types of traffic are allowed. An ACL typically references a port number of the service or application that is allowed or denied.

Boundary routers communicate with external hosts so that external hosts are able to connect to internal hosts. Internal routers communicate with internal hosts so that they can connect to other internal hosts. The security configuration of boundary routers is more vital to help filter external traffic and to prevent unwanted communication from reaching the internal network.

Gateway

The term ***gateway*** doesn't refer to a particular device but rather to any device that performs some sort of translation or acts as a control point to entry and exit.

An example of a device performing as a gateway would be an email server. It receives email from all types of email servers (Exchange, IBM Notes, Micro Focus GroupWise) and performs any translation of formats that is necessary between these different implementations.

Another example would be a ***network access server (NAS)*** that controls access to a network. This device would be considered a gateway in that all traffic might need to be authenticated before entry is allowed. This type of server might even examine the computers themselves for the latest security patches and updates before entry is allowed.

Firewalls

The network device that perhaps is most connected with the idea of security is the firewall. ***Firewalls*** can be software programs that are installed over server operating systems, or they can be appliances that have their own operating system. In either case, their job is to inspect and control the type of traffic allowed.

Firewalls can be classified on the basis of their type and their architecture. They can also be physical devices or exist in a virtualized environment. Here, we look at them from all angles.

Firewall Types

When we discuss *types* of firewalls, we are focusing on the differences in the way they operate. Some firewalls make a more thorough inspection of traffic than others. Usually, there is trade-off in the performance of the firewall and the type of inspection that it performs. A deep inspection of the contents of each packet results in the firewall having a detrimental effect on throughput, whereas a more cursory look at each packet has somewhat less of an impact on performance. It is for this reason that we should select what traffic to inspect wisely, keeping this trade-off in mind.

Packet filtering firewalls are the least detrimental to throughput because they inspect only the header of the packet for allowed IP addresses or port numbers. Although even performing this function will slow traffic, it involves looking only at the beginning of the packet and making a quick decision to allow or block traffic.

Although packet filtering firewalls serve an important function, they may fail to prevent many attack types. They cannot prevent IP spoofing, attacks that are specific to an application, attacks that depend on packet fragmentation, or attacks that take advantage of the TCP handshake. More advanced inspection firewall types are required to stop these attacks.

Stateful firewalls are those that are aware of the proper functioning of the TCP handshake, keep track of the state of all connections with respect to this process, and can recognize when packets that are trying to enter the network don't make sense in the context of the TCP three-way handshake. We discussed how the TCP three-way handshake occurs in the "Transport Layer" section (under "TCP/IP Model"), earlier in this chapter.

To review that process, a packet that has both the SYN flag and the ACK flag set should never arrive at a firewall for delivery unless it is part of an existing handshake process, and it should be in response to a packet sent from inside the network with the SYN flag set. This is the type of packet that the stateful firewall would disallow. It also can recognize other attack types that attempt to misuse this process. It does this by maintaining a state table about all current connections and the status of each connection process. This information allows it to recognize any traffic that doesn't make sense with the current state of the connection. Of course, maintaining this table and referencing the table cause this firewall type to have more effect on performance than a packet filtering firewall.

Proxy firewalls actually stand between each connection from the outside to the inside and make the connection on behalf of the endpoints. Therefore, there is no direct connection. The proxy firewall acts as a relay between the two endpoints, as displayed in Figure 4-33. Proxy firewalls can operate at two different layers of the OSI model, as discussed next.

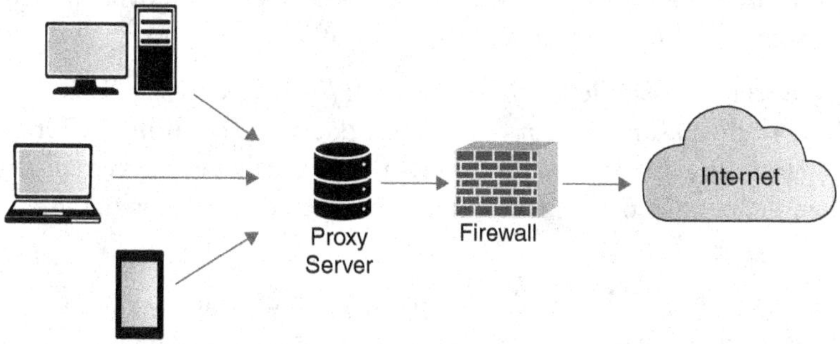

Figure 4-33 Proxy Firewall

Circuit-level proxies operate at the Session layer (Layer 5) of the OSI model. They make decisions based on the protocol header and Session layer information. Because they do not do deep packet inspection (at Layer 7, or the Application layer, of the

OSI model), they are considered application-independent and can be used for wide ranges of Layer 7 protocol types.

A ***Socket Secure (SOCKS) firewall*** is an example of a circuit-level firewall. It requires a SOCKS client on the computers. Many vendors have integrated their software with SOCKS to make using this type of firewall easier. SOCKS routes network packets through a proxy server. SOCKS v5 added authentication to the process. A SOCKS firewall works at the Session layer (Layer 5).

Application-level proxies perform deep packet inspection. This type of firewall understands the details of the communication process at Layer 7 for the application of interest. An application-level firewall maintains a different proxy function for each protocol. For example, for HTTP the proxy will be able to read and filter traffic based on specific HTTP commands. Operating at this layer requires each packet to be completely opened and closed, making this firewall the most impactful on performance.

Dynamic packet filtering, rather than describing a different type of firewall, describes functionality that a firewall might or might not possess. When an internal computer attempts to establish a session with a remote computer, it places both a source port number and a destination port number in the packet. For example, if the computer is making a request of a web server, because HTTP uses port 80, the destination port will be 80.

The source computer selects the source port at random from the numbers available above the well-known port numbers, or above 1023. Because predicting what that random number will be is impossible, creating a firewall rule that anticipates and allows traffic back through the firewall on that random port is impossible. A ***dynamic packet filtering firewall*** will keep track of that source port and dynamically add a new access control rule to the list to allow return traffic to that port.

A ***kernel proxy firewall*** is an example of a *fifth-generation firewall*. It inspects the packet at every layer of the OSI model but does not introduce the performance hit that an Application layer firewall will because it does this inspection at the kernel layer. It also follows the proxy model in that it stands between the two systems and creates connections on their behalf.

Unified threat management (UTM) provides multiple layers of security, and its functionality includes content filtering, web filtering, and antivirus (see Figure 4-34). UTM devices are marketed as network security appliances, which can be network hardware appliances, virtual appliances, or cloud services. Unified threat management can include intrusion detection and intrusion prevention technologies. For example, UTM may detect an attack based on malware signatures or other anomalies. UTM also supports VPN functionality. In terms of web filtering for content, some UTMs can scan websites for security vulnerabilities that may be harmful to the requesting computer.

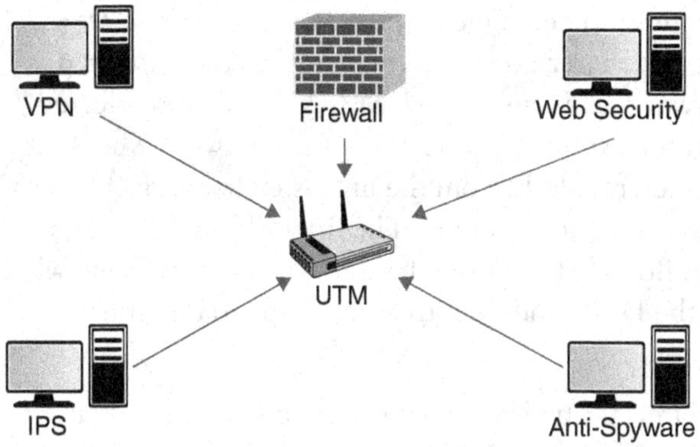

Figure 4-34 Unified Threat Management (UTM)

Firewall Architecture

Firewall architecture refers to the way in which the firewall or firewalls are deployed in the network to form a system of protection. Here, we look at the various ways firewalls can be deployed and what the names of these various configurations are.

Although *bastion hosts* are included in this discussion regarding firewalls, a bastion host might or might not be a firewall. The term actually refers to the position of a device. If it is exposed directly to the Internet or to any untrusted network, it is called a ***bastion host***. All standard hardening procedures are especially important for these exposed devices. Any unnecessary services should be stopped, all unneeded ports should be closed, and all security patches must be up to date. These procedures are said to *reduce the attack surface*. If a bastion host is deployed, it is the only host on the internal network that is exposed to the Internet or untrusted networks. If the bastion host is deployed separately from the firewall, it is placed outside the firewall or on the public side of the ***demilitarized zone (DMZ)***. The bastion host filters all incoming traffic. Firewalls and routers can be configured to be bastion hosts. A DMZ separates a LAN from an untrusted network. The DMZ provides an additional layer of security by restricting access to the LAN from the Internet.

A ***dual-homed firewall***, also referred to as a dual-homed host, has two network interfaces via the installation of two NICs, each on a separate network. In many cases, automatic routing between these interfaces is turned off. The firewall software allows or denies traffic between the two interfaces based on the firewall rules configured by the administrator. The danger of relying on a single dual-homed firewall is that there is a single point of failure. If this device is compromised, the network can also be compromised sooner or later. If it suffers a denial-of-service (DoS) attack, no traffic will pass. Neither is a good situation.

In some cases, a firewall may be multihomed. One popular type is the ***three-legged firewall***. This configuration has three interfaces: one connected to the untrusted network, one to the internal network, and one to the DMZ. A DMZ, also referred to as a ***perimeter network*** or ***screened subnet***, is a portion of the network where systems are placed that will be accessed regularly from the untrusted network. These might be web servers or an email server, for example. The firewall can then be configured to control the traffic that flows between the three networks, being somewhat careful with traffic destined for the DMZ and then treating traffic to the internal network with much more suspicion.

Although the firewalls discussed thus far typically connect directly to the untrusted network (at least one interface does), a ***screened host*** is a firewall that is between the final router and the internal network. When traffic comes into the router and is forwarded to the firewall, it will be inspected before going into the internal network.

Taking this concept a step further is a screened subnet. In this case, two firewalls are used, and traffic must be inspected at both firewalls to enter the internal network. It is called a screened subnet because there will be a subnet between the two firewalls that can act as a DMZ for resources from the outside world.

In the real world, the discussed approaches are mixed and matched to meet requirements, so you might find elements of all these architectural concepts being applied to a specific situation.

Proxy Server

Proxy servers can be appliances, or they can be software that is installed on a server operating system. These servers act like a proxy firewall in that they create the web connection between systems on their behalf, but they can typically allow and disallow traffic on a more granular basis. For example, a proxy server might allow the Sales group to go to certain websites while not allowing the Data Entry group access to the same sites. The functionality of proxy servers can extend beyond HTTP to other traffic types, such as FTP and others.

Proxy servers can provide an additional beneficial function called *web caching*. When a proxy server is configured to provide web caching, it saves a copy of all web pages that have been delivered to internal computers in a web cache. If any user requests the same page later, the proxy server has a local copy and need not spend the time and effort to retrieve it from the Internet. This function greatly improves web performance for frequently requested pages.

PBX

A ***private branch exchange (PBX)*** is a private telephone switch that resides on the customer premises. It has a direct connection to the telecommunication provider's switch. It performs call routing within the internal phone system. This is how a company can have two "outside" lines but 50 internal phones. The call comes in on one of the two outside lines, and the PBX routes it to the proper extension. Sometimes the system converts analog to digital, but not always.

The security considerations with these devices revolve around their default configurations. They typically are configured with default administrator passwords that should be changed, and they often contain backdoor connections that can be used by vendor support personnel to connect in and help with problems. These backdoors are usually well known and should be disabled until they are needed.

There are different types of PBX fraud. In one scenario, a hacker calls a number in a company and gains access to an employee's voicemail by successfully guessing the user's PIN. The fraudster then uses the call forwarding feature to forward calls to a premium telephone number that the attacker has set up earlier. The fraudster then continually calls that same number to rack up charges from calls forwarded to a premium number. Because the company manages the PBX and not the telecom provider, the company can be liable for tens of thousands of dollars in charges to the premium number. PBX is a legacy term and today has been replaced by terms like VoIP (Voice over Internet Protocol) instead.

Honeypot

Honeypots are systems that are configured to be attractive to hackers and lure them into spending time attacking them while information is gathered about the attack. In some cases, entire networks called ***honeynets*** are attractively configured for this purpose. These types of approaches should be undertaken only by companies with the skill to properly deploy and monitor them.

Care should be taken that the honeypots and honeynets do not provide direct connections to any important systems and do not provide hackers with a jumping-off point to other areas of the good network. The ultimate purpose of honeypot systems is to divert hackers from more valuable resources and to gather as much information about an attack as possible. The related term *tarpit* is a type of honeypot designed to provide a very slow connection to hackers so that the attack can be analyzed.

IDS

An intrusion detection system (IDS) is a system responsible for detecting unauthorized access or attacks against systems and networks. It can verify, itemize, and characterize threats from outside and inside the network. Most IDSs are programmed to react certain ways in specific situations. Event notifications and alerts are crucial to an IDS. They inform administrators and security professionals when and where attacks are detected.

The most common way to classify an IDS is based on its information source: network-based or host-based.

A network-based IDS (NIDS) is the most common IDS and monitors network traffic on a local network segment. To monitor traffic on the network segment, the NIC must be operating in promiscuous mode. An NIDS can monitor only the network traffic. It cannot monitor any internal activity that occurs within a system, such as an attack against a system that is carried out by logging on to the system's local terminal. An NIDS is affected by a switched network because generally an NIDS monitors only a single network segment.

A ***Network Node Intrusion Detection System (NNIDS)*** is used to monitor traffic between a network and a host. One example of an NNIDS would be used for monitoring traffic connected to a VPN.

A host-based IDS (HIDS) monitors traffic on a single system. Its primary responsibility is to protect the system on which it is installed. An HIDS uses information from the operating system audit trails and system logs. The detection capabilities of an HIDS are limited by how complete the audit logs and system logs are.

IDS implementations are further divided into the following categories:

Key Topic

- **Signature-based:** This type of IDS analyzes traffic and compares it to known attack patterns, called signatures, that reside within the IDS database. It is also referred to as a misuse-detection system. Although this type of IDS is popular, it can only recognize attacks as compared with its database and is only as effective as the signatures provided. Frequent updates are necessary to prevent newly discovered attacks. The two main types of signature-based IDSs are
  - **Pattern-matching:** The IDS compares traffic to a database of attack patterns. The IDS carries out specific steps when it detects traffic that matches an attack pattern.
  - **Stateful-matching:** The IDS records the initial operating system state. Any changes to the system state that specifically violate the defined rules result in an alert or notification being sent.
- **Anomaly-based:** This type of IDS analyzes traffic and compares it to normal traffic to determine whether said traffic is a threat. It is also referred to as a

behavior-based or profile-based system. The problem with this type of system is that any traffic outside of expected norms is reported, resulting in more false positives than signature-based systems. The three main types of anomaly-based IDSs are

- **Statistical anomaly-based:** The IDS samples the live environment to record activities. The longer the IDS is in operation, the more accurate a profile that will be built. However, developing a profile that will not have a large number of false positives can be difficult and time-consuming. Thresholds for activity deviations are important in this IDS. Lower thresholds may result in more false positives, whereas too high a threshold may result in more false negatives.
- **Protocol anomaly-based:** The IDS has knowledge of the protocols that it will monitor. A profile of normal usage is built and compared to activity.
- **Traffic anomaly-based:** The IDS tracks traffic pattern changes. All future traffic patterns are compared to the sample. Changing the threshold will reduce the number of false positives or negatives. This type of filter is excellent for detecting unknown attacks, but user activity might not be static enough to effectively implement this system.

- **Rule- or heuristic-based:** This type of IDS is an expert system that uses a knowledge base, inference engine, and rule-based programming. The knowledge is configured as rules. The data and traffic are analyzed, and the rules are applied to the analyzed traffic. The inference engine uses its intelligent software to "learn." If characteristics of an attack are met, alerts or notifications trigger. This is often referred to as an IF/THEN or expert system.

An application-based IDS is a specialized IDS that analyzes transaction log files for a single application. This type of IDS is usually provided as part of the application or can be purchased as an add-on.

When implementing and managing IDSs, administrators must understand the difference between a false positive and a false negative. A false positive occurs when an IDS identifies an activity as an attack but the activity is acceptable behavior. A false negative occurs when the IDS does not identify malicious activity. Although a false positive is a false alarm, a false negative is a dangerous state because the security professional may not be aware that an attack already took place or is currently taking place.

Tools that can complement an IDS include vulnerability analysis systems, honeypots, and padded cells. As described earlier, honeypots are systems that are configured with reduced security to entice attackers so that administrators can learn about attack techniques. Padded cells are special hosts to which an attacker is transferred during an attack.

IPS

An intrusion prevention system (IPS) is a system responsible for preventing attacks. When an attack begins, an IPS takes actions to prevent and contain the attack. An IPS can be network- or host-based, like an IDS. Although an IPS can be signature- or anomaly-based, it can also use a rate-based metric that analyzes the volume of traffic as well as the type of traffic.

In most cases, implementing an IPS is more costly than an IDS because of the added security of preventing attacks versus simply detecting attacks. In addition, running an IPS can cause greater performance load than running an IDS.

Endpoint Detection and Response

Endpoint Detection and Response (EDR) is a tool for monitoring threats on network hosts and then automatically responding to certain types of attacks. The power of EDR lies in its tremendous logging capabilities, which benefit incident responders. The cost of EDR can, however, be prohibitively expensive for most companies. A software agent is installed on each host system (or endpoint) on the network. EDR tracks processes, changes to file registries (Windows configuration files), file system activity, and network connections on each host. Endpoint and network events are collected and stored in a database. EDR is different from IDS or IPS because EDR is more focused on endpoints. Many companies use both EDR and IDS/IPS.

Mobile Devices

Mobile devices—including laptops, tablets, smartphones, e-readers, and wearable technology devices—have quickly become the most widely used devices. An organization should adopt a formal mobile device security policy and a bring-your-own-device (BYOD) security policy if personal devices will be permitted to join the network. The organization may also want to consider deploying a network access control (NAC) server to ensure that any devices that join the network meet minimum security requirements and quarantine any devices that do not meet minimum security requirements.

NIST SP 800-124 Revision 2 provides guidelines for managing the security of mobile devices in the enterprise. According to NIST SP 800-124 Rev. 2, organizations should implement the following guidelines to improve the security of their mobile devices:

- Organizations deploying mobile devices should consider the merits of each provided security service, determine which services are needed for their environment, and then design and acquire one or more solutions that collectively provide the necessary services. Most organizations do not need all of the possible security services provided by mobile device solutions. Categories of services to be considered include the following:

- **General policy:** Enforcing enterprise security policies on the mobile device, such as restricting access to hardware and device features, managing wireless network interfaces, detecting changes to approved security baseline, and limiting or denying access to devices with an unapproved OS (including jailbroken/rooted devices).
- **Data communication and storage:** Supporting strongly encrypted data communications and data storage, wiping the device before reissuing it, and remotely wiping the device if it is lost or stolen and is at risk of having its data recovered by an untrusted party.
- **User and device authentication:** Requiring device authentication and/or other authentication before accessing organization resources, resetting forgotten passwords remotely, automatically locking idle devices, and remotely locking devices suspected of being left unlocked in an unsecured location.
- **Applications:** Restricting which app stores may be used and which applications may be installed, restricting the permissions assigned to each application, installing and updating applications, restricting the use of synchronization services, verifying digital signatures on applications, and distributing the organization's applications from a dedicated mobile application store.

- Organizations should implement and test a pilot of their mobile device solution before putting the solution into production. Aspects of the solution that should be evaluated for each type of mobile device include connectivity, protection, authentication, application functionality, solution management, logging, and performance. Another important consideration is the security of the mobile device implementation itself; at a minimum, all components should be updated with the latest patches and configured following sound security practices. Also, use of jailbroken or rooted mobile devices should be automatically detected when feasible. Finally, administrators should ensure that the mobile device solution does not unexpectedly "fall back" to default settings for interoperability or other reasons.
- Organizations should fully secure each organization-issued mobile device before allowing a user to access it. This ensures a basic level of trust in the device before it is exposed to threats. For any already-deployed organization-issued mobile device with an unknown security profile (e.g., an unmanaged device), organizations should fully secure them to a known good state (for example, through deployment and use of enterprise mobile device

management technologies). Supplemental security controls should be deployed as risk merits, such as antivirus software and data loss prevention (DLP) technologies.

- Organizations should regularly maintain mobile device security. Helpful operational processes for maintenance include checking for upgrades and patches, and acquiring, testing, and deploying them; ensuring that each mobile device infrastructure component has its clock synced to a common time source; reconfiguring access control features as needed; and detecting and documenting anomalies within the mobile device infrastructure, including unauthorized configuration changes to mobile devices. Other helpful maintenance processes are keeping an active inventory of each mobile device, its user, and its applications; revoking access to or deleting an application that has already been installed but has subsequently been assessed as too risky to use; and scrubbing sensitive data from mobile devices before reissuing them to other users. Also, organizations should periodically perform assessments to confirm that their mobile device policies, processes, and procedures are being followed properly. Assessment activities may be passive, such as reviewing logs, or active, such as performing vulnerability scans and penetration testing.

The main threats when dealing with mobile devices include

- Lack of physical security controls
- Use of untrusted mobile devices
- Use of untrusted networks
- Use of untrusted applications
- Interaction with other systems
- Use of untrusted content
- Use of location services

NIST SP 800-124 Rev. 2 makes several recommendations for mobile devices. General policy restrictions of particular interest for mobile device security include the following:

- Restrict user and application access to hardware, such as the digital camera, GPS, Bluetooth interface, USB interface, and removable storage.
- Restrict user and application access to native OS services, such as the built-in web browser, email client, calendaring, contacts, application installation services, and so on.

- Manage wireless network interfaces (Wi-Fi, Bluetooth, and so on).
- Automatically monitor, detect, and report when policy violations occur, such as changes from the approved security configuration baseline, and automatically take action when possible and appropriate.
- Limit or prevent access to enterprise services based on the mobile device's operating system version (including whether the device has been rooted/jailbroken), vendor/brand, model, or mobile device management software client version (if applicable). Note that this information may be spoofable.

Data communication and storage restrictions for mobile device security include the following:

- Strongly encrypt data communications between the mobile device and the organization.
- Strongly encrypt stored data on both built-in storage and removable media storage.
- Wipe the device (to scrub its stored data) before reissuing it to another user, retiring the device, and so on.
- Remotely wipe the device (to scrub its stored data) if it is suspected that the device has been lost, stolen, or otherwise fallen into untrusted hands and is at risk of having its data recovered by an untrusted party.

User and device authentication restrictions for mobile device security include the following:

- Require a device password/passcode and/or other authentication (e.g., token-based authentication, network-based device authentication, domain authentication) before accessing the organization's resources.
- If device account lockout is enabled or the device password/passcode is forgotten, an administrator can reset it remotely to restore access to the device.
- Have the device automatically lock itself after it is idle for a period (e.g., 5 minutes).
- Under the direction of an administrator, remotely lock the device if it is suspected that the device has been left in an unlocked state in an unsecured location.
- After a certain number of unsuccessful attempts to authenticate, then the device should be wiped.

Application restrictions for mobile device security include the following:

- Restrict which app stores may be used.
- Restrict which applications may be installed through whitelisting (preferable) or blacklisting.
- Restrict the permissions (e.g., camera access, location access) assigned to each application.
- Install, update, and remove applications. Safeguard the mechanisms used to perform these actions.
- Restrict the use of operating system and application synchronization services (e.g., local device synchronization, remote synchronization services, and websites).
- Distribute the organization's applications from a dedicated mobile application store.

For more information on mobile device security recommendations, download NIST SP 800-124 Rev. 2 from https://nvlpubs.nist.gov/nistpubs/SpecialPublications/NIST.SP.800-124r2.pdf.

Network Routing

Routing occurs at Layer 3 of the OSI model, which is also the layer at which IP operates and where the source and destination IP addresses are placed in the packet. Routers are devices that transfer traffic between systems in different IP networks. When computers are in different IP networks, they cannot communicate unless a router is available to route the packets to the other networks.

Routers keep information about the paths to other networks in a routing table. These tables can be populated in several ways. Administrators manually enter these routes, or dynamic routing protocols allow the routers running the same protocol to exchange routing tables and routing information. Manual configuration, also called static routing, has the advantage of avoiding the additional traffic created by dynamic routing protocols and allows for precise control of routing behavior, but it requires manual intervention when link failures occur. Dynamic routing protocols create traffic but are able to react to link outages and reroute traffic without manual intervention.

From a security standpoint, routing protocols introduce the possibility that routing update traffic might be captured, allowing hackers to gain valuable information about the layout of the network. Moreover, Cisco devices (perhaps the most widely used) by default also use a proprietary Layer 2 protocol, called Cisco Discovery Protocol (CDP), to inform each other about their capabilities. If the CDP packets are captured, additional information can be obtained that can be helpful to mapping the network in advance of an attack.

In the following sections, we compare and contrast routing protocols.

Distance Vector, Link State, or Hybrid Routing

Routing protocols have different capabilities and operational characteristics that impact when and where they are utilized. Routing protocols come in two basic types: interior and exterior. Interior routing protocols are used within an autonomous system, which is a network managed by one set of administrators, typically a single enterprise. Exterior routing protocols route traffic between systems or company networks. An example of this type of routing is what occurs on the Internet.

Routing protocols also can fall into three categories that describe their operations more than their scope: distance vector, link state, and hybrid (or advanced distance vector). The difference in them mostly revolves around the amount of traffic created and the method used to determine the best path out of possible paths to a network. The value used to make this decision is called a metric, and each routing protocol category has a different way of calculating the metric and thus determining the best path.

Distance vector protocols share their entire routing table with their neighboring routers on a schedule, thereby creating the most traffic of the three categories. They also use a metric called *hop count*. Hop count is simply the number of routers a packet traverses from the source to get to a destination.

Link state protocols share network changes (link outages and recoveries) only with neighbors, thereby greatly reducing the amount of traffic generated. They also use a much more sophisticated metric that is based on many factors, such as the bandwidth of each link on the path and the congestion on each link. Therefore, when using one of these protocols, a path might be chosen as best even though it has more hops because the path chosen has better bandwidth, meaning less congestion.

Hybrid or advanced distance vector protocols exhibit characteristics of both types. EIGRP, discussed a bit later, is the only example of this type. In the past, EIGRP was referred to as a hybrid protocol, but in the last several years, Cisco (which created IGRP and EIGRP) has been calling this an advanced distance vector protocol, so both terms might be used. In the following sections, we briefly discuss several of the most common routing protocols.

RIP

Routing Information Protocol (RIP) is a standards-based distance vector protocol that has two versions: RIPv1 and RIPv2. It operates at Layer 3 (Network layer).

Both use hop count as a metric and share their entire routing tables every 30 seconds. Although RIP is the simplest to configure, it has a maximum hop count of 15, so it is useful only in very small networks. The biggest difference between the two versions is that RIPv1 can only perform classful routing, whereas RIPv2 can route in a network where CIDR has been implemented.

Unlike RIPv1, RIPv2 carries a subnet mask. It supports password authentication security and specifies the next hop.

OSPF

Open Shortest Path First (OSPF) is a standards-based link state protocol. It uses a metric called cost that is calculated based on many considerations. It operates at Layer 3 (Network layer). OSPF makes much more sophisticated routing decisions than a distance vector routing protocol such as RIP. To take full of advantage of OSPF, a much deeper knowledge of routing and OSPF itself is required. It can scale successfully to very large networks because it has no minimum hop count.

OSPFv2 allows routers to communicate with other routers regarding the routes they know. Link state advertisements (LSAs) are used to communicate the routes between the routers.

IGRP

Interior Gateway Routing Protocol (IGRP) is an obsolete classful Cisco-proprietary routing protocol that is not likely used in the real world because of its inability to operate in an environment where CIDR has been implemented. It has been replaced with the classless version Enhanced IGRP (EIGRP), discussed next.

EIGRP

Enhanced IGRP (EIGRP) is a classless Cisco-proprietary routing protocol that is considered a hybrid or advanced distance vector protocol. It exhibits some characteristics of both link state and distance vector operations. It also has no limitations on hop count and is much simpler to implement than OSPF. It does, however, require that all routers be Cisco.

VRRP

When a router goes down, all hosts that use that router for routing will be unable to send traffic to other networks. ***Virtual Router Redundancy Protocol (VRRP)*** is not really a routing protocol but rather is used to provide multiple gateways to clients for fault tolerance in the case of a router going down. All hosts in a network are set with the IP address of the virtual router as their default gateway. Multiple physical routers are mapped to this address, so there will be an available router even if one goes down.

IS-IS

Intermediate System to Intermediate System (IS-IS) is a complex interior routing protocol that is based on OSI protocols rather than IP. It is a link state protocol. The TCP/IP implementation is called Integrated IS-IS. OSPF has more functionality, but IS-IS creates less traffic than OSPF and is much less widely implemented than OSPF.

BGP

Border Gateway Protocol (BGP) is an exterior routing protocol considered to be a path vector protocol. It routes between autonomous systems (ASs) or gateway hosts and is used on the Internet. It has a rich set of attributes that administrators can manipulate to control path selection and to control the exact way in which traffic enters and exits the AS. However, it is one of the most complex to understand and configure. BGP is an Application layer (Layer 7 of OSI) protocol.

Transmission Media

The transmission media used on a network is the cabling that is used to transmit network traffic. Each of the different transmission media has a maximum speed, maximum distance, different security issues, and different environment. In the following sections, we discuss the cabling, network topologies, network performance metrics, network technologies, and WAN technologies that are covered in the CISSP exam.

Cabling

Although it's true that a cabled network is easier to secure from eavesdropping than a wireless network, security professionals must still be aware of some security issues. They should also understand some general behaviors of cabling that affect performance and ultimately can affect availability. As discussed in the previous chapters, maintaining availability to the network is also one of the goals of CIA. Therefore, performance characteristics of cabling that can impact availability are also discussed.

Noise is a term used to cover several types of interference that can be introduced to the cable and cause problems. In general, noise is defined as any unwanted information. Noise can be from large electrical motors, other computers, lighting, and other sources. This noise combines with the data signals (packets) on the line and distorts the signal. When even a single bit in a transmission is misread (read as a 1 when it should be a 0 or vice versa), corrupted data is received, and retransmissions must occur. Retransmissions lead to lower throughput and in some cases no throughput whatsoever.

In any case, where noise becomes a problem, the simplest way to mitigate the problem is to use shielded cabling. In cases where the noise is still present, locating the specific source and taking measures to remove it (or at least the interference it is generating) from the environment might be necessary.

Although cabling is a bounded media and much easier to secure than wireless, eavesdropping can still occur. All cabling that depends on electrical voltages, such as coaxial and twisted pair, can be tapped or monitored with the right equipment. The least susceptible to eavesdropping (although not completely immune) is fiber optic cabling because it doesn't use electrical voltages, but rather light waves. In any situation where eavesdropping is a concern, using fiber optic cabling can be a measure that will at least drastically raise the difficulty of eavesdropping. The real solution is ensuring physical security of the cabling. The cable runs should not be open, visible, and available to attackers.

Cabling resides at the physical layer of the OSI model and simply provides a medium by which data can be transferred. The vast majority of data is transferred across cables of various types, including coaxial, fiber optic, and twisted pair. Some of these cables represent the data in terms of electrical voltages, whereas fiber cables manipulate light to represent the data. Here, we discuss each type.

Attenuation is the weakening of the signal as it travels down the cable and meets resistance. In the discussion on cabling earlier in this chapter, you learned that all cables have a recommended maximum length. When a cable that is longer than its recommended length is used, attenuation weakens the signal to the point it cannot be read correctly, resulting in the same problem that is the end result of noise. The data must be sent again, lowering throughput.

The solution to this problem is in design. Follow the cable length recommendations listed in the section on cables earlier in this chapter with any type of cabling. This includes coaxial, twisted pair, and fiber optic. All types have maximum lengths that should not be exceeded without risking attenuation.

Another important point of comparison between cable types is their data rate, which describes how much data can be sent through the cable per second. This area has seen great improvement over the years, going from rates of 10 Mbps in a LAN to 1000 Mbps and even 10 Gbps in today's networks (and even higher rates in data centers).

Another consideration when selecting a cable type is the ease of installation. Some cable types are easier than others to install, and fiber optic cabling requires a special skill set to install, raising its price of installation.

Finally (and most importantly for this discussion) is the security of the cable. Cables can leak or radiate information. Hackers can also tap into them if they have physical access to the cables. Just as the cable types can vary in allowable length and capacity, they can also vary in their susceptibility to these types of data losses.

Coaxial

One of the earliest cable types to be used for networking was ***coaxial***, the same basic type of cable that brought cable TV to millions of homes. Although coaxial cabling is still used, due to its low capacity and the adoption of other cable types, its use is almost obsolete now in LANs.

Coaxial cabling comes in two types or thicknesses. The thicker type, called ***Thicknet***, has the official name 10BASE-5. This naming system, used for other cable types as well, imparts several facts about the cable. In the case of 10BASE-5, it means that it is capable of transferring 10 Mbps and can go roughly 1,640 feet. Thicknet uses two types of connectors: a vampire tap (named thusly because it has a spike that pierces the cable) and N-connectors.

Thinnet, or 10BASE-2, also operates at 10 Mbps. When it was named, it was anticipated to be capable of running 200 feet, but this distance was later reduced to 185 feet. Both types are used in a bus topology (more on topologies in the section "Network Topologies," later in this chapter). Thinnet uses two types of connectors: BNC connectors and T-connectors.

Coaxial has an outer cylindrical covering that surrounds either a solid core wire (Thicknet) or a braided core (Thinnet). This type of cabling has been replaced over time with more capable twisted pair and fiber optic cabling. Coaxial cabling can be tapped, so physical access to this cabling should be restricted or prevented if possible. It should be out of sight if it is used. Figure 4-35 shows the structure of a coaxial cable.

Key Topic

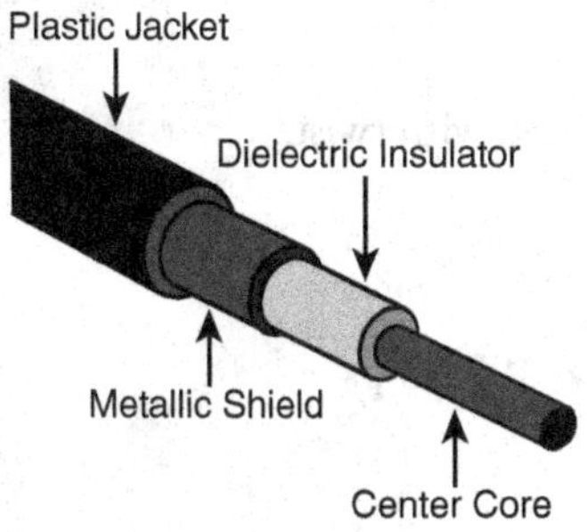

Figure 4-35 Coaxial Cabling

Another security problem with coax in a bus topology is that it is broadcast-based, which means a sniffer attached anywhere in the network can capture all traffic. In switched networks (more on that topic earlier in this chapter, in the section "Network Devices"), this is not a consideration.

Twisted Pair

The most common type of network cabling found today is called ***twisted pair*** cabling. It has this name because inside the cable are four pairs of smaller wires that are braided or twisted. This twisting is designed to eliminate a phenomenon called ***crosstalk***, which occurs when wires that are inside a cable interfere with one another. The number of wire pairs that are used depends on the implementation. In some implementations, only two pairs are used, and in others, all four wire pairs are used. Figure 4-36 shows the structure of a twisted pair cable.

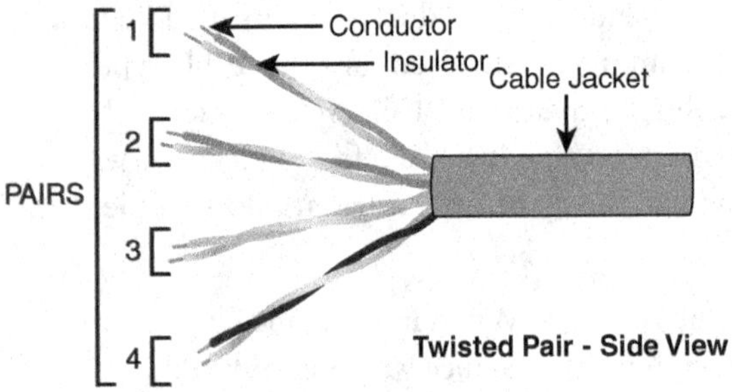

Figure 4-36 Twisted Pair Cabling

Twisted pair cabling comes in shielded (STP) and unshielded (UTP) versions. Nothing is gained from the shielding except protection from ***radio frequency interference (RFI)*** and ***electromagnetic interference (EMI)***. RFI is interference from radio sources in the area, whereas EMI is interference from power lines. A common type of EMI is called common mode noise, which is interference that appears on both signal leads (signal and circuit return) or the terminals of a measuring circuit and ground. If neither EMI nor RFI is a problem, nothing is gained by using STP, and it costs more.

The same naming system used with coaxial and fiber is used with twisted pair. The following are the major types of twisted pair:

- **10BASE-T:** Operates at 10 Mbps
- **100BASE-T:** Also called Fast Ethernet; operates at 100 Mbps

- **1000BASE-T:** Also called Gigabit Ethernet; operates at 1000 Mbps
- **10GBASE-T:** Operates at 10 Gbps

Twisted pair cabling comes in various capabilities and is rated in categories. Table 4-9 lists the major types and their characteristics. Regardless of the category, twisted pair cabling can be run about 100 meters before attenuation degrades the signal.

Key Topic

Table 4-9 Twisted Pair Categories

Name	Maximum Transmission Speed
Cat3	10 Mbps
Cat4	16 Mbps
Cat5	100 Mbps
Cat5e	100 Mbps
Cat6	1 Gbps
Cat6a	10 Gbps
Cat7	10 Gbps
Cat7a	10 Gbps; 40 Gbps (50 meters); 100 Gbps (15 meters)

Fiber Optic

Fiber optic cabling transmits light beams that are transmitted through an inner glass or plastic core of the cable. This core is covered by cladding that causes light to be confined to the core of the fiber. It is often used as the network backbone and may even be seen in home Internet, phone, and cable TV implementations. Figure 4-37 shows the structure of a fiber optic cable.

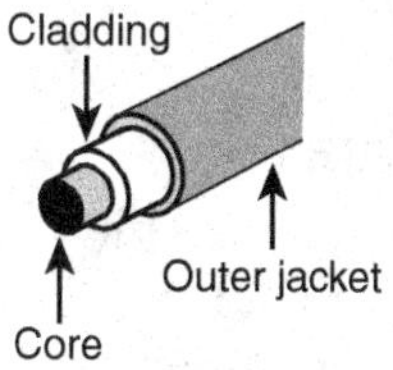

Figure 4-37 Fiber Optic Cabling

Fiber optic cabling manipulates light such that it can be interpreted as binary data ones and zeros. Because it is not electrically based, it is totally impervious to EMI,

RFI, and crosstalk. Moreover, although not impossible, tapping or eavesdropping on a fiber cable is much more difficult. In most cases, attempting to tap into it results in a failure of the cable, which then becomes quite apparent to all.

Fiber comes in single- and multimode formats. The single mode uses a single beam of light provided by a laser, goes the farthest of the two, and is the most expensive. Multimode uses several beams of light at the same time, uses LEDs, will not go as far, and is less expensive. Either type goes much farther than electrical cabling in a single run and also typically provides more capacity. Fiber cabling has its drawbacks, however. It is the most expensive to purchase and the most expensive to install. Table 4-10 shows some selected fiber specifications and their theoretical maximum distances.

Table 4-10 Selected Fiber Specifications

Standard	Distance
100BASE-FX	Maximum length is 400 meters for half-duplex connections (to ensure collisions are detected) or 2 kilometers for full-duplex
1000BAASE-SX	550 meters
1000BASE-LX	***Multimode fiber*** (up to 550 meters) or ***single-mode fiber*** (up to 2 kilometers; can be optimized for longer distances, up to 10 kilometers)
10GBASE-LR	10 kilometers
10GBASE-ER	40 kilometers

Network Topologies

Networks can be described by their logical topology (the data path used) and by their physical topology (the way in which devices are connected to one another). In most cases (but not all), the logical topology and the physical topology will be the same. Next, we discuss both logical and physical network topologies.

Ring

A physical ***ring topology*** is one in which the devices are daisy-chained one to another in a circle or ring. If the network is also a logical ring, the data circles the ring from one device to another. Two technologies use this topology: FDDI and Token Ring. Both of these technologies are discussed in detail in the upcoming section "Network Technologies." Figure 4-38 shows a typical ring topology.

One of the drawbacks of the ring topology is that if a break occurs in the line, all systems will be affected because the ring will be broken. As described in the section "Network Technologies," an FDDI network addresses this issue with a double ring for fault tolerance.

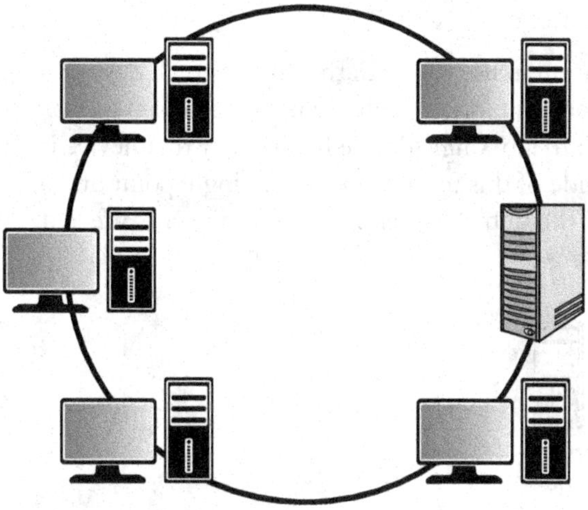

Figure 4-38 Ring Topology

Bus

The ***bus topology*** was the earliest Ethernet topology used. In this topology, all devices are connected to a single line that has two definitive endpoints. The bus network does *not* loop back and form a ring. This topology is broadcast-based, which can be a security issue in that a sniffer or protocol analyzer connected at any point in the network bus will be capable of capturing all traffic. From a fault tolerance standpoint, the bus topology suffers the same danger as a ring. If a break occurs anywhere in the line, all devices are affected. Moreover, a requirement specific to this topology is that each end of the bus must be terminated. This requirement prevents signals from "bouncing" back on the line, causing collisions. (More on collisions later, but collisions require the collided packets to be sent again, lowering overall throughput.) If this termination is not done properly, the network will not function correctly. Figure 4-39 shows a bus topology.

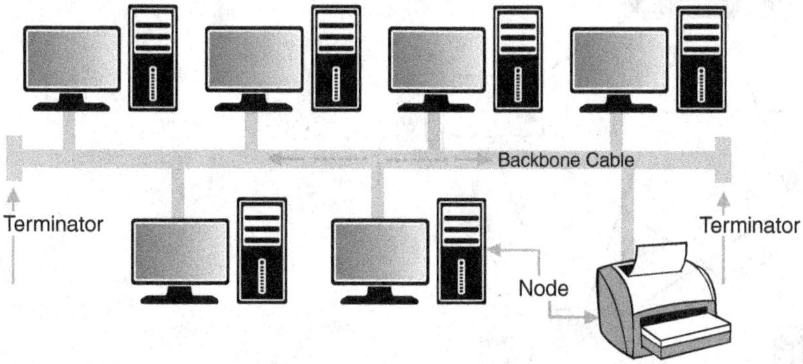

Figure 4-39 Bus Topology

Star

The ***star topology*** is the most common in use today. In this topology, all devices are connected to a central device (either a hub or a switch). One of the advantages of this topology is that if a connection to any single device breaks, *only* that device is affected and no others. The downside of this topology is that a single point of failure (the hub or switch) exists. If the hub or switch fails, all devices are affected. Figure 4-40 shows a star topology.

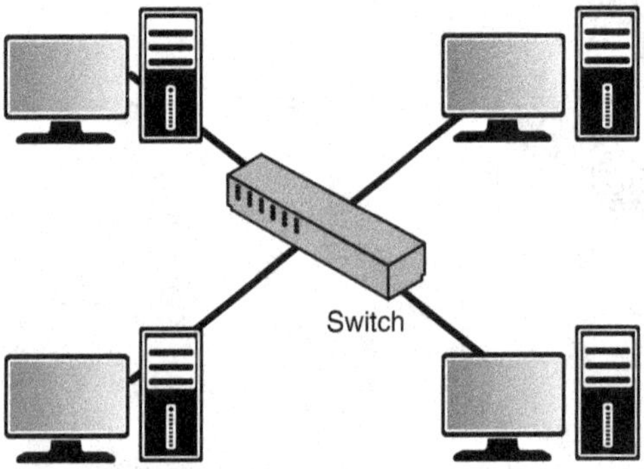

Figure 4-40 Star Topology

Mesh

Although the ***mesh topology*** is the most fault tolerant of any discussed thus far, it is also the most expensive to deploy. In this topology, all devices are connected to all other devices. This provides complete fault tolerance but also requires multiple interfaces and cables on each device. For that reason, it is deployed only in rare circumstances where such an expense is warranted. Figure 4-41 shows a mesh topology.

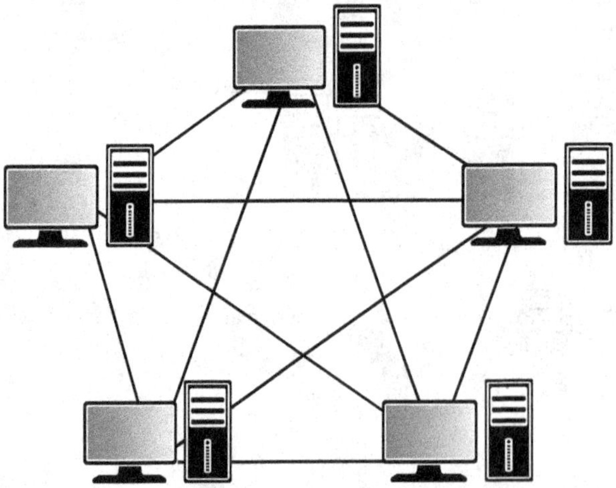

Figure 4-41 Mesh Topology

Hybrid

In many cases, an organization's network is a combination of these network topologies, or a ***hybrid*** network. For example, one section might be a star that connects to a bus network or a ring network. Figure 4-42 shows an example of a hybrid network.

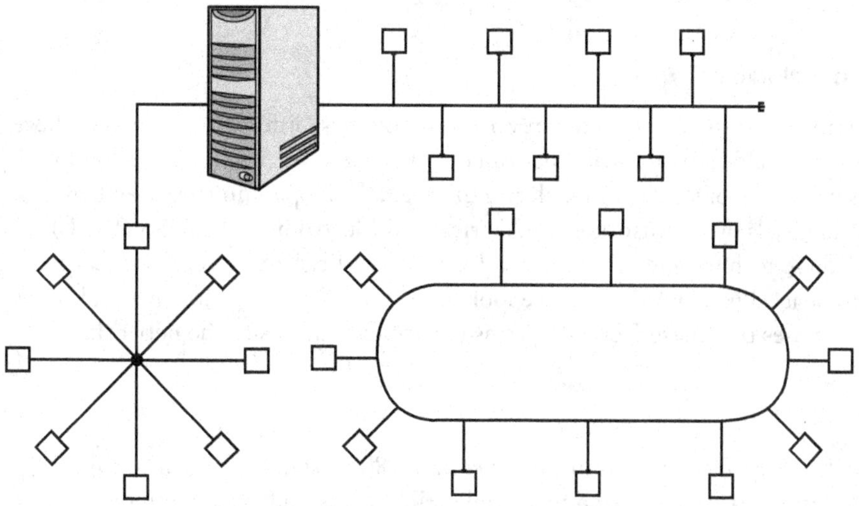

Figure 4-42 Hybrid Topology

Performance Metrics

Several performance metrics are used to measure network reliability, quality of service, and speed. One such metric is ***bandwidth***, which measures the capacity of a wired or wireless network. More specifically, bandwidth refers to the number of bits, kilobits, megabits, or gigabits that can be sent within a set time, usually per second. The greater the bandwidth the more data that can be sent per second. ***Latency*** refers to the time it takes for data to be transmitted from one endpoint to another endpoint on a network, and is measured in milliseconds. Consequently, latency impacts the user experience; higher latency means that it takes the user longer to see a response to a request on a network. In an age where we rely more on the cloud for storage, data is often physically further away from a client computer. Therefore, a response to a data request can take more time to be completed, which means greater latency. ***Jitter*** refers to disruption or uneven intervals between data packets being transmitted—sometimes referred to as packet delay variation (PDV). Jitter can occur with real-time applications, such as video streaming and VoIP calls, where speed of delivery is prioritized over the negative effects of jitter. There are several services that perform Internet service speed tests that indicate jitter in milliseconds. ***Throughput*** measures how much data was actually transmitted from a source to a destination, within a specified timeframe. This is different from bandwidth, which is a theoretical measurement (i.e., how much data could potentially be transferred). Throughput is often measured in bits per second. ***Signal-to-noise ratio (SNR)*** is a comparison between the power of a signal (or amplitude) and unwanted noise. This measurement is often denoted in decibels (dB), and the higher the SNR the better. As previously noted, noise refers to background noise, such as people talking in the background.

Network Technologies

Just as a network can be connected in various topologies, different technologies have been implemented over the years that run over those topologies. These technologies operate at Layer 2 of the OSI model, and their details of operation are specified in various standards by the Institute of Electrical and Electronics Engineers (IEEE). Some of these technologies are designed for LAN applications, whereas others are meant to be used in a WAN. Next, we look at the main LAN technologies and some of the processes that these technologies use to arbitrate access to the network.

Ethernet 802.3

The IEEE specified the details of ***Ethernet*** in the 802.3 standard. Prior to this standardization, Ethernet existed in several earlier forms, the most common of which was called Ethernet II or DIX Ethernet (DIX stands for the three companies that collaborated on its creation, DEC, Intel, and Xerox).

As discussed in the section on the OSI model, the PDU created at Layer 2 is called a frame. Because Ethernet is a Layer 2 protocol, the individual Ethernet packets are referred to as *frames*. There are small differences in the frame structures of Ethernet II and 802.3, although they are compatible in the same network. Figure 4-43 shows a comparison of the two frames. The significant difference is that during the IEEE standardization process, the Ethernet Type field was changed to a (data) length field in the 802.3 standard. For purposes of identifying the data type, another field called the 802.2 header was inserted to contain that information.

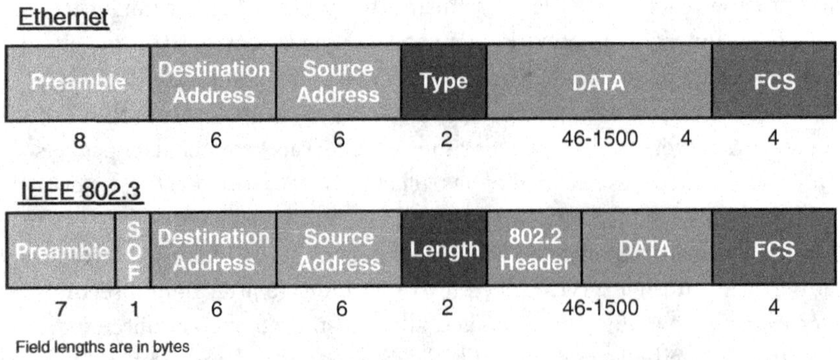

Figure 4-43 Ethernet II and 802.3

Ethernet has been implemented on coaxial, fiber, and twisted pair wiring. Table 4-11 lists some of the more common Ethernet implementations.

Table 4-11 Ethernet Implementations

Ethernet Type	Cable Type	Speed
10BASE-2	Coaxial	10 Mbps
10BASE-5	Coaxial	10 Mbps
10BASE-T	Twisted pair	10 Mbps
100BASE-TX	Twisted pair	100 Mbps
1000BASE-T	Twisted pair	1000 Mbps
1000BASE-X	Fiber	1000 Mbps
10GBASE-T	Twisted pair	10 Gbps

NOTE Despite the fact that 1000BASE-T and 1000BASE-X are faster, 100BASE-TX is called *Fast Ethernet*. Also, both 1000BASE-T and 1000BASE-X are usually referred to as Gigabit Ethernet.

Ethernet calls for devices to share the medium on a frame-by-frame basis. It arbitrates access to the media using a process called Carrier Sense Multiple Access/Collision Detection (CSMA/CD). This process is discussed in detail in the upcoming section "CSMA/CD Versus CSMA/CA," where it is contrasted with the method used in 802.11 wireless networks.

Token Ring 802.5

Ethernet is the most common Layer 2 protocol, but it has not always been that way. An example of a proprietary Layer 2 protocol that enjoyed some small success is IBM ***Token Ring***. This protocol operates using specific IBM connective devices and cables, and the nodes must have Token Ring network cards installed. It can operate at 16 Mbps, which at the time of its release was impressive, but the proprietary nature of the equipment and the soon-to-be faster Ethernet caused Token Ring to fall from favor.

As mentioned earlier, in most cases the physical network topology is the same as the logical topology. Token Ring is the exception to that general rule. It is logically a ring and physically a star. It is a star in that all devices are connected to a central device called a media access unit (MAU), but the ring is formed in the MAU, and the flow of the data goes from one device to another in a ring design by entering and exiting each port of the MAU, as shown in Figure 4-44.

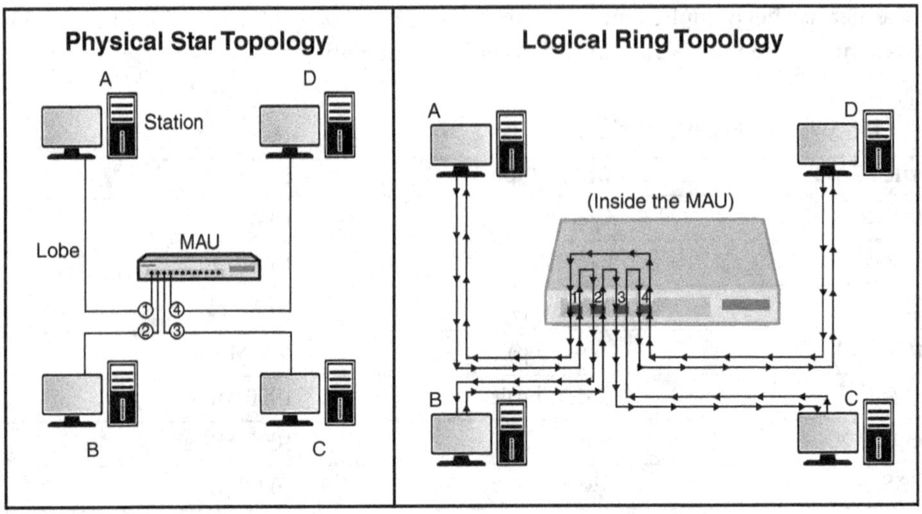

Figure 4-44 Token Ring

FDDI

Another Layer 2 protocol that uses a ring topology is ***Fiber Distributed Data Interface (FDDI)***. Unlike Token Ring, it is both a physical and a logical ring. It is actually a double ring, each going in a different direction to provide fault tolerance. It also is implemented with fiber cabling. In many cases, it is used for a network backbone and is then connected to other network types, such as Ethernet, forming a hybrid network. It is also used in metropolitan-area networks (MANs) because it can be deployed up to 100 kilometers.

Figure 4-45 shows an example of an FDDI ring.

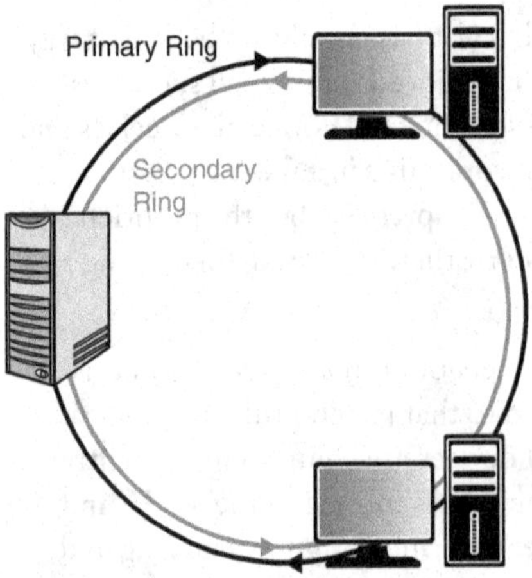

Figure 4-45 FDDI

Contention Methods

Regardless of the Layer 2 protocol in use, some method must be used to arbitrate the use of the shared media. Four basic processes have been employed to act as the traffic cop, so to speak:

- CSMA/CD
- CSMA/CA
- Token passing
- Polling

In the following sections, we compare and contrast each and provide examples of technologies that use each.

CSMA/CD Versus CSMA/CA

To appreciate ***Carrier Sense Multiple Access with Collision Detection (CSMA/CD)*** and ***Carrier Sense Multiple Access with Collision Avoidance (CSMA/CA)***, you must understand the concept of collisions and collision domains in a shared network medium. Collisions occur when two devices send a frame at the same time, causing the frames and their underlying electrical signals to collide on the wire. When this situation occurs, both signals and the frames they represent are destroyed or at the very least corrupted such that they are discarded when they reach the destination. Frame corruption or disposal causes both devices to resend the frames, resulting in a drop in overall throughput.

Collision Domains

A collision domain is any segment of the network where the possibility exists for two or more devices' signals to collide. In a bus topology, that would constitute the entire network because the entire bus is a shared medium. In a star topology, the scope of the collision domain or domains depends on the central connecting device. Central connecting devices include hubs and switches. Hubs and switches are discussed in more detail in the earlier section "Network Devices," but here we need to discuss their differences with respect to collision domains.

A hub is an unintelligent junction box into which all devices plug. All the ports in the hub are in the same collision domain because when a hub receives a frame, the hub broadcasts the frame out all ports. So logically, the network is still a bus.

A star topology with a switch in the center does not operate this way. A switch has the intelligence to record the MAC address of each device on every port. After all the devices' MAC addresses are recorded, the switch sends a frame *only* to the port on which the destination device resides. Because each device's traffic is then segregated from any other device's traffic, each device is considered to be in its own collision domain.

This segregation provided by switches has both performance and security benefits. From a performance perspective, it greatly reduces the number of collisions, thereby significantly increasing overall throughput in the network. From a security standpoint, it means that a sniffer connected to a port in the switch will capture *only* traffic destined for that port, not all traffic. Compare this security to a hub-centric network. When a hub is in the center of a star network, a sniffer will capture all traffic regardless of the port to which it is connected because all ports are in the same collision domain.

In Figure 4-46, a switch has several devices and a hub connected to it, with each collision domain marked to show how the two devices create collision domains. Note that each port on the switch is a collision domain, whereas the entire hub is a single collision domain.

Collision Domains

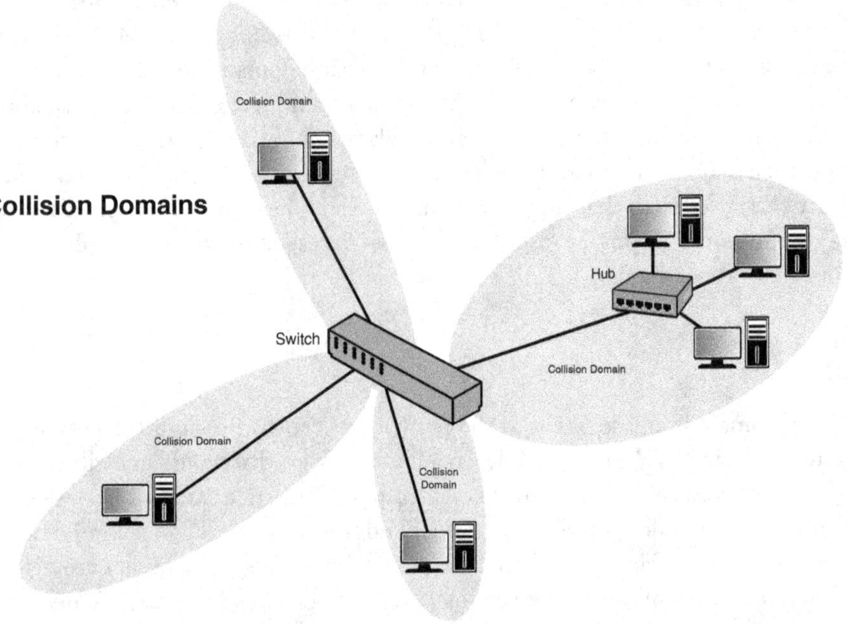

Figure 4-46 Collision Domains

CSMA/CD

In 802.3 networks, a mechanism called Carrier Sense Multiple Access/Collision Detection (CSMA/CD) is used when a shared medium is in use to recover from inevitable collisions. This process is a step-by-step mechanism that each station follows every time it needs to send a single frame. The steps to the process are as follows:

1. When a device needs to transmit, it checks the wire for existing traffic. This process is called carrier sense.
2. If the wire is clear, the device transmits and continues to perform carrier sense.
3. If a collision is detected, both devices issue a jam signal to all the other devices, which indicates to them to *not* transmit. Then both devices increment a retransmission counter. This is a cumulative total of the number of times this frame has been transmitted and a collision occurred. There is a maximum number at which it aborts the transmission of the frame.
4. Both devices calculate a random amount of time (called a random back-off) and wait that amount of time before transmitting again.
5. In most cases, because both devices choose random amounts of time to wait, another collision will not occur. If it does, the procedure repeats.

CSMA/CA

In 802.11 wireless networks, CSMA/CD cannot be used as an arbitration method because, unlike when using bounded media, the devices cannot detect a collision. The method used is called Carrier Sense Multiple Access/Collision Avoidance (CSMA/CA). This process is much more laborious because each station must acknowledge each frame that is transmitted.

The "Wireless Networks" section (earlier in this chapter) covers 802.11 network operations in more detail, but for the purposes of understanding CSMA/CA, we must at least lay some groundwork. The typical wireless network contains an access point (AP) and at least one or more wireless stations. In this type of network (called an infrastructure mode wireless network), traffic never traverses directly between stations but is always relayed through the AP. The steps in CSMA/CA are as follows:

1. Station A has a frame to send to Station B. It checks for traffic in two ways. First, it performs carrier sense, which means it listens to see whether any radio waves are being received on its transmitter. Second, after the transmission is sent, it will continue to monitor the network for possible collisions.
2. If traffic is being transmitted, Station A decrements an internal countdown mechanism called the random back-off algorithm. This counter would have started counting down after the last time this station was allowed to transmit. All stations will count down their own individual timers. When a station's timer expires, it is allowed to send.

3. If Station A performs carrier sense, there is no traffic, and its timer hits zero, it sends the frame.
4. The frame goes to the AP.
5. The AP sends an acknowledgment back to Station A. Until that acknowledgment is received by Station A, all other stations must remain silent. For each frame that the AP needs to relay, it must wait its turn to send using the same mechanism as the stations.
6. When its turn comes up in the cache queue, the frame from Station A is relayed to Station B.
7. Station B sends an acknowledgment back to the AP. Until that acknowledgment is received by the AP, all other stations must remain silent.

As you can see, these processes create a lot of overhead but are required to prevent collisions in a wireless network.

Token Passing

Both FDDI and Token Ring networks use a process called ***token passing***. In this process, a special packet called a token is passed around the network. A station cannot send until the token comes around and is empty. Using this process, no collisions occur because two devices are never allowed to send at the same time. The problem with this process is that the possibility exists for a single device to gain control of the token and monopolize the entire network.

Polling

The final contention method to discuss is ***polling***. In this system, a primary device polls every other device to see whether it needs to transmit. In this way, known as round robin, each device gets a transmit opportunity. This method is common in the mainframe environment.

WAN Technologies

Many different technologies have evolved for delivering WAN access to a LAN. They differ in capacity, availability, and, of course, cost. In the following sections, we compare the various technologies.

T Lines

T-carriers are dedicated lines to which the subscriber has private access and does not share with another customer. Customers can purchase an entire T1, or they can purchase a part of a T1 called a ***fractional T1***. T1 lines consist of 24 channels, each capable of 64 Kbps. This means a T1 has a total capacity of 1.544 Mbps. The T1 is split into channels through a process called time-division multiplexing (TDM).

The drawback of a T1 is that the customer is buying the full capacity of the number of channels purchased, and any capacity left unused is wasted. This inflexibility and the high cost have made this option less appealing than it was at one time. The cost is a function of not only the number of channels but the distance of the line as well.

T-carriers also come in larger increments. Table 4-12 shows a summary of T-carriers and their capacity.

Table 4-12 T-Carriers

Carrier	Number of Channels	Speed (Mbps)
Fractional	1	0.064
T1	24	1.544
T2	96	6.312
T3	672	44.736
T4	4,032	274.176
T5	5,760	400.352

E Lines

In Europe, a similar technology to T-carrier lines exists called ***E-carriers***. With this technology, 30 channels are bundled rather than 24. These technologies are not compatible, and the available sizes are a bit different. Table 4-13 shows some selected increments of E-carriers.

Table 4-13 E-Carriers

Signal	Rate
E0	64 Kbps
E1	2.048 Mbps
E2	8.448 Mbps
E3	34.368 Mbps
E4	139.264 Mbps
E5	565.148 Mbps

OC Lines (SONET)

Synchronous Optical Networking (SONET) uses fiber-based links that operate over lines measured in optical carrier (OC) transmission rates. These lines are defined by an integer value of the basic unit of rate. The basic OC-1 rate is 55.84 Mbps, and all other rates are multiples of that. For example, an OC-3 yields 155.52 Mbps. Table 4-14 shows some of these rates. A company might use the smaller increments, whereas a service provider would use the larger pipes.

Table 4-14 Carrier Rates

Optical Carrier	Speed
OC-3	155 Mbps
OC-12	622 Mbps
OC-48	2.5 Gbps
OC-192	9.6 Gbps

CSU/DSU

A discussion of WAN connections would not be complete without discussing a device that many customers connect to for their WAN connection. A ***channel service unit/data service unit (CSU/DSU)*** connects a LAN to a WAN. This device performs a translation of the information from a format that is acceptable on the LAN to one that can be transmitted over the WAN connection.

The CSU/DSU is considered a data communications equipment (DCE) device, and it provides an interface for the router, which is considered a data terminal equipment (DTE) device. The CSU/DSU will most likely be owned by the telco, but not always, and in some cases this functionality might be built into the interface of the router, making a separate device unnecessary.

Circuit Switching Versus Packet Switching

On the topic of WAN connections, discussing the types of networks that these connections might pass through is also helpful. Some are circuit-switched, whereas others are packet-switched. ***Circuit-switching networks*** (such as the telephone) establish a set path to the destination and use only that path for the entire communication. It results in a predictable operation with fixed delays. These networks usually carry voice-oriented traffic.

Packet-switching networks (such as the Internet or a LAN) establish an optimal *path-per-packet*. This means each packet might go a different route to get to the destination. The traffic on these networks experiences performance bursts, and the amount of delay can vary widely. These types of networks usually carry data-oriented traffic.

Frame Relay

Frame Relay is a Layer 2 (OSI model) protocol used for WAN connections. Therefore, when Ethernet traffic must traverse a Frame Relay link, the Layer 2 header of the packet will be completely re-created to conform to Frame Relay. When the Frame Relay frame arrives at the destination, a new Ethernet Layer 2 header will be placed on the packet for that portion of the network.

When Frame Relay connections are provisioned, the customer pays for a minimum amount of bandwidth called the Committed Information Rate (CIR). That will be the floor of performance. However, because Frame Relay is a packet-switched network using Frame Relay switches, the actual performance will vary based on conditions. Customers are sharing the network rather than having a dedicated line, such as a T1 or Integrated Services Digital Network (ISDN) line. So in many cases, the actual performance will exceed the CIR.

ATM

Asynchronous Transfer Mode (ATM) is a cell-switching technology. It transfers fixed-size cells of 53 bytes rather than packets, and after a path is established, it uses the same path for the entire communication. The use of a fixed path makes performance more predictable, making it a good option for voice and video, which need such predictability. Where IP networks depend on the source and destination devices to ensure data is properly transmitted, this responsibility falls on the shoulders of the devices between the two in the ATM world.

ATM is used mostly by carriers and service providers for their backbones, but some companies have implemented their own ATM backbones and ATM switches. This allows them to make an ATM connection to the carrier, which can save money over a connection with a T link because the ATM connection cost will be based on usage, unlike the fixed cost of the T1.

X.25

X.25 is somewhat like Frame Relay in that traffic moves through a packet-switching network. It charges by bandwidth used. The data is divided into 128-byte High-Level Data Link Control (HDLC) frames. It is, however, an older technology created in a time when noisy transmission lines were a big concern. Therefore, it has many built-in error-checking mechanisms that make it very inefficient.

Switched Multimegabit Data Service

Switched Multimegabit Data Service (SMDS) is a connectionless, packet-switched technology that communicates across an established public network. It has been largely repacked with other WAN technologies. It can provide LAN-like performance to a WAN. It is generally delivered over a SONET ring with a maximum effective service radius of around 30 miles.

Point-to-Point Protocol

Point-to-Point-Protocol (PPP) is a Layer 2 protocol that performs framing and encapsulation of data across point-to-point connections. These are connections to the ISP where only the customer device and the ISP device reside on either end. It can encapsulate several different LAN protocols such as TCP/IP. It does this by using a Network Core Protocol (NCP) for each of the LAN protocols in use.

Along with the use of multiple NCPs, it uses a single Link Control Protocol (LCP) to establish the connection. PPP provides the ability to authenticate the connection between the devices using either Password Authentication Protocol (PAP) or Challenge Handshake Authentication Protocol (CHAP). Whereas PAP transmits the credentials in cleartext, CHAP does *not* send the credentials across the line and is much safer.

High-Speed Serial Interface

High-Speed Serial Interface (HSSI) is one of the many physical implementations of a serial interface. Because these interfaces exist on devices, they are considered to operate at Layer 1 of the OSI model. The Physical layer is the layer that is concerned with the signaling of the message and the interface between the sender or receiver and the medium. Examples of other serial interfaces are

- X.25
- V.35
- X.21

The HSSI interface is found on both routers and multiplexers and provides a connection to services such as Frame Relay and ATM. It operates at speeds up to 52 Mbps.

PSTN (POTS, PBX)

Probably the least attractive WAN connection available, at least from a performance standpoint, is the ***public switched telephone network (PSTN)***. Also referred to as the

plain old telephone service (POTS), this is the circuit-switched network that has been used for analog phone service for years and is now mostly a digital operation.

This network can be utilized using modems for an analog line or with ISDN for digital phone lines. Both of these options are discussed in more detail in the section "Remote Connection Technologies" (later in this chapter) because that is their main use. In some cases, these connections might be used between offices but, due to the poor performance, typically only as a backup solution in case a more capable option fails. These connections must be established each time they are used as opposed to "always on" solutions, such as cable or DSL.

PBX devices are discussed in the earlier section "Network Devices."

VoIP

Although voice over the PSTN is circuit-switched, voice can also be encapsulated in packets and sent across packet-switching networks. When this is done over an IP network, it is called ***Voice over IP (VoIP)***. Where circuit-switching networks use the ***Signaling System 7 (SS7)*** protocol to set up, control, and disconnect a call, VoIP uses ***Session Initiation Protocol (SIP)*** to break up the call sessions. In VoIP implementations, QoS is implemented to ensure that certain traffic (especially voice) is given preferential treatment over the network.

SIP is an Application layer protocol that can operate over either TCP or UDP. Addressing is in terms of IP addresses, and the voice traffic uses the same network used for regular data. Because latency is always possible on these networks, protocols have been implemented to reduce the impact. Applications such as voice and video need to have protocols and devices that can provide an isochronous network. Isochronous networks guarantee continuous bandwidth without interruption. They do not use an internal clock source or start and stop bits. All bits are of equal importance and are anticipated to occur at regular intervals.

VoIP is also prone to attacks and can be secured by taking the following measures:

- Create a separate VLAN or subnet for the IP phones and prevent access to this VLAN by other computers.
- Deploy a VoIP-aware firewall at the perimeter.
- Ensure that all passwords related to VoIP are strong.
- Secure the Network layer with IPsec.

Network Access Control Devices

Key Topic

Network access control (NAC) is a service that goes beyond authentication of the user and includes an examination of the state of the computer the user is introducing to the network when making a remote access or VPN connection to the network.

The Cisco world calls these services Network Admission Control, and the Microsoft world calls them Network Access Protection (NAP). Regardless of the term used, the goals of the features are the same: to examine all devices requesting network access for malware, missing security updates, and any other security issues the devices could potentially introduce to the network.

The steps that occur in Microsoft NAP are shown in Figure 4-47. The health state of the device requesting access is collected and sent to the Network Policy Server (NPS), where the state is compared to requirements. If requirements are met, access is granted.

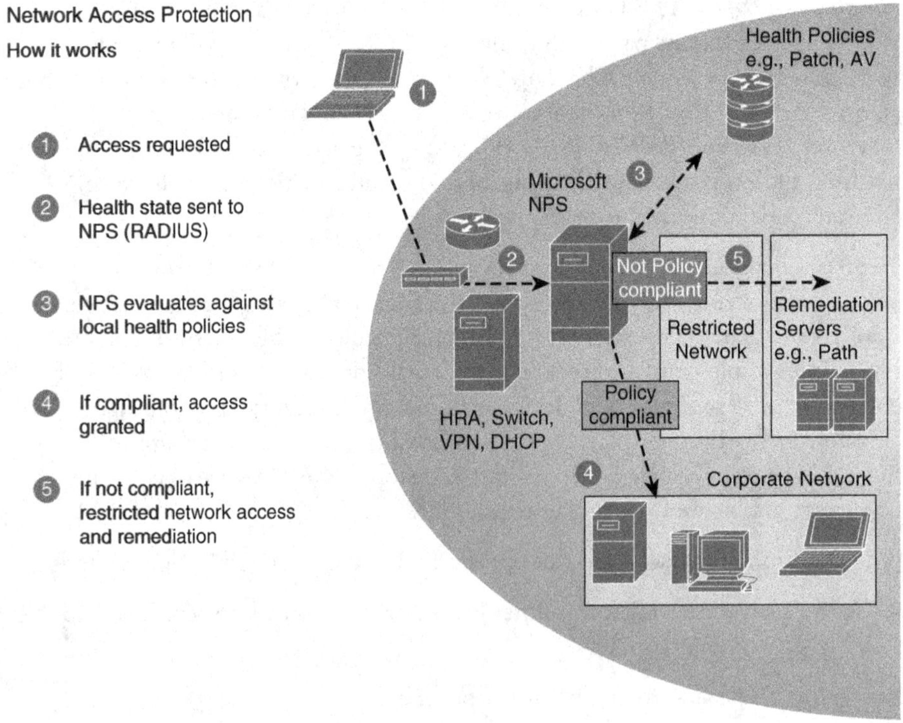

Figure 4-47 NAP Steps

These are the limitations of using NAC or NAP:

- They work well for company-managed computers but less so for an organization's guests.

- They tend to react only to known threats and not new threats.
- The return on investment is still unproven.
- Some implementations involve confusing configuration.

Quarantine/Remediation

If you examine step 5 in the process shown in Figure 4-46, you see that a device that fails examination is placed in a restricted network until it can be remediated. A remediation server addresses the problems discovered on the device. It may remove the malware, install missing operating system updates, or update virus definitions. When the remediation process is complete, the device is granted full access to the network.

Firewalls/Proxies

Firewalls and proxies can be used as part of NAC deployment. Firewalls enforce security rules by filtering incoming traffic by source address, destination address, or service. It is important that the rules be configured correctly to ensure that access to the network is not granted to malicious traffic or users. Proxies act as mediators between trusted and untrusted clients or servers. When proxies are deployed, it appears that all packets sent to the untrusted clients or servers originate with the proxies, thereby allowing all internal hosts to hide behind one public IP address.

NOTE Firewalls and proxies are discussed in more detail earlier in this chapter, in the "Hardware" section.

Network Access Control Systems

Network access control (NAC) systems allow organizations to enforce security policies to endpoints across the network. With the growth of Internet of Things (IoT) devices, such as smart thermostats, smart cameras, and Internet connected medical devices, there are more and more devices connecting to organizational networks, which puts these networks at risk—especially since many of these devices are inherently insecure and maintain poor security protocols. Additionally, as described earlier in the "Mobile Devices" sections, organizations are allowing more personal devices (e.g., mobile phones and tablets), referred to as BYOD, to access their network resources, which adds to the organization's network security risk.

NAC allows the organization to implement an enterprise security strategy that applies to IoT and BYOD. Consequently, a NAC system can deny IoT and BYOD devices access to network devices, or limited access to network resources, if they are deemed noncompliant with the organization's security policies, thereby reducing risk. Often a NAC system will allow a device to access the enterprise network once it becomes compliant with mandated protocols. For example, a mobile device updates its operating system or mobile application (app) to the latest version. A NAC system not only profiles and examines the device connecting to its network but also profiles the user of the device—meaning that there are different access privileges for employees versus contractors versus vendors versus partners or visitors.

Endpoint Security

Endpoint security is a field of security that attempts to protect individual systems in a network by staying in constant contact with these individual systems from a central location. Endpoint security typically works on a client/server model in that each system will have software that communicates with the software on the central server. The functionality provided can vary.

In its simplest form, this functionality includes monitoring and automatic updating and configuration of security patches and personal firewall settings. In more advanced systems, it might include an examination of the system each time it connects to the network to ensure that all security patches are up to date, and in even more advanced scenarios, it could automatically provide remediation to the computer. In either case, the computer would not be allowed to connect to the network until the problem is resolved, either manually or automatically. Other measures include using device or drive encryption, enabling remote management capabilities (such as remote wiping and remote location), and implementing device ownership policies and agreements so that the organization can manage or seize the device.

NIST SP 800-128 discusses implementing endpoint protection platforms (EPPs). According to NIST SP 800-128, endpoints (personal computers, mobile devices, etc.) are a fundamental part of any organization's information system. They are an important source of connecting end users to networks and information systems, and are also a major source of vulnerabilities and a frequent target of attackers looking to penetrate a network. User behavior is difficult to control and hard to predict, and user actions, whether it is clicking on a link that executes malware or changing a security setting to improve the usability of their PC, frequently allow exploitation of vulnerabilities. Commercial vendors offer a variety of products to improve security at the "endpoints" of a network.

NIST SP 800-128 describes these EPPs as including the following:

- **Anti-malware:** Anti-malware applications are part of the common secure configurations for system components. Anti-malware software employs a wide range of signatures and detection schemes, automatically updates signatures, disallows modification by users, runs scans on a frequently scheduled basis, has an auto-protect feature set to scan automatically when a user action is performed (e.g., opening or copying a file), and may provide protection from zero-day attacks. For platforms for which anti-malware software is not available, other forms of anti-malware such as rootkit detectors may be employed.

- **Personal firewalls:** Personal firewalls provide a wide range of protection for host machines, including restriction on ports and services, control against malicious programs executing on the host, control of removable devices such as USB devices, and auditing and logging capability.
- **Host-based intrusion detection and prevention system (HIDPS):** HIDPS is an application that monitors the characteristics of a single host and the events occurring within that host to identify and stop suspicious activity. This is distinguished from network-based IDPS, which is an intrusion detection and prevention system that monitors network traffic for particular network segments or devices and analyzes the network and application protocol activity to identify and stop suspicious activity.
- **Restrictions on the use of mobile code:** Organizations exercise caution in allowing the use of "mobile code" such as ActiveX, Java, and JavaScript. An attacker can easily attach a script to a URL in a web page or email that, when clicked, will execute malicious code within the computer's browser.

Security professionals may also want to read NIST SP 800-111, which provides guidance to storage encryption technologies for end-user devices. In addition, NIST provides checklists for implementing different operating systems according to the United States Government Configuration Baseline (USGCB).

Content-Distribution Networks

A ***content-distribution network (CDN)***, also referred to as a content delivery network, is a distributed network of servers that is usually located in multiple data centers connected over the Internet. The content contained on the CDN can include text, graphics, applications, streaming media, and other content that is critical to users. CDNs are highly scalable to allow owners to quickly adjust to the demands of the end users. CDN examples include Microsoft Azure CDN, Netflix video streaming, and Amazon CloudFront.

CDNs use caching to distribute the static content to the CDN. When a request is sent, the geographically closest point of presence (POP) to the requestor provides the cached static content. During the transaction, the POP queries the server for updated content. When content that has not been cached on local servers is requested, the CDN will request the content from the origin server and save a cached copy.

Secure Communication Channels

Organizations must ensure that communication channels are secured. The following sections discuss voice, multimedia collaboration, remote access, data communications, and virtualized networks.

Voice

Voice communication channels include PSTN, POTS, and PBX systems that are used to manage most voice communications over telecommunications networks. POTS systems use analog communication, whereas PSTN was originally analog but has transitioned to use mostly digital communication.

Analog communication supports voice quality and basic phone features, including phone transfer. Digital communication goes beyond analog to support music on hold, VoIP integration, and alarms. In addition, digital systems do not rely on the copper wiring used by analog systems.

Multimedia Collaboration

In today's modern enterprises, the sharing of multimedia during both web presentations or meetings and instant messaging programs has exploded. Note that not all collaboration tools and products are created equally in regard to the security. Many were built with an emphasis on ease of use rather than security. This is a key issue to consider when choosing a product. For both the presenter and the recipient, the following security requirements should be met:

- Data confidentiality
- Origin authentication
- Identity confidentiality
- Data integrity
- Repudiation of transmission
- Non-repudiation of transmission
- Availability to present
- Availability to receive

Peer-to-peer (P2P) applications are used more frequently today. However, many organizations are concerned about their use because it is very easy to share intellectual property over these applications. P2P applications are often used to violate intellectual property laws. Because P2P applications are associated with piracy and copyright violations, organizations should include these applications in their security policies. Because these applications can be used as a means to gain entry to an organization's network, it is usually best to implement policies and rules to prevent P2P applications.

Remote Meeting Technology

Many companies offer technologies and services that allow virtual meetings to occur over the Internet. In most cases, they use browser extensions on the host computer and permit desktop sharing and remote control. If organizations plan to implement remote meeting technology, security professionals should fully research any possible options and the security included as part of the remote meeting technology, specifically authentication and encryption. In addition, any personnel who will be hosting virtual meetings should be trained on the proper use of such applications and any security policies that affect their usage.

Remote collaboration and virtual meetings have been important to organizations for many years. The COVID-19 pandemic increased the need for remote collaboration using voice and video applications, such as Zoom and Teams. However, the increased use of these virtual meeting applications prompted IT staff to reevaluate the security of different applications, especially after several unauthorized access incidents. With advancements in artificial intelligence (AI), there is the threat of impersonation, with phony voice and video interactions now possible. Security of these platforms has improved, but it is important to ensure that you update your application when new updates become available, add a complex password to prevent unauthorized access, and, if possible, have participants pre-register and be approved for admittance.

There are notable differences, in terms of security, across these platforms, and therefore price should not be the only determining factor in adopting one application over another. Sometimes, government agencies and government contractors can provide invaluable advice about which communication platforms they trust the most.

Instant Messaging

While instant messaging applications make communicating with each other much easier, they can also include features that many organizations consider security risks. Instant message applications usually use peer-to-peer systems, server-oriented systems, or brokered systems. The organization would have to allow the use of the appropriate instant messaging protocol for the application that the organization implements. Protocols that are used include Extensible Messaging and Presence Protocol (XMPP) and Internet Relay Chat (IRC).

Keep in mind that user identification is easily falsified in instant messaging applications. All messages are sent in cleartext, including any file transfer operations. Many instant messaging applications also allow scripting, which means that users can easily be tricked into executing a command that they think is a valid part of the application but that is a malicious script inserted by an attacker.

Remote Access

As the world becomes more virtual, remote access technologies are becoming increasingly important to organizations. These technologies allow personnel to work from virtually anywhere in the world, provided that they have some means of connecting to the Internet or other network. In the following sections, we discuss remote connection technologies, VPN screen scrapers, virtual applications/desktops, and telecommuting.

Remote Connection Technologies

In many cases, connections must be made to the main network from outside the network. The reasons for these connections are varied. In some cases, it is for the purpose of allowing telecommuters to work on the network as if sitting in the office with all network resources available to them. In another instance, it is for the purposes of managing network devices, whereas in others, it could be to provide connections between small offices and the main office.

Here, we discuss some of these connection types along with the security measures that go hand in hand with them. These measures include both encryption mechanisms and authentication schemes.

Dial-up

A ***dial-up connection*** is one that uses the PSTN. If it is initiated over an analog phone line, it requires a modem that converts the digital data to analog on the sending end with a modem on the receiving end converting it back to digital. These lines operate up to 56 Kbps.

Dial-up connections can use either ***Serial Line Internet Protocol (SLIP)*** or Point-to-Point Protocol (PPP) at Layer 2. SLIP is an older protocol that has been made obsolete by PPP. PPP provides authentication and multilink capability. The caller is authenticated by the remote access server. This authentication process can be centralized by using either a TACACS+ or RADIUS server. These servers are discussed more fully later.

Some basic security measures that should be in place when using dial-up are

- Have the remote access server call back the initiating caller at a preset number. Do *not* allow call forwarding because it can be used to thwart this security measure.

- Set modems to answer after a set number of rings to thwart war dialers (more on them later).
- Consolidate the modems in one place for physical security, and disable modems not in use.
- Use the strongest possible authentication mechanisms.

If the connection is done over a digital line, it can use ISDN. It also must be dialed up to make the connection but offers much more capability, and the entire process is all digital.

ISDN

Integrated Services Digital Network (ISDN) is sometimes referred to as digital dial-up. The really big difference between ISDN and analog dial-up is the performance. ISDN can be provisioned in two ways:

- ***Basic Rate Interface (BRI)*:** Provides three channels—two B channels that provide 64 Kbps each and a D channel that is 16 Kbps, for a total of 144 Kbps.
- ***Primary Rate Interface (PRI)*:** Can provide up to 23 B channels and a D channel for a total of 1.544 Mbps.

Although ISDN is typically now used only as a backup connection solution and many consider ISDN to be a dedicated connection and thus safe, attacks can be mounted against ISDN connections, including

- **Physical attacks:** These are attacks by persons who are able to physically get to network equipment. With regard to ISDN, shared telecom closets can provide an AP. Physical security measures to follow are described in Chapter 7, "Security Operations."
- **Router attacks:** If a router can be convinced to accept an ISDN call from a rogue router, it might allow an attacker access to the network. Routers should be configured to authenticate with one another before accepting call requests.

DSL

Digital Subscriber Line (DSL) is a popular option that provides a high-speed connection from a home or small office to the ISP. Although DSL uses the existing phone lines, it is an always-on connection. By using different frequencies than the voice transmissions over the same copper lines, talking on the phone and using the data network (Internet) at the same time is possible.

DSL also is many times faster than ISDN or dial-up. It comes in several variants, some of which offer the same speed uploading and downloading (which is called symmetric service) while most offer better download performance than upload performance (called asymmetric service). Some possible versions are

- ***Symmetric DSL (SDSL)*:** Usually provides from 192 Kbps to 1.1 Gbps in both directions. It is usually used by businesses.
- ***Asymmetric DSL (ADSL)*:** Usually provides uploads from 128 Kbps to 384 Kbps and downloads up to 768 Kbps. It is usually used in homes.
- ***High Bit-Rate DSL (HDSL)*:** Provides T1 speeds.
- ***Very High Bit-Rate DSL (VDSL)*:** Is capable of supporting high-definition TV (HDTV) and VoIP.

Unlike cable connections, DSL connections are dedicated links, but there are still security issues to consider. The PCs and other devices that are used to access the DSL line should be set with the following options in Internet Options:

- Check for publisher's certificate revocation.
- Enable memory protection to help mitigate online attacks.
- Enable SmartScreen Filter.
- Use SSL 3.0.
- Use TLS 1.1 or higher.
- Warn about certificate address mismatch.
- Warn if POST submittal is redirected to a zone that does not permit posts.

Another issue with DSL is the fact that it is always connected and the device typically keeps the same or a static IP address. A static IP address provides a fixed target for the attacker. Therefore, taking measures such as implementing a NAT helps hide the true IP address of the device to the outside world.

Cable

Getting connections to the ISP using the same cabling system used to deliver cable TV is also possible. ***Cable modems*** can provide 250 Mbps and higher over the coaxial cabling used for cable TV. Cable modems conform to the ***Data-Over-Cable Service Interface Specifications (DOCSIS)*** standard. DOCSIS 4.0 has and a maximum upstream capacity of 6 Gbps.

A security and performance concern with cable modems is that each customer is on a shared line with neighbors. This means performance varies with the time of day and congestion and the data is traveling over a shared medium. For this reason, many cable companies now encrypt these transmissions.

Broadband cable requires a cable modem at the customer's location and a cable modem termination system at the cable company facility, typically a cable television headend. The two are connected via coaxial cable or a hybrid fiber coaxial (HFC) plant. They can typically operate up to 160 kilometers between the modem and the termination system. Downstream bit rates to the customer vary but generally run in the 300 Mbps area and higher. Upstream traffic to the provider usually only provides up to 20 Mbps.

VPN

Virtual private network (VPN) connections provide protection of information through strong authentication protocols and encryption mechanisms. Although we typically use the most untrusted network, the Internet, as the classic example, and most VPNs do travel through the Internet, they can be used with interior networks as well whenever traffic needs to be protected from prying eyes.

When discussing VPN connections, many new to the subject become confused by the number and type of protocols involved. Let's break down which protocols are required, which are optional, and how they all play together. Recall how the process of encapsulation works. Earlier we discussed this concept when we discussed packet creation, and in that context, we applied it to how one layer of the OSI model "wraps around" or encapsulates, the other data already created at the other layers.

In VPN operations, entire protocols encapsulate other protocols. They include

- A LAN protocol (required)
- A remote access or line protocol (required)
- An authentication protocol (optional)
- An encryption protocol (optional)

Let's start with the original packet before it is sent across the VPN. This is a LAN packet, probably a TCP/IP packet. The change that will be made to this packet is that it will be wrapped in a line or remote access protocol. This protocol's only job is to carry the TCP/IP packet still fully intact across the line and then, just like a ferry boat drops a car at the other side of a river, it de-encapsulates the original packet and delivers it to the destination LAN unchanged.

Several of these remote access or line protocols are available. Among them are

- ***Point-to-Point-Tunneling Protocol (PPTP)***
- ***Layer 2 Tunneling Protocol (L2TP)***

PPTP is a Microsoft protocol based on PPP. It uses built-in Microsoft Point-to-Point Encryption (MPPE) and can use a number of authentication methods, including CHAP, MS-CHAP, and EAP-TLS. One shortcoming of PPTP is that it works only on IP-based networks. If a WAN connection that is not IP-based is in use, L2TP must be used.

MS-CHAP comes in two versions. Both versions can be susceptible to password attacks. Version 1 is inherently insecure and should be avoided. Version 2 is much safer but can still suffer brute-force attacks on the password, although such attacks usually take up to 23 hours to crack the password. Moreover, the MPPE used with MS-CHAP can suffer attacks on the RC4 algorithm on which it is based. Although PPTP is a better solution, it also has been shown to have known vulnerabilities related to the PPP authentication protocols used and is no longer recommended by Microsoft.

Although EAP-TLS is superior to both MS-CHAP and PPTP, its deployment requires a public key infrastructure (PKI), which often is impractical because the network team either does not have the technical capabilities to implement it or does not have sufficient resources to maintain it.

L2TP is a newer protocol that operates at Layer 2 of the OSI model. It can use various authentication mechanisms such as PPTP but does not provide any encryption. It is typically used with IPsec, a very strong encryption mechanism.

With PPTP, the encryption is included, and the only remaining choice to be made is the authentication protocol. These authentication protocols are discussed later in the section "Remote Authentication Protocols."

With L2TP, both encryption and authentication protocols, if desired, must be added. IPsec can provide encryption, data integrity, and system-based authentication, which makes it a flexible and capable option. When certain parts of the IPsec suite are implemented, these features can be used or not.

IPsec is actually a suite of protocols in the same way that TCP/IP is. It includes the following components:

- ***Authentication Header (AH)*:** Provides data integrity, data origin authentication, and protection from replay attacks.
- ***Encapsulating Security Payload (ESP)*:** Provides all that AH does as well as data confidentiality.

- ***Internet Security Association and Key Management Protocol (ISAKMP):*** Handles the creation of a security association for the session and the exchange of keys.
- ***Internet Key Exchange (IKE)*, also sometimes referred to as IPsec Key Exchange:** Provides the authentication material used to create the keys exchanged by ISAKMP during peer authentication. This was proposed to be performed by a protocol called Oakley that relied on the Diffie-Hellman algorithm, but Oakley has been superseded by IKE.

IPsec is a framework, which means it does not specify many of the components used with it. These components must be identified in the configuration, and they must match for the two ends to successfully create the required security association (SA) that must be in place before any data is transferred. The selections that must be made are

- The encryption algorithm (encrypts the data)
- The hashing algorithm (ensures the data has not been altered and verifies its origin)
- The mode (tunnel or transport)
- The protocol (AH, ESP, or both)

All these settings must match on both ends of the connection. It is not possible for the systems to make these selections on the fly. They must be preconfigured correctly to match.

When the tunnel is configured in tunnel mode, the tunnel exists only between the two gateways, and all traffic that passes through the tunnel is protected. This is normally used to protect all traffic between two offices. The SA is between the gateways between the offices. This is the type of connection that would be called a site-to-site VPN.

The SA between the two endpoints is made up of the security parameter index (SPI) and the AH/ESP combination. The SPI, a value contained in each IPsec header, helps the devices maintain the relationship between each SA (of which there could be several happening at once) and the security parameters (also called the transform set) used for each SA. The SA is a simplex (or one-way channel); if two endpoints need to communicate in both directions, they need two different SAs.

Each session has a unique session value, which helps to prevent

- Reverse engineering
- Content modification
- Factoring attacks (the attacker tries all the combinations of numbers that can be used with the algorithm to decrypt ciphertext)

With respect to authenticating the connection, the keys can be pre-shared or derived from a PKI. A PKI creates a public/private key pair that is associated with individual users and computers that use a certificate. These key pairs are used in the place of pre-shared keys in that case. Certificates that are not derived from a PKI can also be used.

In transport mode, the SA is either between two end stations or between an end station and a gateway or remote access server. In this mode, the tunnel extends from computer to computer or from computer to gateway. This is the type of connection that would be used for a remote access VPN. This is but one application of IPsec. It is also used in other applications such as a General Packet Radio Service (GPRS), a VPN solution for devices using a 3G or 4G cell phone network.

When the communication is from gateway to gateway or host to gateway, either transport or tunnel mode can be used. If the communication is computer to computer, the tunnel must be in transport mode. If the tunnel is configured in transport mode from gateway to host, the gateway must operate as a host.

The most effective attack against IPsec VPNs is a man-in-the-middle attack. In this attack, the attacker proceeds through the security negotiation phase until the key negotiation when the victim reveals its identity. In a well-implemented system, the attacker will fail when the attacker cannot likewise prove their identity.

RADIUS and TACACS+

When users are making connections to the network through a variety of mechanisms, they should be authenticated first. These users could be accessing the network through

- Dial-up remote access servers
- VPN access servers
- Wireless access points
- Security-enabled switches

At one time, each of these access devices would perform the authentication process locally on the device. The administrators would need to ensure that all remote access policies and settings were consistent across them all. When a password required changing, it had to be done on all devices.

Remote Authentication Dial-In User Service (RADIUS) and ***Terminal Access Controller Access-Control System Plus (TACACS+)*** are networking protocols that provide centralized authentication and authorization. These services can be run at a central location, and all the access devices (AP, remote access, VPN, and so on) can be made clients of the server. Whenever authentication occurs, the TACACS+ or

RADIUS server performs the authentication and authorization. This setup provides one location to manage the remote access policies and passwords for the network. Another advantage of using these systems is that the audit and access information (logs) is not kept on the access server.

TACACS and TACACS+ are Cisco-proprietary services that operate in Cisco devices, whereas RADIUS is an RFC standard defined. Cisco has implemented several versions of TACACS over time. It went from TACACS to XTACACS to the latest version, TACACS+. The latest version provides authentication, accounting, and authorization, which is why it is sometimes referred to as an AAA service. TACACS+ employs tokens for two-factor, dynamic password authentication. It also allows users to change their passwords.

RADIUS is designed to provide a framework that includes three components: a supplicant, an authenticator, and a RADIUS server. The supplicant is the device seeking authentication. The authenticator is the device to which the supplicant is attempting to connect (AP, switch, remote access server), and the RADIUS server is the authentication server. With regard to RADIUS, the device seeking entry is *not* the RADIUS client. The ***authenticating server*** is the RADIUS server, and the authenticator (AP, switch, remote access server) is the RADIUS client.

In some cases, a RADIUS server can be the client of another RADIUS server. In that case, the RADIUS server acts as a proxy client for its RADIUS clients.

Diameter is another authentication protocol based on RADIUS and is *not* compatible with RADIUS. Diameter has a much larger set of attribute/value pairs (AVPs) than RADIUS, allowing more functionality and services to communicate, but has not been widely adopted.

Remote Authentication Protocols

Earlier we said that one of the protocol choices that must be made when provisioning a remote access solution is the authentication protocol. Here, we discuss some of the most important of those protocols:

- ***Password Authentication Protocol (PAP)***: PAP provides authentication, but the credentials are sent in cleartext and can be read with a sniffer.
- ***Challenge Handshake Authentication Protocol (CHAP)***: CHAP solves the cleartext problem by operating without sending the credentials across the link. The server sends the client a set of random texts called a challenge. The client encrypts the text with the password and sends it back. The server then decrypts the text with the same password and compares the result with what was sent originally. If the results match, then the server can be assured that the user or system possesses the correct password without ever needing to send it across the untrusted network.

- ***Extensible Authentication Protocol (EAP)*:** EAP is not a single protocol but a framework for port-based access control that uses the same three components that are used in RADIUS. A wide variety of these implementations can use all sorts of authentication mechanisms, including certificates, a PKI, or even simple passwords.

Telnet

Telnet is a remote access protocol used to connect to a device for the purpose of executing commands on the device. It can be used to access servers, routers, switches, and many other devices for the purpose of managing them. Telnet is not considered a secure remote management protocol because, like another protocol used with Unix-based systems, rlogin, it transmits all information including the authentication process in cleartext. Alternatives such as SSH have been adopted to perform the same function while providing encryption. Telnet and rlogin connections are connection-oriented, so they use TCP as the transport protocol.

Remote Log-in (rlogin), Remote Shell (rsh), and Remote Copy (rcp)

The rlogin/rsh/rcp family of protocols allows users to connect remotely, execute commands, and copy data to Unix-based computers. Authentication is based on the host or IP address. If an organization needs to allow this access, SSHv2 should be implemented with these protocols.

TLS/SSL

Transport Layer Security/Secure Sockets Layer (TLS/SSL) is another option for creating secure connections to servers. It works at the Application layer of the OSI model. It is used mainly to protect HTTP traffic or web servers. Its functionality is embedded in most browsers, and its use typically requires no action on the part of the user. It is widely used to secure Internet transactions. It can be implemented in two ways:

- **SSL portal VPN:** A user has a single SSL connection used to access multiple services on the web server. After being authenticated, the user is provided a page that acts as a portal to other services.
- **SSL tunnel VPN:** Users use an SSL tunnel to access services on a server that is not a web server. An SSL tunnel VPN uses custom programming to provide access to non-web services through a web browser.

TLS and SSL are similar but not the same. TLS 1.0 and higher are based on the SSL 3.0 specification, but they are not operationally compatible. Both implement confidentiality, authentication, and integrity above the Transport layer. The server is always authenticated, and optionally, the client also can be. SSL v2 must be used for client-side authentication. When SSL is configured, a session key length must be designated. The two options are 40-bit and 128-bit. SSL prevents man-in-the-middle attacks by using self-signed certificates to authenticate the server public key.

VPN Screen Scraper

A VPN ***screen scraper*** is an application that allows an attacker to capture what is on the user's display. Attackers can use screen scrapers to obtain user credentials, PIN sequences, proprietary or confidential data, and any other information displayed.

Virtual Application/Desktop

Although virtualization is becoming increasingly popular, organizations do not always consider securing the communication channels used by virtualization applications. With virtualization, remote users are able to execute desktop commands as if they were sitting at the virtual computer to which they are connecting. Security professionals should research all virtual application options to ensure that the application chosen provides the organization with all the capabilities needed while at the same time ensuring that the selected solution provides the appropriate level of security. When using virtualization, security professionals should ensure that the same security measures that are implemented on the host computer are also implemented on each virtual machine. For example, antivirus software should be installed on the host computer and on each virtual machine running on the computer.

Telecommuting/Teleworking

Organizations have had to adapt their work environments to meet the ever-changing needs of the technologically advancing world. Many organizations today have trouble recruiting the talent they need to fill available positions. COVID-19 also prompted more telecommuting. Consequently, telecommuting or working remotely is increasingly being used to help with recruitment, ensure that skilled employees are employed, and keep employees safe.

Organizations must ensure that remote workers are fully trained in all security policies, particularly policies regarding VPN access and confidential information access and storage. It is also suggested that you implement remote wiping capabilities and full device encryption on any organization-issued devices. Finally, users must understand the implications of accessing organizational resources from public places.

Data Communications

In securing communication networks, organizations must understand the importance of protecting data communications. Data communication involves any digital transmission of data over a network and is discussed throughout this book.

Virtualized Networks

In securing communication networks, organizations must understand the effects of virtualized networks on security. In this section, we cover the following concepts related to virtualized networks: SDN, VPC, VSAN, guest operating systems, port isolation, and FIM.

Software-Defined Networking

Key Topic

Software-defined networking (SDN) accelerates software deployment and delivery, thereby reducing IT costs through policy-enabled workflow automation. It enables cloud architectures by providing automated, on-demand application delivery and mobility at scale.

SDN allows for the physical separation of the network control plane from the forwarding plane, and the control plane can control several devices. Administrators can therefore separate traditional network traffic, both wired and wireless, into three components: raw data, method of transmission, and data purpose. An SDN includes three architecture layers:

- **Infrastructure layer:** Includes switches, routers, and data and the data forwarding process. Also referred to as the data plane.
- **Control layer:** Includes device intelligence that determines traffic flow. Also referred to as the control plane.
- **Application layer:** Includes network services, utilities, and applications. Also referred to as the application plane.

Because of these layers, hardware that is handling the network traffic does not need to direct the traffic.

SDN may be particularly helpful with cloud and virtualization by allowing them to be more efficient, reliable, and simplified.

SDN is comprised of data, control, and management planes. The data plane refers to the transmission of data packets through a networking device. The control plane manages network routing protocols and facilitates communication between devices. These protocols can include Border Gateway Protocol, Enhanced Interior Gateway Routing Protocol, or Open Shortest Pathway First. The management plane is responsible for transmitting and receiving data packets and includes protocols such as Telnet, SSH, and SNMP.

Switching describes the process of transmitting data between local-area networks, using switches. Store-and-forward switching occurs when the switching device receives an entire frame and then stores the frame in buffer memory. The frame is then checked for errors using cyclic redundancy check (CRC). Cut-through switching occurs when the switching device simply forwards a data packet as soon as the destination address is received. In other words, unlike store-and-forward, cut-through does not perform error checking. Furthermore, frames are not stored by the switching device.

Virtual Private Cloud (VPC)

Hosted within a public cloud and hosted by a public cloud service, a virtual private cloud (VPC) is isolated and allows a VPC customer to host websites, run code, and store data securely. Figure 4-48 shows an example of a VPC. A public cloud is shared by many customers, but a VPC within that public cloud is not shared.

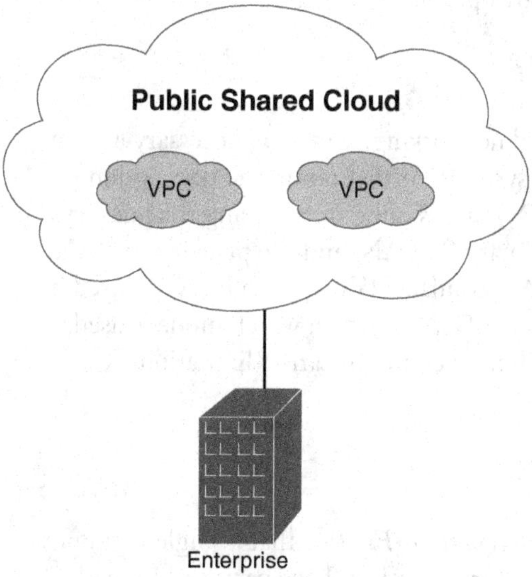

Figure 4-48 Virtual Private Cloud (VPC)

A VPC is secured using a dedicated subnet and a virtual local-area network (VLAN); a subnet is a range of IP addresses used within a network, and a VLAN is a logical group of devices on a network that is partitioned using network switches and/or software. A virtual private network (VPN) provides additional security for a customer accessing resources on a VPC.

Network access control lists (ACLs) are rules governing which users have access to a subnet within a VPC. Furthermore, VPN software can be hosted on a VPC, for added security. A VPC can also utilize identity and access management (IAM) as another layer of security. A network firewall may also be used with a VPC to monitor inbound and outbound network traffic. As with all networks, it is important to collect logs of inbound and outbound network traffic. These logs should in turn be analyzed regularly.

Virtual SAN

A ***virtual storage-area network (VSAN)*** is a software-defined storage method that allows pooling of storage capabilities and instant and automatic provisioning of virtual machine storage. This is a method of software-defined storage (SDS). It usually includes dynamic tiering, QoS, caching, replication, and cloning. Data availability is ensured through the software, not by implementing redundant hardware. Administrators are able to define policies that allow the software to determine the best placement of data. By including intelligent data placement, software-based controllers, and software RAID, a VSAN can provide better data protection and availability than traditional hardware-only options.

Guest Operating Systems

If an organization implements virtualized networking, it may be necessary at some point to grant access to guest operating systems. At that point, the best option would be to configure a private VLAN (PVLAN) that is only for accessing the guest system. The first created PVLAN is the primary PVLAN, and the primary PVLAN can include many secondary PVLANs. A secondary PVLAN can be configured in promiscuous, isolated, or community mode. Depending on which mode is used, nodes within a PVLAN in that mode will have communication limitations. Using a PVLAN is also known as ***port isolation***.

Federated Identity with a Third Party

The idea behind ***Federated Identity Management (FIM)*** is that a single login provides access to multiple trusted networks. Organizations have partnerships with other enterprises, which are referred to as trust domains. These trust domains maintain their own identity management but will also use a third party that will store user credentials as part of FIM. This third party is known as an identity broker or an identity provider, and that organization is responsible for access control. FIM means that authentication with one trusted domain provides access to other partner networks that comprise the FIM.

Single sign-on (SSO) provides access to multiple systems, using the same credentials. SSO works within one organization, whereas FIM allows the same credentials to be used with federated partners. A federated partner can be a vendor or an email service, such as Gmail.

Network Attacks

Key Topic

Before security professionals can address network security threats, they must be aware of the threats, understand how they work, and know the measures to take to prevent the attacks from succeeding. The following sections cover a wide variety of attack types along with measures that should be taken to prevent them from occurring.

Network Component Attacks

Network components are often attack targets because many organizations use the same devices. Security professionals must understand attacks against these devices, including non-blind spoofing, blind spoofing, man-in-the-middle attacks, MAC flooding attacks, 802.1Q and Inter-Switch Link protocol tagging attacks, double-encapsulated 802.1Q/nested VLAN attacks, and ARP attacks.

Non-Blind Spoofing

A non-blind spoofing attack occurs when an attacker is on the same subnet as the victim. This attack sniffs the sequence and acknowledgment numbers and uses them to hijack the session.

To prevent these attacks, security professionals may want to consider the following measures:

- Using ingress filtering on packets to filter the inbound traffic
- Deploying protocols through a number sequence that is used to create a secure connection to other systems
- Configuring the network to reject packets from the network that claim to originate from a local address
- Enabling encryption sessions at the router if allowing outside connections from trusted hosts

Blind Spoofing

In a blind spoofing attack, the sequence and acknowledgment numbers cannot be attained. Packets are sent to the target to obtain a sampling of the sequence numbers so that the attacker can generate a valid sequence number for the attack. This approach usually works best on older systems because they use an exact formula for determining sequence numbers. However, most of today's modern operating systems use random sequence number generation.

The mitigations listed for non-blind spoofing attacks also apply to blind spoofing attacks.

Man-in-the-Middle Attack

A man-in-the-middle (MITM) attack intercepts legitimate traffic between two entities. The attacker can control information flow and can eliminate or alter the communication between the two parties. Both non-blind spoofing and blind spoofing are types of MITM attacks.

Some MITM attacks can be mitigated by encrypting the messages. Other defenses include using secure DNS extensions, PKI, stronger mutual authentication, and second secure channel verification.

MAC Flooding Attack

Because switches and bridges are limited in terms of the number of entries that can be contained in the MAC table, attackers can flood such a device with traffic to turn the device into a dumb pseudo-hub, thereby ensuring that the attackers can sniff all the traffic on the device. Using port security, 802.1X, and dynamic VLANs can help to prevent this attack.

802.1Q and Inter-Switch Link Protocol (ISL) Tagging Attack

Tagging attacks occur when a user on a VLAN gets unauthorized access to another VLAN. Preventing this type of attack usually involves either setting Dynamic Trunking Protocol (DTP) to off on all nontrusted ports or following simple configuration guidelines for the switch.

Double-Encapsulated 802.1Q/Nested VLAN Attack

In a double-encapsulated 802.1Q/nested VLAN attack, attackers can cause traffic to hop VLANs by injecting packets that are double-tagged in an 802.1Q VLAN. This attack can be prevented by clearing the native VLAN from all 802.1Q trunks or picking an unused VLAN as the native VLAN.

ARP Attack

Within a VLAN, ARP poisoning attacks are used to fool routers into learning the identities of counterfeited devices. An attacker then poses as that device and performs an MITM attack. Prevention of this attack is best carried out by blocking direct communication at Layer 2 between the attacker and attacked device or by using ARP inspection or some similar mechanism in the devices.

ICMP Attacks

Earlier in this chapter we described the Internet Control Message Protocol (ICMP), one of the protocols in the TCP/IP suite. Devices use this protocol to send error messages to sending devices when transmission problems occur and also when either the **ping** command or the **traceroute** command is used for troubleshooting. Like many tools and utilities that were created for good purposes, this protocol can also be used by attackers who take advantage of its functionality.

In the following sections, we cover ICMP-based attacks. One of the ways to prevent ICMP-based attacks is to disallow its use by blocking the protocol number for ICMP, which is 1. Many firewall products also have the capability to block only certain types of ICMP messages as opposed to prohibiting its use entirely. We also discuss some of these problematic ICMP message types here.

Ping of Death

A ping of death is an attack that takes advantage of the normal behavior of devices that receive oversized ICMP packets. ICMP packets are normally a predictable 65,536 bytes in length. Hackers have learned how to insert additional data into ICMP packets. A ***ping of death attack*** sends several of these oversized packets, which can cause the victim system to be unstable at the least and possibly freeze up. That results in a denial-of-service attack because it makes the target system less able or even unable to perform its normal function in the network.

Smurf

The ***smurf attack*** is a denial-of-service attack that uses a type of ping packet called an ICMP ECHO REQUEST. This attack is an example of a distributed denial-of-service (DDoS) attack in that the perpetrator enlists the aid of other machines in the network.

When a system receives an ICMP ECHO REQUEST packet, it attempts to answer this request with an ICMP ECHO REPLY packet (usually four times by default). Normally, this reply is sent to a single sending system. In this attack, the ECHO REQUEST has its destination address set to the network broadcast address of the network in which the target system resides, and the source address is set to the target system. When every system in the network replies to the request, it overwhelms the target device, causing it to freeze or crash.

Fraggle

Although not really an ICMP attack because it uses UDP, the fraggle attack is a DDoS attack with the same goal and method as the smurf attack. In this attack, an attacker sends a large amount of UDP echo traffic to an IP broadcast address, all of it having a fake source address, which will, of course, be the target system. When all systems in the network reply, the target is overwhelmed.

ICMP Redirect

One of the many types of error messages that ICMP uses is called an ICMP redirect or an ICMP packet type 5. ICMP redirects are used by routers to specify better routing paths out of one network. When ICMP does this, it changes the path that the packet will take.

By crafting ICMP redirect packets, the attacker alters the route table of the host that receives the redirect message. This alteration changes the way packets are routed in the network to the attacker's advantage. After its routing table is altered, the host will continue to use the path for 10 minutes. For this reason, ICMP redirect packets might be one of the types you might want to disallow on the firewall.

Ping Scanning

ICMP can be used to scan the network for live or active IP addresses. This attack, known as ***ping scanning***, basically pings every IP address and keeps track of which IP addresses respond to the ping. This attack is usually accompanied or followed by a ***port scan***, covered later in this chapter.

Traceroute Exploitation

Traceroute is used to determine the path that a packet travels between a source and destination. Attackers can use traceroute to map a network to better understand packet routing. They can also use traceroute with Nmap, as discussed later in this chapter, to determine firewall rules.

DNS Attacks

As mentioned in the discussion of DNS earlier in this chapter, DNS resolves computer and domain names to IP addresses. It is a vital service to the network, and for that reason, multiple DNS servers are always recommended for fault tolerance. DNS servers are a favorite target of DoS and DDoS attacks because of the mayhem caused by taking them down or causing the DNS servers to malfunction.

DNS servers also can be used to divert traffic to the attacker by altering DNS records. In the following sections, we cover all types of DNS attacks, along with practices that can eliminate or mitigate the effect of these attacks.

DNS Cache Poisoning

DNS clients send requests for name-to-IP address resolution (called queries) to a DNS server. The search for the IP address that goes with a computer or domain name usually starts with a local DNS server that is not authoritative for the DNS domain in which the requested computer or website resides. When this situation occurs, the local DNS server makes a request of the DNS server that does hold the record in question. After the local DNS server receives the answer, it returns the answer to the local DNS client. After this, the local DNS server maintains that record in its DNS cache for a period called the Time to Live (TTL), which is usually an hour but can vary.

In a ***DNS cache poisoning attack***, the attacker attempts to refresh or update that record when it expires with a different address than the correct address. If the attacker can convince the DNS server to accept this refresh, the local DNS server will then be responding to client requests for that computer with the address inserted by the attacker. Typically, the address they now receive is for a fake website that appears to look in every way like the site the client is requesting. The hacker can then harvest all the name and password combinations entered on the fake site.

To prevent this type of attack, the DNS servers should be limited in the updates they accept. In most DNS software, network administrators can restrict the DNS servers from which a server will accept updates. This can help prevent the server from accepting these false updates.

DoS

DNS servers are a favorite target of denial-of-service (DoS) attacks. The reason is that the loss of DNS service in the network typically brings the network to a halt because many network services depend on its functioning. Any of the assorted types of DoS attacks discussed in this book can be targeted to DNS servers. For example, a ping of death might be the attack of choice.

DDoS

Any of the assorted DoS attacks can be amplified by the attacker by recruiting other devices to assist in the attack. Some examples of these attacks are the smurf and fraggle attacks (covered earlier). A ***distributed denial-of-service (DDoS) attack*** occurs when more than one system or device floods the bandwidth of a targeted system or network.

In some cases, the attacker might have used malware to install software on thousands of computers (called zombies) to which commands are sent at a given time, instructing all the devices to launch the attack. Not only does this amplify the attack, but it also helps to hide the source of the attack because it appears to come from many places at once. In terms of the CIA triad, availability is the biggest problem associated with DDoS, as this persistent attack may render a network resource, such as a web server, unavailable.

DNSSEC

One of the newer approaches to preventing DNS attacks is a stronger authentication mechanism called ***Domain Name System Security Extensions (DNSSEC)***. Many current implementations of DNS software contain this functionality. It uses digital signatures to validate the source of all messages to ensure they are not spoofed.

The problem with DNSSEC illustrates the classic trade-off between security and simplicity. To deploy DNSSEC, a PKI must be built and maintained to issue, validate, and renew the public/private key pairs and certificates that must be issued to all the DNS servers. (PKI is covered more fully in Chapter 3.) Moreover, for complete security of DNS, all the DNS servers on the Internet would also need to participate, which complicates the situation further. The work on this continues today.

URL Hiding

An alternate and in some ways simpler way for an attacker to divert traffic to a fake website is a method called ***URL hiding***. This attack takes advantage of the ability to embed URLs in web pages and email. The attacker might refer to the correct name of the website in the text of the web page or email, but when inserting the URL that goes with the link, the attacker inserts the URL for the fake site. The best protection against this issue is to ask users to not click links on unknown or untrusted websites.

Domain Grabbing

Domain grabbing occurs when individuals register a domain name of a well-known company before the company has the chance to do so. Then later the individuals hold the name hostage until the company becomes willing to pay to get the domain name. In some cases, these same individuals monitor the renewal times for well-known websites and register the name before the company has a chance to perform the renewal. Some practices that can help to prevent this situation are to register domain names for longer periods of time and to register all permutations of the chosen domain name (misspellings and so on).

Cybersquatting

When domain names are registered with no intent to use them but with intent to hold them hostage (as described in the preceding section), it is called ***cybersquatting***. The same practices to prevent domain grabbing are called for to prevent the company from becoming a victim of cybersquatting.

Email Attacks

One of the most popular avenues for attacks is a tool many people use every day—email. In the following sections, we cover several attacks that use email as the vehicle. In most cases, the best way to prevent these attacks is user training and awareness because many of these attacks are based on poor security practices on the part of the user.

Email Spoofing

Email spoofing is the process of sending an email that appears to come from a reliable source when it really comes from another. It is made possible by altering the fields of email headers such as From, Return Path, and Reply-to. Its purpose is to convince the receiver to trust the message and reply to it with some sensitive information that the receiver would not have shared unless it was a trusted message.

Often this spoofing is one step in an attack designed to harvest usernames and passwords for banking or financial sites. This attack can be mitigated in several ways. One is SMTP authentication, which, when enabled, disallows the sending of an email by a user who cannot authenticate with the sending server.

Another possible mitigation technique is to implement the ***Sender Policy Framework (SPF)***. The SPF is an email validation system that works by using DNS to determine whether an email sent by someone has been sent by a host sanctioned by that domain's administrator. If that email can't be validated, it is not delivered to the recipient's box.

A review of the email header information can validate whether the email sender's name and email address have been spoofed. There are certain validation indicators to look for, some of which are displayed in Figure 4-49.

Original message	
Message ID	<c9f46151-08d1-4b43-9225-5c3571e7f985@Spark>
Created on:	26 March 2021 at 08:39 (Delivered after 13 seconds)
From:	Ross Lou[redacted]d.ie>
To:	Darren Hayes [redacted]
Subject:	Re: Re: Server Upgrade
SPF:	PASS with IP 209.85.2[redacted]
DKIM:	'PASS' with domain [redacted].com Learn more
DMARC:	'PASS' Learn more

Figure 4-49 Email Header

The ***Message-ID*** is a unique hash that represents the underlying email message. This ID is defined by the IETF in RFC 2822. The Sender Policy Framework (SPF) is used to check whether a specific IP address is authorized to send mail from a specific domain (RFC 7208). The ***DKIM (DomainKeys Identified Mail)*** refers to a pair of cryptographic keys that are used to sign an outgoing message, while validating incoming messages (RFC 6376). ***DMARC (Domain-based Message Authentication, Reporting & Conformance)*** provides the sender with an option that lets the recipient know if the email was protected by SPF or DKIM. ***ARC (Authenticated Receive Chain)*** is a standard, created in 2016, that helps to improve how DKIM and SPF results are passed from one mail server to the next during forwarding.

Spear Phishing

Phishing is a social engineering attack where a recipient is convinced to click a link in an email that appears to go to a trusted site but in fact goes to the hacker's site. This attack is used to harvest usernames and passwords.

Spear phishing is the process of foisting this attack on a specific person, such as a company manager or human resources manager rather than a random set of people. The attack might be made more convincing by learning details about the person through social media that the email might reference to boost its appearance of legitimacy.

Whaling

Just as spear phishing is a subset of phishing, ***whaling*** is a subset of spear phishing. It targets a single person, and in the case of whaling, that person is someone of significance or importance. It might be a CEO, CFO, CSO, COO, or CTO, for example. The attack is based on the assumption that these people have more sensitive information to divulge.

Spam

No one enjoys how email boxes fill up every day with unsolicited emails, usually trying to sell something. In many cases, users cause themselves to receive this email by not paying close attention to all the details when buying something or visiting a site. When email is sent out on a mass basis that is not requested, it is called ***spam***.

Spam is more than an annoyance because it can clog email boxes and cause email servers to spend resources delivering it. Sending spam is illegal, so many spammers try to hide the source of the spam by relaying through other corporations' email servers. Not only does this practice hide the true source of the email, but it can cause the relaying company to get in trouble.

Today's email servers can deny relaying to any email servers that are not specified. This solution can prevent an organization's email system from being used as a spamming mechanism. This type of relaying should be disallowed on the organization's email servers. In addition, spam filters can be implemented on personal email, such as web-based email clients.

Wireless Attacks

Wireless attacks are some of the hardest to prevent because of the nature of the medium. If you want to make radio transmissions available to users, you must make them available to anyone else in the area. Moreover, there is no way to determine when someone is capturing radio waves! You might be able to prevent someone from connecting to or becoming a wireless client on the network, but you cannot stop them from using a wireless sniffer to capture the packets. In the following sections, we cover some of the more common attacks and also discuss some mitigation techniques.

Wardriving

Wardriving is the process of driving around a neighborhood with a wireless device connected to a high-power antenna searching for WLANs. It could be for the purpose of obtaining free Internet access, or it could be to identify any open networks vulnerable to an attack.

Warchalking

Warchalking is a practice that typically accompanies wardriving. When a wardriver locates a WLAN, that attacker indicates in chalk on a sidewalk or building the SSID and the types of security used on the network. This activity has gone mostly online now because many sites are dedicated to compiling lists of found WLANs and their locations.

Remote Attacks

Although all attacks, such as DoS attacks, DNS poisoning, port scanning, and ICMP attacks, are remote in the sense that they can be launched from outside the network, remote attacks can also be focused on remote access systems such as VPN servers or dial-up servers. As security practices have evolved, these types of attacks have somewhat diminished.

Wardialing is not the threat that it once was simply because organizations don't use modems and modem banks as much as they used to. In this attack, software programs attempt to dial large lists of phone numbers for the purpose of identifying numbers attached to modems. When a person or fax machine answers, it records that fact, and when a modem answers, it attempts to make a connection. If this connection is successful, the hacker now has an entryway into the network.

Other Attacks

In these final sections of the chapter, we cover some other attacks that might not fall into any of the other categories discussed thus far.

SYN ACK Attacks

The ***SYN ACK attack*** takes advantage of the TCP three-way handshake, covered in the "Transport Layer" section (under "TCP/IP Model"), earlier in this chapter.

In this attack, the hacker sends many packets with the SYN flag set, which causes the receiving computer to set aside memory for each ACK packet it expects to receive in return. These packets never come, and at some point, the resources of the receiving computer are exhausted, making this a form of DoS attack.

Session Hijacking

In a ***session hijacking attack***, the hacker attempts to place himself in the middle of an active conversation between two computers for the purpose of taking over the session of one of the two computers, thus receiving all data sent to that computer. Juggernaut and the Hunt Project allow the attacker to spy on the TCP session between the computers. Then the hacker uses some sort of DoS attack to remove one of the two computers from the network while spoofing the IP address of that computer and replacing that computer in the conversation. This results in the hacker receiving all traffic that was originally intended for the computer that suffered the DoS attack.

Port Scanning

ICMP can also be used to scan the network for unused or open ports. Open ports indicate services that might be running and listening on a device that might be susceptible to being used for an attack. This attack basically pings every address and port number combination and keeps track of which ports are open on each device as the pings are answered by open ports with listening services and not answered by closed ports.

Nmap is one of the most popular port scanning tools used today. Security professionals must understand NULL, FIN, and XMAS scans performed by Nmap. Any packet not containing SYN, RST, or ACK bits will return a response if the port is closed. If the port is open, a response will not be sent. A NULL scan does not send any bits. A FIN scan sets the FIN bit. An XMAS scan sets the FIN, PSH, and URG flags. Two advantages of these scan types are that they can sneak through certain non-stateful firewalls and packet filtering routers, and they are stealthier than even a SYN scan.

Organizations can perform their own port scanning or use a third-party security consultant to identify open ports that may cause vulnerabilities. Using port scanning tools can also inform an organization which ports are open and should be closed because they are unneeded. An effective firewall can also prevent unauthorized access. The firewall can control ports, indicate how these ports can be viewed, and identify when port scanning occurs.

Teardrop

A ***teardrop*** attack is a type of fragmentation attack. The maximum transmission unit (MTU) of a section of the network might cause a packet to be broken up or fragmented, which requires the fragments to be reassembled when received. The hacker sends malformed fragments of packets that, when reassembled by the receiver, cause the receiver to crash or become unstable.

IP Address Spoofing

IP address spoofing is one of the techniques used by hackers to hide their trail or to masquerade as another computer. The hacker alters the IP address as it appears in the packet. This can sometimes allow the packet to get through an ACL that is based on IP addresses. It also can be used to make a connection to a system that only trusts certain IP addresses or ranges of IP addresses.

Zero-Day

A zero-day exploit refers to a software vulnerability for which no patch currently exists because that vulnerability is yet to be known by the developer. A zero-day attack refers to an attack that utilizes a zero-day exploit.

Ransomware

Ransomware is malicious software that uses cryptography to encrypt and block access to an organization's data unless a ransom is paid. The attacker holds the decryption key that is required to unlock the data. Most attackers request payment in the form of cryptocurrency, such as Bitcoin, to obfuscate the attacker's identity. Certain variants of ransomware are used to target specific industries. Therefore, sharing threat intelligence with peer companies can be beneficial, such as through an Information Sharing and Analysis Center (ISAC). Companies can also view the NIST Cybersecurity Framework as well as access helpful resources from StopRansomware.gov. It is also recommended that organizations contact law enforcement when a ransomware attack occurs. In the United States, organizations should contact their local FBI field office or the Internet Crime Complaint Center (IC3). Other helpful resources include the Cybersecurity and Infrastructure Security Agency (CISA), Cyber Fraud Task Force (CFTF), and European Cybercrime Centre (EC3). The website https://nomoreransom.org also provides helpful tips to mitigate risk or determine if there is a solution to a ransomware variant available.

A ransomware attack may be perpetrated by using an email link (phishing), or using a remote access Trojan (RAT), unpatched software, or through other means.

Many organizations today run tabletop exercises in which they simulate a ransomware attack and detail how they will react to such an attack. These exercises can help to identify how to react, identify gaps in security, and delineate roles for key players. Creating regular backups that are stored on an air-gapped system or a separate network store is critical to continuity planning. Cyber insurance may help to recoup any incurred losses, although policies have been continually changing because of an increased exposure to ransomware attacks and the potential for huge losses.

It is important for organizations to keep track of legislation to determine their options. North Carolina, for example, became the first state to prohibit ransomware payments. Pennsylvania introduced legislation that bars state and local governments from using taxpayer money to pay a ransom. Texas introduced a similar bill. Therefore, it is important for organizations to be aware of new legislation being introduced.

Even after a ransom has been paid, there is no guarantee that the organization's data will be decrypted, and sometimes the organization will be hit with ransomware again by the same attacker(s) or a different perpetrator. With a double extortion ransomware attack, the criminals copy and exfiltrate company data and then encrypt the organization's data. The threat actor then demands a ransom to decrypt the data and a second ransom to prevent the stolen data from being leaked on the Web.

Exam Preparation Tasks

As mentioned in the section "About the *CISSP Cert Guide*, Fifth Edition" in the Introduction, you have a couple of choices for exam preparation: the exercises here, Chapter 9, "Final Preparation," and the exam simulation questions in the Pearson Test Prep practice test software.

Review All Key Topics

Review the most important topics in this chapter, noted with the Key Topic icon in the outer margin of the page. Table 4-15 lists a reference of these key topics and the page numbers on which each is found.

Key Topic

Table 4-15 Key Topics for Chapter 4

Key Topic Element	Description	Page Number
Figure 4-1	Protocol Mappings	396
Figure 4-2	OSI and TCP/IP Models	397
Figure 4-4	TCP Three-Way Handshake	400
Figure 4-6	Encapsulation	403
Table 4-1	Common TCP/UDP Port Numbers	404
Table 4-2	Classful IP Addressing	407
Table 4-3	Private IP Address Ranges	408
Table 4-4	Differences Between IPv4 and IPv6	417
Figure 4-17	Comparison of IPv4 and IPv6 Addressing	424
Section	Multilayer Protocols	442
Section	Converged Protocols	443
Table 4-7	WPA and WPA2	464
Table 4-8	EAP Type Comparison	466
List	IDS implementations	486
Figure 4-35	Coaxial Cabling	497
Table 4-9	Twisted Pair Categories	499
Paragraph	Network access control (NAC)	516
Paragraph	Software-defined networking (SDN)	532
Section	Network Attacks	535

Define Key Terms

Define the following key terms from this chapter and check your answers in the glossary:

5G; 802.11a; 802.11ac; 802.11ax; 802.11b; 802.11be; 802.11bn; 802.11g; 802.11n; 802.1X; access point (AP); Ad Hoc mode; Address Resolution Protocol (ARP); Application layer (Layer 7); application-level proxy; Asymmetric DSL (ADSL); Asynchronous Transfer Mode (ATM); asynchronous transmission; attenuation; Authenticated Receive Chain (ARC); authenticating server; Authentication Header (AH); authenticator; Automatic Private IP Addressing (APIPA); bandwidth; baseband; Basic Rate Interface (BRI); bastion host; Bluejacking; Bluesnarfing; Bluetooth; Border Gateway Protocol (BGP); broadband; broadcast; bus topology; cable modem; campus-area network (CAN); capacity management; Carrier Sense Multiple Access/Collision Avoidance (CSMA/CA); Carrier Sense Multiple Access/Collision Detection (CSMA/CD); Challenge Handshake Authentication Protocol (CHAP); channel service unit/data service unit (CSU/DSU); circuit-level proxy; circuit-switching network; cloud computing; coaxial; code-division multiple access (CDMA); Compute Express Link (CXL); content-distribution network (CDN); Control and User Plane Separation (CUPS); control plane; crosstalk; cybersquatting; Data Link layer (Layer 2); Data-Over-Cable Service Interface Specifications (DOCSIS); data plane; dedicated short-range communications (DSRC); demilitarized zone (DMZ); demultiplexer; device-to-device (D2D) communication; dial-up connection; digital; Digital Subscriber Line (DSL); direct-sequence spread spectrum (DSSS); distance vector protocol; distributed denial-of-service (DDoS) attack; Distributed Network Protocol version 3 (DNP3); Domain-based Message Authentication, Reporting & Conformance (DMARC); DNS cache poisoning attack; domain grabbing; Domain Name System (DNS); Domain Name System Security Extensions (DNSSEC); DomainKeys Identified Mail (DKIM); dual-homed firewall; Dynamic Host Configuration Protocol (DHCP); dynamic NAT; dynamic packet filtering firewall; E-carriers; electromagnetic interference (EMI); email spoofing; Encapsulating Security Payload (ESP); encapsulation; Endpoint Detection and Response (EDR); endpoint security; Enhanced IGRP (EIGRP); Ethernet; Extensible Authentication Protocol (EAP); extranet; Extremely High Throughput (EHT); fault detection and handling; Federated Identity Management (FIM); Fiber Distributed Data Interface (FDDI); fiber optic; Fibre Channel over Ethernet (FCoE); File Transfer Protocol (FTP); firewall; fractional T1; frequency-division multiple access (FDMA); frequency-division multiplexing (FDM); frequency-hopping spread spectrum (FHSS); FTPS; gateway; Global System for Mobile communications (GSM); High-Bit-Rate DSL (HDSL); High-Speed Serial Interface (HSSI); honeynet; honeypot; HTTP-Secure (HTTP-S); hub; hybrid; hybrid or advanced distance vector protocol; Hypertext Transfer

Protocol (HTTP); Hypertext Transfer Protocol Secure (HTTPS); InfiniBand; infrared; Infrastructure mode; Integrated Services Digital Network (ISDN); Intermediate System to Intermediate System (IS-IS); Internet Control Message Protocol (ICMP); Internet Group Management Protocol (IGMP); Internet Key Exchange (IKE); Internet Message Access Protocol (IMAP); Internet Protocol (IP); Internet Protocol Security (IPsec); Internet Security Association and Key Management Protocol (ISAKMP); Internet Small Computer System Interface (iSCSI); intranet; IP address spoofing; IP convergence; Isochronous Channels (ISOC); jitter; kernel proxy firewall; Label Distribution Protocol (LDP); latency; Layer 2 Tunneling Protocol (L2TP); Layer 3 switch; Layer 4 switch; link state protocol; local-area network (LAN); media access control (MAC) address; mesh topology; Message-ID; Metro Ethernet; metropolitan-area network (MAN); mobile IPv6 (MIPv6); multicast; Multi-access Edge Computing (MEC); multi-mode fiber; multiple input, multiple output (MIMO); multiplexer; Multiprotocol Label Switching (MPLS); multi-user multiple input, multiple output (MU MIMO); Near Field Communication (NFC); network access control (NAC); network access server (NAS); Network Address Translation (NAT); Network layer (Layer 3); Network Node Intrusion Detection System (NNIDS); network observability; network monitoring; noise; Open Shortest Path First (OSPF); Open Systems Interconnection (OSI) model; orthogonal frequency-division multiplexing (OFDM); packet filtering firewall; packet-switching network; Password Authentication Protocol (PAP); patch panel; perimeter network; personal-area network (PAN); phishing; Physical layer (Layer 1); ping of death attack; ping scanning; plain old telephone service (POTS); Point-to-Point Protocol (PPP); Point-to-Point Tunneling Protocol (PPTP); polling; Port Address Translation (PAT); port isolation; port scan; Post Office Protocol (POP); Presentation layer (Layer 6); Primary Rate Interface (PRI); private branch exchange (PBX); private IP address; proxy firewall; public switched telephone network (PSTN); radio frequency interference (RFI); remote access; Remote Authentication Dial-In User Service (RADIUS); reverse ARP (RARP); ring topology; router; Routing Information Protocol (RIP); screen scraper; screened host; screened subnet; secure HTTP (S-HTTP); Secure Sockets Layer (SSL); Sender Policy Framework (SPF); Serial Line Internet Protocol (SLIP); service set identifier (SSID); session hijacking attack; Session Initiation Protocol (SIP); Session layer (Layer 5); signal-to-noise ratio (SNR); Signaling System 7 (SS7); Simple Mail Transfer Protocol (SMTP); Simple Network Management Protocol (SNMP); single-mode fiber; smurf attack; Socket Secure (SOCKS) firewall; software-defined networking (SDN); spam; spear phishing; SSH File Transfer Protocol (SFTP); star topology; stateful firewall; stateful NAT (SNAT); static NAT; storage-area network (SAN); supplicant; Switched Multimegabit Data Service (SMDS); switch; SYN ACK attack; Synchronous Optical Networking (SONET); synchronous transmission; T-carrier; TCP three-way handshake; teardrop; Telnet; Terminal Access

Controller Access-Control System Plus (TACACS+); Thicknet; Thinnet; three-legged firewall; throughput; time-division multiplexing (TDM); token passing; Token Ring; traffic shaping; Transport layer (Layer 4); Transport Layer Security (SSL); twisted pair; unicast; unified threat management (UTM); URL hiding; Very High Bit-Rate DSL (VDSL); virtual local-area network (VLAN); virtual private network (VPN); Virtual Router Redundancy Protocol (VRRP); virtual storage-area network (VSAN); Voice over 5G (Vo5G); Voice over IP (VoIP); Voice over LTE (VoLTE); Voice over New Radio (VoNR); warchalking; war-driving; whaling; wide-area network (WAN); Wi-Fi 4; Wi-Fi 5; Wi-Fi 6; Wi-Fi 7; Wi-Fi 8; Wi-Fi Protected Access (WPA); Wired Equivalent Privacy (WEP); wireless access in vehicle environments (WAVE); wireless local-area network (WLAN); WPA2; X.25

Answer Review Questions

1. At which layer of the OSI model does the encapsulation process begin?
   a. Transport
   b. Application
   c. Physical
   d. Session

2. Which layers of the OSI model are equivalent to the Link layer of the TCP/IP model? (Choose two.)
   a. Data Link
   b. Physical
   c. Session
   d. Application
   e. Presentation

3. Which of the following represents the range of port numbers that is referred to as "well-known" port numbers?
   a. 49152–65535
   b. 0–1023
   c. 1024–49151
   d. All above 500

4. What is the port number for Hypertext Transfer Protocol (HTTP)?
   a. 23
   b. 443
   c. 80
   d. 110

5. What protocol in the Transmission Control Protocol/Internet Protocol (TCP/IP) suite resolves IP addresses to MAC addresses?
   a. ARP
   b. TCP
   c. IP
   d. ICMP

6. How many bits are contained in an IPv4 address?
   a. 128
   b. 48
   c. 32
   d. 64

7. Which of the following is a Class C IPv4 address?
   a. 172.16.5.6
   b. 192.168.5.54
   c. 10.6.5.8
   d. 224.6.6.6

8. Which of the following is a valid private IP address?
   a. 10.2.6.6
   b. 172.15.6.6
   c. 191.6.6.6
   d. 223.54.5.5

9. Which service converts private IP addresses to public IP addresses?
   a. DHCP (Dynamic Host Configuration Protocol)
   b. DNS (Domain Name System)
   c. NAT (Network Address Translation)
   d. WEP (Wired Equivalent Privacy)

10. Which of the following transmission types uses stop and start bits in its communication?
    a. Asynchronous
    b. Unicast
    c. Multicast
    d. Synchronous

11. Which protocol encapsulates Fibre Channel frames over Ethernet networks?
    a. MPLS (Multiprotocol Label Switching)
    b. FCoE (Fibre Channel over Ethernet)
    c. iSCSI (Internet Small Computer Systems Interface)
    d. VoIP (Voice over Internet Protocol)

12. Which protocol uses port number 143?
    a. Remote Desktop Protocol (RDP)
    b. Apple Filing Protocol (AFP)
    c. Internet Message Access Protocol (IMAP)
    d. Secure Shell Protocol (SSH)

13. Which of the following best describes NFS?
    a. An email protocol
    b. A directory query protocol that is based on X.500
    c. An Application layer protocol that is used to retrieve information from network devices
    d. A client/server file-sharing protocol used in Unix/Linux

14. Which of the following is a multilayer protocol that is used between components in process automation systems generally used in electric and water companies?
    a. DNP3 (Distributed Network Protocol 3)
    b. VoIP (Voice over Internet Protocol)
    c. WPA (Wi-Fi Protected Access)
    d. WPA2 (Wi-Fi Protected Access 2)

15. Which wireless communication standard includes multi-user, multiple input, multiple output (MU-MIMO)?
    a. 802.11a
    b. 802.11ac
    c. 802.11g
    d. 802.11n

16. Which of the following is a service that goes beyond authentication of the user and examines the state of the computer that the user is introducing to the network when making a remote access or VPN (virtual private network) connection to the network?
    a. NAC (network access control)
    b. SNAT (stateful network address translation)
    c. LDP (Label Distribution Protocol)
    d. RARP (Reverse Address Resolution Protocol)

17. Which of the following assigns an IP address to a device if the device is unable to communicate with the DHCP server in a Windows-based network?
    a. NFC (Near Field Communication)
    b. Dynamic NAT (Network Address Translation)
    c. APIPA (Automatic Private IP Addressing)
    d. Mobile IPv6

18. Which of the following is a field of security that attempts to protect individual systems in a network by staying in constant contact with them from a central location?
    a. IP convergence
    b. Remote access
    c. Static NAT
    d. Endpoint security

19. Which of the following accelerates software deployment and delivery, thereby reducing IT costs through policy-enabled workflow automation?
    a. Virtual storage-area network (VSAN)
    b. Internet Group Management Protocol (IGMP)
    c. Transport Layer Security/Secure Sockets Layer (TLS/SSL)
    d. Software-defined networking (SDN)

20. Which of the following types of Extensible Authentication Protocol (EAP) is *not* recommended for WLAN implementations because it supports one-way authentication and may allow the user's password to be derived?

    a. EAP-Message Digest 5 (EAP-MD5)

    b. EAP-Transport Layer Security (EAP-TLS)

    c. EAP-Tunneled TLS (EAP-TTLS)

    d. Protected EAP (PEAP)

21. Which of the following is considered the wireless access point during the 802.1X authentication process?

    a. Supplicant

    b. Authenticator

    c. Authentication server

    d. Multimedia collaborator

22. During a routine network security audit on a local network, you suspect the presence of several rogue wireless access points (WAPs). What should you do first to identify if and where any rogue WAPs have been deployed on the network?

    a. Adjust the power levels on all valid WAPs to decrease the coverage radius.

    b. Replace all valid WAP directional antennas with omnidirectional antennas.

    c. Perform a wireless site survey.

    d. Ensure that all valid WAPs are using WPA2.

23. Which of the following would be considered a valid IPv6 address?

    a. 192.72.103

    b. 11011000.00000101.000011

    c. 1.1.193.62

    d. 2001:0db8:0055:0000:cd23:0000:0000:0205/48

24. What type of attack occurs when more than one system or device floods the bandwidth of a targeted system or network?

    a. Domain Name System Security Extensions (DNSSEC)

    b. Domain grabbing

c. Cybersquatting

d. Distributed denial-of-service (DDoS)

25. What type of attack is occurring when the attacker intercepts legitimate traffic between two entities?

    a. Man-in-the-middle (MITM)

    b. Smurf

    c. Bluejacking

    d. Bluesnarfing

Answers and Explanations

1. **b.** The Application layer (Layer 7) is the place where the encapsulation process begins. This layer receives the raw data from the application in use and provides services such as file transfer and message exchange to the application (and thus the user).
2. **a, b.** The Link layer of the TCP/IP model provides the services provided by both the Data Link and the Physical layers in the OSI model.
3. **b.** The port numbers in the range 0 to 1023 are the well-known ports, or system ports. They are assigned by the IETF for standards-track protocols, as per RFC 6335.
4. **c.** The listed port numbers are as follows:

   23—Telnet

   443—HTTPS

   80—HTTP

   110—POP3
5. **a.** Address Resolution Protocol (ARP) resolves IP addresses to MAC addresses.
6. **c.** IPv4 addresses are 32 bits in length and can be represented in either binary or in dotted-decimal format. IPv6 addresses are 128 bits in length and are composed of hexadecimal characters.
7. **b.** The IP Class C range of addresses is from 192.0.0.0 to 223.255.255.255.
8. **a.** Valid private IP address ranges are

Class	Range
Class A	10.0.0.0–10.255.255.255
Class B	172.16.0.0–172.31.255.255
Class C	192.168.0.0–192.168.255.255

9. **c.** Network Address Translation (NAT) is a service that can be supplied by a router or by a server. The device that provides the service stands between the local LAN and the Internet. When packets need to go to the Internet, the packets go through the NAT service first. The NAT service changes the private IP address to a public address that is routable on the Internet. When the response is returned from the Web, the NAT service receives it and translates the address back to the original private IP address and sends it back to the originator.

10. **a.** With asynchronous transmission, the systems use start and stop bits to communicate when each byte is starting and stopping. This method also uses what are called parity bits to be used for the purpose of ensuring that each byte has not changed or been corrupted en route. This introduces additional overhead to the transmission.

11. **b.** Fibre Channel over Ethernet (FCoE) encapsulates Fibre Channel frames over Ethernet networks.

12. **c.** IMAP uses port 143. RDP uses port 3389. AFP (Apple Filing Protocol) uses port 548. SSH uses port 22.

13. **d.** NFS is a client/server file-sharing protocol used in Unix/Linux.

14. **a.** DNP3 is a multilayer protocol that is used between components in process automation systems in electric and water companies.

15. **b.** 802.11ac includes multi-user multiple-input, multiple-output (MU MIMO).

16. **a.** Network access control goes beyond authentication of the user and includes an examination of the state of the computer the user is introducing to the network when making a remote access or VPN connection to the network. Stateful NAT (SNAT) implements two or more NAT devices to work together as a translation group. One member provides network translation of IP address information. The other member uses that information to create duplicate translation table entries. Label Distribution Protocol (LDP) allows routers capable of Multiprotocol Label Switching (MPLS) to exchange label mapping information. Reverse ARP (RARP) resolves MAC addresses to IP addresses.

17. **c.** Automatic Private IP Addressing (APIPA) assigns an IP address to a device if the device is unable to communicate with the DHCP server; APIPA is primarily implemented in Windows. The range of IP addresses assigned is 169.254.0.1 to 169.254.255.254 with a subnet mask of 255.255.0.0. Near Field Communication (NFC) is a set of communication protocols that allow two electronic devices, one of which is usually a mobile device, to establish communication by bringing them within 2 inches of each other. With dynamic NAT, multiple internal private IP addresses are given access to multiple external public IP addresses. This is considered a many-to-many mapping. Mobile IPv6 (MIPv6) is an enhanced protocol supporting roaming for a mobile node

so that it can move from one network to another without losing IP-layer connectivity (as defined in RFC 3775).

18. **d.** Endpoint security is a field of security that attempts to protect individual systems in a network by staying in constant contact with these individual systems from a central location. IP convergence involves carrying different types of traffic over one network. The traffic includes voice, video, data, and images. It is based on the Internet Protocol (IP) and supports multimedia applications. Remote access allows users to access an organization's resources from a remote connection. These remote connections can be direct dial-in connections but more commonly use the Internet as the network over which the data is transmitted. With static NAT, an internal private IP address is mapped to a specific external public IP address. This is considered a one-to-one-mapping.

19. **d.** Software-defined networking (SDN) accelerates software deployment and delivery, thereby reducing IT costs through policy-enabled workflow automation. It enables cloud architectures by providing automated, on-demand application delivery and mobility at scale. A virtual storage-area network (VSAN) is a software-defined storage method that allows pooling of storage capabilities and instant and automatic provisioning of virtual machine storage. Internet Group Management Protocol (IGMP) provides multicasting capabilities to devices. Multicasting allows devices to transmit data to multiple recipients. IGMP is used by many gaming platforms. Transport Layer Security/Secure Sockets Layer (TLS/SSL) is used for creating secure connections to servers. It works at the Application layer of the OSI model. It is used mainly to protect HTTP traffic or web servers.

20. **a.** EAP-Message Digest 5 (EAP-MD5) provides base-level EAP support using one-way authentication. This method is not recommended for WLAN implementations because it may allow the user's password to be derived. EAP-Transport Layer Security (EAP-TLS) uses certificates to provide mutual authentication of the client and the network. The certificates must be managed on both the client and server side. EAP-Tunneled TLS (EAP-TTLS) provides for certificate-based, mutual authentication of the client and network through an encrypted channel (or tunnel). It requires only server-side certificates. Protected EAP (PEAP) securely transports authentication data, including legacy password-based protocols, via 802.11 Wi-Fi networks using tunneling between PEAP clients and an authentication server (AS). It uses only server-side certificates.

21. **b.** There are three basic entities during 802.1X authentication:

    - **Supplicant:** A software client running on the Wi-Fi workstation
    - **Authenticator:** The wireless access point
    - **Authentication server (AS):** A server that contains an authentication database, usually a RADIUS server

22. **c.** Administrators perform a site survey prior to deploying a new wireless network to determine the standard and possible channels deployed. After a wireless network is deployed, site surveys are used to determine whether rogue access points have been deployed or to determine where new access points should be deployed to increase the range of the wireless network. Although adjusting all WAP power levels, replacing all antennas, and ensuring WPA2 is being used are all related to WAPs, they are not the best solution to the question presented.

23. **d.** 2001:0db8:0055:0000:cd23:0000:0000:0205/48 is a valid IPv6 address that can be compressed to 2001:db8:55:0:cd23::205/48.

24. **d.** A distributed denial-of-service (DDoS) attack occurs when more than one system or device floods the bandwidth of a targeted system or network. A newer approach to preventing DNS attacks is a stronger authentication mechanism called Domain Name System Security Extensions (DNSSEC). Many current implementations of DNS software contain this functionality. It uses digital signatures to validate the source of all messages to ensure they are not spoofed. Domain grabbing occurs when individuals register a domain name of a well-known company before the company has the chance to do so. Then later the individuals hold the name hostage until the company becomes willing to pay to get the domain name. When domain names are registered with no intent to use them but with intent to hold them hostage, it is called cybersquatting.

25. **a.** A man-in-the-middle (MITM) attack intercepts legitimate traffic between two entities. The attacker can control information flow and can eliminate or alter the communication between the two parties. A smurf attack is a denial-of-service (DoS) attack that uses a type of ping packet called an ICMP ECHO REQUEST. Bluejacking occurs when an unsolicited message is sent to a Bluetooth-enabled device, often for the purpose of adding a business card to the victim's contact list. This attack can be prevented by placing the device in non-discoverable mode. Bluesnarfing is the unauthorized access to a device using the Bluetooth connection. In this case, the attacker is trying to access information on the device rather than send messages to the device.

This chapter covers the following topics:

- **Access Control Process:** Concepts discussed include the steps of the access control process.
- **Physical and Logical Access to Assets:** Concepts discussed include access control administration, information access, systems access, device access, facilities access, application access, and service access.
- **Identification and Authentication Concepts:** Concepts discussed include knowledge factors, ownership factors, characteristic factors, location factors, time factors, single- versus multifactor authentication, device authentication, password-less authentication, and groups and roles.
- **Identification and Authentication Implementation:** Concepts discussed include authentication, authorization, and accounting (AAA); separation of duties; least privilege/need-to-know; default to no access; directory service; single sign-on; federated identity management (IdM); session management; registration proof and registration of identity; credential management systems; Remote Authentication Dial-In User Service (RADIUS); Terminal Access Controller Access Control System Plus (TACACS+); and just-in-time (JIT).
- **Identity as a Service (IDaaS) Implementation:** Concepts discussed include the considerations when implementing IDaaS.
- **Third-Party Identity Services Integration:** This section details how to integrate third-party identity services in an enterprise, including on-premises, cloud, federated, and hybrid identity services.
- **Authorization Mechanisms:** This section covers permissions, rights, and privileges; access control models; and access control policies.
- **Provisioning Life Cycle:** This section describes the provisioning life cycle; identity and account management; user, system, and service account access review; account transfers; account revocation; role definition and transition; and privilege escalation.
- **Access Control Threats:** Concepts discussed include password threats, social engineering threats, DoS/DDoS, buffer overflow, mobile code, malicious software, spoofing, sniffing and eavesdropping, emanating, backdoor/trapdoor, access aggregation, and advanced persistent threat (APT).
- **Prevent or Mitigate Access Control Threats:** This section describes ways to prevent or mitigate access control threats.

CHAPTER 5

Identity and Access Management (IAM)

Identity and access management (IAM) is mainly concerned with controlling access to assets and managing identities. These assets include computers, equipment, networks, and applications. Security professionals must understand how to control physical and logical access to the assets and manage identification, authentication, and authorization systems. Finally, the access control threats must be addressed.

Identity and access management involves how access management works, why IAM is important, and how IAM components and devices work together in an enterprise. ***Access control*** allows only properly authenticated and authorized users, applications, devices, and systems to access enterprise resources and information. It includes facilities, support systems, information systems, network devices, and personnel. Security professionals use access controls to specify which users can access a resource, which resources can be accessed, which operations can be performed, and which actions will be monitored with or without giving an advanced warning.

Foundation Topics

Access Control Process

Although many approaches to implementing access controls have been designed, all the approaches generally involve the following steps:

Key Topic

1. Identify resources.
2. Identify users.
3. Identify the relationships between the resources and users.

Identify Resources

This first step in the access control process involves identifying all resources in the IT infrastructure by deciding which entities need to be protected. When identifying these resources, you must also consider how the resources will be accessed. You can use the following questions as a starting point during resource identification:

- Will this information be accessed by members of the general public?
- Should access to this information be restricted to employees only?
- Should access to this information be restricted to a smaller subset of employees?

Keep in mind that data, applications, services, servers, and network devices are all considered resources. Resources are any organizational asset that users can access or request access to. In access control, resources are often referred to as objects, and the requesting service or person as a subject.

Identify Users

After identifying the resources, an organization should identify the users who need access to the resources. The organization may also identify devices and services that will need access to resources. A typical security professional must manage multiple levels of users who require access to organizational resources. During this step, only identifying the users, devices, and services is important. The level of access these users will be given will be analyzed further in the next step. In access control, users, devices, and services are often referred to as subjects.

As part of this step, you must analyze and understand the users' needs and then measure the validity of those needs against organizational needs, policies, legal issues, data sensitivity, and risk.

Remember that any access control strategy and the system deployed to enforce it should avoid complexity. The more complex an access control system is, the harder that system is to manage and implement security. In addition, anticipating security issues that could occur in more complex systems is much harder. As a security professional, you must balance the organization's security needs and policies with the needs of the users. If a security mechanism that you implement causes too much difficulty for the user, the user might engage in practices that subvert the mechanisms that you implement. For example, if you implement a password policy that requires a very long, complex password, users might find remembering their passwords to be difficult. Users might then write their passwords on sticky notes that are attached to their monitor or keyboard.

Identify the Relationships Between Resources and Users

The final step in the access control process is to define the access control levels that need to be in place for each resource and the relationships between the resources and users, devices, and services. For example, if an organization has defined a web server as a resource, general employees might need a less restrictive level of access to the resource than the public and a more restrictive level of access to the resource than the web development staff. In addition, the web service may need access to certain resources, such as a database, to provide customers with the appropriate data after proper authentication. Access controls should be designed to support the business functionality of the resources that are being protected. Controlling the actions that can be performed for a specific resource based on a user's, device's, or service's role is vital.

Physical and Logical Access to Assets

Access control is all about using physical or logical controls to control who or what has access to a network, system, or device. It also involves what type of access is given to the information, network, system, device, facility, or services. Access control is primarily provided using physical and logical controls.

NOTE Physical and logical access controls are covered in more depth in Chapter 1, "Security and Risk Management."

Physical access focuses on controlling access to a network, system, or device. In most cases, physical access involves using access control to prevent users from being able to touch network components (including wiring), systems, or devices. Although locks are the most popular physical access control method to prevent access to devices in a data center, other ***physical controls***, such as guards and biometrics, should also be considered, depending on the needs of the organization and the value of the asset being protected.

Logical controls, also known as technical controls, limit the access a user has through software or hardware components. Authentication, logs, and encryption are examples of logical controls.

When installing an access control system, security professionals should understand who needs access to the asset being protected and how those users actually access the asset. When multiple users need access to an asset, the organization should implement defense in depth using a multilayer access control system. For example, users wanting access to the building may only need to sign in with a security guard. However, to access the locked data center within the same building, users would need a smart card. Both of these examples would be physical access controls. To protect data on a single server within the building (but not in the data center), the organization would need to deploy such mechanisms as authentication, encryption, and ***access control lists (ACLs)*** as logical access controls but could also place the server in a locked server room to provide physical access control.

When deploying physical and logical access controls, security professionals must understand the access control administration methods and the different assets that must be protected and their possible access controls.

Access Control Administration

Access control administration occurs in two basic manners: centralized and decentralized.

Centralized

In ***centralized access control***, a central department or personnel oversee the access for all organizational resources. This administration method ensures that user access is controlled in a consistent manner across the entire enterprise and applies to every single employee, including the CEO. However, centralized access control can be slow because all access requests have to be processed by the central entity. Any hack or disruption in the central entity's security can also disrupt the entire organization.

Decentralized

In ***decentralized access control***, personnel closest to the resources, such as department managers and data owners, oversee the access control for individual resources. This administration method ensures that those who know the data control the access rights to the data. However, decentralized access control can be hard to manage because there is no single entity responsible for configuring access rights. Decentralized access control thereby loses the uniformity and fairness of security.

Some companies may implement a hybrid approach that includes both centralized and decentralized access control. In this deployment model, centralized administration is used for basic access, but granular access to individual assets, such as data on a departmental server, is handled by the data owner as decentralized access.

Information

To fully protect information that is stored on an organization's network, servers, or other devices, security professionals must provide both physical and logical access controls. The physical access controls, such as placing devices in a locked room, protect the devices on which the information resides. The logical access controls—such as deploying data or drive encryption, transport encryption, ACLs, and firewalls—protect the data from unauthorized access.

The value of the information being protected will likely determine the controls that an organization is willing to deploy. For example, regular correspondence on a client computer will likely not require the same controls as financial data stored on a server. For the client computer, the organization may simply deploy a local software firewall and appropriate ACL permissions on the local folders and files. For the server, the organization may need to deploy more complex measures, including drive encryption, transport encryption, ACLs, and other measures.

Systems

To fully protect the systems that the organization uses, including client and server computers, security professionals may rely on both physical and logical access controls. However, some systems, like client computers, may be deployed in such a manner that only minimal physical controls are used. If a user is granted access to a building, that user may find client computers being used in nonsecure cubicles throughout the building. For these systems, a security professional must ensure that the appropriate authentication mechanisms are deployed. If confidential information is stored on the client computers, data encryption should also be deployed. But only the organization can best determine which controls to deploy on individual client computers.

When it comes to servers, determining which access controls to deploy is usually a more complicated process. Security professionals should work with the server owner, whether it is a department head or an IT professional, to determine the value of the asset and the needed protection. Of course, most servers should be placed in a locked room that has restricted access. In many cases, this will be a data center or server room. However, servers can be deployed in regular locked offices if necessary. In addition, other controls should be deployed to ensure that the system is fully protected. The access control needs of a file server are different from those of a web server or database server. It is vital that the organization perform a thorough assessment of the data that is being processed and stored on the system before determining which access controls to deploy. If limited resources are available, security professionals must ensure that their most important systems have more access controls than other systems.

Devices

As with systems, physical access to devices is best provided by placing the devices in a secure room. Logical access to devices is provided by implementing the appropriate ACL or rule list, authentication, and encryption, as well as securing any remote interfaces that are used to manage the device. In addition, security professionals should ensure that the default accounts and passwords are changed or disabled on all devices.

For any IT professionals that need to access the device, a user account should be configured for the professional with the appropriate level of access needed. If a remote interface is used, make sure to enable encryption, such as SSL, to ensure that communication via the remote interface is not intercepted and read. Security professionals should closely monitor vendor announcements for any devices to ensure that the devices are kept up to date with the latest security patches and firmware updates.

Facilities

With facilities, the primary concern is physical access, which can be provided using locks, fencing, bollards, guards, and closed-circuit television (CCTV). Many organizations think that such measures are enough. But with today's advanced industrial control systems and the Internet of Things (IoT), organizations must also consider any devices involved in facility security. If an organization has an alarm/security system that allows remote viewing access from the Internet, the appropriate logical controls must be in place to prevent a malicious user from accessing the system and changing its settings or from using the system to gain inside information about the facility layout and day-to-day operations. If the organization uses an industrial control system (ICS), logical controls should also be a priority. Security professionals must work with organizations to ensure that physical and logical controls are implemented appropriately to ensure that the entire facility is protected.

Applications

Applications are installed digitally on devices. Logical access involves controlling who can digitally access or install applications on a device. For organizations, these applications may require that security professionals use IAM solutions to permit or deny access to users and roles. Permission may be limited to using the application or may be as expansive as allowing the users to install applications. These applications may use enterprise IAM or an in-application mechanism. Security professionals may need to use group policies to control the ability to install the applications on Windows devices. Physical access to applications is a slightly different matter. Some applications are installed via digital media. Security professionals should ensure that the media is stored in a secured location, such as a locked filing cabinet. Physical access to an application can also be obtained by gaining physical access to a device on which the application is installed. Devices should be configured to enter sleep or standby mode after a certain amount of user inactivity. In addition, users should be trained to digitally lock their devices when they leave their desks. This would ensure that an unauthorized user is not able to access the application.

Security professionals should help establish the appropriate physical and logical controls for all applications.

Services

Services refer to various forms of software and hardware functionalities that are essential for the operations of an organization's IT environment. These can include:

- Software services: These are programs or processes that run in the background and perform specific tasks required by other software applications or the operating system itself. Examples include database services, web server services, and email services.
- Hardware services: This refers to the functionalities provided by physical devices, which can include network interface cards, network routers, switches, and firewalls. These devices often run their own software services to manage data routing, network security, and connection management.
- Cloud services: These services are offered over the Internet by cloud service providers, including Software as a Service (SaaS), Infrastructure as a Service (IaaS), and Platform as a Service (PaaS).

Services will need their own service account that can be used to manage the service's access. When using services, security professionals must fully assess the purpose of the service and deploy the appropriate controls to provide the following:

- Authentication and Authorization: Access to services is typically controlled through authentication (verifying the identity of a user or service) and authorization (determining if an authenticated entity has the right to access a service). This can involve mechanisms like passwords, tokens, digital certificates, and multifactor authentication (MFA).

- Role-Based Access Control (RBAC): This model restricts access to services based on the roles of individual users within an organization. It ensures that only authorized users can access specific services based on their job functions.
- Least Privilege Principle: This principle involves granting users or services the minimum levels of access needed to perform their functions. This reduces the risk of unauthorized access to sensitive services and minimizes the potential damage from a compromise.
- Network Segmentation and Firewalls: These are used to control access to services by separating networks into different segments and restricting access between them. Firewalls can block or allow traffic to services based on predefined security rules.
- Service Configuration Management: Properly configuring services to disable unnecessary functionalities, close unused ports, and apply the latest security patches is crucial for reducing vulnerabilities and controlling access.
- Monitoring and Logging: Continuous monitoring of service access and maintaining logs are essential for detecting unauthorized access attempts, ensuring compliance with access policies, and facilitating forensic analysis in case of security incidents.

Controlling physical and logical access to services is foundational to protecting an organization's assets. Security professionals must be adept at implementing and managing access control mechanisms to ensure that only authorized users and systems can access critical services. This involves a thorough understanding of the services running within the organization's environment, the potential vulnerabilities associated with these services, and the best practices for securing them against unauthorized access. By effectively controlling access to services, security professionals help maintain the security and integrity of the organization's information systems and data, aligning with the core goals of information security management.

Identification and Authentication Concepts

To be able to access a resource, a user, device, or service must profess an identity, provide the necessary credentials, and have the appropriate rights to perform the tasks to be completed. The first step in this process is called ***identification***, which is the act of a user, device, or service professing an identity to an access control system. Often, this is part of the hiring process, whereby a user provides a photo ID for identity verification. Identification allows an account to be created for the user in the enterprise.

Authentication, the second part of the process, is the act of validating a user, device, or service with a unique identifier by providing the appropriate credentials. When trying to differentiate between the two, security professionals should know that *identification* identifies the user, device, or service and *authentication* verifies that the identity provided by the user, device, or service is valid. Authentication is usually implemented through a password or one-time code provided at login. When a user, device, or service logs in to a system, the login process should validate the login after the user, device, or service supplies all the input data.

After a user, device, or service is authenticated, the user, device, or service must be granted the rights and permissions to resources. The process is referred to as ***authorization***.

The most popular forms of user identification—either issued by an organization or self-generated by users—include user IDs or user accounts, account numbers, and personal identification numbers (PINs).

NIST SP 800-63

NIST Special Publication (SP) 800-63 provides a suite of technical requirements for federal agencies implementing digital identity services, including an overview of identity frameworks, using authenticators, credentials, and assertions in digital systems. In July 2017, NIST finalized the four-volume SP 800-63 entitled "Digital Identity Guidelines." The four volumes in this SP are as follows:

- **SP 800-63 Digital Identity Guidelines:** Provides the risk assessment methodology and an overview of general identity frameworks, using authenticators, credentials, and assertions together in a digital system, and a risk-based process of selecting assurance levels. SP 800-63 contains both normative and informative material.
- **SP 800-63A Enrollment and Identity Proofing:** Addresses how applicants can prove their identities and become enrolled as valid subjects within an identity system. It provides requirements for processes by which applicants can both proof and enroll at one of three different levels of risk mitigation in both remote and physically present scenarios. SP 800-63A contains both normative and informative material.
- **SP 800-63B Authentication and Life Cycle Management:** Addresses how an individual can securely authenticate to a credential service provider (CSP) to access a digital service or set of digital services. This volume also describes the process of binding an authenticator to an identity. SP 800-63B contains both normative and informative material.

- **SP 800-63C Federation and Assertions:** Provides requirements on the use of federated identity architectures and assertions to convey the results of authentication processes and relevant identity information to an agency application. Furthermore, this volume offers privacy-enhancing techniques to share information about a valid, authenticated subject, and describes methods that allow for strong multifactor authentication (MFA) while the subject remains pseudonymous to the digital service. SP 800-63C contains both normative and informative material.

Specifically in SP 800-63B, passwords fall into the category of memorized secrets. Memorized secrets and other password guidelines are given that may or may not differ greatly from those that were given in the past and we are following today:

- Memorized secrets should be at least 8 characters in length if chosen by the subscriber or at least 6 characters in length if chosen randomly by the CSP or verifier.
- Verifiers should require subscriber-chosen memorized secrets to be at least 8 characters in length and should be allowed to include all printing ASCII characters, the space character, and Unicode characters.
- Memorized secrets that are randomly chosen by the CSP or by the verifier should be at least 6 characters in length and should be generated using an approved random bit generator.
- Memorized secret verifiers should not permit the subscriber to store a "hint" that is accessible to an unauthenticated claimant. Verifiers should not prompt subscribers to use specific types of information (e.g., "What was the name of your first pet?") when choosing memorized secrets.
- When processing requests to establish and change memorized secrets, verifiers should compare the prospective secrets against a list that contains values known to be commonly used, expected, or compromised. For example, the list *may* include but is not limited to passwords obtained from previous breach corpuses, dictionary words, repetitive or sequential characters (e.g., "aaaaaa" or "1234abcd"), and context-specific words, such as the name of the service, the username, and derivatives thereof.
- Verifiers should offer guidance to the subscriber, such as a password-strength meter, to assist the user in choosing a strong memorized secret.
- Verifiers should implement a rate-limiting mechanism that effectively limits the number of failed authentication attempts that can be made on the subscriber's account.

- Verifiers should not impose other composition rules (e.g., requiring mixtures of different character types or prohibiting consecutively repeated characters) for memorized secrets. Verifiers should not require memorized secrets to be changed arbitrarily (e.g., periodically). However, verifiers should force a change if there is evidence of compromise of the authenticator.
- Verifiers should permit claimants to use "paste" functionality when entering a memorized secret, thereby facilitating the use of password managers, which are widely used and in many cases increase the likelihood that users will choose stronger memorized secrets.
- To assist the claimant in successfully entering a memorized secret, the verifier should offer an option to display the secret—rather than a series of dots or asterisks—until it is entered.
- The verifier should use approved encryption and an authenticated protected channel when requesting memorized secrets to provide resistance to eavesdropping and man-in-the-middle attacks.
- Verifiers should store memorized secrets in a form that is resistant to offline attacks. Memorized secrets should be salted and hashed using a suitable one-way key derivation function. The salt should be at least 32 bits in length and be chosen arbitrarily so as to minimize salt value collisions among stored hashes. Both the salt value and the resulting hash should be stored for each subscriber using a memorized secret authenticator.

According to NIST SP 800-63B, passwords remain a very widely used form of authentication despite widespread frustration with the use of passwords from both a usability and security standpoint. Humans, however, have only a limited ability to memorize complex, arbitrary secrets, so they often choose passwords that can be easily guessed. To address the resultant security concerns, online services have introduced rules in an effort to increase the complexity of these memorized secrets. The most notable form of these is composition rules, which require the user to choose passwords constructed using a mix of character types, such as at least one digit, uppercase letter, and symbol. However, analyses of breached password databases reveal that the benefit of such rules is not nearly as significant as initially thought, although the impact on usability and memorability is severe. A different and somewhat simpler approach, based primarily on password length, is presented in SP 800-63B.

Many attacks associated with the use of passwords are not affected by password complexity and length. Keystroke logging, phishing, and social engineering attacks are as equally effective on lengthy, complex passwords as simple ones.

Password length has been found to be a primary factor in characterizing password strength. Passwords that are too short yield to brute-force attacks as well as to dictionary attacks using words and commonly chosen passwords.

The minimum password length that should be required depends to a large extent on the threat model being addressed. Online attacks where the attacker attempts to log in by guessing the password can be mitigated by limiting the rate of login attempts permitted. To prevent an attacker (or a persistent claimant with poor typing skills) from easily inflicting a denial-of-service attack on the subscriber by making many incorrect guesses, passwords need to be complex enough that rate limiting does not occur after a modest number of erroneous attempts but does occur before there is a significant chance of a successful guess.

Users should be encouraged to make their passwords as lengthy as they want, within reason. Since the size of a hashed password is independent of its length, there is no reason not to permit the use of lengthy passwords (or passphrases) if the user wishes. Extremely long passwords (perhaps megabytes in length) could conceivably require excessive processing time to hash, so it is reasonable to have some limit.

Composition rules are commonly used in an attempt to increase the difficulty of guessing user-chosen passwords. Research has shown, however, that users respond in very predictable ways to the requirements imposed by composition rules. For example, a user who might have chosen the word "password" as a password may choose "Password1" if required to include an uppercase letter and a number, or "Password1!" if a symbol is also required.

Users also express frustration when attempts to create complex passwords are rejected by online services. Many services reject passwords with spaces and various special characters. In some cases, not accepting certain special characters might be an effort to avoid attacks, like SQL injection, that use the characters as reserved words in SQL programming language. But a properly hashed password would not be sent intact to a database in any case, so such precautions are unnecessary. Spaces themselves add little to the complexity of passwords and may introduce usability issues (e.g., the undetected use of two spaces rather than one), so it may be beneficial to remove repeated spaces in typed passwords prior to verification.

Most users' password choices can be somewhat predictable depending on their hobbies and social interactions, so attackers are likely to guess passwords that have been successful in the past. They include dictionary words and passwords from previous breaches, such as the "Password1!" discussed in the previous example. For this reason, it is recommended that passwords chosen by users be compared against a "blacklist" of unacceptable passwords that the organization has adopted and documented. This list should include passwords from previous breach corpuses, dictionary words, and specific words (such as the name of the service itself) that users are likely to choose. Because user choice of passwords will also be governed by a minimum length requirement, this dictionary need only include entries meeting that requirement.

Highly complex memorized secrets introduce a new potential vulnerability: they are less likely to be memorable, and it is more likely that they will be written down or stored electronically in an unsafe manner. Although these practices are not necessarily vulnerable, statistically some methods of recording such secrets will be. Preventing such a vulnerability is an additional motivation not to require excessively long or complex memorized secrets.

Another factor that determines the strength of memorized secrets is the process by which they are generated. Secrets that are randomly chosen (in most cases by the verifier and are uniformly distributed) will be more difficult to guess or brute-force attack than user-chosen secrets meeting the same length and complexity requirements.

Five Factors for Authentication

After establishing the user, device, or service identification method, an organization must decide which authentication method to use.

Authentication methods are divided into five broad categories:

Key Topic

- ***Knowledge factor authentication***: Something a person knows
- ***Ownership factor authentication***: Something a person has or possesses
- ***Characteristic factor authentication***: Something a person is
- ***Location factor authentication***: Somewhere a person is
- ***Time factor authentication***: The time a person is authenticating

NOTE Originally, there were three factors (something you know, something you have, and something you are). They were referred to as Type I, Type II, and Type III factors, respectively. However, modern technology has forced the security field to recently recognize two additional factors: somewhere you are and the time of authentication.

Knowledge Factors

As briefly described in the preceding section, knowledge factor authentication is authentication that is provided based on something that a person knows. Although the most popular form of authentication used by this category is password authentication, other knowledge factors can be used, including date of birth, mother's maiden name, key combination, or PIN.

Password Types and Management

As mentioned earlier, password authentication is the most popular authentication method implemented today. However, password types can vary from system to system. Understanding all the types of passwords that can be used is vital. Passwords and other knowledge factors are referred to as memorized secrets in NIST SP 800-63.

The types of passwords that you should be familiar with include

Key Topic

- **Standard word or simple passwords:** As the name implies, these passwords consist of single words that often include a mixture of upper- and lowercase letters and numbers. The advantage of this password type is that it is easy to remember. A disadvantage of this password type is that it is easy for attackers to crack or break, resulting in a compromised account.
- **Combination passwords:** This password type uses a mix of dictionary words, usually two unrelated words. These are also referred to as composition passwords. Like standard word passwords, they can include upper- and lowercase letters and numbers. An advantage of this password is that it is harder to break than simple passwords. A disadvantage is that it can be hard to remember.
- **Static passwords:** This password type is the same for each login. It provides a minimum level of security because the password never changes. It is most often seen in peer-to-peer networks.
- **Complex passwords:** This password type forces a user to include a mixture of upper- and lowercase letters, numbers, and special characters. For many organizations today, this type of password is enforced as part of the organization's password policy. An advantage of this password type is that it is very hard to crack. A disadvantage is that it is harder to remember and can often be much harder to enter correctly than standard or combination passwords.
- **Passphrase passwords:** This password type requires that a long phrase be used. Because of the password's length, it is easier to remember but much harder to attack, both of which are definite advantages. Incorporating upper- and lowercase letters, numbers, and special characters in this type of password can significantly increase authentication security.
- **Cognitive passwords:** This password type is a piece of information that can be used to verify an individual's identity. This information is provided to the system by answering a series of questions based on the user's life, such as

favorite color, pet's name, mother's maiden name, and so on. An advantage to this type is that users can usually easily remember this information. The disadvantage is that someone who has intimate knowledge of the person's life (spouse, child, sibling, and so on) might be able to provide this information as well.

- **One-time passwords:** Also called a dynamic password, this type of password is used only once to log in to the access control system. This password type provides the highest level of security because the one-time passwords can be used just once and discarded within a certain timeframe or after they are used.
- **Graphical passwords:** Also called CAPTCHA, which stands for Completely Automated Public Turing test to tell Computers and Humans Apart, passwords, this type of password uses graphics as part of the authentication mechanism. One popular implementation requires a user to enter a series of characters in the graphic displayed. This implementation ensures that a human is entering the password, not a robot. Another popular implementation requires users to select the appropriate graphic for their accounts from a list of graphics shown to the users. The list changes dynamically every time a user tries to log in.
- **Numeric passwords:** This type of password includes only numbers. Keep in mind that the choices of a password are limited by the number of digits allowed. For example, if all passwords are four digits, then the maximum number of password possibilities is 10,000, from 0000 through 9999. After an attacker realizes that only numbers are used, cracking user passwords would be much easier because all the possibilities for a certain number of digits can be easily known.

Passwords are considered weaker than passphrases, one-time passwords, token devices, and login phrases. After an organization has decided which type of password to use, the organization must establish its password management policies.

Password management considerations include

Key Topic

- **Password life:** How long the password will be valid. For many organizations, passwords are valid for 60 to 90 days. This setting is adjustable based on organizational needs.
- **Password history:** How long before a password can be reused. Password policies usually remember a certain number of previously used passwords.
- **Authentication period:** How long a user can remain logged in. If a user remains logged in for the period without activity, the user will be automatically logged out.

- **Password complexity:** How the password will be structured. Most organizations require upper- and lowercase letters, numbers, and special characters.
- **Password length:** How long the password must be. Most organizations require longer passwords and set their own length.
- ***Password masking*:** Prevents a password from being learned through shoulder surfing by obscuring the characters entered.

As part of password management, organizations should establish a procedure for changing passwords. Most organizations implement a service that allows users to automatically reset their password before the password expires. In addition, most organizations should consider establishing a password reset policy in cases where users have forgotten their password or passwords have been compromised. A self-service password reset approach allows users to reset their own passwords without the assistance of help desk employees. An assisted password reset approach requires that users contact help desk personnel for help in changing their passwords.

Password reset policies can also be affected by other organizational policies, such as account lockout policies. Account lockout policies are security policies that organizations implement to protect against attacks that are carried out against passwords. Organizations often configure account lockout policies so that user accounts are locked after a certain number of unsuccessful login attempts. If an account is locked out, the system administrator might need to unlock or re-enable the user account. Security professionals should also consider encouraging organizations to require users to reset their passwords if their accounts have been locked or after a password has been used for a certain amount of time (often 90 days). For most organizations, all the password policies, including account lockout policies, are implemented at the enterprise level on the servers that manage the network. Account lockout policies are most often used to protect against brute-force or dictionary attacks.

NOTE An older term that you might need to be familiar with is *clipping level*. A clipping level is a configured baseline threshold above which violations will be recorded. For example, an organization might want to start recording any unsuccessful login attempts after the first one, with account lockout occurring after five failed attempts. This concept is referred to as rate limiting in NIST SP 800-63, which is discussed later in this chapter.

Depending on which servers are used to manage the enterprise, security professionals must be aware of the security issues that affect user account and password management. Two popular server operating systems are Linux and Windows.

For Linux, passwords are stored in the */etc/passwd* or */etc/shadow* file. Because the */etc/passwd* file is a text file that can be easily accessed using administrative-level accounts, you should ensure that any Linux servers use the */etc/shadow* file where the passwords in the file can be protected using a hash. The *root* user in Linux is a default account that is given administrative-level access to the entire server. If the *root* account is compromised, all passwords should be changed. Access to the *root* account should be limited only to system administrators, and root login should be allowed only via a local system console, not remotely.

For Windows computers that are in workgroups, the Security Accounts Manager (SAM) stores user passwords in a hashed format. However, known security issues exist with a SAM, including the ability to dump the password hashes directly from the registry. You should take all Microsoft-recommended security measures to protect this file. If you manage a Windows network, you should change the name of the default Administrator account or disable it. If this account is retained, make sure that you assign it a password. The default Administrator account might have full access to a Windows server.

Ownership Factors

Ownership factor authentication is authentication that is provided based on something that a person has. Ownership factors can include token devices, memory cards, phones, keys, fobs, and smart cards.

Synchronous and Asynchronous Token Devices

The token device (often referred to as a password generator) is a handheld device that presents the authentication server with the one-time password. If the authentication method requires a token device, the user must be in physical possession of the device to authenticate. So, although the token device provides a password to the authentication server, the token device is considered an ownership authentication factor because its use requires ownership of the device.

Two basic token device authentication methods are used: synchronous or asynchronous. A synchronous token generates a unique password at fixed time intervals with the authentication server. An asynchronous token generates the password based on a challenge/response technique with the authentication server, with the token device providing the correct answer to the authentication server's challenge.

A token device is usually implemented only in very secure environments because of the cost of deploying the token device. In addition, token-based solutions can experience problems if they include a battery because of the battery lifespan of the token device.

Memory Cards

A memory card is a swipe card that is issued to valid users. The card contains user authentication information. When the card is swiped through a card reader, the information stored on the card is compared to the information that the user enters. If the information matches, the authentication server approves the login. If it does not match, authentication is denied.

Because the card must be read by a card reader, each computer or access device must have its own card reader. In addition, the cards must be created and programmed. Both of these steps add complexity and cost to the authentication process. However, it is often worth the extra complexity and cost for the added security it provides, which is a definite benefit of this system. However, the data on the memory cards is not protected, a weakness that organizations should consider before implementing this type of system. Memory-only cards can be counterfeited.

Smart Cards

Similar to a memory card, a smart card accepts, stores, and sends data but can hold more data than a memory card. Smart cards, often known as integrated circuit cards (ICCs), contain memory like a memory card but also contain an embedded chip like bank or credit cards. Smart cards use card readers. However, the data on the smart card is used by the authentication server without user input. To protect against lost or stolen smart cards, most implementations require the user to input a secret PIN, meaning the user is actually providing both a knowledge (PIN) and ownership (smart card) authentication factor.

Two basic types of smart cards are used: contact cards and contactless cards. Contact cards require physical contact with the card reader, usually by swiping. Contactless cards, also referred to as proximity cards, simply need to be in close proximity to the reader. Hybrid cards are available that allow a card to be used in both contact and contactless systems.

For comparative purposes, security professionals should remember that smart cards have processing power due to the embedded chips. Memory cards do not have processing power. Smart card systems are much more reliable than memory card systems.

Smart cards are even more expensive to implement than memory cards. Many organizations prefer smart cards over memory cards because they are harder to counterfeit and the data on them can be protected using a variety of encryption methods.

Characteristic Factors

Characteristic factor authentication is authentication that is provided based on something that a person is. Biometric technology is the technology that allows users to be authenticated based on physiological or behavioral characteristics. Physiological characteristics include any unique physical attribute of the user, including iris, retina, and fingerprints. Behavioral characteristics measure a person's actions in a situation, including voice patterns and data entry characteristics.

Biometric technologies are now common in some of the most popular operating systems. Examples include Windows Hello and Apple's Touch ID and Face ID technologies. As a security professional, you need to be aware of such new technologies as they are deployed to provide added security. Educating users on these technologies should also be a priority to ensure that users adopt these technologies as they are deployed.

Physiological Characteristics

Physiological systems use a biometric scanning device to measure certain information about a physiological characteristic. Keep in mind that any changes to the physiological characteristics can affect authentication. For example, if a facial scan system is used and a user undergoes facial surgery, often a new stored scan will need to be performed so that the user can be authenticated.

You should understand the following physiological biometric systems:

Key Topic

- Fingerprint
- Finger scan
- Hand geometry
- Hand topography
- Palm or hand scans
- Facial scans
- Retina scans
- Iris scans
- Vascular scans

A fingerprint scan usually scans the ridges of a finger for matching. A special type of fingerprint scan called minutiae matching is more microscopic in that it records the bifurcations and other detailed characteristics. Minutiae matching requires more authentication server space and more processing time than ridge fingerprint scans. Fingerprint scanning systems have a lower user acceptance rate than many systems because users are concerned with how the fingerprint information will be used and shared.

A finger scan extracts only certain features from a fingerprint. Because a limited amount of the fingerprint information is needed, finger scans require relatively less server space or processing time than any type of fingerprint scan.

A hand geometry scan usually obtains size, shape, or other layout attributes of a user's hand but can also measure bone length or finger length. Two categories of hand geometry systems are mechanical and image-edge detective systems. Regardless of which category is used, hand geometry scanners require less server space and processing time than fingerprint or finger scans.

A hand topography scan records the peaks and valleys of the hand and its shape. This system is usually implemented in conjunction with hand geometry scans because hand topography scans are not unique enough if used alone.

A palm or hand scan combines fingerprint and hand geometry technologies. It records fingerprint information from every finger as well as hand geometry information.

A facial scan records facial characteristics, including bone structure, eye width, and forehead size. This biometric method uses eigenfeatures or eigenfaces. Neither of these methods actually captures a real picture of a face. With eigenfeatures, the distance between facial features is measured and recorded. With eigenfaces, measurements of facial components are gathered and compared to a set of standard eigenfaces. For example, a person's face might be composed of the average face plus 21 percent from eigenface 1, 83 percent from eigenface 2, and –18 percent from eigenface 3. Many facial scan biometric devices use a combination of eigenfeatures and eigenfaces for better security.

A retina scan scans the retina's blood vessel pattern. A retina scan is considered more intrusive than an iris scan.

An iris scan scans the colored portion of the eye, including all rifts, coronas, and furrows. Iris scans have a higher accuracy than any other biometric scan.

A vascular scan scans the pattern of veins in the user's hand or face. Although this method can be a good choice because it is not very intrusive, physical injuries to the hand or face, depending on which the system uses, could cause false rejections.

Users are often afraid of eye scans. It is important to educate your users about them to ensure user acceptance. Otherwise, the organization may want to choose another method.

Behavioral Characteristics

Key Topic

Behavioral systems use a biometric scanning device to measure a person's actions. You should understand the following behavioral biometric systems:

- Signature dynamics
- Keystroke dynamics
- Voice pattern or print

Signature dynamics measure stroke speed, pen pressure, and acceleration and deceleration while users write their signatures. Dynamic signature verification (DSV) analyzes signature features and specific features of the signing process.

Keystroke dynamics measure the typing pattern that a user uses when inputting a password or other predetermined phrase. In this case, even if the correct password or phrase is entered but the entry pattern on the keyboard is different, the user will be denied access. *Flight time*, a term associated with keystroke dynamics, is the amount of time it takes to switch between keys. *Dwell time* is the amount of time you hold down a key.

Voice pattern or print measures the sound pattern of a user stating a certain word. When the user attempts to authenticate, that user will be asked to repeat those words in different orders. If the pattern matches, authentication is allowed. These may be unreliable due to mimicry.

Biometric Considerations

Key Topic

When considering biometric technologies, security professionals should understand the following terms:

- **Enrollment time:** The process of obtaining the sample that is used by the biometric system. This process requires actions that must be repeated several times.
- **Feature extraction:** The approach to obtaining biometric information from a collected sample of a user's physiological or behavioral characteristics.
- ***Biometric accuracy*:** The most important characteristic of biometric systems. It is how correct the overall readings will be. However, no biometric system is 100% accurate.
- ***Biometric throughput rate*:** The rate at which the biometric system will be able to scan characteristics and complete the analysis to permit or deny access. The acceptable rate is 6–10 subjects per minute. A single user should be able to complete the process in 5–10 seconds.
- ***Biometric acceptability*:** The likelihood that users will accept and follow the system.

- ***False rejection rate (FRR)*:** A measurement of valid users that will be falsely rejected by the system. This is called a Type I error.
- ***False acceptance rate (FAR)*:** A measurement of the percentage of invalid users that will be falsely accepted by the system. This is called a Type II error. Type II FAR errors are more dangerous than Type I FRR errors.
- ***Crossover error rate (CER)*:** The point at which FRR equals FAR. Expressed as a percentage, this is the most important metric. It shows the accuracy at which the system functions.

When analyzing biometric systems, security professionals often refer to a Zephyr chart that illustrates the comparative strengths and weaknesses of biometric systems. However, you should also consider how effective each biometric system is and its level of user acceptance. The more popular biometric methods are ranked here by effectiveness, with the most effective being first:

1. Iris scan
2. Retina scan
3. Fingerprint
4. Handprint
5. Hand geometry
6. Voice pattern
7. Keystroke pattern
8. Signature dynamics

The more popular biometric methods ranked by user acceptance follow, with the methods that are ranked more popular by users being first:

1. Voice pattern
2. Keystroke pattern
3. Signature dynamics
4. Hand geometry
5. Handprint
6. Fingerprint
7. Iris scan
8. Retina scan

When considering FAR, FRR, and CER, smaller values are better. FAR errors are more dangerous than FRR errors. Security professionals can use the CER for comparative analysis when helping their organization decide which system to implement. For example, voice print systems usually have higher CERs than iris scans, hand geometry, or fingerprints.

Figure 5-1 shows the biometric enrollment and authentication process.

Key Topic

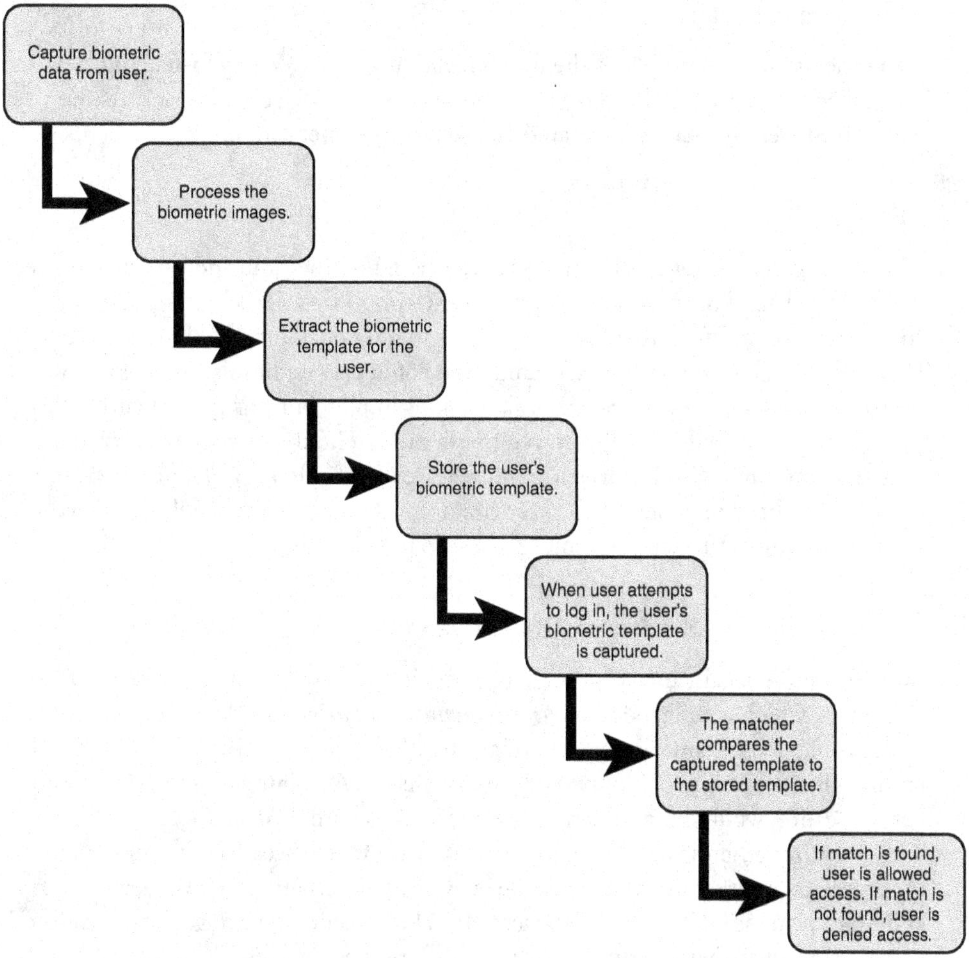

Figure 5-1 Biometric Enrollment and Authentication Process

Location Factors

Location factor authentication provides a means of authenticating the user based on the location from which the user is authenticating. This could include the computer or device the person is using or the geographic location based on GPS coordinates. The primary appeal to this type of authentication is that it limits the user to logging in from those certain locations only. This type of authentication is particularly useful in large manufacturing environments for users who should log in to only certain terminals in the facility.

Geo-fencing is one example of the use of location factors. With geo-fencing, devices operate correctly within the geo-fence boundaries. If a device enters or exits the geo-fenced area, an alert is generated and sent to the operator.

Time Factors

Time factor authentication authenticates a user based on the time and/or date the user is authenticating. For example, if certain users work only a set schedule, you can configure their accounts to allow them to log in only during those set work hours. However, keep in mind that such a limitation could cause administrative issues if overtime hours are allowed. Some organizations implement this type of authentication effectively by padding the allowed hours with an hour or two leeway for the start and end times. Credit cards use this feature effectively to protect their customers. If transactions take place in a short timeframe from geographically dispersed locations, credit cards will often block the second transaction.

Single-Factor Versus Multifactor Authentication

Authentication usually ensures that a user provide at least one factor from the five categories, which is referred to as ***single-factor authentication***. An example would be providing a username and password at login. Two-factor authentication (2FA) ensures that the user provides two of the five factors. An example of two-factor authentication would be providing a username, password, and smart card at login. Three-factor authentication ensures that a user provides three factors. An example of three-factor authentication would be providing a username, password, smart card, and fingerprint at login. For authentication to be considered strong authentication, a user must provide factors from at least two different categories. (Note that the username is the identification factor, not an authentication factor.)

The term ***multifactor authentication (MFA)*** is used when more than one authentication factor is used. So, two-factor or three-factor authentication may be referred to as multifactor authentication.

You should understand that providing multiple authentication factors from the same category is still considered single-factor authentication. For example, if a user provides a username, password, and the user's mother's maiden name, single-factor authentication is being used. In this example, the user is still only providing factors that are something a person knows.

Device Authentication

Device authentication, also referred to as endpoint authentication, is a form of authentication that relies on the identity of the device as part of the authentication process. With device authentication, the identity of the device from which a user logs in is included as part of the authentication process, thereby providing two-factor authentication using the device and user's credentials. If the user then attempts to log in from a different device, the authentication system recognizes that a new device is being used and asks the user to provide extra authentication verification information, usually an answer to a security question. The user is usually then given the option to include this device in the authentication (if the device is a private device) or not (if the device is a public device). In this manner, the device itself becomes a security token and, as such, becomes a "something you have" authentication factor.

Security professionals should not confuse device authentication with a system that uses a known mobile device or email to provide a one-time password or PIN needed for authentication. When a system transmits the one-time password or PIN that must be used as part of authentication to a mobile device or via email, this is just another authentication factor, not device authentication. With this system, the user registers a mobile device number or email address with the authentication system. When the user logs in, that user usually provides two factors of authentication. After authentication of the initial factors is completed, the one-time password or PIN is transmitted to the known device or email, which the user must input as part of a second authentication interface.

Password-Less Authentication

Password-less authentication is an authentication method that does not require users to remember or enter a password to gain access to systems or services. Instead, it relies on alternative mechanisms to verify identity. Password-less authentication methods are designed to enhance security while also improving user convenience and reducing the risks associated with password management.

Password-less authentication can be implemented using various methods, including:

- Biometric Authentication: Uses unique physical characteristics, such as fingerprints, facial recognition, or iris scans, to verify identity.
- Security Tokens: Hardware devices, such as USB tokens, or software-based tokens generate a one-time use authentication code.

- Mobile Device Authentication: Utilizes a smartphone app to confirm identity through push notifications, QR codes, or location-based methods.
- SMS or Email Verification: Sends a one-time code to the user's registered phone number or email address, which they then use to log in.

Password-less authentication methods are often considered more secure than traditional password-based systems, which are vulnerable to phishing, brute force, and social engineering attacks. By eliminating passwords, organizations reduce the risk of password-related breaches.

Password fatigue is a common issue in security, where users are overwhelmed by the need to remember multiple complex passwords. Password-less systems simplify the login process, improving user satisfaction and compliance with security policies.

Password-less methods can be integrated into MFA strategies, serving as one of the factors in a multifactor approach. This aligns with the principle of layering security controls to create a more robust defense.

When designing an identification and authentication strategy that includes password-less methods, security professionals should consider:

- Technology and Infrastructure Requirements: Implementing password-less authentication may require new technologies or infrastructure changes. Security professionals must evaluate the compatibility, costs, and deployment challenges associated with these methods.
- User Education and Acceptance: Transitioning to password-less systems may require user training and awareness programs to ensure smooth adoption and to maximize the security benefits.
- Regulatory and Compliance Impacts: Security professionals must ensure that the chosen password-less methods comply with all relevant laws, regulations, and industry standards.
- Recovery and Backup Mechanisms: Even in password-less systems, there needs to be a secure method for account recovery and authentication backup in case the primary method is unavailable.

Password-less authentication offers a promising alternative to traditional password-based systems, providing enhanced security and user convenience. Security professionals must carefully design and implement these systems, considering the unique needs and constraints of their organizations, to effectively secure access to assets.

Groups and Roles

Understanding the concepts of groups and roles is fundamental to effectively managing access control and security policies within an organization. These concepts streamline the process of granting appropriate access rights and permissions to users, devices, and services based on their functions, responsibilities, or characteristics.

In cybersecurity and access management, a group is a collection of users, devices, or other entities that share common access requirements to resources and services. Groups simplify access management by allowing administrators to assign permissions and access rights to a collective entity rather than individually. This is particularly useful in large organizations where managing access rights individually would be impractical and time-consuming.

A role represents a set of permissions and access rights tied to the job functions or responsibilities within an organization. Roles are assigned to users based on their job duties and what access they need to perform their tasks. Roles support the implementation of the principle of least privilege by ensuring that users receive only the access necessary to fulfill their job functions, no more, no less. This minimizes the risk of unauthorized access and limits the potential damage from insider threats or compromised accounts.

Groups and roles are used in the following manners:

- Access Control: Implementing RBAC systems is a common practice where roles are defined with specific permissions, and users are then assigned to these roles. This methodology streamlines the process of granting appropriate access to resources, ensuring users can perform their jobs without unnecessary access that could pose a security risk.

- Security Policy Enforcement: Groups and roles are used to enforce security policies consistently across the organization. For example, a group might be created for all users who require access to a particular system, and a role might define what actions users can take within that system. This helps in maintaining a secure and controlled environment.

- Efficiency and Scalability: Using groups and roles allows for more efficient management of user access rights and can easily scale as the organization grows. Adding a new user to a group or assigning them a role automatically grants them the access they need without the need to configure permissions individually.

For security professionals tasked with designing identification and authentication strategies, understanding and effectively utilizing groups and roles is essential. This involves:

- Identifying and defining roles based on job functions and responsibilities within the organization.

- Grouping entities (users, devices, and services) with similar access needs and collectively managing their access rights.

- Implementing RBAC or similar access control models to ensure that access to resources is granted based on the roles that entities hold, supporting the principle of least privilege and reducing the attack surface by limiting unnecessary access.

Furthermore, in the context of devices and services, groups and roles can help manage machine identities and service accounts, ensuring that automated processes and system-to-system interactions are securely authenticated and authorized according to the defined security policies.

Identification and Authentication Implementation

Identification and authentication are necessary steps to providing authorization. Authorization is the point after identification and authentication at which a user is granted the rights and permissions to resources. The next sections cover important components in identification and authentication: authentication, authorization, and accounting (AAA); separation of duties; least privilege/need-to-know; default to no access; directory services; single sign-on (including Kerberos, SESAME, federated identity management, and security domains); session management; registration, proof, and registration of identity; and credential management systems.

Authentication, Authorization, and Accounting (AAA)

Authentication, Authorization, and Accounting (AAA) are foundational security concepts that form the cornerstone of access control and security policies within organizations. Understanding and implementing AAA frameworks is crucial for security professionals, especially when designing identification and authentication strategies. These concepts ensure that only legitimate users (or devices) gain access to an organization's resources and that their activities are appropriately tracked and managed.

Authentication

Authentication is the process of verifying the identity of a user, device, or entity. It ensures that the entity requesting access is who it claims to be.

Authentication can be implemented through the five factors of authentication discussed earlier in this chapter. Multifactor authentication (MFA) combines two or more of these methods to enhance security.

Designing an effective authentication strategy involves selecting appropriate authentication mechanisms based on the level of security required, the type of resources being accessed, and the user or device context. Security professionals must balance security needs with usability to ensure that authentication measures do not impede legitimate access.

Authorization

Authorization occurs after authentication and determines which resources a user, device, or entity is permitted to access and what actions they are allowed to perform.

Authorization is often implemented through access control models such as discretionary access control (DAC), mandatory access control (MAC), or role-based access control (RBAC), discussed later in this chapter. These models define policies for granting or denying access to resources based on the authenticated entity's attributes, roles, or security classifications.

In designing identification and authentication strategies, security professionals must ensure that authorization mechanisms are properly aligned with organizational policies and the principle of least privilege. This involves defining clear roles and permissions and ensuring that access rights are accurately assigned and enforced.

Accounting

Accounting, in the context of AAA, refers to the tracking and recording of user activities. This includes logging access attempts, actions performed, resources used, and the duration of each session. Accounting may sometimes be referred to as auditing.

Accounting is typically achieved through logging and monitoring systems that capture detailed information about user interactions with IT resources. These logs can be analyzed to detect security incidents, policy violations, or operational issues.

Designing a strategy that includes robust accounting measures allows security professionals to ensure accountability, perform forensic analysis in the event of security incidents, and comply with legal and regulatory requirements. Effective accounting practices also enable the organization to review access patterns, identify potential security weaknesses, and improve overall security posture.

Organizations could implement any combination of the following components:

- **Strong identification:** All users should have their own accounts. Group or role accounts cannot be traced back to a single individual.
- **Strong authentication:** Multifactor authentication is best. At minimum, two-factor authentication should be implemented.

- **Monitoring:** User actions should be monitored, including login, privilege use, and other actions. Users should be warned as part of a no-expectation-of-privacy statement that all actions can be monitored.
- **Audit logs:** Audit logs should be maintained and stored according to organizational security policies. Administrators should periodically review these logs and adjust authorizations of users accordingly.

Although organizations should internally implement these accountability mechanisms, they should also periodically have a third party perform audits and tests. Third-party audit is important because the third party that is not part of the organization can provide objectivity that internal personnel often may fail to provide.

Auditing and reporting ensure that users are held accountable for their actions, but an auditing mechanism can report only on events that it is configured to monitor. Reporting is a separate process of checking the auditing logs and preparing a report based on the findings. In addition, logging alerts can also be created that automatically perform certain actions, such as sending an email to an administrator. Security professionals should monitor network events, system events, application events, user events, and keystroke activity. Keep in mind that any auditing activity might impact the performance of the system being monitored. Organizations must find a balance between auditing important events and activities and ensuring that device performance is maintained at an acceptable level. Also, organizations must ensure that any monitoring that occurs is in compliance with all applicable laws and the auditors are given written permission before an audit is conducted.

When designing an auditing mechanism, security professionals should remember the following guidelines:

Key Topic

- Develop an audit log management plan that includes mechanisms to control the log size, backup processes, and periodic review plans.
- Establish an organizational policy for log preservation that ensures the logs are preserved or backed up as needed.
- Ensure that the ability to delete an audit log is a two-person control that requires the cooperation of at least two administrators. This strategy ensures that a single administrator is not able to delete logs that might hold incriminating evidence.
- Monitor all high-privilege accounts (including all root users and administrative-level accounts).
- Ensure that the audit trail includes who processed the transaction, when the transaction occurred (date and time), where the transaction occurred (which system), and whether the transaction was successful or not.

- Ensure that deleting the log and deleting data within the logs cannot occur unless the user has the appropriate administrative-level permissions.

NOTE *Scrubbing* is the act of deleting incriminating data within an audit log.

Audit trails detect computer penetrations and reveal actions that identify misuse. As a security professional, you should use the audit trails to review patterns of access to individual objects. To identify abnormal patterns of behavior, you should first identify normal patterns of behavior. Also, you should establish the clipping level, which is a baseline of user errors above which violations will be recorded. For example, your organization might choose to ignore the first invalid login attempt, knowing that initial failed login attempts are often due to user error. Any further invalid login attempts after the first would be recorded because they could be a sign of an attack. A common clipping level that is used is three failed login attempts. For security purposes, any failed login attempt above the limit of three would be considered malicious. In most cases, a lockout policy would lock out a user's account after this clipping level is reached.

Audit trails deter attacker attempts to bypass the protection mechanisms that are configured on a system or device. As a security professional, you should specifically configure the audit trails to track system/device rights or privileges being granted to a user, and data additions, deletions, or modifications.

Finally, audit trails must be monitored, and automatic notifications should be configured. If no one monitors the audit trail, then the data recorded in the audit trail is useless. Certain actions should be configured to trigger automatic notifications. For example, you might want to configure an email alert to occur after a certain number of invalid login attempts because invalid login attempts might be a sign that a brute-force password attack is occurring.

Separation of Duties

Separation of duties is an important concept to keep in mind when designing an organization's authentication and authorization policies. Separation of duties prevents fraud by distributing tasks and their associated rights and privileges between two or more users. This separation helps deter fraud and collusion because any fraudulent act can occur only if there is collusion. A good example of separation of duties is authorizing one person to manage backup procedures and another to manage restore procedures.

Separation of duties is associated with dual controls and split knowledge. With dual controls, two or more users are authorized and required to perform certain functions. For example, a retail establishment might require two managers to open the safe.

Split knowledge ensures that no single user has all the information to perform a particular task. An example of a split control is the military's requiring a committee to approve missile firing and then two individuals to each enter a unique combination to initiate a missile firing.

Least Privilege/Need-to-Know

The principle of ***least privilege*** requires that a user or process is given only the minimum required access needed to perform a particular task. Its main purpose is to ensure that users have access only to the resources they need and are authorized to perform only the tasks they need to perform. To properly implement the least privilege principle, organizations must identify all users' jobs and restrict users only to the identified privileges.

The ***need-to-know*** principle is closely associated with the privilege allocation given to the users. Although least privilege seeks to reduce access to a minimum, the need-to-know principle actually defines what the minimum privileges for each job or business function are. Excessive privileges become a problem when a user has more rights, privileges, and permissions than that user needs to do the job. Excessive privileges are hard to control in large environments.

In a common implementation of the least privilege and need-to-know principles, for example, a system administrator is issued both an administrative-level account and a normal user account. In most day-to-day functions, the administrator should use the normal user account. When needing to perform administrative-level tasks, the system administrator should use the administrative-level account. If the administrator uses the administrative-level account while performing routine tasks, the admin risks compromising the security of the system and user accountability because the administrative-level account is more susceptible to theft.

Organizational rules that support the principle of least privilege include the following:

- Keep the number of administrative accounts to a minimum.
- Administrators should use normal user accounts when performing routine operations.
- Permissions on tools that are likely to be used by attackers should be as restrictive as possible.

To more easily support the least privilege and need-to-know principles, users should be divided into groups to facilitate the confinement of information to a single group or area. This process is referred to as compartmentalization.

Default to No Access

During the authorization process, you should configure an organization's access control mechanisms so that the default level of security is to default to *no access*. This means that if nothing has been specifically allowed for a user or group, then the user or group cannot access the resource. The best security approach is to start with no access and add rights based on a user's need to know and least privilege needed to accomplish their daily tasks.

Directory Services

A directory service is a database designed to centralize data management regarding network subjects and objects. A typical directory contains a hierarchy that includes users, groups, systems, servers, client workstations, and so on. Because the directory service contains data about users and other network entities, it can be used by many applications that require access to that information.

The most common directory service standards are

- X.500
- ***Lightweight Directory Access Protocol (LDAP)***
- X.400
- Active Directory Domain Services (AD DS)

X.500 uses the Directory Access Protocol (DAP). In X.500, the distinguished name (DN) provides the full path in the X.500 database where the entry is found. The relative distinguished name (RDN) in X.500 is an entry's name without the full path.

Based on X.500's DAP, LDAP is simpler than X.500. LDAP supports DN and RDN, but includes more attributes such as the common name (CN), domain component (DC), and organizational unit (OU) attributes. Using a client/server architecture, LDAP uses TCP port 389 to communicate. If advanced security is needed, LDAP over SSL communicates via TCP port 636.

X.400 is mainly for message transfer and storage. It uses elements to create a series of name/value pairs separated by semicolons. X.400 has gradually been replaced by Simple Mail Transfer Protocol (SMTP) implementations.

Microsoft's implementation of LDAP is Active Directory Domain Services (AD DS), which stores and organizes directory data into trees and forests. It also manages logon processes and authentication between users and domains and allows administrators to logically group users and devices into organizational units.

Single Sign-on

In a ***single sign-on (SSO)*** environment, a user enters login credentials once and can access all resources in the network. The Open Group Security Forum has defined many objectives for an SSO system. Some of the objectives for the user sign-on interface and user account management include the following:

- The interface should be independent of the type of authentication information handled.
- The creation, deletion, and modification of user accounts should be supported.
- Support should be provided for a user to establish a default user profile.
- Accounts should be independent of any platform or operating system.

NOTE To obtain more information about the Open Group's Single Sign-On Standard, you should access the website at www.opengroup.org/security/sso_scope.htm.

Key Topic

SSO provides many advantages and disadvantages when it is implemented.

Advantages of an SSO system include

- Users are able to use stronger passwords.
- User and password administration is simplified.
- Resource access is much faster.
- User login is a one-time effort and can be more efficient.
- Users need to remember only one set of login credentials.

Disadvantages of an SSO system include

- After obtaining system access through the initial SSO login, a user is able to access all resources to which that user is granted access. Although this is also an advantage for the user (only one login needed), it is also considered a disadvantage because only one sign-on can compromise all the systems that participate in the SSO network.
- If a user's credentials are compromised, attackers will have access to all resources to which the user has access.

Although the discussion on SSO so far has been mainly about how it is used for networks and domains, SSO can also be implemented in web-based systems. Enterprise access management (EAM) provides access control management for web-based enterprise systems. Its functions include accommodation of a variety of authentication methods and role-based access control.

SSO can be implemented in Kerberos, SESAME, OpenID Connect (OIDC)/Open Authorization (OAuth), Security Assertion Markup Language (SAML), and federated identity management environments. Security domains can then be established to assign SSO rights to resources.

Kerberos

Kerberos is an authentication protocol that uses a client/server model developed by MIT's Project Athena. It is the default authentication model in recent editions of Windows Server and is also used in Apple, Oracle, and Linux operating systems. Kerberos is an SSO system that uses symmetric key cryptography, and it provides confidentiality and integrity.

Kerberos assumes that messaging, cabling, and client computers are not secure and are easily accessible. In a Kerberos exchange involving a message with an authenticator, the authenticator contains the client ID and a timestamp. Because a Kerberos ticket is valid for a certain time, the timestamp ensures the validity of the request.

In a Kerberos environment, the Key Distribution Center (KDC) is the repository for all user and service secret keys. The client sends a request to the authentication server (AS), which might or might not be the KDC. The AS forwards the client credentials to the KDC. The KDC authenticates clients to other entities on a network and facilitates communication using session keys. The KDC provides security to clients or principals, which are users, network services, and software. Each principal must have an account on the KDC. The KDC issues a ticket-granting ticket (TGT) to the principal. The principal will send the TGT to the ticket-granting service (TGS) when the principal needs to connect to another entity. The TGS then transmits a ticket and session keys to the principal. The set of principles for which a single KDC is responsible is referred to as a realm.

Some advantages of implementing Kerberos include the following:

Key Topic

- User passwords do *not* need to be sent over the network.
- Both the client and server authenticate each other.
- The tickets passed between the server and client are time-stamped and include lifetime information.
- The Kerberos protocol uses open Internet standards and is not limited to proprietary codes or authentication mechanisms.

Some disadvantages of implementing Kerberos include the following:

- KDC redundancy is required if providing fault tolerance is a requirement. The KDC is a single point of failure.

- The KDC must be scalable to ensure that performance of the system does not degrade.
- Session keys on the client machines can be compromised.
- Kerberos traffic needs to be encrypted to protect the information over the network.
- All systems participating in the Kerberos process must have synchronized clocks.
- Kerberos systems are susceptible to password-guessing attacks.

Figure 5-2 shows the ticket-issuing process for Kerberos.

Key Topic

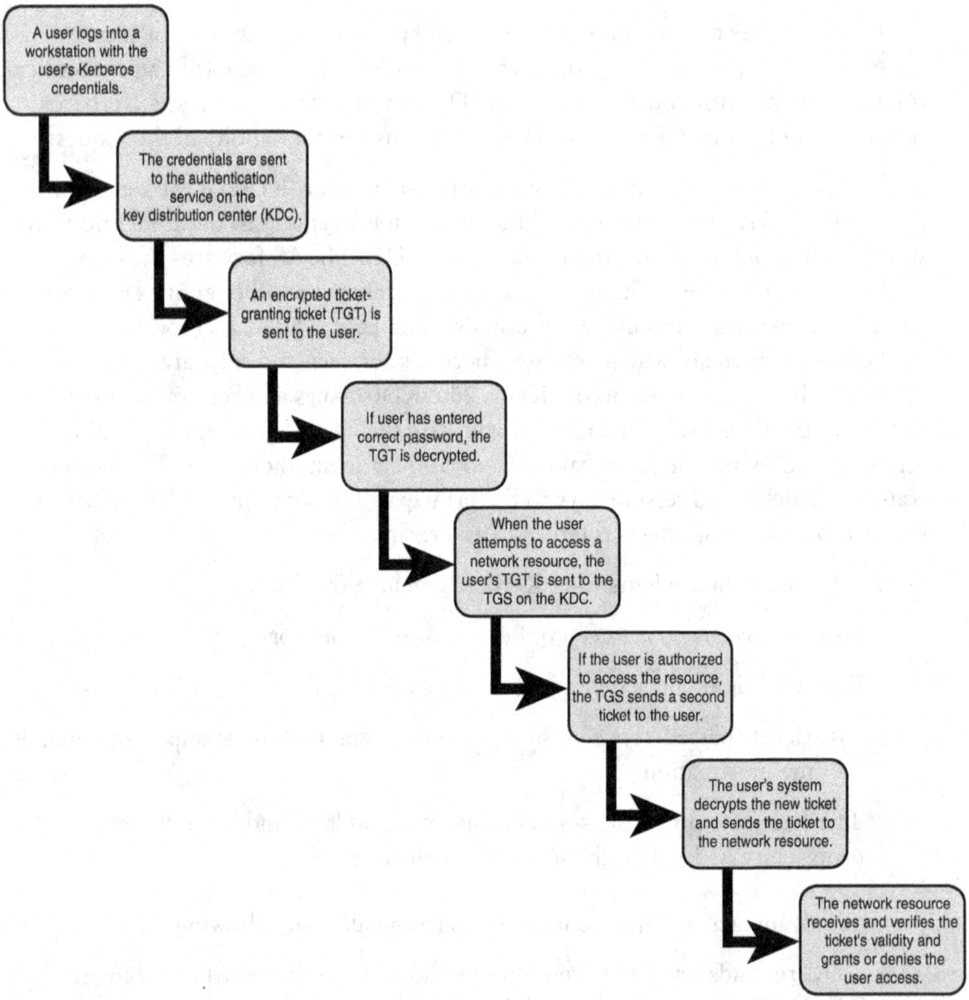

Figure 5-2 Kerberos Ticket-Issuing Process

SESAME

The ***Secure European System for Applications in a Multi-vendor Environment (SESAME)*** project extended the functionality of Kerberos to fix its weaknesses. SESAME uses both symmetric and asymmetric cryptography to protect interchanged data. SESAME uses a trusted authentication server at each host.

SESAME uses Privileged Attribute Certificates (PACs) instead of tickets. It incorporates two certificates: one for authentication and one for defining access privileges. The trusted authentication server is referred to as the Privileged Attribute Server (PAS), which performs roles similar to the KDC in Kerberos. SESAME can be integrated into a Kerberos system.

OpenID Connect (OIDC)/Open Authorization (OAuth)

Open Authorization (OAuth) is an access delegation standard that applications can use to ensure secure delegated access over HTTPS. It authorizes devices, APIs, servers, and applications with access tokens rather than credentials. OAuth allows an end user's account information to be used by third-party services, such as a social media application, without exposing the user's password. OAuth uses JavaScript Object Notation (JSON) data interchange.

OpenID Connect (OIDC) is an identity layer built on top of the OAuth 2.0 framework. It allows third-party applications to verify the identity of the end user and to obtain basic user profile information.

Whereas OAuth 2.0 is about resource access and sharing, OIDC is about user authentication.

Security Assertion Markup Language (SAML)

Security Assertion Markup Language (SAML) allows users to access multiple web applications using one set of login credentials, thereby providing SSO. It passes authentication data in a set format between two parties, usually an identity provider (IdP) and a web application. SAML uses Extensible Markup Language (XML) format.

In a comparison of SAML and OAuth, SAML provides more control to enterprises to keep their SSO logins more secure, whereas OAuth is better on mobile devices.

Federated Identity Management (IdM)

A federated identity is a portable identity that can be used across businesses and domains. In ***federated identity management (FIM)***, each organization that joins the federation agrees to enforce a common set of policies and standards. These policies and standards define how to provision and manage user identification, authentication, and authorization. Federated identity management uses two basic models for linking organizations within the federation: the cross-certification model and trusted third-party (or bridge) model. Through this model, an SSO system can be implemented.

In the ***cross-certification federated identity model***, each organization certifies that every other organization is trusted. This trust is established when the organizations review each other's standards. Each organization must verify and certify through due diligence that the other organizations meet or exceed standards. One disadvantage of cross certification is that the number of trust relationships that must be managed can become a problem. In addition, verifying the trustworthiness of other organizations can be time-consuming and resource intensive.

In the trusted third-party (or bridge) federated identity model, each organization subscribes to the standards of a third party. The third party manages verification, certification, and due diligence for all organizations. This model is usually the best if an organization needs to establish federated identity management relationships with a large number of organizations.

Security Assertion Markup Language (SAML) 2.0 is an SAML standard that exchanges authentication and authorization data between organizations or security domains. It uses an XML-based protocol to pass information about a principal between an SAML authority and a web service via security tokens. In SAML 2.0, there are three roles: the principal or user, the identity provider, and the service provider. The service provider requests identity verification from the identity provider. SAML is very flexible because it is based on XML. If an organization implements enterprise SAML identity federation, the organization can select which identity attributes to share with another organization.

Security Domains

A domain is a set of resources that is available to a subject over a network. Subjects that access a domain include users, processes, and applications. A ***security domain*** is a set of resources that follows the same security policies and is available to a subject. The domains are usually arranged in a hierarchical structure of parent and child domains.

NOTE Do not confuse the term *security domain* with protection domain. Although a security domain usually encompasses a network, a protection domain resides within a single resource. A *protection domain* is a group of processes that shares access to the same resource.

Session Management

Session management ensures that any instance of identification and authentication to a resource is managed properly. This process includes managing desktop sessions and remote sessions.

Desktop sessions should be managed through a variety of mechanisms. Screen locks allow computers to be automatically locked if left idle for a certain period of time. To reactivate a computer, the user must log back in. Screensavers are one kind of timeout mechanism, and other timeout features may also be used, such as shutting down or placing a computer in hibernation after a certain period. Session or logon limitations allow organizations to configure how many concurrent sessions a user can have. Schedule limitations allow organizations to configure the time during which a user can access a computer.

Remote sessions usually incorporate some of the same mechanisms as desktop sessions. However, remote sessions do not occur at the computer itself. Rather, they are carried out over a network connection. Remote sessions should always use secure connection protocols. In addition, if users will only be connecting remotely from certain computers, the organization may want to implement some type of rule-based access that allows only certain connections.

Registration, Proof, and Establishment of Identity

A proof of identity process involves collecting and verifying information about an individual to prove that the person who has a valid account is who that person claims to be. Establishment is the process of determining what that user's identity will be. Proofing is the act of ensuring that a person is who that person claims to be, and registration is the act of entering the identity into the IAM solution. The most basic method of proof of identity is providing a driver's license, passport, or some other government-issued identification. Proof of identity is performed before user account creation. Once proof of identity is completed, the user is issued a credential, and authentication factors are determined and recorded, which is referred to as identity establishment. Setting up the user's account in the IAM solution, such as Active Directory, is an example of registration. From that point forward, authentication occurs each time the user logs in using the issued credential.

The National Institute of Standards and Technology (NIST) has issued documents that provide guidance on proof of identity:

- FIPS Publication 201-2, "Personal Identity Verification (PIV) of Federal Employees and Contractors": This document specifies the architecture and technical requirements for a common identification standard for federal employees and contractors. This publication includes identification, security, and privacy requirements and personal identity verification system guidelines.

- NIST SP 800-79-2, "Guidelines for the Authorization of Personal Identity Verification Card Issuers (PCI) and Derived PIV Credential Issuers (DPCI)": This document includes preparation guidelines, issuer control implementation guidelines, and issuer control life cycle guidelines.

Both of these NIST publications are intended to guide federal government agencies in their proof of identity efforts and can also be used by private organizations to aid in the development of their own systems.

Credential Management Systems

Users are often required to remember usernames, passwords, and other authentication information for a variety of organizations. They often use the same authentication credentials across multiple platforms, which makes online identity theft and fraud easier to commit. After a set of credentials has been discovered on one online system, attackers often use the same set of credentials on another organization's systems to see if they can gain access. Along with this problem comes an organization's own internal issue for maintaining different credentials for users needing access to multiple systems with different credentialing systems. Factor in the increasing use of mobile devices, and you have a recipe for disaster.

Credential management systems, sometimes referred to as password vaults, allow organizations to establish an enterprisewide user authentication and authorization framework. These credential management systems store all user credentials and passwords needed to access any systems to which the user needs access. The user only needs to remember the master password, often a very long password, to access the credentials stored in the system. When the user needs to log into a device or application, the credentials needed are retrieved from the credential management system after successful login.

Organizations should employ security professionals to design, deploy, and manage secure credential management systems. The business requirements for a credential management system should include individual privacy protection guidelines, automated identity solutions, security, and innovation. Some of the guidelines of a credential management system include the following:

- Use a long and strong password for system or vault access.
- Use strong passwords for all stored credentials within the credential management system.
- Automatically generate complex passwords.
- Implement password history.
- Use access control mechanisms, including the who, what, how, and when of access.

- Implement auditing.
- Implement backup and restore mechanisms for data integrity.
- Implement redundant systems within the credential management systems to ensure 24/7/365 access.
- Implement credential management group policies or other mechanisms offered by operating systems.

When an organization implements a credential management system, separation of duties becomes even more important because the centralized credential management system can be used to commit fraud. Security professionals should provide guidance on how the separation should occur to best protect the organization and its assets.

Remote Authentication Dial-In User Service (RADIUS)/Terminal Access Controller Access Control System Plus (TACACS+)

RADIUS authenticates and logs remote network users, while TACACS+ most commonly provides administrator access to network devices, like routers and switches. Both protocols provide centralized authentication, authorization, and accounting (AAA) services on a network.

NOTE RADIUS and TACACS+ are covered in more detail in Chapter 4, "Communication and Network Security."

TACACS+ is more reliable than RADIUS. It supports authorization of commands. Finally, all TACACS+ communication is encrypted, whereas RADIUS authentication encrypts only the password.

However, RADIUS is an open standard and can be used with all types of devices, while TACACS+ works only with Cisco products. The accounting support in RADIUS is more robust than that provided by TACACS+.

Just-In-Time (JIT)

Just-In-Time (JIT) access enables organizations to grant access to applications or systems for predetermined periods of time, on an as-needed basis. With JIT provisioning, if a user does not already have an account in a target application, the IAM system creates the account for a user on the fly when the user first accesses the application. JIT uses the SAML protocol to transmit information from the identity provider to the web application. The web application receives the information from the identity provider via SAML assertions.

Using a cloud identity provider with JIT is the most streamlined approach because admins can configure application permissions by role or group and revoke application access from one central location. Although setting up a JIT configuration between the identity and service providers can be tedious, administrative effort will be saved in the long run when each user is provisioned automatically.

Identity as a Service (IDaaS) Implementation

Identity as a Service (IDaaS) provides a set of identity and access management functions to target systems on customers' premises and/or in the cloud. IDaaS includes identity governance and administration (IGA), which provides the ability to provision identities held by the service to target applications. It includes user authentication, single sign-on (SSO), and authorization enforcement. IDaaS services are divided into two categories: web access software for cloud-based applications and cloud-delivered legacy identity management services. Web IDaaS applications do not work with on-premises applications. Most IDaaS deployments offer SSO authentication, federated identities, remote administration, and internal directory service integration. IDaaS is different from identity and access management (IAM) solutions, which are operated from within the organization's own network via bundled software and hardware. IAM solutions may use Active Directory and LDAP.

If organizations consider IDaaS deployment, they should primarily be concerned with service availability, identity data protection, and trusting a third party with a critical business function. They should also be concerned with regulatory compliance. Moving identity management to the cloud brings up a whole host of questions for the organization regarding auditing, ensuring compliance of regulations, and what happens if disclosures occur.

An organization should perform a comprehensive risk analysis prior to implementing and deploying any IDaaS service. After performing the risk analysis, the organization should determine which identities should be placed on the IDaaS solution.

Third-Party Identity Services Integration

If an organization decides to deploy a third-party identity service, including cloud computing solutions, security practitioners must be involved in the integration of that implementation with internal services and resources. This integration can be complex, especially if the provider solution is not fully compatible with existing internal systems. Most third-party identity services provide cloud identity, directory synchronization, and federated identity. Examples of these services include the Amazon Web Services (AWS) Identity and Access Management (IAM) service and Oracle Identity Management.

Third-party identity services include on-premises, cloud, federated, and hybrid services. These three service types are discussed throughout this chapter.

Authorization Mechanisms

Authorization mechanisms are systems an organization deploys to control which systems a user or device can access. Authorization mechanisms include access control models and access control policies.

Permissions, Rights, and Privileges

Permissions are granted or denied at the file, folder, or other object level. Common permission types include Read, Write, Execute, and Full Control. Data custodians or administrators will grant users permissions on a file or folder based on the owner's request to do so.

Rights allow administrators to assign specific privileges and logon rights to groups or users. Rights manage who is allowed to perform certain operations on an entire computer or within a domain, rather than a particular object within a computer. While user permissions are granted by an object's owner, user rights are assigned using a computer's local security policy or a domain security policy. User rights apply to user accounts, whereas permissions apply to objects.

Rights include the ability to log on to a system interactively, which is a logon right, or the ability to back up administrative-level files, which is considered a privilege. (Users should be able to only back up files that they own.) User rights are divided into two categories: privileges and logon rights. Privileges are the right of an account, such as a user or group account, to perform various system-related operations on the local computer, such as shutting down the system, loading device drivers, or changing the system time. Logon rights control how users are allowed access to the computer, including logging on locally or through a network connection or whether as a service or as a batch job.

Conflicts can occur in situations where the rights that are required to administer a system overlap the rights of resource ownership. When rights conflict, a privilege is allowed to override a permission.

Access Control Models

An access control model is a formal description of an organization's security policy. Access control models are implemented to simplify access control administration by grouping objects and subjects. Subjects are entities that request access to an object or data within an object. Users, programs, and processes are subjects. Objects are entities that contain information or functionality. Computers, databases, files, programs, directories, and fields are objects. A secure access control model must ensure that secure objects cannot flow to a less secure subject.

The access control models and concepts that you need to understand include the following:

- Discretionary access control
- Mandatory access control
- Role-based access control
- Rule-based access control
- Attribute-based access control
- Content-dependent versus context-dependent access control
- Risk-based access control
- Access control matrix
- Capabilities table
- ACL

Discretionary Access Control

In ***discretionary access control (DAC)***, the owner of the object specifies which subjects can access the resource. DAC is typically used in local, dynamic situations. The access is based on the subject's identity, profile, or role. DAC is considered to be a need-to-know control.

DAC can be an administrative burden because the data owner grants access privileges to the users and then the data custodian must configure the privileges. Under DAC, a subject's rights must be terminated when the subject leaves the organization. Identity-based access control is a subset of DAC and is based on user identity or group membership. However, implementing DAC is usually necessary, especially for large organizations.

Nondiscretionary access control is the opposite of DAC. In nondiscretionary access control, access controls are configured by a security administrator or other authority. The central authority decides which subjects have access to objects based on the organization's policy. In nondiscretionary access control, the system compares the subject's identity with the objects' access control list.

Mandatory Access Control

In ***mandatory access control (MAC)***, subject authorization is based on security labels. MAC is often described as prohibitive because it is based on a security label system. Under MAC, all that is not expressly permitted is forbidden. Only administrators can change the category of a resource.

MAC is more secure than DAC. DAC is more flexible and scalable than MAC. Because of the importance of security in MAC, labeling is required. Data classification reflects the data's sensitivity. In a MAC system, a clearance is a subject's privilege. Each subject and object is given a security or sensitivity label. The security labels are hierarchical. For commercial organizations, the levels of security labels could be confidential, proprietary, corporate, sensitive, and public. For government or military institutions, the levels of security labels could be top secret, secret, confidential, and unclassified.

In MAC, the system makes access decisions when it compares the subject's clearance level with the object's security label.

Role-Based Access Control

In ***role-based access control (RBAC)***, each subject is assigned to one or more roles. Roles are hierarchical. Access control is defined based on the roles. RBAC can be used to easily enforce minimum privileges for subjects. An example of RBAC is implementing one access control policy for bank tellers and another policy for loan officers.

RBAC is not as secure as the previously mentioned access control models because security is based on roles. RBAC usually has a much lower cost to implement than the other models and is popular in commercial applications. It is an excellent choice for organizations with high employee turnover. RBAC can effectively replace DAC and MAC because it allows you to specify and enforce enterprise security policies in a way that maps to the organization's structure.

RBAC is managed in four ways: non-RBAC, limited RBAC, hybrid RBAC, and full RBAC. In non-RBAC, no roles are used. In limited RBAC, users are mapped to single application roles, but some applications do not use RBAC and require identity-based access. In hybrid RBAC, each user is mapped to a single role, which gives them access to multiple systems, but each user can be mapped to other roles that have access to single systems. In full RBAC, users are mapped to a single role as defined by the organization's security policy, and access to the systems is managed through the organizational roles.

Rule-Based Access Control

Rule-based access control facilitates frequent changes to data permissions and is defined in RFC 2828. Using this method, a security policy is based on global rules imposed for all users. Profiles are used to control access. Many routers and firewalls use this type of access control and define which packet types are allowed on a network. Rules can be written allowing or denying access based on packet type, port number used, MAC address, and other parameters. Rules can be added, edited, or deleted as required.

Attribute-Based Access Control

Attribute-based access control (ABAC) grants or denies user requests based on arbitrary attributes of the user and arbitrary attributes of the object, and environment conditions that may be globally recognized. NIST SP 800-162 was published to define and clarify ABAC.

According to NIST SP 800-162, ABAC is an access control method where subject requests to perform operations on objects are granted or denied based on assigned attributes of the subject, assigned attributes of the object, environment conditions, and a set of policies that are specified in terms of those attributes and conditions. An operation is the execution of a function at the request of a subject upon an object. Operations include read, write, edit, delete, copy, execute, and modify. A policy is the representation of rules or relationships that make it possible to determine whether a requested access should be allowed, given the values of the attributes of the subject, object, and possibly environment conditions. Environment conditions are the operational or situational context in which access requests occur. Environment conditions are detectable environmental characteristics. Environment characteristics are independent of subject or object, and may include the current time, day of the week, location of a user, or the current threat level.

Figure 5-3 shows a basic ABAC scenario according to NIST SP 800-162.

As specified in NIST SP 800-162, there are characteristics or attributes of a subject such as name, date of birth, home address, training record, and job function that may, either individually or when combined, comprise a unique identity that distinguishes that person from all others. These characteristics are often called subject attributes.

Like subjects, each object has a set of attributes that help describe and identify it. These traits are called object attributes and are sometimes referred to as resource attributes. Object attributes are typically bound to their objects through reference, by embedding them within the object, or through some other means of assured association such as cryptographic binding.

Key Topic

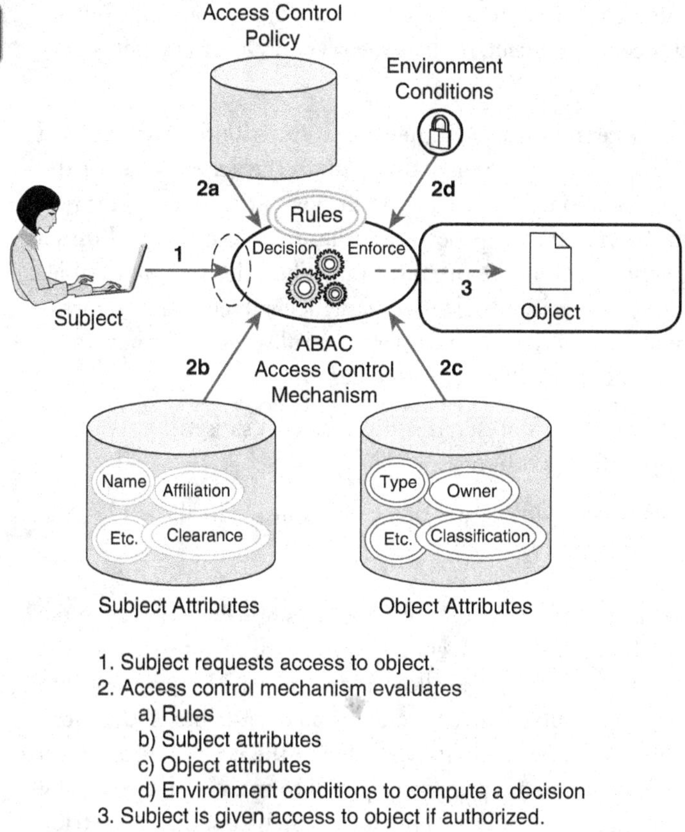

Figure 5-3 NIST SP 800-162 Basic ABAC Scenario

ACLs and RBAC are in some ways special cases of ABAC in terms of the attributes used. ACLs work on the attribute of "identity." RBAC works on the attribute of "role." The key difference with ABAC is the concept of policies that express a complex Boolean rule set that can evaluate many different attributes. While it is possible to achieve ABAC objectives using ACLs or RBAC, demonstrating access control requirements compliance is difficult and costly due to the level of abstraction required between the access control requirements and the ACL or RBAC model. Another problem with ACL or RBAC models is that if the access control requirements need to be changed depending on business demands or user changes, it may be difficult to identify all the places where the ACL or RBAC implementation needs to be updated.

ABAC relies on the assignment of attributes to subjects and objects, and the development of policy that contains the access rules. Each object within the system must be assigned specific object attributes that characterize the object. Some attributes pertain to the entire instance of an object, such as the owner. Other attributes may apply only to parts of the object.

Each subject that uses the system must be assigned specific attributes. Every object within the system must have at least one policy that defines the access rules for the allowable subjects, operations, and environment conditions to the object. This policy is normally derived from documented or procedural rules that describe the business processes and allowable actions within the organization. The rules that bind subject and object attributes indirectly specify privileges (i.e., which subjects can perform which operations on which objects). Allowable operation rules can be expressed through many forms of computational language such as

- A Boolean combination of attributes and conditions that satisfy the authorization for a specific operation
- A set of relations associating subject and object attributes and allowable operations

After object attributes, subject attributes, and policies are established, objects can be protected using ABAC. Access control mechanisms mediate access to the objects by limiting access to allowable operations by allowable subjects. The access control mechanism assembles the policy, subject attributes, and object attributes; then it renders and enforces a decision based on the logic provided in the policy. Access control mechanisms must be able to manage the process required to make and enforce the decision, including determining what policy to retrieve, which attributes to retrieve in what order, and where to retrieve attributes. The access control mechanism must then perform the computation necessary to render a decision.

The policies that can be implemented in an ABAC model are limited only to the degree imposed by the computational language and the richness of the available attributes. This flexibility enables the greatest breadth of subjects to access the greatest breadth of objects without having to specify individual relationships between each subject and each object.

While ABAC is an enabler of information sharing, the set of components required to implement ABAC gets more complex when deployed across an enterprise. At the enterprise level, the increased scale requires complex and sometimes independently established management capabilities necessary to ensure consistent sharing and use of policies and attributes and the controlled distribution and employment of access control mechanisms throughout the enterprise.

Content-Dependent Versus Context-Dependent

Content-dependent access control makes access decisions based on the data contained within the object. With this access control, the data that a user sees might be different from the actual data, based on the policy and access rules that are applied.

Context-dependent access control is based on subject or object attributes or environmental characteristics. These characteristics can include location or time of day. An example of context-dependent access control is administrators implementing a security policy that checks to see whether a user can log in only from a particular workstation and during certain hours of the day.

Security experts consider a constrained user interface as another method of access control. An example of a constrained user interface is a shell, which is a software interface to an operating system that implements access control by limiting the system commands that are available. Another example is database views that are filtered based on user or system criteria. Constrained user interfaces can be content- or context-dependent based on how the administrator constrains the interface.

Risk-Based Access Control

Risk-based access control uses risk probability to make access decisions. It performs a risk analysis to estimate the risk value related to each access request. The estimated risk value is then compared against access policies to determine the access decision.

With risk-based access control, the access granted can be based on the risk factors of the individual connection. For example, a user connecting to a resource via the local network would not be considered as risky as a user connecting via a mobile device connected to a coffee shop wireless network. If risk-based access control were deployed, it would see the mobile device as a greater risk and could require another authentication factor than that required for a local connection. In addition, with risk-based access control, an organization could allow the system to learn about user patterns and behaviors and thereby lessen stringent controls over time based on that data.

Risk-based access includes an external authorization service (EAS), a runtime authorization service, and an attribute collection service. The EAS provides policy enforcement by taking the request data and sending an authorization decision request to the risk-based access authorization service. The runtime authorization service stores the policy, calculates the risk score, and makes the access decision. The attribute collection service collects web browser and location attributes from the user.

Let's look at an example. Suppose a company employee named Michael works normal Monday through Friday business hours from the central office. He always accesses the corporate network using his company-issued laptop or mobile phone. This connection would be seen as a low-risk connection, and normal organizational username/password authentication would suffice. However, when Michael travels for business and attempts to connect to the corporate network from his hotel via a free Wi-Fi, risk-based access control policies could request secondary authentication factors from Michael based on this new Internet connection. Even if the new connection were from the same device, the policy could notice several risks, including a new location or new login hours.

For organizations with a large enterprise, security professionals should provide guidance on those times when risk-based access control should be considered and how it could benefit these organizations.

Access Control Matrix

An ***access control matrix*** is a table that consists of a list of subjects, a list of objects, and a list of the actions that a subject can take upon each object. The rows in the matrix are the subjects, and the columns in the matrix are the objects. Common implementations of an access control matrix include a capabilities table and an ACL.

Capabilities Table

A capability corresponds to a subject's row from an access control matrix. A ***capability table*** lists the access rights that a particular subject has to objects. A capability table is about the subject.

ACL

An ACL corresponds to an object's column from an access control matrix. An ACL lists all the access rights that subjects have to a particular object; an ACL is about the object.

Figure 5-4 shows an access control matrix and how a capability and ACL are part of it.

Subject	File 1	File 2	Printer 1	Printer 2
John	Read	Read, Write	Print	Full Control
Sally	Full Control	Read	Full Control	Print
George	No Access	Full Control	No Access	Print

Figure 5-4 Access Control Matrix

Access Control Policies and Policy Enforcement

An ***access control policy*** defines the method for identifying and authenticating users and the level of access that is granted to users. Organizations should put access control policies in place to ensure that access control decisions for users are based on formal guidelines. If an access control policy is not adopted, organizations will have trouble assigning, managing, and administering access management.

Access policy enforcement is a critical component in the realm of information security as it involves the use of specialized systems to define, administer, and enforce security policies that control access to resources. Two key concepts in this area are the policy decision point (PDP) and policy enforcement point (PEP), which work together to ensure that access control policies are correctly applied.

The PDP is the component within a system that makes decisions regarding access control policies. It evaluates requests against established policies to determine whether the request should be granted or denied. When a request for access is made, the PDP assesses this request based on the rules and policies with which it has been configured. It considers the credentials provided, the resource being accessed, and the context of the request (such as the time of day or the requestor's location).

The PEP is the mechanism that actually enforces the decisions made by the PDP. It sits at the point of access to resources and ensures that only requests approved by the PDP are allowed. Upon receiving a decision from the PDP, the PEP either grants or denies access based on that decision. The PEP is responsible for intercepting all access requests, querying the PDP for a decision, and then enforcing that decision.

For security professionals, understanding the role of the PDP and PEP is crucial in designing and implementing effective authorization mechanisms. They must ensure that the PDP has access to up-to-date and comprehensive policy rules and that it can accurately evaluate access requests in real time. Security professionals must ensure that PEPs are correctly positioned within the system architecture to effectively control access to resources. They also need to ensure that PEPs can securely communicate with PDPs to receive access decisions.

The integration of PDP and PEP is essential for dynamic and effective access control within an organization's IT environment. This model allows for centralized policy management (via the PDP) and decentralized policy enforcement (via the PEP), providing a scalable and flexible approach to access control.

Security professionals must adhere to the following guidelines when implementing these systems:

- Ensure that the PDP and PEP architecture can scale to meet the organization's needs, handling a large number of access requests across diverse resources.
- Secure the communication between PEPs and PDPs to prevent interception or tampering with access decisions.
- Design the system to minimize latency in the decision-making process, ensuring that access control does not hinder user productivity or system performance.
- Implement logging and monitoring of decisions and enforcement actions to support auditing, compliance, and forensic analysis.

Understanding and implementing the concepts of PDP and PEP are fundamental to developing robust authorization mechanisms. These components enable organizations to enforce access policies effectively, ensuring that resources are protected from unauthorized access while facilitating legitimate use. Security professionals play a key role in designing, configuring, and managing these systems to uphold the security and integrity of organizational assets.

Key Topic

Provisioning Life Cycle

Organizations should create a formal process for creating, changing, and removing users, which is the ***provisioning life cycle***. This process includes user approval, user creation, user creation standards, and authorization. Users should sign a written statement that explains the access conditions, including user responsibilities. Finally, access modification and removal procedures should be documented.

User accounts are not the only types of accounts security professionals may need to provision. Security professionals also need to understand systems and service accounts.

A system account is generally thought of in two ways. System accounts are often created for actual devices or services, including computers, routers, and firewalls. These system accounts allow organizations to track the devices and assign them security policies and directory service policies. In addition, a system account is an account created during operating system installation. It is considered a user account but often performs operating system functions. System administrators also log in to some system accounts, such as the Windows Administrator account or the UNIX/Linux root account. System accounts are generally privileged accounts. Security professionals should, at minimum, rename these default admin and operating system accounts and ensure that the default password is changed.

A service account is an account created explicitly to provide a security context for services running on Windows or Unix computers. The security context determines the service's ability to access local and network resources. Services that need accounts include Domain Name System (DNS), HyperText Transfer Protocol (HTTP), File Transfer Protocol (FTP), and Dynamic Host Configuration Protocol (DHCP). Services that should not be running on a computer should be disabled and have the service accounts deleted.

Provisioning

User ***provisioning*** policies should be integrated as part of human resources management. Human resources policies should include procedures whereby the human resources department formally requests the creation or deletion of a user account when new personnel are hired or terminated.

Identity and Account Management

Identity and account management is vital to any authentication process. As a security professional, you must ensure that your organization has a formal procedure to control the creation and allocation of access credentials or identities. If invalid accounts are allowed to be created and are not disabled, security breaches will occur. Most organizations implement a method to review the identification and authentication process to ensure that user accounts are current. Questions that are likely to help in the process include

- Is a current list of authorized users, devices, and services and their access maintained and approved?
- Are passwords changed at least every few days (e.g., 90 days) or earlier if needed?
- Are inactive user, device, and service accounts disabled after a specified period of inactivity?

Any identity management procedure must include processes for creating (provisioning), changing and monitoring (reviewing), and removing users, devices, and services from the access control system (revoking). This procedure is referred to as the provisioning life cycle. When initially establishing a user account, new users should be required to provide valid photo identification and should sign a statement regarding password confidentiality. For device and service accounts, the device or service owner should request account creation. User, device, and service accounts must be unique. Policies should be in place that standardize the structure of user, device, and service accounts. For example, all user accounts should be *firstname.lastname* or some other structure. This structure ensures that users within an organization will be able to determine a new user's identification, mainly for communication purposes. Device and service naming conventions should also be adopted.

After creation, accounts should be monitored to ensure that they remain active. Inactive accounts should be automatically disabled after a certain period of inactivity based on business requirements. In addition, any termination policy should include formal procedures to ensure that all accounts are disabled or deleted. Elements of proper account management include the following:

- Establish a formal process for establishing, issuing, and closing accounts.
- Periodically review accounts.
- Implement a process for tracking access authorization.
- Periodically rescreen personnel in sensitive positions.
- Periodically verify the legitimacy of accounts.

Account reviews are a vital part of account management. Accounts should be reviewed for conformity with the principle of least privilege. (The principle of least privilege is explained earlier in this chapter.) Account reviews can be performed on an enterprisewide, systemwide, or application-by-application basis. The size of the organization will greatly affect which of these methods to use. As part of account reviews, organizations should determine whether all accounts are active.

User, System, and Service Account Access Review

Account review should be performed periodically to determine that all accounts that have been created are still being used. If a user, system, or service account is inactive for a certain period, it is always best to disable that account and wait for a user request to renew. When no requests for renewal are made, the disabled accounts are usually deleted after a certain period. After an account is deleted, any objects owned by the account may remain in the current state, meaning no new users can be given permissions nor can current permissions be changed. Having this period when an account is disabled prior to deletion allows administrators to identify those objects and transfer their ownership to another user or system account.

Account Transfers

Accounts, particularly user accounts, may need to be periodically transferred within an organization. This is most often the case when personnel move from one department or role to another. Procedures should be written so that the user account is granted the appropriate permissions for the new department or role. In addition, any unneeded permissions from the old department or role should be revoked. Following this procedure ensures that privilege creep does not occur. ***Privilege creep***, also referred to as permissions creep, occurs when an employee moves between roles in an organization and keeps the access or permissions of the previous role.

Account Revocation

Account ***revocation***, also referred to as ***deprovisioning***, is the process of removing an account from a device or enterprise. Because accounts are assigned unique IDs in most operating systems, it is very important that security professionals ensure that accounts are no longer needed prior to deletion. Countless stories exist where accounts were deleted and then access to certain resources was lost. Even if an administrator re-creates an account with the same account name, it will not have the same unique ID that was assigned to the original account. Therefore, the administrator would still be unable to access resources owned by the original account.

Organizations should adopt formal policies on account revocation. These policies should be implemented as part of any employee termination policy.

Role Definition and Transition

Role definition is the process of establishing what roles are needed and documenting the permissions and privileges of those roles. Roles may be organizational or departmental. Roles will then need to be created and assigned the appropriate rights.

After roles are defined and created, user or group accounts must be assigned to the roles. It is important that security professionals ensure that appropriate procedures are in place for adding users or groups to roles. However, having procedures in place for removing users or groups from roles is just as important. These procedures also act as a protection against privilege creep, mentioned earlier.

Role transition is the process of moving an account to another role. In most cases, the account is added to the new role and then removed from the previous role. Role transition generally occurs when personnel are transferred to another department or when personnel receive promotions or demotions within the organization. Security professionals should ensure that the appropriate processes are in place to ensure proper role transitioning with the principle of least privilege in mind.

Regular monitoring of the roles should occur to ensure that a particular role is assigned only to those accounts that belong in that role and that all created roles are still valid. Roles can be created in applications, devices, and computers.

Privilege Escalation

Privilege escalation, also referred to as *privilege creep* or *permissions creep*, is a situation in which a user account has accumulated permissions over time, thereby resulting in an account with unnecessary elevated permissions and privileges. It most often is the result of a user being granted new permissions without having current permissions examined and revoked as needed. User accounts with this condition are a security hole just waiting for an attacker to exploit. Privilege escalation is prevented when an organization has the appropriate processes in place for role transition, as discussed above.

Two types of privilege escalation can occur: horizontal and vertical. In horizontal privilege escalation, a hacker uses the privilege escalation account to access other accounts that have the same permissions. In vertical privilege escalation, a valid user or hacker uses the privilege escalation account to obtain less or more privileges, such as through a system or administrative account. This is the most worrying form of privilege escalation because the hacker can cause immense system damage, change account settings, access sensitive and confidential information, and even disseminate malware throughout the network. It might be necessary to access an account with lower privileges to reach a certain resource.

Managed service accounts should be carefully monitored for privilege escalation. Because these accounts are critical to the operation of the service, security administrators are often reluctant to remove permissions.

In addition, privilege escalation may result in the compromise of an administrator-level account. It is important that users use their account with administrator-level permissions only when tasks that require those permissions must be completed. In other cases, they should use the lower-level account. This includes the default Administrator account in Windows and the root account in Linux.

When it comes to working with Linux, there are two ways to run administrative applications: (1) change over to the super user, also known as the root account, using the **su** command with a known password for the root or super user account, or (2) use the **sudo** command. With the **sudo** command, the user uses their regular or another user account but with root privilege. However, with the **su** command, the user is actually logged in to the root account. Also, the root privilege in the **sudo** command is valid only for a temporary amount of time. When that time expires, the user has to input a password again to regain root privilege.

Security professionals should ensure that use of the **su** command is greatly restricted. While the **sudo** command is a better choice, users should still use it only when it is strictly necessary.

Service Account Management

Service account management is a critical aspect of IAM strategies. Service accounts are special types of accounts used by applications, services, and automated processes to interact with the operating system or other services, often requiring privileged access to perform their functions. Proper management of these accounts is essential for maintaining security and operational efficiency within an organization.

Service account management includes:

- Identification and Inventory: The first step is identifying all service accounts within an organization and maintaining an inventory. This includes understanding the purpose of each account, the systems and data it has access to, and the level of privileges granted.
- Provisioning and Deprovisioning: Like user accounts, service accounts must be carefully provisioned and deprovisioned. Provisioning involves setting up accounts with the minimum necessary privileges (following the principle of least privilege) and configuring them according to security best practices. Deprovisioning is equally important to remove access when a service account is no longer needed, to prevent unused accounts from becoming security vulnerabilities.
- Password Management: Service accounts often have passwords that are rarely changed due to the potential disruption of services. Automating password changes and using complex, unique passwords are essential practices. In some cases, deploying solutions that enable password-less authentication for service accounts can enhance security.
- Access Control and Monitoring: Regularly reviewing and auditing the access rights of service accounts helps ensure they only have access to necessary resources. Continuous monitoring for anomalous activities associated with service accounts can detect potential security incidents or misconfigurations.
- Documentation and Policy Enforcement: Documenting service accounts, including their purpose, associated services, and access rights, supports effective management and audit processes. Establishing policies for the creation, maintenance, and retirement of service accounts is crucial for security and compliance.

Service account management plays a pivotal role in the broader scope of IAM, emphasizing the need to manage not just user identities but also non-human identities represented by service accounts. Security professionals are expected to:

- Develop and implement service account policies.
- Ensure security and compliance for protecting access to sensitive data and systems through service accounts.
- Leverage automation and to reduce the risk of human error and improve operational efficiency.
- Conduct regular audits to identify and remediate potential security issues, such as excessive privileges or inactive accounts.

By ensuring that service accounts are properly managed throughout their life cycle, organizations can significantly reduce their attack surface, comply with regulatory requirements, and maintain the integrity of their critical systems and data.

Access Control Threats

Access control threats directly impact the confidentiality, integrity, and availability of organizational assets. The purpose of most access control threats is to cause harm to an organization. Because harming an organization is easier to do from within its network, outsiders usually first attempt to attack any access controls that are in place.

Access control threats that security professionals should understand include

- Password threats
- Social engineering threats
- DoS/DDoS
- Buffer overflow
- Mobile code
- Malicious software
- Spoofing
- Sniffing and eavesdropping
- Emanating
- Backdoor/trapdoor

Password Threats

A password threat is any attack that attempts to discover user passwords. The most popular password threats are dictionary attacks, brute-force attacks, birthday attacks, rainbow table attacks, and sniffer attacks.

The best countermeasures against password threats are to implement complex password policies, require users to change passwords on a regular basis, employ account lockout policies, encrypt password files, and use password-cracking tools to discover weak passwords.

Dictionary Attack

A ***dictionary attack*** occurs when attackers use a dictionary of common words to discover passwords. An automated program uses the hash of the dictionary word and compares this hash value to entries in the system password file. Although the program comes with a dictionary, attackers also use extra dictionaries that are found on the Internet.

You should implement a security rule that says that a password must *not* be a word found in the dictionary file to protect against these attacks. You can also implement an account lockout policy so that an account is locked out after a certain number of invalid login attempts.

Brute-Force Attack

Brute-force attacks are more difficult to carry out because they work through all possible combinations of numbers and characters. A brute-force attack is also referred to as an exhaustive attack. It carries out password searches until a correct password is found. These attacks are also very time-consuming.

Birthday Attack

A ***birthday attack*** compares the values that attackers have against a set of password hashes for which they know the passwords. Eventually, the attackers will find a password that matches. To protect against birthday attacks, implement encryption on the transmission. The attack gets its name from the likelihood of a group of users using the same password, similar to the likelihood of a group of users assembled in a room, having the same birthday, often referred to as the birthday paradox.

Rainbow Table Attack

A ***rainbow table attack*** is similar to a birthday attack in that comparisons are used against known hash values. However, in a rainbow table attack, a rainbow table is used that contains the cryptographic hashes of passwords. Using an up-to-date hashing algorithm (versus one that is outdated) is the first step in protecting against this type of attack. Salting is the process of randomizing each hash by adding random data that is unique to each user to their password hash, so even the same password has a unique hash.

Sniffer Attack

A ***sniffer attack*** in the context of password attacks simply uses a sniffer to capture an unencrypted or plaintext password. Security professionals should periodically use sniffers to see whether they can determine passwords using these tools. Encryption of the password transmission prevents this type of attack.

Social Engineering Threats

Social engineering attacks occur when attackers use believable language and user gullibility to obtain user credentials or some other confidential information. Social engineering threats that you should understand include phishing/pharming, shoulder surfing, identity theft, and dumpster diving.

The best countermeasure against social engineering threats is to provide user security awareness training. This training should be required and must occur on a regular basis because social engineering techniques evolve constantly.

Phishing/Pharming

Phishing is a social engineering attack in which attackers try to learn personal information, including credit card information and financial data. This type of attack is usually carried out by implementing a fake website that very closely resembles a legitimate website. Users enter data, including credentials, on the fake website, allowing the attackers to capture any information entered. Spear phishing is a phishing attack carried out against a specific target by learning about the target's habits and likes. Spear phishing attacks take longer to carry out than phishing attacks because of the information that must be gathered. ***Whaling*** is a type of phishing that specifically targets high-level executives or other high-profile individuals. ***Vishing*** is a type of phishing that uses a phone system or VoIP technologies. The user initially receives a call, text, or email that says to call a specific number and provide personal information such as name, birth date, Social Security number, and credit card information.

Pharming is similar to phishing, but it actually pollutes the contents of a computer's DNS cache so that requests to a legitimate site are actually routed to an alternate site.

Caution users against using any links embedded in email messages, even if the message appears to have come from a legitimate entity. Users should also review the address bar any time they access a site where their personal information is required to ensure that the site is correct and that SSL is being used, which is indicated by an HTTPS designation at the beginning of the URL address.

These attacks can be carried out via phone, email, and text messages.

Shoulder Surfing

Shoulder surfing occurs when an attacker watches a user enter login or other confidential data. To avoid the attack, a corporation should encourage users to always be aware of who is observing their actions. Implementing privacy screens helps to ensure that data entry cannot be recorded.

Identity Theft

Identity theft occurs when someone obtains personal information, including driver's license number, bank account number, and Social Security number, and uses that information to assume the identity of the individual whose information was stolen. After the identity is assumed, the attack can go in any direction. In most cases, attackers open financial accounts in the user's name. Attackers also can gain access to the user's valid financial accounts where government identification is usually required.

Dumpster Diving

Dumpster diving occurs when attackers examine garbage contents to obtain confidential information, such as personnel information, account login information, network diagrams, and organizational financial data.

Organizations should implement policies for shredding documents that contain this information.

DoS/DDoS

A denial-of-service (DoS) attack occurs when attackers flood a device with enough requests to degrade the performance of the targeted device. Some popular DoS attacks include SYN floods and teardrop attacks.

A distributed DoS (DDoS) attack is a DoS attack that is carried out from multiple attack locations. Vulnerable devices are infected with software agents, called zombies. They turn the vulnerable devices into botnets, which then carry out the attack. Because of the geographically distributed bots and the very nature of the attack, identifying all the attacking botnets is virtually impossible. The botnets also help to hide the original source of the attack.

Buffer Overflow

Buffers are portions of system memory that are used to store information. A ***buffer overflow*** occurs when the amount of data that is submitted to the application is larger than the buffer can handle. Typically, this type of attack is possible because of poorly written application or operating system code. This attack can result in an injection of malicious code.

To protect against this issue, organizations should ensure that all operating systems and applications are updated with the latest service packs, updates, and patches. In addition, programmers should properly test all applications to check for overflow conditions. Finally, programmers should use input validation to ensure that the data submitted is not too large for the buffer.

Mobile Code

Mobile code is any software that is transmitted across a network to be executed on a local system. Examples of mobile code include Java applets, JavaScript code, and ActiveX controls. Mobile code includes security controls, Java sandboxes, and ActiveX digital code signatures. Malicious mobile code can be used to bypass access controls.

Organizations should ensure that users understand the security concerns of malicious mobile code. Users should download mobile code only from legitimate sites and vendors.

NOTE For more information about mobile code, see the section, "Mobile Code," in Chapter 8, "Software Development Security."

Malicious Software

Malicious software, also called malware, is any software that is designed to perform malicious acts.

The following are the five classes of malware you should understand:

Key Topic

- ***Virus***: Any malware that attaches itself to another application to replicate or distribute itself.
- ***Worm***: Any malware that replicates itself, meaning that it does not need another application or human interaction to propagate.
- ***Trojan horse***: Any malware that disguises itself as a needed application while carrying out malicious actions.

- ***Spyware***: Any malware that collects private user data, including browsing history login credentials, website data, or keyboard input.
- ***Ransomware***: Any malware that prevents or limits users' access to their systems or devices. Usually, it forces victims to pay the ransom for the return of system access.

The best defense against malicious software is to implement antivirus and anti-malware software. Today most vendors package these two types of software in the same package. Keeping antivirus and anti-malware software up to date is vital. Doing so includes ensuring that the latest virus and malware definitions are installed.

Spoofing

Spoofing, also referred to as masquerading, occurs when communication from an attacker appears to come from trusted sources. Spoofing examples include IP spoofing and hyperlink spoofing. The goal of this type of attack is to obtain access to credentials or other personal information.

A man-in-the-middle attack uses spoofing as part of the attack. Some security professionals consider phishing attacks as a type of spoofing attack.

Sniffing and Eavesdropping

Sniffing, also referred to as eavesdropping, occurs when an attacker inserts a device or software into the communication medium that collects all the information transmitted over the medium. Network sniffers are used by both legitimate security professionals and attackers.

Organizations should monitor and limit the use of sniffers. To protect against their use, you should encrypt all inbound and outbound traffic on the network.

Emanating

Emanations are electromagnetic signals that are emitted by an electronic device. Attackers can target certain devices or transmission mediums to eavesdrop on communication without having physical access to the device or medium.

The TEMPEST program, initiated by the United States and the United Kingdom, researches ways to limit emanations and standardizes the technologies used. Any equipment that meets TEMPEST standards suppresses signal emanations using shielding material. Devices that meet TEMPEST standards usually implement an outer barrier or coating, called a Faraday cage or Faraday shield. TEMPEST devices are most often used in government, the military, or in law enforcement.

Backdoor/Trapdoor

A ***backdoor*** or ***trapdoor*** is a mechanism implemented in many devices or applications that gives the user who uses the backdoor unlimited access to the device or application. Privileged backdoor accounts are the most common method of backdoor that you will see today.

Most established vendors no longer release devices or applications with this security issue. You should be aware of any known backdoors in the devices or applications you manage.

Access Aggregation

Access aggregation is a term that is often used synonymously with privilege creep. Access aggregation occurs when users gain more access across more systems. It can be intentional, as when single sign-on is implemented, or unintentional, when users are granted more rights without first checking and considering the rights that they already have. Privilege or authorization creep occurs when users are given new rights without having their old rights revoked. So, privilege creep is actually a subset of access aggregation.

To protect against access aggregation, organizations should implement permissions/rights policies that review an account when permissions or rights changes—both in escalation and de-escalation—are requested. Administrators should ensure that any existing permissions or rights that the user no longer needs are removed. For example, if a user is moving from the accounting department to the sales department, the user account should no longer have permissions or rights to accounting resources.

Security professionals should work with data owners and data custodians to ensure that the appropriate policies are implemented.

Advanced Persistent Threat

An ***advanced persistent threat (APT)*** is an attack in which an unauthorized person gains access to a network and remains for a long period of time with the intention being to steal data. An APT does not aim to cause damage to the network or organization. Its main aim is to gain access to valuable information.

After attackers gain access to the network, they usually set up a backdoor. To prevent discovery, the attackers may erase audit logs (also known as covering their tracks), rewrite code, and employ other sophisticated evasion techniques. Some APTs are so complex that they require a full-time administrator. The attackers will work to establish backdoors with each successful breach of an internal system.

The best method to detect APTs is to look for anomalies or large amounts of data transfers in outbound data.

Prevent or Mitigate Access Control Threats

Because access control threats are so widespread, organizations must do all they can to protect their access control systems, including deploying anti-malware, firewalls, intrusion detection and prevention, and other defense tools. Security professionals should encourage their organizations to deploy the following measures to prevent or mitigate access control threats:

- Deploy physical access controls for all systems and devices.
- Control and monitor access to password files.
- Encrypt password files.
- Deploy an enterprisewide strong password policy.
- Deploy password masking on all operating systems and applications.
- Deploy multifactor authentication.
- Deploy account lockout on prolonged inactivity.
- Deploy auditing for access controls.
- Deploy a user account management policy to ensure that user accounts are created and removed as necessary.
- Provide user security awareness training that specifically focuses on access control.

Exam Preparation Tasks

As mentioned in the section "About the *CISSP Cert Guide*, Fifth Edition" in the Introduction, you have a couple of choices for exam preparation: the exercises here, Chapter 9, "Final Preparation," and the exam simulation questions in the Pearson Test Prep practice test software.

Review All Key Topics

Review the most important topics in this chapter, noted with the Key Topic icon in the outer margin of the page. Table 5-1 lists a reference of these key topics and the page numbers on which each is found.

Key Topic

Table 5-1 Key Topics for Chapter 5

Key Topic Element	Description	Page Number
List	Access control process	562
List	Five factors for authentication	573
List	Password types	574
List	Password management considerations	575
List	Physiological characteristics	579
Section	Behavioral Characteristics	581
Section	Biometric Considerations	581
Figure 5-1	Biometric Enrollment and Authentication Process	583
Lists	Advantages and disadvantages of SSO	590
Lists	Advantages and disadvantages of Kerberos	594
Figure 5-2	Kerberos Ticket-Issuing Process	595
List	Auditing mechanism guidelines	596
Figure 5-3	NIST SP 800-162 Basic ABAC Scenario	607
Section	Provisioning Life Cycle	612
List	Five classes of malware	622

Define Key Terms

Define the following key terms from this chapter and check your answers in the glossary:

access aggregation; access control; access control list (ACL); access control matrix; access control policy; advanced persistent threat (APT); attribute-based access control (ABAC); authentication; authorization; backdoor; biometric acceptability; biometric accuracy; biometric throughput rate; birthday attack; brute-force attack; buffer overflow; capability table; centralized access control; characteristic factors; context-dependent access control; cross-certification federated identity model; crossover error rate (CER); decentralized access control; device authentication; deprovisioning; dictionary attack; discretionary access control (DAC); dumpster diving; false acceptance rate (FAR); false rejection rate (FRR); federated identity management (FIM); identification; Identity as a Service (IDaaS); Kerberos; knowledge factors; least privilege; Lightweight Directory Access Protocol (LDAP); location factors; logical control; mandatory access control (MAC); multifactor authentication (MFA); need-to-know; ownership factors; password masking; pharming; phishing; physical control; privilege creep; provisioning; provisioning life cycle; rainbow table attack; ransomware; revocation; role-based access control (RBAC); rule-based access control; Secure European System for Applications in a Multi-vendor Environment (SESAME); Security Assertion Markup Language (SAML); security domain; separation of duties; shoulder surfing; single-factor authentication; single sign-on (SSO); sniffer attack; spyware; trapdoor; Trojan horse; virus; vishing; whaling; worm

Answer Review Questions

1. Which of the following is *not* an example of a knowledge authentication factor?
   a. Password
   b. Mother's maiden name
   c. City of birth
   d. Smart card
2. Which of the following statements about memory cards and smart cards is false?
   a. A memory card can be a swipe card that contains user authentication information.
   b. Memory cards are also known as integrated circuit cards (ICCs).
   c. Smart cards contain memory and an embedded chip.
   d. Smart card systems are more reliable than memory card systems.
3. Which biometric method is most effective as far as accuracy?
   a. Iris scan
   b. Retina scan
   c. Fingerprint
   d. Handprint
4. What is a Type I error in a biometric authentication system?
   a. Crossover error rate (CER)
   b. False rejection rate (FRR)
   c. False acceptance rate (FAR)
   d. Throughput rate

5. Which access control model is a desirable model used by routers and firewalls to control access to secure networks?
   a. Discretionary access control
   b. Mandatory access control
   c. Role-based access control
   d. Rule-based access control

6. Which threat is *not* considered a social engineering threat?
   a. Phishing
   b. Pharming
   c. DoS attack
   d. Dumpster diving

7. Which of the following statements best describes an IDaaS implementation?
   a. Ensures that any instance of identification and authentication to a resource is managed properly.
   b. Collects and verifies information about an individual to prove that the person who has a valid account is who that person claims to be.
   c. Provides a set of identity and access management functions to target systems on customers' premises and/or in the cloud.
   d. Exchanges authentication and authorization data between organizations or security domains.

8. Which of the following is an example of multifactor authentication?
   a. Username and password
   b. Username, retina scan, and smart card
   c. Retina scan and finger scan
   d. Smart card and security token

9. You decide to implement an access control policy that requires that users only log on from certain workstations within your organization's facility. Which type of authentication factor are you implementing?
   a. Knowledge factor
   b. Location factor
   c. Ownership factor
   d. Characteristic factor

10. Which threat is considered a password threat?
    a. Buffer overflow
    b. Sniffing
    c. Spoofing
    d. Brute-force attack

11. Which session management mechanisms are often used to manage desktop sessions?
    a. Screensavers and timeouts
    b. FIPS 201.2 and NIST SP 800-79-2
    c. Bollards and locks
    d. KDC, TGT, and TGS

12. Which of the following is a major disadvantage of implementing an SSO system?
    a. Users are able to use stronger passwords.
    b. Users need to remember the login credentials for a single system.
    c. User and password administration is simplified.
    d. If a user's credentials are compromised, an attacker can access all resources.

13. Which type of attack is carried out from multiple locations using zombies and botnets?
    a. TEMPEST
    b. DDoS
    c. Backdoor
    d. Emanating

14. Which type of attack is one in which an unauthorized person gains access to a network and remains for a long period of time with the intention of stealing data?
    a. APT
    b. ABAC
    c. Access aggregation
    d. FIM

15. Which of the following is a formal process for creating, changing, and removing users that includes user approval, user creation, user creation standards, and authorization?
    a. NIST SP 800-63
    b. Centralized access control
    c. Decentralized access control
    d. Provisioning life cycle

Answers and Explanations

1. **d.** Knowledge factors are something a person knows, including passwords, mother's maiden name, city of birth, and date of birth. Ownership factors are something a person has, including a smart card.
2. **b.** Memory cards are *not* also known as integrated circuit cards (ICCs). Smart cards are also known as ICCs.
3. **a.** Iris scans are considered more effective as far as accuracy than retina scans, fingerprints, and handprints.
4. **b.** A Type I error in a biometric system is false rejection rate (FRR). A Type II error in a biometric system is false acceptance rate (FAR). Crossover error rate (CER) is the point at which FRR equals FAR. Throughput rate is the rate at which users are authenticated.
5. **d.** Rule-based access control is a desirable model used by routers and firewalls to control access to networks. The other three types of access control models are not usually implemented by routers and firewalls.
6. **c.** A denial-of-service (DoS) attack is not considered a social engineering threat. The other three options are considered to be social engineering threats.
7. **c.** An Identity as a Service (IDaaS) implementation provides a set of identity and access management functions to target systems on customers' premises and/or in the cloud. Session management ensures that any instance of identification and authentication to a resource is managed properly. A proof of identity process collects and verifies information about an individual to prove that the person who has a valid account is who that person claims to be.
8. **b.** Using a username, retina scan, and smart card is an example of multifactor authentication. The username is something you know, the retina scan is something you are, and the smart card is something you have.
9. **b.** You are implementing a location factor, which is based on where a person is located when logging in.

10. **d.** A brute-force attack is considered a password threat.
11. **a.** Desktop sessions can be managed through screensavers, timeouts, logon, and schedule limitations. FIPS PUB 201.2 and NIST SP 800-79-2 are documents that provide guidance on proof of identity. Physical access to facilities can be provided securely using locks, fencing, bollards, guards, and CCTV. In Kerberos, the Key Distribution Center (KDC) issues a ticket-granting ticket (TGT) to the principal. The principal sends the TGT to the ticket-granting service (TGS) when the principal needs to connect to another entity.
12. **d.** If a user's credentials are compromised in a single sign-on (SSO) environment, attackers have access to all resources to which the user has access. All other choices are advantages to implementing an SSO system.
13. **b.** A distributed DoS (DDoS) attack is a DoS attack that is carried out from multiple attack locations. Vulnerable devices are infected with software agents, called zombies. They turn the vulnerable devices into botnets, which then carry out the attack. Devices that meet TEMPEST standards implement an outer barrier or coating, called a Faraday cage or Faraday shield. A backdoor or trapdoor is a mechanism implemented in many devices or applications that gives the user who uses the backdoor unlimited access to the device or application. Emanations are electromagnetic signals that are emitted by an electronic device. Attackers can target certain devices or transmission mediums to eavesdrop on communication without having physical access to the device or medium.
14. **a.** An advanced persistent threat (APT) is an attack in which an unauthorized person gains access to a network and remains for a long period of time with the intention of stealing data. Attribute-based access control (ABAC) grants or denies user requests based on arbitrary attributes of the user and arbitrary attributes of the object, and environment conditions that may be globally recognized. Access aggregation is a term that is often used synonymously with privilege creep. Access aggregation occurs when users gain more access across more systems. In federated identity management (FIM), each organization that joins the federation agrees to enforce a common set of policies and standards. These policies and standards define how to provision and manage user identification, authentication, and authorization.
15. **d.** The provisioning life cycle is a formal process for creating, changing, and removing users. This process includes user approval, user creation, user creation standards, and authorization. Users should sign a written statement that explains the access conditions, including user responsibilities. NIST SP 800-63 provides a suite of technical requirements for federal agencies implementing digital identity services, including an overview of identity frameworks; and using authenticators, credentials, and assertions in digital systems.

In centralized access control, a central department or personnel oversee the access for all organizational resources. This administration method ensures that user access is controlled in a consistent manner across the entire enterprise. In decentralized access control, personnel closest to the resources, such as department managers and data owners, oversee the access control for individual resources.

This chapter covers the following topics:

- **Design and Validate Assessment and Testing Strategies:** Concepts discussed include the use of assessment, test, and audit strategies, including internal, external, and third-party strategies, and the effect location has on the testing.
- **Conduct Security Control Testing:** Concepts discussed include the security control testing process, including vulnerability assessments, penetration testing, log reviews, synthetic transactions, code review and testing, misuse case testing, test coverage analysis, and interface testing.
- **Collect Security Process Data:** Concepts discussed include NIST SP 800-137, account management, management review and approval, key performance and risk indicators, backup verification data, training and awareness, and disaster recovery and business continuity.
- **Analyze Test Outputs and Generate a Report:** Concepts discussed include the importance of analyzing and reporting test outputs, including automatic and manual reports.
- **Conduct or Facilitate Security Audits:** Concepts discussed include the internal, external, and third-party auditing processes and the three types of SOC reports.

CHAPTER 6

Security Assessment and Testing

Security assessment and testing covers designing, performing, and analyzing security testing. Security professionals must understand these processes to protect their assets from attacks.

Security assessment and testing requires a number of testing methods to determine an organization's vulnerabilities and risks. It assists an organization in managing the risks in planning, deploying, operating, and maintaining systems and processes. Its goal is to identify any technical, operational, and system deficiencies early in the process, before those deficiencies are deployed. The earlier you can discover those deficiencies, the cheaper it is to fix them.

This chapter discusses assessment and testing strategies; security control testing; collection of security process data; analysis and reporting of test outputs; and internal, external, and third-party audits.

Foundation Topics

Design and Validate Assessment and Testing Strategies

Security professionals must ensure that their organization plans, designs, executes, and validates appropriate security assessment, testing, and audit strategies to ensure that risks are mitigated. Security professionals must take a lead role in helping the organization implement the appropriate security assessment, testing, and auditing strategies. The organization should rely on industry best practices, national and international standards, and vendor-recommended practices and guidelines to ensure that the strategies are planned and implemented appropriately.

Organizations with IT assets will most likely establish a team that will be responsible for executing any assessment, testing, and auditing strategies. The team should consist of individuals who understand security assessment, testing, and auditing but should also include representatives from other areas of the organization. Verifying and validating security are ongoing activities that never really stop. But security professionals should help guide an organization in terms of when a particular type of assessment or testing is best performed.

Security Testing

Security testing ensures that a control is functioning properly. Both manual and automatic security testing can be performed. Security testing should be carried out on a regular basis and should be performed on all types of devices.

When performing security testing, security professionals should understand that testing will affect the performance of the devices involved in the security tests. Security testing cannot always be performed during nonpeak hours. Performing this testing only during nonpeak hours could also result in skewed results.

Security professionals should consider the following factors when performing security testing:

- Impact on performance
- Difficulty of testing method
- Time needed
- Changes that could affect the performance
- System risk
- System criticality
- Security test availability

- Information sensitivity level
- Likelihood of technical failure or misconfiguration

Permission must be obtained prior to performing any tests. After security tests are performed, security professionals should analyze the results and make appropriate recommendations based on those results. In addition, the security testing tools themselves can be configured to send alerts or messages based on preconfigured triggers or filters. Without proper analysis, reporting, and remediation, security testing does not provide a benefit to the organization.

Security Assessments

Security assessments are the reviews of the security status and reports for a system, application, or other environment. During this assessment, a security professional will review the results of the security tests, identify any vulnerabilities, and make recommendations for remediation. Security testing leads to security assessments.

Security professionals should prepare a formal security assessment report that includes all of the identified issues and recommendations. Also, they should document the actions taken based on the recommendations.

Red Team versus Blue Team

Penetration testing sometimes involves Red Team versus Blue Team exercises. The ***Red Team*** simulates attacks on a network, whereas the ***Blue Team*** is responsible for defending the network. Some Red Team–Blue Team exercises may include physical security tests, which means that a team may also try to social engineer its way into a "secure" facility—perhaps dressed up as a courier. Generally, a Red Team is more effective when it is composed of external consultants (see Figure 6-1).

Red Team	Blue Team
• Ethical Hacking	• Defensive Security
• Penetration Testing	• Incident Response
• Black Box Testing	• Triage
• Social Engineering	• Digital Forensics
• Web App Vulnerability Testing	

Figure 6-1 Red Team versus Blue Team Activities

Some organizations use a Purple Team instead of Red Team versus Blue Team. In a Purple Team, the Red Team and Blue Team come together to align their strategies and expertise (see Figure 6-2). The Purple Team will develop both offensive and defensive exercises.

Figure 6-2 Red and Blue Mixed Equals Purple (the Same Team Develops Offensive and Defensive Tactics)

Security Auditing

According to the National Institute of Standards and Technology (NIST), a security audit is an "[i]ndependent review and examination of a system's records and activities to determine the adequacy of system controls, ensure compliance with established security policy and procedures, detect breaches in security services, and recommend any changes that are indicated for countermeasures." Like security assessment and testing, it can be performed internally, externally, and via a third party. Security auditing is covered in more detail later in this chapter and in Chapter 7, "Security Operations."

Internal, External, and Third-party Security Assessment, Testing, and Auditing

Security assessment, testing, and auditing occur in three manners: internal, external, and third-party.

Internal assessment, testing, and auditing are carried out by personnel within the organization. Internal assessments are within the organization's control. External assessment, testing, and auditing are carried out by a vendor or contractor that is engaged by the company or by an authorized entity, usually an attacker. External assessments are outside the organization's control, although the organization may be informed of the assessment if it is by a vendor or contractor.

Sometimes third-party assessment, testing, and auditing are performed by a party completely unrelated to the company and not previously engaged by it. This scenario often arises as a result of having to comply with some standard or regulation or when accreditation or certification is involved. Many certifying or regulating bodies may require engagement of a third party that has not had a previous relationship with the organization being assessed. In this case, the certifying body will work with the organization to engage an approved third party. These assessments are considered as being outside of enterprise control, although the organization may know it will occur. Often they do not know when.

Companies should ensure that, at a minimum, internal and external testing and assessments are completed on a regular basis. It is important that all testing obtain prior approval, be carefully planned, and be announced to end users as the testing may affect performance.

Location

Security assessment, testing, and auditing can be carried out on a variety of locations, including on-premises, cloud, and hybrid, depending on the organization's deployment of resources. When implementing a known internal or external assessment, the team is often given the location within which they must operate.

On-premises assessments are carried out to test the resources within the organization's facilities and networks. Depending on the size of the organization, this could be for the entire network, a section of the network (for example, certain subnets or virtual local area networks), or even a branch office when an organization has multiple physical locations. Those authorized to perform the assessment must ensure they understand the boundaries, if any, of the assessment.

Cloud assessments are carried out to test the organization's resources deployed in the cloud. If cloud assessments will be completed, the organization should notify the cloud service provider (CSP) to ensure that the CSP's team knows that assessments will be completed. Again, understanding the boundaries of the assessment is vital for the assessment team.

Hybrid assessments generally include both on-premises and cloud assessments. In addition, in some cases, hybrid assessments may only be for a specific location, for example, a branch office or single department, and involve both on-premises and cloud-deployed devices.

Conduct Security Control Testing

Organizations must manage the security control testing that occurs to ensure that all security controls are tested thoroughly by authorized individuals. The facets of security control testing that organizations must include are vulnerability assessments, penetration testing, log reviews, synthetic transactions, code review and testing, misuse case testing, test coverage analysis, and interface testing.

Vulnerability Assessment

A ***vulnerability assessment*** helps to identify the areas of weakness in a network, device, technology, or application. It can also help to determine asset prioritization within an organization. A comprehensive vulnerability assessment is part of the risk management process. But for access control, security professionals should use vulnerability assessments that specifically target the access control mechanisms.

Vulnerability assessments usually fall into one of three categories:

Key Topic

- **Personnel testing:** Reviews standard practices and procedures that users follow.
- **Physical testing:** Reviews facility and perimeter protections.
- **System and network testing:** Reviews systems, devices, and network topology.

The security analyst who will be performing a vulnerability assessment must understand the systems and devices that are on the network and the jobs they perform. The analyst needs this information to be able to assess the vulnerabilities of the systems and devices based on the known and potential threats to the systems and devices.

After gaining knowledge regarding the systems and devices, the security analyst should examine existing controls in place and identify any threats against these controls. The security analyst can then use all the information gathered to determine which automated tools to use to search for vulnerabilities. After the vulnerability analysis is complete, the security analyst should verify the results to ensure that they are accurate and then report the findings to management, with suggestions for remedial action. With this information in hand, the analyst should carry out threat modeling to identify the threats that could negatively affect systems and devices and the attack methods that could be used.

Vulnerability assessment applications include Nessus, Open Vulnerability Assessment System (OpenVAS), Core Impact, Nexpose, GFI LanGuard, and Qualys Cloud Platform. Of these applications, OpenVAS is free.

When selecting a vulnerability assessment tool, you should research the following metrics: accuracy, reliability, scalability, and reporting. Accuracy is the most important metric. A false positive generally results in time spent researching an issue that does not exist. A false negative is more serious, because it means the scanner failed to identify an issue that poses a serious security risk.

Network Discovery Scan

A ***network discovery scan*** examines a range of IP addresses to determine which ports are open. This type of scan only shows a list of systems on the network and the ports in use on the network. It does not actually check for any vulnerabilities.

Topology discovery entails determining the devices in the network, their connectivity relationships to one another, and the internal IP addressing scheme in use. Any combination of these pieces of information allows hackers to create a "map" of the network, which aids them tremendously in evaluating and interpreting the data they gather in other parts of the hacking process. If attackers are completely successful, they will end up with a diagram of the network. Your challenge as a security professional is to determine whether such a mapping process is possible, using the same tools as the attackers. Based on your findings, you should determine steps to take that make topology discovery either more difficult or, better yet, impossible.

Operating system fingerprinting is the process of using some method to determine the operating system running on a host or a server. By identifying the OS version and build number, hackers can identify common vulnerabilities of that OS using readily available documentation from the Internet. While many of the issues will have been addressed in subsequent updates, service packs, and hotfixes, there might be zero-day weaknesses (issues that have not been identified or addressed by the vendor) that hackers can leverage in the attack. Moreover, if any of the relevant security patches have not been applied, the weaknesses the patches were intended to address will exist on the machine. Therefore, the purpose of attempting OS fingerprinting during an assessment is to assess the relative ease with which it can be done and identify methods to make it more difficult.

Operating systems have well-known and extensively documented vulnerabilities, and so do common services. By determining the services that are running on a system, attackers also can discover potential vulnerabilities of the service of which they may attempt to take advantage. This is typically done with a port scan, in which all "open" or "listening" ports are identified. Once again, the lion's share of these issues will have been mitigated with the proper security patches, but that is not always the case; it is not uncommon for security analysts to find that systems that are running vulnerable services are missing the relevant security patches. Consequently, when performing service discovery, you should check patches on systems found to have open ports. It is also advisable to close any ports not required, or ports that are open by default but not used, for the system to do its job.

Network discovery tools can perform the following types of scans:

- **TCP SYN scan:** Sends a packet to each scanned port with the SYN flag set. If a response is received with the SYN and ACK flags set, the port is open.
- **TCP ACK scan:** Sends a packet to each port with the ACK flag set. If no response is received, then the port is marked as filtered. If an RST response is received, then the port is marked as unfiltered.
- **Xmas scan:** Sends a packet with the FIN, PSH, and URG flags set. If the port is open, there is no response. If the port is closed, the target responds with an RST/ACK packet. These attacks are so named because they light up alternating, blinking bits to resemble a Christmas tree.

The result of this type of scan is primarily for security professionals to determine whether ports are open that should be closed.

The most widely used network discovery scanning tool is Nmap.

Network Vulnerability Scan

Network vulnerability scans perform more complex scans of the network than network discovery scans. These scans will probe a targeted system or network to identify vulnerabilities. The tools used in these types of scans will contain a database of known vulnerabilities and will identify whether a specific ***vulnerability*** exists on each device.

There are two types of vulnerability scanners:

- **Passive vulnerability scanners:** A ***passive vulnerability scanner (PVS)*** monitors network traffic at the packet layer to determine topology, services, and vulnerabilities. It avoids the instability that can be introduced to a system by actively scanning for vulnerabilities.

  PVS tools analyze the packet stream and look for vulnerabilities through direct analysis. They are deployed in much the same way as intrusion detection systems (IDSs) or packet analyzers. A PVS can pick a network session that targets a protected server and monitor it as much as needed. The biggest benefit of a PVS is its ability to do its work without impacting the monitored network. Some examples of PVSs are the Nessus Network Monitor (formerly Tenable PVS) and NetScanTools Pro.

- **Active vulnerability scanners:** Whereas passive scanners can only gather information, ***active vulnerability scanners (AVSs)*** can take action to block an attack, such as blocking an unknown or unidentified IP address that sends suspicious commands. They can also be used to simulate an attack to assess readiness. They operate by sending transmissions to nodes and examining the responses. As a result, these scanners may disrupt network traffic. Active scanning should not begin until end users are notified about upcoming testing and the potential for network downtime. Examples include Nessus, Burp Suite, and IBM Security QRadar.

Regardless of whether it's active or passive, a vulnerability scanner cannot replace the expertise of trained security personnel. Moreover, these scanners are only as effective as the signature databases on which they depend, so the databases must be updated regularly. Finally, scanners require bandwidth and can potentially slow the network.

For best performance, you can place a vulnerability scanner in a subnet that needs to be protected. You can also connect a scanner through a firewall to multiple subnets; doing so complicates the configuration and requires opening ports on the firewall, which could be problematic and could impact the performance of the firewall.

The most popular network vulnerability scanning tools include Qualys, Nessus, and Tripwire IP360.

Vulnerability scanners can use agents that are installed on the devices, or they can be agentless. While many vendors argue that using agents is always best, there are advantages and disadvantages to both, as presented in Table 6-1.

Key Topic

Table 6-1 Server-Based vs. Agent-Based Scanning

Type	Technology	Characteristics
Agent-based	Pull technology	Can get information from disconnected machines or machines in the DMZ
		Ideal for remote locations that have limited bandwidth
		Less dependent on network connectivity
		Based on policies defined in the central console
Server-based	Push technology	Good for networks with plentiful bandwidth
		Dependent on network connectivity
		Central authority does all the scanning and deployment

Some scanners can do both agent-based and server-based scanning (also called agentless or sensor-based scanning).

Web Application Vulnerability Scan

A web application is a computer program that uses a web browser and web technologies to perform tasks on websites. Web applications reside on web servers. Examples of web applications include webmail and document sharing applications, such as Gmail and Google Docs. The benefit of using a web application is that the user does not need to download an application locally or be concerned about software updates. However, companies that utilize third-party web applications have little control over their security and depend on the vendor for patching vulnerabilities. Because web applications are widely used today, organizations must ensure that their web applications remain secure and free of vulnerabilities. Web application vulnerability scanners are special tools that examine web applications for known vulnerabilities.

Popular web application vulnerability scanners include Grabber and Vega.

Penetration Testing

The goal of penetration testing, which also relates to ethical hacking, is to simulate an attack to identify any threats that can stem from internal or external resources planning to exploit the vulnerabilities of a system or device.

The steps in performing a ***penetration test*** are as follows:

Key Topic

1. Plan for the penetration test.
2. Obtain written consent from management.
3. Document information about the target system or device.
4. Gather information about attack methods against the target system or device. This step includes performing port scans.
5. Identify the known vulnerabilities of the target system or device.
6. Execute attacks against the target system or device to gain user and privileged access.
7. Document the results of the penetration test and report the findings to management, with suggestions for remedial action.

Both internal and external tests should be performed. Internal tests occur from within the network, whereas external tests originate outside the network and target the servers and devices that are publicly visible.

Strategies for penetration testing are based on the testing objectives defined by the organization. The strategies that you should be familiar with include the following:

Key Topic

- ***Blind test***: The testing team is provided with limited knowledge of the network systems and devices that use publicly available information. The organization's security team knows in advance about a simulated attack (or attacks). This test requires more effort by the testing team, and the team must simulate an actual attack.
- ***Double-blind test***: This test is like a blind test except that the organization's security team does *not* know that an attack is coming. Only a few individuals in the organization know about the attack, and they do not share this information with the security team. This test usually requires equal effort for both the testing team and the organization's security team.
- ***Target test***: Both the testing team and the organization's security team are given maximum information about the network and the type of attack that will occur. This test is the easiest to complete but does not provide a full picture of the organization's security.

Penetration testing is also divided into categories based on the amount of information to be provided. The main categories that you should be familiar with include the following:

Key Topic

- **Zero-knowledge test:** The testing team is provided with no knowledge regarding the organization's network map. The testing team can use any means available to obtain information about the organization's network. This type is also referred to as closed, or black-box, testing.

- ***Partial-knowledge test*:** The testing team is provided with public knowledge regarding the organization's network. Boundaries might be set for this type of test. It is also referred to as gray-box testing.

- ***Full-knowledge test*:** The testing team is provided with all available knowledge regarding the organization's network, map, and its topology. This test is focused more on what attacks can be carried out. It is also referred to as white-box testing.

Penetration testing applications include Metasploit, Wireshark, Core Impact, Nessus, Cain & Abel, Kali Linux, and John the Ripper. When selecting a penetration testing tool, you should first determine which systems you want to test. Then research the different tools to discover which can perform the tests that you want to perform for those systems and research the tools' methodologies for testing. In addition, the organization needs to select the correct individual to carry out the test. Remember that penetration tests should include manual methods as well as automated methods because relying on only one of these two will not yield a thorough result.

Table 6-2 compares vulnerability assessments and penetration tests.

Key Topic

Table 6-2 Comparison of Vulnerability Assessments and Penetration Tests

	Vulnerability Assessment	Penetration Test
Purpose	Identifies vulnerabilities that may result in compromise of a system.	Identifies ways to exploit vulnerabilities to circumvent the security features of systems.
When	After significant system changes. Schedule at least quarterly thereafter.	After significant system changes. Schedule at least annually thereafter.
How	Use automated tools with manual verification of identified issues.	Use both automated and manual methods to provide a comprehensive report.
Reports	Potential risks posed by known vulnerabilities, ranked using base scores associated with each vulnerability. Both internal and external reports should be provided.	Description of each issue discovered, including specific risks the issue may pose and specifically how and to what extent it may be exploited.
Duration	Typically, several seconds to several minutes per scanned host.	Days or weeks, depending on the scope and size of the environment to be tested. Tests may grow in duration if efforts uncover additional scope.

Log Reviews

A ***log*** is a physical or electronic recording of events that occur on an organizational asset, including systems, networks, devices, and facilities. Each entry in a log covers a single event that occurs on the asset. In most cases, there are separate logs for different event types, including security logs, operating system logs, and application logs. Because so many logs are generated on a single device, many organizations have trouble ensuring that the logs are reviewed in a timely manner. ***Log review***, however, is probably one of the most important steps an organization can take to ensure that issues are detected before they become major problems.

Computer security logs are particularly important because they can help an organization identify security incidents, policy violations, and fraud. Log management ensures that computer security logs, whether they show any errors or have normal operational procedures, are stored in sufficient detail for an appropriate period of time so that auditing, forensic analysis, investigations, baselines, trends, and long-term problems can be identified.

NIST has provided two special publications that relate to log management: NIST SP 800-92, "Guide to Computer Security Log Management," and NIST SP 800-137, "Information Security Continuous Monitoring (ISCM) for Federal Information Systems and Organizations." Although both of these special publications are primarily used by federal government agencies and organizations, other organizations may want to use them as well because of the wealth of information they provide. The following section covers NIST SP 800-92, and NIST SP 800-137 is discussed later in this chapter.

NIST SP 800-92

NIST SP 800-92 makes the following recommendations for more efficient and effective log management:

Key Topic

- Organizations should establish policies and procedures for log management. As part of the planning process, an organization should
  - Define its logging requirements and goals.
  - Develop policies that clearly define mandatory requirements and suggested recommendations for log management activities.
  - Ensure that related policies and procedures incorporate and support the log management requirements and recommendations.
- Management should provide the necessary support for the efforts involving log management planning, policy, and procedures development.

- Organizations should prioritize log management appropriately throughout the organization.
- Organizations should create and maintain a log management infrastructure.
- Organizations should provide proper support for all staff with log management responsibilities.
- Organizations should establish standard log management operational processes. This includes ensuring that administrators
    - Monitor the logging status of all log sources.
    - Monitor log rotation and archival processes.
    - Check for upgrades and patches to logging software and acquire, test, and deploy them.
    - Ensure that each logging host's clock is synchronized to a common time source.
    - Reconfigure logging as needed based on policy changes, technology changes, and other factors.
    - Document and report anomalies in log settings, configurations, and processes.

According to NIST SP 800-92, common log management infrastructure components include general functions (log parsing, event filtering, and event aggregation), storage (log rotation, log archival, log reduction, log conversion, log normalization, and log file integrity checking), log analysis (event correlation, log viewing, and log reporting), and log disposal (log clearing.)

Syslog provides a simple framework for log entry generation, storage, and transfer that any operating system, security software, or application could use if designed to do so. Many log sources either use syslog as their native logging format or offer features that allow their log formats to be converted to syslog format. Each syslog message has only three parts. The first part specifies the facility and severity as numerical values. The second part of the message contains a timestamp and the hostname or IP address of the source of the log. The third part is the actual log message content.

No standard fields are defined within the message content; it is intended to be human-readable and not easily machine-parsable. This protocol provides tremendous flexibility for log generators, which can place whatever information they deem important within the content field, but it makes automated analysis of the log data very challenging. A single source may use many different formats for its log message content, so an analysis program would need to be familiar with each format and be able to extract the meaning of the data within the fields of each format. This problem becomes much more challenging when log messages are generated by many sources. It might not be feasible to understand the meaning of all log messages, so analysis might be limited to keyword and pattern searches. Some organizations design their syslog infrastructures so that similar types of messages are grouped together or assigned similar codes, which can make log analysis automation easier to perform.

As log security has become a greater concern, several implementations of syslog have been created that place greater emphasis on security. Most have been based on IETF's RFC 3195, which was designed specifically to improve the security of syslog. Implementations based on this standard can support log confidentiality, integrity, and availability through several features, including reliable log delivery, transmission confidentiality protection, and transmission integrity protection and authentication.

Security information and event management (SIEM) products allow administrators to consolidate all security information logs. This consolidation ensures that administrators can perform analysis on all logs from a single resource rather than having to analyze each log on its separate resource. Most SIEM products support two ways of collecting logs from log generators:

- **Agentless:** The SIEM server receives data from the individual hosts without needing to have any special software installed on those hosts. Some servers pull logs from the hosts, which is usually done by having the server authenticate to each host and retrieve its logs regularly. In other cases, the hosts push their logs to the server, which usually involves each host authenticating to the server and transferring its logs regularly. Regardless of whether the logs are pushed or pulled, the server then performs event filtering and aggregation and log normalization and analysis on the collected logs.
- **Agent-based:** An agent program is installed on the host to perform event filtering and aggregation and log normalization for a particular type of log. The host then transmits the normalized log data to the SIEM server, usually on a real-time or near-real-time basis for analysis and storage. Multiple agents may need to be installed if a host has multiple types of logs of interest. Some SIEM products also offer agents for generic formats such as syslog and Simple Network Management Protocol (SNMP). A generic agent is used primarily to get log data from a source for which a format-specific agent and an agentless method are not available. Some products also allow administrators to create custom agents to handle unsupported log sources.

There are advantages and disadvantages to each method. The primary advantage of the agentless approach is that agents do not need to be installed, configured, and maintained on each logging host. The primary disadvantage is the lack of filtering and aggregation at the individual host level, which can cause significantly larger amounts of data to be transferred over networks and increase the amount of time it takes to filter and analyze the logs. Another potential disadvantage of the agentless method is that the SIEM server may need credentials for authenticating to each logging host. In some cases, only one of the two methods is feasible; for example, there might be no way to remotely collect logs from a particular host without installing an agent onto it.

SIEM products usually include support for several dozen types of log sources, such as OSs, security software, application servers (e.g., web servers, email servers), and even physical security control devices such as badge readers. For each supported log source type, except for generic formats such as syslog, the SIEM products typically know how to categorize the most important logged fields. This approach significantly improves the normalization, analysis, and correlation of log data over that performed by software with a less granular understanding of specific log sources and formats. Also, the SIEM software can perform event reduction by disregarding data fields that are not significant to computer security, potentially reducing the SIEM software's network bandwidth and data storage usage. Setting up and maintaining SIEM needs both human and monetary resources to organize and manage the logs. The logs are kept for a certain time period for audit/legal purposes as the organizational policies indicate.

Typically, system, network, and security administrators are responsible for managing logging on their systems, performing regular analysis of their log data, documenting and reporting the results of their log management activities, and ensuring that log data is provided to the log management infrastructure in accordance with the organization's policies. In addition, some of the organization's security administrators act as log management infrastructure administrators, with responsibilities such as the following:

- Contact system-level administrators to get additional information regarding an event or to request that they investigate a particular event.
- Identify changes needed to system logging configurations (e.g., which entries and data fields are sent to the centralized log servers, what log format should be used) and inform system-level administrators of the necessary changes.
- Initiate responses to events, including incident handling and operational problems (e.g., a failure of a log management infrastructure component).
- Ensure that old log data is archived to removable media and disposed of properly when it is no longer needed.
- Cooperate with requests from legal counsel, auditors, and others.

- Monitor the status of the log management infrastructure (e.g., failures in logging software or log archival media, failures of local systems to transfer their log data) and initiate appropriate responses when problems occur.
- Test and implement upgrades and updates to the log management infrastructure's components.
- Maintain the security of the log management infrastructure.

Organizations should develop and enforce policies that clearly define mandatory requirements and suggested recommendations for several aspects of log management, including log generation, log transmission, log storage and disposal, and log analysis. Table 6-3 gives examples of logging configuration settings that an organization can use. The types of values defined in Table 6-3 should only be applied to the hosts and host components previously specified by the organization as ones that must or should log security-related events.

Key Topic

Table 6-3 Examples of Logging Configuration Settings

Category	Low-Impact Systems	Moderate-Impact Systems	High-Impact Systems
Log retention duration	1–2 weeks	1–3 months	3–12 months
Log rotation	Optional (if performed, at least every week or every 25 MB)	Every 6–24 hours or every 2–5 MB	Every 15–60 minutes or every 0.5–1.0 MB
Log data transfer frequency (to SIEM)	Every 3–24 hours	Every 15–60 minutes	At least every 5 minutes
Local log data analysis	Every 1–7 days	Every 12–24 hours	At least 6 times a day
File integrity check for rotated logs?	Optional	Yes	Yes
Encrypt rotated logs?	Optional	Optional	Yes
Encrypt log data transfers to SIEM?	Optional	Yes	Yes

Synthetic Transactions

Synthetic transaction monitoring, which is a type of proactive monitoring, is often preferred for websites and applications. Synthetic transaction monitoring is sometimes referred to as synthetic benchmarking. It provides insight into the availability and performance of an application and warns of any potential issue before users experience any degradation in application behavior. It uses external agents to run scripted transactions against an application. For example, Microsoft's System Center Operations Manager uses synthetic transactions to monitor databases, websites, and TCP port usage.

In contrast, ***real user monitoring (RUM)***, which is a type of passive monitoring, captures and analyzes every transaction of every application or website user. Unlike synthetic monitoring, which attempts to gain performance insights by regularly testing synthetic interactions, RUM cuts through the guesswork by seeing exactly how users are interacting with the application.

Code Review and Testing

Code review and testing must occur throughout the entire system or application development life cycle. The goal of ***code review and testing*** is to identify bad programming patterns, security misconfigurations, functional bugs, and logic flaws.

In the planning and design phase, code review and testing include architecture security reviews and threat modeling. In the development phase, code review and testing include static source code analysis, manual code review, static binary code analysis, and manual binary review. After an application is deployed, code review and testing involve penetration testing, vulnerability scanning, and fuzz testing.

Formal code review involves a careful and detailed process with multiple participants and multiple phases. In this type of code review, software developers attend meetings where each line of code is reviewed, usually using printed copies. Lightweight code review typically requires less overhead than formal code inspections, though it can be equally effective when done properly. Code review is helpful to detect logic bombs written into the code by disgruntled employees or inadvertent mistakes by new programmers. It also helps in creating a better documented code. Code review methods include the following:

- **Over-the-shoulder:** One developer looks over the author's shoulder as the author walks through the code.
- **Email pass-around:** Source code is emailed to reviewers automatically after the code is checked in.
- **Pair programming:** Two authors develop code together at the same workstation.
- **Tool-assisted code review:** Authors and reviewers use tools designed for peer code review.
- ***Black-box testing*, or *zero-knowledge testing*:** The team is provided with no knowledge regarding the organization's application. The team can use any means at its disposal to obtain information about the organization's application. This is also referred to as closed testing.
- ***White-box testing*:** The team goes into the process with a deep understanding of the application or system. Using this knowledge, the team builds test cases to exercise each path, input field, and processing routine.

- ***Gray-box testing***: The team is provided more information than in black-box testing, while not as much as in white-box testing. Gray-box testing has the advantage of being nonintrusive while maintaining the boundary between developer and tester. On the other hand, it may uncover some of the problems that might be discovered with white-box testing.

Table 6-4 compares black-box, gray-box, and white-box testing.

Key Topic

Table 6-4 Black-Box, Gray-Box, and White-Box Testing

Black Box	Gray Box	White Box
Internal workings of the application are not known.	Internal workings of the application are somewhat known.	Internal workings of the application are fully known.
Also called closed-box, data-driven, and functional testing.	Also called translucent testing, as the tester has partial knowledge.	Also known as clear-box, structural, or code-based testing.
Performed by end users, testers, and developers.	Performed by end users, testers, and developers.	Performed by testers and developers.
Least time-consuming.	More time-consuming than black-box testing but less so than white-box testing.	Most exhaustive and time-consuming.

Other types of testing include dynamic versus static testing and manual versus automatic testing.

Code Review Process

The code review process varies from organization to organization. Fagan inspections are the most formal code reviews that can occur and should adhere to the following process:

1. Plan
2. Overview
3. Prepare
4. Inspect
5. Rework
6. Follow-up

Most organizations do not strictly adhere to the Fagan inspection process. Each organization should adopt a code review process fitting for its business requirements. The more restrictive the environment, the more formal the code review process should be.

Static Testing

Static testing analyzes software security without actually running the software. This analysis is usually provided by reviewing the source code or compiled application. Automated tools are used to detect common software flaws. Static testing has code available for review and can find if almost all requirements are met. Static testing tools should be available throughout the software design process.

Dynamic Testing

Dynamic testing analyzes software security in the runtime environment. With this testing, the tester does not have access to the application's source code. Dynamic testing can only find whether functional requirements are met or not.

Dynamic testing often includes the use of synthetic transactions, which are scripted transactions that have an expected outcome. These synthetic transactions are executed against the code to be tested, and the output is then compared to the expected output. Any discrepancies between the two outputs should be investigated for possible source code flaws.

Fuzz Testing

Fuzz testing is a dynamic testing tool that provides input to the software to test the software's limits and discover flaws. The input provided can be randomly generated by the tool or specially created to test for known vulnerabilities.

Fuzz testers include Untidy and Peach Fuzzer.

Misuse Case Testing

Misuse case testing, also referred to as ***negative testing***, tests an application to ensure that the application can handle invalid input or unexpected behavior. This testing is completed to ensure that an application will not crash and to improve the quality of an application by identifying its weak points. When misuse case testing is performed, organizations should expect to find issues. Misuse case testing should include testing that looks for the following:

- Required fields must be populated.
- Fields with a defined data type can only accept data that is the required data type.

- Fields with character limits allow only the preconfigured number of characters.
- Fields with a defined data range accept only data within that range.
- Fields accept only data that has been validated.

NOTE Fields that contain passwords or personally identifiable information (PII) should be masked so that their contents cannot be read by unauthorized users.

Test Coverage Analysis

Test coverage analysis uses test cases that are written against the application requirements specifications. Individuals involved in this analysis do not need to see the code to write the test cases. Once a document that describes all the test cases is written, test groups refer to a percentage of the test cases that were run, that passed, that failed, and so on. The application developer usually performs test coverage analysis as a part of unit testing. Quality assurance groups use overall test coverage analysis to indicate test metrics and coverage according to the test plan.

Test coverage analysis creates additional test cases to increase coverage. It helps developers find areas of an application not exercised by a set of test cases. It helps in determining a quantitative measure of code coverage, which indirectly measures the quality of the application or product.

One disadvantage of code coverage measurement is that it measures coverage of what the code covers but cannot test what the code does not cover or what has not been written. In addition, this analysis looks at a structure or function that already exists and not those that do not yet exist.

Interface Testing

Interface testing evaluates whether an application's systems or components correctly pass data and control to one another. It verifies whether module interactions from various libraries, interfaces, and links are working properly and errors are handled correctly. Interfaces that should be tested include client interfaces, server interfaces, remote interfaces, graphical user interfaces (GUIs), application programming interfaces (APIs), external and internal interfaces, and physical network interfaces.

GUI testing involves testing a product's GUI to ensure that it meets its specifications through the use of test cases. API testing tests APIs directly in isolation and as part of the end-to-end transactions exercised, during integration testing, to determine whether the APIs return the correct responses.

Collect Security Process Data

After security controls are tested, organizations must ensure that they collect the appropriate security process data. ***NIST SP 800-137*** provides guidelines for developing an ***information security continuous monitoring (ISCM)*** program. Security professionals should ensure that security process data that is collected includes account management, management review, key performance and risk indicators, backup verification data, training and awareness, and disaster recovery and business continuity.

NIST SP 800-137

According to NIST SP 800-137, *ISCM* is defined as maintaining ongoing awareness of information security, vulnerabilities, and threats to support organizational risk management decisions.

Organizations should take the following steps to establish, implement, and maintain ISCM:

Key Topic

1. Define an ISCM strategy based on risk tolerance that maintains clear visibility into assets, awareness of vulnerabilities, up-to-date threat information, and mission/business impacts.
2. Establish an ISCM program that includes metrics, status monitoring frequencies, control assessment frequencies, and an ISCM technical architecture.
3. Implement an ISCM program and collect the security-related information required for metrics, assessments, and reporting. Automate collection, analysis, and reporting of data where possible.
4. Analyze the data collected, report findings, and determine the appropriate responses. The organization may need to collect additional information to clarify or supplement existing monitoring data.
5. Respond to findings with technical, management, and operational mitigating activities or acceptance, transference/sharing, or avoidance/rejection.
6. Review and update the monitoring program, adjusting the ISCM strategy and maturing measurement capabilities to increase visibility into assets and awareness of vulnerabilities, further enable data-driven control of the security of an organization's information infrastructure, and increase organizational resilience.

Account Management

Account management is important because it involves the addition and deletion of accounts that are granted access to systems or networks. But account management also involves changing the permissions or privileges granted to those accounts. If account management is not monitored and recorded properly, organizations may discover that accounts have been created by unauthorized persons or those with misused privileges for the sole purpose of carrying out fraudulent or malicious activities. Two-person controls should be used with account management, often involving one administrator who creates accounts and another who assigns those accounts the appropriate permissions or privileges.

Escalation and *revocation* are two terms that are important to security professionals. Account privilege escalation occurs when a user account is granted more permissions based on new job duties or a complete job change. Security professionals should fully analyze a user's needs prior to changing the current permissions or privileges, making sure to grant only permissions or privileges that are needed for the new task and to remove those that are no longer needed. Without such analysis, users may be able to retain permissions that cause possible security issues because separation of duties is no longer retained. For example, suppose a user is hired in the accounts payable department to print out all vendor checks. Later this user receives a promotion to approve payment for the same accounts. If this user's old permission to print checks is not removed, this single user would be able to both approve the checks and print them, which is a direct violation of separation of duties. Moreover, when an employee moves from one department to another and the employee's old (unneeded) access privileges are not rescinded, this is referred to as escalating privileges, which poses a serious risk to the organization. Today, many managers and supervisors are required to review and approve system access for each of their employees—often on an annual basis.

Account revocation occurs when a user account is revoked because a user is no longer with an organization. Security professionals must keep in mind that there will be objects that belong to this user. If the user account is simply deleted, access to the objects owned by the user may be lost. A better plan may be to disable the account for a certain period. Account revocation policies should also distinguish between revoking an account for a user who resigns from an organization or moves to another unrelated department/branch and revoking an account for a user who is terminated.

Management Review and Approval

Management review of security process data should be mandatory, followed by recommendations. No matter how much data an organization collects about its security processes, the data is useless if an administrator never reviews it. Guidelines and procedures should be established to ensure that management review occurs in a timely manner. Without regular review, even the most minor security issue can be quickly turned into a major security breach.

Management review should include an approval process whereby the management team reviews any recommendations from security professionals and approves or rejects the recommendations based on the data given. If alternatives are given, management should examine all alternatives and approve the alternative that best satisfies the organizational needs. Security professionals should ensure that the reports provided to management are as comprehensive as possible so that all the data can be analyzed to ensure the most appropriate solution is selected.

Key Performance and Risk Indicators

By using key performance and risk indicators of security process data, organizations better identify when security risks are likely to occur. Key performance indicators (KPIs) allow organizations to determine whether levels of performance are below or above established norms. Key risk indicators (KRIs) allow organizations to identify whether certain risks are more or less likely to occur.

NIST has released the *Framework for Improving Critical Infrastructure Cybersecurity*, also known as the Cybersecurity Framework, which focuses on using business drivers to guide cybersecurity activities and considering cybersecurity risks as part of the organization's risk management processes. The framework consists of three parts: the Framework Core, the Framework Profiles, and the Framework Implementation Tiers.

The Framework Core is a set of cybersecurity activities, outcomes, and informative references that are common across critical infrastructure sectors, providing the detailed guidance for developing individual organizational profiles. The Framework Core consists of five concurrent and continuous functions: identify, protect, detect, respond, and recover.

After each function is identified, categories and subcategories for each function are recorded. The Framework Profiles are developed based on the business needs of the categories and subcategories. Through use of the Framework Profiles, the framework helps an organization align its cybersecurity activities with its business requirements, risk tolerances, and resources.

The Framework Implementation Tiers provide a mechanism for organizations to view and understand the characteristics of their approach to managing cybersecurity risk. The following tiers are used: Tier 1, partial; Tier 2, risk informed; Tier 3, repeatable; and Tier 4, adaptive.

Organizations will continue to have unique risks—different threats, different vulnerabilities, and different risk tolerances—and how they implement the practices in the framework will vary. Ultimately, the framework is aimed at reducing and better managing cybersecurity risks and is not a one-size-fits-all approach to managing cybersecurity.

Backup Verification Data

Any security process data that is collected should also be backed up. Security professionals should ensure that their organization has the appropriate backup and restore guidelines in place for all security process data. If data is not backed up properly, a failure can result in vital data being lost forever. In addition, personnel should test the restore process on a regular basis to make sure it works as it should. If an organization is unable to properly restore a system from a backup, the organization might as well not have the backup.

It is important to note here that data from decommissioned assets may still need to be kept for legal purposes. This data needs to be fully tested to ensure recoverability. The backup media needs to be carefully documented to ensure that systems exist that still use that media. For example, if CD/DVD backups exist of a decommissioned system, the organization must ensure that a CD/DVD reader is still available.

Training and Awareness

All personnel must understand any security assessment and testing strategies that an organization employs. Technical personnel may need to be trained in the details about security assessment and testing, including security control testing and collecting security process data. Other personnel, however, only need to be given more awareness training on this subject. Security professionals should ensure that all personnel are aware and understand what type of assessment and testing occurs, what is captured by this process, and why this is important to the organization. Management must fully support the security assessment and testing strategy and must communicate in advance to all personnel and stakeholders the importance of this program.

Disaster Recovery and Business Continuity

Any disaster recovery and business continuity plans that an organization develops must consider security assessment and testing, security control testing, and security process data collection. Often when an organization goes into disaster recovery mode, personnel do not think about these processes. As a matter of fact, ordinary security controls often fall by the wayside at such times. A security professional is responsible for ensuring that this does not happen. Security professionals involved in developing the disaster recovery and business continuity plans must cover all these areas, which can be done with table-top exercises. These plans should be tested at least once a year with all personnel involved and documented with dates of testing and updates to procedures, if any.

Analyze Test Outputs and Generate a Report

Personnel should understand the automated and manual reporting that can be done as part of security assessment and testing. In addition, they should be training to review these reports to determine if any actions need to be taken. Output must be reported in a timely manner to management in order to ensure that they understand the value of this process. Personnel may need to provide different reports depending on the level of audience understanding. For example, high-level management may need only a summary of findings. But technical personnel should be given details of the findings to ensure that they can implement the appropriate controls to mitigate or prevent any risks found during security assessment and testing.

Personnel may need special training on how to run manual reports and how to analyze the report outputs.

Conduct or Facilitate Security Audits

Organizations should conduct internal, external, and third-party audits as part of any security assessment and testing strategy. These audits should test all security controls that are currently in place. The following are some guidelines to consider as part of a good security audit plan:

- At minimum, perform annual audits to establish a security baseline.
- Determine your organization's objectives for the audit and share them with the auditors.
- Set the ground rules for the audit, including the dates/times of the audit, before the audit starts.
- Choose auditors who have security experience.
- Involve business unit managers early in the process.
- Ensure that auditors rely on experience, not just checklists.
- Ensure that the auditor's report reflects risks that the organization has identified.

- Ensure that the audit is conducted properly.
- Ensure that the audit covers all systems and all policies and procedures.
- Examine the report when the audit is complete.

Remember that internal audits are performed by personnel within the organization and are within the organization's control. External or third-party audits are performed by individuals outside the organization or another company and are outside the organization's control. Audits may also be location-based, including on-premises, cloud, or hybrid audits. All types of audits should be conducted to ensure that all vulnerabilities are discovered and the appropriate controls can be deployed. External audits are the best because they avoid any bias toward the organization. Internal audit findings may not match what an external auditor finds.

Many regulations today require that audits occur. Organizations used to rely on Statement on Auditing Standards (SAS) 70, which provided auditors information and verification about data center controls and processes related to data center users and their financial reporting. A SAS 70 audit verified that the controls and processes set in place by a data center are actually followed. The Statement on Standards for Attestation Engagements (SSAE) 16, Reporting on Controls at a Service Organization, is a standard that verifies the controls and processes and also requires a written assertion regarding the design and operating effectiveness of the controls being reviewed.

An SSAE 16 audit results in a Service Organization Control (SOC) 1 report. This report focuses on internal controls over financial reporting. There are two types of SOC 1 reports:

Key Topic

- **SOC 1, Type 1 report:** Focuses on the auditors' opinion of the accuracy and completeness of the data center management's design of controls, system, and/or service.
- **SOC 1, Type 2 report:** Includes the Type 1 report as well as an audit of the effectiveness of controls over a certain time period, normally between six months and a year.

Two other report types are also available: SOC 2 and SOC 3. Both of these audits provide benchmarks for controls related to the security, availability, processing integrity, confidentiality, or privacy of a system and its information. A SOC 2 report includes service auditor testing and results, and a SOC 3 report provides only the system description and auditor opinion. A SOC 3 report is for general use and provides a level of certification for data center operators that assures data center users of facility security, high availability, and process integrity. Table 6-5 briefly compares the three types of SOC reports.

Key Topic

Table 6-5 SOC Reports Comparison

	What It Reports On	Who Uses It
SOC 1	Internal controls over financial reporting	User auditors and controller office
SOC 2	Security, availability, processing integrity, confidentiality, or privacy controls	Management, regulators, and others; shared under nondisclosure agreement (NDA)
SOC 3	Security, availability, processing integrity, confidentiality, or privacy controls	Publicly available to anyone

Exam Preparation Tasks

As mentioned in the section "About the *CISSP Cert Guide*, Fifth Edition" in the Introduction, you have a couple of choices for exam preparation: the exercises here, Chapter 9, "Final Preparation," and the exam simulation questions in the Pearson Test Prep Software Online.

Review All Key Topics

Review the most important topics in this chapter, noted with the Key Topic icon in the outer margin of the page. Table 6-6 lists a reference of these key topics and the page numbers on which each is found.

Key Topic

Table 6-6 Key Topics for Chapter 6

Key Topic Element	Description	Page Number
List	Three categories of vulnerability assessments	640
Table 6-1	Server-Based vs. Agent-Based Scanning	643
List	Steps in a penetration test	644
List	Strategies for penetration testing	644
List	Penetration testing categories	644
Table 6-2	Comparison of Vulnerability Assessments and Penetration Tests	645
List	NIST SP 800-92 recommendations for log management	646
Table 6-3	Examples of Logging Configuration Settings	650
Table 6-4	Black-Box, Gray-Box, and White-Box Testing	652
List	Steps to establish, implement, and maintain ISCM	655
List	Types of SOC 1 reports	660
Table 6-5	SOC Reports Comparison	661

Define Key Terms

Define the following key terms from this chapter and check your answers in the glossary:

account management; active vulnerability scanner (AVS); black-box testing; blind test; Blue Team; code review and testing; double-blind test; dynamic testing; full-knowledge test; fuzz testing; gray-box testing; information security continuous monitoring (ISCM); interface testing; log; log review; misuse case testing; negative testing; network discovery scan; network vulnerability scan; NIST SP 800-137; NIST SP 800-92; operating system fingerprinting; partial-knowledge test; passive vulnerability scanner (PVS); penetration test; real user monitoring (RUM); Red Team; static testing; synthetic transaction monitoring; target test; test coverage analysis; topology discovery; vulnerability; vulnerability assessment; white-box testing; zero-knowledge test

Answer Review Questions

1. For which of the following penetration tests does the testing team have limited knowledge of the network systems and devices with only access to publicly available information?
   a. Target test
   b. Physical test
   c. Blind test
   d. Double-blind test

2. Which of the following is *not* a guideline according to NIST SP 800-92?
   a. Organizations should establish policies and procedures for log management.
   b. Organizations should create and maintain a log management infrastructure.
   c. Organizations should prioritize log management appropriately throughout the organization.
   d. Choose auditors with security experience.

3. According to NIST SP 800-92, which of the following are facets of log management infrastructure? (Choose all that apply.)
   a. General functions (log parsing, event filtering, and event aggregation)
   b. Storage (log rotation, log archival, log reduction, log conversion, log normalization, log file integrity checking)

c. Log analysis (event correlation, log viewing, log reporting)
d. Log disposal (log clearing)

4. What are the two ways of collecting logs using security information and event management (SIEM) products, according to NIST SP 800-92?
   a. Passive and active
   b. Agentless and agent-based
   c. Push and pull
   d. Throughput and rate

5. Which monitoring method MOST likely captures and analyzes every transaction of every application or website user when configured correctly?
   a. RUM
   b. Synthetic transaction monitoring
   c. Code review and testing
   d. Misuse case testing

6. Which type of testing is also known as negative testing?
   a. RUM (real user monitoring)
   b. Synthetic transaction monitoring
   c. Code review and testing
   d. Misuse case testing

7. What is the first step of the information security continuous monitoring (ISCM) plan, according to NIST SP 800-137?
   a. Establish an ISCM program.
   b. Define the ISCM strategy.
   c. Implement an ISCM program.
   d. Analyze the data collected.

8. What is the second step of the information security continuous monitoring (ISCM) plan, according to NIST SP 800-137?
   a. Establish an ISCM program.
   b. Define the ISCM strategy.
   c. Implement an ISCM program.
   d. Analyze the data collected.

9. Which of the following is *not* a guideline for internal, external, and third-party audits?
   a. Choose auditors with security experience.
   b. Involve business unit managers early in the process.
   c. At a minimum, perform biannual audits to establish a security baseline.
   d. Ensure that the audit covers all systems and all policies and procedures.

10. Which SOC (Service Organization Control) report can be shared with the general public WITHOUT causing any harm to the organization?
    a. SOC 1, Type 1
    b. SOC 1, Type 2
    c. SOC 2
    d. SOC 3

11. Which of the following is the last step in performing a penetration test?
    a. Document the results of the penetration test and report the findings to management, with suggestions for remedial action.
    b. Gather information about attack methods against the target system or device.
    c. Document information about the target system or device.
    d. Execute attacks against the target system or device to gain user and privileged access.

12. In which of the following does the testing team have zero knowledge of the organization's network?
    a. Gray-box testing
    b. Black-box testing
    c. White-box testing
    d. Physical testing

13. Which of the following is defined as a dynamic testing tool that tests the software's limits and may discover flaws?
    a. Interface testing
    b. Static testing
    c. Test coverage analysis
    d. Fuzz testing

14. Which factors should security professionals follow when performing security testing? (Choose all that apply.)
    a. Changes that could affect the performance
    b. System risk
    c. Information sensitivity level
    d. Likelihood of technical failure or misconfiguration

15. Which of the following can a hacker use to identify common vulnerabilities in an operating system running on a host or server?
    a. Operating system fingerprinting
    b. Network discovery scan
    c. Key performance and risk indicators
    d. Third-party audits

Answers and Explanations

1. **c.** With a blind test, the testing team knows an attack is coming and has limited knowledge of the network systems and devices and publicly available information. A target test occurs when the testing team and the organization's security team are given maximum information about the network and the type of attack that will occur. A physical test is not a type of penetration test. It is a type of vulnerability assessment. A double-blind test is like a blind test except that the organization's security team does not know an attack is coming.
2. **d.** NIST SP 800-92 does not include any information regarding auditors. So, the "Choose auditors with security experience" option is *not* a guideline according to NIST SP 800-92.
3. **a, b, c, d.** According to NIST SP 800-92, log management functions should include general functions (log parsing, event filtering, and event aggregation), storage (log rotation, log archival, log reduction, log conversion, log normalization, log file integrity checking), log analysis (event correlation, log viewing, log reporting), and log disposal (log clearing).
4. **b.** The two ways of collecting logs using security information and event management (SIEM) products, according to NIST SP 800-92, are agentless and agent-based.
5. **a.** Real user monitoring (RUM) captures and analyzes every transaction of every application or website user.
6. **d.** Misuse case testing is also known as negative testing.

7. **b.** The steps in an ISCM program, according to NIST SP 800-137, are
    1. Define an ISCM strategy.
    2. Establish an ISCM program.
    3. Implement an ISCM program and collect the security-related information required for metrics, assessments, and reporting.
    4. Analyze the data collected, report findings, and determine the appropriate responses.
    5. Respond to findings.
    6. Review and update the monitoring program.
8. **a.** The steps in an ISCM program, according to NIST SP 800-137, are
    1. Define an ISCM strategy.
    2. Establish an ISCM program.
    3. Implement an ISCM program and collect the security-related information required for metrics, assessments, and reporting.
    4. Analyze the data collected, report findings, and determine the appropriate responses.
    5. Respond to findings.
    6. Review and update the monitoring program.
9. **c.** The following are guidelines for internal, external, and third-party audits:
    - At minimum, perform annual audits to establish a security baseline.
    - Determine your organization's objectives for the audit and share them with the auditors.
    - Set the ground rules for the audit, including the dates/times of the audit, before the audit starts.
    - Choose auditors who have security experience.
    - Involve business unit managers early in the process.
    - Ensure that auditors rely on experience, not just checklists.
    - Ensure that the auditor's report reflects risks that the organization has identified.
    - Ensure that the audit is conducted properly.
    - Ensure that the audit covers all systems and all policies and procedures.
    - Examine the report when the audit is complete.

10. **d.** SOC 3 is the only SOC report that should be shared with the general public.

11. **a.** The steps in performing a penetration test are as follows:

    1. Document information about the target system or device.
    2. Gather information about attack methods against the target system or device. This step includes performing port scans.
    3. Identify the known vulnerabilities of the target system or device.
    4. Execute attacks against the target system or device to gain user and privileged access.
    5. Document the results of the penetration test and report the findings to management, with suggestions for remedial action.

12. **b.** In black-box testing, or zero-knowledge testing, the testing team is provided with no knowledge regarding the organization's network. In white-box testing, the testing team goes into the testing process with a deep understanding of the application or system. In gray-box testing, the testing team is provided more information than in black-box testing, while not as much as in white-box testing. Gray-box testing has the advantage of being nonintrusive while maintaining the boundary between developer and tester. Physical testing reviews facility and perimeter protections.

13. **d.** Fuzz testing is a dynamic testing tool that provides input to the software to test the software's limits and discover flaws. The input provided can be randomly generated by the tool or specially created to test for known vulnerabilities. Interface testing evaluates whether an application's systems or components correctly pass data and control to one another. It verifies whether module interactions are working properly and errors are handled correctly. Static testing analyzes software security without actually running the software. This is usually provided by reviewing the source code or compiled application. Test coverage analysis uses test cases that are written against the application requirements specifications.

14. **a, b, c, d.** Security professionals should consider the following factors when performing security testing:

    - Impact
    - Difficulty
    - Time needed
    - Changes that could affect the performance
    - System risk
    - System criticality

- Security test availability
- Information sensitivity level
- Likelihood of technical failure or misconfiguration

15. **a.** Operating system fingerprinting is the process of using some method to determine the operating system running on a host or a server. By identifying the OS version and build number, hackers can identify common vulnerabilities of that OS using readily available documentation from the Internet. A network discovery scan examines a range of IP addresses to determine which ports are open. This type of scan only shows a list of systems on the network and the ports in use on the network. It does not actually check for any vulnerabilities. By using key performance and risk indicators of security process data, organizations better identify when security risks are likely to occur. Key performance indicators allow organizations to determine whether levels of performance are below or above established norms. Key risk indicators allow organizations to identify whether certain risks are more or less likely to occur. Organizations should conduct internal, external, and third-party audits as part of any security assessment and testing strategy.

This chapter covers the following topics:

- **Investigations:** Concepts discussed include forensic and digital investigations and procedures; reporting and documentation; investigative techniques; evidence collection and handling; digital forensics tools, tactics, and procedures; and artifacts.
- **Logging and Monitoring Activities:** Concepts discussed include audit and review, intrusion detection and prevention, security information and event management, Security Orchestration and Automated Response, continuous monitoring and tuning, egress monitoring, log management, threat intelligence, and user and entity behavior analytics (UEBA).
- **Configuration and Change Management:** Concepts discussed include configuration management and change management, resource provisioning, baselining, and automation.
- **Security Operations Concepts:** Concepts discussed include need to know/least privilege; account, group, and role management; separation of duties and responsibilities; privileged account management; job rotation and mandatory vacation; two-person control; sensitive information procedures; record retention; information life cycle; and service-level agreements.
- **Resource Protection:** Concepts discussed include protecting tangible and intangible assets, protecting data at rest and data in transit. and managing media, hardware, and software assets.
- **Incident Management:** Concepts discussed include event versus incident, incident response team and incident investigations, rules of engagement, authorization, scope, incident response procedures, incident response management, and the steps in the incident response process.
- **Detective and Preventive Measures:** Concepts discussed include IDS/IPS, firewalls, whitelisting/blacklisting, third-party security services, sandboxing, honeypots/honeynets, anti-malware/antivirus, clipping levels, deviations from standards, unusual or unexplained events, unscheduled reboots, unauthorized disclosure, trusted recovery, trusted paths, input/output controls,

system hardening, vulnerability management systems, and machine learning and artificial intelligence (AI) based tools.

- **Patch and Vulnerability Management:** Concepts discussed include the enterprise patch management process.
- **Recovery Strategies:** Concepts discussed include creating recovery strategies; backup storage strategies; recovery and multiple site strategies; redundant systems, facilities, and power; fault-tolerance technologies; insurance; data backup; fire detection and suppression; high availability; quality of service; and system resilience.
- **Disaster Recovery:** Concepts discussed include response, personnel, communications, assessment, restoration, training and awareness, and lessons learned.
- **Testing Disaster Recovery Plans:** Concepts discussed include read-through test, checklist test, table-top exercise, structured walk-through test, simulation test, parallel test, full-interruption test, functional drill, and evacuation drill.
- **Business Continuity Planning and Exercises:** Concepts discussed include business continuity planning and exercises.
- **Physical Security:** Concepts discussed include perimeter security controls and internal security controls.
- **Personnel Safety and Security:** Concepts discussed include duress, travel, monitoring, emergency management, and security training and awareness.

CHAPTER 7

Security Operations

Security operations involves ensuring that all operations within an organization are carried out in a secure manner. It is concerned with investigating, managing, and preventing events or incidents. It also covers logging activities as they occur, provisioning and protecting resources as needed, managing events and incidents, recovering from events and disasters, and providing physical security. Ultimately, security operations involves the day-to-day operation of an organization. Security professionals should receive the appropriate training in these areas or employ experts in them to ensure that the organization's assets are properly protected.

The Security Operations domain within CISSP addresses a broad array of topics, including investigations, logging, monitoring, provisioning, security operations concepts, resource protection, incident management, detective and preventive measures, patch and vulnerability management, change management, disaster recovery, business continuity, physical security, and personnel safety. The Security Operations domain carries an average weight of 13 percent of the CISSP certification exam, which is the third highest weight of all the eight domains and is tied with two other domains. So, pay close attention to the many details in this chapter!

Foundation Topics

Investigations

Investigations must be carried out in the appropriate manner to ensure that any evidence collected can be used in court. Without proper investigations and evidence collection, attackers will not be held responsible for their actions. In the following sections, we discuss forensic and digital investigations and evidence.

Forensic and Digital Investigations

Computer investigations require different procedures than regular investigations because the timeframe for the investigator is compressed, and a security or other technical expert might be required to assist in the investigation. Also, computer information is intangible and often requires extra care to ensure that the data is retained in its original format. Finally, the evidence in a computer crime is much more difficult to gather.

After a decision has been made to investigate a computer crime, you, as a security professional, should follow standardized procedures, including the following:

- Identify what type of system is to be investigated.
- Identify the investigation team members.
- Determine the risk that the suspect will destroy evidence.

After law enforcement has been informed of a computer crime, the organization's investigator's constraints are increased. You might need to turn the investigation over to law enforcement to ensure that evidence is preserved properly.

In the investigation of a computer crime, evidentiary rules must be addressed. Computer evidence should prove a fact that is material to the case and must be reliable. The chain of custody must be maintained, as described later in the chapter. Computer evidence is less likely to be admitted in court as evidence if the process for producing the evidence has not been properly documented.

NOTE Although the majority of the discussion of investigations focuses on ***criminal investigations***, organizations must also consider investigating the actions of personnel that may violate corporate policies. For example, organizations might want to monitor personnel to ensure that the acceptable use policy (AUP) is not being violated. Security professionals should ensure that these investigations are coordinated to include required human resources personnel. Internal investigations often can be just as important as criminal investigations.

Any forensic investigation involves the following steps:

Key Topic

1. Identification
2. Preservation
3. Collection
4. Examination
5. Analysis
6. Presentation
7. Decision

The forensic investigation process is shown in Figure 7-1.

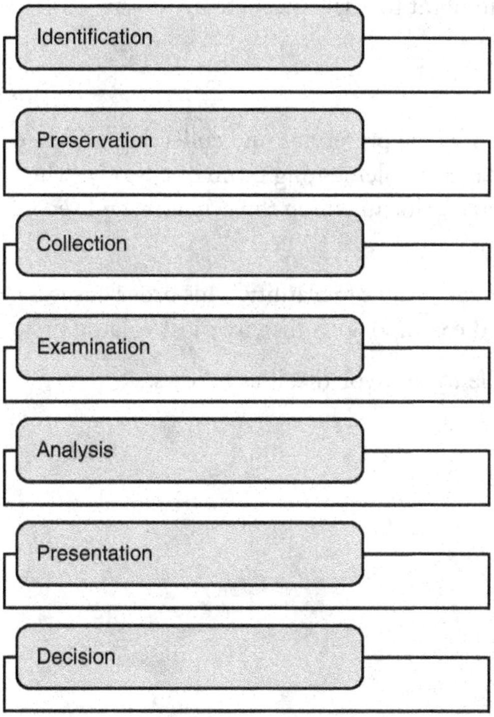

Figure 7-1 Forensic Investigation Process

The following sections cover these forensic investigation steps in detail as well as explain forensic procedures, reporting and documentation, IOCE/SWGDE and NIST, the crime scene, MOM, the chain of custody, interviewing, and investigative techniques.

Identify Evidence

The first step in any forensic investigation is to identify and secure the crime scene and identify the evidence. The evidence is identified by reviewing audit logs, monitoring systems, analyzing user complaints, and analyzing detection mechanisms. Initially, the investigators might be unsure of which evidence is important. Preserving evidence that you might not need, which is the next step in the process, is always better than wishing you had evidence that you did not retain. Therefore, a logical first step in any investigation is identifying the evidence and securing the crime scene.

In digital investigations, the attacked system and its environment (the devices through which the attack occurred) are considered the crime scene. In some cases, the system from which the attack originated can also be considered part of the crime scene. However, fully capturing the attacker's systems may not always be possible. For this reason, you should ensure that you capture any data, such as IP addresses, usernames, and other identifiers, that can point to a specific system.

Preserve and Collect Evidence

The next steps in forensic investigations include preserving and collecting evidence. This process involves making system images, implementing chain of custody (which is discussed in detail in its own section later), documenting the evidence, and recording timestamps.

Before collecting any evidence, consider the order of volatility. This order ensures that investigators collect evidence from the components that are most volatile first.

The order of volatility, from most volatile to least volatile, is as follows:

Key Topic

1. Memory contents
2. Swap files
3. Network processes
4. System processes
5. File system information
6. Raw disk blocks

To make system images, you need to use a tool that creates a bit-level copy of the system. In most cases, you must isolate the system and remove it from production or the live environment to create this bit-level copy. You should ensure that two copies of the image are retained. One copy of the image will be stored to ensure that an undamaged, accurate copy is available as evidence. The other copy will be used during the examination and analysis steps. Message digests and other hash algorithms are generally useful to ensure data integrity of the preserved image of the bit-level copy.

Although the system image is usually the most important piece of evidence, it is not the only piece of evidence you need. You might also need to capture data that is stored in cache, process tables, memory, and the registry. When documenting a computer attack, you should use a bound notebook to keep notes.

Remember that you might need to include experts in digital investigations to ensure that evidence is properly preserved and collected. Investigators usually assemble a field kit to help in the investigation process. This kit might include tags and labels, disassembly tools, and tamper-evident packaging. Commercial field kits are available, or you could assemble your own based on organizational needs.

Examine and Analyze Evidence

After evidence has been preserved and collected, the investigator then needs to examine and analyze the evidence. While examining evidence, any characteristics, such as timestamps and identification properties, should be determined and documented. After the evidence has been fully analyzed using scientific methods, the full incident should be reconstructed and documented.

Present Findings

After an examination and analysis of the evidence, it must be presented in a format that is acceptable to the court system or judge as evidence in court. In most cases when presenting evidence in court, presenting the findings in a format the audience can understand is best. Although an expert should be used to testify as to the findings, it is important that the expert be able to articulate to a nontechnical audience the details of the evidence.

Decide

At the end of the court proceeding, a decision will be made by the judge or jury as to the guilt or innocence of the accused party. At that time, evidence may no longer need to be retained, provided there is no possibility of an appeal. However, documenting any lessons learned from the incident is important to avoid the same mistakes in the future and to learn from the courtroom experience. Any individuals involved in any part of the investigation should be a part of this lessons-learned session.

Forensic Procedures

Collecting digital evidence is trickier than collecting physical evidence and must be completed by trained forensic technicians and investigators. These individuals must stay abreast of the latest tools and technologies that can be used to investigate a computer crime.

Technicians and investigators must follow established forensic procedures to ensure that any evidence collected will be admissible in a court of law. It is the trained individual's responsibility to ensure that the procedures they use follow established standards. Organizations, such as the National Institute of Standards and Technology (NIST) and the International Organization for Standardization and the International Electrotechnical Commission (ISO/IEC), establish standards that help to guide organizations in the proper establishment of these and other procedures. Always consult with these standards prior to performing any investigation to determine whether suggested procedures have changed or if new tools are available.

Reporting and Documentation

After any investigation is over, security professionals should provide reports and documentation to management regarding the incident. This report should be presented to management as quickly as possible so that management can determine whether controls need to be implemented to prevent the incident. This submission to management will often happen prior to the presentation of any legal findings in a court of law. Organizations should establish procedures for ensuring that individuals to whom the reports are submitted have the appropriate clearance. It may also be necessary to redact certain parts of the report to ensure that any criminal cases are not negatively affected.

Although internal reporting is important, security professionals should also have guidelines for when to report incidents to law enforcement. The earlier that law enforcement is involved, the more likely that evidence will be admissible in a court of law. However, most local law enforcement personnel do not have the knowledge or skills to carry out a full digital investigation. If the organization does not have properly trained personnel, a third-party forensic investigator will need to be called in to perform the investigation. Legal professionals should also be brought in to help.

Proper documentation must be maintained throughout the investigation and include logs, chain of custody forms, and documented procedures and guidelines.

IOCE/SWGDE and NIST

The International Organization on Computer Evidence (IOCE) and Scientific Working Group on Digital Evidence (SWGDE) are two groups that study digital forensics and help to establish standards for digital investigations. Both groups release guidelines on many formats of digital information, including computer data, mobile device data, automobile computer systems data, and so on. Any investigators should ensure that they comply with the principles from these groups.

Although the IOCE is no longer a functioning evidence body, it did establish some principles that are still applicable today. The main principles as documented by IOCE are as follows:

Key Topic

- The general rules of evidence should be applied to all digital evidence.
- Upon the seizure of digital evidence, any actions taken to preserve the evidence should not change that evidence in any way.
- When a person needs to access original digital evidence, that person should be suitably trained and authorized for the purpose.
- All activity relating to the seizure, access, storage, or transfer of digital evidence must be fully documented, preserved, and available for review.
- An individual is responsible for all actions taken with respect to digital evidence while the digital evidence is in that individual's possession.
- Any agency that seizes, accesses, stores, or transfers digital evidence is responsible for compliance with IOCE principles.

NIST SP 800-86, "Guide to Integrating Forensic Techniques into Incident Response," provides guidelines on the data collection, examination, analysis, and reporting related to digital forensics. It explains the use of forensic investigators, IT staff, and incident handlers as part of any forensic investigation. It discusses how cost, response time, and data sensitivity should affect any forensic investigation.

Crime Scene

A ***crime scene*** is the environment in which potential evidence exists. After the crime scene has been identified, steps should be taken to ensure that the environment is protected, including both the physical and virtual environment. To secure the physical crime scene, an investigator might need to isolate the systems involved by removing them from a network. However, the systems should *not* be powered down until the investigator is sure that all digital evidence has been captured. Remember: Live computer data is dynamic and is possibly stored in several volatile locations.

In response to a possible crime, it is important to ensure that the crime scene environment is protected using the following steps:

Key Topic

1. Identify the crime scene.
2. Protect the entire crime scene.
3. Identify any pieces of evidence or potential sources of evidence that are part of the crime scene.

4. Collect all evidence at the crime scene.
5. Minimize contamination by properly securing and preserving all evidence.

Remember that there can be more than one crime scene, especially in digital crimes. If an attacker breaches an organization's network, all assets that were compromised are part of the crime scene, and any assets that the attacker used are also part of the crime scene.

Access to the crime scene should be tightly controlled and limited only to individuals who are vital to the investigation. As part of the documentation process, make sure to note anyone who has access to the crime scene. After a crime scene is contaminated, no way exists to restore it to the original condition that existed immediately following the attack. It is important that the crime scene evidence be appropriately captured.

MOM

Documenting motive, opportunity, and means (MOM) is the most basic strategy for determining suspects. ***Motive*** is all about why the crime was committed and who committed the crime. ***Opportunity*** is all about where and when the crime occurred. ***Means*** is all about how the crime was carried out by the suspect. Any suspect who is considered must possess all three of these qualities. For example, a suspect might have a motive for a crime (being dismissed from the organization) and an opportunity for committing the crime (user accounts were not disabled properly) but might not possess the means to carry out the crime.

Understanding MOM can help any investigator narrow down the list of suspects.

Chain of Custody

At the beginning of any investigation, you should ask the questions who, what, when, where, and how. These questions can help you get all the data needed for the chain of custody. The ***chain of custody*** shows who controlled the evidence, who secured the evidence, and who obtained the evidence. It is a signed document that shows the entire history of the piece of evidence. Each piece of evidence will have its own chain of custody. A proper chain of custody must be preserved to successfully prosecute a suspect. To preserve a proper chain of custody, you must collect the evidence following predefined procedures in accordance with all laws and regulations.

Chain of custody forms should be used to track who has access to the evidence, when that access occurs, and other valuable details based on the organization's or investigation's needs. This chain of custody form should be kept with the evidence at all times. For example, if a forensic investigator plans to analyze the contents of a digital log, that investigator should complete the appropriate information on the chain of custody form to indicate when a copy of the digital log was obtained, the type of analysis being performed, and other details.

The primary purpose of the chain of custody is to ensure that evidence is admissible in court. Law enforcement officers emphasize chain of custody in any investigations that they conduct. Involving law enforcement early in the process during an investigation can help to ensure that the proper chain of custody is followed.

Interviewing

An investigation often involves interviewing suspects and witnesses. One person should be in charge of all interviews. Because evidence needs to be obtained, ensuring that the interviewer understands what information needs to be obtained and all the questions to cover is important. Reading rights to a suspect is necessary *only* if law enforcement is performing the interview. Recording the interview might be a good idea to provide corroboration later when the interview is used as evidence.

If an employee is suspected of a computer crime involving the organization's computers, a representative of the human resources department should be involved in any interrogation of the suspect. The employee should be interviewed only by an individual who is senior to that employee.

Investigative Techniques

A computer crime involves the use of investigative techniques, which include interviewing (discussed above), surveillance, forensics, and undercover operations.

Surveillance includes both physical surveillance and computer surveillance. Physical surveillance uses security cameras, wiretaps, and visual tracking to monitor movement. Computer surveillance monitors elements of computer use and online behavior. It may also include sting operations, like setting up a honeypot or honeynet.

After interviews are completed and surveillance gathers enough evidence, investigators will want to perform advanced forensic analysis. Organizations can do this by continually monitoring activity, but if law enforcement is involved, a warrant will need to be obtained that will allow forensic analysis of identified computers and devices. Investigators should follow the electronic trail wherever it leads, looking for digital fingerprints in emails, files, and web-browsing histories.

In some cases, crimes may require investigators to go undercover, adopting fake online personae to trap criminals. In this case, investigators should log all interactions as evidence and may even arrange a face-to-face meeting to arrest the perpetrator.

Evidence Collection and Handling

For evidence to be admissible, it must be relevant, legally permissible, reliable, properly identified, and properly preserved. *Relevant* means that it must prove a material fact related to the crime in that it shows a crime has been committed, can provide information describing the crime, can provide information regarding the perpetrator's motives, or can verify what occurred. *Legally permissible* means that evidence is deemed by the judge to be useful in helping the jury or judge reach a decision and cannot be objected to on the basis that it is irrelevant, immaterial, or violates the rules against hearsay and other objections. *Reliability* means that it has not been tampered with or modified. *Properly identified* means that the evidence is labeled appropriately and entered into the evidence log. *Preservation* means that the evidence is not damaged, modified, or corrupted in anyway.

All evidence must be tagged. When creating evidence tags, be sure to document the mode and means of transportation, a complete description of evidence including quality, who received the evidence, and who had access to the evidence.

Any investigator must ensure that evidence adheres to the five rules of evidence (see the following section). In addition, the investigator must understand each type of evidence that can be obtained and how each type can be used in court. Investigators must follow surveillance, search, and seizure guidelines. Finally, investigators must understand the differences among media, software, network, and hardware/embedded device analysis.

Five Rules of Evidence

When gathering evidence, an investigator must ensure that the evidence meets the five rules that govern it:

Key Topic

- Be authentic.
- Be accurate.
- Be complete.
- Be convincing.
- Be admissible.

Because digital evidence is more volatile than other evidence, it still must meet these five rules.

Types of Evidence

An investigator must be aware of the types of evidence used in court to ensure that all evidence is admissible. Sometimes the type of evidence determines its admissibility.

The types of evidence that you should understand are as follows:

Key Topic

- Best evidence
- Secondary evidence
- Direct evidence
- Conclusive evidence
- Circumstantial evidence
- Corroborative evidence
- Opinion evidence
- Hearsay evidence

Best Evidence

The ***best evidence rule*** states that when evidence, such as a document or recording, is presented, only the original will be accepted unless a legitimate reason exists for why the original cannot be used. In most cases, digital evidence is not considered best evidence because investigators must capture *copies* of the original data and state.

However, courts can apply the best evidence rule to digital evidence on a case-by-case basis, depending on the evidence and the situation. In this situation, the copy must be proved by an expert witness who can testify as to the contents and confirm that it is an accurate copy of the original.

Secondary Evidence

Secondary evidence has been reproduced from an original or substituted for an original item. Copies of original documents and oral testimony are considered secondary evidence.

Direct Evidence

Direct evidence proves or disproves a fact through oral testimony based on information gathered through the witness's senses. A witness can testify on what he saw, smelled, heard, tasted, or felt. This is considered direct evidence. Only the witness can give direct evidence. No one else can report on what the witness told them because that is considered hearsay evidence.

Conclusive Evidence

Conclusive evidence does not require any other corroboration and cannot be contradicted by any other evidence.

Circumstantial Evidence

Circumstantial evidence provides inference of information from other intermediate relevant facts. This evidence helps a jury come to a conclusion by using a fact to imply that another fact is true or untrue. An example is implying that a former employee committed an act against an organization due to his dislike of the organization after his dismissal. Circumstantial evidence is often dismissed or never presented, although it is impossible to control the behavior of jurors in this regard once they start deliberation.

Corroborative Evidence

Corroborative evidence supports another piece of evidence. For example, if a suspect produces a receipt to prove she was at a particular restaurant at a certain time and then a waiter testifies that he waited on the suspect at that time, then the waiter provides corroborating evidence through his testimony.

Opinion Evidence

Opinion evidence is based on what the witness thinks, feels, or infers regarding the facts. A witness in opinion evidence is not normally an expert because if an expert witness is used, that expert is able to testify on a fact based on knowledge in a certain area. For example, a psychiatrist can testify as to conclusions on a suspect's state of mind. Expert testimony is not considered opinion evidence because of the expert's knowledge and experience.

Hearsay Evidence

Hearsay evidence is evidence that is secondhand, where the witness does not have direct knowledge of the fact asserted but knows it only from being told by someone. In some cases, computer-based evidence is considered hearsay, especially if an expert cannot testify as to the accuracy and integrity of the evidence.

Surveillance, Search, and Seizure

Surveillance, search, and seizure are important facets of any investigation. ***Surveillance*** is the act of monitoring behavior, activities, or other changing information, usually of people. ***Search*** is the act of pursuing items or information. ***Seizure*** is the act of taking custody of physical or digital components.

Investigators use two types of surveillance: physical surveillance and computer surveillance. Physical surveillance occurs when a person's actions are reported or captured using cameras, direct observance, or closed-circuit TV (CCTV). Computer surveillance occurs when a person's actions are reported or captured using digital information, such as audit logs.

A search warrant is required in most cases to actively search a private site for evidence. For a search warrant to be issued, probable cause that a crime has been committed must be proven to a judge. The judge must also be given corroboration regarding the existence of evidence. The only time a search warrant does not need to be issued is during exigent circumstances, which are emergency circumstances that are necessary to prevent physical harm, the destruction of evidence, the suspect's escape, or some other consequence improperly frustrating legitimate law enforcement efforts. Exigent circumstances will have to be proven when the evidence is presented in court.

Seizure of evidence can occur only if the evidence is specifically listed as part of the search warrant unless the evidence is in plain view. Evidence specifically listed in the search warrant can be seized, and the search can occur only in areas specifically listed in the warrant.

Search and seizure rules do not apply to private organizations and individuals provided the organization or individual is not guilty of violating a criminal law. Most organizations warn their employees that any files stored on organizational resources are considered property of the organization. This is usually part of any no-expectation-of-privacy policy.

A discussion of evidence would be incomplete without discussing jurisdiction. Because computer crimes can involve assets that cross jurisdictional boundaries, investigators must understand that the civil and criminal laws of countries can differ greatly. It is always best to consult local law enforcement personnel for any criminal or ***civil investigation*** and follow any advice they give for investigations that cross jurisdictions.

Media Analysis

Investigators can perform many types of media analysis, depending on the media type. A media recovery specialist may be employed to provide a certified forensic image, which is an expensive process. An ***artifact*** in a digital forensics investigation includes things like registry keys, files, timestamps, and event logs. These are the traces security professionals follow in digital forensic work. They will vary depending on the device type, operating system, and other factors.

The following types of media analysis can be used:

Key Topic

- ***Disk imaging*:** Creates an exact image of the contents of the hard drive.
- ***Slack space analysis*:** Analyzes the slack (marked as empty or reusable) space on the drive to see whether any old (marked for deletion) data can be retrieved.
- ***Content analysis*:** Analyzes the contents of the drive and gives a report detailing the types of data by percentage.
- ***Steganography analysis*:** Analyzes the files on a drive to see whether the files have been altered.

Software Analysis

Software analysis is a little more difficult to perform than media analysis because it often requires the input of an expert on software code, including source code, compiled code, or machine code. It often involves decompiling or reverse engineering. This type of analysis is often used during malware analysis and copyright disputes.

Software analysis techniques include the following:

Key Topic

- **Content analysis:** Analyzes the content of software, particularly malware, to determine for which purpose the software was created.
- **Reverse engineering:** Retrieves the source code of a program to study how the program performs certain operations.
- **Author identification:** Attempts to determine the software's author.
- **Context analysis:** Analyzes the environment the software was found in to discover clues to determining risk.

Network Analysis

Network analysis involves the use of networking tools to preserve logs and activity for evidence.

Network analysis techniques include the following:

Key Topic

- **Communications analysis:** Analyzes communication over a network by capturing all or part of the communication and searching for particular types of activity.

- **Log analysis:** Analyzes network traffic logs.
- **Path tracing:** Traces the path of a particular traffic packet or traffic type to discover the route used by the attacker.

Hardware/Embedded Device Analysis

Hardware/embedded device analysis involves using the tools and firmware provided with devices to determine the actions that were performed on and by the device. The techniques used to analyze the hardware/embedded device vary based on the device. In most cases, the device vendor can provide advice on the best technique to use depending on what information you need. Log analysis, operating system analysis, and memory inspections are some of the general techniques used.

This type of analysis is used when mobile devices are analyzed. For performing this type of analysis, NIST makes the following recommendations:

- Any analysis should not change the data contained on the device or media.
- Only competent investigators should access the original data and must explain all actions they took.
- Audit trails or other records must be created and preserved during all steps of the investigation.
- The lead investigator is responsible for ensuring that all these procedures are followed.
- All activities regarding digital evidence, including its seizure, access to it, its storage, or its transfer, must be documented, preserved, and available for review.

Digital Forensic Tools, Tactics, and Procedures

For evidence collection, investigators will need a digital toolkit. The following should be included as part of any digital toolkit:

- Forensic laptops and power supplies
- Tool sets
- Digital camera
- Case folder
- Blank forms
- Evidence collection and packaging supplies

- Software
- Air card for Internet access
- Cables for data transfer (network, crossover, USB, and so on)
- Blank hard drives and other media
- Hardware write blockers

The digital toolkit should contain forensic tools that will enable an investigator to obtain data that can be used as evidence. The tools used by investigators are classified according to the type of information they obtain, as shown in the following list:

- Disk and data capture tools
- File viewers
- File analysis tools
- Registry analysis tools
- Internet analysis tools
- Email analysis tools
- Mobile device analysis tools
- macOS analysis tools
- Network forensic tools
- Database forensic tools

Many of the tools available today can provide services in multiple areas listed here. Investigators should obtain training in the proper usage of these tools.

Tools that can be included in a digital forensic toolkit include the following:

- Digital Forensics Framework (DFF)
- Open Computer Forensics Architecture (OCFA)
- Computer Aided INvestigative Environment (CAINE)
- X-Ways Forensics
- SANS Investigative Forensics Toolkit (SIFT)
- EnCase Forensic
- Registry Recon
- The Sleuth Kit (TSK)

- LibForensics
- Volatility
- WindowsSCOPE
- The Coroner's Toolkit (TCT)
- Oxygen Forensic Suite
- Bulk_Extractor
- Xplico
- RedLine
- Computer Online Forensic Evidence Extractor (COFEE)
- PlainSight
- XRY
- Helix3
- UFED

Investigators must also be familiar with the proper digital forensic tactics and procedures that are commonly used. For this reason, investigators should be properly trained to ensure that the tools, tactics, and procedures are followed so that evidence collected will be admissible in court. Keep in mind that you should not be tested on the functionality of the individual tools or the digital forensics tactics and procedures on the CISSP exam; however, you should understand that these tools, tactics, and procedures provide digital forensic investigation automation and investigatory standards compliance. A CISSP candidate's job role is not defined as performing individual forensic investigation tasks; however, the CISSP professional should be familiar with the tools, tactics, and procedures available to ensure that an organization's investigator obtains the appropriate tools to perform digital investigations and follows appropriate tactics and procedures.

NOTE Investigation types are discussed in detail in Chapter 1, "Security and Risk Management."

Artifacts

Artifacts, in the context of digital forensics and cybersecurity investigations, refer to pieces of digital evidence that are collected during an investigation. These artifacts can come from various sources, including data files, computer systems, networks, and mobile devices. Each type of artifact can provide valuable insights into the activities that have taken place within a system or network and can be critical in understanding the scope, method, and impact of a cybersecurity incident.

Data artifacts include any data that can provide information about the incident, such as logs (system logs, application logs, security logs), documents, emails, and encrypted files. Analyzing these artifacts can reveal the timeline of events, actions taken by users, and possible data exfiltration.

Computer artifacts refer to digital evidence found on computer systems, including files and folders, system registry information, installed applications, and system configuration settings. They can also include memory dumps that provide information on the processes and activities that were running at a particular point in time.

NOTE Because logs, documents, emails, and most computer data can exist in files, these can be treated as both data artifacts and computer artifacts.

Network artifacts are derived from network equipment and monitoring tools, including packet captures, firewall and router logs, intrusion detection system (IDS) alerts, and Domain Name System (DNS) logs. Network artifacts are crucial for understanding the communications that have occurred, both internally and externally, which might indicate data transfers, command and control (C2) communication, or unauthorized access attempts.

With the increasing use of mobile devices and even personal devices in business operations, artifacts from mobile devices, such as call logs, text messages, app data, and location information, have become increasingly important in investigations. Mobile device forensics can uncover a wealth of information regarding the actions and movements of individuals involved in an incident.

In cybersecurity investigations, artifacts are invaluable sources of evidence that can provide detailed insights into security incidents. Security professionals must be adept at managing the entire life cycle of these artifacts—from identification and collection through analysis and reporting—while ensuring compliance with legal and organizational standards. Understanding how to effectively work with different types of artifacts is essential for conducting thorough investigations and supporting organizational security objectives.

Logging and Monitoring Activities

As part of operations security, administrators must ensure that user activities are logged and monitored regularly. These activities include audit and review, intrusion detection and prevention, security information and event management, continuous monitoring, egress monitoring, log management, threat intelligence, and user and entity behavior analytics (UEBA).

Audit and Review

Accountability is impossible without a record of activities and review of those activities. Capturing and monitoring audit logs provide the digital proof when someone who is performing certain activities needs to be identified. This goes for both the good guys and the bad guys. In many cases it is required to determine who misconfigured something rather than who stole something. Audit trails based on access and identification codes establish individual accountability. The questions to address when reviewing audit logs include the following:

- Are users accessing information or performing tasks that are unnecessary for their jobs?
- Are repetitive mistakes (such as deletions) being made?
- Do too many users have special rights and privileges?

The level and amount of auditing should reflect the security policy of the company. Audits can be either self-audits or performed by a third party. Self-audits always introduce the danger of subjectivity to the process. Logs can be generated on a wide variety of devices including IDSs, servers, routers, and switches. In fact, a host-based IDS makes use of the operating system logs of the host machine.

When assessing controls over audit trails or logs, address the following questions:

- Does the audit trail provide a trace of user actions?
- Is access to online logs strictly controlled?
- Is there separation of duties between security personnel who administer the access control function and those who administer the audit trail?

Keep and store logs in accordance with the retention policy defined in the organization's security policy. They must be secured to prevent modification, deletion, and destruction. When auditing is functioning in a monitoring role, it supports the *detection* security function in the *technical* category. When formal review of the audit logs takes place, it is a form of *detective administrative* control. Reviewing audit data should be a function separate from the day-to-day administration of the system.

Log Types

Key Topic

Logging is the process of recording event information to a log file or database. It captures system events, changes, messages, and other information that shows the activities that occur on a system or device. The different types of logs that security professionals use include security logs, systems logs, application logs, firewall logs, proxy logs, and change logs.

Security logs record access to resources, including access to files, folders, and printers. They can record when a user accesses, modifies, or deletes a file or folder. Although most systems will record when key files are accessed, it is often necessary for an administrator to enable auditing on other resources, such as data folders or network printers. When auditing is running on a device, it will affect the performance of that device. For this reason, security professionals should configure auditing only when necessary based on the organization's security policies.

System logs record system events, such as system and service startup and shutdown. They can help a security professional to determine the actions taken by a malicious user.

Applications logs record actions that occur within a specific application. Security professionals should work with application developers or vendors to determine which type of information should be logged.

Firewall logs record network traffic information, including incoming and outgoing traffic. This usually includes important data, such as IP addresses and port numbers that can be used to determine the origin of an attack.

Proxy logs record details on the Internet traffic that passes through the proxy server, including the sites being visited by users, how much time is being spent on those sites, and if attempts are being made to access prohibited sites.

Change logs report changes made to a specific device or application as part of the change management process.

Audit Types

When auditing is enabled, administrators can select individual events to monitor to ensure user accountability. Audit types include access review audits, user privilege audits, and privileged group audits.

Access review audits ensure that object access and user account management practices adhere to the organization's security policy. User privilege audits monitor right and permission usage for all users. Privileged group audits monitor when high-level groups and administrator accounts are used.

Intrusion Detection and Prevention

IDSs alert organizations when unauthorized access or actions occur, while intrusion prevention systems (IPSs) monitor the same kind of activity but actually work to prevent the actions from being successful. IDS and IPS devices can be used during investigations to provide information regarding traffic patterns that occur just before an attack succeeds. Security professionals must constantly tune IDS and IPS devices to ensure that the correct activity is being detected or prevented. In some cases, these two functions are included in the same system and referred to as intrusion detection and prevention systems (IDPS). As changes occur in the way that attacks are carried out, these systems must be adjusted, fine-tuned, or re-programmed to capture any new attacks or threats.

NOTE IDS and IPS devices are discussed in more detail later in this chapter and also in Chapter 4, "Communication and Network Security."

Security Information and Event Management (SIEM)

SIEM can collect log and system information to comply with regulatory requirements, provide internal accountability, provide risk management, and perform monitoring and trending. SIEM stores raw information from various systems and devices and aggregates that information into a single database. Security professionals must work together to ensure that the appropriate actions will be monitored and to ensure that the correct examinations of the records occur. Because SIEM systems are centralized repositories of security information, organizations should take particular care to provide adequate security for these systems to ensure that attackers cannot access or alter the records contained in them.

NOTE SIEM is discussed in more detail in Chapter 6, "Security Assessment and Testing."

Security Orchestration and Automated Response (SOAR)

Security Orchestration and Automated Response (SOAR) integrates a series of different security tools to collect data and security alerts and bring all of that information into one platform, which is referred to as security orchestration. These security tools (or applications) can include firewalls and IDPSs.

The second part of SOAR refers to the automated response to security incidents. SOAR benefits both a security operations center (SOC) and incident response (IR) by producing a faster response than a person or a team can produce through automation. Furthermore, a SOC and IR face continuous challenges with hiring and maintaining skilled staff; therefore, SOAR can alleviate the demands of these functional areas. SOAR can automate threat intelligence, malware analysis, vulnerability management, and responses to phishing attacks, to name but a few. Machine learning (ML) can benefit incident response by learning from historical data and providing an automated response to security threats.

SOAR can also be beneficial to organizations by providing a comprehensive dashboard of security threats and generating reports for various organizational stakeholders.

Continuous Monitoring and Tuning

Continuous monitoring and tuning enable organizations to keep pace with the dynamic nature of cyber threats and the ever-evolving IT landscape.

Continuous monitoring involves the ongoing observation and analysis of system, network, and application activity to identify unusual behavior or potential security incidents. This process relies on various tools and technologies, including SIEM systems, IDSs, and IPSs. The key aspects of continuous monitoring include:

- **Log Collection:** Aggregating logs from various sources, such as servers, network devices, security appliances, and applications, to provide a comprehensive view of organizational activities and potential security events.
- **Real-time Analysis:** Employing automated tools to analyze logs and monitor events in real-time, enabling immediate detection of suspicious activities or deviations from normal patterns.
- **Alerting:** Configuring alerts based on predefined criteria or thresholds to notify security personnel of potential security incidents or system malfunctions that require immediate attention.

Tuning is the process of adjusting monitoring and security tools to reduce false positives and false negatives, ensuring that the security team can focus on genuine threats. Effective tuning requires an understanding of the organization's network architecture, normal traffic patterns, and legitimate system behavior. Key aspects of tuning include:

- **Configuration Adjustments:** Refining the configuration settings of monitoring tools and security systems to better align with the specific environment and security policies of the organization. This may involve adjusting thresholds for alerts, updating rule sets for IDS/IPS, or customizing SIEM correlation rules.
- **Whitelisting and Blacklisting:** Identifying and approving (whitelisting) legitimate activities or entities that should not trigger alerts, while blocking (blacklisting) known malicious IP addresses, domains, and applications to prevent security breaches.

- **Regular Reviews:** Periodically reviewing the performance and effectiveness of monitoring tools to ensure they are accurately identifying relevant security events without overwhelming the team with false alarms. This also involves updating the monitoring configuration to adapt to changes in the network environment or threat landscape.

Continuous monitoring and tuning are integral to maintaining a robust security posture, allowing organizations to detect and respond to threats in real time while minimizing the distraction of irrelevant alerts. For security professionals, mastering these processes is essential for conducting effective logging and monitoring activities, ensuring the security and resilience of information systems against the backdrop of a constantly evolving cyber threat landscape.

Egress Monitoring

To understand egress monitoring, security professionals must first understand data egress and ingress. The main difference between egress and ingress is the direction of data flow. Ingress refers to data entering a system or network, while egress refers to data leaving a system or network.

Egress monitoring occurs when an organization monitors the outbound flow of information from one network to another. The most popular form of egress monitoring is carried out using firewalls that monitor and control outbound traffic.

Data leakage occurs when sensitive data is disclosed to unauthorized personnel either intentionally or inadvertently. ***Data loss prevention (DLP) software*** attempts to prevent data leakage. It does this by maintaining awareness of actions that can and cannot be taken with respect to a digital file. For example, it might allow printing of a file but only at the company office. It might also disallow sending the digital file through email. DLP software uses ingress and egress filters to identify sensitive data that is leaving the organization and can prevent such leakage.

Another scenario might be the release of product plans that should be available only to the Sales group. A security professional could set a policy like the following for that document:

- It cannot be emailed to anyone other than Sales group members.
- It cannot be printed.
- It cannot be copied.

A DLP can be implemented in two locations:

- **Network DLP:** Installed at network egress points near the perimeter, network DLP analyzes network traffic.
- **Endpoint DLP:** Endpoint DLP runs on end-user workstations or servers in the organization.

You can use both precise and imprecise methods to determine what is sensitive:

- **Precise methods:** These methods involve content registration and trigger almost zero false-positive incidents.
- **Imprecise methods:** These methods can include keywords, lexicons, regular expressions, extended regular expressions, metadata tags, Bayesian analysis, and statistical analysis.

The value of a DLP system lies in the level of precision with which it can locate and prevent the leakage of sensitive data.

NOTE Steganography and watermarking are sometimes part of egress monitoring. Both of these cryptographic tools are discussed in Chapter 3, "Security Architecture and Engineering."

Log Management

Log management is the process of storing and handling log events generated by applications, devices, and infrastructure components. It includes collecting, aggregating, parsing, storing, analyzing, searching, archiving, and disposing of logs. The goal of log management is to use the events entered in the logs for troubleshooting.

Log files contain a record of events and are often divided into categories. Through log management, an administrator can gather the event data in one place and examine it together, thereby allowing the administrator to analyze the data and identify issues and patterns. Log management provides improved monitoring and troubleshooting, operations, resource usage, and security.

Log management includes five key functions:

- Log collection
- Log aggregation
- Log search and analysis
- Log monitoring and alerting
- Log visualization and reporting

Organizations should adopt a log management policy. This policy should include guidelines on what to log, where to store logs, how long to store logs, how often logs should be reviewed, and whether logs should be encrypted or archived for audit purposes.

Threat Intelligence

Threat intelligence is threat information that allows organizations to implement controls to protect against the threats. A ***threat intelligence feed (TI feed)***, also referred to as a ***threat feed***, is an ongoing stream of data related to identified potential threats to an organization's security, usually provided by threat intelligence sources. ***Threat intelligence sources*** include open-source intelligence (OSINT), social media intelligence, human intelligence, and technical intelligence, including intelligence from the dark web. ***Threat hunting*** is a cyber defense activity that proactively and iteratively searches networks to detect and isolate advanced threats that evade existing security solutions. The actual process of threat hunting is beyond the scope of the CISSP exam with its management focus. Threat hunting requires that an organization employs an experienced cybersecurity analyst or firm to use manual or machine-based techniques to proactively identify threats that currently deployed automated detection methods did not catch.

User and Entity Behavior Analytics (UEBA)

User and entity behavior analytics (UEBA), also known as ***user behavior analytics (UBA)***, is the process of gathering data regarding daily user network events so that normal conduct by users is understood. Organizations can use UEBA to detect compromised credentials, lateral movement, and other malicious behavior. UEBA is often added on as a layer to existing SIEM deployments. The key to UEBA is detecting behavior anomalies that could be indicative of a threat.

Configuration and Change Management

Configuration management specifically focuses on bringing order out of the chaos that can occur when multiple engineers and technicians have administrative access to the computers and devices that make the network function.

Configuration management documents the setup for computers and devices, including operating system and firmware versions. Change management provides the mechanism whereby the configuration can be changed through formal approval. Some standards consider configuration management a subset of change management, whereas others say change management is a subset of configuration management. It is just as important to recognize that there is a relationship between the two.

Configuration management documents the configuration items (CIs) that can then be changed via the change management process.

The following are the functions of configuration management:

Key Topic

- Report the status of change processing.
- Document the functional and physical characteristics of each CI.
- Perform information capture and version control.
- Control changes to the CIs, and issue versions of CIs from the software library.

NOTE In the context of configuration management, a *software library* is a controlled area accessible only to approved users who are restricted to the use of an approved procedure. A *configuration item* is a uniquely identifiable subset of the system that represents the smallest portion to be subject to an independent configuration control procedure. When an operation is broken into individual CIs, the process is called *configuration identification*.

Examples of these types of changes are

- Operating system configuration
- Software configuration
- Hardware configuration

From a CISSP perspective, the biggest contribution of configuration management control is ensuring that changes to the system do not unintentionally diminish security. It is the main reason why all changes must be documented, and all network diagrams, both logical and physical, *must* be updated regularly and consistently to accurately reflect the state of each CI *currently* and not as it was a few months or years ago. Verifying that all configuration management policies are being followed should be an ongoing process.

In many cases, it is beneficial to form a configuration control board. The tasks of the configuration control board can include

- Ensuring that changes made are approved, tested, documented, and implemented correctly.
- Meeting periodically to discuss configuration status accounting reports.
- Maintaining responsibility for ensuring that changes made do not jeopardize the soundness of the verification system.

In summary, the components of configuration management are

- Configuration control
- Configuration status accounting
- Configuration audit

All networks and devices evolve, grow, and change over time. Companies and their processes also evolve and change, which is a good thing. But organizations should manage change in a structured way so as to maintain a common sense of purpose about the changes. By following recommended steps in a formal process, change can be prevented from becoming a small element that controls the larger process. The following are guidelines to include as a part of any change control policy:

- All changes should be formally requested. Change logs should be maintained.
- Each request should be analyzed to ensure that it supports all goals and policies. This analysis includes baselining and security impact analysis.
- Prior to formal approval, all costs and effects of the methods of implementation should be reviewed. Using the collected data, changes should be approved or denied.
- After they're approved, the change steps should be developed.
- During implementation, incremental testing should occur, and it should rely on a predetermined fallback strategy if necessary. Versioning should be used to effectively track and control changes to a collection of entities. Change managers should ensure that fallback or rollback strategies exist.
- Complete documentation should be produced and submitted with a formal report to management.

One of the key benefits of following this method is the ability to make use of the documentation in future planning. Lessons learned can be applied and even the process itself can be improved through analysis.

Resource Provisioning

Resource provisioning is a process in security operations which ensures that an organization deploys only the assets it currently needs. Resource provisioning must follow the organization's resource life cycle. To properly manage the resource life cycle, an organization must maintain an accurate asset inventory and use appropriate configuration management processes. Resources that are involved in provisioning include physical assets, virtual assets, cloud assets, and applications.

Asset Inventory and Management

An ***asset*** is any item of value to an organization, including physical devices and digital information. Recognizing when assets are stolen or improperly deployed is impossible if no item count or inventory system exists or if the inventory is not kept updated. All equipment should be inventoried, and all relevant information about each device should be maintained and kept up to date. Each asset should be fully documented, including serial numbers, model numbers, firmware version, operating system version, responsible personnel, and so on. The organization should maintain this information both electronically and in hard copy. Maintaining this inventory will aid in determining when new assets should be deployed or when currently deployed assets should be decommissioned.

Security devices, such as firewalls, network address translation (NAT) devices, and IDSs and IPSs, should receive the most attention because they relate to physical and logical security. Beyond this, devices that can easily be stolen, such as laptops, tablets, and smartphones, should be locked away. If that is not practical, then consider locking these types of devices to stationary objects (for example, using cable locks with laptops).

When the technology is available, tracking of small devices can help mitigate the loss of both devices and their data. Many smartphones now include tracking software that allows you to locate a device after it has been stolen or lost by using either cell tower tracking or GPS. Deploy the device tracking technology when available.

Another useful feature available on many smartphones and other portable devices is a remote wiping feature. This allows the user to send a signal to a stolen device, instructing it to wipe out all the data contained on the device. Similarly, these devices typically also come with the ability to be remotely locked when misplaced or stolen.

Strict control of the use of portable media devices can help prevent sensitive information from leaving the network or office premises. These devices include CDs, DVDs, flash drives, and external hard drives. Although written rules should be in effect about the use of these devices, using security policies to prevent the copying of data to these media types is also possible. Allowing the copying of data to these drive types as long as the data is encrypted is also possible. If these functions are provided by the network operating system, you should deploy them.

It should not be possible for unauthorized persons to access and tamper with any devices. Tampering includes defacing, damaging, or changing the configuration of a device. Organizations should use integrity verification programs to look for evidence of data tampering, errors, and omissions. Devices that should be secured should be stored in locked closets or drawers.

Encrypting sensitive data stored on devices can help prevent the exposure of data in the event of a theft or in the event of inappropriate access of the device.

Physical Assets

Physical assets include servers, desktop computers, laptops, mobile devices, and network devices that are deployed in the enterprise. Physical assets should be deployed and decommissioned based on organizational need. For example, suppose an organization deploys a wireless access point (WAP) and allows a third-party auditor to use it. Proper resource provisioning should ensure that the third-party auditor's access is revoked when access is no longer needed. Without proper inventory and configuration management, the WAP may remain deployed and can be used at some point to carry out a wireless network attack.

Virtual Assets

Virtual assets include software-defined networks, virtual storage-area networks (VSANs), guest operating systems deployed on virtual machines (VMs), and virtual routers. As with physical assets, the deployment and decommissioning of virtual assets should be tightly controlled as part of configuration management because virtual assets, just like physical assets, can be compromised. For example, a Windows 10 VM deployed on a Windows Server system should be retained only until it is no longer needed. As long as the VM is being used, it is important to ensure that the appropriate updates, patches, and security controls are deployed on it as part of configuration management. When users no longer access the VM, it should be removed.

Virtual storage occurs when physical storage (including hard drives, DVDs, and other storage media) from multiple network devices is compiled into a single logical space and appears as a single drive to the regular user. Block virtualization separates the logical storage from the physical storage. File virtualization eliminates the dependency between data accessed at the file level and the physical storage location of the files. Host-based virtual storage requires software running on the host. Storage device–based virtual storage runs on a storage controller and allows other storage controllers to be attached. Network-based virtual storage uses network-based devices, such as iSCSI or Fibre Channel, to create a storage solution.

Cloud Assets

Cloud assets include cloud services, virtual machines, storage networks, and other cloud services contracted through a cloud service provider. Cloud assets are usually billed based on usage and should be carefully provisioned and monitored to prevent the organization from paying for portions of service that it does not need. Configuration management should ensure that the appropriate monitoring policies are in place to make certain that only resources that are needed are deployed.

Applications

Applications include commercial applications that are locally installed, web services, and any cloud-deployed application services, such as Software as a Service (SaaS). The appropriate number of licenses should be maintained for all commercial applications. An organization should periodically review its licensing needs. For cloud deployments of software services, configuration management should be used to ensure that only personnel who have valid needs for the software are given access to it.

Baselining

Baselining is the process of documenting the attributes of a CI at a point in time, which serves as a basis for defining change. Configuration baselines should be documented for all CIs. If a change is approved and completed to a CI, then the baseline of the CI needs to be adjusted based on the changes made.

Baseline configurations should be maintained over time. This requires creating new baselines as organizational information systems change.

Automation

Automation software reduces cost, complexity, and errors in configuration management by maintaining a CI database. With automation tools, CI baselines can be saved. Then if a change has unanticipated consequences, administrators can simply roll the CI back to the saved baseline.

Automation tools allow administrators to make changes and deployments faster and remove the potential for administrator error. They also allow administrators to track the state of resources, preventing duplicated effort by attempting to install something that is already deployed to a CI. Finally, configuration management tools can audit an organization's CIs so that administrators can easily pinpoint CIs with certain issues or needs.

Security Operations Concepts

Key Topic

Throughout this book, you've seen references made to policies and principles that can guide all security operations. In the following sections, we review some concepts more completely that have already been touched on and introduce some new issues concerned with maintaining security operations.

Need to Know/Least Privilege

With regard to allowing access to resources and assigning rights to perform operations, always apply the concepts of ***least privilege*** and ***need to know***. Under the principle of least privilege, users should only have the specific permissions necessary to perform their duties—no more, no less. On the other hand, using the need to know principle, users would only be given access to sensitive information relevant to their duties, not to other information stored by the company.

Discretionary access control (DAC) and role-based access control (RBAC) are examples of systems based on a user's need to know. To ensure least privilege requires that the user's job be identified and each user be granted the lowest clearance required for their tasks.

Managing Accounts, Groups, and Roles

Devices, computers, and applications implement user and group accounts and roles to allow or deny access. User accounts are created for each user needing access. Group accounts are used to configure permissions on resources. User accounts are added to the appropriate group accounts to inherit the permissions granted to that group. User accounts can also be assigned to roles. Roles are most often used by applications.

Security professionals should understand the following accounts:

- **Root or built-in administrator accounts:** These are the most powerful accounts on the system. Root accounts are used in Linux-based systems, whereas administrator accounts are used in Windows-based systems. It is best to disable such an account after you have created another account with the same privileges, because most of these account names are well known and can be used by attackers. If you decide to keep these accounts, most vendors suggest that you change the account name and give it a complex password. Root or administrator accounts should be used only when performing administrative duties, and use of these accounts should always be audited.

- **Service accounts:** These accounts are used to run system services and applications. Therefore, security professionals can limit the service account's access to the system. Always research the default user accounts that are used. Make sure that you change the passwords for these accounts on a regular basis. Use of these accounts should always be audited.

- **Regular administrator accounts:** These administrator accounts are created and assigned only to a single individual. Any user who has an administrative account should also have a regular/standard user account to use for normal day-to-day operations. Administrative accounts should be used only when performing administrative-level duties, and use of these accounts should always be audited.

- **Power user accounts:** These accounts have more privileges and permissions than normal user accounts. These accounts should be reviewed on a regular basis to ensure that only users who need the higher-level permissions have these accounts. Most modern operating systems limit the abilities of the power users or even remove this account type entirely.
- **Regular/standard user accounts:** These are the accounts users use while performing their normal everyday job duties. These accounts must strictly follow the principle of least privilege.

NOTE Administrative-level, service, and power user accounts usually have higher privileges and can do more damage. These account types should be regularly audited to monitor their usage.

Separation of Duties and Responsibilities

The concept of ***separation of duties*** prescribes that sensitive operations be divided among multiple users so that no one user has the rights and access to carry out the operation alone. Separation of duties and responsibilities is valuable in deterring fraud by ensuring that no single individual can compromise a system. It is considered a *preventive* administrative control. An example would be one person initiating a request for a payment and another authorizing that payment to be made.

Privilege Account Management

Security professionals should ensure that organizations establish the proper account, group, and role life cycle management procedures to ensure they are properly created, managed, and removed. The provisioning life cycle is covered in more detail in Chapter 5, "Identity and Access Management (IAM)."

Inevitably, some users, especially supervisors or those in the IT support department, will require special rights and privileges that other users do not possess. For example, one requirement might be that a set of users who work the help desk might need to be able to reset passwords or perhaps make changes to user accounts. These types of rights carry with them a responsibility to exercise the rights responsibly and ethically.

Although in a perfect world we would like to assume that we can expect ethical and secure behavior from all users, in the real world we know this is not always true.

Therefore, one of the things to monitor is the use of these privileges and privileged accounts. Although security professionals should be concerned with the amount of monitoring performed and the amount of data produced by the monitoring of privilege usage, recording the exercise of special privileges or the use of privileged accounts should not be sacrificed, even if it means regularly saving the data as a log file and clearing the event gathering system.

Job Rotation and Mandatory Vacation

From a security perspective, ***job rotation*** refers to the training of multiple users to perform the duties of a position to help prevent fraud by any individual employee. The idea is that by making more than one person familiar with the legitimate functions of the position, the higher the likelihood that unusual activities by any one person will be noticed. This approach is often used in conjunction with *mandatory vacations*, in which all users are required to take time off, allowing another to fill their position while gone, which enhances the opportunity to discover unusual activity. Beyond the security aspects of job rotation, additional benefits include

- Trained backup in case of emergencies
- Protection against fraud
- Cross training of employees

Rotation of duties, separation of duties, and mandatory vacations are all administrative controls.

Two-Person Control

A ***two-person control***, also referred to as a two-man rule, occurs when certain access and actions require the presence of two authorized people at all times. Common examples are the requirement for two people to sign and approve checks over a certain dollar amount or for two people to be present to perform a certain activity, such as opening a safe.

Sensitive Information Procedures

Access control and its use in preventing unauthorized access to sensitive data are important for organizational security. It follows that the secure handling of sensitive information is critical. Although we tend to think in terms of the company's information, it is also critical that the company protect the private information of its customers and employees. A leak of users' and customers' personal information causes, at a minimum, embarrassment for the company and possibly fines and lawsuits.

Regardless of whether the aim is to protect company data or personal data, the key is to apply the access control principles to both sets of data. When you are examining access control procedures and policies, the following questions need to be answered:

- Are data or privileges available to the user that are not required for the job?
- How many users have access to sensitive data, and why?

Record Retention

Proper access control is not possible without auditing. It allows us to track activities and discover problems before they are fully realized. Because this analysis can sometimes lead to a mountain of data to analyze, you should monitor only the most sensitive of activities, and retain and review all records. Moreover, in many cases companies are required by law or regulation to maintain records of certain data.

Most auditing systems allow for the configuration of data retention options. In some cases, the default operation is to start writing over the older records in the log when the maximum log size is full. Regularly clearing and saving the log can prevent this from happening and avoid the loss of important events. In cases of extremely sensitive data, having a server shut off access when a security log is full and cannot record any more events is even advisable.

Information Life Cycle

In security operations, security professionals must understand the life cycle of information, which includes creation/reception, distribution, usage, maintenance, and disposal of information. After information is gathered, it must be classified to ensure that only authorized personnel can access the information.

NOTE For more information on the information life cycle, refer to Chapter 2, "Asset Security."

Service-Level Agreements

Service-level agreements (SLAs) are agreements about the ability of the support system to respond to problems within a certain timeframe while providing an agreed-upon level of service. SLAs can be internal between departments or external to a service provider. When parties agree on the speed and accuracy with which various problems related to the provided service are addressed, some predictability is introduced to the response to problems, which ultimately supports the maintenance of access to resources.

An SLA should contain a description of the services to be provided and the service levels and metrics that the customer can expect. It also includes the duties and responsibilities of each party of the SLA. It lists the service specifics, exclusions, service levels, escalation procedures, and cost. It should include a clause regarding payment to the customers resulting from a breach of the SLA. Although SLAs can be transferable, they are not transferable by law. Most SLAs also contain a transfer clause, whereby a service provider can take over an SLA if the customer is unhappy with the original service provider. Metrics that should be measured include service availability, service levels, defect rates, technical quality, and security. SLAs should be periodically reviewed to ensure that the business needs, technical environment, or workloads have not changed. In addition, metrics, measurement tools, and processes should be reviewed to see if they have improved.

Resource Protection

Enterprise resources include both assets you can see and touch (tangible), such as computers and printers, and assets you cannot see and touch (intangible), such as trade secrets and processes. Although typically you would think of resource protection as preventing the corruption of digital resources and as the prevention of damage to physical resources, this concept also includes maintaining the availability of those resources. In the following sections, we discuss both aspects of resource protection.

Protecting Tangible and Intangible Assets

In some cases, among the most valuable assets of a company are ***intangible assets*** such as secret recipes, formulas, and trade secrets. In other cases, the value of the company is derived from its physical assets such as facilities, equipment, and the talents of its people. All are considered resources and should be included in a comprehensive resource protection plan. Next, we explore some specific concerns with these various types of resources.

Facilities

Usually, the largest tangible asset an organization has is the building in which it operates and the surrounding land. Physical security is covered later in this chapter, but it bears emphasizing that vulnerability testing (discussed more fully in Chapter 6) ought to include the security controls of the facility itself. Some examples of vulnerability testing as it relates to facilities include

- Do doors close automatically, and does an alarm sound if they are held open too long?

- Are the protection mechanisms of sensitive areas, such as server rooms and wiring closets, sufficient and operational?
- Does the fire suppression system work?
- Are sensitive documents shredded as opposed to being thrown in the dumpster?

Beyond the access issues, the main systems that are needed to ensure operations are not disrupted include fire detection/suppression, HVAC (including temperature and humidity controls), water and sewage systems, power/backup power, communications equipment, and intrusion detection.

Hardware

Another of the more ***tangible assets*** that must be protected is all the hardware that makes the network operate. This hardware includes not only the computers and printers with which the users directly come in contact but also the infrastructure devices that they never see such as routers, switches, and firewall appliances. Maintaining access to these critical devices from an availability standpoint is covered later in the sections “Redundancy and Fault Tolerance” and “Backup and Recovery Systems.”

From a management standpoint, these devices are typically managed remotely. Special care must be taken to safeguard access to these management features as well as protect the data and commands passing across the network to these devices. Some specific guidelines include

- Change all default administrator passwords on the devices to comply with the organization’s password policies.
- Limit the number of users who have remote access to these devices.
- Rather than Telnet (which sends commands in cleartext), use an encrypted command-line tool such as Secure Shell (SSH).
- Manage critical systems locally.
- Limit physical access to these devices.

Software

Software assets include any propriety application, scripts, or batch files that have been developed in house that are critical to the operation of the organization. Secure coding and development practices can help to prevent weaknesses in these systems. Security professionals also must pay attention to preventing theft of these assets.

Moreover, closely monitoring the use of commercial applications and systems in the enterprise can prevent unintentional breach of licensing agreements. One of the benefits of giving users only the applications they require to do their job is that it limits the number of users that have an application, helping to prevent exhaustion of licenses for software.

NOTE Software development security is discussed in detail in Chapter 8, "Software Development Security."

Information Assets

Information assets are the last asset type that needs to be discussed, but by no means are they the least important. The *primary* purpose of ***operations security*** is to safeguard information assets that are resident in the system. These assets include recipes, processes, trade secrets, product plans, and any other type of information that enables the enterprise to maintain competitiveness within its industry. The principles of data classification and access control apply most critically to these assets. In some cases, the dollar value of these assets might be difficult to determine, although it might be clear to all involved that the asset is critical. For example, the secret formula for Coca-Cola has been closely guarded for many years due to its value to the company.

Protecting Data at Rest and Data in Transit

Protecting data at rest and data in transit are two fundamental aspects of information security that are crucial for resource protection. This protection emphasizes the importance of safeguarding information regardless of its state—whether it's stored on a device (data at rest) or being transmitted over a network (data in transit). Each state poses unique security challenges and requires specific protection strategies to mitigate the risk of unauthorized access, disclosure, alteration, or destruction.

Data at rest refers to any data stored on physical or digital media. This includes data stored on hard drives, solid state drives (SSDs), USB drives, backup tapes, and databases. Protecting data at rest is essential to prevent unauthorized access and leaks of sensitive information. The primary methods for protecting data at rest include:

- **Encryption:** Encrypting the data stored on physical or digital media so that it is unreadable to unauthorized users. Even if an attacker gains physical access to the storage media, the data will remain protected if encrypted properly.
- **Access Controls:** Implementing robust access control mechanisms to ensure that only authorized personnel can access sensitive data. This includes the use of strong authentication methods and permissions settings that restrict access based on user roles.

- **Data Masking:** Applying data masking techniques to hide sensitive information within a dataset, ensuring that unauthorized individuals cannot view the actual data even if they can access the dataset.
- **Physical Security:** Ensuring physical security measures are in place to protect the storage media from theft, tampering, or destruction. This includes secure facilities, locked storage cabinets, and surveillance systems.

Data in transit refers to data actively moving from one location to another, such as across the Internet or through a private network. Data in transit is vulnerable to interception, modification, and eavesdropping, making its protection critical. Key strategies for protecting data in transit include:

- **Encryption:** Using encryption protocols such as Transport Layer Security (TLS) or Internet Protocol Security (IPsec) to encrypt data while it is being transmitted. This ensures that even if data is intercepted, it cannot be read by unauthorized parties.
- **Secure Protocols:** Employing secure communication protocols (e.g., HTTPS, SFTP, and SSH) that provide encryption and secure authentication mechanisms to protect data during transmission.
- **Virtual Private Networks (VPNs):** Utilizing VPNs to create a secure and encrypted connection over a public network, ensuring that data transmitted between the VPN client and server is protected from eavesdropping or interception.
- **Email Security:** Implementing secure email gateways and encryption for emails to protect sensitive information sent via email from unauthorized access or disclosure.

Protecting data at rest and data in transit are critical components of a comprehensive cybersecurity strategy. By implementing appropriate security measures, organizations can safeguard sensitive information from unauthorized access, ensuring the confidentiality, integrity, and availability of data. For security professionals, understanding and applying these protection strategies is essential for meeting the objective of resource protection and maintaining a secure information environment.

Asset Management

In the process of managing these assets, several issues must be addressed. Certainly, access to the asset must be closely controlled to prevent its deletion, theft, or corruption (in the case of digital assets) and from physical damage (in the case of physical assets). Moreover, the asset must remain available when needed. This section covers methods of ensuring availability, authorization, and integrity.

Redundancy and Fault Tolerance

One way to provide uninterrupted access to information assets is through redundancy and fault tolerance. ***Redundancy*** refers to providing multiple instances of either a physical or logical component such that a second component is available if the first fails. ***Fault tolerance*** is a broader concept that includes redundancy but refers to any process that allows a system to continue making information assets available in the case of a failure.

In some cases, redundancy is applied at the physical layer, such as network redundancy provided by a dual backbone in a local network environment or by using multiple network cards in a critical server. In other cases, redundancy is applied logically such as when a router knows multiple paths to a destination in case one fails.

Fault tolerance countermeasures are designed to combat threats to design reliability. Although fault tolerance can include redundancy, it also refers to systems such as Redundant Array of Independent Disks (RAID) in which data is written across multiple disks in such a way that a disk can fail and the data can be quickly made available from the remaining functioning disks in the array without resorting to backup media. Be familiar with a number of RAID types because not all provide fault tolerance. Regardless of the technique employed for fault tolerance to operate, a system must be capable of detecting and correcting the fault.

Backup and Recovery Systems

Although comprehensive coverage of backup and recovery systems is found throughout this chapter, it is important to emphasize here the role of operations in carrying out those activities. After the backup schedule has been designed, there will be daily tasks associated with carrying out the plan. One of the most important parts of this system is an ongoing testing process to ensure that all backups are usable in case a recovery is required. In addition, the organization needs to ensure that they retain the devices needed to successfully restore the backups. The time to discover that a backup did not succeed is during testing and not during a live recovery.

Identity and Access Management

From an operations perspective, it is important to realize that managing these things is an ongoing process that might require creating accounts, deleting accounts, creating and populating groups, and managing the permissions associated with all of these concepts. An essential task is ensuring that the rights to perform these actions are tightly controlled and that a formal process is established for removing permissions when they are no longer required and disabling accounts that are no longer needed.

Another area to focus on is the control of the use of privileged accounts or accounts that have rights and permissions that exceed those of a regular user account. Although this control obviously applies to built-in administrator, root, or supervisor accounts (which in some operating systems are called root accounts) that have vast permissions, it also applies to any account that confers special privileges to the user.

Moreover, as a security professional, you should maintain the same tight control over the numerous built-in groups that exist in Windows to grant special rights to the group members. When using these groups, make note of any privileges held by the default groups that are not required for your purposes. You might want to remove some of the privileges from the default groups to support the concept of least privilege. You learn more about identity and access management in Chapter 5.

Media Management

Media management is an important part of operations security because media is where data is stored. Media management includes RAID, SAN, NAS, and HSM.

RAID

Redundant Array of Independent Disks (RAID) refers to a system whereby multiple hard drives are used to provide either a performance boost or fault tolerance for the data. When we speak of fault tolerance in RAID, we mean maintaining access to the data even in a drive failure without restoring the data from backup media. The following are the types of RAID with which you should be familiar.

RAID 0, also called disk striping, writes the data across multiple drives or disks. Although it improves performance, it does not provide fault tolerance. Figure 7-2 depicts RAID 0.

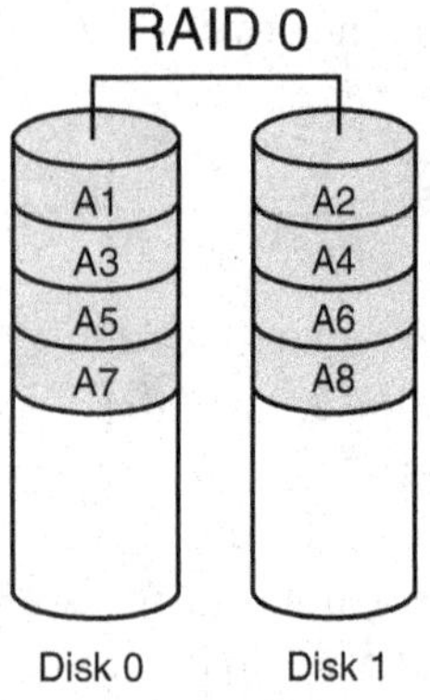

Figure 7-2 RAID 0

RAID 1, also called disk mirroring, uses two drives or disks and writes a copy of the data to both disks, providing fault tolerance in the case of a single drive failure. Figure 7-3 depicts RAID 1.

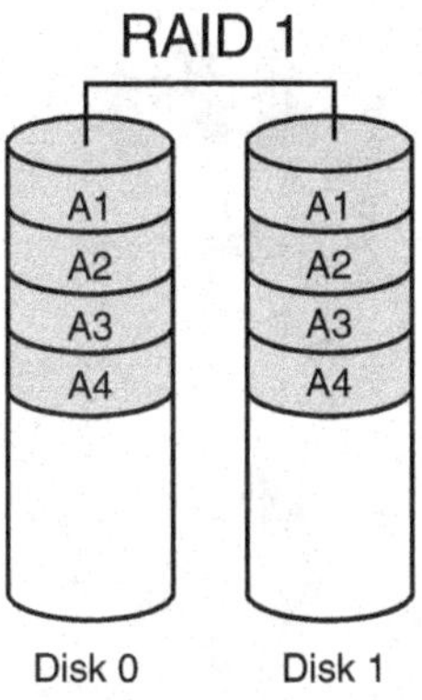

Figure 7-3 RAID 1

RAID 3, requiring at least three drives or disks, also requires that the data is written across all drives like striping and then *parity information* is written to a single dedicated drive. The parity information is used to regenerate the data in the case of a single drive failure. The downfall is that the parity drive is a single point of failure if it goes bad. Figure 7-4 depicts RAID 3.

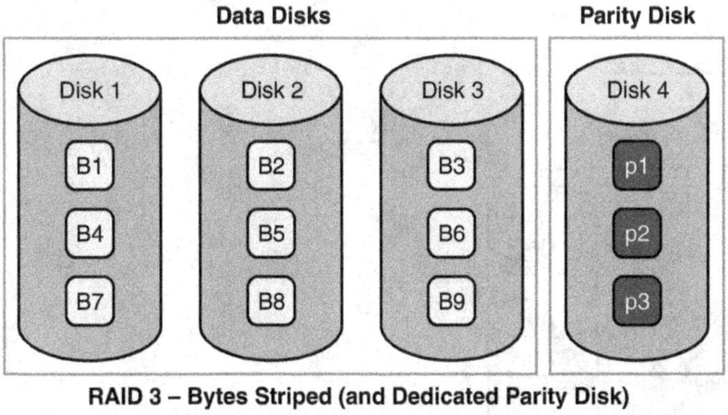

Figure 7-4 RAID 3

RAID 5, requiring at least three drives or disks, also requires that the data is written across all drives like striping and then parity information also is written across all drives. The parity information is used in the same way as in RAID 3, but it is not stored on a single drive so there is no single point of failure for the parity data. With hardware RAID level 5, the spare drives that replace the failed drives are usually hot swappable, meaning they can be replaced on the server while it is running. Figure 7-5 depicts RAID 5.

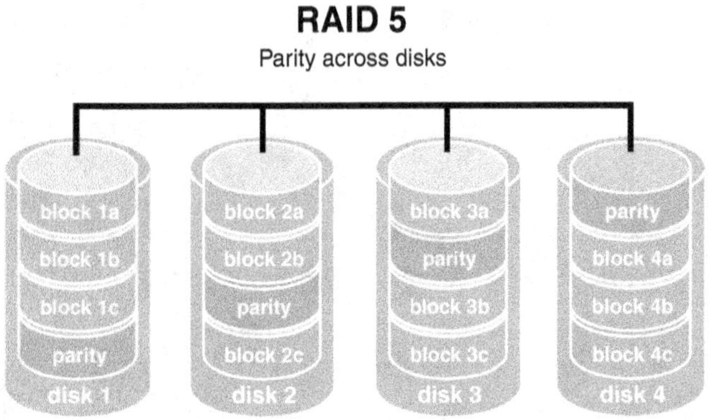

Figure 7-5 RAID 5

RAID 10, which requires at least four drives or disks, is a combination of RAID 0 and RAID 1. First, a RAID 1 volume is created by mirroring two drives together. Then a RAID 0 stripe set is created on each mirrored pair. Figure 7-6 depicts RAID 10.

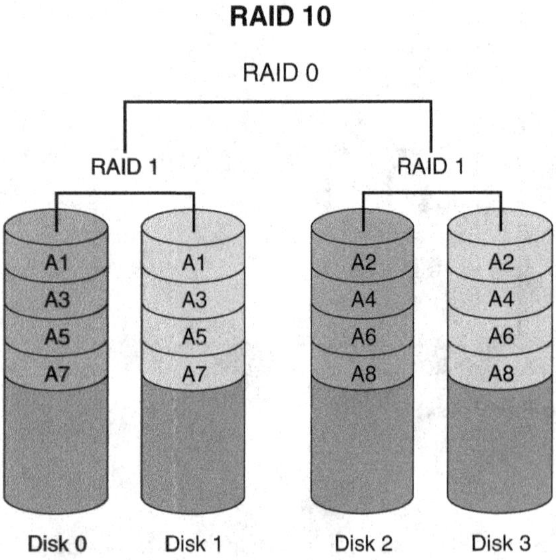

Figure 7-6 RAID 10

Although RAID can be implemented with software or with hardware, certain types of RAID are faster when implemented with hardware. When software RAID is used, it is a function of the operating system. Both RAID 3 and 5 are examples of RAID types that are faster when implemented with hardware. Simple striping or mirroring (RAID 0 and 1), however, tend to perform well in software because they do not use the hardware-level parity drives. Table 7-1 summarizes the RAID types.

Key Topic

Table 7-1 RAID Levels

RAID Level	Minimum Number of Drives or Disks	Description	Strengths	Weaknesses
RAID 0	2	Data striping without redundancy	Highest performance	No data protection; one drive fails, all data is lost
RAID 1	2	Disk mirroring	Very high performance; very high data protection; very minimal penalty on write performance	High redundancy cost overhead; because all data is duplicated, twice the storage capacity is required
RAID 3	3	Byte-level data striping with dedicated parity drive	Excellent performance for large, sequential data requests	Not well suited for transaction-oriented network applications; single parity drive does not support multiple, simultaneous read and write requests
RAID 5	3	Block-level data striping with distributed parity	Best cost/performance for transaction-oriented networks; very high performance, very high data protection; supports multiple simultaneous reads and writes; can also be optimized for large, sequential requests	Write performance is slower than RAID 0 or RAID 1
RAID 10	4	Disk mirroring with striping	Same fault tolerance as RAID 1; same overhead as with mirroring; provides high I/O rates; can sustain multiple simultaneous drive failures	Very expensive; all drives must move in parallel to properly track, which reduces sustained performance; very limited scalability at a very high cost

SAN

Storage-area networks (SANs) are composed of high-capacity storage devices that are connected by a high-speed private network (separate from the LAN) using storage-specific switches. This storage information architecture addresses the collection, management, and use of data.

NAS

Network-attached storage (NAS) serves the same function as SAN, but clients access the storage in a different way. In a NAS, almost any machine that can connect to the LAN (or is interconnected to the LAN through a WAN) can use protocols such as NFS, CIFS, or HTTP to connect to a NAS and share files. In a SAN, only devices that can use the Fibre Channel SCSI network can access the data, so it is typically done though a server that has this capability. Figure 7-7 shows a comparison of the two systems.

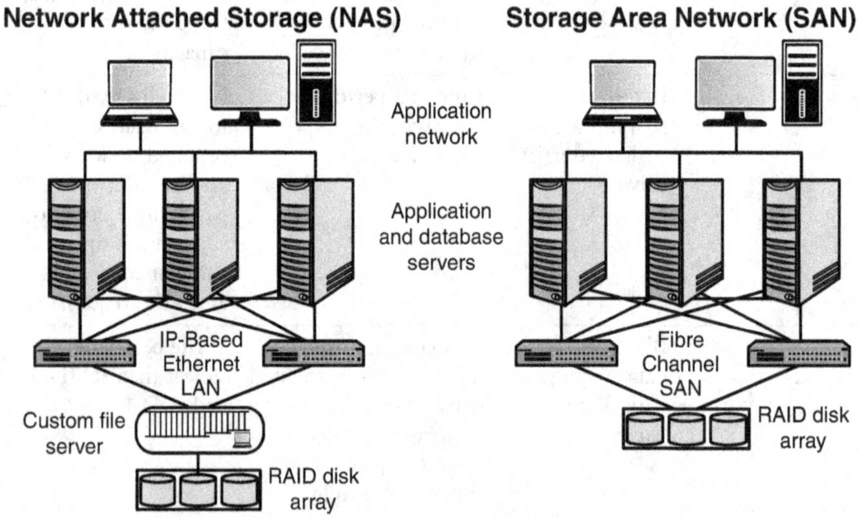

Figure 7-7 NAS and SAN

HSM

A ***hierarchical storage management (HSM)*** system is a type of backup management system that provides a continuous online backup by using optical or tape "jukeboxes." It operates by automatically moving data between high-cost and low-cost storage media as the data ages. When continuous availability (24-hours-a-day processing) is required, HSM provides a good alternative to tape backups. It also strives to use the proper media for the scenario. For example, a rewritable (CD-R/W) optical disc is sometimes used for backups that require short-time storage for changeable data but require faster file access than tape.

NOTE Don't confuse the acronym *HSM*. HSM can also refer to hardware security module, which is a device that manages and protects digital keys for strong authentication.

Media History

Security professionals must accurately maintain media library logs to keep track of the history of the media. This task is important in that all media types have a maximum number of times they can safely be used. A log should be kept by a media librarian. This log should track all media (backup and other types such as OS installation discs and USB thumb drives). With respect to the backup media, use the following guidelines:

- Track all instances of access to the media.
- Track the number and location of backups.
- Track age of media to prevent loss of data through media degeneration.
- Inventory the media regularly.

Media Labeling and Storage

All forms of storage media (tapes, optical, USB thumb drives, and so on) should be labeled plainly and stored safely. Some guidelines in the area of media control are to

- Accurately and promptly mark all data storage media.
- Ensure proper environmental storage of the media.
- Ensure the safe and clean handling of the media.
- Log data media to provide a physical inventory control.

The environment where the media will be stored is also important. For example, damage starts occurring to magnetic media above 100 degrees. The *Forest Green Book* is a Rainbow Series book that defines the secure handling of sensitive or classified automated information system memory and secondary storage media, such as degaussers, magnetic tapes, hard disks, and cards. The Rainbow Series is discussed in more detail in Chapter 3.

Sanitizing and Disposing of Media

During media disposal, you must ensure no data remains on the media. The most reliable, secure means of removing data from magnetic storage media, such as a magnetic tape cassette, is through degaussing, which exposes the media to a powerful, alternating magnetic field. It removes any previously written data, leaving the media in a magnetically randomized (blank) state. Some other disposal terms and concepts with which you should be familiar are

- ***Data purging***: Using a method such as degaussing to make the old data unavailable even with forensics. Degaussing only works with magnetic drives. Purging renders information unrecoverable against laboratory attacks (forensics).
- ***Data clearing***: Rendering information unrecoverable by a keyboard. This attack extracts information from data storage media by executing software utilities, keystrokes, or other system resources executed from a keyboard.
- ***Remanence***: Any data left after the media has been erased.

Network and Resource Management

Although the Security Operations domain focuses on providing confidentiality and integrity of data, availability of the data is also one of its goals. This means designing and maintaining processes and systems that maintain availability to resources despite hardware or software failures in the environment. The following principles and concepts are available to assist in maintaining access to resources:

- **Redundant hardware:** Failures of physical components, such as hard drives and network cards, can interrupt access to resources. Providing redundant instances of these components can help to ensure a faster return to access. In some cases, changing out a component might require manual intervention, but in many cases these items are hot swappable (they can be changed with the device up and running), in which case a momentary reduction in performance might occur rather than a complete disruption of access.
- **Fault-tolerant technologies:** Taking the idea of redundancy to the next level are technologies that are based on multiple computing systems working together to provide uninterrupted access even in the event of a failure of one of the systems. Clustering of servers and grid computing are both great examples of this approach.
- **Service-level agreements (SLAs):** SLAs are agreements about the capability of the support system to respond to problems within a certain timeframe while providing an agreed level of service. They can be internal between

departments or external to a service provider. By agreeing on the quickness with which various problems are addressed, some predictability is introduced to the response to problems, which ultimately supports the maintenance of access to resources.

- **MTBF and MTTR:** Although SLAs are appropriate for services that are provided, a slightly different approach to introducing predictability can be used with regard to physical components that are purchased. Vendors typically publish values for a product's mean time between failure (MTBF), which describes how often a component fails on average. Another valuable metric typically provided is the mean time to repair (MTTR), which describes the average amount of time it will take to get the device fixed and back online.
- **Single point of failure (SPOF):** Though not actually a strategy, it is worth mentioning that the ultimate goal of any of these approaches is to avoid an SPOF in a system. All components and groups of components and devices should be examined to discover any single element that could interrupt access to resources if a failure occurs. Each SPOF should then be mitigated in some way.

Incident Management

Incident response and management are vital to every organization to ensure that any security incidents are detected, contained, and investigated. Incident response is the beginning of any investigation. After an incident has been discovered, incident response personnel perform specific tasks. During the entire incident response, the incident response team must ensure that they follow proper procedures to ensure that evidence is preserved. Incident management ensures that the incident response team manages an incident and returns service to normal as quickly as possible after the incident.

As part of incident response, security professionals must understand the difference between events and incidents (see the following section). The incident response team must have the appropriate incident response procedures in place to ensure that the incident is handled, but the procedures must not hinder any forensic investigations that might be needed to ensure that parties are held responsible for any illegal actions. Security professionals must understand the rules of engagement and the authorization and scope of any incident investigation.

Event Versus Incident

With regard to incident response, a basic difference exists between events and incidents. An ***event*** is a noticeable change of state that occurs. Whereas events include both negative and positive events, incident response focuses more on negative events—events that have been deemed as negatively impacting the organization. An ***incident*** is a series of events that negatively impact an organization's operations and security.

Events can be detected only if an organization has established the proper auditing and security mechanisms to monitor activity. A single negative event might occur. For example, the auditing log might show that an invalid login attempt occurred. By itself, this login attempt is not a security concern. However, if many invalid login attempts occur over a period of a few hours, the organization might be undergoing an attack. The initial invalid login is considered an event, but the series of invalid login attempts over a few hours would be an incident, especially if it is discovered that the invalid login attempts all originated from the same IP address.

Incident Response Team and Incident Investigations

When establishing the incident response team, organizations must consider the technical knowledge of each individual. The members of the team must understand the organization's security policy and have strong communication skills. Members should also receive training in incident response and investigations.

When an incident has occurred, the primary goal of the team is to contain the attack and repair any damage caused by the incident. Security isolation of an incident scene should start immediately when the incident is discovered. Evidence must be preserved, and the appropriate authorities should be notified.

The incident response team should have access to the incident response plan. This plan should include the list of authorities to contact, team roles and responsibilities, an internal contact list, procedures for securing and preserving evidence, and a list of investigation experts who can be contacted for help. A step-by-step manual should be created that the incident response team must follow to ensure that no steps are skipped. After the incident response process has been engaged, all incident response actions should be documented.

If the incident response team determines that a crime has been committed, senior management and the proper authorities should be contacted immediately.

Rules of Engagement, Authorization, and Scope

An organization ought to document the rules of engagement, authorization, and scope for the incident response team. The rules of engagement define which actions are acceptable and unacceptable if an incident has occurred. The authorization and scope provide the incident response team with the authority to perform an investigation and with the allowable scope of any investigation they must undertake.

The rules of engagement act as a guideline for the incident response team to ensure that they do not cross the line from enticement into entrapment. Enticement occurs when the opportunity for illegal actions is provided (luring) but attackers make their own decision to perform the action, and entrapment means to encourage someone to commit a crime that the individual might have had no intention of committing. Enticement is legal but does raise ethical arguments and might not be admissible in court. Conversely, entrapment is illegal.

An example of enticement is when a legitimate software company offers a free trial of its antivirus software to users who sign up with their email addresses. However, buried in the terms and conditions is permission for the company to collect extensive personal data from the user's device, including browsing history, location data, and contact information. While the free trial entices users to try out the software, they may not be fully aware of the extent of data collection, leading to accusations of enticement.

An example of entrapment is when a reputable online retailer offers a "limited-time offer" on a popular smart home device, enticing customers to make a quick purchase. However, upon receiving the device, customers realize that it requires a paid subscription to access essential features or security updates. The retailer failed to disclose these additional costs upfront, leading customers to feel entrapped into purchasing a product under false pretenses.

In both scenarios, the actions of the legitimate companies could be perceived as manipulative or deceptive, resulting in accusations of enticement or entrapment from customers or regulatory authorities.

Incident Response Procedures

When performing incident response, the incident response team must follow incident response procedures. Depending on where you look, you might find different steps or phases included as part of the incident response process.

For the CISSP exam, you need to remember the following steps:

Key Topic

1. Detect the incident.
2. Respond to the incident.
3. Mitigate the effects of the incident.
4. Report the incident to the appropriate personnel.
5. Recover from the incident.
6. Remediate all components affected by the incident to ensure that all traces of the incident have been removed.
7. Review the incident, and document all findings as lessons learned.

The actual investigation of the incident occurs during the respond, mitigate, report, and recover steps. Following appropriate forensic and digital investigation processes during the investigation can ensure that evidence is preserved.

The incident response process is shown in Figure 7-8.

Figure 7-8 Incident Response Process

Incident Response Management

Security events will inevitably occur, and the response to these events says much about how damaging the events will be to the organization. Incident response policies should be formally designed, well communicated, and followed. They should specifically address cyberattacks against an organization's IT systems.

Detect

The first step in the incident response process is to detect the incident. Prior to any incident response investigation, security professionals must first perform the appropriate triage for the affected assets. This process includes initially detecting the incident and determining how serious the incident is. In some cases, during the triage phase, security professionals may determine that a false positive has occurred, meaning that an attack really did not occur, even though an alert indicated that it did. If an attack is confirmed, then the incident response will progress into investigative actions.

All detective controls, such as auditing, discussed in Chapter 1, are designed to provide this capability. The worst sort of incident is the one that goes unnoticed.

Respond

The response to the incident should be appropriate for the type of incident. Denial-of-service (DoS) attacks against the web server would require a quicker and different response than a missing mouse in the server room. Establish standard responses and response times ahead of time.

Response involves containing the incident and quarantining the affected assets, thus preventing other assets from being affected and reducing the potential impact. Different methods can be used, depending on the category of the attack, the asset affected, and the data criticality or infection risk.

After an attack is contained or isolated, analysts should work to examine and analyze the cause of the incident. This analysis includes determining where the incident originated. Security professionals should use experience and formal training to make the appropriate conclusions regarding the incident. After the root cause has been determined, security professionals should follow incident handling policies that the organization has in place.

Mitigate

Mitigation includes limiting the scope of what the attack might do to the organization's assets. If damage has occurred or the incident may broaden and affect other assets, proper mitigation techniques ensure that the incident is contained to within a certain scope of assets. Mitigation options vary, depending on the kind of attack that has occurred. Security professionals should develop procedures in advance that detail how to properly mitigate any attacks that occur against organizational assets. Preparing these mitigation procedures in advance ensures that they are thorough and gives personnel a chance to test the procedures.

Report

All incidents should be reported within a timeframe that reflects the seriousness of the incident. In many cases, establishing a list of incident types and the person to contact when that type of incident occurs is helpful. Exercising attention to detail at this early stage while time-sensitive information is still available is critical.

Recover

Recovery involves a reaction designed to make the network or system that is affected functional again; it includes repair of the affected assets and prevention of similar incidents in the future. Exactly what recovery means depends on the circumstances and the recovery measures that are available. For example, if fault-tolerance measures are in place, the recovery might consist of simply allowing one server in a cluster to fail over to another. In other cases, recovery could mean restoring the server from a recent backup. The main goal of this step is to make all resources available again. Delay putting any asset back into operation until it is at least protected from the incident that occurred. Thoroughly test assets for vulnerabilities and weaknesses before reintroducing them into production.

Remediate

The remediation step involves eliminating any residual danger or damage to the network that still might exist. For example, in the case of a virus outbreak, it could mean scanning all systems to root out any additional affected machines. These measures are designed to make a more detailed mitigation when time allows.

Review and Lessons Learned

Finally, security professionals should review each incident to discover what could be learned from it. Changes to procedures might be called for. Lessons learned should be shared with all personnel who might encounter this type of incident again. Complete documentation and analysis are the goal of this step.

Detective and Preventive Measures

As you have probably gathered by now, a wide variety of security threats faces those charged with protecting the assets of an organization. Luckily, a wide variety of tools is available to use to accomplish this task. The following sections cover some common threats and mitigation approaches.

IDS/IPS

Setup, configuration, and monitoring of any intrusion detection and intrusion prevention systems (IDS/IPS) are also ongoing responsibilities of operations security. Many of these systems must be updated on a regular basis with the attack signatures that enable them to detect new attack types. The analysis engines that they use also sometimes have updates that need to be applied.

Moreover, the log files of systems that are set to log certain events rather than take specific actions when they occur need to have those logs archived and analyzed on a regular basis. Spending large sums of money on software that gathers important log information and then disregarding that log information makes no sense.

IDS and IPS are discussed in more detail earlier in this chapter and in Chapter 4.

Intrusion response is just as important as intrusion detection and prevention. Intrusion response is about responding appropriately to any intrusion attempt. Most systems use alarms and signals to communicate with the appropriate personnel or systems when an intrusion has been attempted. An organization must respond to alerts and signals in a timely manner.

Firewalls

Firewalls can be implemented on multiple levels to allow or prevent communication based on a variety of factors. If personnel discover that certain types of unwanted traffic are occurring, it is often fairly simple to configure a firewall to prevent that type of traffic. Firewalls can protect the boundaries between networks, traffic within a subnetwork, or a single system. Make sure to keep firewalls fully updated per the vendor's security patches. Firewalls are discussed in more depth in Chapter 4.

Whitelisting/Blacklisting

Whitelisting occurs when a list of acceptable email addresses, Internet addresses, websites, applications, or some other identifier is configured as good senders or as allowed. ***Blacklisting*** identifies bad senders. ***Graylisting*** is somewhere in between the two, listing entities that cannot be identified as whitelist or blacklist items. In the case of graylisting, the new entity must pass through a series of tests to determine whether it will be whitelisted or blacklisted.

Whitelisting, blacklisting, and graylisting are commonly used with spam filtering tools.

Third-Party Security Services

Security professionals may need to rely on third-party security services to find threats in the enterprise. Some common third-party security services include malware/virus detection and honeypots/honeynets. It is often easier to rely on a solution developed by a third party than to try to develop your own in-house solution. Always research the features provided with a solution to determine if it meets the needs of your organization. Compare the different products available to ensure that the organization purchases the best solution for its needs.

Sandboxing

Sandboxing is a software virtualization technique that allows applications and processes to run in an isolated virtual environment. Applications and processes in the sandbox are not allowed to make permanent changes to the system and its files outside the sandbox.

Some malware attempts to delay or stall code execution, allowing the sandbox to time out. A sandbox can use hooks and environmental checks to detect malware. These methods do not prevent many types of malware. For this reason, third-party security services are important.

Honeypots/Honeynets

Honeypots are systems that are configured with reduced security to entice attackers so that administrators can learn about attack techniques. In some cases, entire networks called ***honeynets*** are attractively configured for this purpose. These types of approaches should be undertaken only by companies with the skill to properly deploy and monitor them. Some third-party security services can provide this function for organizations.

Anti-malware/Antivirus

All updates of antivirus and anti-malware software are the responsibility of operations security. It is important to deploy a comprehensive anti-malware/antivirus solution for the entire enterprise.

Clipping Levels

Clipping levels set a baseline for normal user errors, and violations exceeding that threshold will be recorded for analysis of why the violations occurred. When clipping levels are used, a certain number of occurrences of an activity might generate no information, whereas recording of activities begins when a certain level is exceeded.

Clipping levels are used to

- Reduce the amount of data to be evaluated in audit logs.
- Provide a baseline of user errors above which violations will be recorded.

NOTE Clipping levels are also covered in Chapter 5.

Deviations from Standards

One of the methods that you can use to identify performance problems that arise is to develop standards or baselines for the performance of certain systems. After these benchmarks have been established, deviations for the standards can be identified. This information is especially helpful in identifying certain types of DoS attacks as they occur. Beyond the security benefit, identifying these problems also aids in identifying systems that might need upgrading before the situation affects productivity.

Unusual or Unexplained Events

In some cases, events occur that appear to have no logical cause. That type of answer should never be accepted when problems occur. Although the focus is typically on getting systems up and running again, the root causes of issues must be identified. You should avoid the temptation to implement a quick workaround (often at the expense of security). When time permits, using a methodical approach to find exactly why the event happened is best, because inevitably the problem will come back if the root cause has not been addressed.

Unscheduled Reboots

When systems reboot on their own, this behavior is typically a sign of hardware problems of some sort. Reboots should be recorded and addressed. Overheating or other environmental changes is a common cause of many reboots. Sometimes reboots may also be the result of a DoS attack. You should have system monitoring in place to record all system reboots and investigate any that are not initiated by a human or have occurred as a result of an automatic upgrade.

Unauthorized Disclosure

The unauthorized disclosure of information is a large threat to organizations. It includes destruction of information, interruption of service, theft of information, corruption of information, and improper modification of information. Enterprise solutions must be deployed to monitor for any potential disclosure of information.

Trusted Recovery

When an application or operating system suffers a failure (crash, freeze, and so on), it is important that the system respond in a way that leaves the system in a secure state or that it makes a ***trusted recovery***. A trusted recovery ensures that security is not breached when a system crash or other system failure occurs. You might recall from Chapter 3 that the *Orange Book* requires a system be capable of a trusted recovery for all systems rated B3 or A1.

Trusted Paths

A ***trusted path*** is a communication channel between the user or the program through which that user is working and the trusted computer base (TCB). The TCB provides the resources to protect the channel and prevent it from being compromised. Conversely, a communication path that is not protected by the system's normal security mechanisms is called a *covert channel*. Taking this a step further, if the interface offered to the user is secured, it is referred to as a *trusted shell*.

Operations security must ensure that trusted paths are validated. This validation occurs using log collection, log analysis, vulnerability scans, patch management, and system integrity checks.

Input/Output Controls

The main thrust of input/output control is to apply controls or checks to the input that is allowed to be submitted to the system. Performing input validation on all information accepted into the system can ensure that it is of the right data type and format and that it does not leave the system in an insecure state.

Also, secure output of the system (printouts, reports, and so on) should be ensured. All sensitive output information should require a receipt before release and have proper access controls applied regardless of its format.

System Hardening

Another of the ongoing goals of operations security is to ensure that all systems have been hardened to the extent that is possible and still provide functionality. The hardening can be accomplished both on a physical basis and on a logical basis. Physical security of systems is covered in detail later in this chapter. From a logical perspective,

- Remove unnecessary applications.
- Disable unnecessary services.
- Block unrequired ports.
- Tightly control the connecting of external storage devices and media if it's allowed at all.

Vulnerability Management Systems

The importance of performing vulnerability and penetration testing has been emphasized throughout this book. A vulnerability management system is software that centralizes, and to a certain extent automates, the process of continually monitoring and testing the network for vulnerabilities. These systems can scan the network for vulnerabilities, report them, and in many cases remediate the problem without human intervention. Although they're a valuable tool in the toolbox, these systems, regardless of how sophisticated they might be, cannot take the place of vulnerability and penetration testing performed by trained professionals.

Machine Learning and Artificial Intelligence (AI)-Based Tools

Machine learning and artificial intelligence (AI)-based tools are tools that give systems the ability to learn and improve without much human input. Artificial intelligence is any technology that enables a machine to simulate human behavior. A type of AI, machine learning allows a machine to learn from what is happening and make decisions based on what it sees.

Using these technologies in a security context means that data can be used to detect threats and compile investigative information. These tools help cybersecurity professionals find, contextualize, and organize relevant data at any stage in the threat intelligence life cycle. With machine learning and AI, organizations can process the data much faster than if actual human effort was involved.

Patch and Vulnerability Management

Patch management is often seen as a subset of configuration management. *Software patches* are updates released by vendors that either fix functional issues with or close newly discovered security loopholes in operating systems, applications, and versions of firmware that run on the network devices.

To ensure that all devices have the latest patches installed, deploy a formal system to make certain that all systems receive the latest updates *after* thorough testing in a nonproduction environment. It is not always possible for a vendor to anticipate every possible impact a change might have on business-critical systems in the network. The enterprise is responsible for ensuring that patches do not adversely impact operations.

The patch management life cycle includes the following steps:

Key Topic

1. **Patch prioritization and scheduling:** Determine the priority of the patches and schedule the patches for deployment.
2. **Patch testing:** Test the patches prior to deployment to ensure that they work properly and do not cause system or security issues.
3. **Patch installation:** Install the patches in the live environment.
4. **Patch assessment and audit:** After patches are deployed, ensure that the patches work properly.

Many organizations deploy a centralized patch management system to ensure that patches are deployed in a timely manner. With this system, administrators can test and review all patches before deploying them to the systems they affect. Administrators can schedule the updates to occur during nonpeak hours.

Vulnerability management identifies, classifies, remediates, and mitigates vulnerabilities in systems and applications. Vulnerability management tools, also referred to as vulnerability scanners, should be used to regularly assess the network, systems, and applications. Any identified vulnerabilities should be investigated and the appropriate remediation or mitigation steps taken. Nessus is a popular open-source vulnerability scanner in use today. As with patch management systems and antivirus applications, it is necessary to ensure that vulnerability scanners have the latest signature files.

Recovery Strategies

Identifying the preventive controls is the third step of the business continuity steps as outlined in NIST SP 800-34 R1. If preventive controls are identified in the business impact analysis (BIA), disasters or disruptive events might be mitigated or eliminated. These preventive measures deter, detect, and/or reduce impacts to the system. Preventive methods are preferable to actions that might be necessary to recover the system after a disruption if the preventive controls are feasible and cost effective.

The following sections discuss the primary controls that organizations can implement as part of business continuity and disaster recovery, including redundant systems, facilities, and power; fault-tolerance technologies; insurance; data backup; fire detection and suppression; high availability; quality of service; and system resilience.

Create Recovery Strategies

Organizations must create recovery strategies for all assets that are vital to successful operation. *Higher-level* recovery strategies identify the order in which processes and functions are restored. *System-level* recovery strategies define how a particular system is to be restored. Keep in mind those individuals who best understand the system should define system recovery strategies. Although the business continuity planning (BCP) committee probably can develop the prioritized recovery lists and high-level recovery strategies, system administrators and other IT personnel need to be involved in the development of recovery strategies for IT assets.

Disaster recovery tasks include recovery procedures, personnel safety procedures, and restoration procedures. The overall business recovery plan should require a committee to be formed to decide the best course of action. This recovery plan committee receives its direction from the BCP committee and senior management.

All decisions regarding recovery should be made in advance and incorporated into the disaster recovery plan (DRP). Any plans and procedures that are developed should refer to functions or processes, not specific individuals. As part of the disaster recovery planning, the recovery plan committee should contact critical vendors ahead of time to ensure that any equipment or supplies can be replaced in a timely manner.

When a disaster or disruptive event has occurred, the organization's spokesperson should report the bad news in an emergency press conference before the press learns of the news through another channel. The DRP should detail any guidelines for handling the press. The emergency press conference site should be planned ahead of time.

When resuming normal operations after a disruptive event, the organization should conduct a thorough investigation if the cause of the event is unknown. Personnel should account for all damage-related costs that occur as a result of the event. In addition, appropriate steps should be taken to prevent further damage to property.

The commonality between all recovery plans is that they all become obsolete. For this reason, they require testing and updating.

The following sections include a discussion of categorizing asset recovery priorities, business process recovery, facility recovery, supply and technology recovery, user environment recovery, data recovery, and training personnel.

Categorize Asset Recovery Priorities

As discussed in Chapter 1, the recovery time objective (RTO), work recovery time (WRT), and recovery point objective (RPO) values determine what recovery solutions are selected. An RTO stipulates the amount of time an organization will need to recover from a disaster, and an RPO stipulates the amount of data an organization can lose when a disaster occurs. The RTO, WRT, and RPO values are derived during the BIA process.

In developing the recovery strategy, the recovery plan committee takes the RTO, WRT, and RPO values and determines the recovery strategies that should be used to ensure that the organization meets these BIA goals.

Critical devices, systems, and applications need to be restored earlier than devices, systems, or applications that do not fall into this category. Keep in mind when classifying systems that most critical systems cannot be restored using manual methods. The recovery plan committee must understand the backup/restore solutions that are available and implement the system that will provide recovery within the BIA values and cost constraints. The window of time for recovery of data-processing capabilities is based on the criticality of the operations affected.

Business Process Recovery

As part of the DRP, the recovery plan committee must understand the interrelationships between the processes and systems. A business process is a collection of tasks that produces a specific service or product for a particular customer or customers.

For example, if the organization determines that an accounting system is a critical application and the accounting system relies on a database server farm, the DRP needs to include the database server as a critical asset. Although restoring the entire database server farm to restore the critical accounting system might not be necessary, at least one of the servers in the farm is necessary for proper operation.

Workflow documents should be provided to the recovery plan committee for each business process. As part of recovering the business processes, the recovery plan committee must also understand the process's required roles and resources, input and output tools, and interfaces with other business processes.

Supply and Technology Recovery

Although facility recovery is not often a concern with smaller disasters or disruptive events, almost all recovery efforts usually involve the recovery of supplies and technology. Organizations must ensure that any DRPs include guidelines and procedures for recovering supplies and technology. As part of supply and technology recovery, the DRP should include all pertinent vendor contact information in the event that new supplies and technological assets must be purchased.

The DRP must include recovery information on the following assets that must be restored:

- Hardware backup
- Software backup
- Human resources
- Heating, ventilation, and air conditioning (HVAC)
- Supplies
- Documentation

Hardware Backup

Hardware that must be included as part of the DRP includes client computers, server computers, routers, switches, firewalls, and any other hardware that is running on the organization's network. The DRP must include not only guidelines and procedures for restoring all the data on each of these devices, but also information regarding restoring these systems manually if the systems are damaged or completely destroyed. Legacy devices that are no longer available in the retail market should also be identified.

As part of preparing the DRP, the recovery plan team must determine the amount of time that it will take the hardware vendors to provide replacements for any damaged or destroyed hardware. Without this information documented, any recovery plans might be ineffective due to lack of resources. Organizations might need to explore other options, including purchasing redundant systems and storing them at an alternate location, if vendors are unable to provide replacement hardware in a timely manner. When replacement of legacy devices is possible, organizations should take measures to replace them before the disaster occurs.

Software Backup

Even if an organization has every device needed to restore its infrastructure, those devices are useless if the applications and software that run on the devices are not available. The applications and software include any operating systems, databases, and utilities that need to be running on the device.

Many organizations might think that this requirement is fulfilled if they have a backup on either tape, DVD, flash drive, hard drive, or other media of all their software. But all software that is backed up usually requires at least an operating system to be running on the device on which it is restored. These data backups often also require that the backup management software is running on the backup device, whether that is a server or dedicated device.

All software installation media, service packs, and other necessary updates should be stored at an alternate location. In addition, all license information should be documented as part of the DRP. Finally, frequent backups of applications should be taken, whether this is through the application's internal backup system or through some other organizational backup. A backup is useful only if it can be restored, so the DRP should fully document all the steps involved.

In many cases, applications are purchased from a software vendor, and only the software vendor understands the coding that occurs in the applications. Because there are no guarantees in today's market, some organizations might decide that they need to ensure that they are protected against a software vendor's demise. A software escrow is an agreement whereby a third party is given the source code of the software to ensure that the customer has access to the source code if certain conditions for the software vendor occur, including bankruptcy and disaster.

Human Resources

No organization is capable of operating without personnel. An occupant emergency plan specifically addresses procedures for minimizing loss of life or injury when a threat occurs. The human resources team is responsible for contacting all personnel in the event of a disaster. Contact information for all personnel should be stored onsite and offsite. Multiple members of the HR team should have access to the personnel contact information. Remember that personnel safety is always the primary concern. All other resources should be protected only after the personnel are safe.

After the initial event is over, the HR team should monitor personnel morale and guard against employee stress and burnout during the recovery period. If proper cross-training has occurred, multiple personnel can be rotated in during the recovery process. Any DRP should take into consideration the need to provide adequate periods of rest for any personnel involved in the disaster recovery process. It should also include guidelines on how to deal with situations where any personnel fall victims of a disaster.

The organization must ensure that salaries and other funding to personnel continue during and after the disaster. Because funding can be critical both for personnel and for resource purchases, authorized, signed checks should be securely stored offsite. Lower-level management with the appropriate access controls should have the ability to disperse funds using these checks in the event that senior management is unavailable.

An executive succession plan should also be created to ensure that the organization follows the appropriate steps to protect itself and continue operation.

Supplies

Often disasters affect the ability to supply an organization with its needed resources, including paper, cabling, and even water. The organization should document any resources that are vital to its daily operations and the vendors from which these resources can be obtained. Because supply vendors can also be affected by the disaster, alternative suppliers should be identified.

Documentation

For disaster recovery to be a success, the personnel involved must be able to complete the appropriate recovery procedures. Although the documentation of all these procedures might be tedious, it is necessary to ensure that recovery occurs. In addition, each department within the organization should be asked to decide what departmental documentation is needed to carry out day-to-day operations. This documentation should be stored in a central location onsite, and a copy should be retained offsite also. Specific personnel should be tasked with ensuring that this documentation is created, stored, and updated as appropriate.

User Environment Recovery

All aspects of the end-user environment recovery must be included as part of the DRP to ensure that the end users can return to work as quickly as possible. As part of this user environment recovery, end-user notification must occur. Users must be notified of where and when to report after a disaster occurs.

The actual user environment recovery should occur in stages, with the most critical functions being restored first. User requirements should be documented to ensure that all aspects of the user environment are restored. For example, users in a critical department might all need their own client computers. These same users might also need to access an application that is located on a server. If the server is not restored, the users will be unable to perform their job duties even if their client computers are available.

Finally, manual steps that can be used for any function should be documented. Because we are so dependent on technology today, we often overlook the manual methods of performing our job tasks. Documenting these manual methods might ensure that operations can still occur, even if they occur at a decreased rate.

Data Recovery

In most organizations, the data is one of the most critical assets when recovering from a disaster. The BCPs and DRPs must include guidelines and procedures for recovering data. However, the operations teams must determine which data is backed up, how often the data is backed up, and the method of backup used. So although we discuss data backup, remember that BCP teams do not actually make any data backup decisions. The BCP teams are primarily concerned with ensuring that the data that is backed up can be restored in a timely manner.

Next, we discuss the data backup types and schemes that are used as well as electronic backup methods that organizations can implement.

Data Backup Types and Schemes

To design an appropriate data recovery solution, security professionals must understand the different types of data backups that can occur and how these backups are used together to restore the live environments.

For the CISSP exam, you must understand the following data backup types and schemes:

Key Topic

- Full backup
- Differential backup
- Incremental backup
- Copy backup
- Daily backup
- Transaction log backup
- First in, first out rotation scheme
- Grandfather/father/son rotation scheme

The three main data backups are full backups, differential backups, and incremental backups. To understand these three data backup types, you must understand the concept of archive bits. When a file is created or updated, the archive bit for the file is enabled. If the archive bit is cleared, the file will not be archived during the next backup. If the archive bit is enabled, the file will be archived during the next backup.

With a ***full backup***, all data is backed up. During the full backup process, the archive bit for each file is cleared. A full backup takes the longest time and the most space to complete. However, if an organization uses only full backups, then only the latest full backup needs to be restored. Any differential or incremental backup will first start with a full backup as its baseline. A full backup is the most appropriate for offsite archiving.

In a ***differential backup***, all files that have been changed since the last full backup will be backed up. During the differential backup process, the archive bit for each file is not cleared. A differential backup might vary from taking a short time and a small amount of space to growing in both the backup time and amount of space it needs over time. Each differential backup will back up all the files in the previous differential backup if a full backup has not occurred since that time. In an organization that uses a full/differential scheme, the full backup and only the most recent differential backup must be restored, meaning only two backups are needed.

An ***incremental backup*** backs up all files that have been changed since the last backup of any type. During the incremental backup process, the archive bit for each file is cleared. An incremental backup usually takes the least amount of time and space to complete. In an organization that uses a full/incremental scheme, the full backup and each subsequent incremental backup must be restored. The incremental backups must be restored in order. If your organization completes a full backup on Sunday and an incremental backup daily Monday through Saturday, up to seven backups could be needed to restore the data. Figure 7-9 compares the different types of backups.

Backup Type	Data Backed Up	Backup Time	Restore Time	Storage Space
Full Backup	All Data	Slowest	Fast	High
Incremental Backup	Only New/Modified Files/Folders	Fast	Moderate	Lowest
Differential Backup	All Data Since Last Full	Moderate	Fast	Moderate

Figure 7-9 Backup Types Comparison

Copy and daily backups are two special backup types that are not considered part of any regularly scheduled backup scheme because they do not require any other backup type for restoration. ***Copy backups*** are similar to normal backups but do not reset the file's archive bit. ***Daily backups*** use a file's timestamp to determine whether it needs archiving. Daily backups are popular in mission-critical environments where multiple daily backups are required because files are updated constantly.

Transaction log backups are used only in environments where capturing all transactions that have occurred since the last backup is important. Transaction log backups help organizations to recover to a particular point in time and are most commonly used in database environments.

Although magnetic tape drives are still used to back up data, organizations today may back up their data to optical discs, including CD-ROMs, DVDs, and Blu-ray discs; high-capacity, high-speed magnetic drives; flash-based media; or even network storage. No matter the media used, retaining backups both onsite and offsite is important. Store onsite backup copies in a waterproof, heat-resistant, fire-resistant safe or vault.

Electronic Backup

Electronic backup solutions back up data more quickly and more accurately than the normal data backups and are best implemented when information changes often.

For the CISSP exam, you should be familiar with the following electronic backup terms and solutions:

- ***Electronic vaulting***: Copies files as modifications occur. This method occurs in real time.
- **Remote journaling:** Copies the journal or transaction log offsite on a regular schedule. This method occurs in batches.
- **Tape vaulting:** Creates backups over a direct communication line on a backup system at an offsite facility.
- **Hierarchical storage management (HSM):** Stores frequently accessed data on faster media and less frequently accessed data on slower media.
- **Optical jukebox:** Stores data on optical disks and uses robotics to load and unload the optical disks as needed. This method is ideal when 24/7 availability is required.
- **Replication:** Copies data from one storage location to another. Synchronous replication uses constant data updates to ensure that the locations are close to the same, whereas asynchronous replication delays updates to a predefined schedule.

Many companies use cloud backup or replication solutions. Any organization considering a cloud solution should research the full security implications of this type of deployment.

Training Personnel

Even if an organization takes the steps to develop the most thorough BCPs and DRPs, these plans are useless if the organization's personnel do not have the skills to completely recover the organization's assets when a disaster occurs. Personnel should be given the appropriate time and monetary resources to ensure that adequate training occurs. This includes allowing personnel to test any DRPs.

Training should be obtained from both internal and external sources. When job duties change or new personnel are hired, policies should be in place to ensure the appropriate transfer of knowledge occurs.

Backup Storage Strategies

As part of any backup plan, an organization should also consider the backup storage strategy or rotation scheme that it will use. Cost considerations and storage considerations often dictate that backup media is reused after a period of time. If this reuse is not planned in advance, media can become unreliable due to overuse. Two of the most popular backup rotation schemes are first in, first out and grandfather/father/son.

In the ***first in, first out (FIFO)*** scheme, the newest backup is saved to the oldest media. Although this is the simplest rotation scheme, it does not protect against data errors. If an error in data exists, the organization might not have a version of the data that does not contain the error.

In the ***grandfather/father/son (GFS)*** scheme, three sets of backups are defined. Most often these three definitions are daily, weekly, and monthly. The daily backups are the sons, the weekly backups are the fathers, and the monthly backups are the grandfathers. Each week, one son advances to the father set. Each month, one father advances to the grandfather set.

Figure 7-10 displays a typical 5-day GFS rotation using 21 backup media. The daily backups are usually differential or incremental backups. The weekly and monthly backups must be a full backup.

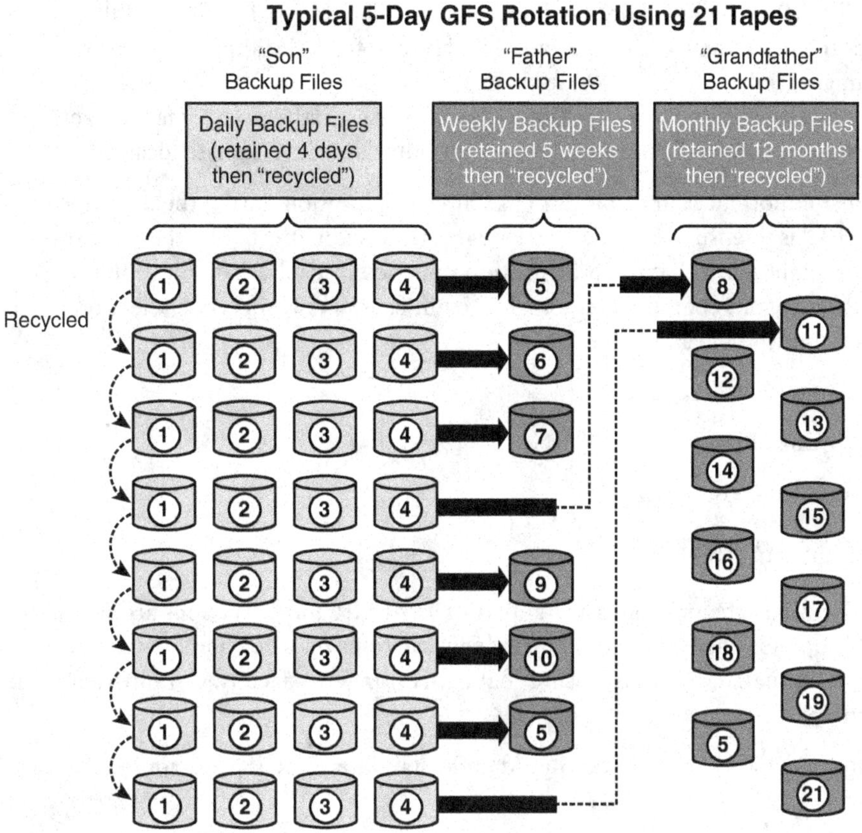

Figure 7-10 Grandfather/Father/Son Backup Rotation Scheme

Once the rotation scheme is determined, security professionals should work with other IT staff to determine which backups will be stored onsite, offsite, or in the cloud. Keep in mind that the availability and restorability of any onsite backups can be affected by incidents at the primary site and the duration of the incident. Offsite storage should be far enough away as to not be affected by the same incidents or in a more protected environment, such as a safe. Cloud storage is an excellent alternative, but requires an Internet connection for access.

Recovery and Multiple Site Strategies

When dealing with an event that either partially or fully destroys the primary facility, the organization will need an alternate location from which to operate until the primary facility is restored. The DRP should define the alternate location and its recovery procedures, often referred to as a recovery site strategy.

The DRP should include not only how to bring the alternate location to full operation but also how the organization will return from the alternate location to the primary facility after it is restored. Also, for security purposes, the DRP should include details on the security controls that were used at the primary facility and guidelines on how to implement these same controls at the alternate location.

The most important factor in locating an alternate location during the development of the DRP is to ensure that the alternate location is not affected by the same disaster. This might mean that the organization must select an alternate location that is in another city or geographic region. The main factors that affect the selection of an alternate location include the following:

- Geographic location
- Organizational needs
- Location's cost
- Location's restoration effort

Testing an alternate location is a vital part of any DRP. Some locations are easier to test than others. The DRP should include instructions on when and how to periodically test alternate facilities to ensure that the contingency facility is compatible with the primary facility.

The alternate locations that you should understand for the CISSP exam include the following:

- Hot site
- Cold site
- Warm site
- Tertiary site
- Reciprocal agreements
- Redundant sites
- Resource capacity agreement

Hot Site

A ***hot site*** is a leased facility that contains all the resources needed for full operation. This environment includes computers, raised flooring, full utilities, electrical and communications wiring, networking equipment, and UPSs. The only resource that must be restored at a hot site is the organization's data, often only partially. It should take only a few minutes to hours to bring a hot site to full operation.

Although a hot site provides the quickest recovery, it is the most expensive to maintain due to the ready-to-use asset conditions. In addition, it can be administratively hard to manage if the organization requires proprietary hardware or software. A hot site requires the same security controls as the primary facility and full redundancy, including hardware, software, and communication wiring.

Cold Site

A ***cold site*** is a leased facility that contains only electrical and communications wiring, air conditioning, plumbing, and raised flooring. No communications equipment, networking hardware, or computers are installed at a cold site until it is necessary to bring the site to full operation. For this reason, a cold site takes much longer to bring to full operation than a hot or warm site.

Although a cold site provides the slowest recovery, it is the least expensive to maintain. It is also the most difficult to test.

Warm Site

A ***warm site*** is a leased facility that contains electrical and communications wiring, full utilities, and networking equipment. In most cases, the only devices that are not included in a warm site are the computers. A warm site takes longer to restore than a hot site but less than a cold site.

A warm site is somewhere between the restoration time and cost of a hot site and cold site. It is the most widely implemented alternate leased location. Although testing a warm site is easier than testing a cold site, a warm site requires much more effort for testing than a hot site.

Figure 7-11 compares the components deployed in these three sites.

Key Topic

	Hot Site	Warm Site	Cold Site
Electrical Connection	Yes	Yes	Yes
Peripherals	Yes	Some	None
Networking	Yes	None	None
Servers and Other Hardware	Yes	None	None
Applications	Yes	None	None

Figure 7-11 Hot Site, Warm Site, and Cold Site Comparison

Tertiary Site

A ***tertiary site*** is a secondary backup site that provides an alternate in case the hot site, warm site, or cold site is unavailable. Many large companies implement tertiary sites to protect against catastrophes that affect large geographic areas.

For example, if an organization requires a data center that is located on the coast, the organization might have its primary location in New Orleans, Louisiana, and its hot site in Mobile, Alabama. This organization might consider locating a tertiary site in Omaha, Nebraska, because a hurricane can affect both the Louisiana and Alabama Gulf coast.

Reciprocal Agreements

A ***reciprocal agreement*** is an agreement between two organizations that have similar technological needs and infrastructures. In the agreement, both organizations agree to act as an alternate location for the other if either one of the organization's primary facilities is rendered unusable. Unfortunately in most cases, these agreements are hard to enforce due to various legalities.

A disadvantage of this alternate site is that it might not be capable of handling the required workload and operations of the other organization.

NOTE A mutual-aid agreement is a prearranged agreement between two organizations in which each organization agrees to provide assistance to the other in the event of a disaster.

Redundant Sites

A ***redundant site*** (or mirrored site) is one that is identically configured as the primary site. A redundant or mirrored site is not a leased site but is usually owned by the same organization that owns the primary site. The organization is responsible for maintaining the redundant site. Multiple processing sites can also be configured to serve as operationally redundant sites.

Although redundant sites are expensive to maintain, many organizations today see them as a necessary expense to ensure that uninterrupted service can be provided.

Resource Capacity Agreement

A resource capacity agreement is a formal agreement or contract that specifies the resources and services provided by a disaster recovery (DR) site in the event of a primary site failure or disaster. These resources can include hardware, software, networking equipment, and facilities necessary to restore and continue business operations. This agreement is crucial for ensuring that the recovery site has the minimum capacity to meet the organization's needs during a disaster recovery operation.

Resource capacity agreements should include clauses that cover the following:

- Availability of Resources: The agreement defines the specific resources that will be available to the organization in the event of a disaster. This includes computing power, storage capacity, network bandwidth, and any other critical infrastructure components required for recovery.
- Service Levels: It outlines the service levels or performance metrics that the recovery site must meet, such as recovery time objectives (RTOs) and recovery point objectives (RPOs). These metrics are essential for planning and executing a successful recovery strategy.
- Costs and Fees: The agreement details the costs associated with activating and using the recovery site, including any fees for maintaining standby resources or for actual usage during a disaster recovery operation.
- Roles and Responsibilities: It specifies the responsibilities of both the organization and the recovery site provider, including who is responsible for managing the recovery process, restoring data, and ensuring the continuity of operations.
- Duration and Terms: The duration of the agreement and the terms under which it can be activated, extended, or terminated are clearly defined. This includes conditions under which the agreement can be reviewed and updated to reflect changes in the organization's requirements or the provider's offerings.
- Testing and Auditing: The agreement may include provisions for regular testing and auditing of the recovery site's capabilities to ensure that it can meet the agreed-upon service levels and resource requirements in the event of a disaster. In most cases, the type of testing that must be completed is specifically mentioned in the agreement.

Resource capacity agreements are critical for ensuring that an organization can recover from a disaster with minimal downtime and data loss, and they play a key role in risk management and mitigation strategies. Security professionals must be familiar with the components of such agreements and how they fit into the broader context of recovery site strategies, including hot sites, cold sites, and warm sites, as well as how they align with the organization's overall business continuity and disaster recovery objectives.

Redundant Systems, Facilities, and Power

In anticipation of disasters and disruptive events, organizations should implement redundancy for critical systems, facilities, and power and assess any systems that have been identified as critical to determine whether implementing redundant systems is cost effective. Implementing redundant systems at an alternate location often ensures that services are uninterrupted. Redundant systems include redundant servers, redundant routers, redundant internal hardware, and even redundant backbones. Redundancy occurs when an organization has a secondary component, system, or device that takes over when the primary unit fails.

Redundant facilities ensure that the organization maintains a facility at whatever level it chooses to ensure that the organizational services can continue when a disruptive event occurs.

Power redundancy is implemented using uninterruptible power supplies (UPSs) and power generators.

Redundancy on individual components can also be provided. The spare components are either cold spares, warm spares, or hot spares. A cold spare is not powered up but can be inserted into the system if needed. A warm spare is in the system but does not have power unless needed. A hot spare is in the system and powered on, ready to become operational at a moment's notice.

Fault-Tolerance Technologies

Fault tolerance enables a system to continue operation in the event of the failure of one or more components. Fault tolerance within a system can include fault-tolerant adapter cards and fault-tolerant storage drives. One of the most well-known fault-tolerant systems is RAID, which is discussed earlier in this chapter.

By implementing fault-tolerant technologies, an organization can ensure that normal operation occurs if a single fault-tolerant component fails.

Insurance

Although redundancy and fault tolerance can actually act as preventive measures against failures, insurance is not really a preventive measure. If an organization purchases insurance to provide protection in the event of a disruptive event, the insurance has no power to protect against the event itself. The purpose of the insurance is to ensure that the organization will have access to additional financial resources to help in the recovery.

Keep in mind that recovery efforts from a disruptive event can often incur large financial costs. Even some of the best estimates might still fall short when the actual recovery must take place. By purchasing insurance, the organization can ensure that key financial transactions, including payroll, accounts payable, and any recovery costs, are covered.

Insurance actual cost valuation (ACV) compensates property based on the value of the item on the date of loss plus 10 percent. Insurance also considers depreciation unless the insurance is for the actual cost of resources. However, keep in mind that insurance on any printed materials covers only inscribed, printed, or written documents, manuscripts, or records. It does not cover money and securities. A special type of insurance called *business interruption insurance* provides monetary protection for expenses and lost earnings.

Organizations should annually review insurance policies and update them as necessary.

Data Backup

Data backup provides prevention against data loss but not prevention against disruptive events. All organizations should ensure that all systems that store important files are backed up in a timely manner. Users should also be encouraged to back up personal files that they might need. In addition, periodic testing of the restoration process should occur to ensure that the files can be restored.

Data recovery, including backup types and schemes and electronic backup, was covered in detail earlier in this chapter.

Fire Detection and Suppression

Organizations should implement fire detection and suppression systems as part of any BCP. Fire detection and suppression systems vary based on the method of detection/suppression used and are discussed in greater detail in the "Environmental Security and Issues" section of Chapter 3.

High Availability

High availability in data recovery is a concept which ensures that data is always available using redundancy and fault tolerance. Most organizations implement high-availability solutions as part of any DRP.

High-availability terms and techniques that you must understand include the following:

- **Redundant Array of Independent Disks (RAID):** A hard-drive technology in which data is written across multiple disks in such a way that a disk can fail and the data can be quickly made available from the remaining disks in the array without restoring from a backup tape or other backup media.

- ***Storage-area network (SAN)*****:** High-capacity storage (several petabytes) devices that are connected by a high-speed private network using storage-specific switches.
- ***Failover*****:** The capacity of a system to switch over to a backup system if a failure in the primary system occurs.
- ***Failsoft*****:** The capability of a system to terminate noncritical processes when a failure occurs.
- **Clustering:** A capability of a software product that provides load-balancing services. With clustering, one instance of an application server acts as a master controller and distributes requests to multiple instances using round-robin, weighted round-robin, or least-connections algorithms.
- **Load balancing:** A capability of a hardware product that provides load-balancing services. Application delivery controllers (ADCs) support the same algorithms but also use complex number-crunching processes, such as per-server CPU and memory utilization, fastest response times, and so on, to adjust the balance of the load. Load-balancing solutions are also referred to as farms or pools.

Quality of Service

Quality of service (QoS) is a technology that manages network resources to ensure a predefined level of service. It assigns traffic priorities to the different types of traffic or protocols on a network. QoS deploys when a bottleneck occurs and decides which traffic is more important than the rest. Exactly what traffic is more important than other traffic is based on rules the administrator supplies. Importance can be based on IP address, MAC address, and even service name. However, QoS works only when a bottleneck occurs in the appropriate location and the settings are bandwidth declarations. For example, if the QoS settings are set beyond the ISP's bandwidth, traffic will not be prioritized if a router thinks there is enough available bandwidth. But what if the ISP's maximums are being met, and the ISP decides what is or is not important? The key to any QoS deployment is to tweak the settings and observe the network over time.

System Resilience

System resilience is the ability of a system, device, or data center to recover quickly and continue operating after an equipment failure, a power outage, or another disruption. It involves the use of redundant components or facilities. When one component fails or is disrupted, the redundant component takes over seamlessly and continues to provide services to the users.

Disaster Recovery

Disaster recovery involves restoring services and systems from a contingency state, or the temporary state that operations may be in where they are running but not at the primary facility or on the optimum resources. The DRP is discussed in detail in Chapter 1. In this chapter, we discuss the disaster recovery process further, in terms of response, personnel, communications, assessment, restoration, and training and awareness.

Response

After an event has occurred, the appropriate personnel should be contacted to initiate the communications that alert the appropriate recovery team and the affected personnel of the event. All the teams listed in the personnel section then need to perform their duties. A process hierarchy must be developed so that each team performs its duties as part of the disaster recovery process in the correct order.

Personnel

Although the number one and number two priorities when a disaster occurs are personnel safety and health and damage mitigation, respectively, recovering from a disaster quickly becomes an organization's priority after these two are handled. However, no organization can recover from a disaster if the personnel are not properly trained and prepared. To ensure that personnel can perform their duties during disaster recovery, they must know and understand their job tasks.

During any disaster recovery, financial management is important. Financial management usually includes the chief financial officer and any other key accounting personnel. This group must track the recovery costs and assess the cash flow projections. They formally notify any insurers of claims that will be made. Finally, this group is responsible for establishing payroll continuance guidelines, procurement procedures, and emergency costs tracking procedures.

Organizations must decide which teams are needed during a disaster recovery and ensure that the appropriate personnel are placed on each of these teams. The disaster recovery manager directs the short-term recovery actions immediately following a disaster.

Organizations might need to implement the following teams to provide the appropriate support for the DRP:

- Damage assessment team
- Legal team
- Media relations team

- Recovery team
- Relocation team
- Restoration team
- Salvage team
- Security team

Damage Assessment Team

The damage assessment team is responsible for determining the disaster's cause and the amount of damage that has occurred to organizational assets. It identifies all affected assets and the critical assets' functionality after the disaster. The damage assessment team determines which assets will need to be restored and replaced and contacts the appropriate teams that need to be activated.

Legal Team

The legal team deals with all legal issues immediately following the disaster and during the disaster recovery. The legal team oversees any public relations events that are held to address the disaster, although the media relations team will actually deliver the message. The legal team should be consulted to ensure that all recovery operations adhere to federal and state laws and regulations.

Media Relations Team

The media relations team informs the public, personnel, and media whenever emergencies extend beyond the organization's facilities according to the guidelines given in the DRP. The emergency press conference site should be planned ahead. When issuing public statements, the media relations team should be honest and accurate about what is known about the event and its effects. The organization's response to the media during and after the event should be unified.

A credible, knowledgeable, experienced, and informed spokesperson appointed by the company should deliver the organization's response. When dealing with the media after a disaster, the spokesperson should report bad news before the media discovers it through another channel. Anyone making disaster announcements to the public should understand that the audience for such announcements includes the media, unions, stakeholders, neighbors, employees, contractors, and even competitors.

Recovery Team

The recovery team's primary task is recovering the critical business functions at the alternate facility. This task mostly involves ensuring that the physical assets are in place, including computers and other devices, wiring, and so on. The recovery team usually oversees the relocation and restoration teams.

Relocation Team

The relocation team oversees the actual transfer of assets between locations. This task includes moving assets from the primary site to the alternate site and then returning those assets when the primary site is ready for operation.

Restoration Team

The restoration team actually ensures that the assets and data are restored to operations. The restoration team needs access to the backup media.

Salvage Team

The salvage team recovers all assets at the disaster location and ensures that the primary site returns to normal if this is possible. The salvage team manages the cleaning of equipment, oversees the rebuilding of the original facility if possible, and identifies any experts to employ in the recovery process. In most cases, the salvage team can decide when operations at the disaster site can resume.

Security Team

The security team is responsible for managing the security at both the disaster site and any alternate location that the organization uses during the recovery. Because the geographic area that the security team must manage after the disaster is often much larger, the security team might need to hire outside contractors to aid in this process. Using these outside contractors to guard the physical access to the sites and internal resources to provide security inside the facilities is always a better approach because the reduced state might make issuing the appropriate access credentials to contractors difficult.

Communications

Communication during disaster recovery is important to ensure that the organization recovers in a timely manner. It is also important to ensure that no steps are omitted and that the steps occur in the correct order. Communication with personnel depends on who is being contacted about the disaster. Personnel who are affected by a disaster should receive communications that list the affected systems, the projected outage time, and any contingencies they should follow in the meantime. The different disaster recovery teams should receive communications that pertain to their duties during the recovery from the disaster.

Communications methods should include both a primary and secondary communication method, including phone calls, emails, and text messages, as not all methods of communication may be readily available, depending on what has occurred. Security professionals should ensure that the organization documents and regularly updates the methods whereby personnel are contacted. Because issues could occur with Internet access, traditional land line access should be documented if available.

During recovery, security professionals should work closely with the different teams to ensure that all assets remain secure. All teams involved in the process should also communicate often with each other to update each other on the progress.

Assessment

When an event occurs, personnel need to assess the event's severity and impact. Doing so ensures that the appropriate response is implemented. Most organizations establish event categories, including nonincident, incident, and severe incident. Each organization should have a disaster recovery assessment process in place to ensure that personnel properly assess each event.

Restoration

The restoration process involves restoring the primary systems and facilities to normal operation. The personnel involved in this process depend on the assets that were affected by the event. Any teams involved in the recovery of assets should carefully coordinate their recovery efforts. Without careful coordination, recovery could be negatively impacted. For example, if full recovery of a web application requires that the database servers be operational, the database administrator must work closely with the web application and system administrators to ensure that both web applications and computer servers are returned to normal function.

Training and Awareness

Personnel at all levels need to be given the proper training on the disaster recovery process. Regular users just need to be given awareness training so that they understand the complexity of the process. Leadership needs training on how to lead the organization during a crisis. Technical teams need training on the recovery procedures and logistics. Security professionals need training on how to protect assets during recovery.

Most organizations include business continuity and disaster recovery awareness training as part of the initial training given to personnel when they are hired. Organizations should also periodically update personnel to ensure that they do not forget about disaster recovery.

Lessons Learned

Documenting lessons learned is the process of gathering information that reflects both the positive and negative experiences of a project, incident, or disaster recovery effort. The purpose of documenting lessons learned at the end of a disaster is to use the lessons to refine the disaster recovery plan and to provide future disaster recovery teams with information to increase efficiency.

By properly documenting these lessons, team members ensure that their experiences are carried forward to aid future teams.

NOTE Business continuity and disaster recovery are covered in more detail in Chapter 1.

Testing Disaster Recovery Plans

After the BCP is fully documented, an organization must take measures to ensure that the plan is maintained and kept up to date. At a minimum, an organization must evaluate and modify the BCP and DRP on an annual basis. This evaluation usually involves some sort of test to ensure that the plans are accurate and thorough. Testing frequently is important because any plan is not viable unless testing has occurred. Organizations should stipulate how often and what type of testing should occur. Through testing, inaccuracies, deficiencies, and omissions are detected.

Testing the BCP and DRP prepares and trains personnel to perform their duties. It also ensures that the alternate backup site can perform as needed. When testing occurs, the test is probably flawed if no issues with the plan are found.

Communications regarding disaster recovery testing are crucial. Management will need a full report of any findings obtained during the disaster recovery test. Stakeholders will likely need fewer details than company management. Regulators may also need a report of the findings of the disaster recovery test. The test status should be included as part of any testing report (for example, test completed, test in progress, test unsuccessful). Keep in mind the audience for any report and their needs, as reports to different audiences likely need to contain different details.

The types of tests that are commonly used to assess the BCP and DRP include the following:

Key Topic

- Read-through test
- Checklist test
- Table-top exercise
- Structured walk-through test
- Simulation test
- Parallel test
- Full-interruption test
- Functional drill
- Evacuation drill

Read-Through Test

A ***read-through test*** involves the teams that are part of any recovery plan. These teams read through the plan that has been developed and attempt to identify any inaccuracies or omissions in the plan.

Checklist Test

The ***checklist test*** occurs when managers of each department or functional area review the BCP. These managers make note of any modifications to the plan. The BCP committee then uses all the management notes to make changes to the BCP.

Table-Top Exercise

A ***table-top exercise*** is the most cost-effective and efficient way to identify areas of overlap in the plan before conducting higher-level testing. A table-top exercise is an informal brainstorming session that encourages participation from business leaders and other key employees. In a table-top exercise, the participants are given roles and responsibilities and agree to a particular disaster scenario on which they will focus.

Structured Walk-Through Test

The ***structured walk-through test*** involves representatives of each department or functional area thoroughly reviewing the BCP's accuracy. This type of test is the most important one to perform prior to a live disaster.

Simulation Test

In a ***simulation test***, the operations and support personnel execute the DRP in a role-playing scenario. This test identifies omitted steps and threats.

Parallel Test

A ***parallel test*** involves bringing the recovery site to a state of operational readiness but maintaining operations at the primary site.

Full-Interruption Test

A ***full-interruption test*** involves shutting down the primary facility and bringing the alternate facility up to full operation. This is a hard switchover in which all processing occurs at the primary facility until the "switch" is thrown. Switchover should be close to immediate. This type of test requires full coordination between all the parties and includes notifying users in advance of the planned test. An organization should perform this type of test only when all other tests have been implemented and are successful.

Functional Drill

A functional drill tests a single function or department to see whether the function's DRP is complete. This type of drill requires the participation of the personnel who perform the function.

Evacuation Drill

In an evacuation drill, personnel follow the evacuation or shelter-in-place guidelines for a particular disaster type. In this type of drill, personnel must understand the area to which they are to report when the evacuation occurs. All personnel at the facility being tested should be accounted for at that time.

Business Continuity Planning and Exercises

After a test is complete, all test results should be documented, and the plans should be modified to reflect those results. The list of successful and unsuccessful activities from the tests will be the most useful to management when maintaining the BCP. All obsolete information in the plans should be deleted, and any new information should be added. In addition, modifying current information based on new regulations, laws, or protocols might be necessary.

Version control of the plans should be managed to ensure that the organization always uses the most recent version. In addition, the BCP should be stored in multiple locations to ensure that it is available if a location is destroyed by the disaster. Multiple personnel should have the latest version of the plans to ensure that the plans can be retrieved if primary personnel are unavailable when the plan is needed.

Physical Security

Physical security involves using the appropriate security controls to protect all assets from physical access. Perimeter security involves implementing the appropriate perimeter security controls, including gates and fences, perimeter intrusion detection, lighting, patrol force, and access control, to prevent access to the perimeter of a facility. Building and internal security involves implementing the appropriate building and internal security controls.

Key Topic

Perimeter Security Controls

When considering the perimeter security of a facility, taking a holistic approach, sometimes known as the *concentric circle* approach, is sometimes helpful (see Figure 7-12). This approach relies on creating layers of physical barriers to information.

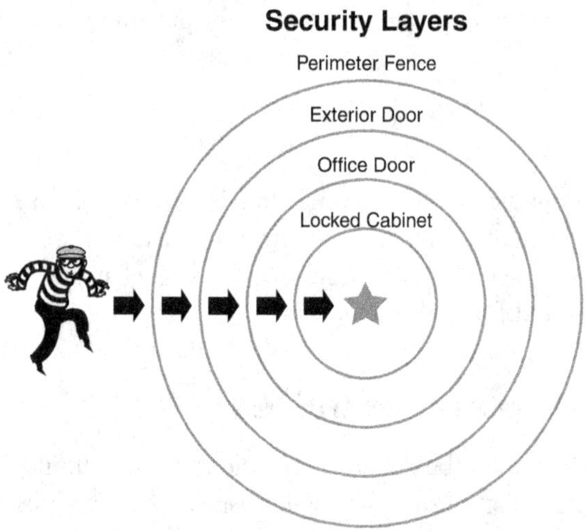

Figure 7-12 Concentric Circle Approach

Next, we look at implementing this concept in detail.

Gates and Fences

The outermost ring in the concentric circle approach is composed of the gates and fences that surround the facility. Within that are interior circles of physical barriers, each of which has its own set of concerns. Here, we cover considerations for barriers (bollards), fences, gates, and walls.

Bollards

Barriers called ***bollards*** have become quite common around the perimeter of new office and government buildings. These short vertical posts placed at the building's entrance way and lining sidewalks help to provide protection from vehicles that might either intentionally or unintentionally crash into or enter the building or injure pedestrians. They can be made of many types of materials. The ones shown in Figure 7-13 are stainless steel.

Figure 7-13 Stainless Steel Bollards

Fences

Fencing is the first line of defense in the concentric circle paradigm. When selecting the type of fencing to install, consider the determination of the individuals you are trying to discourage from entry. Use the following guidelines with respect to height:

- Fences 3 to 4 feet tall deter only casual intruders.
- Fences 6 to 7 feet tall are too tall to climb easily.
- Fences 8 feet and taller deter more determined intruders, especially when these fences are augmented with razor wire.

A geo-fence is a geographic area within which devices are managed using some sort of radio frequency communication. For example, a geo-fence could be set up in a radius around a store or point location or within a predefined set of boundaries, such as around a school zone. It is used to track users or devices entering or leaving the geo-fence area. Alerts could be configured to message the device's user and the geo-fence operator of the device's location.

Gates

Gates can be weak points in a fence if not handled correctly. Gates are rated by the Underwriters Laboratory (UL) in the following way. Each step up in class requires additional levels of protection:

- ***Class 1 gate*:** Residential use
- ***Class 2 gate*:** Commercial usage
- ***Class 3 gate*:** Industrial usage
- ***Class 4 gate*:** Restricted area

Walls

In some cases, walls might be called for around a facility. When that is the case, and when perimeter security is critical, perimeter intrusion detection systems, discussed next, can be deployed to alert security personnel of any breaching of the walls.

Perimeter Intrusion Detection

Regardless of whether an organization uses fences or walls, or even decides to deploy neither of these impediments, it can significantly reduce exposure by deploying one of the following types of perimeter intrusion detection systems. All the systems described next are considered physical intrusion detection methods.

Infrared Sensors

Passive infrared (PIR) systems operate by identifying changes in heat waves in an area. Because the presence of an intruder would raise the temperature of the surrounding air particles, this system alerts or sounds an alarm when this occurs.

Electromechanical Systems

Electromechanical systems operate by detecting a break in an electrical circuit. For example, the circuit might cross a window or door and when the window or door is opened, the circuit is broken, setting off an alarm of some sort. Another example might be a pressure pad placed under the carpet to detect the presence of individuals.

Photoelectric Systems

Photometric systems (or photoelectric systems) operate by detecting changes in the light and thus are used in windowless areas. They send a beam of light across the area, and if the beam is interrupted (by a person or a stray animal, for example), the alarm is triggered.

Acoustical Detection Systems

Acoustical systems use strategically placed microphones to detect any sound made during a forced entry. These systems work well only in areas where there is not a lot of surrounding noise. They are typically very sensitive, which would cause many false alarms in a loud area, such as a door next to a busy street.

Wave Motion Detector

Wave motion devices generate a wave pattern in the area and detect any motion that disturbs the wave pattern. When the pattern is disturbed, an alarm sounds.

Capacitance Detector

Capacitance detectors emit a magnetic field and monitor that field. If the field is disrupted, which will occur when a person enters the area, the alarm will sound.

CCTV

A ***closed-circuit television (CCTV) system*** uses sets of cameras that can either be monitored in real time or can record days' worth of activity that can be viewed as needed at a later time. In very high-security facilities, these systems are usually monitored. One of the main benefits of using CCTV is that it increases a guard's visual capabilities. Guards can monitor larger areas at once from a central location. CCTV is a category of physical surveillance, not computer/network surveillance.

Camera types include outdoor, infrared, fixed-position, pan/tilt, dome, and Internet Protocol (IP) cameras. When implementing cameras, organizations need to select the appropriate lens, resolution, frames per second (FPS), and compression. In addition, analysis of the lighting requirements of the different cameras must be understood; a CCTV system should work in the amount of light that the location provides. In addition, an organization must understand the different types of monitor displays, including single-image, split-screen, and large-format displays. Finally, storage space will be required, whether the videos are digital format and stored on a server or physical format and stored on physical tapes. Storage can be a particular concern when continuous monitoring is implemented.

NOTE Organizations need to post alerts in prominent locations informing individuals within the facility that they are being recorded by CCTV.

Lighting

One of the best ways to deter crime and mischief is to shine a light on areas of concern. Next, we look at some types of lighting and some lighting systems that have proven to be effective. Lighting is considered a physical control for physical security.

Types of Systems

The security professional must be familiar with several types of lighting systems:

- **Continuous lighting:** An array of lights that provide an even amount of illumination across an area.
- ***Standby lighting*:** A type of system that illuminates only at certain times or on a schedule.
- ***Movable lighting*:** Lighting that can be repositioned as needed.
- ***Emergency lighting*:** Lighting systems with their own power source to use when power is out.

Types of Lighting

A number of options are available when choosing the illumination source or type of light. The following are the most common choices:

- ***Fluorescent*:** A very low-pressure mercury-vapor gas-discharge lamp that uses fluorescence to produce visible light.
- ***Mercury vapor*:** A gas-discharge lamp that uses an electric arc through vaporized mercury to produce light.
- ***Sodium vapor*:** A gas-discharge lamp that uses sodium in an excited state to produce light.
- ***Quartz lamp*:** A lamp consisting of an ultraviolet light source, such as mercury vapor, contained in a fused-silica bulb that transmits ultraviolet light with little absorption.
- ***Light-emitting diode (LED)*:** Consumes less power. Brighter and longer-working than other options.

Regardless of the light source, it will be rated by its ***feet of illumination***. When positioning the lights, you must take this rating into consideration. For example, if a controlled light fixture mounted on a 5-meter pole can illuminate an area 30 meters in diameter, for security lighting purposes, the distance between the fixtures should be 30 feet. Moreover, there should be extensive exterior perimeter lighting of entrances or parking areas to discourage prowlers or casual intruders.

Patrol Force

An excellent augmentation to all other detection systems is the presence of a guard patrolling the facility. This option offers the most flexibility in reacting to whatever occurs. One of the keys to success is adequate training of guards so that they are prepared for any eventuality. There should be a prepared response for any possible occurrence. One of the main benefits of this approach is that guards can use discriminating judgment based on the situation, which automated systems cannot do.

The patrol force can be internally hired, trained, and controlled or can be outsourced to a contract security company. An organization can control the training and performance of an internal patrol force. However, some organizations outsource the patrol force to ensure impartiality and cost savings.

Access Control

When physical access to the facility is granted, a number of guidelines should be followed with respect to recordkeeping. Every successful and unsuccessful attempt to enter or exit the facility, including those instances where admission was granted, should be recorded as follows:

- Date and time
- Specific entry point
- User ID employed during the attempt

Building and Internal Security Controls

Building and internal security involves the locks, keys, and escort requirements/visitor controls that organizations should consider. Building and internal security is covered in detail in Chapter 3.

Personnel Safety and Security

The human resources are the first priority for any organization to protect under all circumstances. In the event of a fire, the first action to always take is to evacuate all personnel. Their safety comes before all other considerations. Although equipment and, in most cases the data, can be recovered, human beings and their skillset can neither be backed up nor replaced.

An Occupant Emergency Plan (OEP) provides coordinated procedures for minimizing loss of life or injury and protecting property damage in response to a physical threat. In a disaster of any type, personnel safety is the first concern.

The organization is responsible for protecting the privacy of each individual's information, especially as it relates to personnel and medical records. Although this expectation of privacy does not necessarily and usually does not extend to their activities on the network, both federal and state laws hold organizations responsible for the release of this type of information, with violations resulting in heavy fines and potential lawsuits if the company is found liable.

Organizations should develop policies for dealing with employee duress, travel, monitoring, emergency management, and security training and awareness.

Duress

Employee ***duress*** occurs when an employee is coerced to commit an action by another party. This is a particular concern for high-level management or employees with high security clearances because they have access to extra assets. Organizations should train employees on what to do when under duress. For any security codes, PINs, or passwords that are used, it is a good policy to implement a secondary duress code. Then, if personnel are under duress, they use the duress code to access the systems, facilities, or other assets. Security personnel are alerted that the duress code has been used. Organizations should stress to personnel that the protection of life should trump any other considerations.

Employees can be both enticed and entrapped to commit actions against their employer. Here are examples of how employees could be enticed or entrapped by hackers:

- Enticement
    - Opportunities, such as investment schemes or job offers, to entice employees into disclosing sensitive information or performing unauthorized actions.
    - Exploiting employees' personal vulnerabilities or desires, such as offering fake promotions or career opportunities, to manipulate them into divulging confidential company information or compromising security controls.
- Entrapment
    - Coercive tactics, where hackers threaten employees with physical harm, financial loss, or reputational damage if they refuse to comply with their demands, forcing them to participate in criminal activities against their employer.
    - Blackmail or extortion schemes, where hackers obtain compromising information about employees through illicit means, such as hacking personal devices or social media accounts, and then use this information to coerce them into assisting with cyberattacks or providing access to company systems.
    - Manipulating employees into unwittingly aiding in cyberattacks by exploiting their lack of awareness or understanding of cybersecurity risks, such as using pretexting techniques to deceive them into disclosing sensitive information or executing malicious actions on behalf of the attacker.

In these scenarios, hackers exploit human vulnerabilities and psychological tactics to entice or entrap employees into aiding them in their malicious activities. It underscores the importance of cybersecurity awareness training for employees and implementing robust security measures to prevent such tactics from succeeding.

Travel

Employees often travel for business purposes and take their organization-issued assets while traveling. Employees must be given the proper training to ensure that they keep organization-issued assets safe during the travel period and to be particularly careful when in public. They should also receive instructions and training on properly reporting lost or stolen assets.

Monitoring

Employee actions on organizational assets may need to be monitored, particularly for personnel with high clearance levels. However, it is important that personnel understand that they are being monitored. Organizations that will monitor employees should issue a no-expectation-of-privacy statement. Employees should be given a copy of this statement when hired and should sign a receipt for the statement. In addition, periodic reminders of this policy should be placed in prominent locations, including on bulletin boards, login screens, and websites.

For any monitoring to be effective, organizations should capture baseline behavior for users.

Emergency Management

Organizations should have specific emergency management policies and procedures in place. Emergency management teams should be formed to document the types of emergencies that could occur and prepare the appropriate emergency plans to be used if a specific emergency occurs.

These plans should be periodically tested to ensure that personnel understand what to do in the event of an emergency and revised based on the results of these tests.

Emergencies that should be anticipated include weather events (such as tornadoes, hurricanes, and winter storms), active shooter situations, and power outages. Emergency management oftentimes leads to business continuity and disaster recovery if the effects of the emergency are long term. Emergency management is concerned with the immediate reaction to the emergency. While business continuity and disaster recovery are focused on the recovery of the organization to normal operations, not every emergency will require full disaster recovery. For example, if an organization is notified that a tornado warning has been issued, the organization should implement the emergency plan for tornadoes. If the tornado does not affect the facility, operations can return to normal as soon as the warning expires and the tornado passes. If the tornado affects the facility, however, it might be necessary to implement the business continuity and disaster recovery plans.

Security Training and Awareness

Personnel should receive security training and awareness regularly. Security training and awareness are covered in detail in Chapter 1.

Exam Preparation Tasks

As mentioned in the section "About the *CISSP Cert Guide*, Fifth Edition" in the Introduction, you have a couple of choices for exam preparation: the exercises here, Chapter 9, "Final Preparation," and the exam simulation questions in the Pearson Test Prep Software Online.

Review All Key Topics

Review the most important topics in this chapter, noted with the Key Topic icon in the outer margin of the page. Table 7-2 lists a reference of these key topics and the page numbers on which each is found.

Key Topic

Table 7-2 Key Topics for Chapter 7

Key Topic Element	Description	Page Number
List	Forensic investigation steps	675
List	Order of volatility	676
List	IOCE principles	679
List	Crime scene steps	679
List	Five rules of evidence	682
List	Types of evidence	683
List	Media analysis types	686
List	Software analysis techniques	686
List	Network analysis techniques	686
Section	Log Types	691
List	Functions of configuration management	698
Section	Security Operations Concepts	702
Table 7-1	RAID Levels	715
List	Incident response steps	721
List	Patch management life cycle steps	729
List	Data backup types and schemes	735
Figure 7-11	Hot Site, Warm Site, and Cold Site Comparison	741
List	Types of tests used to assess BCP and DRP	752
Section	Perimeter Security Controls	754

Define Key Terms

Define the following key terms from this chapter and check your answers in the glossary:

acoustical systems; artifact; asset; baselining; best evidence rule; blacklisting; bollards; chain of custody; checklist test; circumstantial evidence; civil investigation; Class 1 gate; Class 2 gate; Class 3 gate; Class 4 gate; clipping levels; closed-circuit television (CCTV) system; cold site; conclusive evidence; content analysis; continuous lighting; copy backup; corroborative evidence; crime scene; criminal investigation; daily backup; data clearing; data loss prevention (DLP) software; data purging; differential backup; direct evidence; disk imaging; duress; egress monitoring; electronic vaulting; emergency lighting; event; failover; failsoft; fault tolerance; feet of illumination; first in, first out (FIFO); fluorescent; full backup; full-interruption test; grandfather/father/son (GFS); graylisting; hearsay evidence; hierarchical storage management (HSM) system; high availability; honeynet; honeypot; hot site; incident; incremental backup; intangible assets; job rotation; least privilege; log management; means; mercury vapor; motive; movable lighting; need to know; network-attached storage (NAS); operations security; opinion evidence; opportunity; passive infrared (PIR) system; photometric system; quality of service (QoS); quartz lamp; parallel test; RAID 0; RAID 1; RAID 3; RAID 5; RAID 10; read-through test; reciprocal agreement; redundancy; redundant site; regulatory investigation; remanence; resource provisioning; sandboxing; search; seizure; secondary evidence; separation of duties; service-level agreement (SLA); simulation test; slack space analysis; sodium vapor; standby lighting; steganography analysis; storage-area network (SAN); structured walk-through test; surveillance; system resilience; table-top exercise; tangible assets; tertiary site; threat intelligence; threat intelligence feed (TI feed); threat feed; threat intelligence sources; threat hunting; transaction log backup; trusted path; trusted recovery; two-person control; user and entity behavior analytics (UEBA); user behavior analytics (UBA); warm site; whitelisting

Answer Review Questions

1. What is the first step of the incident response process?
   a. Respond to the incident.
   b. Detect the incident.
   c. Report the incident.
   d. Recover from the incident.

2. What is the second step of the forensic investigations process?
   a. Identification
   b. Collection
   c. Preservation
   d. Examination

3. Which of the following is *not* one of the five rules of evidence?
   a. Be accurate.
   b. Be complete.
   c. Be admissible.
   d. Be volatile.

4. Which of the following refers to allowing access to users only to the minimum resources required to do their jobs?
   a. Job rotation
   b. Separation of duties
   c. Least privilege
   d. Mandatory vacation

5. Which of the following is an example of an intangible asset?
   a. Disc drive
   b. Recipe
   c. People
   d. Windows server

6. Which of the following is *not* a step in incident response management?
   a. Detect
   b. Respond
   c. Monitor
   d. Report

7. Which of the following is *not* a backup type?
   a. Full
   b. Incremental
   c. Grandfather/father/son
   d. Transaction log

8. Which term is used for a facility that contains all the resources needed for full operation?
   a. Cold site
   b. Hot site
   c. Warm site
   d. Tertiary site

9. Which electronic backup type stores data on optical discs and uses robotics to load and unload the optical disks as needed?
   a. Optical jukebox
   b. Hierarchical storage management
   c. Tape vaulting
   d. Replication

10. What is failsoft?
    a. The capacity of a system to switch over to a backup system if a failure in the primary system occurs
    b. The capability of a system to terminate noncritical processes when a failure occurs
    c. A software product that provides load-balancing services
    d. High-capacity storage devices that are connected by a high-speed private network using storage-specific switches

11. An organization's firewall is monitoring the outbound flow of information from one network to another. What specific type of monitoring is this?
    a. Egress monitoring
    b. Continuous monitoring
    c. CMaaS
    d. Resource provisioning

12. Which of the following are considered virtual assets? (Choose all that apply.)
    a. Software-defined networks
    b. Virtual storage-area networks
    c. Guest OSs deployed on VMs
    d. Virtual routers

13. Which of the following describes the ability of a system, device, or data center to recover quickly and continue operating after an equipment failure, power outage, or other disruption?
    a. Quality of service (QoS)
    b. Recovery time objective (RTO)
    c. Recovery point objective (RPO)
    d. System resilience

14. Which of the following are the main factors that affect the selection of an alternate location during the development of a DRP? (Choose all that apply.)
    a. Geographic location
    b. Organizational needs
    c. Location's cost
    d. Location's restoration effort

15. Which of the following is a hard-drive technology in which data is written across multiple disks in such a way that when one disk fails, data can be made available from other functioning disks?
    a. RAID
    b. Clustering
    c. Failover
    d. Load balancing

16. You need to record incoming and outgoing network traffic information in order to determine the origin of an attack. Which of the following logs would be appropriate for this purpose?
    a. System log
    b. Application log
    c. Firewall log
    d. Change log

17. What should you perform on all information accepted into a system to ensure that it is of the right data type and format and that it does not place the system in an insecure state?
    a. Clipping levels
    b. Two-person control

c. Access review audits

d. Input validation

18. Which of the following defenses would you implement to discourage a determined intruder?

    a. 3 to 4 feet tall fence

    b. 6 to 7 feet tall fence

    c. 8 feet and taller fence

    d. Geo-fence

19. Which of the following actions could you perform to logically harden a system? (Choose all that apply.)

    a. Remove unnecessary applications.

    b. Disable unnecessary services.

    c. Block unused ports.

    d. Tightly control the connecting of external storage devices and media.

Answers and Explanations

1. **b.** The steps of the incident response process are as follows:

    1. Detect the incident.
    2. Respond to the incident.
    3. Report the incident to the appropriate personnel.
    4. Recover from the incident.
    5. Remediate all components affected by the incident to ensure that all traces of the incident have been removed.
    6. Review the incident and document all findings.

2. **c.** The steps of the forensic investigation process are as follows:

    1. Identification
    2. Preservation
    3. Collection
    4. Examination
    5. Analysis
    6. Presentation
    7. Decision

3. **d.** The five rules of evidence are as follows:
   - Be authentic.
   - Be accurate.
   - Be complete.
   - Be convincing.
   - Be admissible.
4. **c.** When security professionals allow access to resources and assign rights to perform operations, the concept of least privilege should always be applied. In the context of resource access, this means the default level of access should be no access. Users should be given access only to resources required to do their jobs, and that access should require manual implementation after the requirement is verified by a supervisor.
5. **b.** In many cases, some of the most valuable assets for a company are intangible ones, such as secret recipes, formulas, and trade secrets.
6. **c.** The steps in incident response management are
   1. Detect the incident.
   2. Respond to the incident.
   3. Mitigate the incident.
   4. Report the incident.
   5. Recover from the incident.
   6. Remediate the incident.
   7. Review and document lessons learned.
7. **c.** Grandfather/father/son is not a backup type; it is a backup rotation scheme.
8. **b.** A hot site is a leased facility that contains all the resources needed for full operation.
9. **a.** An optical jukebox stores data on optical discs and uses robotics to load and unload the optical discs as needed.
10. **b.** Failsoft is the capability of a system to terminate noncritical processes when a failure occurs.
11. **a.** Egress monitoring occurs when an organization monitors the outbound flow of information from one network to another. The most popular form of egress monitoring is carried out using firewalls that monitor and control outbound traffic. Continuous monitoring and Continuous Monitoring as a Service (CMaaS) are not specific enough to answer this question. Any logging and monitoring activities should be part of an organizational continuous monitoring program. The continuous monitoring program must be designed to

meet the needs of the organization and implemented correctly to ensure that the organization's critical infrastructure is guarded. Organizations may want to look into CMaaS solutions deployed by cloud service providers. Resource provisioning is the process in security operations that ensures that the organization deploys only the assets that it currently needs.

12. **a, b, c, d.** Virtual assets include software-defined networks (SDNs), virtual storage-area networks (VSANs), guest operating systems deployed on virtual machines (VMs), and virtual routers. As with physical assets, the deployment and decommissioning of virtual assets should be tightly controlled as part of configuration management because virtual assets, like physical assets, can be compromised.

13. **d.** System resilience is the ability of a system, device, or data center to recover quickly and continue operating after an equipment failure, power outage, or other disruption. It involves the use of redundant components or facilities. Quality of service (QoS) is a technology that manages network resources to ensure a predefined level of service. It assigns traffic priorities to the different types of traffic on a network. A recovery time objective (RTO) stipulates the amount of time an organization needs to recover from a disaster, and a recovery point objective (RPO) stipulates the amount of data an organization can lose when a disaster occurs.

14. **a, b, c, d.** The main factors that affect the selection of an alternate location during the development of a disaster recovery plan (DRP) include the following:

    - Geographic location
    - Organizational needs
    - Location's cost
    - Location's restoration effort

15. **a.** Redundant Array of Independent Disks (RAID) is a hard-drive technology in which data is written across multiple disks in such a way that a disk can fail and the data can be quickly made available from remaining disks in the array without restoring from a backup tape or other backup media. Clustering refers to a software product that provides load-balancing services. With clustering, one instance of an application server acts as a master controller and distributes requests to multiple instances using round-robin, weighted round-robin, or least-connections algorithms. Failover is the capacity of a system to switch over to a backup system if a failure in the primary system occurs. Load balancing refers to a hardware product that provides load-balancing services. Application delivery controllers (ADCs) support the same algorithms but also use complex number-crunching processes, such as per-server CPU and memory

utilization, fastest response times, and so on, to adjust the balance of the load. Load-balancing solutions are also referred to as farms or pools.

16. **c.** Firewall logs record network traffic information, including incoming and outgoing traffic. This usually includes important data, such as IP addresses and port numbers that can be used to determine the origin of an attack. System logs record system events, such as system and service startup and shutdown. Applications logs record actions that occur within a specific application. Change logs report changes made to a specific device or application as part of the change management process.

17. **d.** The main thrust of input/output control is to apply controls or checks to the input that is allowed to be submitted to the system. Performing input validation on all information accepted into the system can ensure that it is of the right data type and format and that it does not leave the system in an insecure state. Clipping levels set a baseline for normal user errors, and violations exceeding that threshold will be recorded for analysis of why the violations occurred. A two-person control, also referred to as a two-man rule, occurs when certain access and actions require the presence of two authorized people at all times. Access review audits ensure that object access and user account management practices adhere to the organization's security policy.

18. **c.** Fencing is the first line of defense in the concentric circle paradigm. When selecting the type of fencing to install, consider the determination of the individuals you are trying to discourage. Use the following guidelines with respect to height:

    - Fences 3 to 4 feet tall deter only casual intruders.
    - Fences 6 to 7 feet tall are too tall to climb easily.
    - Fences 8 feet and taller deter more determined intruders, especially when those fences are augmented with razor wire.

    A geo-fence is a geographic area within which devices are managed using some sort of radio frequency communication. It is used to track users or devices entering or leaving the geo-fence area.

19. **a, b, c, d.** An ongoing goal of operations security is to ensure that all systems have been hardened to the extent that is possible and still provide functionality. The following actions can be performed to logically harden a system:

    - Remove unnecessary applications.
    - Disable unnecessary services.
    - Block unused ports.
    - Tightly control the connecting of external storage devices and media if it's allowed at all.

This chapter covers the following subjects:

- **Software Development Concepts:** Concepts discussed include software architectures and languages used to implement them.
- **Security in the System and Software Development Life Cycle:** Concepts discussed include the System Development Life Cycle; the Software Development Life Cycle; software development methods and maturity models; operation and maintenance; change management; and the integrated product team.
- **Security Controls in Development:** Concepts discussed include software development security best practices, software environment security, source code issues, source code analysis tools, code repository security, application programming interface security, software threats, and software protection mechanisms.
- **Assess Software Security Effectiveness:** Concepts discussed include auditing and logging, risk analysis and mitigation, and regression and acceptance testing.
- **Security Impact of Acquired Software:** Concepts discussed include the acquired software life cycle and the security impact of acquired software.
- **Secure Coding Guidelines and Standards:** Concepts discussed include security weaknesses and vulnerabilities at the source code level, security of application programming interfaces, and secure coding practices.

CHAPTER 8

Software Development Security

Software development security covers all the security issues and controls that security professionals must understand when dealing with commercial or in-house-developed software. They should understand the software development life cycle and be able to assess software security effectiveness and the impact of software.

Software is at the heart of all functionality in computer systems. Various types of software, including operating systems, applications, and utilities, work together to deliver instructions from a human to hardware. All these instructions are created with the intent of making some operation possible.

When software is written and developed, the focus can be placed on its functionality and ease of use or on its security. In many cases, the two goals might work at cross purposes. Giving inadequate attention to the security of a piece of software results in software that can introduce security issues to both the application and the systems on which it is run. Moreover, some types of software are intentionally developed to create security vulnerabilities in a network or system. This chapter discusses software development methodology, best practices for secure development, and types of malware and methods of mitigating the effects of malware.

Foundation Topics

Software Development Concepts

Software comprises the written instructions that allow humans to communicate with the computer hardware. These instructions are written in various *programming languages*. As programming has evolved over the years, each successive language has delivered more functionality to programmers. Programming languages can be classified in categories based on the types of instructions they create and to which part of the system they speak. The following sections cover the main categories.

Machine Languages

Machine languages are those that deliver instructions directly to the processor. This was the only type of programming done in the 1950s and uses basic binary instructions without a compiler or interpreter (programs that convert higher language types to a form that can be executed by the processor). This type of programming is both time-consuming and prone to errors. Most of these programs were very rudimentary due to the need to keep a tight rein on their length.

Assembly Languages and Assemblers

Considered to be "one step above" machine languages, ***assembly languages*** use symbols or mnemonics to represent sections of complicated binary code. Consequently, these languages use an assembler to convert the code to machine level. Although this tool greatly simplifies and shortens the code, it still requires extensive knowledge of the computer's architecture. It also means that any code written in these languages will be hardware specific. Although assembly language is simpler to write than machine language, it is not as easy to create as the high-level languages discussed next.

High-Level Languages, Compilers, and Interpreters

In the 1960s, a third level of language emerged, called ***high-level languages***. These instructions use abstract statements (for example, IF–THEN–ELSE), and some of these languages are processor independent. They are easier to work with, and their syntax is more similar to human language. This code uses either assemblers or compilers to convert the instructions into machine code. The end result is a decrease in the total number of code writers required for a particular project.

A fourth generation of languages, called ***very-high-level languages***, focuses on abstract algorithms that hide some of the complexity from the programmer. These algorithms free programmers to focus on the real-world problems they are trying to solve rather than the details that go on behind the scenes.

Finally, in the 1990s, a fifth generation of languages began to emerge, called ***natural languages***. The goal is to use these languages to create software that can solve problems on its own rather than require a programmer to create code to deal with the problem. Although this goal is not fully realized, using knowledge-based processing and artificial intelligence is worth pursuing.

A significant distinction exists with respect to security between compiled programs and interpreted programs. Because a compiled program has already been translated to binary language (machine code), detecting malicious code inside an application is very difficult. Interpreted code, on the other hand, uses a language interpreter, which is a piece of software that translates high-level code, line-by-line, each time a program is executed (run). In this case, spotting malicious code is somewhat easier because the code is a bit more readable by humans.

Object-Oriented Programming

In classic software development, data is input into a program, the program manages the data from beginning to end, and a result is returned. ***Object-oriented programming (OOP)*** supplies the same functionality, but it is more efficiently introduced through different techniques. In OOP, *objects* are organized in a hierarchy of *classes* with characteristics called *attributes* attached to each class. OOP emphasizes the employment of objects and methods rather than types or transformations.

The programmer creates the classes of objects but not necessarily the objects themselves. Software in the program allows for objects to be created on demand when needed through requests. When a request comes in, usually from an existing object for a new object to carry out some function, it is built (instantiated) with necessary code. It does not matter whether objects are written in a different programming language as long as the objects have the ability to communicate with one another, a process usually made possible through an application programming interface (API).

Moreover, because objects are organized in hierarchical classes, object *methods* (functions or procedures) have the ability to be passed when required from a class to a subclass through a process called *inheritance*. The objects contain or *encapsulate* attribute *values*. Objects communicate with messages sent to another object's API. Different objects might react differently to the same message, which is called the object's *behavior*. The code that defines how an object will behave with respect to a message is called its *method*.

Some parts of an object can be defined as private, which means its internal data and operation are not visible to other objects. This privacy is provided through the encapsulation process and is sometimes called *data hiding*. *Abstraction* is the ability to suppress these unnecessary internal details. Other objects, subjects, and applications can make use of objects' functionality through standardized interfaces without worrying about the details of the functionality.

OOP uses data types with defined ranges. Programmers must identify all data objects and their relationships through a process called data modeling. The object is then generalized into an object class and is defined as part of a logic sequence, also called a method, used to manipulate the object. An object can be used in different applications.

Examples of OOP languages are C++, Java, Simula 67, and Smalltalk. The many advantages to this OOP include

- Modularity in design through autonomous objects
- Definition of internal components without impacting other parts of the system
- Reusability of objects and their components
- The capability to more readily map to business needs

Polymorphism

In an object-oriented system, ***polymorphism*** denotes objects of many different classes that are related by some common superclass; thus, any object denoted by this name can respond to some common set of operations in a different way. Polymorphism is the ability of different objects with a common name to react to the same message or input and produce a different output. For example, three objects can be created to receive the string "Toyota Corolla" as input. One object's output might be "subcompact," another's might be "uses regular fuel," and another's might be "costs $18,000." In some cases, these differences derive from the fact that the objects have inherited different characteristics from their parent classes.

Polyinstantiation

Polyinstantiation prevents low-level objects from gaining information from a higher security level. Objects may act differently depending on the data they contain. For this reason, it may be difficult to determine whether inherited security properties are valid. Polyinstantiation prevents inference database attacks.

Encapsulation

Encapsulation protects objects by preventing direct access to data that is in the object. It ensures that private data is protected. However, encapsulation makes it hard to apply the appropriate security policies to an object because it is hard to determine what the object contains.

Cohesion

Cohesion is a term used to describe program organization. It is how an object functions independently by itself. If it is completely independent, it is said to have *high cohesion*. High cohesion is good in that changes can be made to the model without affecting other modules. It also makes reusing the module easier. The highest cohesion is provided by limiting the scope of a module's operation.

Coupling

Coupling describes how much interaction one module requires from another module to function in the overall programming. Low or loose coupling indicates that a module does not need much help from other modules, whereas high coupling indicates the opposite. If Module A needs to wait on results from messages it sent to three other modules before it can proceed, it is said to have high coupling. Low coupling, in other words, indicates how independent a class is from other classes. The best programming provides high cohesion and low coupling.

Data Structures

Data structure refers to the logical relationship between elements of data. It describes the extent to which elements, methods of access, and processing alternatives are associated and the organization of data elements. These relationships can be simple or complex. From a security standpoint, these relationships or the way in which various software components communicate and the data formats that they use must be well understood to understand the vulnerabilities that might be exposed by these data structures.

Distributed Object-Oriented Systems

When an application operates in a client/server framework, as many do, the solution is performing *distributed computing*. This means that components on different systems must be able to both locate each other and communicate on a network. Typically, the bulk of the solution is on the server, and a smaller piece is located on the client. Therefore, some architecture is required to support this process-to-process communication. Several ***distributed object-oriented systems*** can be used, as discussed in the next sections.

CORBA

Common Object Request Broker Architecture (CORBA) is an open object-oriented standard developed by the Object Management Group (OMG). This standard uses a component called the Object Request Broker (ORB) to implement exchanges among objects in a heterogeneous, distributed environment.

The ORB manages all communication between components. It accepts requests for service from the client application, directs the request to the server, and then relays the response back to the client application. The ORB makes communication possible locally or remotely. This communication is even possible between components that are written in different languages because they use a standard interface to communicate with the ORB.

The ORB is responsible for enforcing the security policy, which describes what the users and system are allowed to do and what actions are restricted. It provides four types of policies: access control, data protection, nonrepudiation, and auditing.

COM and DCOM

Component Object Model (COM) is a model for communication between processes on the same computer, whereas, as its name implies, the ***Distributed Component Object Model (DCOM)*** is a model for communication between processes in different parts of the network. DCOM works as the middleware between these remote processes (called interprocess communication [IPC]).

DCOM provides the same services as those provided by the ORB in the CORBA framework—that is, data connectivity, message service, and distributed transaction service. All of these functions are integrated into one technology that uses the same interface as COM.

OLE

Object Linking and Embedding (OLE) is a method for sharing objects on a local computer that uses COM (Component Object Model) as its foundation. In fact, OLE is sometimes described as the predecessor of COM. It allows objects to be embedded in documents (spreadsheets, graphics, and so on). The term *linking* refers to the relationship between one program and another, and the term *embedding* refers to the placement of data into a foreign program or document. One example of OLE is including an Excel worksheet in a Microsoft Word document.

Java

Java Platform, Enterprise Edition (Java EE), is another distributed component model that relies on the Java programming language. It is a framework used to develop software that provides APIs for networking services and uses an interprocess communication process that is based on Common Object Request Broker

Architecture (CORBA). Its goal is to provide a standardized method of providing back-end code that carries out business logic for enterprise applications.

SOA

A newer approach to providing a distributed computing model is the ***service-oriented architecture (SOA)***. It operates on the theory of providing web-based communication functionality without each application requiring redundant code to be written per application. It uses standardized interfaces and components called service brokers to facilitate communication among web-based applications.

Mobile Code

Mobile code is a type of code that can be transferred across a network and then executed on a remote system or device. The security concerns with mobile code revolve around preventing the execution of malicious code without the knowledge of the user. The following sections cover the two main types of mobile code, Java applets and ActiveX applets, and the way they operate.

Java Applets

A ***Java applet*** is a small application written in Java that is run from a web page. It is platform independent and compiles to byte code that is not processor-specific. When the applet downloads to the computer, the Java virtual machine (JVM), which must be present on the destination computer, converts the byte code to machine code.

The JVM executes the applet in a protected environment called a *sandbox*. This critical security feature, called the Java Security Model (JSM), helps mitigate the extent of damage that could be caused by the applet if it has any malicious code. However, it does not eliminate the problem with hostile applets (also called active content modules), so Java applets should still be regarded with suspicion because they might launch an intentional attack after being downloaded from the Internet. Java applets have largely been phased out.

ActiveX

ActiveX is a Microsoft technology that uses OOP (object-oriented programming) and is based on the COM and DCOM. These self-sufficient programs, called controls, become a part of the operating system after they're downloaded. The problem is that these controls execute under the security context of the current user, which in many cases has administrator rights without knowing and by default. This means that a malicious ActiveX control will download and automatically run with administrative privileges and could do some serious damage.

ActiveX uses Authenticode technology to digitally sign the controls. This system has been shown to have significant flaws, and ActiveX controls are generally regarded with more suspicion than Java applets. First, a malicious website could prompt you to install a malicious ActiveX control, and it was very easy for Internet Explorer users to agree to the prompt and install it. Second, a bug in a legitimate ActiveX control, which was a common problem, could cause a vulnerability. ActiveX is being phased out and is not supported by Microsoft's Edge web browser.

NIST SP 800-163

NIST SP 800-163 Rev. 1, "Vetting the Security of Mobile Applications," was written to help organizations (1) understand the process for vetting the security of mobile applications, (2) plan for the implementation of an application (app) vetting process, (3) develop app security requirements, (4) understand the types of app vulnerabilities and the testing methods used to detect those vulnerabilities, and (5) determine whether an app is acceptable for deployment on the organization's mobile devices.

To provide software assurance for apps, organizations should develop security requirements that specify, for example, how data used by an app should be secured, the environment in which an app will be deployed, and the acceptable level of risk for an app. To help ensure that an app conforms to such requirements, a process for evaluating the security of apps should be performed. This process is referred to as an app vetting process. An ***app vetting*** process is a sequence of activities that aims to determine whether an app conforms to the organization's security requirements. This process is performed on an app after the app has been developed and released for distribution but prior to its deployment on an organization's mobile device. Thus, an app vetting process is distinguished from software assurance processes that may occur during the software development life cycle of an app. Note that an app vetting process typically involves analysis of an app's compiled, binary representation but can also involve analysis of the app's source code if it is available.

An app vetting process comprises a sequence of two main activities: ***app testing*** and ***app approval/rejection***.

According to NIST SP 800-163 Rev. 1, an app vetting process begins when an app is submitted by a mobile device administrator to one or more analyzers for testing. Apps that are submitted by an administrator for testing will typically be acquired from an app store or an app developer, each of which may be internal or external to the organization. An analyzer is a service, tool, or human that tests an app for specific software vulnerabilities and may be internal or external to the organization. After an app has been received and preprocessed by an analyzer, the analyzer then tests the app for the presence of software vulnerabilities. Such testing may include a wide variety of tests including static and dynamic analyses and may be performed in an automated or manual fashion. Note that the tests performed by an analyzer are aimed at identifying software vulnerabilities that may be common across different apps. After testing an app, an analyzer generates a report that identifies detected software vulnerabilities. In addition, the analyzer generates a risk assessment that estimates the likelihood that a detected vulnerability will be exploited and the impact that the detected vulnerability may have on the app or its related device or network. Risk assessments are typically represented as ordinal values indicating the severity of the risk (for example, low-, moderate-, and high-risk).

After the report and risk assessment are generated by an analyzer, they are made available to one or more auditors of the organization. The auditor inspects reports and risk assessments from one or more analyzers to ensure that an app meets the security requirements of the organization. The auditor also independently evaluates additional criteria to determine whether the app violates any organization-specific security requirements that could not be ascertained by the analyzers. After evaluating all reports, risk assessments, and additional criteria, the auditor then collates this information into a single report and risk assessment and derives a recommendation for approving or rejecting the app based on the overall security posture of the app. This recommendation is then made available to an approver. An approver uses the recommendations provided by one or more auditors that describe the security posture of the app as well as other non-security-related criteria to determine the organization's official approval or rejection of an app. If an app is approved it is then permitted to deploy the app on the organization's mobile devices. If, however, the app is rejected, the organization will follow specified procedures for identifying a suitable alternative app or rectifying issues with the problematic app.

According to NIST SP 800-163 Rev. 1, before an organization can implement an app vetting process, it is necessary for the organization to (1) develop app security requirements, (2) understand the limitations of app vetting, and (3) procure a budget and staff for supporting the app vetting process.

A general requirement is an app security requirement that specifies a software characteristic or behavior that an app should exhibit to be considered secure. General app security requirements include

- **Enabling authorized functionality:** The app must work as described; all buttons, menu items, and other interfaces must work. Error conditions must be handled gracefully, such as when a service or function is unavailable (for example, disabled, unreachable, and so on).
- **Preventing unauthorized functionality:** Unauthorized functionality, such as data exfiltration performed by malware, must not be supported.
- **Limiting permissions:** Apps should have only the minimum permissions necessary and should grant other applications only the necessary permissions.

- **Protecting sensitive data:** Apps that collect, store, and transmit sensitive data should protect the confidentiality and integrity of sensitive data. This category includes preserving privacy, such as asking permission to use personal information and using it only for authorized purposes.
- **Securing app code dependencies:** If the app has any dependencies, such as on libraries, they should be used in a reasonable manner and not for malicious purposes.
- **Testing app updates:** New versions of the app must also be tested on a separate device to identify any new weaknesses. The implication is that when an existing app is updated, the updated app is not automatically approved.

A context-sensitive requirement is an app security requirement that specifies how the organization should use apps to ensure that organization's security posture. For an app, the satisfaction or violation of context-sensitive requirements cannot be determined by analyzers but instead must be determined by an auditor using organization-specific vetting criteria. Such criteria include

- **Requirements:** The pertinent requirements, security policies, privacy policies, acceptable use policies, and social media guidelines that are applicable to the organization.
- **Provenance:** The identity of the developer, the developer's organization, the developer's reputation, date received, marketplace/app store consumer reviews, and so on.
- **Data sensitivity:** The relative sensitivity of the data collected, stored, and/or transmitted by the app.
- **App criticality:** How critical the app is to the organization's business processes.
- **Target users:** The intended set of users of the app.
- **Target hardware:** The intended hardware platform and configuration on which the app will be deployed.
- **Target environment:** The intended operational environment of the app (e.g., general public use versus sensitive military environment).
- **Digital signature:** Digital signatures applied to the app binaries or packages.
- **App documentation:**
  - **User guide:** When available, the app's user guide assists testing by specifying the expected functionality and expected behaviors. This guide is simply a statement from the developer describing what they claim their app does and how it does it.

- **Test plans:** Reviewing the developer's test plans may help focus app vetting by identifying any areas that have not been tested or were tested inadequately. A developer could opt to submit a test oracle in certain situations to demonstrate its internal test effort.
- **Testing results:** Code review results and other testing results will indicate which security standards were followed. For example, if an application threat model was created, this model should be submitted. It will list weaknesses that were identified and should have been addressed during design and coding of the app.
- **Service-level agreement:** If an app was developed for an organization by a third party, a service-level agreement (SLA) may have been included as part of the vendor contract. This contract should require the app to be compatible with the organization's security policy.

Security in the System and Software Development Life Cycle

When writing code for new software, developers must ensure that the appropriate security controls are implemented and that the code is properly secured. The following sections cover the System Development Life Cycle; the Software Development Life Cycle; software development methods and maturity models; operation and maintenance; change management; and the integrated product team.

System Development Life Cycle

When an organization defines new functionality that must be provided either to its customers or internally, it must create systems to deliver that functionality. Many decisions have to be made, and a logical process should be followed in making those decisions. This process is called the ***System Development Life Cycle (SDLC)***. Rather than being a haphazard approach, the SDLC provides clear and logical steps to follow to ensure that the system that emerges at the end of the development process provides the intended functionality with an acceptable level of security.

SP 800-37 Rev. 2, "Risk Management Framework for Information Systems and Organizations: A System Life Cycle Approach for Security and Privacy," is an important publication for security professionals to review. This paper provides guidance on managing security and privacy risk as it relates to the SDLC.

The System Development Life Cycle includes the following phases:

Key Topic

1. Initiate
2. Acquire/Develop

3. Implement
4. Operate/Maintain
5. Dispose/Decommission

Next, we explain these five phases in the SDLC.

Initiate

In the Initiate phase, the realization is made that a new feature or functionality is desired or required in an existing piece of software. This new feature might constitute an upgrade to an existing product or the development of a whole new piece of software. In either case, the Initiate phase includes making a decision on whether to purchase or develop the product internally.

In this stage, an organization must also give thought to the security requirements of the solution. A *preliminary risk assessment* can be created to detail the confidentiality, integrity, and availability (CIA) requirements and concerns. Identifying these issues at the outset is important so these considerations can guide the purchase or development of the solution. The earlier in the System Development Life Cycle that the security requirements are identified, the more likely that the issues can be successfully addressed in the final product.

Acquire/Develop

In the Acquire/Develop stage of the System Development Life Cycle, a series of activities takes place that provides input to facilitate making a decision about acquiring or developing the solution; the organization then makes a decision on the solution. The activities are designed to get answers to the following questions:

- What functions does the system need to perform?
- What are the potential risks to CIA exposed by the solution?
- What protection levels must be provided to satisfy legal and regulatory requirements?
- What tests are required to ensure that security concerns have been mitigated?
- How do various third-party solutions address these concerns?
- How do the security controls required by the solution affect other parts of the company security policy?
- What metrics will be used to evaluate the success of the security controls?

The answers to these questions should guide the acquisition or develop the decision as well as the steps that follow this stage of the System Development Life Cycle.

Implement

In the Implement stage, the solution is introduced to the live environment but not without its completing both certification and accreditation. ***Certification*** is the process of technically verifying the solution's effectiveness and security. The ***accreditation*** process involves a formal authorization to introduce the solution into the production environment by management.

Operate/Maintain

After the system is operating in the environment, the process does not end. Doing a performance baseline is important so that continuous monitoring can take place. The baseline ensures that performance issues can be quickly determined. Any changes over time (addition of new features, patches to the solution, and so on) should be closely monitored with respect to the effects on the baseline.

Instituting a formal ***change management process*** ensures that all changes are both approved and documented. Because changes can affect both security and performance, special attention should be given to monitoring the solution after any changes.

Finally, vulnerability assessments and penetration testing after the solution is implemented can help discover any security or performance problems that might either be introduced by a change or arise as a result of a new threat.

Dispose/Decommission

The Dispose/Decommission stage consists of removing the solution from the environment when it reaches the end of its usefulness. When this situation occurs, an organization must consider certain issues. They include

- Does removal or replacement of the solution introduce any security holes in the network?
- How can the system be terminated in an orderly fashion so as not to disrupt business continuity?
- How should any residual data left on any systems be removed?
- How should any physical systems that were a part of the solution be disposed of safely?
- Are there any legal or regulatory issues that would guide the destruction of data?

Software Development Life Cycle

The Software Development Life Cycle (SDLC) can be seen as a subset of the System Development Life Cycle in that any system under development could (but does not necessarily) include the development of software to support the solution. The goal of the SDLC is to provide a predictable framework of procedures designed to identify all requirements with regard to functionality, cost, reliability, and delivery schedule and ensure that each is met in the final solution. Here, we break down the steps in the Software Development Life Cycle and describe how each step contributes to this ultimate goal. Keep in mind that steps in the Software Development Life Cycle can vary based on the provider, and this is but one popular example.

The following sections outline the SDLC steps in detail:

Key Topic

1. Plan/Initiate Project
2. Gather Requirements
3. Design
4. Develop
5. Test/Validate
6. Release/Maintain
7. Certify/Accredit
8. Change Management and Configuration Management/Replacement

Plan/Initiate Project

In the Plan/Initiate Project phase of the Software Development Life Cycle, the organization decides to initiate a new software development project and formally plans the project. Security professionals should be involved in this phase to determine whether information involved in the project requires protection and whether the application needs to be safeguarded separately from the data it processes. Security professionals need to analyze the expected results of the new application to determine whether the resultant data has a higher value to the organization and, therefore, requires higher protection.

Any information that is handled by the application needs a value assigned by its owner, and any special regulatory or compliance requirements need to be documented. For example, healthcare information is regulated by several federal laws and must be protected. The classification of all input and output data of the application needs to be documented, and the appropriate application controls should be documented to ensure that the input and output data are protected.

Data transmission must also be analyzed to determine the types of networks used. All data sources must also be analyzed. Finally, the effects of the application on organizational operations and culture need to be analyzed.

Gather Requirements

In the Gather Requirements phase of the Software Development Life Cycle, both the functionality and the security requirements of the solution are identified. These requirements could be derived from a variety of sources, such as evaluating competitor products for a commercial product or surveying the needs of users for an internal solution. In some cases, these requirements could come from a direct request from a current customer. There are also user requirements, functional requirements, and security requirements.

From a security perspective, an organization must identify potential vulnerabilities and threats. When this assessment is performed, the intended purpose of the software and the expected environment must be considered. Moreover, the data that will be generated or handled by the solution must be assessed for its sensitivity. Assigning a privacy impact rating to the data to help guide measures intended to protect the data from exposure might be useful.

Design

In the Design phase of the Software Development Life Cycle, an organization develops a detailed description of how the software will satisfy all functional and security goals. It attempts to map the internal behavior and operations of the software to specific requirements to identify any requirements that have not been met prior to implementation and testing.

During this process, the state of the application is determined in every phase of its activities. The state of the application refers to its functional and security posture during each operation it performs. Therefore all possible operations must be identified. This is done to ensure that at no time does the software enter an insecure state or act in an unpredictable way.

Identifying and mapping the attack surface is also a part of this analysis. The attack surface describes what is available to be leveraged by an attacker. The amount of attack surface might change at various stages of the application, but at no time should the attack surface provided violate the security needs identified in the Gather Requirements stage.

Develop

The Develop phase involves writing the code or instructions that make the software work. The emphasis of this phase is strict adherence to secure coding practices. Some models that can help promote secure coding are covered later in this chapter, in the section "Software Development Security Best Practices."

Many security issues with software are created through insecure coding practices, such as lack of input validation or data type checks. Organizations need to identify these issues in a code review that attempts to assume all possible attack scenarios and their impact on the code. Not identifying these issues can lead to attacks such as buffer overflows and injection and to other error conditions, which are covered later in this chapter, in the section "Security Weaknesses and Vulnerabilities at the Source Code Level."

Test/Validate

In the Test/Validate phase, several types of testing should occur, including ways to identify both functional errors and security issues. The auditing method that assesses the extent of the system testing and identifies specific program logic that has not been tested is called the *test data method*. This method tests not only expected or valid input but also invalid and unexpected values to assess the behavior of the software in both instances. An active attempt should be made to ethically attack the software, including attempts at buffer overflows and denial-of-service (DoS) attacks. Some goals of testing performed at this time are

- **Verification testing:** Determines whether the original design specifications have been met.
- **Validation testing:** Takes a higher-level view and determines whether the original purpose of the software has been achieved.

Software is typically developed in pieces or modules of code that are later assembled to produce the final product. Each module should be tested separately, in a procedure called *unit testing*. Having development staff carry out this testing is critical, but using a different group of engineers than the ones who wrote the code can ensure that an impartial process occurs. This is a good example of the concept of separation of duties.

The following should be characteristics of the unit testing:

- The test data is part of the specifications.
- Testing should check for out-of-range values and out-of-bounds conditions.
- Correct test output results should be developed and known beforehand.

Live or actual field data is *not* recommended for use in the unit testing procedures.

Additional testing that is recommended includes

- **Integration testing:** Assesses the way in which the modules work together and determines whether functional and security specifications have been met.
- ***Acceptance testing*:** Ensures that the customer (either internal or external) is satisfied with the functionality of the software.
- **Regression testing:** Takes place after changes are made to the code to ensure the changes have reduced neither functionality nor security and did not create new errors or issues.

Release/Maintenance

The Release/Maintenance phase includes the implementation of the software into the live environment and the continued monitoring of its operation. Finding additional functional and security problems at this point, as the software begins to interface with other elements of the network, is not unusual.

In many cases, vulnerabilities are discovered in the live environments for which no current fix or patch exists. Such a vulnerability is referred to as a *zero-day vulnerability*. It is, of course, better for an organization to have supporting development staff discover these issues than to have people who are looking to exploit vulnerabilities find them.

Certify/Accredit

Certification is the process of evaluating software or a system for its security effectiveness with regard to the customer's needs. Ratings can certainly be an input to this but are not the only consideration. *Accreditation* is the formal acceptance of the adequacy of a system's overall security by the management. Provisional accreditation is given for a specific amount of time and lists required changes to applications, systems, or accreditation documentation. Full accreditation grants accreditation without any required changes. Provisional accreditation becomes full accreditation after all the changes are completed, analyzed, and approved by the certifying body.

Although certification and accreditation are related, they are not considered to be two steps in a process.

Change Management and Configuration Management/Replacement

After a solution is deployed in a live production environment, additional changes may be made to the software due to security issues that are discovered. In some cases, the software might have to be altered to enhance or increase its functionality. In either case, changes must be handled through a formal change and configuration management process.

The purpose of the change management process is to ensure that all changes to the configuration of the source code and the source code itself are approved by the proper personnel and are implemented in a safe and logical manner. This process should always ensure continued functionality in the live environment, and changes should be documented fully, including all changes to hardware and software.

In some cases, it may be necessary to completely replace applications or systems. Although some failures may be fixed with enhancements or changes, a failure may occur that can be solved only by completely replacing the application.

DevSecOps

DevSecOps is short for development, security, operations, which is a methodology that focuses on integrating security during each stage of the Software Development Life Cycle. Prior to DevSecOps, security was added in the latter stages of the development life cycle. When security is integrated at all stages, it becomes a shared responsibility for developers, operations, and IT security. Ultimately, the goal is to deliver more secure code faster.

Static Application Security Testing (SAST) and Dynamic Application Security Testing (DAST)

Application testing is a critical part of software development, with the goal of identifying security vulnerabilities. As you have just learned from DevSecOps, security testing should be integrated in every phase of the development life cycle, which means that application security testing should begin early in application development.

Static Application Security Testing (SAST), also referred to as white-box testing, is the analysis of code at rest. This type of security testing goes through the code line-by-line to identify security vulnerabilities. Unlike SAST, DAST does not have access to the source code during security testing.

Dynamic Application Security Testing (DAST), also referred to as black-box testing, refers to application testing by simulating attacks on the application while the application is running. DAST is often associated with web application vulnerability scanning. Much of this testing checks for vulnerabilities that have been publicized by organizations such as OWASP (Open Web Application Security Project) and CISA (Cybersecurity & Infrastructure Security Agency). An example of an application vulnerability that DAST may identify is SQL injection. Again, the goal is to identify security vulnerabilities that may be related to application configuration or authentication protocols.

DAST can occur when the application is in production, but more commonly this security testing takes place during the quality assurance phase of development. Keep in mind that DAST should be used throughout the life cycle of the application.

Interactive Application Security Test (IAST)

Interactive Application Security Testing (IAST) is a modern approach to application security testing that combines elements of SAST and DAST methodologies to identify vulnerabilities in web applications and services. IAST operates from within the application or runtime environment, providing real-time feedback on security issues as the application is used or tested during the development and testing phases.

IAST tools are designed to be integrated into the application or its environment, monitoring the application's behavior and data flow in real time. They can be deployed alongside the application in test environments or during quality assurance processes. As the application runs, the IAST tool analyzes its operations, including interactions with databases, file systems, and external services, to detect security vulnerabilities and logical flaws.

IAST tools provide immediate feedback on security issues as they are identified, allowing developers to address vulnerabilities early in the development process. By incorporating aspects of both SAST and DAST, IAST can offer comprehensive coverage of security vulnerabilities, including those that are only detectable during runtime.

Because IAST tools have insight into the application's runtime behavior, they can provide more accurate findings with fewer false positives compared to other testing methodologies. IAST can analyze not only custom code but also interactions with third-party libraries and frameworks, providing a broader view of an application's security posture.

Software Composition Analysis

Software Composition Analysis (SCA) is a critical tool to identify and evaluate the security, licensing, and operational risks associated with open-source and third-party components in a software project. As modern software development increasingly relies on open-source components and third-party libraries to speed up development and leverage existing solutions, it becomes essential to manage the risks associated with these components.

SCA tools scan a project's codebase to identify open-source and third-party components and their versions. They then cross reference this information against databases of known vulnerabilities, such as the National Vulnerability Database (NVD), to identify any components that are vulnerable to exploitation.

In addition to security vulnerabilities, SCA tools analyze the licenses associated with each open-source or third-party component used within a software project. This helps organizations ensure that they comply with the legal requirements of these licenses, avoiding potential legal issues related to copyright infringement or non-compliance with open-source licenses.

SCA provides visibility into the dependencies of a software project, helping developers understand how different components are connected and the potential impact of upgrading or removing specific components. This is crucial for maintaining the integrity and security of the software over time.

SCA tools can be integrated into the continuous integration/continuous deployment (CI/CD) pipeline, allowing for automated and continuous analysis of software components as part of the development process. This ensures that vulnerabilities and license compliance issues can be addressed early in the development life cycle, before deployment.

NOTE CI/CD is covered in detail later in this chapter.

Integrating SCA into the software development ecosystem supports security control implementation, risk management and mitigation, security best practices, and regulatory compliance.

Software Development Methods and Maturity Models

In the course of creating software in the past, developers learned many things about the development process. As development projects have grown from a single developer to small teams to now large development teams working on massive projects with many modules that must securely interact, development models have been created to increase the efficiency and success of these projects. A new "lessons learned" phase has been incorporated into these models and methods. The following sections cover some of the common models, along with concepts and practices that must be understood to implement them.

Next, we discuss the following software development methods and maturity models:

Key Topic

- Build and Fix Model
- Waterfall Model

- V-shaped Model
- Prototype Model
- Modified Prototype Model
- Incremental Model
- Spiral Model
- Agile Model
- Scaled Agile Framework (SAFe)
- Continuous Integration and Continuous Delivery (CI/CD)
- Rapid Application Development (RAD) Model
- Joint Analysis Development (JAD) Model
- Cleanroom Model
- Structured Programming Development Model
- Exploratory Model
- Computer-Aided Software Engineering (CASE) Model
- Component-Based Development Model
- Capability Maturity Model Integration (CMMI)
- ISO 9001:2015/90003:2014
- IDEAL Model

Build and Fix Model

Although it's not a formal model, the ***Build and Fix*** approach describes a method that, while certainly used in the past, has been largely discredited and is now used as a template for how *not* to manage a development project. Simply put, in this method, the software is developed as quickly as possible and released.

No formal control mechanisms are used to provide feedback during the process. The product is rushed to market, and problems are fixed on an as-discovered basis with patches and service packs. Although this approach gets the product to market faster and cheaper, in the long run the costs involved in addressing problems and the collateral damage to the product in the marketplace outweigh any initial cost savings.

Despite the fact that this model still seems to be in use today, most successful developers have learned to implement one of the other models discussed here so that the initial product, though not necessarily perfect, comes much closer to meeting all the functional and security requirements of the design. Moreover, using these models helps to identify and eliminate as many bugs as possible without using the customer as "quality control."

In this simplistic model of the software development process, certain unrealistic assumptions are made, including

- Each step of development can be completed and finalized without affecting later stages that might require rework.
- Iteration (reworking and repeating) among the steps in the process that is typically called for in other models is not stressed in this model.
- Phases are not seen as individual milestones as in some other models discussed here.

Waterfall Model

The original ***Waterfall model*** breaks the development process into distinct phases. Although this model uses somewhat of a rigid approach, the basic process is as a sequential series of steps that are followed without going back to earlier steps. This approach is called *incremental development*. Figure 8-1 is a representation of the Waterfall process.

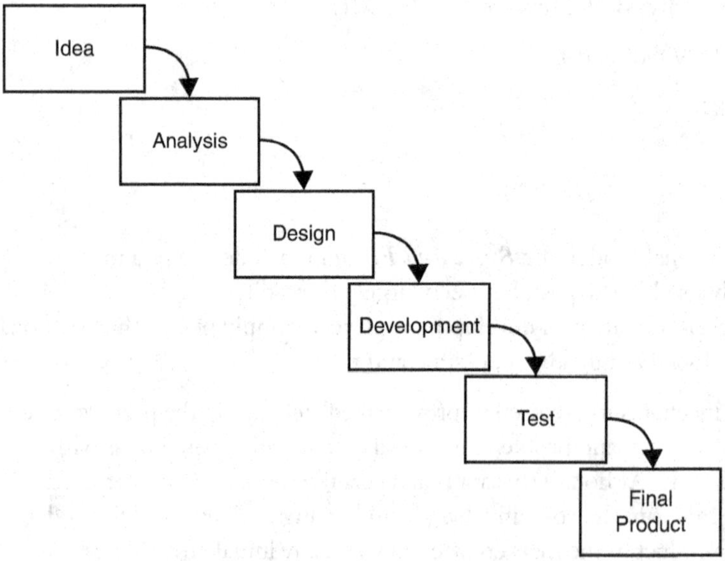

Figure 8-1 Waterfall Model

In the *modified* Waterfall model, each phase in the development process is considered its own milestone in the project management process. Unlimited backward iteration (returning to earlier stages to address problems) is not allowed in this model. However, product verification and validation are performed in this model. Problems that are discovered during the project do *not* initiate a return to earlier stages but rather are dealt with after the project is complete.

V-shaped Model

The ***V-shaped model*** is also somewhat rigid but differs primarily from the Waterfall method in that verification and validation are performed at each step. Although this model can work when all requirements are well understood up front (frequently not the case) and potential scope changes are small, it does not provide for handling events concurrently because it is also a sequential process like the Waterfall. It does build in a higher likelihood of success because it performs testing at every stage. Figure 8-2 is a representation of this process.

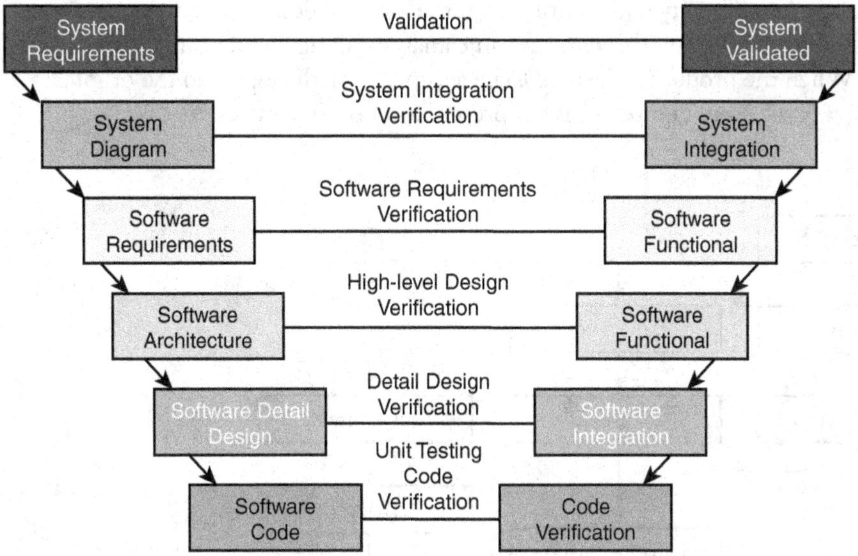

Figure 8-2 V-shaped Model

Prototyping

Although it's not a formal model unto itself, ***prototyping*** is the use of a sample of code to explore a specific approach to solving a problem before extensive time and cost have been invested in the approach. This technique allows the team to both identify the utility of the sample code and identify design problems with the approach. Prototype systems can provide significant time and cost savings because the whole final product does not have to be made to begin testing it.

Modified Prototype Model (MPM)

MPM is a prototyping method that is used with minimal requirements. The client provides feedback, and then a fully functioning prototype is developed and used as the basis for the final product.

Incremental Model

The ***Incremental model*** is a refinement to the basic Waterfall model, which states that software should be developed in increments of functional capability. In this model, a working version or iteration of the solution is produced, tested, and redone until the final product is completed. You could think of it as a series of waterfalls. After each iteration or version of the software is completed, testing occurs to identify gaps in functionality and security from the original design. Then the gaps are addressed by proceeding through the same analysis, design, code, and test stages again. When the product is deemed to be acceptable with respect to the original design, it is released. Figure 8-3 is a representation of this process.

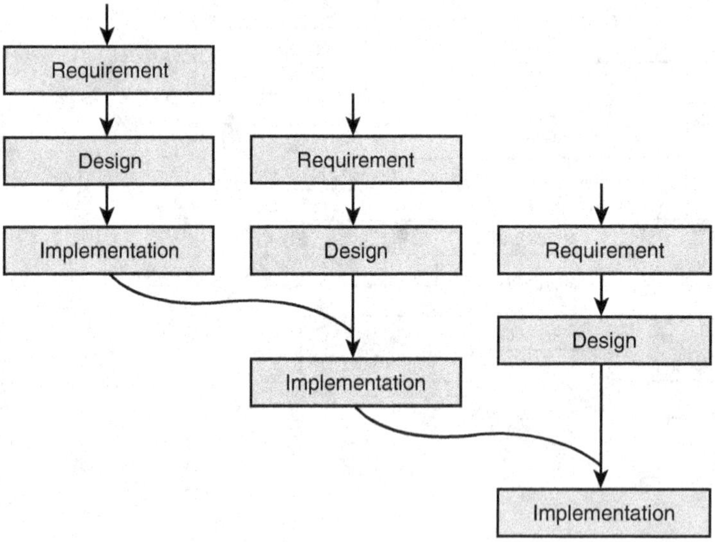

Figure 8-3 Incremental Model

Spiral Model

The ***Spiral model*** is actually a meta-model that incorporates a number of the software development models. It is also an iterative approach but places more emphasis on risk analysis at each stage. Prototypes are produced at each stage, and the process can be seen as a loop that keeps circling back to take a critical look at risks that have been addressed while still allowing visibility into new risks that might have been created in the last iteration.

This model assumes that knowledge will be gained at each iteration and should be incorporated into the design as it evolves. Some cases even involve the customer making comments and observations at each iteration. Figure 8-4 is a representation of this process. The radial dimension of the diagram represents cumulative cost, and the angular dimension represents progress made in completing each cycle. It is a continuously evolving model.

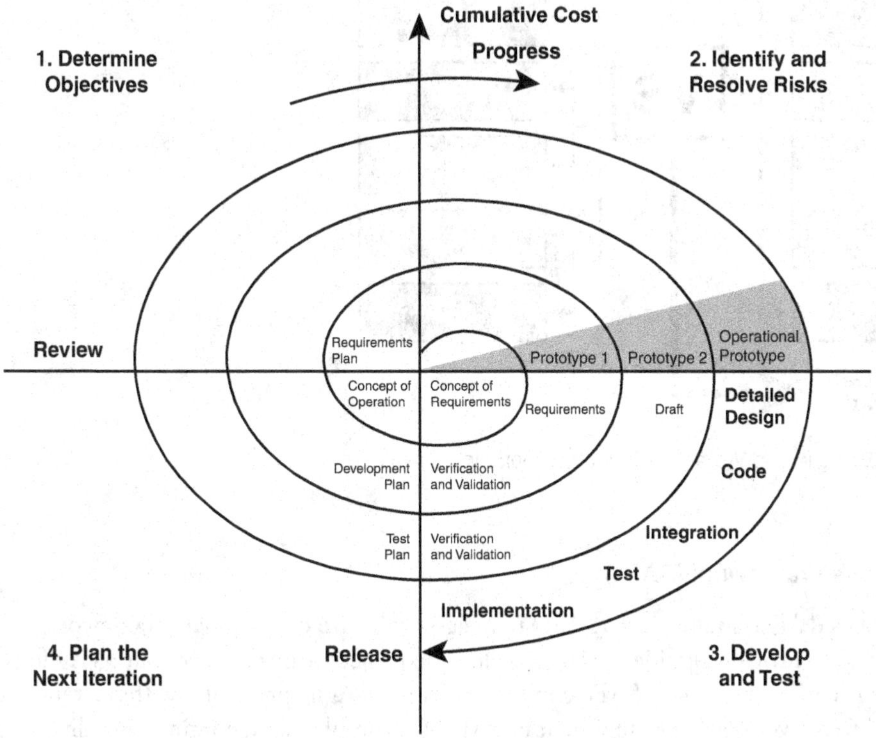

Figure 8-4 Spiral Model

Agile Model

Many of the processes or models discussed thus far rely on rigid adherence to process-oriented models. In many cases, the focus is more on following procedural steps than on reacting to changes quickly and increasing efficiency. The ***Agile*** model puts more emphasis on continuous feedback and cross-functional teamwork.

This model attempts to be nimble enough to react to situations that arise during development. Less time is spent on the upfront analysis and more emphasis is placed on learning from the process and incorporating lessons learned in real time. There is also regular and active interaction with the customer throughout the process. Figure 8-5 compares the Agile model with the Waterfall model.

Key Topic

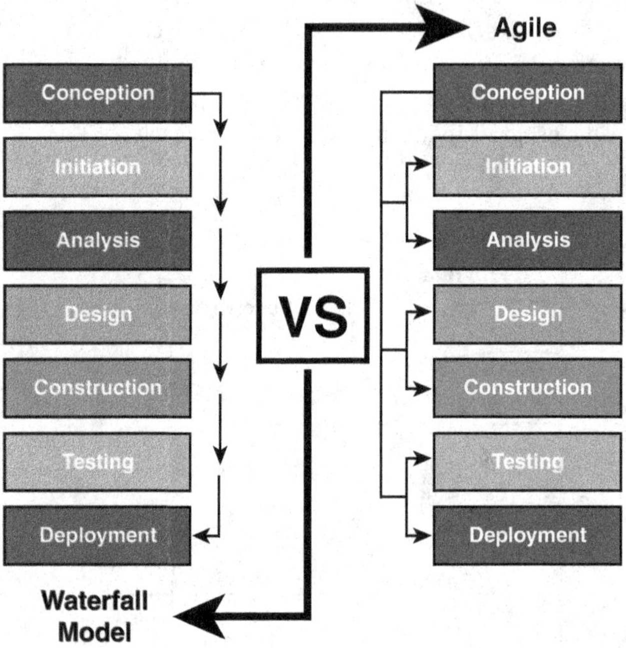

Figure 8-5 Agile and Waterfall Model Comparison

Scaled Agile Framework (SAFe)

The Scaled Agile Framework (SAFe) is an agile software development framework designed to provide a guide for large-scale agile project teams to carry out an Agile transformation seamlessly. SAFe combines Lean and Agile principles within a templated framework. A key component of SAFe is its emphasis on continuous delivery and improvement, aligning development efforts with business needs while maintaining a high level of flexibility and responsiveness to change. Each stage provides a working application, but not the final product.

SAFe principles emphasize building quality into the product from the beginning of the development process. Integrating security as a component of quality ensures that security measures are considered at each stage of the SDLC, rather than being an afterthought.

SAFe's foundation on Lean-Agile principles promotes adaptive planning, evolutionary development, early delivery, and continuous improvement, which are conducive to incorporating security practices in a flexible and responsive manner. Security requirements and considerations can be adapted as the project evolves, rather than being rigidly defined from the outset.

SAFe includes a continuous delivery pipeline that represents the workflows, activities, and automation needed to move new functionality from ideation to release and operation. Integrating security activities, such as static and dynamic code analysis, vulnerability assessments, and security testing, into this pipeline ensures continuous security assessment and improvement.

SAFe promotes cross-functional teams that include all necessary skills to define, build, and test increments of value in a short time frame. Including security professionals or empowering team members with security skills ensures that security considerations are included in daily activities and decision-making processes.

SAFe involves program increment (PI) planning, which is a routine, face-to-face event where all team members establish the objectives for the upcoming increment. Security objectives, such as compliance goals, risk mitigation strategies, and security feature development, can be integrated into PI planning to ensure they are prioritized and aligned with business objectives.

For security professionals, understanding how to integrate security into SAFe and other development methodologies is crucial for ensuring that software products are designed, developed, and deployed securely. They must work to embed security practices throughout the SDLC, from initial planning to deployment and maintenance, leveraging the principles and structure provided by frameworks like SAFe to facilitate this integration.

Continuous Integration and Continuous Delivery (CI/CD)

Continuous integration (CI) refers to the process of frequently integrating code changes and updates, provided by the development team, during software development. These changes may occur several times a day. Automated testing of the code is built into the CI process. ***Continuous delivery (CD)*** refers to the frequent transfer of changes through the process to production. These changes may include bug fixes or configuration changes. During the CD process, code can be deployed at any time, provided that automated test cases were successful. Development implements changes that are then pushed to testing. Testing verifies changes and tests the product to approve changes to be pushed to production.

Rapid Application Development (RAD) Model

In the ***Rapid Application Development (RAD) model***, less time is spent up front on design, and emphasis is placed on rapidly producing prototypes with the assumption that crucial knowledge can be gained only through trial and error. This model is especially helpful when requirements are not well understood at the outset and are developed as issues and challenges arise during the building of prototypes. Figure 8-6 compares the RAD model to traditional models, where the project is completed fully and then verified and validated.

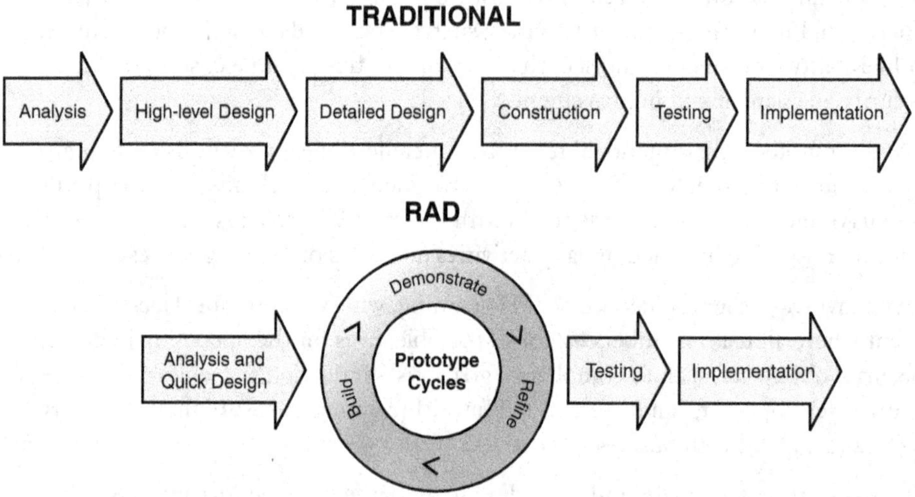

Figure 8-6 Traditional and RAD Models

Joint Analysis Development (JAD) Model

The ***Joint Analysis Development (JAD) model*** uses a team approach. It uses workshops to both agree on requirements and resolve differences. JAD is based on the theory that bringing all parties together at all stages usually results in a better product to emerge at the end of the process.

Cleanroom Model

In contrast to the JAD model, the ***Cleanroom model*** strictly adheres to formal steps and a more structured method. It attempts to prevent errors and mistakes through extensive testing. This method works well in situations where high quality is a must, the application is mission critical, or the solution must undergo a strict certification process.

Structured Programming Development Model

In the Structured Programming Development model, programmers write programs while allowing influence on the quality of the finished products. It is one of the most widely known development models and requires defined processes. The product is reviewed at the end of each phase for approval. Security is added in a formalized, structured manner.

Exploratory Model

In the Exploratory model, requirements are based on what is currently available. Assumptions are documented about how the system might work. To create a usable system, other insights and suggestions are incorporated as they are discovered. In this model, security will probably not have priority over enhancements. As a result, security controls are often added on an ad hoc basis.

Computer-Aided Software Engineering (CASE)

The CASE method uses computers and computer utilities to help analyze, design, develop, implement, and maintain software. It requires that you build and maintain software tools and training for developers. CASE tools are divided into the following categories:

- Business and analysis modeling
- Development
- Verification and validation
- Configuration management
- Metrics and measurement
- Project management

Component-Based Development

The Component-Based Development method uses building blocks to assemble an application rather than building the application itself from scratch. The advantage of this method in regards to security is that the components are tested for security prior to being used in the application.

CMMI

The ***Capability Maturity Model Integration (CMMI)*** is a comprehensive set of guidelines that addresses all phases of the Software Development Life Cycle.

It describes a series of stages or maturity levels that a development process can advance through as it goes from the ad hoc (Build and Fix) model to one that incorporates a budgeted plan for continuous improvement. Figure 8-7 shows its five maturity levels and explains each one.

Key Topic

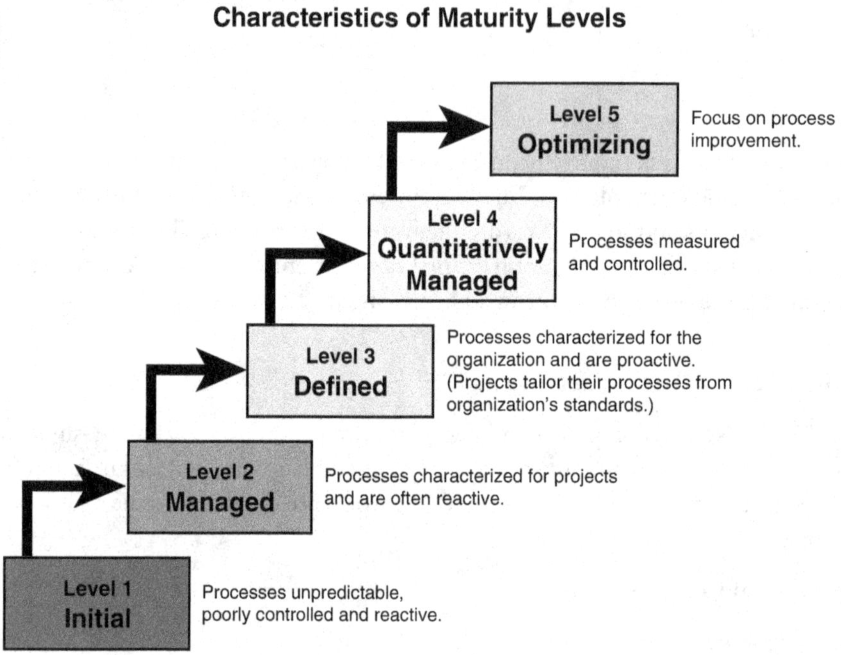

Figure 8-7 CMMI Maturity Levels

ISO 9001:2015/90003:2014

ISO 9001:2015 is a quality management systems standard. It specifies requirements for a quality management system when an organization (1) needs to demonstrate its ability to consistently provide products and services that meet customer and applicable statutory and regulatory requirements, and (2) aims to enhance customer satisfaction through the effective application of the system, including processes for improvement of the system and the assurance of conformity to customer and applicable statutory and regulatory requirements.

All the requirements of ISO 9001:2015 are generic and are intended to be applicable to any organization, regardless of its type or size and regardless of what products and services it provides.

ISO 90003:2014 guides organizations in the application of ISO 9001:2015 in terms of the acquisition, supply, development, operation, and maintenance of computer software and related support services. It does not add to or otherwise change the requirements of ISO 9001:2015.

The application of ISO/IEC 90003:2014 is appropriate to software that is part of a commercial contract with another organization, a product available for a market sector, used to support the processes of an organization, embedded in a hardware product, or related to software services. Some organizations may be involved in all of these activities; others may specialize in one area. Whatever the situation, the organization's quality management system should cover all aspects (software related and non-software related) of the business.

ISO/IEC 90003:2014 identifies the issues that should be addressed and is independent of the technology, life cycle models, development processes, sequence of activities, and organizational structure used by an organization. Additional guidance and frequent references to the ISO/IEC JTC 1/SC 7 software engineering standards are provided to assist in the application of ISO 9001:2015, in particular ISO/IEC 12207:2017. ISO 9001:2015 is about quality management systems, and ISO/IEC 12207:2017 is about systems and software engineering and software life cycle processes. The entire scope of these two standards is not important for security professionals. However, security professionals should ensure that the software development team understands and follows these standards.

IDEAL Model

The ***IDEAL model*** was developed by the Software Engineering Institute to provide guidance on software development. Its name is an acronym that stands for the five phases:

1. **Initiate:** Outline the business reasons behind the change, build support for the initiative, and implement the infrastructure needed.
2. **Diagnose:** Analyze the current organizational state and make change recommendations.
3. **Establish:** Take the recommendations from the previous phase and use them to develop an action plan.
4. **Act:** Develop, test, refine, and implement the solutions according to the action plan from the previous phase.
5. **Learn:** Use the quality improvement process to determine whether goals have been met and develop new actions based on the analysis.

Figure 8-8 shows the steps involved in each of the phases of the IDEAL model.

Key Topic

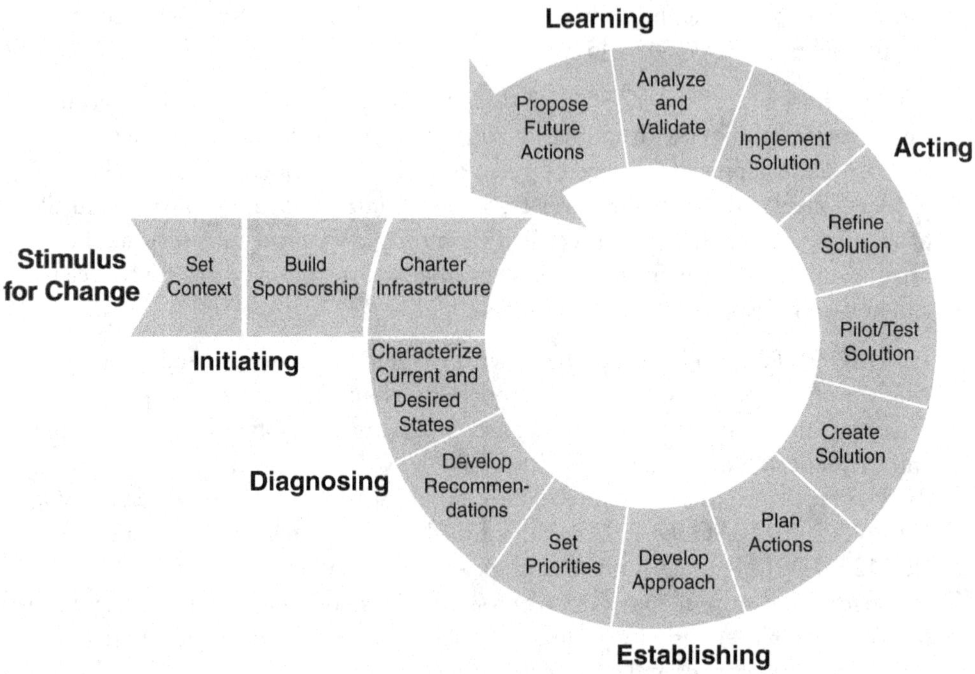

Figure 8-8 Phases and Steps of the IDEAL Model

Operation and Maintenance

Operation and maintenance ensure that the information system is fully functional and performs optimally until the system reaches its end of life. This process includes managing changes to the system to support end users, monitoring system performance, performing required security activities (such as backups, contingency planning, and audits), and providing end-user support through training and documentation.

This process often includes the development of the following deliverables:

- **Standard operating procedures:** Defines the business processes related to the operations and maintenance of the system.
- **Performance reports:** Tracks routine metrics to act as system performance indicators.
- **Issue reports:** Provides details regarding issues and system incidents.

Integrated Product Team

Integrated Product and Process Development (IPPD) integrates all essential acquisition activities through the use of multidisciplinary teams to optimize the design, manufacturing, and supportability processes. IPPD facilitates meeting cost and performance objectives from product conception through production, including field support. One of the key IPPD tenets is multidisciplinary teamwork through integrated product teams (IPTs). It is based on a U.S. Department of Defense (DoD) handbook.

The acquisition process is typically divided into five stages, with the first four formal phases separated by milestone decision points. These are the five stages:

1. Phase 0: Concept Exploration (CE)
2. Phase I: Program Definition and Risk Reduction (PDRR)
3. Phase II: Engineering and Manufacturing Development (EMD)
4. Phase III: Production, Fielding/Deployment, and Operational Support (PFDOS)
5. Demilitarization and Disposal (DD)

The DoD handbook says the IPT should function efficiently and effectively. The important point to remember is that each IPT in IPPD has a mission to develop and deliver a product and its associated processes. At the program level, IPT characteristics include

- Responsibility for a defined product or process
- Authority over the resources and personnel
- An agreed schedule for delivery of the defined product
- An agreed level of risk to deliver the defined product
- An agreed-upon set of measurable metrics

IPTs are an integral part of the acquisition oversight and review process. There are generally two levels of IPTs: the working-level integrated product team (WIPT) and the overarching integrated product team (OIPT). Each program should have one OIPT and at least one WIPT. A WIPT should focus on a particular topic, such as cost/performance, program baseline, acquisition strategy, test and evaluation (or contracting). An integrating integrated product team (IIPT), which is a type of a WIPT, should coordinate WIPT efforts and cover all program topics, including those not otherwise assigned to another IPT. IPT participation is the primary way for any organization to be part of the acquisition program. IIPTs are essential in that they facilitate staff-level program insight into programs at the program level and provide the requisite input to the OIPT.

DevOps (development operations) emphasizes the collaboration and communication of both software developers and other IT professionals while automating the process of software delivery and infrastructure changes. It aims to ensure that building, testing, and releasing software can happen more quickly, more often, and more reliably.

Security Controls in Development

Security controls in software development must be properly implemented to ensure that security issues with software do not become problematic for the organization. To provide security controls, developers must

- Understand current industry's best practices for software development security and software environment security.
- Recognize source code issues and know which source code analysis tools are available and what they do to resolve source code issues.
- Provide code repository security.
- Implement application programming interface security.
- Understand software threats and software protection mechanisms.

Software Development Security Best Practices

To support the goal of ensuring that software is soundly developed with regard to both functionality and security, a number of organizations have attempted to assemble a set of software development best practices. First, we look at some of those organizations, and then we look at a number of their most important recommendations.

WASC

The ***Web Application Security Consortium (WASC)*** is an organization that provides best practices for web-based applications along with a variety of resources, tools, and information that organizations can make use of in developing web applications.

One of the functions undertaken by WASC is continual monitoring of attacks leading to the development and maintenance of an up-to-date list of top attack methods that are currently known. This list can aid in ensuring that organizations not only are aware of the latest attack methods and how widespread these attacks are but also can make the proper precautions and care to their web applications to mitigate these attack types.

OWASP

The ***Open Web Application Security Project (OWASP)*** is another group that monitors attacks, specifically web attacks. OWASP maintains a list of top 10 attacks on an ongoing basis. This group also holds regular meetings at chapters throughout the world, providing resources and tools including testing procedures, code review steps, and development guidelines.

BSI

The Department of Homeland Security (DHS) also has become involved in promoting software security best practices. The ***Build Security In (BSI)*** initiative promotes a process-agnostic approach that makes security recommendations with regard to architectures, testing methods, code reviews, and management processes. The DHS Software Assurance program addresses ways to reduce vulnerabilities, mitigate exploitations, and improve the routine development and delivery of software solutions. Although the BSI initiative is considered defunct, security professionals should still be aware of its existence.

ISO/IEC 27000

The International Organization for Standardization (ISO) and the International Electrotechnical Commission (IEC) created the 27034 standard, which is part of a larger body of standards called the ***ISO/IEC 27000*** series. These standards provide guidance to organizations in integrating security into the development and maintenance of software applications. These suggestions are relevant not only to the development of in-house applications but also to the safe deployment, distribution, and management of third-party solutions in an enterprise.

Software Environment Security

The software environment, also referred to as a software library, includes code, classes, procedures, scripts, configuration data, subroutines, macro definitions, global variables, and templates. Software libraries must be built using safe coding practice and implemented properly. Also, they must be kept up to date with updates and security patches. Finally, they must include a feedback feature to address any identified issues. Common programming language libraries include C, C++, Java Class Library (JCL), and the Ruby standard.

Security professionals do not always have the skills necessary to ensure that developed software has the appropriate security implemented. For this reason, they should work to improve security awareness and identify experts who can ensure that secure programming practices are followed.

Source Code Analysis Tools

Source code analysis tools analyze ***source code*** or compiled versions of code to locate security flaws. While these tools do not usually find every security flaw, and often tag as flaws some elements that are not actually flaws, they still provide help to programmers in targeting the security-relevant code. Security professionals should work closely with programmers to ensure that source code analysis tools are used throughout the Software Development Life Cycle.

Source code analysis tools work with many kinds of software and can be run often. They are very good at detecting common issues, such as buffer overflows and SQL injections. They also highlight the exact source files and line numbers where the possible flaws are located. However, they may not always find all security issues because many issues are hard to detect. These tools often report a high number of false positives and frequently may not be able to identify configuration issues. Importantly, many source code analysis tools cannot analyze code that cannot be compiled.

Common open-source code analysis tools include .NET analyzers for Microsoft, CodeSearchDiggity for Google, and FindBugs for Java. Commercial tools are also available.

NOTE A list of tools is available at https://samate.nist.gov/index.php/Source_Code_Security_Analyzers.html.

Code Repository Security

Security professionals must be concerned with the security of code while it is being developed, used, and stored in the enterprise. Security professionals should establish security measures to provide physical, system, operational, and software security. In addition, guidelines for communication should be established, including guidelines for the use of encryption. Backups should be performed regularly and securely stored. A limited number of employees should be given access to the ***code repository***. More than one copy of code should be stored. Sub-versions should be stored with the date captured in separate locations for retrieval when required. This ensures recovery should the organization decide to roll back changes.

Software Threats

Software threats, or malicious software, can also be created in the way software is coded or developed. Following development best practices can help prevent this inadvertent creation of security issues when creating software. Software threats also can be introduced through malware. In the following sections, we discuss malware and software coding issues as well as options to mitigate the threat. Some of these topics are discussed in Chapter 5, "Identity and Access Management (IAM)," and they are covered more extensively in this chapter.

Malware

Malicious software (or ***malware***) is any software that intends to harm a computer, modifies/corrupts/deletes data, or takes actions the user did not authorize. It includes a wide array of malware types, including ones you have probably heard of, such as viruses, and many you might not have heard of but of which you should be aware.

Some of the malware that security professionals need to understand includes the following:

Key Topic

- Virus
  - Boot sector virus
  - Parasitic virus
  - Stealth virus
  - Polymorphic virus
  - Macro virus
  - Multipartite virus
- Worm
- Trojan horse
- Logic bomb
- Spyware/adware
- Botnet
- Rootkit
- Ransomware
- Keylogger
- Mobile Malware

Virus

A ***virus*** is a software program that infects and causes the other genuine software to malfunction. It uses a host application to reproduce and deliver its malware and typically attaches itself to a file. It differs from a worm (described below) in that it usually requires some action on the part of the user to help it spread to other computers.

Following are the virus types along with a brief description of each:

- ***Boot sector virus***: This type of malware infects the boot sector of a computer and either overwrites files or installs code into the sector so the virus initiates at startup.
- ***Parasitic virus***: This type of virus attaches itself to a file, usually an executable file, and then delivers the payload when the program is used.
- ***Stealth virus***: This type of virus is difficult for a system to detect.
- ***Polymorphic virus***: This type of virus makes copies of itself, and then makes changes to those copies, thereby morphing into a new form. It does so in hopes of avoiding detection from antivirus software.
- ***Macro virus***: This type of virus infects programs written in Word, Basic, Visual Basic, or VBScript that are used to automate functions. These viruses infect Microsoft Office files and are easy to create because the underlying language is simple and intuitive to apply. They are especially dangerous in that they infect the operating system itself. They also can be transported between different operating systems because the languages are platform independent.
- ***Multipartite virus***: Originally, this type of virus could infect both program files and boot sectors. This term now means that the virus can infect more than one type of object or can infect in more than one way.
- **File or system infector:** File infectors program files, and system infectors infect system program files.
- **Companion virus:** This type of virus does not physically touch the target file. It is also referred to as a spawn virus.
- **Email malware:** This type of malware specifically uses an email system to spread itself because it is aware of the email system functions. Knowledge of such email system functions allows this virus to take advantage of all email system capabilities.
- **Script malware:** This type of malware is a stand-alone file that can be executed by an interpreter.

Worm

A ***worm*** is a type of malware that can spread without the assistance of the user. It is a small program that, like a virus, is used to deliver a payload. One way to help mitigate the effects of worms is to place limits on sharing, writing, and executing programs.

Trojan Horse

A ***Trojan horse*** is a program or rogue application that appears to, or is purported to do, one thing but actually does another when executed. For example, what appears to be a screensaver program might really be a Trojan horse. When the user unwittingly uses the program, it executes its payload, which in turn could delete files or create backdoors. Backdoors are alternative ways to access the computer undetected in the future.

One type of Trojan targets and attempts to access and make use of smart cards. A countermeasure to prevent this attack is to use "single-access device driver" architecture. Using this approach, the operating system allows only one application to have access to the serial device (and thus the smart card) at any given time. Another way to prevent the attack is by using a smart card that enforces a "one private key usage per PIN entry" policy model. In this model, the user must enter a PIN every single time the private key is used, and therefore, the Trojan horse would not have access to the key.

Trojans do one thing on the front to the user and a second simultaneous thing on the back without the user noticing.

Logic Bomb

A ***logic bomb*** is a type of malware that executes when a particular event takes place. It is a purposeful malware programming script written by a developer to cause trouble based on certain logic, like a certain day or when a certain event occurs. For example, that event could be a time of day or a specific date, or it could be the first time you open notepad.exe. Some logic bombs execute when digital forensics is being conducted, and in that case the bomb might delete all digital evidence.

Spyware/Adware

Adware doesn't actually steal anything, but it tracks Internet usage in an attempt to tailor ads and junk email to a user's interests. ***Spyware*** also tracks activities and can also gather personal information that could lead to identity theft. In some cases, spyware can even direct the computer to install software and change settings.

Botnet

A bot is a type of malware that installs itself on large numbers of computers through infected emails, downloads from websites, Trojan horses, and shared media. After it's installed, the bot can connect back to the hacker's computer. After a connection is successfully established, the hacker's server controls all the bots located on these machines. At a set time, the hacker might direct the bots to take some action, such as direct all the machines to send out spam messages, initiate a distributed denial-of-service (DDoS) attack, send phishing emails, or do any number of malicious acts. The collection of computers that act together is called a ***botnet***, and the individual computers are called *zombies*. The attacker's computer that manages the botnet is often referred to as the bot herder or bot master. Figure 8-9 shows this relationship.

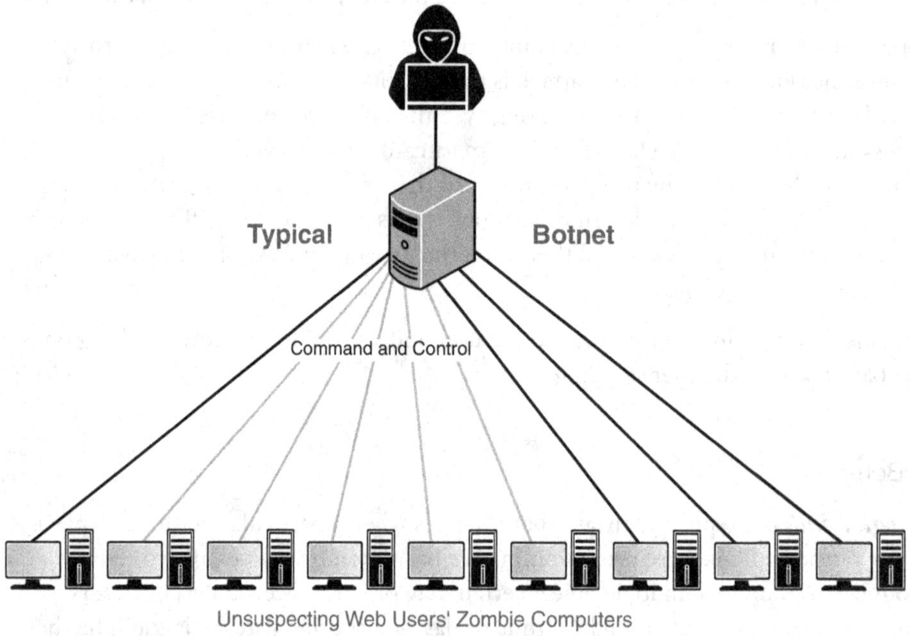

Figure 8-9 Botnet

Rootkit

A rootkit is a set of tools that a hacker can use on a computer after managing to gain access and elevating privileges to administrator. It gets its name from the root account, the most powerful account in UNIX-based operating systems. The rootkit tools might include a backdoor for the hacker to access. This is one of the hardest types of malware to remove, and in many cases only a reformat of the hard drive will completely remove it.

The following are some of the actions a rootkit can take:

- Install a backdoor.
- Remove all entries from the security log (log scrubbing).
- Replace default tools with compromised versions (Trojaned programs).
- Make malicious kernel changes.

Ransomware

Ransomware is malware that prevents or limits users from accessing their systems. It is called ransomware because it forces its victims to pay a ransom through certain online payment methods to be given access to their systems again or to get their data back. Generally, the hacker will demand a ransom (or payment) in cryptocurrency within a short space of time; after the deadline, the ransom goes up, thereby forcing an organization to make a quick decision. An organization should view the resources available at nomoreransom.org first in case an existing solution is available to remove the ransomware. The organization should also consider cyber insurance to prepare for a potential ransomware or other major cyberattack.

The best protection against ransomware is frequent backups.

Keylogger

A ***keylogger*** is malware that records a user's keystrokes. After these keystrokes are sent back to the hacker can in turn use those recorded keystrokes to log into the website using the user's credentials.

Mobile Malware

The huge growth in mobile devices, such as smartphones, has meant that there has been tremendous growth in mobile malware. ***Mobile malware*** can include mobile banking Trojans—that is, a link to a mobile application installation, which is malicious. The majority of mobile malware is found on Android devices.

Malware Protection

Organizations and individuals are not totally helpless in the fight against malware. Programs and practices can help to mitigate the damage malware can cause. Here, we discuss some of the ways to protect a network from malware.

Antivirus Software

The first line of defense is antivirus software. This software is designed to identify viruses, Trojans, and worms and delete them, or at least quarantine them until they can be removed. This identification process requires that the software's definition files, the files that make it possible for the software to identify the latest viruses, are updated frequently. If a new virus is created that has not yet been identified in the list, the computer will not be protected until the virus definition is added and the new definition file is downloaded.

Anti-malware Software

Closely related to antivirus software and in some cases part of the same software package, anti-malware software focuses on other types of malware, such as adware and spyware. An important way to help prevent malware infection is to train users on appropriate behavior when using the Internet. For that reason, user education in safe practices is a necessary part of preventing malware. This practice should be a part of security policies.

Scanning Types

Three major types of scanning for malware or viruses occur: known signature scanning, activity monitoring, and change detection. With known signature scanning, a database of malware signatures is maintained. When scans occur, they are looking for matches to a signature in the database. With activity monitoring, the monitor watches for suspicious activity. With change detection, the detector examines files and configuration, stores the information, and compares the stored information against the configuration at a later date. It usually involves checksum values.

Security Policies

Security policies are covered in detail in Chapter 1, "Security and Risk Management," but it is important to mention here that encouraging or requiring safe browsing and data handling practices should be formalized into the security policy of the organization. Some of the items to stress in this policy and perhaps include in training for users are the importance of the following:

- Antivirus and anti-malware updates
- Reporting any error message concerning an update failure on the user machine
- Reporting any strange computer behavior that might indicate a virus infection

Software Protection Mechanisms

In 1972, the U.S. government commissioned the Computer Security Technology Planning Study to outline the basic and foundational security requirements of systems purchased by the government. This study eventually led to the Trusted Computer System Evaluation Criteria, or *Orange Book* (discussed in more detail in Chapter 3, "Security Architecture and Engineering"). This section defines some of the core tenets in the Orange Book:

- **Trusted computer base (TCB):** The TCB comprises the components (hardware, firmware, and/or software) that are trusted to enforce the security policy of the system and that, if compromised, jeopardize the security properties of the entire system. The reference monitor is a primary component of the TCB. This term is derived from the Orange Book. All changes to the TCB should be audited and controlled, which is an example of a configuration management control.

- **Security perimeter:** This is the dividing line between the trusted parts of the system and the parts that are untrusted. According to security design best practices, components that lie within this boundary (which means they lie within the TCB) should never permit untrusted components to access critical resources in an insecure manner.
- **Reference monitor:** A reference monitor is a system component that enforces access controls on an object. It is an access control concept that refers to an abstract machine that mediates all accesses to objects by subjects. It was introduced for circumventing difficulties in classic approaches to computer security by limiting damages produced by malicious programs. The security risk created by a *covert channel* is that it bypasses the reference monitor functions. The reference monitor should exhibit isolation, completeness, and verifiability. Isolation is required because of the following:
    - The reference monitor can't be available for public access. The less access, the better.
    - The reference monitor must have a sense of completeness to provide the whole information and process cycles.
    - The reference monitor must be verifiable, to provide security, audit, and accounting functions.
- **Security kernel:** A security kernel is the hardware, firmware, and software elements of a TCB that implements the reference monitor concept. It is an access control concept, not an actual physical component. The security kernel should be as small as possible so that it can be easily verified. The security kernel implements the authorized access relationship between subjects and objects of a system as established by the reference monitor. While it is performing this role, all accesses must be meditated, protected from modification, and verifiable.

Assess Software Security Effectiveness

Regardless of whether a software program is purchased from a third party or developed in-house, being able to verify and prove how secure the application is can be useful. The two ways to approach this task are auditing the program's actions and determining whether it performs any insecure actions, or assessing it through a formal process.

Auditing and Logging

One approach, and a practice that should continue after the software has been introduced to the environment, is continual auditing of its actions and regular reviewing of the audit data. By monitoring the audit logs, a security professional can identify security weaknesses that might not have been apparent in the beginning or that might have gone unreported until now. In addition, any changes that are made are recorded by the audit log and then can be checked to ensure that no security issues were introduced with the change.

Risk Analysis and Mitigation

Risk analysis and mitigation were covered thoroughly in Chapter 1. Because risk management is an ongoing process, it must also be incorporated as part of any software development. Risk analysis determines the risks that can occur, whereas risk mitigation takes steps to reduce the effects of the identified risks. Security professionals should do the following as part of a software development risk analysis and mitigation strategy:

- Integrate risk analysis and mitigation in the Software Development Life Cycle.
- Use qualitative, quantitative, and hybrid risk analysis approaches based on standardized risk analysis methods.
- Track and manage weaknesses that are discovered throughout risk assessment, change management, and continuous monitoring.

Because software often contains vulnerabilities that are not discovered until the software is operational, security professionals should ensure that a patch management process is documented and implemented when necessary to provide risk mitigation. This task includes using a change control process, testing any newly released patches on an independent device, keeping a working backup, scheduling production downtime to apply the new patches, and establishing a back-out plan. Prior to deploying any patches, security professionals should notify helpdesk personnel and key user groups. When patches are deployed, the least critical computers and devices should receive the patch first, moving up through the hierarchy until the most critical computers and devices are patched.

When mitigations (patches) are deployed, the mitigations must be tested and verified, usually as part of quality assurance and testing. Any risk mitigation that has been completed must be verified by an independent party that is not the developer or system owner. Developers should be encouraged to use code signing to ensure code integrity, to determine who developed code, and to determine the code's purpose. Code-signing certificates are digital certificates which ensure that code has not been changed. By signing code, organizations can determine whether the code has been modified by an entity other than the signer. Code signing primarily covers running code, not stored code. While code signing verifies code integrity, it cannot guarantee freedom from security vulnerabilities or that an app will not load unsafe or unaltered code during execution.

Regression and Acceptance Testing

Any changes or additions to software must undergo regression and acceptance testing. Regression testing verifies that the software behaves the way it should. Regression testing may identify bugs that may have been accidentally introduced into the new build or release candidate. Acceptance testing verifies whether the software is doing what the end user expects it to do. Acceptance testing is more formal in nature and actually tests the functionality for users based on a functional/user requirement.

Security Impact of Acquired Software

Organizations often purchase commercial software or contract with other organizations to develop customized software. Security professionals should ensure that organizations understand the security impact of any acquired software. This includes commercial off-the-shelf (COTS), open-source, and third-party applications, managed services (like enterprise applications and cloud services).

The process to acquire software has the following four phases:

Key Topic

1. **Planning:** During this phase, the organization performs a needs assessment, develops the software requirements, creates the acquisition strategy, and develops evaluation criteria and a plan.
2. **Contracting:** Once planning has been completed, the organization creates a request for proposal (RFP) or other supplier solicitation forms, evaluates the supplier proposals, and negotiates the final contract with the selected seller.
3. **Monitoring and accepting:** After a contract is in place, the organization establishes the contract work schedule, implements change control procedures, and reviews and accepts the software deliverables. Somewhere around this step, the organization downloads the software, tests on an isolated machine, and certifies for use.
4. **Follow-up:** When the software is in place, the organization must sustain the software, including managing risks and changes. At some point, the organization may need to decommission or upgrade the software.

A security professional should be involved in the software assurance process to ensure that unintentional errors, malicious code, information theft, and unauthorized product changes or inserted agents are detected.

COTS software refers to ready-made products available in the commercial market and designed to be used "as is." These products are developed for a mass market, rather than tailored for a specific customer or organization. While COTS products are professionally developed and may undergo rigorous testing, they can still contain vulnerabilities. Because the source code is usually not available, relying on the vendor for patches and updates is necessary. Security assessments might include evaluating the vendor's reputation, the frequency and transparency of their security updates, and known vulnerabilities reported in their products.

Open-source software is characterized by its publicly available source code, allowing anyone to inspect, modify, and suggest enhancements to the software. The open nature of the source code can be a double-edged sword; it allows for greater transparency and the potential for widespread review, which can lead to more secure software. However, it also means that vulnerabilities can be discovered and exploited by malicious actors. Assessing the security impact of open-source software involves reviewing the project's activity level, community responsiveness to security issues, and the regularity of security patches.

Third-party software refers to any software developed outside the organization but integrated into the organization's systems or processes. This category can overlap with COTS and open-source software but also includes solutions developed by external entities specifically for the organization. The main concerns include the third party's development and security practices, the nature of data access the software requires, and how updates are managed. Assessing third-party software often involves conducting security audits, reviewing compliance with security standards, and understanding the contractual obligations related to security updates and vulnerability disclosures. Any software development agreements will need to include provisions for auditing, patching, and regular updates.

Managed services involve external providers delivering and managing applications and services. This model can include Software as a Service (SaaS) applications, cloud-based solutions, and outsourced IT services. The security impact of using managed services is influenced by the service provider's security policies, data protection measures, and the ability to respond to incidents. Evaluating managed services includes understanding the data privacy practices, the provider's compliance with relevant regulations and standards, service-level agreements (SLAs) related to security, and mechanisms for monitoring and auditing service performance and security.

For security professionals, assessing the security impact of acquired software requires:

- Due Diligence and Risk Assessment: Conducting thorough due diligence to understand the security posture and practices of the software or service provider. This includes risk assessments to identify potential vulnerabilities and impacts on the organization's security posture.

- Compliance and Regulation Review: Ensuring that the software or services comply with applicable laws, regulations, and industry standards, especially those related to data protection and privacy.
- Vendor Management: Establishing strong vendor management practices, including setting clear security requirements and regularly reviewing vendors' adherence to these requirements.
- Security Integration and Monitoring: Integrating acquired software into the organization's broader security framework, including implementing necessary controls and continuously monitoring for new vulnerabilities or security issues.

Understanding and applying these considerations helps security professionals mitigate the risks associated with acquired software, ensuring that the organization's security posture is maintained and enhanced.

Secure Coding Guidelines and Standards

Security professionals must ensure that developers within their organization understand secure coding guidelines and standards. This includes understanding security weaknesses and vulnerabilities at the source code level, security of application programming interfaces, and secure coding practices. A major risk today is that developers will often reuse existing code and functionality, or third-party libraries, that may have untested, unknown security vulnerabilities.

Security Weaknesses and Vulnerabilities at the Source Code Level

Many security issues with software have their roots in poor development practices. A number of threats can be minimized by following certain established software coding principles. Here, we discuss source code issues, along with some guidelines for secure development processes.

Buffer Overflow

As discussed in Chapter 5, a buffer is an area of memory where commands and data are placed until they can be processed by the CPU. A ***buffer overflow*** occurs when too much data is accepted as input to a specific process. Hackers can take advantage of this phenomenon by submitting too much data, which can cause an error or, in some cases, execute commands on the machine if the hackers can locate an area where commands can be executed. Not all attacks are designed to execute commands. Some just lock up the computer and are used as DoS attacks.

A packet containing a long string of *no-operation instructions* (NOPs) followed by a command is usually indicative of a type of buffer overflow attack called an NOP slide. The purpose is to get the CPU to locate where a command can be executed. The following is an example of a packet as seen from a sniffer, showing a long string of 90s in the middle of the packet that pads the packet and causes it to overrun the buffer:

```
TCP Connection Request
---- 14/03/2018 15:40:57.910
68.144.193.124 : 4560 TCP Connected ID = 1
---- 14/03/2018 15:40:57.910
Status Code: 0 OK
68.144.193.124 : 4560 TCP Data In Length 697 bytes
MD5 = 19323C2EA6F5FCEE2382690100455C17
---- 14/03/2018 15:40:57.920
0000 90 90 90 90 90 90 90 90 90 90 90 90 90 90 90 90 ................
0010 90 90 90 90 90 90 90 90 90 90 90 90 90 90 90 90 ................
0020 90 90 90 90 90 90 90 90 90 90 90 90 90 90 90 90 ................
0030 90 90 90 90 90 90 90 90 90 90 90 90 90 90 90 90 ................
0040 90 90 90 90 90 90 90 90 90 90 90 90 90 90 90 90 ................
0050 90 90 90 90 90 90 90 90 90 90 90 90 90 90 90 90 ................
0060 90 90 90 90 90 90 90 90 90 90 90 90 90 90 90 90 ................
0070 90 90 90 90 90 90 90 90 90 90 90 90 90 90 90 90 ................
0080 90 90 90 90 90 90 90 90 90 90 90 90 90 90 90 90 ................
0090 90 90 90 90 90 90 90 90 90 90 90 90 90 90 90 90 ................
00A0 90 90 90 90 90 90 90 90 90 90 90 90 90 90 90 90 ................
00B0 90 90 90 90 90 90 90 90 90 90 90 90 90 90 90 90 ................
00C0 90 90 90 90 90 90 90 90 90 90 90 90 90 90 90 90 ................
00D0 90 90 90 90 90 90 90 90 90 90 90 90 90 90 90 90 ................
00E0 90 90 90 90 90 90 90 90 90 90 90 90 90 90 90 90 ................
00F0 90 90 90 90 90 90 90 90 90 90 90 90 90 90 90 90 ................
0100 90 90 90 90 90 90 90 90 90 90 90 90 4D 3F E3 77 ............M?.w
0110 90 90 90 90 FF 63 64 90 90 90 90 90 90 90 90 90 .....cd.........
0120 90 90 90 90 90 90 90 90 90 90 90 90 90 90 90 90 ................
0130 90 90 90 90 90 90 90 90 EB 10 5A 4A 33 C9 66 B9 ..........ZJ3.f.
0140 66 01 80 34 0A 99 E2 FA EB 05 E8 EB FF FF FF 70 f..4...........p
0150 99 98 99 99 C3 21 95 69 64 E6 12 99 12 E9 85 34 .....!.id......4
0160 12 D9 91 12 41 12 EA A5 9A 6A 12 EF E1 9A 6A 12 ....A....j....j.
0170 E7 B9 9A 62 12 D7 8D AA 74 CF CE C8 12 A6 9A 62 ...b....t......b
0180 12 6B F3 97 C0 6A 3F ED 91 C0 C6 1A 5E 9D DC 7B .k...j?.....^..{
0190 70 C0 C6 C7 12 54 12 DF BD 9A 5A 48 78 9A 58 AA p....T....ZHx.X.
01A0 50 FF 12 91 12 DF 85 9A 5A 58 78 9B 9A 58 12 99 P.......ZXx..X..
```

```
01B0 9A 5A 12 63 12 6E 1A 5F 97 12 49 F3 9A C0 71 E5 .Z.c.n._..I...q.
01C0 99 99 99 1A 5F 94 CB CF 66 CE 65 C3 12 41 F3 9D ...._...f.e..A..
01D0 C0 71 F0 99 99 99 C9 C9 C9 C9 F3 98 F3 9B 66 CE .q............f.
01E0 69 12 41 5E 9E 9B 99 9E 24 AA 59 10 DE 9D F3 89 i.A^....$.Y.....
01F0 CE CA 66 CE 6D F3 98 CA 66 CE 61 C9 C9 CA 66 CE ..f.m...f.a...f.
0200 65 1A 75 DD 12 6D AA 42 F3 89 C0 10 85 17 7B 62 e.u..m.B......{b
0210 10 DF A1 10 DF A5 10 DF D9 5E DF B5 98 98 99 99 .........^......
0220 14 DE 89 C9 CF CA CA CA F3 98 CA CA 5E DE A5 FA ............^...
0230 F4 FD 99 14 DE A5 C9 CA 66 CE 7D C9 66 CE 71 AA ........f.}.f.q.
0240 59 35 1C 59 EC 60 C8 CB CF CA 66 4B C3 C0 32 7B Y5.Y.`....fK..2{
0250 77 AA 59 5A 71 62 67 66 66 DE FC ED C9 EB F6 FA w.YZqbgff.......
0260 D8 FD FD EB FC EA EA 99 DA EB FC F8 ED FC C9 EB ................
0270 F6 FA FC EA EA D8 99 DC E1 F0 ED C9 EB F6 FA FC ................
0280 EA EA 99 D5 F6 F8 FD D5 F0 FB EB F8 EB E0 D8 99 ................
0290 EE EA AB C6 AA AB 99 CE CA D8 CA F6 FA F2 FC ED ................
02A0 D8 99 FB F0 F7 FD 99 F5 F0 EA ED FC F7 99 F8 FA ................
```

In many cases, the key to preventing buffer overflow attacks is ***input validation***. This method requires that any input be checked for format and length at the application before it is used. Buffer overflows and boundary errors (when input exceeds the boundaries allotted for the input) are considered to be a family of error conditions called input validation errors.

Malformed input is the category in which all buffer overflow attacks fit. Malformed input is any attack in which the input is configured in an unusual way.

Escalation of Privileges

Privilege escalation is the process of exploiting a bug or weakness in an operating system to allow users to receive privileges to which they are not entitled. These privileges can be used to delete files, view private information, or install unwanted programs such as viruses.

Backdoor

Backdoors and ***trapdoors*** have been mentioned in passing several times in this book (for example, Chapter 5). A backdoor is a piece of software installed by hackers, using one of the delivery mechanisms previously discussed, that allows them to return later and connect to the computer without going through the normal authentication process. A backdoor normally bypasses access control measures. Some commercial applications inadvertently include backdoors because programmers forget to remove them before release to market. In many cases, the backdoor program is listening on a specific port number, and when attackers attempt to connect to that port, they are allowed to connect without authentication. An example is Back Orifice 2000 (BO2K), an application-level Trojan horse used to give an attacker backdoor network access.

Rogue Programmers

It is becoming commonplace for regular computer users to create utilities and scripts for performing their day-to-day duties. Unfortunately, these rogue programmers do not fully understand the security issues that can arise with the use of such tools. If possible, an organization should forbid the usage of any utilities or scripts that are not created by trained programmers. However, if an organization allows casual programming, security professionals should ensure that the people who are writing utilities and scripts receive the appropriate training in system development practices. Regular code review should be included as part of the development process to fix any rogue code.

Covert Channel

A covert channel occurs when two processes transfer information in a manner that violates a system's security policy. Two types of covert channels can occur:

- **Storage:** Involves direct or indirect storage location reading by multiple processes. It usually occurs at a memory location or disk sector shared by two subjects at different security levels.
- **Timing:** Involves one process being able to influence the rate at which another process can acquire CPU, memory, or I/O resources.

Object Reuse

Memory is allocated to a process, de-allocated to a process, and then allocated to another process. Sometimes data from an old process remains behind (in RAM or cache or on the hard drive), and this old data causes a security violation. If the memory is not zeroed out or overwritten by the operating system, this remaining data is carried over into a new process and may be reused. Object reuse can also occur on a hard drive or a paging or swap file.

Mobile Code

As previously mentioned, mobile code is executable content that transmits across a network from a remote source to a local host and is executed on the local host. Mobile code can come from a variety of sources, including web pages and email messages.

Local execution of remotely sourced code is a security concern for every organization today. Mobile code presents a unique security issue because often one subject is acting on behalf of another or itself. Security controls must be implemented to define which of these requests will be allowed or denied.

Time of Check/Time of Use (TOC/TOU)

A TOC or TOU attack occurs when a control changes between the time when a variable's contents are changed and the time when the variable is actually used. For example, say that a user logs on in the morning and is given all the permissions needed at login. Later in the day, the user is moved to another position in the company, and that user's permissions are changed in the system. However, the user does not log out and therefore still has the old permissions, based on the original login. To prevent this type of problem, security professionals should implement periodic mandatory authentication to ensure that users and systems are re-authenticated at regular intervals throughout the day.

Security of Application Programming Interfaces

Even the most secure devices have some sort of application programming interface (API) that is used to perform tasks. Unfortunately, untrustworthy people use those same APIs to perform unscrupulous tasks. APIs are used in the Internet of Things (IoT) so that devices can speak to each other without users even knowing they are there. APIs are used to control and monitor things people use every day, including fitness bands, home thermostats, lighting, and automobiles. Comprehensive security must protect the entire spectrum of devices in the digital workplace, including apps and APIs. API security is critical for an organization that is exposing digital assets.

Guidelines for providing API security include

- Use the same security controls for APIs as for any web application in the enterprise.
- Use Hash-based Message Authentication Code (HMAC).
- Use encryption when passing static keys.
- Use a framework or an existing library to implement security solutions for APIs.
- Implement password encryption instead of single key-based authentication.

Secure Coding Practices

Developers should follow secure coding practices. Earlier in this chapter, we covered software development security best practices. In addition to those best practices, developers should keep in mind the secure coding best practices covered in the following sections.

Validate Input

Developers should be sure to validate any input into an application from all untrusted data sources. Proper input validation can eliminate the vast majority of software vulnerabilities. Most external data sources, including command-line arguments, network interfaces, environmental variables, and user-controlled files, should be considered untrusted.

Heed Compiler Warnings

When developers use a compiler, they should compile the code using the highest warning level available in the compiler. Then they should work to eliminate any warnings they receive by modifying the code. Both static and dynamic analysis tools should be used to detect and eliminate additional security flaws.

Design for Security Policies

Developers should design software to implement and enforce security policies. The design should be kept as simple and small as possible. The likelihood that errors exist in implementation, configuration, and use increases when developers use complex designs. As security mechanisms become more complex, the developer effort needed to achieve an appropriate level of assurance increases dramatically.

Implement Default Deny

Security professionals should ensure that, by default, access is denied and the protection scheme identifies conditions under which access is permitted.

Adhere to the Principle of Least Privilege, and Practice Defense in Depth

Every software action should execute with the least set of privileges necessary to complete the job. Any elevated permission should be granted for the minimum period of time necessary. This approach reduces the chance that an attacker can execute arbitrary code with elevated privileges.

Implement multiple defensive strategies, also known as defense in depth. Doing so ensures that if one layer of defense turns out to be inadequate, another layer of defense can prevent a security flaw from becoming an exploitable vulnerability and/or limit the consequences of a successful exploit.

Sanitize Data Prior to Transmission to Other Systems

Sanitize all data passed to other systems, including command shells, processes, relational databases, and application components. Attackers may be able to invoke unused functionality in these systems using SQL, command, or other injection attacks. This is not necessarily an input validation problem because the system being invoked does not understand the context in which the call is made.

Exam Preparation Tasks

As mentioned in the section "About the *CISSP Cert Guide*, Fifth Edition" in the Introduction, you have a couple of choices for exam preparation: the exercises here, Chapter 9, "Final Preparation," and the exam simulation questions in the Pearson Test Prep Software Online.

Review All Key Topics

Review the most important topics in this chapter, noted with the Key Topic icon in the outer margin of the page. Table 8-1 lists a reference of these key topics and the page numbers on which each is found.

Key Topic

Table 8-1 Key Topics for Chapter 8

Key Topic Element	Description	Page Number
List	System Development Life Cycle	783
List	Software Development Life Cycle	786
List	Software development methods and maturity models	792
Figure 8-5	Agile and Waterfall Model Comparison	798
Figure 8-7	CMMI Maturity Levels	802
Figure 8-8	Phases and Steps of the IDEAL Model	804
List	Malware	809
List	Acquired software life cycle	817

Define Key Terms

Define the following key terms from this chapter and check your answers in the glossary:

acceptance testing; accreditation; ActiveX; adware; Agile; app vetting; app testing; app approval/rejection; assembly languages; backdoor; boot sector malware;

botnet; buffer overflow; Build and Fix; Build Security In (BSI); Capability Maturity Model Integration (CMMI); certification; change management process; Cleanroom model; code repository; cohesion; Common Object Request Broker Architecture (CORBA); Component Object Model (COM); Continuous Integration and Continuous Delivery (CI/CD); coupling; data structure; DevSecOps; Distributed Component Object Model (DCOM); distributed object-oriented systems; Dynamic Application Security Testing (DAST); high-level languages; IDEAL model; Incremental model; input validation; ISO/IEC 27000; Java applet; Java Platform, Enterprise Edition (Java EE); Joint Analysis Development (JAD) model; keylogger; logic bomb; machine languages; macro virus; malware; mobile code; mobile malware; multipartite virus; natural languages; Object Linking and Embedding (OLE); object-oriented programming (OOP); Open Web Application Security Project (OWASP); parasitic virus; polyinstantiation; polymorphic virus; polymorphism; privilege escalation; prototyping; Rapid Application Development (RAD); Security Orchestration and Automated Response (SOAR); service-oriented architecture (SOA); Software Development Life Cycle; source code; Spiral model; spyware; stealth virus; Static Application Security Testing (SAST); System Development Life Cycle (SDLC); trapdoor; Trojan horse; very-high-level languages; virus; V-shaped model; Waterfall model; Web Application Security Consortium (WASC); worm

Answer Review Questions

1. Which of the following is the last step in the System Development Life Cycle?
    a. Operate/Maintain
    b. Dispose
    c. Acquire/Develop
    d. Initiate

2. In which of the following stages of the Software Development Life Cycle is the software actually coded?
    a. Gather Requirements
    b. Design
    c. Develop
    d. Test/Validate

3. Which of the following initiatives was developed by the Department of Homeland Security?
   a. WASC (Web Application Security Consortium)
   b. BSI (Build Security In)
   c. OWASP (Open Web Application Security Project)
   d. ISO (International Organization for Standardization)

4. Which of the following development models includes no formal control mechanisms to provide feedback?
   a. Waterfall
   b. V-shaped
   c. Build and Fix
   d. Spiral

5. Which language type delivers instructions directly to the processor?
   a. Assembly languages
   b. High-level languages
   c. Machine languages
   d. Natural languages

6. Which term describes the degree to which elements in a module are related to one another?
   a. Polymorphism
   b. Cohesion
   c. Coupling
   d. Data structures

7. Which term describes a standard for communication between processes on the same computer?
   a. CORBA (Common Object Request Broker Architecture)
   b. DCOM (Distributed Component Object Model)
   c. COM (Component Object Model)
   d. SOA (service-oriented architecture)

8. Which of the following is a Microsoft technology?
   a. ActiveX
   b. Java
   c. SOA (service-oriented architecture)
   d. CORBA (Common Object Request Broker Architecture)

9. Which of the following is the dividing line between the trusted parts of the system and those that are untrusted?
   a. Security perimeter
   b. Reference monitor
   c. Trusted computer base (TCB)
   d. Security kernel

10. Which of the following is a system component that enforces access controls on an object?
    a. Security perimeter
    b. Reference monitor
    c. Trusted computer base (TCB)
    d. Security kernel

11. Which of the following tests ensures that the customer (either internal or external) is satisfied with the functionality of the software?
    a. Integration testing
    b. Acceptance testing
    c. Regression testing
    d. Accreditation

12. In which of the following software development models is less time spent on the upfront analysis and more emphasis placed on learning from the process feedback and incorporating lessons learned in real time?
    a. Agile Development
    b. Rapid Application Development
    c. Cleanroom Model
    d. Modified Waterfall

13. Which of the following software development risk analysis and mitigation strategy guidelines should security professionals follow? (Choose all that apply.)
    a. Integrate risk analysis and mitigation in the Software Development Life Cycle.
    b. Use qualitative, quantitative, and hybrid risk analysis approaches based on standardized risk analysis methods.
    c. Track and manage weaknesses that are discovered throughout risk assessment, change management, and continuous monitoring.
    d. Encapsulate data to make it easier to apply the appropriate policies to objects.

14. Which of the following are valid guidelines for providing application programming interface (API) security? (Choose all that apply.)
    a. Use the same security controls for APIs as for any web application in the enterprise.
    b. Use Hash-based Message Authentication Code (HMAC).
    c. Use encryption when passing static keys.
    d. Implement password encryption instead of single key-based authentication.

15. Which of the following is *not* one of the four phases of acquiring software?
    a. Planning
    b. Contracting
    c. Development
    d. Monitoring and accepting

16. Which of the following are considered secure coding best practices that developers and security professionals should adhere to? (Choose all that apply.)
    a. Sanitize all data passed to other systems.
    b. Implement default deny.
    c. Validate input.
    d. Heed compiler warnings.

17. Which of the following is a sequence of activities that aims to determine whether an application conforms to the organization's security requirements?
    a. Component-Based Development
    b. Change management process
    c. IDEAL (Initiate, Diagnose, Establish, Act, Learn) phases
    d. Application vetting process

Answers and Explanations

1. **b.** The five steps in the System Development Life Cycle are as follows:
   1. Initiate
   2. Acquire/Develop
   3. Implement
   4. Operate/Maintain
   5. Dispose
2. **c.** The Develop stage involves writing the code or instructions that make the software work. The emphasis of this phase is strict adherence to secure coding practices.
3. **b.** The Department of Homeland Security (DHS) is involved in promoting software security best practices. The Build Security In (BSI) initiative promotes a process-agnostic approach that makes security recommendations with regard to architectures, testing methods, code reviews, and management processes.
4. **c.** Though it's not a formal model, the Build and Fix approach describes a method that has been largely discredited and is now used as a template for how not to manage a development project. Simply put, in this method, the software is developed as quickly as possible and released.
5. **c.** Machine languages deliver instructions directly to the processor. This was the only type of programming done in the 1950s and uses basic binary instructions, compiler or interpreter. (These programs convert higher language types to a form that can be executed by the processor.)
6. **b.** Cohesion describes how many different tasks a module can carry out. If a module is limited to a small number or a single function, it is said to have high cohesion. Coupling describes how much interaction one module requires from another module to do its job. Low or loose coupling indicates that a module does not need much help from other modules, whereas high coupling indicates the opposite.

7. **c.** Component Object Model (COM) is a model for communication between processes on the same computer, while, as the name implies, the Distributed Component Object Model (DCOM) is a model for communication between processes in different parts of the network.
8. **a.** ActiveX is a Microsoft technology that uses object-oriented programming (OOP) and is based on the COM and DCOM.
9. **a.** The security perimeter is the dividing line between the trusted parts of the system and those that are untrusted. According to security design best practices, components that lie within this boundary (which means they lie within the TCB) should never permit untrusted components to access critical resources in an insecure manner.
10. **b.** A reference monitor is a system component that enforces access controls on an object. It is an access control concept that refers to an abstract machine that mediates all accesses to objects by subjects.
11. **b.** Acceptance testing ensures that the customer (either internal or external) is satisfied with the functionality of the software. Integration testing assesses how the modules work together and determines whether functional and security specifications have been met. Regression testing takes place after changes are made to the code to ensure that the changes have reduced neither functionality nor security. Accreditation is the formal acceptance of the adequacy of a system's overall security by management.
12. **a.** With the Agile model, less time is spent on upfront analysis, and more emphasis is placed on learning from the process and incorporating lessons learned in real time. There is also more interaction with the customer throughout the process. In the Rapid Application Development (RAD) model, less time is spent up front on design, while emphasis is placed on rapidly producing prototypes with the assumption that crucial knowledge can only be gained through trial and error. In contrast to the JAD model, the Cleanroom model strictly adheres to formal steps and a more structured method. It attempts to prevent errors and mistakes through extensive testing. In the modified Waterfall model, each phase in the development process is considered its own milestone in the project management process. Unlimited backward iteration (returning to earlier stages to address problems) is not allowed in this model.
13. **a, b, c.** Security professionals should ensure that the software development risk analysis and mitigation strategy follows these guidelines:
    - Integrate risk analysis and mitigation in the Software Development Life Cycle.

- Use qualitative, quantitative, and hybrid risk analysis approaches based on standardized risk analysis methods.
- Track and manage weaknesses that are discovered throughout risk assessment, change management, and continuous monitoring.

14. **a, b, c, d.** Comprehensive security must protect the entire spectrum of devices in the digital workplace, including apps and APIs. API security is critical for an organization that is exposing digital assets. Guidelines for providing API security include
    - Use the same security controls for APIs as for any web application in the enterprise.
    - Use Hash-based Message Authentication Code (HMAC).
    - Use encryption when passing static keys.
    - Use a framework or an existing library to implement security solutions for APIs.
    - Implement password encryption instead of single key-based authentication.
15. **c.** In the Software Development Life Cycle, the code or instructions that make the software work are written in the Develop phase. The process of acquiring software has the following four phases:
    1. **Planning:** During this phase, the organization performs a needs assessment, develops the software requirements, creates the acquisition strategy, and develops evaluation criteria and a plan.
    2. **Contracting:** When planning is complete, the organization creates a request for proposal (RFP) or other supplier solicitation forms, evaluates the supplier proposals, and negotiates the final contract with the selected seller.
    3. **Monitoring and accepting:** When a contract is in place, the organization establishes the contract work schedule, implements change control procedures, and reviews and accepts the software deliverables.
    4. **Follow-up:** When the software is in place, the organization must sustain the software, including managing risks and changes. At some point, the organization may need to decommission the software.
16. **a, b, c, d.** Developers and security professionals should adhere to the following secure coding best practices:
    - Sanitize all data passed to other systems, including command shells, processes, relational databases, and application components.

- Security professionals should ensure that, by default, access is denied and the protection scheme identifies conditions under which access is permitted.
- Developers should validate any input into an application from all untrusted data sources.
- When developers use a compiler, they should compile the code using the highest warning level available in the compiler.
- Design software to implement and enforce security policies.
- Adhere to the principle of least privilege, and practice defense in depth.

17. **d.** An app vetting process is a sequence of activities that aims to determine whether an app conforms to the organization's security requirements. An app vetting process comprises a sequence of two main activities: *app testing* and *app approval/rejection*. The Component-Based Development method uses building blocks to assemble an application instead of build it. The advantage of this method in regard to security is that the components are tested for security prior to being used in the application. The purpose of the change management process is to ensure that all changes to the configuration of the source code and to the source code itself are approved by the proper personnel and are implemented in a safe and logical manner. The IDEAL model was developed by the Software Engineering Institute to provide guidance on software development. Its name is an acronym that stands for the five phases:

    1. **Initiate:** Outline the business reasons behind the change, build support for the initiative, and implement the infrastructure needed.
    2. **Diagnose:** Analyze the current organizational state and make change recommendations.
    3. **Establish:** Take the recommendations from the previous phase and use them to develop an action plan.
    4. **Act:** Develop, test, refine, and implement the solutions according to the action plan from the previous phase.
    5. **Learn:** Use the quality improvement process to determine whether goals have been met and develop new actions based on the analysis.

CHAPTER 9

Final Preparation

The first eight chapters of this book cover the technologies, protocols, design concepts, and considerations required to be prepared to pass the ISC^2 Certified Information Systems Security Professional (CISSP) exam. While these chapters supply the detailed information, most people need more preparation than just reading the first eight chapters of this book. This chapter details a set of tools and a study plan to help you complete your preparation for the exams.

This short chapter has two main sections. The first section lists the exam preparation tools useful at this point in the study process. The second section lists a suggested study plan now that you have completed all the earlier chapters in this book.

NOTE Appendix A, "Memory Tables," and Appendix B, "Memory Tables Answer Key," exist as soft-copy appendixes on the companion website for this book, which you can access by going to www.informit.com/register, registering your book, and entering this book's ISBN: 9780137507474.

Tools for Final Preparation

This section provides information about the available tools and how to access the tools.

Pearson Test Prep Practice Test Engine and Questions on the Website

Register this book to get access to the Pearson Test Prep practice test engine (software that displays and grades a set of exam-realistic, multiple-choice questions). Using the Pearson Test Prep practice test engine, you can either study by going through the questions in Study mode or take a simulated (timed) CISSP exam.

The Pearson Test Prep practice test software comes with two full practice exams. These practice tests are available to you either online or as an offline Windows application. To access the practice exams that were developed with this book, please see the instructions in the card inserted in the sleeve in the back of the book. This card includes a unique access code that enables you to activate your exams in the Pearson Test Prep software.

Accessing the Pearson Test Prep Practice Test Software Online

The online version of this software can be used on any device with a browser and connectivity to the Internet, including desktop machines, tablets, and smartphones. To start using your practice exams online, simply follow these steps:

Step 1. Go to https://www.PearsonTestPrep.com.

Step 2. Select **Pearson IT Certification** as your product group.

Step 3. Enter your email/password for your account. If you don't have an account on PearsonITCertification.com or CiscoPress.com, you will need to establish one by going to PearsonITCertification.com/join.

Step 4. In the My Products tab, click the **Activate New Product** button.

Step 5. Enter the access code printed on the insert card in the back of your book to activate your product.

Step 6. The product will now be listed in your My Products page. Click the **Exams** button to launch the exam settings screen and start your exam.

Accessing the Pearson Test Prep Practice Test Software Offline

If you wish to study offline, you can download and install the Windows version of the Pearson Test Prep practice test software. There is a download link for this software on the book's companion website, or you can just enter this link in your browser:

http://www.pearsonitcertification.com/content/downloads/pcpt/engine.zip

To access the book's companion website and the software, simply follow these steps:

Step 1. Register your book by going to PearsonITCertification.com/register and entering the ISBN: 9780137507474.

Step 2. Answer the challenge questions.

Step 3. Go to your account page and click the **Registered Products** tab.

Step 4. Click the **Access Bonus Content** link under the product listing.

Step 5. Click the **Install Pearson Test Prep Desktop Version** link under the Practice Exams section of the page to download the software.

Step 6. After the software finishes downloading, unzip all the files on your computer.

Step 7. Double-click the application file to start the installation, and follow the onscreen instructions to complete the registration.

Step 8. After the installation is complete, launch the application and click the **Activate Exam** button on the My Products tab.

Step 9. Click the **Activate a Product** button in the Activate Product Wizard.

Step 10. Enter the unique access code found on the card in the sleeve in the back of your book and click the **Activate** button.

Step 11. Click **Next**, and then click **Finish** to download the exam data to your application.

Step 12. Start using the practice exams by selecting the product and clicking the **Open Exam** button to open the exam settings screen.

Note that the offline and online versions will sync together, so saved exams and grade results recorded on one version will be available to you on the other as well.

Customizing Your Exams

Once you are in the exam settings screen, you can choose to take exams in one of three modes:

- **Study mode:** Enables you to fully customize your exams and review answers as you are taking the exam. This is typically the mode you would use first to assess your knowledge and identify information gaps.
- **Practice Exam mode:** Locks certain customization options, as it is presenting a realistic exam experience. Use this mode when you are preparing to test your exam readiness.
- **Flash Card mode:** Strips out the answers and presents you with only the question stem. This mode is great for late-stage preparation when you really want to challenge yourself to provide answers without the benefit of seeing multiple-choice options. This mode does not provide the detailed score reports that the other two modes do, so you should not use it if you are trying to identify knowledge gaps.

In addition to these three modes, you will be able to select the source of your questions. You can choose to take exams that cover all of the chapters or you can narrow your selection to just a single chapter or the chapters that make up specific parts in the book. All chapters are selected by default. If you want to narrow your focus to individual chapters, simply deselect all the chapters; then select only those on which you wish to focus in the Objectives area.

You can also select the exam banks on which to focus. Each exam bank comes complete with a full exam of questions that cover topics in every chapter. You can have the test engine serve up exams from all banks or just from one individual bank by selecting the desired banks in the exam bank area.

There are several other customizations you can make to your exam from the exam settings screen, such as the time of the exam, the number of questions served up, whether to randomize questions and answers, whether to show the number of correct answers for multiple-answer questions, and whether to serve up only specific types of questions. You can also create custom test banks by selecting only questions that you have marked or questions on which you have added notes.

Updating Your Exams

If you are using the online version of the Pearson Test Prep practice test software, you should always have access to the latest version of the software as well as the exam data. If you are using the Windows desktop version, every time you launch the software while connected to the Internet, it checks if there are any updates to your exam data and automatically downloads any changes that were made since the last time you used the software.

Sometimes, due to many factors, the exam data may not fully download when you activate your exam. If you find that figures or exhibits are missing, you may need to manually update your exams. To update a particular exam you have already activated and downloaded, simply click the **Tools** tab and click the **Update Products** button. Again, this is only an issue with the desktop Windows application.

If you wish to check for updates to the Pearson Test Prep exam engine software, Windows desktop version, simply click the **Tools** tab and click the **Update Application** button. This ensures that you are running the latest version of the software engine.

Premium Edition

In addition to the free practice exams provided on the book's companion website, you can purchase additional exams with expanded functionality directly from Pearson IT Certification. The Premium Edition of this title contains an additional two full practice exams and an eBook (in both PDF and ePub format). In addition, the Premium Edition title offers remediation for each question by pointing you to the specific part of the eBook that relates to that question.

Because you have purchased the print version of this title, you can purchase the Premium Edition at a deep discount. There is a coupon code in the book sleeve that contains a one-time-use code and instructions for where you can purchase the Premium Edition.

To view the Premium Edition product page, go to www.informit.com/title/9780137507573.

Memory Tables

Like most Pearson Cert Guides, this book purposely organizes information into tables and lists for easier study and review. Rereading these tables can be very useful before the exam. However, it is easy to skim over the tables without paying attention to every detail, especially when you remember having seen the table's contents when reading the chapter.

As an alternative to simply reading the tables in the various chapters, Appendixes A and B give you another review tool. Appendix A lists partially completed versions of many of the tables from the book. You can open Appendix A (a PDF available on the companion website after registering) and print the appendix. For review, you can attempt to complete the tables. This exercise can help you focus on the review. It also exercises the memory connectors in your brain, plus it makes you think about the information without as much contextual information, which forces a little more contemplation about the facts.

Appendix B, also a PDF available on the companion website, lists the completed tables to check yourself. You can also just refer to the tables as printed in the book.

Chapter-Ending Review Tools

Chapters 1 through 8 each have several features in the "Exam Preparation Tasks" and "Review Questions" sections at the end of the chapter. You might have already worked through these in each chapter. It can also be useful to use these tools again as you make your final preparations for the exam.

Suggested Plan for Final Review/Study

This section lists a suggested study plan from the point at which you finish reading through Chapter 8 until you take the CISSP exam. Certainly, you can ignore this plan, use it as is, or just take suggestions from it.

The plan uses four steps:

Step 1. **Review key topics:** You can use the table that lists the key topics in each chapter, or just flip the pages looking for key topics.

Step 2. **Complete memory tables:** Open Appendix A from the companion website and print the entire thing, or print the tables by major part. Then complete the tables.

Step 3. **Review "Review Questions" sections:** Go through the Review Questions sections at the end of each chapter to identify areas in which you need more study.

Step 4. **Use the Pearson Test Prep practice test engine to practice:** The Pearson Test Prep practice test engine can be used to study using a bank of unique exam-realistic questions available only with this book.

Summary

The tools and suggestions listed in this chapter have been designed with one goal in mind: to help you develop the skills required to pass the CISSP exam. This book has been developed from the beginning to not only tell you the facts but also help you learn how to apply the facts. Regardless of your experience level leading up to when you take the exam, it is our hope that the broad range of preparation tools provided in this book, and even the structure of the book, helps you pass the exam with ease. We hope you do well on the exam.

Index

Numbers

A

B

C

E

F

G

H

I

M

N

O

P

Q

R

S

T

U

V

W

X

Y-Z